NCMHCE Study Guide

Latest NCMHCE Review and 750+ Practice Questions with Detailed Explanation for the National Clinical Mental Health Counseling Exam (Contains 5 Full Length Practice Tests)

Julia Presley

Sophie J. Jimenez

© 2024-2025

Printed in USA.

Disclaimer:

CONTENTS

Part A:

Part B:

Effective Tips to pass the NCMHCE exam:

1. Understand the Exam Structure:

Familiarize yourself with the exam structure and content breakdown to focus your study efforts efficiently.

2. Create a Study Plan:

Developing a study plan is essential to organize your review and ensure that you cover all the necessary topics. Set aside dedicated study time each day or week leading up to the exam date. Break down the content into manageable sections and prioritize areas where you need more review.

3. Practice Time Management:

The NCMHCE exam is timed, so practicing time management is crucial for success. During your study sessions, work on answering practice questions within the allotted time frame. This will help you build confidence and improve your ability to pace yourself during the actual exam.

4. Take Practice Exams:

Taking practice exams is an effective way to assess your knowledge, identify areas of weakness, and gauge your readiness for the NCMHCE exam. Practice exams can help you familiarize yourself with the format and difficulty level of the questions. Analyze your performance on practice exams to focus your review on areas that need improvement.

5. Stay Calm and Confident:

On the day of the exam, remember to stay calm and confident. Get a good night's sleep, eat a healthy breakfast, and arrive at the testing center with ample time to spare. Trust in your preparation and ability to succeed, and approach the exam with a positive mindset.

In conclusion, passing the National Clinical Mental Health Counseling (NCMHCE ®) exam requires diligent preparation, dedication, and a solid understanding of the principles. By following these tips and utilizing reliable study resources, you can increase your chances of passing the exam with ease. Good luck on your journey to becoming a NCMHCE!

Why you'll love this book for acing the NCMHCE Exam:

Up-to-Date Content:

Look no further for a comprehensive study guide tailored to the NCMHCE Exam. Packed with the latest information and a multitude of practice questions, this book ensures you're well-prepared to succeed. Regular updates guarantee alignment with the most current exam standards.

Expert Guidance:

Written by seasoned professionals who have successfully tackled the NCMHCE Exam, this book offers invaluable insights and strategies for exam success. Benefit from the authors' wealth of experience and expertise to navigate the exam with confidence.

Insightful Explanations:

Gain a deeper understanding of the material through detailed explanations provided alongside each question. By delving into the rationale behind the answers, you'll enhance your comprehension and be better equipped to tackle challenging questions on exam day.

Reflective of the Exam Format:

Experience the same question format as the actual NCMHCE Exam, allowing you to familiarize yourself with the test structure and boost your confidence. Practice with questions that mirror the exam will prepare you for success on test day.

Enhanced Critical Thinking:

Engaging with the questions, answers, and explanations in this book will sharpen your critical thinking skills and improve your ability to analyze and respond to exam questions effectively. Strengthen your cognitive abilities and enhance your problem-solving skills as you prepare for the NCMHCE Exam.

Clear and Concise Approach:

Written in a straightforward and easy-to-understand style, this NCMHCE Prep simplifies complex concepts and ensures clarity without overwhelming you with technical language. Dive into the material confidently, knowing that this resource will help you grasp key concepts and excel on the exam.

NCMHCE

GUIDE

1   Professional Practice And Ethics:

Professional practice and ethics in mental health counseling encompass the standards and principles that guide counselors in their professional conduct. These guidelines ensure that counselors provide competent, ethical, and culturally sensitive services to clients. Central to this is adherence to the American Counseling Association (ACA) Code of Ethics, which outlines the ethical obligations of counselors in areas such as confidentiality, informed consent, and professional boundaries.

Confidentiality is paramount, requiring counselors to protect client information unless there is a risk of harm or a legal obligation to disclose it. Informed consent involves clearly communicating the nature of counseling services, including potential risks and benefits, to clients before treatment begins. Maintaining professional boundaries ensures a therapeutic relationship free from conflicts of interest or dual relationships that could impair objectivity.

Counselors must also demonstrate cultural competence by understanding and respecting diverse backgrounds and perspectives. This includes ongoing education and self-reflection to mitigate personal biases. Ethical decision-making frameworks are employed when faced with complex situations, ensuring that decisions align with both ethical standards and client welfare.

Continuous professional development through education and supervision is essential for maintaining competence. By adhering to these ethical principles, mental health counselors uphold the integrity of the profession and foster trust with clients, ultimately enhancing therapeutic outcomes.

1.1 Assessing Counselor Competency for Client Work:

Assessing your competency to work with a specific client involves evaluating your skills, knowledge, and experience in relation to the client's unique needs and presenting issues. This self-assessment is crucial for ensuring ethical and effective practice. Competency encompasses an understanding of the cultural, social, and psychological factors that may impact the counseling process. It requires counselors to be aware of their own biases and limitations.

Begin by considering your educational background and clinical training relevant to the client's concerns. Reflect on past experiences with similar cases and whether you have successfully managed such situations. Evaluate your familiarity with evidence-based practices pertinent to the client's issues.

Cultural competence is essential; assess your understanding of the client's cultural background and whether you can approach their situation with sensitivity and respect. If gaps exist in your knowledge or skills, seek supervision or additional training.

Ethically, counselors must recognize when they are not equipped to handle a case and refer the client to another professional if necessary. Continuous professional development is vital to maintaining competency. This includes staying updated with current research, attending workshops, and engaging in peer consultations.

Ultimately, self-assessment of competency ensures that clients receive the highest standard of care, safeguarding their well-being and promoting positive therapeutic outcomes.

1.2 Statistical Concepts and Methods in Research:

Understanding statistical concepts and methods in research is crucial for mental health counselors, as it enables them to critically evaluate research findings and apply evidence-based practices. Statistics in research involves collecting, analyzing, interpreting, and presenting data to draw meaningful conclusions. Key statistical concepts include descriptive statistics, which summarize data through measures such as the mean, median, mode, and standard deviation. These measures provide insights into the central tendency and variability of data.

Inferential statistics allow researchers to make predictions or inferences about a population based on a sample. This involves hypothesis testing, confidence intervals, and p-values to determine the significance of results. Understanding these concepts helps counselors assess the reliability and validity of research studies.

Methods such as correlation and regression analysis are used to explore relationships between variables. Correlation measures the strength and direction of a relationship between two variables, while regression analysis predicts the value of a dependent variable based on one or more independent variables.

Knowledge of statistical methods also includes understanding sampling techniques, ensuring that samples are representative of populations to generalize findings accurately. Mental health counselors must be adept at interpreting statistical data to integrate research into practice effectively, ensuring that interventions are grounded in scientific evidence. This competence enhances their ability to deliver high-quality care.

1.3 Legal and Ethical Counseling Practice:

Legal and ethical counseling practice involves adhering to established laws, regulations, and ethical standards that govern the mental health counseling profession. Counselors must be knowledgeable about federal and state laws, as well as the ethical guidelines set forth by professional organizations such as the American Counseling Association (ACA). These standards are designed to protect client welfare, ensure professional integrity, and promote the efficacy of counseling services.

Key aspects include maintaining confidentiality, obtaining informed consent, and practicing within one's scope of competence. Confidentiality is paramount; counselors must safeguard client information unless disclosure is required by law or necessary to prevent harm. Informed consent involves clearly communicating the nature of counseling services, potential risks, and client rights, ensuring that clients make informed decisions about their treatment.

Counselors must also demonstrate cultural competence, respecting diverse backgrounds and avoiding discrimination. They should engage in continuous professional development to remain current with best practices and legal requirements. Dual relationships, where personal and professional boundaries might overlap, should be avoided to maintain objectivity.

Ethical decision-making models can guide counselors in resolving dilemmas by systematically evaluating options while considering client welfare and professional standards. Adherence to these principles not only upholds the integrity of the profession but also fosters trust and safety in therapeutic relationships.

1.4 Clarify Counselor/Client Roles:

In the context of mental health counseling, clarifying counselor/client roles is a fundamental aspect that establishes the framework for the therapeutic relationship. This process involves defining and communicating the expectations, responsibilities, and boundaries of both the counselor and the client to ensure a clear understanding and effective collaboration throughout the counseling process.

The counselor's role primarily includes providing a safe and supportive environment for the client, facilitating self-exploration, offering insights, and guiding clients toward achieving their therapeutic goals. Counselors are responsible for maintaining professional boundaries, adhering to ethical guidelines, and ensuring confidentiality. They are also tasked with being empathetic listeners who validate clients' experiences while challenging them to foster growth.

Conversely, the client's role involves active participation in the counseling sessions, being open and honest about their thoughts and feelings, and engaging in agreed-upon therapeutic activities. Clients are encouraged to take responsibility for their personal growth by setting goals and working collaboratively with their counselor.

Clarifying these roles at the outset helps prevent misunderstandings, manage expectations, and build trust within the therapeutic relationship. It also empowers clients by making them aware of their active role in their own healing process. Clearly defined roles contribute significantly to the success of therapy by fostering a structured yet flexible environment conducive to personal development.

1.5 Client Rights and Responsibilities:

Client rights and responsibilities form a fundamental component of ethical practice in mental health counseling. Clients have the right to receive services that are respectful, confidential, and culturally sensitive. They are entitled to informed consent, which means they should be fully aware of the nature and purpose of the counseling services, including potential risks and benefits. Clients also have the right to access their records, participate in treatment planning, and refuse or withdraw from treatment at any time.

Counselors must ensure that clients understand these rights by discussing them at the outset of the therapeutic relationship. This discussion should include confidentiality limits, such as the mandatory reporting of abuse or threats to harm oneself or others. Additionally, clients should be informed about their responsibilities, which include providing accurate information to facilitate effective treatment, attending scheduled sessions, and actively participating in their own therapeutic process.

By clearly outlining both rights and responsibilities, counselors empower clients to take an active role in their mental health care while fostering a collaborative therapeutic environment. This transparency not only builds trust but also promotes ethical standards within the profession. Understanding these aspects is crucial for mental health counselors preparing for the NCMHCE exam, as it underscores their commitment to ethical practice and client welfare.

1.6 Discuss Limits Of Confidentiality:

Discuss Limits of Confidentiality:

Confidentiality is a fundamental ethical obligation in mental health counseling, ensuring that client information is protected and only shared with consent. However, there are specific limits to confidentiality that counselors must communicate to clients. These limits are primarily dictated by legal and ethical standards that mandate disclosure under certain circumstances.

Firstly, counselors are required to breach confidentiality if there is an imminent risk of harm to the client or others. This includes situations where a client expresses suicidal ideation or homicidal intent. The duty to warn and protect overrides confidentiality in these cases.

Secondly, reporting is mandatory in instances of suspected child abuse, elder abuse, or abuse of vulnerable individuals. Counselors must report such suspicions to the appropriate authorities as part of their legal obligations.

Additionally, confidentiality may be limited by court orders or subpoenas that require the disclosure of client information. In such cases, counselors should attempt to limit the scope of disclosure and seek legal consultation if necessary.

Finally, clients should be informed that their information might be shared within the counseling team for supervision or consultation purposes, always ensuring that only the minimal necessary information is disclosed.

Counselors must discuss these limits at the outset of the therapeutic relationship to ensure clients understand when and why their confidentiality might be breached, fostering transparency and trust.

1.7 Explain Counselor/agency Policies:

Counselor and agency policies refer to the guidelines and procedures established by counseling agencies to govern the professional conduct, operational practices, and ethical standards expected of mental health counselors. These policies are integral to ensuring that both counselors and clients are aware of their rights, responsibilities, and the scope of services provided. They encompass a wide range of areas, including confidentiality, informed consent, record-keeping, billing practices, and emergency protocols.

An in-depth understanding of these policies is crucial for mental health counselors, as they provide a framework for ethical decision-making and professional behavior. For instance, confidentiality policies outline how client information is protected and under what circumstances it may be disclosed. Informed consent involves educating clients about the counseling process, potential risks, benefits, and alternatives, ensuring that they voluntarily agree to participate in treatment.

Additionally, agency policies may address the handling of dual relationships and conflicts of interest to prevent situations that could impair professional judgment or exploit clients. Adherence to these policies not only protects clients but also safeguards counselors from legal liabilities and allegations of professional misconduct.

For the NCMHCE exam, candidates must demonstrate proficiency in interpreting and applying these policies within various clinical scenarios. This ensures that future counselors are equipped to maintain ethical standards and deliver competent care within their practice settings.

1.8 Payment, Fees, and Insurance Review:

In the context of mental health counseling, reviewing payment, fees, and insurance benefits is a crucial aspect of professional practice and ethics. This process involves understanding and clearly communicating the financial aspects of counseling services to clients. Counselors must establish transparent fee structures that reflect the value of their services and adhere to ethical guidelines. This includes discussing session costs, payment methods, and any sliding scale options available based on the client's financial situation.

Insurance benefits play a significant role in making mental health services accessible. Counselors should be knowledgeable about various insurance plans and their coverage for mental health services. This includes verifying clients' insurance benefits before initiating services to avoid unexpected costs. Counselors must also navigate the complexities of billing insurance companies, which involves submitting accurate claims and understanding reimbursement rates.

Ethically, counselors are obligated to inform clients about their financial responsibilities upfront. This transparency helps build trust and ensures that clients can make informed decisions about their care. Additionally, counselors must maintain confidentiality when handling financial information and comply with all relevant legal and ethical standards.

Overall, effectively managing payment, fees, and insurance benefits is essential for ensuring ethical practice and maintaining a sustainable counseling business while prioritizing client welfare.

1.9 Counseling: Processes, Risks, and Benefits

In the context of mental health counseling, it is imperative for counselors to clearly articulate the counseling processes, procedures, risks, and benefits to their clients. This transparency not only fosters trust but also empowers clients to make informed decisions about their therapeutic journey.

The counseling process involves a series of structured interactions between the counselor and client aimed at facilitating personal growth and addressing psychological issues. This typically begins with an initial assessment to understand the client's concerns, followed by goal setting, intervention strategies, and evaluation of progress.

Procedures in counseling refer to the specific methods and techniques employed during sessions. These can range from cognitive-behavioral techniques to psychodynamic approaches, tailored to meet the individual needs of the client.

Risks associated with counseling may include emotional discomfort as clients confront difficult issues or a temporary worsening of symptoms as underlying problems are addressed. It is crucial for counselors to discuss these potential risks upfront and develop a plan to manage them effectively.

The benefits of counseling are manifold, including improved mental health, enhanced coping strategies, better interpersonal relationships, and increased self-awareness. By understanding both the potential risks and benefits, clients can engage more fully in the therapeutic process, leading to more successful outcomes. As counselors, it is essential to communicate these elements clearly and ethically.

1.10 Social Media: Uses and Limits

Social media in mental health counseling serves as a tool for professional networking, client engagement, and public education. It allows counselors to connect with peers, share resources, and stay informed about the latest developments in mental health practices. Additionally, social media can be used to disseminate educational content, raise awareness about mental health issues, and promote the services offered by counselors.

However, the use of social media in this field is bound by ethical considerations and professional guidelines. Confidentiality is paramount; counselors must avoid sharing any client information that could lead to identification without explicit consent. The boundary between professional and personal life should be maintained to prevent dual relationships and ensure that interactions remain professional.

Counselors should also be aware of the potential for misinterpretation of information shared online and the need to verify the accuracy of content before dissemination. Engaging with clients via social media can blur boundaries and may lead to ethical dilemmas regarding the counselor-client relationship. The American Counseling Association (ACA) Code of Ethics provides guidelines on maintaining professionalism, ensuring confidentiality, and setting clear boundaries when using social media. Counselors must navigate these platforms carefully to protect their integrity and uphold ethical standards in their practice.

1.11 Legal Aspects of Counseling for Clients:

In the realm of mental health counseling, it is imperative for counselors to inform clients about the legal aspects of counseling as part of ethical and professional practice. This involves providing clients with a clear understanding of their rights and the legal parameters within which counseling services operate. Counselors must explain confidentiality, including its limits, such as mandatory reporting laws that require disclosure in cases of abuse or threats to self or others. Clients should be informed about their right to access their records and the circumstances under which these records might be released without consent.

Additionally, counselors need to discuss informed consent, ensuring that clients understand the nature and purpose of counseling, potential risks and benefits, as well as alternative treatments. This process empowers clients to make informed decisions regarding their participation in counseling services.

Counselors should also address issues related to dual relationships and boundaries to prevent conflicts of interest or exploitation. Furthermore, clients must be made aware of the procedure for filing complaints if they believe their rights have been violated.

By thoroughly informing clients about these legal aspects, counselors not only adhere to ethical standards but also foster a transparent and trusting therapeutic relationship, ultimately enhancing client autonomy and safeguarding both parties involved.

1.12 Obtain Informed Consent:

Informed consent is a fundamental ethical and legal requirement in the practice of mental health counseling. It involves providing clients with comprehensive information about the counseling process, including the nature and purpose of the treatment, potential risks and benefits, confidentiality limits, and the right to withdraw consent at any time. The counselor must ensure that the client fully understands this information and voluntarily agrees to participate in the counseling process.

To obtain informed consent, counselors should communicate clearly and use language that is easily understood by the client, taking into account any cultural or language barriers. This process should be documented through a signed consent form, which serves as evidence that the client has been informed and agrees to the terms of counseling.

Informed consent is not a one-time event but an ongoing process. Counselors must revisit consent as therapy progresses, particularly when there are changes in treatment plans or when new issues arise. This ensures that clients remain informed and engaged in their treatment decisions.

Counselors must also be aware of specific legal requirements regarding informed consent, which can vary by jurisdiction. Understanding these requirements is crucial for maintaining ethical standards and protecting both the client's rights and the counselor's professional integrity.

1.13 Confidentiality in Electronic Communication:

Discuss Confidentiality As It Applies To Electronic Communication:

Confidentiality in electronic communication refers to the ethical and legal obligation of mental health counselors to protect client information shared through digital platforms. This includes emails, text messages, video conferencing, and any other form of electronic communication used in the therapeutic process. Counselors must ensure that these communications are secure and that client privacy is maintained.

To uphold confidentiality, counselors should utilize encrypted communication tools and platforms that comply with regulations such as the Health Insurance Portability and Accountability Act (HIPAA). They should inform clients about the potential risks associated with electronic communication, including breaches of privacy and data security. Informed consent should be obtained, detailing how electronic communications will be used and the measures taken to protect client information.

Counselors must also establish clear policies regarding the use of electronic communication, including response times, boundaries around communication outside of scheduled sessions, and procedures for handling emergencies. Regularly updating security protocols and staying informed about technological advancements are essential practices for maintaining confidentiality.

Additionally, it is important for counselors to document all electronic communications as part of the client's record while ensuring that these records are stored securely. By adhering to these practices, mental health counselors can effectively manage confidentiality in the realm of electronic communication.

1.14 Group Rules and Termination Criteria:

Establishing group rules, expectations, and termination criteria is a fundamental aspect of effective group counseling. It involves setting clear guidelines that govern the behavior and interactions of group members to foster a safe and productive therapeutic environment. Group rules are the agreed-upon norms that ensure respect, confidentiality, and active participation. These rules might include maintaining confidentiality, respecting others' opinions, and attending sessions regularly.

Expectations outline what members can anticipate from the group process and from each other. They clarify the roles of both the counselor and the participants, emphasizing mutual support and a commitment to personal growth. Expectations may also address punctuality, engagement levels, and the willingness to provide and receive feedback.

Termination criteria specify the conditions under which a member may leave the group. These criteria help manage transitions smoothly and maintain group integrity. They might include achieving personal goals, completing a predetermined number of sessions, or reaching a consensus with the counselor regarding readiness to leave.

By clearly defining these elements at the outset, counselors create a structured framework that facilitates trust, cohesion, and accountability within the group. This preparation not only enhances therapeutic outcomes but also ensures that all members have a shared understanding of their responsibilities and rights throughout the counseling process.

1.15 Assessing Informed Consent Competency:

In the realm of mental health counseling, assessing a client's competency to provide informed consent is a critical ethical and legal responsibility. Competency refers to the client's ability to understand the information presented, appreciate the consequences of their decisions, and communicate their preferences. Informed consent is a process that ensures clients are fully aware of the nature, purpose, risks, and benefits of treatment before agreeing to participate.

To assess competency, counselors must evaluate several cognitive and emotional factors. First, they should determine whether the client can comprehend information relevant to the treatment, such as understanding the diagnosis and proposed interventions. This involves gauging the client's intellectual capacity and attention span.

Second, counselors must assess the client's ability to appreciate the situation and its potential outcomes. This includes recognizing how treatment may affect their life and weighing risks against benefits.

Third, it is essential for counselors to ensure that clients can reason logically about treatment options. This involves evaluating their decision-making process and ensuring it is not impaired by mental health conditions or external pressures.

Finally, counselors must confirm that clients can express a choice consistently. If any doubts arise regarding competency, seeking further evaluation or involving legal guardians may be necessary to uphold ethical standards. Assessing competency is fundamental to protecting client autonomy and fostering therapeutic trust.

1.16 Monitoring Therapeutic Relationships and Trust:

Monitoring the therapeutic relationship and building trust are essential components of effective counseling. The therapeutic relationship is the professional bond between the counselor and the client, characterized by mutual respect, empathy, and collaboration. To monitor this relationship, counselors must remain attentive to the dynamics at play, such as power imbalances, communication patterns, and emotional responses. Regularly assessing these elements helps identify potential issues that may hinder progress.

Building trust involves creating a safe environment where clients feel understood and respected. This is achieved through consistent, nonjudgmental listening and maintaining confidentiality. Counselors should demonstrate a genuine interest in the client's well-being and validate their experiences. Transparency about the counseling process and setting clear boundaries also reinforce trust.

Counselors should be aware of cultural, social, and individual factors that influence trust-building. Tailoring approaches to meet diverse needs enhances the therapeutic alliance. Addressing ruptures or misunderstandings promptly is crucial for maintaining trust. This requires open dialogue and a willingness to adjust strategies as needed.

Effective monitoring and trust-building contribute to positive therapeutic outcomes by fostering client engagement and promoting self-disclosure. Counselors must continuously refine these skills to adapt to each unique client-counselor relationship, ensuring a supportive framework for personal growth and healing.

1.17 Review Client Records:

Reviewing client records is a critical component of professional practice and ethics in mental health counseling. It involves the systematic examination of documentation related to a client's therapeutic journey, including initial assessments, treatment plans, progress notes, and any correspondence or reports from other professionals involved in the client's care. This process ensures that counselors maintain a comprehensive understanding of the client's history, current concerns, and treatment progress.

The review of client records serves multiple purposes. Firstly, it aids in continuity of care by providing a detailed account of previous interventions and their outcomes, allowing for informed decision-making regarding future therapeutic strategies. Secondly, it ensures compliance with legal and ethical standards, as accurate and up-to-date records are essential for accountability and transparency in clinical practice. Thirdly, reviewing records facilitates effective communication among multidisciplinary teams by offering insights into the client's background and therapeutic needs.

Counselors must approach record review with diligence and confidentiality, ensuring that all information is handled in accordance with privacy regulations such as HIPAA. This process not only enhances the quality of care provided but also reinforces the counselor's commitment to ethical practice by safeguarding client information and fostering trust within the therapeutic relationship. Proper documentation and regular review are integral to successful client outcomes and professional integrity.

1.18 Ensuring Disability Accommodations:

Providing adequate accommodations for clients with disabilities is a critical aspect of ethical mental health counseling practice. This involves ensuring that all clients, regardless of their physical or cognitive limitations, have equal access to therapeutic services. Counselors must be proactive in identifying and addressing barriers that could impede a client's ability to participate fully in counseling sessions.

Accommodations can include physical modifications, such as ensuring wheelchair accessibility or providing assistive listening devices for individuals with hearing impairments. Additionally, counselors should be prepared to offer alternative communication methods, such as sign language interpretation or written materials in Braille, to meet the needs of clients with sensory disabilities.

Mental health professionals are also responsible for creating an inclusive environment that respects the dignity and autonomy of clients with disabilities. This may involve adapting therapeutic techniques to suit the client's unique abilities and preferences, ensuring that they receive personalized care.

Counselors should stay informed about relevant laws and regulations, such as the Americans with Disabilities Act (ADA), which mandates reasonable accommodations in public services. By doing so, they uphold ethical standards and foster an equitable therapeutic environment. Continuous education and collaboration with disability advocacy groups can further enhance a counselor's ability to serve this population effectively.

1.19 Third-Party Information Disclosure:

In the realm of mental health counseling, Provide Information to Third Parties refers to the ethical and legal considerations involved when sharing client information with individuals or entities outside the therapeutic relationship. This process is governed by strict confidentiality protocols to protect client privacy, as outlined by professional ethical standards and legal regulations such as the Health Insurance Portability and Accountability Act (HIPAA).

Counselors must obtain informed consent from clients before disclosing any information to third parties, except in situations where disclosure is mandated by law, such as cases of abuse, imminent harm to self or others, or court orders. Informed consent involves explaining the purpose of disclosure, the nature of the information to be shared, and the potential consequences.

Furthermore, counselors are responsible for ensuring that only necessary information is disclosed and that it is shared with appropriate parties who have a legitimate need to know. This includes other healthcare providers involved in the client's treatment, insurance companies for billing purposes, or legal representatives.

Counselors must document all disclosures accurately in client records, maintaining transparency and accountability. Ethical practice requires ongoing assessment of the necessity and impact of sharing information, always prioritizing client welfare and adhering to professional guidelines. Understanding these parameters is crucial for mental health counselors preparing for the NCMHCE exam.

1.20 Referral Sources for Inadequate Counseling Services:

In the practice of mental health counseling, it is crucial for counselors to recognize when their services may not adequately meet a client's needs or when they are inappropriate due to the counselor's scope of practice or expertise. Providing referral sources is an ethical obligation that ensures clients receive the best possible care tailored to their specific needs.

A comprehensive referral process involves assessing the client's situation and determining the limitations of current counseling services. Counselors must maintain awareness of their professional boundaries and competencies, acknowledging when specialized interventions are required. This may include cases involving severe mental health disorders, substance abuse issues, or legal concerns that fall outside the counselor's expertise.

Once a need for referral is identified, counselors should provide clients with information about alternative resources and professionals who can offer appropriate support. This includes offering details about specialists, community resources, or organizations that can address the client's unique challenges. The referral process should be conducted with sensitivity and respect for the client's autonomy, ensuring they understand their options and feel supported throughout the transition.

Ultimately, providing referral sources safeguards client welfare and upholds ethical standards in mental health counseling, reinforcing the counselor's role as an advocate for effective and appropriate client care.

1.21 Advocacy for Professional and Client Concerns:

Advocacy in mental health counseling involves representing and supporting the needs and rights of clients as well as the profession itself. Counselors act as advocates by working to remove barriers that impede client well-being and access to services. This includes addressing systemic issues such as discrimination, stigma, and inadequate resources. Advocacy can occur on multiple levels: individual, organizational, community, and policy.

At the individual level, counselors empower clients by helping them navigate personal challenges and encouraging self-advocacy skills. On an organizational level, counselors may work to improve agency policies to better serve clients. Community advocacy involves raising awareness about mental health issues and promoting social change to improve conditions for individuals with mental health concerns.

For professional issues, advocacy entails promoting the counseling profession's role within the broader healthcare system. This includes engaging in activities that highlight the importance of mental health services, lobbying for legislative changes that benefit both counselors and clients, and ensuring that ethical standards are upheld across the profession.

Effective advocacy requires counselors to be informed about current issues affecting their clients and the profession, possess strong communication skills, and collaborate with other professionals and stakeholders. By advocating for both professional and client issues, counselors contribute to a more equitable, effective, and responsive mental health care system.

1.22 Supervision:

Supervision in the context of mental health counseling refers to a structured process in which a more experienced practitioner, known as the supervisor, provides guidance, support, and feedback to a less experienced counselor or supervisee. This process is essential for professional development, ensuring ethical practice, and enhancing clinical skills. Supervision serves multiple functions: it is educational, supportive, and administrative.

Educationally, supervision aims to develop the supervisee's competencies by discussing case conceptualization, therapeutic techniques, and theoretical frameworks. It provides a space for reflective practice, enabling counselors to critically analyze their work and improve their clinical acumen. Supportively, supervision offers emotional backing and stress management strategies, helping counselors navigate the emotional demands of their profession. It creates a safe environment where counselors can express concerns and receive validation.

Administratively, supervision ensures adherence to ethical standards and organizational policies. It involves monitoring caseloads, documentation practices, and compliance with legal requirements. Supervisors are responsible for evaluating the supervisee's performance and providing constructive feedback.

Effective supervision is characterized by clear communication, mutual respect, and a collaborative relationship. It requires confidentiality to foster trust and openness. Through regular supervision sessions, mental health counselors enhance their professional identity, ensuring they provide competent and ethical care to clients. This ongoing process is crucial for maintaining high standards in mental health practice.

1.23 Counseling Process Documentation:

Creating and maintaining documentation is a critical component of the counseling process. It involves systematically recording information that reflects the client's journey through therapy. Proper documentation begins with intake forms, which gather essential personal, medical, and psychological history to establish a baseline for treatment. Progress notes are then maintained throughout the therapeutic relationship, detailing session content, therapeutic interventions, client responses, and any changes in treatment plans. These notes should be clear, concise, and objective, adhering to professional standards such as the SOAP (Subjective, Objective, Assessment, Plan) format.

Documentation also includes treatment plans that outline specific goals and objectives tailored to the client's needs. These plans should be regularly reviewed and updated to reflect progress or necessary adjustments. Additionally, informed consent forms and confidentiality agreements must be documented to ensure ethical compliance and protect both the counselor and the client.

Maintaining accurate records is not only a legal obligation but also enhances continuity of care by providing a comprehensive overview of the client's progress. It facilitates communication among healthcare providers if referrals or consultations are needed. Furthermore, thorough documentation serves as a defense in legal or ethical inquiries. Thus, mental health counselors must prioritize meticulous record-keeping to uphold professional integrity and ensure effective client care.

1.24 Self-Care Awareness and Practice:

Awareness and practice of self-care are critical components for mental health counselors to maintain their well-being and effectiveness in their professional roles. Self-care refers to the conscious act of taking care of one's physical, emotional, and mental health. For counselors, this involves recognizing the impact of their work on their personal well-being and taking proactive steps to manage stress and prevent burnout.

Self-care awareness begins with self-reflection and self-assessment, allowing counselors to identify areas where they may be vulnerable to stress or emotional exhaustion. This awareness is crucial for recognizing early signs of burnout, such as fatigue, irritability, or decreased job satisfaction. By understanding these indicators, counselors can implement self-care strategies tailored to their needs.

Effective self-care practices may include regular physical activity, adequate rest, maintaining a balanced diet, engaging in hobbies, seeking supervision or consultation, and setting professional boundaries. Additionally, counselors should prioritize personal therapy or support groups to process their emotions and experiences.

The practice of self-care not only enhances the counselor's well-being but also improves therapeutic outcomes for clients. By modeling healthy self-care behaviors, counselors can encourage clients to adopt similar practices. Ultimately, consistent self-care fosters resilience and longevity in the counseling profession, ensuring that counselors remain empathetic and effective in their roles.

2   Intake, Assessment, And Diagnosis:

The process of intake, assessment, and diagnosis in mental health counseling is a critical foundational stage that guides the therapeutic journey. Intake involves the initial interaction between the counselor and the client, during which essential information is gathered to understand the client's presenting concerns and background. This phase sets the tone for the therapeutic relationship and ensures that the client feels heard and understood.

Assessment is a systematic process in which counselors collect data through various methods, such as interviews, questionnaires, and psychological testing. The aim is to gain a comprehensive understanding of the client's emotional, cognitive, and behavioral functioning. This phase helps identify strengths, weaknesses, and potential areas of concern that require intervention.

Diagnosis involves analyzing the collected data to identify any mental health disorders according to standardized criteria, such as those outlined in the DSM-5 (Diagnostic and Statistical Manual of Mental Disorders). Accurate diagnosis is crucial, as it informs treatment planning and interventions. It requires a thorough understanding of symptomatology, differential diagnosis, and cultural considerations to avoid misdiagnosis.

Throughout these stages, ethical considerations such as informed consent, confidentiality, and cultural competence are paramount. The integration of intake, assessment, and diagnosis forms the backbone of effective counseling practice by providing a structured approach to understanding and addressing clients' mental health needs.

2.1 Conduct A Biopsychosocial Interview:

A biopsychosocial interview is a comprehensive assessment tool utilized by mental health counselors to gather detailed information about a client's biological, psychological, and social factors that may influence their mental health. This multidimensional approach allows the counselor to understand the client's overall functioning and develop an effective treatment plan.

Biologically, the interview explores the client's medical history, including any current or past illnesses, medications, and family health history. This helps identify any physiological factors that might affect mental health. Psychologically, the counselor assesses the client's emotional state, cognitive processes, behavioral patterns, and past psychological issues or treatments. This component aims to uncover underlying psychological conditions or stressors contributing to the client's current concerns.

Socially, the interview examines the client's relationships, support systems, cultural background, socioeconomic status, and environmental influences. Understanding these aspects provides insight into external factors impacting the client's mental well-being and coping mechanisms.

The biopsychosocial interview is structured yet flexible, allowing counselors to tailor questions based on individual client needs. It requires active listening, empathy, and clinical judgment to accurately interpret the gathered information. By conducting a thorough biopsychosocial interview, counselors can formulate a holistic understanding of the client's situation, which is crucial for accurate diagnosis and personalized intervention strategies in mental health counseling.

2.2 Conduct A Diagnostic Interview:

A diagnostic interview is a structured or semi-structured conversation conducted by a mental health counselor to gather comprehensive information about a client's psychological, emotional, and behavioral functioning. This process is essential for identifying mental health disorders and developing an effective treatment plan. During the diagnostic interview, the counselor employs various techniques to assess the client's history, presenting problems, symptomatology, and psychosocial context.

The interview typically begins with establishing rapport and ensuring that the client feels comfortable and understood. Counselors use open-ended questions to explore the client's chief complaints and symptoms in detail. They also inquire about the onset, duration, and intensity of symptoms, as well as any factors that exacerbate or alleviate them. The interview delves into the client's personal history, including developmental milestones, family dynamics, educational background, occupational history, and social relationships.

Additionally, the counselor evaluates risk factors such as substance use, trauma history, and any previous mental health treatments. The diagnostic interview may incorporate standardized assessment tools or questionnaires to support clinical observations. Throughout the process, counselors remain attuned to nonverbal cues and cultural considerations that might influence the client's experiences.

Ultimately, conducting a diagnostic interview enables counselors to formulate an accurate diagnosis in alignment with established criteria such as the DSM-5 or ICD-10, facilitating targeted therapeutic interventions tailored to the client's unique needs.

2.3 Conduct Cultural Formulation Interview:

The Cultural Formulation Interview (CFI) is a structured tool used by mental health counselors to assess the cultural factors influencing a client's psychological state and treatment. It is an integral part of the diagnostic process, ensuring that cultural context is considered in understanding the client's experiences and symptoms. The CFI consists of a series of questions designed to gather information about the individual's cultural identity, cultural explanations of their illness, cultural factors related to the psychosocial environment and levels of functioning, and cultural elements of the relationship between the individual and the clinician.

Conducting a Cultural Formulation Interview involves actively listening to the client and being sensitive to their cultural background. The interview helps identify potential cultural barriers to treatment adherence and engagement. It encourages clients to share their perspectives on their condition, which can reveal culturally specific stressors or supports that may affect their mental health.

The CFI also aids in developing culturally appropriate treatment plans by highlighting the client's values, beliefs, and practices that may influence therapy. By incorporating cultural understanding into diagnosis and treatment, mental health counselors can provide more effective and personalized care, thereby improving therapeutic outcomes. This process underscores the importance of cultural competence in mental health practice.

2.4 Conduct An Initial Interview:

Conducting an initial interview is a critical component of the intake, assessment, and diagnosis process in mental health counseling. This initial interaction sets the foundation for the therapeutic relationship and informs subsequent treatment planning. During the initial interview, the counselor gathers comprehensive information about the client's presenting concerns, psychological history, medical background, and social context. The primary objective is to establish rapport while simultaneously collecting data that will aid in formulating a preliminary diagnosis.

The process involves open-ended questions that encourage clients to share their experiences and feelings freely. It is essential for the counselor to be empathetic and non-judgmental, creating a safe space for the client to express themselves. Key areas explored include the client's current symptoms, the duration and intensity of these symptoms, past mental health issues, family dynamics, occupational functioning, and any potential risk factors such as substance use or suicidal ideation.

Additionally, the counselor assesses the client's cognitive functioning and emotional state through observation and interaction. The initial interview also involves discussing the limits of confidentiality and obtaining informed consent. By meticulously conducting this interview, counselors can develop a holistic understanding of the client's needs, paving the way for accurate diagnosis and effective treatment planning. This foundational step is crucial for achieving successful therapeutic outcomes.

2.5 Determine Diagnosis:

Determining a diagnosis in the context of mental health counseling involves a systematic process of identifying and classifying a client's psychological condition based on observed symptoms, client history, and clinical judgment. This process is critical for developing an effective treatment plan and involves several key steps.

Firstly, counselors gather comprehensive data through interviews, standardized assessments, and collateral information to understand the client's presenting issues. This data collection is crucial to ensure that all relevant factors are considered. Counselors then analyze this information to identify patterns or clusters of symptoms that align with specific diagnostic criteria outlined in the Diagnostic and Statistical Manual of Mental Disorders (DSM-5).

A thorough understanding of differential diagnosis is essential, as it involves distinguishing between disorders with similar presentations to avoid misdiagnosis. Counselors must also consider cultural, social, and environmental factors that may influence symptomatology and presentation.

Furthermore, diagnosing is not a one-time event but an ongoing process that requires continual reassessment as new information emerges or as the client's condition evolves. Ethical considerations are paramount; counselors must ensure that diagnoses are made objectively, without bias, and with the client's best interests in mind.

Ultimately, determining a diagnosis provides a framework for understanding the client's experiences and guides the therapeutic process toward achieving meaningful outcomes.

2.6 Conducting a Mental Status Exam (MSE):

A Mental Status Exam (MSE) is a structured assessment tool used by mental health counselors to evaluate a client's cognitive, emotional, and psychological functioning at a specific point in time. The MSE provides a comprehensive snapshot of the client's current mental state, aiding in diagnosis and treatment planning. It involves direct observation and interaction with the client, focusing on several key domains.

The MSE assesses appearance (grooming, attire), behavior (eye contact, motor activity), speech (rate, volume), mood and affect (emotional state and expression), thought process (coherence, logic), thought content (delusions, obsessions), perception (hallucinations), cognition (orientation, memory, attention), insight (awareness of condition), and judgment (decision-making capacity).

Each domain is evaluated systematically to identify any abnormalities or deviations from typical functioning. For example, an examiner might note if speech is pressured or if mood is incongruent with the situation. This detailed analysis aids in forming a differential diagnosis by highlighting symptoms that align with specific mental health disorders.

The MSE is integral to the intake process, as it provides baseline data against which changes over time can be measured. By mastering the MSE, mental health counselors enhance their clinical acumen, improving their ability to develop effective treatment strategies tailored to the client's unique needs.

2.7 Consider Co-occurring Diagnoses:

Co-occurring diagnoses, also known as comorbid or dual diagnoses, refer to the presence of two or more disorders in an individual simultaneously. In mental health counseling, this typically involves the coexistence of a mental health disorder and a substance use disorder, though it can also encompass multiple mental health conditions. Recognizing and addressing co-occurring diagnoses is crucial because these disorders can interact in complex ways, potentially exacerbating one another and complicating treatment.

When considering co-occurring diagnoses, counselors must conduct comprehensive assessments that include detailed client histories, symptom evaluations, and possibly standardized diagnostic tools. It is essential to discern how these disorders influence each other. For instance, substance use might be a coping mechanism for managing symptoms of depression or anxiety, or conversely, substance abuse might precipitate or worsen psychiatric symptoms.

Treatment planning should be integrated and holistic, addressing all diagnoses concurrently rather than in isolation. This may involve collaboration with other healthcare providers to ensure a multidisciplinary approach. Effective treatment often includes a combination of psychotherapy, medication management, and support groups tailored to address both the mental health and substance use components.

Understanding co-occurring diagnoses enables mental health counselors to provide more effective interventions, ultimately improving client outcomes and promoting sustained recovery.

2.8 Assessing Care Level Requirements:

Determining the level of care needed is a critical component of the intake, assessment, and diagnosis process in mental health counseling. It involves evaluating the severity and complexity of a client's symptoms, their functional impairment, and their support systems to decide on the most appropriate treatment setting. This decision-making process ensures that clients receive care tailored to their specific needs, promoting optimal recovery outcomes.

In practice, determining the level of care requires a thorough assessment of the client's mental health status, including psychiatric history, current symptomatology, risk factors such as suicidal or homicidal ideation, and potential substance use issues. Counselors must also consider environmental factors, including family dynamics, social support networks, and living situations. Tools such as standardized assessment instruments and clinical interviews are often utilized to gather comprehensive data.

The levels of care range from outpatient services for less severe cases to more intensive interventions, such as partial hospitalization or inpatient treatment, for those with acute needs. The goal is to match the client with a setting that provides sufficient structure and support while allowing for independence where appropriate. This decision is revisited regularly throughout treatment to ensure alignment with the client's evolving needs and progress. Accurate determination of the care level is essential for effective treatment planning and resource allocation.

2.9 Choosing the Right Treatment Modality:

Determining the appropriate modality of treatment involves selecting the most effective therapeutic approach based on the client's unique needs, diagnosis, and presenting issues. This process requires a comprehensive understanding of various counseling modalities, including individual therapy, group therapy, family therapy, and couples therapy. Each modality offers distinct advantages and may be more suitable for certain conditions or client preferences.

To determine the appropriate modality, mental health counselors must first conduct a thorough assessment to gather information about the client's history, symptoms, and treatment goals. This assessment involves evaluating factors such as the severity of symptoms, the client's support system, cultural background, and any co-occurring disorders. The counselor must also consider evidence-based practices and current research findings related to specific treatment modalities for particular diagnoses.

Once the assessment is complete, the counselor collaborates with the client to discuss potential treatment options. This collaborative approach ensures that the selected modality aligns with the client's values and preferences, thereby increasing engagement and adherence to the therapeutic process. Additionally, counselors should remain flexible and open to adjusting the treatment plan as needed based on the client's progress and feedback.

Ultimately, determining the appropriate modality of treatment is a dynamic process that requires clinical expertise, client-centered care, and an ongoing commitment to evaluating treatment efficacy.

2.10 Evaluating Presenting Problems and Distress Levels:

Assessing the presenting problem and level of distress is a critical component in the initial stages of mental health counseling. This process involves identifying the client's primary concerns, symptoms, and the degree to which these issues impact their daily functioning. A comprehensive assessment begins with an open-ended inquiry into the client's reasons for seeking therapy, allowing them to express their concerns in their own words. Counselors should actively listen and observe both verbal and non-verbal cues to gather a holistic understanding of the client's experiences.

The level of distress is evaluated by determining the intensity, frequency, and duration of symptoms. Counselors may employ standardized assessment tools, such as the Beck Depression Inventory or the Generalized Anxiety Disorder 7-item scale, to quantify distress levels objectively. Additionally, exploring the client's coping mechanisms, support systems, and previous mental health history provides context for their current state.

Understanding the presenting problem within the client's cultural, social, and personal framework is essential for accurate assessment. The counselor must remain empathetic and nonjudgmental while considering potential biases or assumptions. This assessment guides treatment planning by prioritizing issues that require immediate attention and setting realistic therapeutic goals. Effectively assessing the presenting problem and level of distress ensures that interventions are tailored to meet the client's unique needs, promoting positive therapeutic outcomes.

2.11 Assessing Mental Health Functioning:

Evaluating an individual's level of mental health functioning involves a comprehensive assessment to determine their psychological, emotional, and social well-being. This process is integral to forming an accurate diagnosis and developing an effective treatment plan. Mental health functioning is assessed through various methods, including clinical interviews, standardized assessments, observations, and collateral information.

During the clinical interview, counselors gather detailed information about the individual's history, current symptoms, and overall functioning in daily life. This includes assessing mood, behavior, thought processes, and interpersonal relationships. Standardized assessments may be used to quantify specific aspects of mental health, such as levels of depression or anxiety.

Observations provide insights into the individual's demeanor, communication style, and non-verbal cues that may indicate distress or dysfunction. Collateral information from family members or other healthcare providers can offer additional perspectives on the individual's functioning.

Counselors must consider cultural, social, and environmental factors that may influence mental health. It is essential to evaluate the strengths and resources that the individual can leverage for recovery. The goal is to establish a baseline of functioning to monitor progress over time and adjust interventions as needed. Accurate evaluation supports effective counseling outcomes by tailoring interventions to meet the unique needs of each client.

2.12 Client Service Screening:

Screening clients for appropriate services is a critical process in mental health counseling that involves evaluating a client's needs to determine the most suitable therapeutic interventions and resources. This process begins with an initial assessment, during which the counselor gathers comprehensive information about the client's psychological, emotional, and social functioning. The goal is to identify any presenting issues, such as symptoms of mental disorders, substance use, or life stressors, that may require specialized intervention.

During screening, counselors must consider various factors, such as the severity and duration of symptoms, the client's history, and any co-occurring conditions. It is essential to use standardized screening tools and evidence-based practices to ensure accuracy and objectivity in identifying client needs. Additionally, cultural competence plays a significant role in understanding the client's background and ensuring that services are tailored appropriately.

The outcome of this screening process is a referral or recommendation for specific services that align with the client's identified needs. This could include individual therapy, group counseling, psychiatric evaluation, or community support services. Effective screening ensures that clients receive timely and appropriate care, improving their chances of successful outcomes. Mental health counselors must remain vigilant in updating their knowledge of available resources and maintaining collaborative relationships with other professionals to facilitate comprehensive care for their clients.

2.13 Assessment Instrument Selection and Interpretation:

Selecting, using, and interpreting appropriate assessment instruments are critical skills for mental health counselors, ensuring accurate client evaluation and diagnosis. This process begins with selecting the right assessment tools, which requires an understanding of the client's presenting issues, cultural background, and specific needs. Counselors must be knowledgeable about various assessment instruments, including their validity, reliability, and applicability to different populations.

Using these instruments involves administering them in a standardized manner to gather objective data about the client's mental health status. This step necessitates familiarity with the instrument's instructions and an ethical approach to ensure client comfort and confidentiality throughout the assessment process.

Interpreting the results is a nuanced task that requires integrating assessment data with clinical observations and the client's history. Counselors must consider contextual factors such as cultural influences and situational variables that might affect the results. The interpretation should lead to a comprehensive understanding of the client's condition, facilitating accurate diagnosis and informed treatment planning.

Overall, proficiency in selecting, using, and interpreting assessment instruments enhances a counselor's ability to provide effective care. It ensures that interventions are tailored to individual client needs, ultimately promoting better therapeutic outcomes. Mastery of these skills is essential for success on the NCMHCE and in professional practice.

2.14 Formal vs. Informal Observations:

Formal and informal observations are crucial techniques in the intake, assessment, and diagnosis process for mental health counselors. Formal observations involve structured methods in which specific behaviors or interactions are systematically recorded and analyzed. These observations often utilize standardized tools or checklists to ensure consistency and reliability in data collection. For instance, a counselor may use a behavior rating scale to assess a client's social interactions during a group therapy session.

In contrast, informal observations are less structured and occur naturally during client interactions. These observations allow counselors to gather qualitative data by noting spontaneous behaviors, emotional expressions, and non-verbal cues. For example, a counselor might observe a client's body language or tone of voice during a conversation to gain insights into their emotional state or level of engagement.

Both formal and informal observations provide valuable information that contributes to a comprehensive understanding of the client's psychological functioning. They help in identifying patterns, assessing progress, and tailoring interventions to meet the client's unique needs. Effective use of these observation methods requires counselors to be attentive, unbiased, and culturally sensitive. By integrating both approaches, counselors enhance their ability to make accurate diagnoses and develop effective treatment plans that align with the client's goals and circumstances.

2.15 Assess For Trauma:

Assessing for trauma involves systematically evaluating a client's history and current symptoms to determine the presence and impact of traumatic experiences. Trauma assessment is critical in mental health counseling, as it helps identify potential underlying causes of psychological distress and guides treatment planning.

A comprehensive trauma assessment includes gathering information about the client's exposure to potentially traumatic events, such as physical or sexual abuse, natural disasters, accidents, or witnessing violence. Counselors should employ a trauma-informed approach, ensuring a safe and supportive environment where clients feel comfortable disclosing sensitive information.

Key components of trauma assessment include exploring the client's emotional and physiological responses to these events, identifying any post-traumatic stress symptoms (e.g., flashbacks, hyperarousal, avoidance), and understanding the impact on their daily functioning and relationships. It is essential to assess both recent and past traumas, as unresolved earlier experiences can influence current mental health.

Counselors should use validated assessment tools and structured interviews to obtain reliable data while being mindful of cultural considerations that may affect how trauma is experienced and expressed. The goal is to develop a nuanced understanding of how trauma affects the client, facilitating the creation of an individualized treatment plan that addresses specific needs and promotes healing and resilience.

2.16 Assess Substance Use:

Assessing substance use is a crucial component of the intake, assessment, and diagnosis process in mental health counseling. It involves systematically evaluating an individual's substance use patterns, the impact on their psychological and physical health, and any related behavioral issues. This assessment helps identify the presence of a substance use disorder and informs the development of an appropriate treatment plan.

The assessment process typically begins with a detailed clinical interview, during which counselors gather information about the frequency, quantity, and context of substance use. Counselors may utilize standardized screening tools such as the CAGE questionnaire or the Alcohol Use Disorders Identification Test (AUDIT) to quantify use and identify potential problems. Additionally, assessing co-occurring mental health disorders is essential, as these can influence or exacerbate substance use issues.

Counselors should also explore the individual's motivation for using substances, potential triggers, and any past attempts at cessation or treatment. Understanding the social and environmental factors that contribute to substance use is vital for developing effective interventions.

Furthermore, assessing the client's readiness for change can guide treatment planning and intervention strategies. This comprehensive evaluation not only aids in diagnosing substance use disorders but also supports the creation of personalized, evidence-based treatment plans that address both substance-related and co-occurring mental health issues.

2.17 Obtain Client Self-reports:

Obtaining client self-reports is a critical component of the intake, assessment, and diagnosis process in mental health counseling. It involves gathering subjective information directly from the client about their thoughts, feelings, behaviors, and experiences. This self-reported data is invaluable as it provides insight into the client's perspective, allowing counselors to understand the client's internal world and the context of their presenting issues.

The process typically begins with open-ended questions that encourage clients to share their narratives in their own words. Counselors may use structured interviews or standardized questionnaires to facilitate this process. These tools help obtain detailed information about the client's mental health history, current symptoms, lifestyle factors, and any psychosocial stressors they may be experiencing.

Client self-reports are essential for developing an accurate clinical picture and formulating a working diagnosis. They help identify patterns and triggers related to the client's symptoms and provide a baseline for measuring progress over time. It is important for counselors to create a safe and non-judgmental environment to encourage honest and comprehensive self-disclosure.

While self-reports are subjective, they are complemented by other assessment methods, such as behavioral observations and collateral information from family members or other professionals, to ensure a holistic understanding of the client's mental health status.

2.18 Evaluate Interactional Dynamics:

Evaluating interactional dynamics involves assessing the ways in which individuals interact within their relationships and environments. This process is crucial for mental health counselors, as it provides insight into the relational patterns that may contribute to a client's psychological issues. Interactional dynamics encompass verbal and non-verbal communication, power structures, emotional exchanges, and behavioral patterns within relationships.

To effectively evaluate these dynamics, counselors must observe and analyze how clients communicate with others, respond to conflict, express emotions, and maintain or disrupt relational boundaries. This evaluation often includes exploring family systems, social networks, and cultural contexts that influence the client's interactions. Counselors may use techniques such as role-playing, family mapping, or genograms to identify patterns and themes in interactional dynamics.

Understanding these dynamics allows counselors to identify maladaptive patterns that may be perpetuating distress or dysfunction. For example, a client who consistently assumes a submissive role in relationships may struggle with assertiveness or self-esteem issues. By recognizing such patterns, counselors can tailor interventions to promote healthier communication styles, boundary-setting, and relationship skills.

Ultimately, evaluating interactional dynamics equips counselors with a comprehensive understanding of the relational factors impacting a client's mental health, enabling them to develop effective treatment plans that address both individual and systemic issues.

2.19 Ongoing Assessment of At-Risk Behaviors:

Conducting ongoing assessments for at-risk behaviors involves the continuous evaluation of clients to identify and address potential threats to their safety and the safety of others. This process is critical in mental health counseling to prevent harm and ensure that appropriate interventions are implemented.

When assessing suicide risk, counselors must evaluate ideation, plans, means, and previous attempts. It is essential to explore protective factors such as social support and coping strategies while also considering risk factors like mental illness, substance abuse, and recent life changes. In cases of potential homicide or violence towards others, understanding the client's history of aggression, access to weapons, and specific threats is vital.

Self-injury assessments involve identifying triggers, frequency, methods used, and underlying emotional distress. This behavior often serves as a coping mechanism for emotional pain or distress, necessitating a compassionate and non-judgmental approach.

When assessing relationship violence, counselors should evaluate the dynamics of power and control within relationships, the history of abuse, and any immediate threats to safety. This includes both intimate partner violence and familial abuse.

Ongoing assessments require regular check-ins and the updating of safety plans as needed. Mental health counselors must remain vigilant and responsive to changes in behavior or circumstances that could elevate risk levels. Collaboration with other professionals and involving support systems can enhance client safety and well-being.

2.20 Assessing Outcomes with Pre- and Post-Tests:

Pre-test and post-test measures are essential tools in the assessment of therapeutic outcomes, providing a structured approach to evaluating client progress over the course of treatment. Pre-tests are administered at the beginning of therapy to establish a baseline of the client's current functioning, symptoms, and issues. This initial assessment helps identify specific areas of concern and set measurable goals for therapy. Post-tests are conducted after a designated period or at the conclusion of therapy to determine changes in the client's condition or behavior.

These measures can take various forms, including standardized questionnaires, self-report scales, or observational checklists. They offer objective data that can be quantitatively analyzed to assess the effectiveness of therapeutic interventions. By comparing pre-test and post-test results, counselors can identify improvements, stagnations, or regressions in client outcomes.

The use of pre-test and post-test measures also facilitates evidence-based practice by providing empirical support for the efficacy of specific counseling techniques. Furthermore, they enhance client engagement by making progress visible and tangible, thereby boosting motivation and adherence to treatment plans. In clinical settings, these measures contribute to accountability and quality assurance, ensuring that therapeutic practices meet established standards of care.

2.21 Evaluate Counseling Effectiveness:

Evaluating counseling effectiveness is a critical process in mental health counseling that involves assessing the impact and outcomes of therapeutic interventions. This evaluation helps counselors determine whether the goals of therapy are being met and guides any necessary adjustments to the treatment plan. It requires a systematic approach that includes both qualitative and quantitative measures.

Counselors begin by setting clear, measurable objectives with clients at the outset of therapy. These objectives provide a benchmark for assessing progress. Throughout the counseling process, counselors employ various tools and techniques, such as standardized assessments, client self-reports, and observational data, to gather information on client progress.

The evaluation process also involves ongoing feedback from clients about their experiences in therapy. This feedback helps identify which aspects of counseling are effective and which may need modification. Additionally, counselors consider external factors that might influence outcomes, such as changes in the client's environment or life circumstances.

Regularly scheduled reviews of the treatment plan ensure that it remains aligned with the client's evolving needs. Counselors must be adept at interpreting data and making informed decisions based on the evidence collected. Ultimately, evaluating counseling effectiveness ensures that therapeutic interventions are client-centered, goal-oriented, and adaptable, enhancing the overall quality of mental health care provided.

3   Areas Of Clinical Focus:

Areas of Clinical Focus in mental health counseling refer to the specific domains or categories of mental health issues and therapeutic interventions in which counselors are expected to be proficient. These areas encompass a wide range of psychological, emotional, and behavioral issues that clients may present in a clinical setting. For the National Clinical Mental Health Counseling Exam (NCMHCE), understanding these areas is crucial, as they form the foundation of effective assessment, diagnosis, and treatment planning.

Key areas include mood disorders such as depression and bipolar disorder, anxiety disorders including generalized anxiety disorder and panic disorder, trauma and stressor-related disorders like PTSD, substance-related and addictive disorders, and personality disorders. Additionally, counselors must be adept at addressing developmental and life transition challenges, relationship issues, grief and loss, and crisis intervention.

Each area requires knowledge of specific diagnostic criteria, evidence-based therapeutic approaches, and cultural competency to tailor interventions appropriately. Counselors must also demonstrate an understanding of ethical considerations, legal implications, and the ability to integrate various theoretical models to meet the unique needs of each client. Mastery of these clinical focus areas ensures that counselors can provide comprehensive care that promotes mental health recovery and well-being across diverse populations.

3.1 Adjustment to Physical Loss and Illness:

Adjustment related to physical loss, injury, or illness involves the psychological and emotional processes individuals undergo in response to significant changes in their physical health. This adjustment is a multifaceted process that includes coping with the immediate impact of the physical condition, managing ongoing symptoms or disabilities, and integrating these changes into one's self-concept and daily life.

Individuals may experience a range of emotions, such as denial, anger, bargaining, depression, and acceptance, commonly referred to as the stages of grief. These emotional responses can influence their ability to adapt to the new realities imposed by their physical condition. The adjustment process is influenced by several factors, including the severity and prognosis of the condition, individual resilience, available support systems, and pre-existing mental health conditions.

Mental health counselors play a crucial role in facilitating this adjustment by providing therapeutic interventions aimed at enhancing coping strategies, fostering acceptance, and promoting psychological resilience. Techniques such as cognitive-behavioral therapy (CBT), psychoeducation, and supportive counseling are often utilized to help individuals reframe negative thoughts, develop problem-solving skills, and build a supportive network.

Understanding the complexity of adjustment related to physical loss or illness is essential for counselors preparing for the NCMHCE exam, as it equips them with the necessary skills to support clients through challenging transitions in their health journey.

3.2 Aging/geriatric Concerns:

Aging and geriatric concerns encompass the psychological, social, and physiological challenges that individuals face as they age. Mental health counselors must understand these concerns to provide effective support to older adults. Aging often involves dealing with significant life changes such as retirement, the loss of loved ones, and potential declines in physical health, all of which can impact mental well-being.

Cognitive changes are a primary concern; while some memory decline is normal, distinguishing between typical aging and pathological conditions like dementia is crucial. Counselors should be adept at recognizing signs of depression and anxiety, which may manifest differently in older adults compared to younger individuals. Social isolation is another critical issue, as it can exacerbate mental health problems and decrease quality of life.

Counselors must also consider the cultural and individual differences in aging experiences. Some older adults may struggle with identity issues related to their changing roles in society or family dynamics. Ethical considerations are paramount when working with this population, including respecting autonomy and ensuring informed consent.

Overall, mental health counselors should employ a holistic approach that integrates medical, psychological, and social aspects of care to effectively support the unique needs of geriatric clients. Understanding these concerns is essential for promoting resilience and enhancing the quality of life among older adults.

3.3 Behavioral Problems:

Behavioral problems refer to a range of actions or conduct that deviate from societal norms and expectations, often resulting in difficulties in social, academic, or occupational functioning. These problems can manifest as aggression, defiance, hyperactivity, impulsivity, or withdrawal. In the context of mental health counseling, understanding behavioral problems involves recognizing the underlying psychological, environmental, and biological factors that contribute to these behaviors.

Mental health counselors assess behavioral problems by considering the individual's developmental stage, cultural background, and life circumstances. It is crucial to differentiate between behaviors that are developmentally appropriate and those that are indicative of a disorder. For instance, while some level of impulsivity is normal in young children, persistent and severe impulsivity may suggest Attention-Deficit/Hyperactivity Disorder (ADHD).

Effective intervention for behavioral problems often involves a combination of therapeutic techniques, such as Cognitive Behavioral Therapy (CBT), behavior modification strategies, and family therapy. Counselors also work closely with schools and families to create supportive environments that reinforce positive behaviors. Additionally, understanding comorbid conditions like anxiety or depression is essential, as these can exacerbate behavioral issues.

Ultimately, addressing behavioral problems requires a comprehensive approach that includes assessment, intervention planning, and ongoing evaluation to ensure that treatment strategies are effective in promoting adaptive behavior and improving overall functioning.

3.4 Bullying:

Bullying is a form of aggressive behavior characterized by the intentional and repetitive infliction of harm or discomfort upon another individual or group, often involving an imbalance of power. This behavior can manifest physically, verbally, socially, or through digital platforms (cyberbullying). The primary aim of bullying is to assert dominance and control over the victim, causing emotional distress, psychological trauma, and social isolation.

In the context of mental health counseling, understanding bullying is crucial, as it significantly impacts an individual's mental well-being. Victims may experience anxiety, depression, low self-esteem, and, in severe cases, suicidal ideation. Counselors must recognize the signs of bullying, which may include unexplained injuries, changes in behavior such as withdrawal or aggression, and reluctance to attend school or social events.

Effective intervention involves creating a safe environment for disclosure, validating the victim's experiences, and implementing strategies to empower them. Counselors should also work on enhancing resilience and coping skills while collaborating with schools or community resources to address systemic issues contributing to bullying.

For the NCMHCE exam, candidates must demonstrate proficiency in identifying bullying dynamics and developing comprehensive treatment plans that incorporate individual counseling techniques and systemic interventions to mitigate the effects of bullying on mental health.

3.5 Caregiving Concerns:

Caregiving concerns encompass the psychological, emotional, and practical challenges faced by individuals providing care to family members or others with chronic illnesses, disabilities, or age-related conditions. These concerns are significant in the mental health counseling field, as they directly impact the caregiver's well-being and the quality of care provided.

Caregivers often experience high levels of stress, anxiety, and depression due to the demanding nature of caregiving responsibilities. This role can lead to caregiver burnout, characterized by emotional exhaustion, reduced personal accomplishment, and depersonalization. Mental health counselors must recognize these symptoms early to provide effective interventions.

Additionally, caregiving can strain personal relationships and financial resources, leading to feelings of isolation and helplessness. Counselors should assess the caregiver's support systems and encourage the utilization of community resources, such as respite care and support groups.

Understanding cultural factors is crucial, as caregiving roles and expectations vary across different cultures. Counselors should be culturally competent to address these dynamics appropriately.

Interventions may include stress management techniques, cognitive-behavioral strategies to reframe negative thoughts, and the promotion of self-care practices. It is essential for counselors to empower caregivers with coping strategies and resources to maintain their mental health while fulfilling their caregiving duties. This holistic approach ensures both caregiver well-being and effective care for the recipient.

3.6 Cultural Adjustments:

Cultural adjustments refer to the modifications and adaptations individuals make when they encounter different cultural environments, which may include changes in behavior, communication styles, and value systems. For mental health counselors, understanding cultural adjustments is crucial for providing effective and culturally competent care. This involves recognizing how cultural backgrounds influence clients' perceptions of mental health, coping mechanisms, and treatment preferences.

Mental health counselors must be adept at identifying cultural factors that impact a client's mental health, such as beliefs about mental illness, stigma, family dynamics, and societal norms. Counselors should also be aware of their own cultural biases and how these may affect the therapeutic relationship. Employing culturally sensitive assessment tools and interventions is essential for accurately understanding and addressing the client's needs.

Counselors should facilitate an open dialogue about cultural differences with their clients, creating a safe space for clients to express their cultural identities and experiences. This includes being flexible in therapeutic approaches to accommodate diverse cultural perspectives. Furthermore, counselors should engage in continuous education and training to enhance their cultural competence.

In summary, cultural adjustments are vital for mental health counselors to provide effective support that respects and integrates the client's cultural context, thereby promoting better mental health outcomes.

3.7 End-of-life Issues:

End-of-life issues encompass the psychological, emotional, and ethical challenges faced by individuals nearing the end of life, as well as their families and caregivers. These issues are critical for mental health counselors to understand, as they play a pivotal role in providing holistic support during this sensitive period.

Counselors must address anticipatory grief, which involves the emotional preparation for impending loss, both for the dying individual and their loved ones. This process can manifest as anxiety, depression, or denial, requiring counselors to employ empathetic listening and validation techniques to facilitate healthy coping mechanisms.

Ethical considerations often arise concerning autonomy and informed consent in end-of-life care decisions, such as advance directives or do-not-resuscitate orders. Counselors need to navigate these discussions with sensitivity, ensuring that clients' wishes are respected while providing clear information about their options.

Spiritual and existential concerns also surface as individuals confront mortality. Counselors should be prepared to explore clients' beliefs and values, offering support that aligns with their spiritual framework. This may involve collaborating with other professionals, such as chaplains or spiritual advisors.

Furthermore, family dynamics can become strained during this time. Counselors should assist in mediating communication among family members to promote understanding and unity. Overall, addressing end-of-life issues requires a comprehensive approach that respects individual dignity and fosters emotional resilience.

3.8 Fear And Panic:

Fear is an emotional response to a perceived threat that is consciously recognized as danger. It is a natural survival mechanism that triggers the fight-or-flight response, preparing the body to either confront or escape the threat. Fear can be rational and beneficial when it prompts protective actions. However, when fear becomes disproportionate to the actual threat, it can lead to anxiety disorders.

Panic, on the other hand, is an intense and sudden surge of overwhelming fear or anxiety, often accompanied by physical symptoms such as heart palpitations, sweating, trembling, shortness of breath, and dizziness. Panic attacks can occur unexpectedly and may not always be linked to a specific trigger. They are a hallmark feature of panic disorder but can also occur in other anxiety disorders.

In clinical practice, mental health counselors must differentiate between normal fear responses and pathological panic. Effective assessment involves understanding the client's history, identifying triggers, and evaluating the frequency and intensity of panic episodes. Treatment approaches may include cognitive-behavioral therapy (CBT) to modify maladaptive thought patterns and exposure therapy to desensitize clients to feared situations. Pharmacotherapy, such as selective serotonin reuptake inhibitors (SSRIs), may also be considered for managing severe cases. Counselors should provide psychoeducation to help clients understand their symptoms and develop coping strategies for managing fear and panic effectively.

3.9 Financial Issues:

Financial issues in the context of mental health counseling refer to the economic challenges that can significantly impact a client's mental well-being and overall quality of life. These issues may include unemployment, underemployment, debt, lack of access to financial resources, and inadequate financial literacy. Financial stress can exacerbate mental health conditions such as anxiety, depression, and stress-related disorders, creating a cycle that further complicates a client's emotional and psychological state.

As a mental health counselor, it is essential to recognize the interplay between financial issues and mental health. Clients may experience feelings of hopelessness or low self-esteem due to their financial situation, which can hinder their motivation and ability to engage in treatment. Counselors must be equipped to assess the extent to which financial problems are affecting their clients' mental health and incorporate this understanding into their therapeutic approach.

Interventions may involve providing psychoeducation on financial management, collaborating with financial advisors or social services for resource allocation, and developing coping strategies to manage financial stress. By addressing these issues holistically, counselors can help clients regain control over their finances, thereby reducing stress and improving their mental health outcomes. Understanding the nuances of financial issues is crucial for effective clinical practice and for supporting clients in achieving sustainable mental wellness.

3.10 Gender Identity Development:

Gender identity development refers to the process through which individuals come to understand and define their own gender, which may or may not align with the sex assigned at birth. This development typically begins in early childhood and continues into adulthood, influenced by a complex interplay of biological, social, and psychological factors.

In early childhood, children start to form a basic sense of gender identity, often influenced by parental expectations and societal norms. As they grow, children become more aware of gender roles and stereotypes, which can shape their understanding of gender. During adolescence, individuals may explore different aspects of their gender identity more deeply, often experimenting with various expressions and presentations. This period can be marked by questioning and self-discovery, particularly for those whose gender identity does not conform to traditional binary notions.

For some individuals, gender identity development involves recognizing a transgender or non-binary identity. This realization can lead to a need for social or medical transition to align one's outward appearance with their internal sense of self. Mental health counselors play a crucial role in supporting clients through this process by providing a safe space for exploration, offering validation, and assisting with any challenges that arise.

Understanding gender identity development is essential for mental health counselors to provide competent and affirming care to clients navigating their gender journey.

3.11 Grief/loss:

Grief is a natural, multifaceted response to loss, particularly the loss of someone or something with which an individual has formed a significant emotional bond. It encompasses a range of feelings, from deep sadness to anger, and can manifest in physical, emotional, cognitive, and behavioral ways. Loss is not limited to death; it includes any significant change or end in one's life, such as divorce, job loss, or losing a home. Understanding grief involves recognizing its stages denial, anger, bargaining, depression, and acceptance though these stages are not necessarily linear or experienced by everyone.

In clinical practice, mental health counselors must be adept at assessing the impact of grief and loss on clients' mental health and daily functioning. This involves understanding the cultural, social, and personal factors that influence grieving processes. Counselors should provide empathetic support while helping clients navigate their emotions and develop coping strategies. Techniques such as narrative therapy can assist clients in reconstructing their life stories post-loss. It is crucial for counselors to recognize when grief becomes complicated or prolonged, potentially leading to disorders like depression or anxiety, which require more intensive intervention. Effective counseling involves creating a safe space for clients to express their grief while guiding them toward healing and adaptation to their new reality.

3.12 Hopelessness/Depression:

Hopelessness and depression are intricately linked constructs often encountered in clinical mental health settings. Depression is a mood disorder characterized by persistent feelings of sadness, loss of interest or pleasure in activities, and various physical and cognitive symptoms that impair daily functioning. It is a multifaceted condition that can manifest through emotional, cognitive, behavioral, and physiological symptoms.

Hopelessness, on the other hand, is a specific cognitive state often associated with depression. It involves negative expectations about the future and a belief that one's situation will not improve, regardless of efforts to change it. This cognitive distortion can exacerbate depressive symptoms and is considered a significant risk factor for suicidal ideation and behavior.

In clinical practice, understanding the interplay between hopelessness and depression is crucial for effective assessment and intervention. Mental health counselors must be adept at identifying signs of hopelessness in clients with depression, as this can inform treatment planning and risk management strategies. Therapeutic approaches such as Cognitive Behavioral Therapy (CBT) are commonly employed to address these issues by challenging negative thought patterns and fostering a sense of agency and hope.

Recognizing the nuances of hopelessness within the broader context of depression allows counselors to tailor interventions that promote resilience and facilitate recovery, ultimately improving client outcomes.

3.13 Loneliness/attachment:

Loneliness refers to the subjective feeling of being isolated or disconnected from others, despite the potential presence of social relationships. It is a complex emotional state that can significantly impact mental health, leading to conditions such as depression and anxiety. Attachment, on the other hand, is a deep and enduring emotional bond that connects one person to another across time and space. The concept of attachment originates from John Bowlby's attachment theory, which posits that early interactions with caregivers shape an individual's ability to form stable relationships later in life.

In clinical practice, understanding loneliness and attachment is crucial for mental health counselors, as these factors can profoundly influence a client's emotional well-being and interpersonal relationships. Loneliness can arise from inadequate attachment styles developed during childhood, such as anxious or avoidant attachment patterns. These patterns can lead to difficulties in forming secure and trusting relationships in adulthood.

Counselors must assess the client's history of attachment and current experiences of loneliness to develop effective therapeutic interventions. Techniques such as cognitive-behavioral therapy (CBT) can help clients reframe negative thought patterns associated with loneliness. Additionally, fostering secure attachments through therapeutic relationships can enhance clients' relational capacities, thereby reducing feelings of loneliness. Understanding these dynamics is essential for counselors preparing for the NCMHCE exam to effectively support clients in overcoming loneliness and developing healthier attachment styles.

3.14 Hyper/hypo Mental Focus:

Hyper/hypo mental focus refers to the spectrum of attention-related issues where an individual exhibits either excessive (hyper) or insufficient (hypo) levels of concentration and attention. Hyper-focus is characterized by intense, prolonged concentration on a specific task or subject, often to the exclusion of other activities or stimuli. While this can lead to high productivity in certain contexts, it may also result in neglecting essential tasks or responsibilities and can be associated with conditions such as Attention-Deficit/Hyperactivity Disorder (ADHD).

Conversely, hypo-focus involves difficulty in maintaining attention on tasks or activities, leading to frequent distractions and challenges in completing tasks efficiently. This condition can manifest as a symptom of various mental health disorders, including ADHD, depression, and anxiety disorders. Individuals experiencing hypo-focus may struggle with organization, time management, and sustaining attention in both professional and personal settings.

For mental health counselors preparing for the NCMHCE, understanding hyper/hypo mental focus is crucial for accurate assessment and intervention planning. Counselors should be adept at identifying these symptoms through clinical interviews and standardized assessments. Interventions may include cognitive-behavioral strategies, mindfulness practices, and environmental modifications aimed at optimizing the individual's attentional capacity while addressing any underlying psychological conditions contributing to these focus issues.

3.15 Intellectual Functioning Issues:

Intellectual functioning issues refer to challenges related to cognitive abilities that affect an individual's capacity to learn, reason, problem-solve, and adapt to new situations. These issues are often identified through assessments of intelligence quotient (IQ) and can significantly impact daily living, academic performance, and social interactions. Intellectual functioning issues are categorized under neurodevelopmental disorders in the DSM-5 and include conditions such as Intellectual Developmental Disorder (IDD), formerly known as mental retardation.

Individuals with intellectual functioning issues may experience difficulties in abstract thinking, judgment, and decision-making. They might struggle with tasks that require planning, organizing, or understanding complex concepts. These challenges can lead to limitations in adaptive functioning, which encompasses the conceptual, social, and practical skills necessary for independent living.

Assessment of intellectual functioning involves standardized tests administered by professionals trained in psychological evaluation. The results help determine the level of support required for individuals to achieve their full potential. Interventions often include educational support, behavioral therapy, and skill-building activities tailored to the individual's needs.

Understanding intellectual functioning issues is crucial for mental health counselors as they develop treatment plans that accommodate cognitive limitations while promoting strengths and enhancing the quality of life. Counselors play a vital role in advocating for appropriate resources and support systems for individuals facing these challenges.

3.16 Insomnia/Sleep Issues:

Insomnia and sleep issues are prevalent concerns within clinical mental health counseling, often manifesting as difficulties in initiating or maintaining sleep or experiencing non-restorative sleep. Insomnia can be categorized into acute (short-term) or chronic (long-term), with chronic insomnia persisting for at least three nights per week over a period of three months or more. The etiology of insomnia is multifaceted, encompassing psychological factors such as stress, anxiety, and depression, as well as physiological and environmental influences.

Sleep issues can significantly impair daily functioning, cognitive performance, and emotional regulation. They may exacerbate existing mental health disorders or contribute to the development of new ones. Counselors must adopt a biopsychosocial approach to assess the underlying causes of insomnia, considering lifestyle habits, medical history, and psychosocial stressors.

Effective interventions for insomnia include cognitive-behavioral therapy for insomnia (CBT-I), which targets maladaptive thoughts and behaviors associated with sleep disturbances. Additionally, psychoeducation on sleep hygiene practices such as maintaining a consistent sleep schedule, creating a conducive sleep environment, and limiting caffeine intake is crucial. Pharmacotherapy may be considered in conjunction with therapeutic interventions when necessary.

Understanding the complexity of insomnia is essential for mental health counselors to develop tailored treatment plans that address both the symptoms and root causes of sleep disturbances, ultimately enhancing clients' overall well-being and quality of life.

3.17 Maladaptive Eating Behaviors:

Maladaptive eating behaviors are patterns of eating that deviate from typical or healthy eating practices and can negatively impact an individual's physical and mental health. These behaviors often arise as coping mechanisms for emotional distress, anxiety, or stress, and may include binge eating, restrictive dieting, emotional eating, and purging. They are not merely occasional habits but persistent patterns that interfere with daily functioning and well-being.

Binge eating involves consuming large amounts of food in a short period, often accompanied by feelings of loss of control. Restrictive dieting is characterized by limiting food intake to the point where nutritional needs are not met, which can lead to significant weight loss and malnutrition. Emotional eating occurs when individuals eat in response to emotions rather than hunger cues, often choosing high-calorie or comfort foods. Purging involves attempts to rid the body of consumed food through vomiting, excessive exercise, or laxative use.

These behaviors are often linked to underlying psychological issues such as low self-esteem, depression, or anxiety disorders. For mental health counselors, understanding these behaviors is crucial for developing effective treatment plans that address both the psychological and behavioral aspects of maladaptive eating. Interventions may include cognitive-behavioral therapy, mindfulness practices, and nutritional counseling to promote healthier relationships with food.

3.18 Remarriage/Recommitment:

Remarriage or recommitment refers to the process of entering into a new marital relationship after the dissolution of a previous one, whether through divorce, separation, or widowhood. This transition involves complex emotional, psychological, and social dynamics that can impact individuals and their families. Mental health counselors play a crucial role in supporting clients through this life change by addressing various challenges and facilitating healthy adjustments.

In remarriage, individuals may face unresolved issues from previous relationships, such as trust concerns or lingering emotional attachments. Additionally, blending families can introduce unique stressors, including navigating relationships with stepchildren and co-parenting with former spouses. Counselors must be adept at helping clients develop effective communication strategies and conflict resolution skills to foster harmonious family dynamics.

Recommitment also requires individuals to reassess their personal values and expectations within the context of a new partnership. Counselors guide clients in exploring these aspects to ensure alignment with their partner's goals and needs. Furthermore, addressing grief or loss associated with the previous relationship is essential for enabling emotional closure and fostering a positive outlook on the future.

Overall, mental health counselors provide invaluable support in helping clients navigate remarriage or recommitment by promoting self-awareness, enhancing relational skills, and encouraging resilience throughout this transformative journey.

3.19 Developmental Processes/Tasks/Issues:

Developmental processes, tasks, and issues are integral concepts in understanding human growth across the lifespan. These elements encompass the physical, cognitive, emotional, and social changes that individuals experience from infancy through old age. Developmental processes refer to the sequential and predictable patterns of change, such as maturation and learning, which facilitate an individual's adaptation to their environment. Tasks are specific challenges or milestones that individuals are expected to achieve during particular life stages, such as forming an identity in adolescence or achieving intimacy in early adulthood.

Issues in development often arise when there is a disruption or delay in these processes or tasks, potentially leading to psychological distress or maladaptive behaviors. These can include attachment issues in early childhood, identity confusion during adolescence, or role transitions in adulthood. Understanding these developmental concepts is crucial for mental health counselors, as they provide a framework for assessing client concerns and tailoring interventions that align with the client's stage of development.

In clinical practice, counselors must consider how developmental factors influence presenting problems and therapeutic goals. By acknowledging the unique developmental context of each client, counselors can facilitate growth and resilience, helping clients navigate their developmental tasks and effectively overcome related challenges.

3.20 Obsessive Thoughts/behaviors:

Obsessive thoughts and behaviors are hallmark symptoms of Obsessive-Compulsive Disorder (OCD), a mental health condition characterized by persistent, intrusive thoughts (obsessions) and repetitive behaviors or mental acts (compulsions) performed to alleviate the distress caused by these obsessions. Obsessions are unwanted, intrusive thoughts, images, or urges that trigger intensely distressing feelings. Common themes include fears of contamination, harm, or symmetry. Compulsions are behaviors or mental acts that an individual feels driven to perform in response to an obsession or according to rigid rules. These actions are aimed at preventing or reducing anxiety or preventing a feared event; however, they are not realistically connected to what they are designed to neutralize.

From a clinical perspective, it is crucial for mental health counselors to differentiate between normal repetitive behaviors and those indicative of OCD. The key lies in the degree of distress and impairment caused by these obsessions and compulsions. Effective treatment often involves Cognitive Behavioral Therapy (CBT), specifically Exposure and Response Prevention (ERP), which helps individuals confront their fears and reduce their compulsive behaviors. Additionally, pharmacotherapy with selective serotonin reuptake inhibitors (SSRIs) may be prescribed. Understanding the complexity of obsessive thoughts and behaviors is essential for developing a comprehensive treatment plan tailored to the individual needs of clients experiencing OCD symptoms.

3.21 Occupation And Career Development:

Occupation and career development is a critical area of focus for mental health counselors, involving the facilitation of clients' understanding and navigation of their vocational paths. This subtopic encompasses the assessment of clients' interests, skills, values, and personality traits to guide them in making informed career choices that align with their personal goals and life circumstances.

In-depth exploration of this area requires an understanding of various theories and models of career development, such as Holland's RIASEC model, Super's Life-Span, Life-Space Theory, and Krumboltz's Social Learning Theory. Counselors must be adept at utilizing assessments like interest inventories and aptitude tests to aid clients in identifying potential career paths.

Moreover, counselors should be knowledgeable about labor market trends and the impact of economic factors on employment opportunities. They must also consider the role of cultural, social, and psychological factors in the career decision-making process. This includes addressing barriers such as discrimination or lack of resources that may affect clients' career development.

Effective counseling in this domain involves helping clients develop skills for job search strategies, resume writing, and interview preparation. Additionally, counselors support clients in managing work-related stress and achieving work-life balance. Ultimately, the goal is to empower clients to achieve satisfying and sustainable careers that contribute positively to their overall well-being.

3.22 Physical Effects of Anxiety:

Physical issues related to anxiety refer to the physiological symptoms and bodily responses that occur as a result of anxiety disorders. Anxiety triggers the body's fight-or-flight response, leading to various physical manifestations. Common physical symptoms include increased heart rate, palpitations, sweating, trembling, and shortness of breath. These symptoms arise due to the activation of the autonomic nervous system, particularly the sympathetic branch, which prepares the body to respond to perceived threats.

Individuals with anxiety may also experience gastrointestinal disturbances such as nausea, diarrhea, or stomach cramps. Muscle tension is another prevalent symptom, often resulting in headaches or chronic pain. Sleep disturbances, including insomnia or restless sleep, are frequently reported by those suffering from anxiety.

The chronic stress associated with anxiety can contribute to more severe health issues over time. Prolonged activation of the stress response can lead to hypertension and an increased risk of cardiovascular diseases. Additionally, individuals may develop a weakened immune system due to persistent exposure to stress hormones.

Understanding these physical manifestations is crucial for mental health counselors as they assess and develop treatment plans for clients with anxiety disorders. Effective interventions may include cognitive-behavioral therapy (CBT), relaxation techniques, and lifestyle modifications aimed at reducing overall stress levels and alleviating physical symptoms.

3.23 Physical Effects of Depression:

Depression is a multifaceted mental health disorder that not only affects emotional well-being but also manifests in various physical symptoms, significantly impacting an individual's daily functioning. Physical issues related to depression can include chronic pain, fatigue, sleep disturbances, and changes in appetite or weight. These symptoms are often interrelated and can exacerbate the psychological aspects of depression.

Chronic pain, such as headaches, back pain, or muscle aches, is a common physical symptom that can occur without an apparent medical cause. This pain is believed to be linked to the neurotransmitter imbalances associated with depression. Fatigue is another prevalent issue, characterized by persistent tiredness that does not improve with rest. This can lead to decreased motivation and productivity.

Sleep disturbances are also frequently reported by individuals with depression. These may include insomnia, characterized by difficulty falling or staying asleep, or hypersomnia, which involves excessive sleeping. Both can further contribute to feelings of exhaustion and cognitive impairment.

Changes in appetite and weight are additional physical manifestations of depression. Some individuals may experience increased appetite and weight gain, while others may have a reduced appetite leading to significant weight loss. These changes are often tied to mood fluctuations and can affect overall health.

Understanding these physical issues is crucial for mental health counselors as they develop comprehensive treatment plans that address both the psychological and physiological aspects of depression.

3.24 Trauma-Related Physical and Emotional Issues:

Trauma can manifest in both physical and emotional forms, significantly impacting an individual's overall well-being. Physically, trauma may lead to somatic symptoms such as headaches, gastrointestinal disturbances, fatigue, and chronic pain. These symptoms often arise due to the body's heightened stress response, which can result in increased cortisol levels and autonomic nervous system dysregulation. Over time, this physiological stress can contribute to long-term health issues, such as cardiovascular disease or immune system deficiencies.

Emotionally, trauma can cause a wide range of psychological issues, including anxiety, depression, and post-traumatic stress disorder (PTSD). Individuals may experience intrusive thoughts, flashbacks, or nightmares related to the traumatic event. Emotional dysregulation is common, leading to mood swings, irritability, or emotional numbness. Trauma survivors might also struggle with feelings of guilt, shame, or helplessness.

The interplay between physical and emotional symptoms can create a cycle where each exacerbates the other. For instance, chronic pain can lead to increased anxiety or depression, while emotional distress can amplify physical symptoms. Understanding this interconnectedness is crucial for mental health counselors in developing comprehensive treatment plans that address both the physical and emotional aspects of trauma. Effective interventions often include trauma-focused therapy approaches, such as Cognitive Behavioral Therapy (CBT) or Eye Movement Desensitization and Reprocessing (EMDR), which aim to process traumatic memories and reduce symptomatology.

3.25 Process Addictions (pornography, Gambling):

Process addictions, also known as behavioral addictions, refer to compulsive engagement in behaviors that provide short-term rewards but lead to negative consequences in the long run. Unlike substance addictions, process addictions do not involve ingesting a chemical substance; instead, they revolve around behaviors such as pornography use and gambling.

Pornography addiction is characterized by an excessive preoccupation with pornographic material that disrupts daily functioning and relationships. Individuals may experience a loss of control over their viewing habits, leading to significant distress and impairment. This addiction often results in desensitization to sexual stimuli, relationship difficulties, and decreased sexual satisfaction.

Gambling addiction, or pathological gambling, involves persistent and recurrent problematic gambling behavior. It is marked by an inability to control gambling impulses despite adverse consequences such as financial ruin, legal issues, and strained relationships. Individuals with this addiction may chase losses, lie about their gambling activities, and rely on others for financial support.

Both pornography and gambling addictions are maintained through the brain's reward system, which reinforces these behaviors due to the release of dopamine. Treatment typically involves cognitive-behavioral therapy (CBT), which helps individuals identify triggers, develop coping strategies, and restructure maladaptive thought patterns. Understanding these process addictions is crucial for mental health counselors as they work to support clients in achieving recovery and improving their overall well-being.

3.26 Racism/Discrimination/Oppression:

Racism, discrimination, and oppression are interconnected social phenomena that significantly impact mental health. Racism refers to beliefs and practices that assert the superiority of one race over others, often resulting in systemic inequalities. Discrimination involves unjust or prejudicial treatment of individuals based on characteristics such as race, gender, or age. Oppression is the systemic and pervasive mistreatment of individuals within marginalized groups, perpetuating inequality and restricting access to resources and opportunities.

In the context of mental health counseling, it is crucial for counselors to recognize how these factors influence clients' psychological well-being. Racism can lead to chronic stress, anxiety, depression, and trauma, affecting both mental and physical health.

Discrimination can exacerbate feelings of isolation, low self-esteem, and hopelessness. Oppression further compounds these issues by creating barriers to accessing mental health services and support systems.

Counselors must adopt culturally competent practices to effectively address the impacts of racism, discrimination, and oppression. This includes developing an awareness of their own biases, understanding the cultural backgrounds of their clients, and advocating for social justice. By fostering an inclusive therapeutic environment and actively working against systemic inequities, counselors can help mitigate the adverse effects of these social issues on mental health. Understanding these dynamics is essential for those preparing for the NCMHCE exam.

3.27 Religious Values Conflict:
Religious values conflict arises when an individual's religious beliefs or practices clash with their personal values, the values of others, or societal norms. This conflict can manifest in various contexts, such as within familial relationships, workplace settings, or broader community interactions. For mental health counselors, understanding religious values conflict is crucial, as it may significantly impact a client's mental well-being and decision-making processes.

Clients experiencing religious values conflict may struggle with internal dilemmas, such as guilt or anxiety, stemming from perceived contradictions between their faith and personal desires or behaviors. For example, a client might experience distress if their sexual orientation conflicts with their religious teachings. Additionally, external conflicts can occur when a client's religious practices are not accepted by others, leading to social isolation or discrimination.

Counselors must approach these conflicts with cultural competence and sensitivity, ensuring they respect the client's religious beliefs while exploring the impact of these beliefs on their mental health. It is essential to facilitate a safe space for clients to express their concerns and explore potential resolutions that align with both their religious convictions and personal values. By employing empathy and understanding, counselors can help clients navigate these complex conflicts and work towards achieving psychological harmony.

3.28 Retirement Concerns:
Retirement concerns encompass the psychological, emotional, and practical challenges individuals face as they transition from active employment to retirement. This phase of life can trigger anxiety and uncertainty due to significant lifestyle changes, including altered daily routines, loss of professional identity, and shifts in social dynamics. Mental health counselors must understand these multifaceted concerns to effectively support clients navigating this transition.

Financial insecurity is a prevalent concern, as retirees may worry about the adequacy of their savings and the sustainability of their income. Counselors should be prepared to address these anxieties by facilitating discussions around financial planning and connecting clients with appropriate resources.

Additionally, the loss of work-related social interactions can lead to feelings of isolation and loneliness. Mental health counselors can assist clients in identifying and fostering new social connections and activities that provide fulfillment and a sense of purpose.

The transition into retirement may also provoke existential questions about meaning and self-worth. Counselors should encourage clients to explore new interests, hobbies, or volunteer opportunities that align with their values and passions.

By understanding the complexities of retirement concerns, mental health counselors can offer empathetic guidance and practical strategies to help clients adjust successfully to this significant life change.

3.29 Ruminating And/or Intrusive Thoughts:
Ruminating and intrusive thoughts are cognitive phenomena commonly encountered in clinical mental health settings, characterized by repetitive and persistent thought patterns. Rumination involves recurrent thinking about past events or distressing situations, often leading to emotional distress and impaired functioning. These thoughts are typically negative, self-critical, and focused on perceived failures or inadequacies. This pattern of thinking can exacerbate symptoms of depression and anxiety, as individuals become trapped in a cycle of negative reflection without resolution.

Intrusive thoughts, on the other hand, are unwanted and involuntary thoughts that can be distressing or disturbing. These thoughts often intrude into one's consciousness without warning and can be related to fears, obsessions, or traumatic experiences. Unlike rumination, which is more voluntary, intrusive thoughts are often resisted by the individual, causing significant anxiety or discomfort.

Both ruminating and intrusive thoughts can interfere with daily functioning and quality of life. Effective therapeutic interventions may include cognitive-behavioral therapy (CBT), which helps individuals identify and challenge maladaptive thought patterns; mindfulness-based strategies to increase awareness and acceptance of these thoughts without judgment; and exposure-response prevention for those with obsessive-compulsive tendencies. Understanding these thought processes is crucial for mental health counselors to provide appropriate support and treatment to clients struggling with these cognitive challenges.

3.30 Separation From Primary Caregivers:
Separation from primary caregivers refers to the physical and emotional detachment experienced by an individual, typically a child, from their main attachment figures, often parents or guardians. This separation can be temporary or permanent and may occur due to various circumstances, such as parental divorce, death, hospitalization, or foster care placement. The impact of this separation is profound, influencing the individual's emotional, psychological, and social development.

In early childhood, secure attachment to a primary caregiver is crucial for healthy emotional development. When a child is separated from their caregiver, it can lead to anxiety, depression, and attachment disorders. These children may exhibit behaviors such as clinginess, withdrawal, or aggression as they struggle to cope with the loss of security and stability.

Mental health counselors working with individuals who have experienced separation from primary caregivers must assess the extent of the impact on their clients' mental health. Interventions may include therapy focused on building new attachments, enhancing coping mechanisms, and addressing any underlying trauma. Counselors should also work with families to support reunification when possible or help establish stable alternative caregiving arrangements.

Understanding the dynamics of separation from primary caregivers is essential for counselors to provide effective support and facilitate healing and resilience in affected individuals.

3.31 Sexual Functioning Concerns:

Sexual functioning concerns encompass a range of issues related to sexual health, performance, and satisfaction. These concerns can affect individuals of any gender and include problems such as low libido, erectile dysfunction, premature ejaculation, delayed ejaculation, anorgasmia, and pain during intercourse. Mental health counselors must understand that these issues can stem from a variety of causes, including psychological factors like anxiety, depression, stress, or trauma; medical conditions such as diabetes or hormonal imbalances; and relational dynamics like communication problems or lack of intimacy.

When addressing sexual functioning concerns, it is crucial for counselors to adopt a biopsychosocial approach. This involves assessing the biological aspects by collaborating with medical professionals to rule out or address any physiological issues. Psychologically, counselors should explore the client's emotional state, past experiences, and cognitive patterns that may contribute to sexual difficulties. Socially, understanding the client's relationship context and cultural background is essential for providing holistic care.

Counselors should also be aware of the impact of societal norms and expectations on sexual functioning and help clients navigate these pressures. Interventions may include cognitive-behavioral therapy to address maladaptive thoughts, psychoeducation about sexual health, and communication skills training for couples. Ultimately, the goal is to enhance sexual well-being and overall quality of life for clients experiencing these concerns.

3.32 Sleeping Habits:

Sleeping habits refer to the patterns and practices that individuals establish to promote healthy sleep. These habits are crucial for maintaining mental and physical health, as sleep is a fundamental biological process that supports cognitive function, emotional regulation, and overall well-being. Good sleeping habits include maintaining a consistent sleep schedule by going to bed and waking up at the same time every day, even on weekends. This consistency helps regulate the body's internal clock, known as the circadian rhythm.

Creating a restful environment is another essential aspect of healthy sleeping habits. This involves ensuring that the bedroom is quiet, dark, and cool, and using comfortable bedding. Limiting exposure to screens and bright lights before bedtime can also enhance sleep quality by reducing interference with melatonin production, a hormone that regulates sleep-wake cycles.

Additionally, incorporating relaxation techniques such as meditation or deep breathing exercises before bed can help reduce stress and promote better sleep. Avoiding caffeine, nicotine, and heavy meals close to bedtime is also recommended to prevent disruptions in sleep patterns.

Mental health counselors should understand the impact of poor sleeping habits on mental health conditions such as anxiety and depression. Addressing sleep issues can be a critical component of therapeutic interventions aimed at improving clients' overall mental health outcomes.

3.33 Spiritual/existential Concerns:

Spiritual/existential concerns refer to the aspects of an individual's life that pertain to their sense of meaning, purpose, and connection to something greater than themselves. These concerns often emerge during times of crisis or significant life transitions and can manifest as questions about one's purpose, values, beliefs, and identity. In the context of mental health counseling, addressing spiritual/existential concerns involves exploring a client's belief systems and existential questions to facilitate personal growth and psychological well-being.

Counselors must recognize that spiritual and existential issues are deeply personal and can vary widely among individuals. Some clients may find solace in religious practices, while others may seek meaning through philosophical inquiry or connections with nature. It is crucial for counselors to adopt a non-judgmental and open-minded approach, respecting each client's unique perspective.

In therapy, addressing these concerns might involve helping clients articulate their beliefs, examine existential anxieties such as fear of death or feelings of isolation, and explore how these factors influence their mental health. Techniques such as existential therapy, logotherapy, or mindfulness-based interventions can be employed to assist clients in finding meaning and purpose in their lives. Ultimately, addressing spiritual/existential concerns can enhance clients' overall well-being by promoting a sense of coherence and fulfillment.

3.34 Stress Management:

Stress management refers to the techniques and psychotherapeutic strategies aimed at controlling an individual's levels of stress, especially chronic stress, to improve everyday functioning. For mental health counselors, understanding and teaching stress management is crucial, as it directly impacts clients' mental and physical well-being.

Effective stress management involves identifying stressors, which can be both internal (thoughts, beliefs) and external (environmental factors), and developing personalized coping mechanisms. Techniques include cognitive-behavioral strategies that help clients reframe negative thoughts, mindfulness practices that promote present-moment awareness, and relaxation techniques such as deep breathing and progressive muscle relaxation.

Counselors also emphasize the importance of lifestyle modifications, such as regular physical activity, balanced nutrition, adequate sleep, and time management skills to prevent stress accumulation. Encouraging clients to engage in social support networks can provide emotional assistance and practical advice.

Furthermore, counselors may use biofeedback tools to help clients gain awareness of their physiological responses to stress, enabling them to regulate their body's reactions more effectively. By integrating these strategies into therapy, mental health counselors empower clients to build resilience against stressors, enhance their coping skills, and maintain emotional equilibrium. Mastery of these concepts is essential for counselors preparing for the NCMHCE exam, as it demonstrates their ability to facilitate client wellness through comprehensive stress management interventions.

3.35 Substance Use/Addiction Issues:

Substance use and addiction issues encompass a range of maladaptive patterns of substance use, leading to clinically significant impairment or distress. Substance use disorders (SUDs) are characterized by the compulsive use of substances despite adverse consequences, including health problems, disability, and failure to meet major responsibilities at work, school, or home. Addiction is often considered a chronic disease that affects the brain's reward, motivation, and memory circuits, leading to an inability to abstain from the substance and resulting in behavioral control issues.

Mental health counselors must understand the biopsychosocial model of addiction, which recognizes the interplay between biological predispositions, psychological factors such as trauma and stress, and social influences, including peer pressure and cultural norms. Effective assessment involves screening tools like the CAGE questionnaire or the AUDIT (Alcohol Use Disorders Identification Test), which help identify problematic substance use patterns.

Treatment approaches for substance use disorders include evidence-based interventions such as cognitive-behavioral therapy (CBT), motivational interviewing (MI), and contingency management. Additionally, counselors should be knowledgeable about pharmacotherapy options like methadone or buprenorphine for opioid addiction. Understanding co-occurring disorders is crucial, as individuals with SUDs often have concurrent mental health issues that require integrated treatment strategies to address both conditions effectively.

3.36 Suicidal Thoughts/behaviors:
Suicidal thoughts and behaviors encompass a range of actions and ideations that indicate an individual's contemplation or intention to end their life. These thoughts can vary in intensity from fleeting considerations to detailed planning of a suicide attempt. Suicidal behaviors may include gestures, attempts, or even completed suicide. It is crucial for mental health counselors to identify risk factors, which can include psychiatric disorders such as depression, anxiety, or substance abuse, as well as situational stressors like loss, trauma, or significant life changes.

Understanding the warning signs is essential for intervention. These may involve expressions of hopelessness, withdrawal from social interactions, changes in mood or behavior, and verbal cues indicating a desire to die. Counselors must conduct thorough risk assessments to evaluate the immediacy and seriousness of the threat. This involves exploring the individual's intent, plan, means to carry out the plan, and previous suicide attempts.

Intervention strategies should be tailored to the individual's needs and may include crisis intervention, safety planning, cognitive-behavioral therapy (CBT), and ongoing support networks. Collaboration with other healthcare providers and family members is often necessary to ensure comprehensive care. Mental health counselors play a pivotal role in recognizing and addressing suicidal thoughts and behaviors to prevent potential tragedies.

3.37 Terminal Illness Issues:
Terminal illness issues encompass the psychological, emotional, and social challenges faced by individuals diagnosed with a terminal condition. Mental health counselors play a crucial role in supporting these individuals and their families as they navigate the complexities of end-of-life care. Terminal illness often triggers a profound existential crisis, prompting patients to confront their mortality and reevaluate the meaning and purpose of their lives. This can lead to a range of emotional responses, including anxiety, depression, anger, denial, and acceptance.

Counselors must be adept at addressing anticipatory grief, which is the mourning that occurs before an impending loss. They should facilitate open communication between patients and their families to ensure that wishes for end-of-life care are respected and understood. Counselors also help clients explore coping mechanisms, provide psychoeducation about the dying process, and offer support in managing physical symptoms such as pain.

Ethical considerations are paramount in terminal illness counseling, including respecting client autonomy, maintaining confidentiality, and navigating complex family dynamics. Additionally, counselors should be sensitive to cultural and spiritual beliefs that influence how individuals perceive death and dying. By providing empathetic support and fostering resilience, mental health counselors help terminally ill clients achieve a sense of peace and closure during their final stages of life.

3.38 Visual/auditory Hallucinations:
Visual and auditory hallucinations are sensory perceptions that occur in the absence of an external stimulus. These hallucinations are significant clinical symptoms often associated with various psychiatric and neurological disorders. Visual hallucinations involve seeing things that are not present, such as shapes, people, or lights, while auditory hallucinations involve hearing sounds, such as voices or music, that do not have a source in the environment.

In the context of mental health counseling, understanding the underlying causes of hallucinations is crucial. They can be indicative of conditions such as schizophrenia, severe depression with psychotic features, bipolar disorder, or delirium. Substance use disorders and withdrawal from certain substances can also result in hallucinations. Moreover, they may occur in neurological conditions like Parkinson's disease or dementia.

For mental health counselors preparing for the NCMHCE, it is essential to assess the nature, frequency, and content of hallucinations during client evaluations. This involves differentiating between true hallucinations and other perceptual disturbances, such as illusions or misinterpretations. Treatment approaches may include antipsychotic medications, psychotherapy, and addressing any underlying medical or substance-related issues. Understanding cultural contexts is also important, as certain cultures may interpret these experiences differently. Accurate assessment and culturally sensitive interventions are key components in effectively managing clients experiencing visual or auditory hallucinations.

3.39 Worry And Anxiety:
Worry and anxiety are interconnected emotional states often addressed in clinical mental health counseling. Worry is a cognitive process characterized by repetitive, uncontrollable thoughts about potential future threats or negative outcomes. It involves a chain of thoughts that are predominantly verbal in nature, often leading to heightened stress levels. Anxiety, on the other hand, is an emotional response that encompasses feelings of tension, nervousness, and apprehension, often accompanied by physical symptoms such as increased heart rate, sweating, and trembling.

In clinical practice, it is crucial to differentiate between normal anxiety, which serves as an adaptive response to stressors, and pathological anxiety, which impairs functioning and quality of life. Generalized Anxiety Disorder (GAD) is a common manifestation in which excessive worry occurs more days than not for at least six months, affecting various aspects of life.

Mental health counselors employ evidence-based interventions such as Cognitive Behavioral Therapy (CBT) to help clients identify and challenge maladaptive thought patterns associated with worry and anxiety. Techniques such as mindfulness and relaxation exercises are also utilized to reduce physiological arousal and promote emotional regulation. Understanding the underlying cognitive processes and employing appropriate therapeutic strategies are essential for the effective management of worry and anxiety in clients seeking mental health support.

3.40 Adoption Issues:

Adoption issues refer to the psychological and emotional challenges that may arise for individuals involved in the adoption process, including adoptees, birth parents, and adoptive parents. These issues can manifest at various stages of life and often involve complex feelings of identity, belonging, and loss. For adoptees, common concerns include struggles with identity formation, attachment difficulties, and feelings of abandonment or rejection. These issues may be exacerbated during developmental milestones, such as adolescence, where identity exploration is critical.

Birth parents may experience grief and loss following the relinquishment of their child, which can lead to long-term emotional distress. They might also grapple with feelings of guilt or regret. Adoptive parents, on the other hand, may face challenges in establishing a secure attachment with their adopted child and may need to navigate societal perceptions or questions about their family dynamics.

Mental health counselors working with individuals affected by adoption must be sensitive to these unique challenges. They should employ therapeutic strategies that promote open communication, validate feelings of loss or confusion, and support identity exploration. Counselors should also be aware of cultural and transracial adoption considerations, offering culturally competent care that respects the diverse backgrounds and experiences of those involved in adoption. Understanding these complexities is crucial for providing effective support and fostering healthy family relationships.

3.41 Blended Family Issues:

Blended family issues refer to the unique challenges and dynamics that arise when two separate families unite through marriage or cohabitation, often involving children from previous relationships. These families, also known as stepfamilies, face distinct emotional and practical hurdles that mental health counselors must address in therapy.

One of the primary issues in blended families is the adjustment process. Children may struggle with loyalty conflicts between biological and stepparents, leading to feelings of divided allegiance. Additionally, establishing new family roles and boundaries can be challenging as members navigate unfamiliar relationships and expectations. The integration of different parenting styles often results in disagreements and confusion, complicating family cohesion.

Communication is another critical area of concern. Open and effective communication is essential to foster understanding and empathy among family members. Counselors must guide families in developing strategies to enhance dialogue, ensuring that each member feels heard and valued.

Moreover, grief and loss are prevalent themes, as individuals may mourn the loss of their previous family structure while adapting to new dynamics. Addressing these emotions is vital for promoting healing and acceptance within the blended family.

Mental health counselors play a crucial role in assisting blended families in building resilience, developing healthy relationships, and creating a cohesive family unit that respects each member's individuality while fostering unity.

3.42 Child Abuse–related Concerns:

Child abuse-related concerns encompass a range of issues that mental health counselors must address when working with children and families. Child abuse is defined as any act or series of acts of commission or omission by a parent or other caregiver that results in harm, potential harm, or threat of harm to a child. It includes physical abuse, emotional abuse, sexual abuse, and neglect.

Understanding the signs and symptoms of child abuse is crucial for early identification and intervention. Physical indicators may include unexplained injuries, bruises, or burns. Behavioral signs can manifest as withdrawal, anxiety, depression, aggression, or fear of going home. Counselors must be adept at recognizing these indicators and understanding the dynamics of abusive relationships.

Mental health counselors play a vital role in assessing the impact of abuse on a child's psychological well-being. They must evaluate the child's emotional state, cognitive development, and social interactions to determine the extent of the trauma experienced. Interventions may involve individual therapy, family counseling, and collaboration with child protective services to ensure the child's safety.

Moreover, counselors must navigate legal and ethical responsibilities, including mandatory reporting laws that require them to report suspected abuse to authorities. Professional competence in this area is essential for safeguarding children's welfare and promoting their recovery from trauma. Understanding cultural contexts and providing trauma-informed care are also critical components of effective intervention.

3.43 Child Development Issues:

Child development issues encompass a range of challenges that can impede a child's physical, cognitive, emotional, and social growth. These issues can arise from genetic factors, environmental influences, or a combination of both. Mental health counselors must understand these developmental challenges to provide effective interventions. Common child development issues include developmental delays, such as speech and language delays, motor skill deficits, and cognitive impairments. Emotional and behavioral disorders, such as anxiety, depression, ADHD, and autism spectrum disorders, are also prevalent concerns.

Counselors should be adept at recognizing the signs of these issues early to facilitate timely intervention. Early identification is crucial, as it can significantly impact the child's long-term development and quality of life. Interventions may include individual therapy, family counseling, and collaboration with educational professionals to create supportive environments. Understanding ecological systems theory is beneficial in assessing how various environmental factors influence child development.

Moreover, counselors should be aware of cultural considerations and how they affect perceptions of child development and related issues. This holistic understanding enables counselors to tailor their approaches to meet the unique needs of each child and family they serve. Mastery of these concepts is essential for success on the NCMHCE exam and in professional practice.

3.44 Dating/relationship Problems:

Dating and relationship problems refer to the challenges individuals face in forming, maintaining, or ending romantic relationships. These issues can manifest in various ways, including communication breakdowns, trust issues, differing expectations, intimacy concerns, and difficulties with conflict resolution. Mental health counselors must understand these dynamics to effectively support clients navigating these challenges.

Communication is a cornerstone of healthy relationships; thus, ineffective communication can lead to misunderstandings and unresolved conflicts. Trust issues often arise from past betrayals or insecurities and can significantly impact relationship stability. Differing expectations regarding roles, future goals, or commitment levels can create friction if not addressed openly.

Intimacy concerns may involve emotional distance or physical disconnect, often stemming from personal insecurities or past trauma. Difficulties with conflict resolution occur when partners lack the skills to negotiate disagreements constructively, leading to escalated disputes or avoidance behaviors.

Counselors should assess the underlying causes of these problems by exploring clients' relationship histories and attachment styles. Interventions may include improving communication skills, fostering empathy and understanding between partners, and addressing individual psychological factors contributing to relationship distress. Cognitive-behavioral techniques and emotion-focused therapy are effective approaches to helping clients develop healthier relationship patterns. Understanding these dynamics is crucial for counselors preparing for the NCMHCE exam, as they reflect real-world scenarios encountered in clinical practice.

3.45 Divorce:
Divorce is the legal dissolution of a marriage by a court or other competent body. For mental health counselors, understanding divorce involves recognizing its multifaceted impact on individuals and families. Divorce can lead to significant emotional, psychological, and financial stress. It often requires individuals to navigate complex changes in identity, lifestyle, and social dynamics.

Counselors must be adept at identifying common emotional responses to divorce, such as grief, anger, anxiety, and depression. They should also be prepared to address issues related to self-esteem, loneliness, and adjustment to new life circumstances. Children may experience confusion, guilt, or behavioral changes, necessitating specialized interventions to support their well-being.

In therapeutic settings, counselors employ various approaches to assist clients in coping with divorce. Cognitive-behavioral therapy (CBT) can help individuals reframe negative thought patterns and develop healthier coping strategies. Family therapy may be beneficial in facilitating communication and resolving conflicts among family members.

Furthermore, counselors should be knowledgeable about community resources that provide legal advice, financial planning, and support groups. Understanding cultural and societal influences on divorce is crucial for providing culturally competent care. By fostering resilience and promoting adaptive coping mechanisms, counselors play a vital role in helping clients navigate the challenges of divorce and move toward personal growth and healing.

3.46 Family Abuse/violence:
Family abuse, also known as domestic violence or family violence, refers to patterns of behavior within a family that involve physical, emotional, psychological, or sexual harm inflicted by one family member upon another. This form of abuse can occur between partners, parents and children, siblings, or extended family members. It is characterized by an imbalance of power and control, where the abuser uses intimidation, manipulation, or coercion to dominate the victim.

Family abuse can manifest in various forms: physical abuse includes hitting, slapping, or other forms of physical harm; emotional abuse involves verbal assaults, threats, or humiliation; psychological abuse encompasses manipulative tactics that undermine the victim's mental stability; and sexual abuse includes any non-consensual sexual activity. Financial abuse is another aspect in which the abuser controls the victim's access to financial resources.

The impact of family violence is profound and long-lasting. Victims may experience depression, anxiety, post-traumatic stress disorder (PTSD), and other mental health issues. Children who witness family violence are at risk for developmental challenges and may perpetuate the cycle of abuse in their future relationships.

Counselors must be adept at identifying signs of family abuse and providing appropriate interventions. This includes creating safety plans, offering therapeutic support, and connecting clients with community resources to ensure their protection and recovery.

3.46.1 Physical Abuse:
Physical abuse refers to the intentional use of physical force against a person that results in bodily injury, pain, or impairment. This form of abuse can manifest in various ways, including hitting, slapping, punching, kicking, choking, or using objects to cause harm. It is crucial for mental health counselors to recognize the signs and symptoms of physical abuse, which may include unexplained bruises, burns, fractures, or other injuries that are inconsistent with the explanations provided by the victim.

In the context of family dynamics, physical abuse often occurs within intimate relationships or between family members. It is a pattern of behavior used to establish power and control over another individual. The psychological impact on victims can be profound, leading to issues such as anxiety, depression, post-traumatic stress disorder (PTSD), and a diminished sense of self-worth.

Counselors must approach cases of physical abuse with sensitivity and care. Assessment should include a thorough evaluation of the individual's physical safety and an exploration of the underlying dynamics contributing to the abusive behavior. Interventions may involve safety planning, therapeutic support for trauma recovery, and coordination with legal or social services when necessary.

Understanding physical abuse is essential for mental health counselors preparing for the NCMHCE, as they must be equipped to identify and address this critical issue effectively within their practice.

3.46.2 Sexual Abuse/Violence:
Sexual abuse and violence refer to any unwanted sexual activity, with perpetrators using force, making threats, or taking advantage of victims who are unable to give consent. It encompasses a range of actions, including rape, attempted rape, child molestation, and sexual harassment. This form of abuse is a violation of an individual's autonomy and dignity, often resulting in profound psychological trauma.

In the context of family dynamics, sexual abuse can occur within relationships where power imbalances exist, such as between partners or from a parent to a child. It is crucial for mental health counselors to recognize the signs of sexual abuse, which may include physical injuries, sexually transmitted infections, or behavioral changes like withdrawal, anxiety, depression, or inappropriate sexual behaviors.

Counselors must approach cases of sexual abuse with sensitivity and confidentiality, ensuring a safe environment for disclosure. Understanding the complex dynamics at play is essential; victims may experience shame, guilt, or fear of not being believed.

Treatment involves trauma-informed care, focusing on empowering the victim and facilitating recovery through therapy modalities such as cognitive-behavioral therapy (CBT) or eye movement desensitization and reprocessing (EMDR).

Professionals must also be aware of their legal obligations regarding mandatory reporting and work collaboratively with other services to provide comprehensive support for survivors. Addressing sexual abuse effectively requires a nuanced understanding of its impact on individuals and families.

3.46.3   Emotional Abuse:
Emotional abuse, within the context of family abuse and violence, refers to a pattern of behavior that aims to undermine an individual's self-worth and emotional well-being. It is a form of psychological manipulation that can be as damaging as physical abuse, although it often goes unnoticed due to its subtle nature. Emotional abuse can manifest through verbal aggression, intimidation, manipulation, and humiliation. It often involves criticism, belittling, and shaming, which can lead to feelings of worthlessness and helplessness in the victim.

The abuser may employ tactics such as constant criticism, controlling behavior, isolation from friends and family, and threats of harm or abandonment. This type of abuse can erode a person's self-esteem over time and result in long-term psychological trauma. Victims may experience anxiety, depression, chronic stress, and post-traumatic stress disorder (PTSD).

Mental health counselors must be adept at recognizing the signs of emotional abuse in clients. These signs include changes in mood or behavior, withdrawal from social interactions, and expressions of low self-esteem or self-doubt. Effective intervention involves validating the victim's experiences, providing emotional support, and developing strategies to empower them toward safety and recovery. Understanding the dynamics of emotional abuse is crucial for counselors in fostering healing and resilience in affected individuals.

3.47 Interpersonal Partner Violence Concerns:
Interpersonal Partner Violence (IPV) refers to any behavior within an intimate relationship that causes physical, psychological, or sexual harm to those involved. IPV can manifest as physical aggression, sexual coercion, psychological abuse, and controlling behaviors. It is crucial for mental health counselors to recognize the multifaceted nature of IPV and understand its profound impact on individuals' mental health.

Victims of IPV often experience a range of psychological effects, including anxiety, depression, post-traumatic stress disorder (PTSD), and diminished self-esteem. These psychological repercussions can lead to substance abuse and suicidal ideation if not addressed promptly. Mental health counselors must be adept at identifying signs of IPV, which may include unexplained injuries, frequent absences from work or social activities, and changes in personality or mood.

Counselors should create a safe and supportive environment for clients to disclose their IPV experiences. It is essential to develop a comprehensive safety plan tailored to the client's needs and circumstances while maintaining confidentiality. Interventions may include individual therapy focusing on empowerment and coping strategies, as well as referrals to support groups or legal resources.

Understanding cultural and contextual factors is vital in addressing IPV effectively. Counselors must approach each case with cultural sensitivity, recognizing that IPV dynamics can vary significantly across different cultures and communities.

3.48 Marital/partner Communication Problems:
Marital and partner communication problems refer to the difficulties and barriers that couples experience in effectively exchanging thoughts, feelings, and needs with one another. These issues can stem from various factors, including differences in communication styles, a lack of active listening, emotional disconnect, or unresolved conflicts. Ineffective communication can lead to misunderstandings, increased conflict, and emotional distance within the relationship.

A common cause of communication problems is the failure to express oneself clearly or the tendency to make assumptions about a partner's thoughts and intentions. Partners may also engage in negative communication patterns, such as criticism, defensiveness, contempt, or stonewalling, which further erode trust and intimacy. Additionally, external stressors like financial pressures or parenting challenges can exacerbate these issues by reducing the time and energy available for meaningful interaction.

Addressing marital and partner communication problems involves fostering open and honest dialogue, practicing active listening, and developing empathy toward each other's perspectives. Techniques such as I statements can help individuals express their feelings without blaming their partner. Couples therapy can also provide a structured environment for partners to explore underlying issues and learn effective communication strategies. By enhancing their communication skills, couples can strengthen their emotional connection and build a more resilient relationship.

3.49 Parenting/co-parenting Conflicts:
Parenting and co-parenting conflicts refer to disagreements and disputes that arise between parents or guardians responsible for raising a child, whether they are married, divorced, or separated. These conflicts can stem from differing parenting styles, values, beliefs, or priorities regarding the child's upbringing. Such conflicts may manifest in various aspects of parenting, including discipline methods, educational choices, healthcare decisions, and religious upbringing.

In the context of co-parenting, particularly after separation or divorce, these conflicts can become more pronounced due to additional stressors, such as legal custody arrangements and communication barriers. Effective co-parenting requires cooperation and communication between parents to ensure that the child's well-being is prioritized. Unresolved conflicts can lead to negative outcomes for children, including emotional distress, behavioral issues, and academic difficulties.

Counselors play a crucial role in addressing parenting and co-parenting conflicts by facilitating open communication between parents and helping them develop conflict resolution strategies. Techniques such as mediation, counseling sessions focused on effective communication skills, and parenting education programs can be employed to manage and mitigate these conflicts. The goal is to foster a collaborative environment where both parents can work together harmoniously for the benefit of their child, ensuring a stable and supportive family structure despite any personal differences.

3.50 Emotional Dysregulation:
Emotional dysregulation refers to a pattern of emotional responses that are poorly modulated and do not fall within the conventionally accepted range of emotional responses. It is characterized by an inability to manage the intensity and duration of

negative emotions such as fear, sadness, or anger. This condition can manifest in various ways, including mood swings, impulsivity, and difficulty calming down after an emotional experience.

In the context of mental health counseling, understanding emotional dysregulation is crucial, as it often underlies various psychological disorders such as borderline personality disorder, bipolar disorder, and post-traumatic stress disorder (PTSD). Emotional dysregulation may result from genetic predispositions, early childhood trauma, or chronic exposure to stress. It involves disruptions in the neural circuits responsible for emotion regulation, particularly those involving the prefrontal cortex and amygdala.

Counselors must assess the presence and extent of emotional dysregulation in clients to tailor effective therapeutic interventions. Techniques such as Dialectical Behavior Therapy (DBT) and Cognitive Behavioral Therapy (CBT) are commonly employed to help individuals develop skills for emotion regulation. These therapies focus on teaching clients how to identify their emotions, increase emotional awareness, and apply strategies to modulate their emotional responses effectively. By addressing emotional dysregulation, counselors can assist clients in achieving greater emotional stability and improved overall functioning.

4   <u>Treatment Planning:</u>

Treatment planning is a structured and collaborative process in mental health counseling that involves developing a detailed plan of action tailored to meet the specific needs of a client. This process begins with a comprehensive assessment of the client's psychological, emotional, and behavioral issues. The primary objective of treatment planning is to establish clear, measurable goals that guide the therapeutic process and facilitate positive change.

A well-constructed treatment plan includes several key components: problem identification, goal setting, intervention strategies, and evaluation methods. Problem identification involves a thorough analysis of the client's presenting issues, considering both their symptoms and underlying causes. Goal setting is an essential aspect where specific, achievable, and time-bound objectives are established, reflecting both the short-term and long-term aspirations of the client.

Intervention strategies outline the therapeutic approaches and techniques that will be employed to achieve these goals. These strategies are chosen based on evidence-based practices and tailored to align with the client's unique circumstances and preferences. Lastly, evaluation methods are incorporated to monitor progress and adjust the treatment plan as needed, ensuring its effectiveness and relevance.

Effective treatment planning requires collaboration between the counselor and the client, fostering a sense of empowerment and ownership over the therapeutic journey. It is a dynamic process that evolves as the client's needs change, emphasizing flexibility and responsiveness in mental health care.

4.1 <u>Client Collaboration for Treatment Goals:</u>

Collaborating with clients to establish treatment goals and objectives is a fundamental aspect of effective mental health counseling. This process involves engaging clients in a participatory and empowering manner to identify and articulate their personal aspirations for therapy. The counselor's role is to facilitate this dialogue, ensuring that the goals are client-centered, realistic, and achievable within the therapeutic context.

The collaboration begins with a thorough assessment of the client's presenting issues, strengths, and resources. Counselors employ active listening skills and empathetic understanding to ensure that clients feel heard and understood. This fosters a therapeutic alliance where clients feel comfortable expressing their needs and desires.

Treatment goals should be specific, measurable, attainable, relevant, and time-bound (SMART). Objectives serve as the stepping stones toward achieving these goals, breaking down the larger aspirations into manageable tasks. For instance, if a client's goal is to reduce anxiety, an objective might be to practice relaxation techniques daily.

This collaborative process not only enhances client engagement but also increases their motivation and commitment to the therapeutic journey. It empowers clients by giving them ownership of their treatment plan, which is crucial for fostering autonomy and self-efficacy. Ultimately, this approach aligns therapeutic interventions with the client's unique values and life circumstances, enhancing the likelihood of successful outcomes.

4.2 <u>Counseling Goals Aligned with Diagnosis:</u>

Establishing short- and long-term counseling goals that align with a client's diagnosis is a critical component of effective treatment planning in mental health counseling. This process involves collaboratively setting achievable and measurable objectives that address the specific symptoms, challenges, and needs identified during the diagnostic assessment.

Short-term goals are designed to provide immediate relief or improvement in the client's condition. They are typically specific, measurable, attainable, relevant, and time-bound (SMART). These goals focus on addressing acute symptoms or behaviors that can be managed or improved within a relatively short period, such as reducing anxiety levels or improving sleep patterns.

Long-term goals, on the other hand, aim to facilitate sustained change and overall well-being. These goals often involve more comprehensive changes in behavior, thought patterns, or lifestyle adjustments that require ongoing effort and commitment. For example, a long-term goal might involve developing healthier coping mechanisms or improving interpersonal relationships.

The alignment of these goals with the client's diagnosis ensures that the treatment plan is tailored to the individual's unique circumstances and clinical presentation. This alignment also provides a framework for evaluating progress and adjusting interventions as needed. By establishing clear short- and long-term goals, counselors can guide clients toward meaningful and lasting improvements in their mental health.

4.3 <u>Barriers to Client Goal Attainment:</u>

Identifying barriers that affect client goal attainment involves recognizing and understanding the obstacles that hinder a client's progress toward achieving their therapeutic objectives. These barriers can be internal, such as cognitive distortions, lack of motivation, or emotional dysregulation, which may impede a client's ability to engage in or sustain therapeutic efforts. External barriers include environmental factors like socioeconomic constraints, lack of social support, or cultural differences that may affect access to resources and services.

Mental health counselors must conduct thorough assessments to pinpoint these barriers accurately. This process involves active listening, empathy, and the use of validated assessment tools to gather comprehensive information about the client's life circumstances and psychological state. Counselors should consider both conscious and unconscious factors that might influence a client's behavior and attitudes toward therapy.

Once identified, these barriers can be addressed through collaborative treatment planning. This involves setting realistic goals, tailoring interventions to the client's unique needs, and employing strategies such as cognitive-behavioral techniques, motivational interviewing, or psychoeducation to overcome obstacles. Regularly revisiting and adjusting the treatment plan ensures that it remains relevant and effective in helping clients navigate their challenges.

By effectively identifying and addressing these barriers, counselors empower clients to make meaningful progress toward their goals, enhancing therapeutic outcomes and promoting long-term well-being.

4.4 Strengths for Goal Attainment:

Identifying strengths that improve the likelihood of goal attainment is a critical component of effective treatment planning in mental health counseling. This process involves recognizing and leveraging the inherent capabilities, resources, and positive attributes of clients to facilitate their progress toward therapeutic goals. Strengths can include personal traits such as resilience, optimism, or creativity, as well as external resources like supportive relationships, stable employment, or community involvement.

In practice, counselors assess these strengths through comprehensive evaluations and collaborative discussions with clients. By focusing on what clients do well and the resources they have available, counselors can design interventions that are not only empowering but also more likely to succeed. This strengths-based approach shifts the focus from deficits to potentials, fostering a sense of hope and motivation in clients.

Furthermore, identifying strengths helps in tailoring personalized strategies that align with clients' unique contexts and preferences. For example, a client who is naturally empathetic might be encouraged to engage in peer support activities as part of their therapeutic process. By capitalizing on these strengths, counselors can enhance clients' self-efficacy and engagement in therapy, ultimately increasing the likelihood of achieving their desired outcomes. This approach is integral to fostering sustainable change and promoting overall well-being.

4.5 Levels of Treatment Referencing:

Topic: Referring to Different Levels of Treatment

In the context of mental health counseling, Referring to Different Levels of Treatment involves determining and recommending the most appropriate intensity of care for a client based on their specific needs, symptoms, and circumstances. This process is crucial for ensuring that clients receive the right level of support and intervention required for their mental health condition.

Levels of treatment can range from outpatient services to inpatient hospitalization. Outpatient services are typically the least intensive, involving regular therapy sessions while the client continues to live at home. Intensive outpatient programs (IOPs) and partial hospitalization programs (PHPs) offer more structured support, often including multiple therapy sessions per week or day. Residential treatment provides 24-hour care in a non-hospital setting, which is ideal for those needing a stable environment to focus on recovery. Inpatient hospitalization is the most intensive level, providing acute care for clients in crisis or experiencing severe symptoms that require constant medical supervision.

When referring clients to different levels of treatment, counselors must assess factors such as the severity of symptoms, the risk of harm to self or others, co-occurring disorders, and the client's support system. This ensures that clients receive tailored care that maximizes their chances for recovery and stability. Understanding these levels aids counselors in making informed decisions that align with best practices and ethical standards.

4.5.1 Outpatient:

Outpatient treatment refers to a level of care where clients receive mental health services without being admitted to a hospital or residential facility. This form of treatment is suitable for individuals who do not require intensive supervision or 24-hour care, allowing them to maintain their daily routines while receiving therapeutic support. Outpatient services encompass a wide range of interventions, including individual therapy, group therapy, family counseling, psychiatric evaluation, medication management, and psychoeducation.

The primary goal of outpatient treatment is to provide flexible and accessible care that addresses the client's mental health needs while promoting autonomy and community integration. It is often recommended for individuals with mild to moderate mental health issues or those transitioning from inpatient care. The frequency and duration of sessions can vary based on the client's specific needs and treatment plan, typically ranging from weekly to monthly visits.

Outpatient settings can include private practices, community mental health centers, hospitals, and clinics. Mental health counselors play a crucial role in assessing the appropriateness of outpatient care for clients, developing tailored treatment plans, and coordinating with other healthcare providers to ensure comprehensive care. Understanding the nuances of outpatient treatment is essential for counselors preparing for the NCMHCE exam, as it reflects their ability to make informed decisions about client care levels.

4.5.2 Inpatient:

Inpatient treatment refers to a structured and intensive level of care provided within a hospital or specialized facility where individuals reside for a period of time to receive comprehensive mental health services. This level of care is typically recommended for individuals experiencing severe psychiatric symptoms, acute crises, or when outpatient treatment has proven insufficient. Inpatient settings offer 24-hour supervision, medical stabilization, and a multidisciplinary approach involving psychiatrists, psychologists, social workers, and nurses.

The primary goal of inpatient care is to ensure the safety and stabilization of the patient while addressing acute symptoms through medication management, psychotherapy, and other therapeutic interventions. Patients benefit from an environment that minimizes external stressors and provides immediate access to professional support. Treatment plans are individualized, focusing on symptom reduction, coping strategies, and preparation for the transition to less intensive levels of care.

Inpatient facilities may vary in their specialization, with some focusing on specific populations such as adolescents or those with dual diagnoses. The duration of inpatient treatment is often short-term, ranging from a few days to several weeks, depending on the individual's needs and progress. Mental health counselors play a crucial role in facilitating group therapy sessions, conducting individual counseling, and collaborating with the treatment team to develop comprehensive discharge plans that ensure continuity of care post-discharge.

4.5.3 Residential:
Residential treatment is a structured and intensive therapeutic approach designed for individuals who require a higher level of care than outpatient services can provide. This form of treatment involves the individual residing at a facility where they receive 24-hour supervision and support. The environment is typically therapeutic, with a focus on creating a safe and stable space conducive to healing and recovery.

Residential treatment programs are particularly beneficial for individuals dealing with severe mental health disorders, substance abuse issues, or co-occurring disorders that have not responded adequately to less intensive forms of treatment. These programs often integrate various therapeutic modalities, including individual therapy, group therapy, family therapy, and experiential therapies such as art or music therapy.

The primary goal of residential treatment is to stabilize the individual, address underlying psychological issues, and develop coping mechanisms that promote long-term recovery and reintegration into society. Treatment plans are highly individualized, catering to the specific needs of each resident. The multidisciplinary team typically includes psychiatrists, psychologists, counselors, social workers, and other healthcare professionals who collaborate to provide comprehensive care.

For mental health counselors preparing for the NCMHCE exam, understanding the nuances of residential treatment is crucial. This includes recognizing when this level of care is appropriate and how it fits into a continuum of care that supports sustained mental health recovery.

4.6 Concurrent Treatment Referrals:
Referring clients to others for concurrent treatment involves the practice of collaborating with other healthcare professionals to address complex or co-occurring issues that a single mental health counselor may not be fully equipped to manage alone. This approach recognizes the multifaceted nature of mental health and the potential need for specialized care, such as medical, psychiatric, or substance abuse treatment, alongside counseling.

When a counselor identifies that a client's needs extend beyond their expertise or scope of practice, they may refer the client to another professional while continuing their own therapeutic work. This ensures comprehensive care and promotes the client's overall well-being. For instance, a client with severe depression might benefit from both psychotherapy and medication management, necessitating collaboration with a psychiatrist.

Effective concurrent treatment requires clear communication and coordination between the counselor and other professionals involved. This includes sharing relevant information (with the client's consent), aligning treatment goals, and regularly updating each other on the client's progress. Ethical considerations include maintaining confidentiality, obtaining informed consent, and ensuring that referrals are made based on the client's best interests rather than convenience or financial incentives.

Overall, referring clients for concurrent treatment underscores the importance of an integrative approach in mental health care, enhancing treatment efficacy and supporting holistic recovery.

4.7 Guide Treatment Planning:
Guide Treatment Planning refers to the structured process of developing a strategic plan to address a client's mental health needs. This involves a collaborative effort between the counselor and the client, ensuring that the treatment is tailored to the client's unique circumstances, preferences, and goals. The process begins with a thorough assessment of the client's presenting issues, history, and current functioning. Based on this assessment, specific, measurable, achievable, relevant, and time-bound (SMART) goals are established.

The treatment plan outlines the therapeutic interventions that will be employed to achieve these goals. It may include various modalities such as cognitive-behavioral therapy, psychodynamic therapy, or family systems therapy, depending on what is most suitable for the client. Additionally, treatment planning involves identifying potential barriers to progress and strategizing ways to overcome them. Regular reviews and updates of the treatment plan are essential to ensure its effectiveness and relevance as the client's situation evolves.

In preparing for the NCMHCE exam, mental health counselors must demonstrate competence in creating comprehensive treatment plans that are ethically sound and culturally sensitive. They should also be adept at integrating evidence-based practices into their planning process to optimize client outcomes. Understanding this process is crucial for effective clinical practice and successful exam performance.

4.8 Termination Process and Issues Overview:
The termination process in counseling refers to the final stage of the therapeutic relationship, where both the counselor and the client collaboratively conclude their sessions. This process is critical as it signifies the culmination of the therapeutic journey and the client's readiness to apply learned skills independently. Effective termination involves a planned and gradual approach, allowing clients to process their feelings about ending therapy and reinforcing their achievements.

Key issues in termination include timing, client readiness, unresolved issues, and potential feelings of loss or abandonment. Timing is essential; premature termination can hinder progress, while delayed termination may foster dependency. Counselors must assess client readiness by evaluating goal attainment and coping skills. Unresolved issues should be addressed before concluding therapy to prevent regression.

Emotional responses such as sadness or anxiety are common during termination. Counselors should facilitate discussions around these emotions, normalizing them as part of the transition. Additionally, planning for future challenges by creating a relapse prevention plan can empower clients.

Ethical considerations are paramount; counselors must ensure that termination is in the client's best interest, providing referrals if necessary. Documentation of the termination process is also crucial for maintaining professional standards and accountability. Overall, successful termination fosters client autonomy and reinforces therapeutic gains.

4.9 Transitions in Group Membership:
Transitions in group membership refer to the changes that occur when individuals join or leave a therapeutic group. These transitions can significantly impact group dynamics, cohesion, and the therapeutic process. When new members join, the group must integrate them into existing norms and relationships, which can alter the group's established dynamic. This integration

requires careful facilitation by the counselor to ensure that new members feel welcomed and valued while maintaining the group's cohesion and trust.

Conversely, when members leave a group, it can evoke feelings of loss or abandonment among the remaining members. The departure might disrupt established roles and require the group to renegotiate its dynamics. Counselors must address these feelings and facilitate discussions around the departure to help members process their emotions and reinforce the group's stability.

Effective management of transitions involves preparing the group for changes, encouraging open communication about feelings related to membership changes, and reinforcing group norms. Counselors should also be attentive to individual reactions and provide support as needed. Understanding these dynamics is crucial for mental health counselors as they work to maintain a supportive and effective therapeutic environment within group settings. This knowledge is essential for those preparing for the NCMHCE, as it reflects competencies in facilitating group processes and managing interpersonal dynamics.

4.10 Follow Up After Discharge:
Follow-up after discharge is a critical component of the continuum of care for clients transitioning from inpatient or intensive outpatient mental health treatment to community-based settings. It involves scheduled interactions between the client and mental health professionals to ensure continuity of care, monitor progress, and address any emerging issues. The primary goal is to prevent relapse, reduce readmission rates, and support the client's recovery journey.

Effective follow-up care includes a comprehensive discharge plan that outlines the client's ongoing treatment needs, medication management, and referrals to outpatient services or support groups. Mental health counselors play a pivotal role in coordinating these efforts by collaborating with multidisciplinary teams to tailor individualized follow-up strategies.

Counselors assess the client's risk factors, provide psychoeducation on coping skills, and help reinforce therapeutic gains achieved during treatment. They also facilitate communication between the client and their support network, enhancing the client's social support system.

Regular follow-up appointments allow for the early identification of potential setbacks or crises, enabling timely interventions. Counselors may employ various modalities such as telehealth, home visits, or office consultations to maintain engagement. Ultimately, follow-up after discharge is essential for promoting long-term stability, fostering resilience, and empowering clients to achieve their personal recovery goals.

4.11 Enhancing Client Decisions with Assessment Results:
The use of assessment instrument results to facilitate client decision-making involves interpreting and applying data gathered from standardized tools to guide clients in making informed choices about their mental health and treatment options. Mental health counselors employ various assessment instruments, such as personality inventories, behavioral checklists, and diagnostic tests, to gather comprehensive information about a client's psychological functioning, strengths, and areas of concern.

Counselors must possess the skills to accurately interpret these results, considering the cultural, social, and individual factors that may influence the outcomes. This interpretation aids in developing a collaborative understanding with the client regarding their mental health status. By presenting the assessment findings in an understandable manner, counselors empower clients to actively participate in their treatment planning.

The counselor's role is to facilitate a dialogue in which clients can explore the implications of their assessment results on their personal goals and life choices. This process encourages self-awareness and insight, enabling clients to identify potential strategies for change or areas requiring further exploration. Ultimately, the effective use of assessment results supports clients in making well-informed decisions about their therapeutic journey, fostering autonomy and enhancing the likelihood of successful outcomes. This approach aligns with ethical standards by promoting client welfare through informed consent and shared decision-making.

4.12 Treatment Plan Review and Revision:
Reviewing and revising the treatment plan is a critical component of effective mental health counseling. This process involves evaluating the current treatment strategies to determine their effectiveness in meeting the client's goals and making necessary adjustments to optimize outcomes. A comprehensive review includes assessing the client's progress, considering any changes in their circumstances, and reflecting on the therapeutic relationship.

The counselor should systematically analyze whether the client's symptoms have improved, remained stable, or worsened. This analysis involves using both qualitative measures, such as client feedback and self-reports, and quantitative measures like standardized assessments or symptom checklists. Additionally, reviewing the treatment plan requires consideration of any new stressors or life events that may impact the client's mental health.

Revising the treatment plan may involve altering therapeutic techniques, setting new goals, or adjusting the frequency and duration of sessions. It is essential to collaborate with the client during this process to ensure that revisions align with their preferences and needs. This collaboration fosters a sense of ownership and motivation in the client.

Ultimately, reviewing and revising the treatment plan is an ongoing, dynamic process that ensures counseling remains relevant and effective. It reflects a commitment to providing personalized care and demonstrates adaptability in addressing the evolving needs of clients.

4.13 Client Engagement in Treatment Progress Review:
Engaging clients in the review of their progress toward treatment goals is a critical component of effective mental health counseling. This process involves collaboratively evaluating the client's advancement toward their established therapeutic objectives, fostering a sense of ownership and empowerment in the client. It requires counselors to facilitate open discussions that encourage clients to reflect on their achievements, challenges, and any adjustments needed in their treatment plans.

The review process begins with setting clear, measurable goals at the onset of therapy, ensuring that both the counselor and the client have a shared understanding of expected outcomes. Regularly scheduled progress reviews are essential, as they provide an opportunity to assess whether these goals remain relevant or require modification based on the client's evolving needs and circumstances.

During these reviews, counselors employ active listening and empathetic communication to validate the client's experiences and perceptions. They also utilize evidence-based tools and techniques, such as progress notes and outcome assessments, to objectively measure progress. This structured feedback loop not only reinforces the therapeutic alliance but also enhances motivation by highlighting successes and identifying areas for further growth.

Ultimately, engaging clients in this reflective process promotes self-awareness, accountability, and resilience, thereby optimizing therapeutic outcomes and supporting long-term mental health improvements.

4.14 Collaborative Documentation and Reporting:

Collaboration with other providers and client support systems is a critical component of mental health counseling, ensuring comprehensive care for clients. This process involves actively engaging with various stakeholders, such as medical professionals, social workers, educators, and family members, to create a cohesive treatment plan tailored to the client's needs. Effective collaboration requires clear communication and coordination among all parties involved.

Documentation and report writing play a pivotal role in this collaborative process. Accurate and thorough documentation serves as a record of the client's progress, treatment interventions, and any changes in their condition. It ensures continuity of care by providing essential information to other providers who may be involved in the client's treatment. Reports should be concise yet detailed, highlighting key observations, therapeutic goals, and outcomes.

When writing reports, mental health counselors must adhere to ethical and legal standards, maintaining confidentiality while sharing pertinent information necessary for collaborative efforts. Documentation should be objective, free from personal biases, and reflect the counselor's professional judgment.

In summary, collaborating with other providers and support systems through effective documentation and report writing enhances the quality of care provided to clients. It fosters a multidisciplinary approach that addresses various aspects of a client's well-being, ultimately contributing to more successful therapeutic outcomes.

4.15 Client Engagement in Therapeutic Integration:

Discussing the integration and maintenance of therapeutic progress involves guiding clients to incorporate the skills and insights gained during therapy into their daily lives, ensuring long-term benefits. This process begins with reviewing the therapeutic goals achieved and highlighting specific strategies that have proven effective. Counselors work collaboratively with clients to identify potential challenges or triggers that may disrupt progress and develop tailored coping mechanisms to address these challenges.

A crucial aspect is fostering client autonomy by encouraging them to take ownership of their therapeutic journey. This involves teaching self-monitoring techniques, such as journaling or mindfulness practices, to help clients recognize early signs of regression and apply learned strategies proactively. Additionally, counselors emphasize the importance of a support network, guiding clients in seeking ongoing support from friends, family, or support groups.

Counselors also focus on relapse prevention planning, which includes identifying high-risk situations and rehearsing responses to potential setbacks. Regular follow-up sessions may be scheduled to reinforce progress and adjust strategies as needed. By empowering clients with these tools and insights, counselors facilitate the seamless integration of therapeutic gains into everyday life, promoting sustained mental health and resilience. This comprehensive approach ensures that clients are well-equipped to maintain their progress beyond the therapeutic setting.

4.16 Client Education on Treatment Plan Compliance:

Educating clients about the value of treatment plan compliance is a critical component of effective mental health counseling. Treatment plan compliance refers to the client's adherence to the agreed-upon therapeutic interventions, strategies, and schedules that are collaboratively designed by the counselor and client to address specific mental health issues. Emphasizing the importance of compliance involves highlighting how consistent participation in therapy sessions, adherence to medication, and engagement in prescribed activities can significantly contribute to achieving desired therapeutic outcomes.

A comprehensive explanation includes discussing how compliance can lead to symptom reduction, improved coping mechanisms, and enhanced overall well-being. It is essential for counselors to communicate that treatment plans are tailored to meet individual needs and that closely following them increases the likelihood of reaching personal goals. Additionally, counselors should address potential barriers to compliance, such as logistical challenges or motivational issues, and work collaboratively with clients to develop strategies for overcoming these obstacles.

By educating clients on the tangible benefits of compliance, such as faster recovery times and sustained mental health improvements, counselors empower clients to take an active role in their treatment journey. This education fosters a sense of responsibility and collaboration between the client and counselor, ultimately enhancing the effectiveness of the therapeutic process.

5 Counseling Skills And Interventions:

Counseling skills and interventions are fundamental components of effective mental health counseling practice. These skills encompass a range of techniques and strategies that counselors employ to facilitate client growth, resolve psychological issues, and promote emotional well-being. Core counseling skills include active listening, empathy, rapport building, and effective communication. Active listening involves fully concentrating on the client's words, understanding their message, and responding thoughtfully. Empathy requires counselors to genuinely understand and share the feelings of their clients, thereby fostering a supportive therapeutic relationship.

Interventions are structured activities or techniques used to address specific client issues. They can include cognitive-behavioral techniques aimed at altering maladaptive thought patterns or psychodynamic approaches that explore unconscious processes influencing behavior. Other interventions might involve solution-focused strategies that help clients identify and build on their strengths to achieve their goals.

Counselors must be adept at selecting appropriate interventions based on the client's unique needs, cultural background, and presenting problems. This requires a thorough assessment and an understanding of various theoretical orientations. The effective use of counseling skills and interventions can lead to significant positive changes in clients' lives, helping them develop healthier coping mechanisms, improve relationships, and achieve personal growth. Mastery of these elements is crucial for success in the National Clinical Mental Health Counseling Exam (NCMHCE).

5.1 Aligning Interventions with Developmental Levels:

Aligning interventions with a client's developmental level is a critical skill in mental health counseling, ensuring that therapeutic strategies are appropriate and effective for the client's stage of life. This approach requires an understanding of developmental psychology and the recognition that individuals progress through various stages of cognitive, emotional, and social development. Each stage is characterized by distinct challenges and capabilities, which influence how clients perceive and respond to interventions.

For children, interventions might focus on play therapy or behavioral techniques that align with their concrete thinking and reliance on caregivers. Adolescents, grappling with identity and autonomy, may benefit from cognitive-behavioral approaches or group therapy that address peer influences and self-concept. Adults require interventions that consider life transitions, such as career changes or family dynamics, utilizing strategies like existential therapy or solution-focused techniques. For older adults, counseling may incorporate reminiscence therapy or life review to address issues of loss and meaning.

Counselors must assess the client's developmental stage through comprehensive evaluation, considering factors such as age, cultural background, and individual experiences. By tailoring interventions to the client's developmental level, counselors enhance engagement, promote a therapeutic alliance, and facilitate meaningful change. This alignment ensures that interventions are not only age-appropriate but also resonate with the client's current life context and capabilities.

5.2 Aligning Interventions with Counseling Modalities:

Aligning interventions with the appropriate counseling modality involves selecting and tailoring therapeutic strategies to fit the specific needs and dynamics of the client(s) involved, whether they are individuals, couples, families, or groups. This process is crucial for effective therapy and requires a deep understanding of each modality's unique characteristics and goals.

For individual counseling, interventions focus on personal growth, self-awareness, and coping strategies. Techniques such as cognitive-behavioral therapy (CBT) or psychodynamic approaches may be employed to address personal issues like anxiety or depression.

In couple counseling, interventions aim to improve communication, resolve conflicts, and enhance relationship satisfaction. Therapists might use emotionally focused therapy (EFT) or the Gottman Method to help partners understand each other's needs and build stronger connections.

Family counseling interventions address systemic issues affecting the entire family unit. Approaches such as structural family therapy or Bowenian family systems therapy are used to improve family dynamics and communication patterns.

Group counseling involves interventions that leverage group dynamics for healing and support. Techniques like group process observation or psychoeducational groups can help members share experiences and learn from each other in a supportive environment.

Selecting the appropriate intervention requires a comprehensive assessment of client needs and a flexible approach to adapt therapeutic techniques to suit the chosen modality effectively.

5.3 Tailoring Interventions to Client Needs:

Aligning interventions with client populations involves tailoring therapeutic strategies to meet the unique needs, characteristics, and contexts of specific client groups. This process is essential for achieving effective counseling outcomes, as it ensures that interventions are culturally relevant, developmentally appropriate, and responsive to the individual differences within diverse populations.

To align interventions effectively, mental health counselors must first conduct a thorough assessment to understand the client's background, including cultural identity, socioeconomic status, age, gender, sexual orientation, and any other relevant factors. This understanding aids in selecting interventions that are not only evidence-based but also resonate with the client's lived experiences.

For instance, when working with adolescents, counselors might incorporate technology-based interventions that align with their familiarity and comfort with digital tools. Similarly, when dealing with clients from a specific cultural background, integrating culturally congruent practices can enhance engagement and trust.

Moreover, aligning interventions requires ongoing evaluation and flexibility. Counselors must be willing to adapt their approaches as they gain deeper insights into the client's needs and as the therapeutic relationship evolves. This alignment is crucial for fostering a collaborative therapeutic environment where clients feel understood and empowered to engage in the healing process.

Ultimately, aligning interventions with client populations underscores the importance of personalized care in mental health counseling, ensuring that each client receives the most effective support possible.

5.3.1 Veterans:

Veterans are individuals who have served in the armed forces and have been discharged under conditions other than dishonorable. This population often faces unique mental health challenges due to their military experiences, including exposure to combat, trauma, and the stress of transitioning back to civilian life. Mental health counselors working with veterans must be aware of common issues such as post-traumatic stress disorder (PTSD), depression, anxiety, substance use disorders, and traumatic brain injuries (TBI).

Counselors should adopt a culturally competent approach that acknowledges the influence of military culture on the veteran's identity and mental health. Interventions should be tailored to address the specific needs of veterans, incorporating evidence-based practices such as cognitive-behavioral therapy (CBT), eye movement desensitization and reprocessing (EMDR), and prolonged exposure therapy for PTSD.

Additionally, understanding the resources available through the Department of Veterans Affairs (VA) and other veteran support organizations is crucial for effective case management and referral. Building a therapeutic alliance is essential, as trust can be a significant barrier due to experiences of stigma or negative perceptions of mental health care within military contexts.

Overall, mental health counselors must remain sensitive to the complex interplay of psychological, social, and cultural factors affecting veterans to provide effective support and facilitate their reintegration into civilian life.

5.3.2 Minorities:
In the context of mental health counseling, minorities refer to groups within a population that differ in race, ethnicity, culture, or socioeconomic status from the majority group. These groups often face unique challenges and barriers in accessing mental health services, which can include cultural stigma, language barriers, and systemic discrimination. Understanding the specific needs and experiences of minority populations is crucial for counselors to provide effective and culturally competent care.

Minority clients may experience stressors related to acculturation, identity development, and racial or ethnic discrimination. These stressors can contribute to mental health issues such as anxiety, depression, and trauma. Counselors must be sensitive to these experiences and recognize the impact of cultural heritage and values on the client's worldview and mental health.

Effective interventions for minority clients involve culturally adapted therapeutic approaches that respect and incorporate the client's cultural background. This may include using culturally relevant metaphors, addressing cultural taboos, and involving family or community members in the therapeutic process when appropriate.

Counselors should engage in ongoing cultural competence training and self-reflection to address their own biases and improve their ability to serve minority populations. By doing so, they can help bridge the gap in mental health care access and outcomes for minority groups, promoting equity and inclusion within the therapeutic setting.

5.3.3 Disenfranchised:
Disenfranchised individuals are those who experience a lack of power, rights, or recognition within societal structures. This term often applies to groups marginalized due to their race, ethnicity, socioeconomic status, gender identity, sexual orientation, or other characteristics that deviate from dominant cultural norms. In the context of mental health counseling, understanding disenfranchisement is crucial, as it impacts clients' psychological well-being and access to resources.

Disenfranchisement can manifest in various ways, including limited access to healthcare, education, employment opportunities, and legal rights. These systemic barriers contribute to heightened stress levels and exacerbate mental health issues such as anxiety, depression, and trauma. Mental health counselors must recognize the unique challenges faced by disenfranchised populations to provide effective interventions.

Counselors should employ culturally competent practices that validate clients' experiences of disenfranchisement and work toward empowering them. This involves advocating for social justice, promoting inclusivity in treatment approaches, and collaborating with clients to identify strengths and resources within their communities. By acknowledging and addressing the systemic factors contributing to disenfranchisement, counselors can foster resilience and facilitate healing.

In preparation for the NCMHCE exam, candidates should be familiar with the concept of disenfranchisement and its implications for clinical practice. Understanding how to align interventions with the needs of disenfranchised populations is essential for providing ethical and effective mental health care.

5.3.4 Disabled:
The term disabled refers to individuals who experience physical, mental, or sensory impairments that significantly impact their daily functioning and participation in society. Disabilities can be congenital or acquired and may include conditions such as mobility impairments, intellectual disabilities, sensory impairments (e.g., blindness or deafness), and mental health disorders. In the context of mental health counseling, it is crucial to understand that disability is not solely defined by the impairment itself but also by the interaction between the individual and societal barriers that hinder full participation.

Mental health counselors working with disabled clients must adopt a person-centered approach, recognizing each client's unique strengths and challenges. This involves tailoring interventions to accommodate the specific needs of the client, ensuring accessibility in communication and physical environments, and advocating for inclusive practices. Counselors should be knowledgeable about relevant legislation, such as the Americans with Disabilities Act (ADA), which mandates reasonable accommodations to promote equality.

Moreover, counselors should be sensitive to the potential for co-occurring mental health issues among disabled individuals, such as anxiety or depression resulting from social isolation or discrimination. By fostering an empowering therapeutic environment, counselors can support disabled clients in achieving their personal goals and enhancing their quality of life while promoting resilience and self-advocacy skills.

5.4 Individual Counseling in Treatment Plans:
Implementing individual counseling in relation to a treatment plan involves the strategic application of therapeutic interventions tailored to meet the specific needs and goals of the client, as outlined in their individualized treatment plan. This process requires a mental health counselor to integrate theoretical knowledge with practical skills, ensuring that each session is purposefully directed toward achieving the client's therapeutic objectives.

The treatment plan serves as a roadmap, detailing the client's presenting issues, therapeutic goals, and the interventions that will be employed. It is crucial for counselors to continuously assess and adapt these interventions based on the client's progress and evolving needs. This dynamic process involves utilizing evidence-based practices and maintaining a client-centered approach, ensuring that therapy aligns with the client's personal values and cultural context.

Counselors must also establish a strong therapeutic alliance, fostering an environment of trust and collaboration. This relationship is pivotal in motivating clients and facilitating meaningful change. Regular evaluation of the client's progress is essential, allowing for adjustments to be made to the treatment plan as necessary.

In summary, implementing individual counseling in relation to a treatment plan requires a comprehensive understanding of therapeutic techniques, ongoing assessment, and a commitment to providing personalized care that promotes client growth and well-being.

5.5 Establish Therapeutic Alliance:
Establishing a therapeutic alliance is a foundational component of effective counseling, characterized by the collaborative and trusting relationship between the counselor and the client. This alliance is crucial for facilitating positive therapeutic outcomes. It involves mutual respect, empathy, and understanding, allowing clients to feel safe and supported in exploring their thoughts, emotions, and behaviors.

To establish a therapeutic alliance, counselors must demonstrate active listening skills, showing genuine interest in the clients' experiences and concerns. Empathy is key; counselors should strive to understand the client's perspective without judgment. Building rapport involves being present and attentive, validating the client's feelings, and providing consistent support throughout the therapeutic process.

Setting clear boundaries and establishing confidentiality are essential for fostering trust. Counselors should communicate openly about the therapeutic process, goals, and expectations, ensuring that clients are active participants in their treatment. Collaboration is emphasized, with counselors encouraging client input in decision-making to empower them in their healing journey.

Maintaining cultural competence and being aware of potential biases further strengthens the alliance. Counselors should be adaptable to each client's unique needs and backgrounds. By continuously nurturing this alliance, counselors can enhance client engagement, promote self-efficacy, and facilitate meaningful change within the therapeutic context.

5.6 Apply Theory-based Counseling Intervention(s):
Theory-based counseling interventions are structured approaches derived from established psychological theories to facilitate client change and growth. These interventions are grounded in specific theoretical frameworks, such as Cognitive Behavioral Therapy (CBT), Person-Centered Therapy, or Psychodynamic Therapy, among others. Each theory provides a unique lens through which counselors understand client issues and guide the therapeutic process.

Applying theory-based interventions involves several key steps. First, counselors conduct a thorough assessment to understand the client's needs, symptoms, and personal history. This assessment informs the selection of an appropriate theoretical approach. For example, a counselor may choose CBT for a client struggling with anxiety due to its focus on altering negative thought patterns.

Once a theoretical framework is selected, the counselor implements interventions consistent with that theory. In CBT, this might involve cognitive restructuring exercises or exposure therapy. In contrast, a person-centered approach would emphasize creating a non-directive, empathetic environment to facilitate self-exploration and personal growth.

Throughout the intervention process, counselors continuously evaluate the effectiveness of their chosen strategies and make necessary adjustments. This dynamic application ensures that interventions remain relevant and effective in meeting the client's evolving needs. Mastery of theory-based interventions is crucial for mental health counselors, as it enhances their ability to provide targeted and effective therapeutic support.

5.7 Address Addiction Issues:
Addressing addiction issues involves understanding, assessing, and intervening in substance use disorders and behavioral addictions. As a mental health counselor, it is crucial to recognize the complexity of addiction, which can include physical dependency, psychological cravings, and social influences. Effective counseling requires a comprehensive assessment that evaluates the type, extent, and impact of addiction on the individual's life.

In-depth knowledge of various treatment modalities is essential. These can include cognitive-behavioral therapy (CBT), motivational interviewing (MI), and contingency management. Each approach targets different aspects of addiction, such as altering thought patterns, enhancing motivation for change, and reinforcing positive behaviors. Counselors must also be adept at developing individualized treatment plans that consider co-occurring mental health disorders, cultural backgrounds, and personal strengths.

Understanding the stages of change model is vital for guiding clients through the recovery process. This model helps identify a client's readiness to change and tailor interventions accordingly. Additionally, addressing addiction issues requires collaboration with other healthcare professionals to provide a holistic approach to treatment.

Lastly, counselors should advocate for harm reduction strategies when appropriate and support clients in building a robust support network to maintain long-term recovery. Continuous professional development in addiction counseling ensures that counselors remain effective in addressing this multifaceted issue.

5.8 Address Cultural Considerations:
Addressing cultural considerations is a critical component of mental health counseling, requiring counselors to recognize and respect the diverse backgrounds of their clients. This involves understanding how cultural factors such as race, ethnicity, religion, gender identity, sexual orientation, socioeconomic status, and disability can influence an individual's mental health and therapeutic needs. Counselors must be culturally competent, meaning they possess the awareness, knowledge, and skills necessary to work effectively with clients from varied cultural backgrounds.

Cultural competence begins with self-awareness, where counselors examine their own biases and assumptions. It extends to acquiring knowledge about different cultural practices and worldviews. Counselors should engage in continuous education and seek supervision or consultation when working with unfamiliar cultural contexts.

In practice, addressing cultural considerations involves tailoring therapeutic approaches to align with the client's cultural values and beliefs. This might include adapting communication styles, being sensitive to nonverbal cues, and integrating culturally relevant interventions. Counselors should also consider the impact of systemic issues such as discrimination and oppression on the client's mental health.

Ultimately, addressing cultural considerations enhances the therapeutic alliance, fosters trust, and improves treatment outcomes by ensuring that counseling is respectful of and responsive to the unique cultural needs of each client.

5.9 Address Family Composition & Cultural Insights:
In the context of mental health counseling, addressing family composition and cultural considerations involves understanding and integrating the diverse family structures and cultural backgrounds of clients into the therapeutic process. Family composition refers to the makeup of a family unit, which can vary widely and includes nuclear families, single-parent families, extended families, blended families, and chosen families. Each type of family structure presents unique dynamics and influences on an individual's mental health and well-being.

Cultural considerations entail recognizing and respecting the cultural values, beliefs, customs, and traditions that shape a client's worldview and behavior. Culture significantly impacts how individuals perceive mental health issues, express symptoms, seek help, and respond to treatment. Counselors must be culturally competent, meaning they possess the awareness, knowledge, and skills necessary to work effectively with clients from diverse cultural backgrounds.

In practice, this means counselors should conduct thorough assessments that consider family roles, communication patterns, and cultural influences. They should also be mindful of potential cultural biases and stereotypes that could affect the therapeutic relationship. By addressing family composition and cultural considerations, counselors can create a more inclusive and supportive environment that acknowledges each client's unique context, ultimately enhancing the effectiveness of the counseling process.

5.10 Systemic Interaction Patterns Evaluation:

Evaluating and explaining systemic patterns of interaction involves analyzing the interconnected behaviors and communication styles within a system, such as a family or group, to understand how these interactions influence both individual and collective functioning. This process requires mental health counselors to adopt a systems perspective, recognizing that individuals are part of larger relational networks where each member's actions can affect others.

To evaluate systemic patterns, counselors must first identify recurring behaviors and communication sequences within the system. This includes observing both verbal and non-verbal interactions, power dynamics, roles, alliances, and boundaries. Counselors may use genograms, family mapping, or direct observation as tools to visualize these patterns.

Once patterns are identified, counselors explain these interactions by linking them to the issues presented by the client(s). This explanation helps clients understand how their behaviors contribute to maintaining dysfunctions or conflicts within the system. For example, a counselor might elucidate how a parent's over-involvement could inadvertently foster dependency in a child.

By evaluating and explaining these systemic interactions, counselors facilitate insight into relational dynamics, empowering clients to alter maladaptive patterns. This understanding is crucial for promoting healthier communication and relationships, ultimately leading to improved mental health outcomes.

5.11 Explore Family Member Interaction:

Exploring family member interactions involves examining the dynamics, communication patterns, roles, and relationships within a family system. This process is crucial for mental health counselors to understand the underlying issues that may affect an individual's mental health. Family interactions can significantly influence a person's behavior, emotional well-being, and coping mechanisms.

In-depth exploration requires identifying both functional and dysfunctional patterns within the family. Counselors assess how family members communicate, resolve conflicts, express emotions, and fulfill roles. This includes observing verbal and non-verbal communication cues, power dynamics, and emotional bonds. Understanding these interactions helps identify sources of stress or support within the family unit.

Counselors utilize various techniques such as genograms, family mapping, and direct observation to gather information about family interactions. These tools help visualize relationships and identify patterns that may contribute to psychological issues. Additionally, engaging with multiple family members during sessions provides a holistic view of the family's influence on the client.

By exploring family member interactions, counselors can develop effective intervention strategies that address systemic issues rather than focusing solely on the individual. This approach promotes healthier communication, strengthens familial relationships, and supports positive change within the family system. Ultimately, it aids in enhancing the client's overall mental health and well-being.

5.12 Exploring Religious and Spiritual Values:

Exploring religious and spiritual values is a critical component of mental health counseling, as these values can significantly influence a client's worldview, coping mechanisms, and overall well-being. In the context of counseling, religious and spiritual exploration involves understanding the client's beliefs, practices, and experiences related to their faith or spirituality. This exploration is essential because it can provide insight into the client's identity, value system, and sources of support or conflict.

Counselors must approach this exploration with sensitivity and openness, recognizing that religious and spiritual beliefs are deeply personal and can vary widely among individuals. It is important to create a safe space where clients feel comfortable sharing their beliefs without fear of judgment or misunderstanding. This involves actively listening, asking open-ended questions, and demonstrating cultural competence.

Understanding a client's religious and spiritual values can aid in developing tailored interventions that align with their beliefs and enhance therapeutic outcomes. For instance, incorporating spiritual practices such as meditation or prayer into treatment plans can be beneficial for some clients. Additionally, acknowledging these values can strengthen the therapeutic alliance by showing respect for the client's unique perspective.

Ultimately, exploring religious and spiritual values is about recognizing the holistic nature of individuals and integrating this understanding into effective mental health care.

5.13 Empowering Clients: Skill Development Strategies

Guiding clients in developing skills and strategies to address their problems is a fundamental aspect of mental health counseling. This process involves collaborating with clients to identify personal strengths and resources that can be leveraged to overcome challenges. Counselors utilize evidence-based interventions to teach clients effective coping mechanisms, problem-solving techniques, and adaptive behaviors.

A comprehensive approach begins with assessing the client's current skill set and understanding the specific issues they face. The counselor then introduces tailored strategies, such as cognitive-behavioral techniques, which help clients reframe negative thinking patterns and develop healthier responses to stressors. Additionally, counselors may incorporate mindfulness practices to enhance emotional regulation and resilience.

Skill development is an iterative process that requires ongoing support and reinforcement. Counselors encourage clients to practice new skills in real-world situations, providing feedback and adjustments as necessary. This experiential learning fosters self-efficacy and empowers clients to handle future challenges independently.

Furthermore, counselors emphasize the importance of setting realistic goals and creating actionable plans. By breaking down larger problems into manageable steps, clients gain a sense of control and accomplishment. This structured approach not only addresses immediate concerns but also equips clients with lifelong tools for personal growth and well-being.

5.14 Building Client Support Systems:

Developing support systems is a critical component of mental health counseling, as it enhances clients' resilience and promotes recovery. Support systems are networks of individuals or groups that provide emotional, practical, and sometimes financial assistance to clients. These networks can include family members, friends, community groups, and professional services.

Mental health counselors play a vital role in helping clients identify and build these support systems. Initially, counselors assess the client's current support system to understand its strengths and gaps. This involves exploring the client's relationships and their effectiveness in providing support. Counselors then guide clients in identifying potential sources of support, which may involve reconnecting with family members, joining support groups, or engaging with community resources.

Counselors also work with clients to develop the communication skills necessary for maintaining healthy relationships within their support systems. This includes teaching assertiveness, active listening, and conflict resolution skills. Additionally, counselors may facilitate family or group sessions to strengthen these relationships.

The ultimate goal is to empower clients to independently manage their support networks, ensuring they have reliable resources during times of need. Effective support systems can significantly enhance a client's coping mechanisms, reduce feelings of isolation, and contribute to long-term mental health stability.

5.15 Facilitating Client Motivation for Desired Change:

Facilitating clients' motivation to make desired changes is a critical aspect of mental health counseling. This process involves understanding and enhancing a client's intrinsic motivation to pursue personal growth and change. Counselors employ various strategies to support this motivation, often rooted in motivational interviewing techniques. These techniques emphasize collaboration, evocation, and autonomy, empowering clients to explore their ambivalence about change and reinforcing their commitment to desired outcomes.

A key component is the establishment of a strong therapeutic alliance, where the counselor demonstrates empathy, active listening, and unconditional positive regard. This relationship fosters a safe space for clients to express their thoughts and feelings without judgment. Counselors help clients identify discrepancies between their current behaviors and their broader life goals, gently guiding them to recognize the benefits of change.

Additionally, counselors assist clients in setting realistic and achievable goals, breaking down larger objectives into manageable steps. They also work on enhancing clients' self-efficacy by affirming their strengths and past successes. By utilizing open-ended questions, reflective listening, and summarizing statements, counselors encourage clients to articulate their own reasons for change, thereby increasing their motivation.

Ultimately, facilitating motivation is about empowering clients to take ownership of their change process, fostering resilience and sustainable personal development.

5.16 Improve Interactional Patterns:

Improving interactional patterns involves enhancing the ways individuals communicate and relate to one another within their interpersonal relationships. This concept is crucial in mental health counseling, as dysfunctional interactional patterns can contribute to psychological distress and relational conflicts. Counselors work to identify maladaptive communication styles, such as passive-aggressiveness, defensiveness, or avoidance, which may hinder healthy relationship dynamics.

To improve these patterns, counselors employ various therapeutic techniques aimed at fostering open, honest, and assertive communication. Techniques may include role-playing exercises to practice new communication skills in a safe environment, active listening exercises to enhance empathy and understanding, and cognitive restructuring to challenge and change negative thought patterns that influence interactions.

Furthermore, counselors may use systemic approaches to address the broader context of relationships, considering family dynamics and cultural influences that impact interactional patterns. By helping clients develop greater self-awareness and emotional regulation skills, counselors empower them to engage in more constructive and supportive interactions.

Ultimately, improving interactional patterns leads to healthier relationships by promoting mutual respect, understanding, and collaboration. This not only enhances individual well-being but also strengthens the social support systems that are vital for mental health resilience. Mental health counselors play a pivotal role in guiding clients toward achieving these improved interactional outcomes.

5.17 Provide Crisis Intervention:

Crisis intervention is a crucial skill for mental health counselors, involving immediate and short-term psychological care aimed at assisting individuals in crisis situations to restore equilibrium to their biopsychosocial functioning and minimize potential long-term psychological trauma. A crisis can be defined as an acute emotional upset arising from situational, developmental, or societal sources, which results in a temporary inability to cope using usual problem-solving methods.

When providing crisis intervention, counselors must quickly assess the severity of the crisis, the individual's emotional state, and any potential risk factors, such as suicidal or homicidal ideation. The primary goal is to ensure safety while fostering stabilization through active listening, validation of feelings, and the development of coping strategies. Counselors employ various techniques, such as de-escalation, problem-solving, and developing an action plan that includes referrals for further support if necessary.

Effective crisis intervention requires sensitivity to cultural factors and an understanding of the individual's unique circumstances. It also involves collaboration with other professionals and agencies to provide comprehensive support. By empowering individuals to regain control and access resources, mental health counselors play a pivotal role in reducing the impact of crises on clients' lives, ultimately facilitating recovery and resilience.

5.18 Understanding Transference and Defense Mechanisms:

Transference occurs when clients project feelings, desires, and expectations from past relationships onto the therapist. This unconscious redirection can manifest as either positive or negative emotions. Educating clients about transference involves helping them recognize these projections and understand their origins in past experiences. By doing so, clients can gain insight into unresolved issues and patterns in their relationships, allowing for more effective therapeutic work.

Defense mechanisms are unconscious psychological strategies employed by individuals to protect themselves from anxiety and distress. Common defense mechanisms include denial, repression, projection, rationalization, and displacement. Educating clients about these mechanisms involves explaining how they function to shield the ego from uncomfortable emotions or thoughts. For example, repression involves unconsciously blocking distressing memories or feelings from awareness, while projection involves attributing one's own unacceptable thoughts or feelings to others.

By understanding transference and defense mechanisms, clients can become more aware of their unconscious processes and how these influence their behavior and emotional responses. This awareness can lead to greater self-understanding and personal growth. Mental health counselors play a crucial role in guiding clients through this educational process, facilitating self-reflection and encouraging the development of healthier coping strategies that enhance therapeutic outcomes.

5.19 Facilitate Trust And Safety:

Facilitating trust and safety is a fundamental aspect of effective mental health counseling, essential for fostering a therapeutic alliance between the counselor and the client. Trust is established through consistent, reliable, and empathetic interactions, where the counselor demonstrates genuine concern and respect for the client's experiences and perspectives. Safety, both emotional and psychological, is achieved by creating an environment where clients feel secure expressing their thoughts and emotions without fear of judgment or repercussions.

To facilitate trust, counselors must maintain confidentiality, adhere to ethical guidelines, and exhibit cultural competence, ensuring that they respect the diverse backgrounds and values of their clients. Active listening, validation of feelings, and transparency in communication further reinforce trust. Counselors should also be aware of their own biases and remain non-judgmental to support open dialogue.

Safety is bolstered by setting clear boundaries and establishing mutually agreed-upon goals for therapy. This includes discussing the limits of confidentiality and obtaining informed consent. Creating a predictable session structure can also enhance the sense of security.

Ultimately, facilitating trust and safety enables clients to explore sensitive issues more openly, paving the way for meaningful therapeutic progress. It empowers clients to engage actively in the counseling process, fostering resilience and promoting healing.

5.20 Build Communication Skills:

Building communication skills is fundamental for mental health counselors to effectively engage with clients and facilitate therapeutic progress. Communication in counseling involves both verbal and non-verbal interactions that convey empathy, understanding, and support. Counselors must develop active listening skills, which include giving full attention to the client, reflecting on their words, and responding appropriately without judgment or interruption. This ensures that clients feel heard and understood, fostering a safe therapeutic environment.

Moreover, counselors need to master the art of asking open-ended questions to encourage clients to explore their thoughts and feelings more deeply. These questions help clients express themselves freely, providing valuable insights into their mental health concerns. Counselors should also be adept at paraphrasing and summarizing client statements to confirm understanding and demonstrate empathy.

Non-verbal communication skills are equally important. Counselors should be aware of their body language, eye contact, facial expressions, and tone of voice, as these elements significantly impact the counseling relationship. Effective communication also involves cultural competence understanding and respecting cultural differences in communication styles.

By honing these skills, mental health counselors can build strong therapeutic alliances, facilitate meaningful dialogue, and ultimately empower clients on their journey toward mental wellness. Proficiency in communication is crucial for success in the NCMHCE exam and professional practice.

5.21 Develop Conflict Resolution Strategies:

Developing conflict resolution strategies is a critical skill for mental health counselors, as conflicts can arise in various contexts, including therapeutic settings, family dynamics, and organizational environments. Conflict resolution involves identifying the underlying issues, facilitating open communication, and collaboratively finding solutions that satisfy all parties involved.

Effective conflict resolution strategies begin with active listening and empathy, allowing counselors to understand the perspectives and emotions of each party. Counselors must create a safe environment where individuals feel heard and respected. Techniques such as reflective listening and paraphrasing can help clarify misunderstandings and demonstrate understanding.

Counselors should guide clients in exploring the root causes of conflict, encouraging them to express their needs and concerns without blame or judgment. This process may involve helping clients identify their emotional triggers and communication patterns that contribute to conflict.

Once the issues are clearly understood, counselors can facilitate brainstorming sessions to generate potential solutions. It is essential to encourage creativity and openness during this phase. Evaluating the feasibility and potential outcomes of each solution helps in selecting the most appropriate course of action.

Finally, counselors assist in negotiating agreements that are mutually acceptable, ensuring that all parties commit to implementing the chosen solution. Follow-up sessions may be necessary to assess progress and make adjustments as needed.

5.22 Develop Safety Plans:

Developing safety plans is a critical component of mental health counseling, particularly when working with clients who may be at risk of harm to themselves or others. A safety plan is a personalized, practical strategy that helps clients identify and utilize coping mechanisms and resources when they are experiencing a crisis. The primary goal of a safety plan is to prevent the escalation of the crisis and ensure the client's immediate safety.

A comprehensive safety plan includes several key elements: the identification of personal warning signs that indicate a crisis may be developing, internal coping strategies that the client can employ without needing to contact another person, social settings and individuals who can provide distraction or support, and family members or friends who can help resolve a crisis. Additionally, it involves identifying professionals or agencies to contact during an emergency, along with steps to make the environment safe, such as removing potential means of self-harm.

Counselors must collaborate with clients to tailor the safety plan to their specific needs and circumstances. This process involves active listening, empathy, and clear communication to ensure that clients understand and feel comfortable with each component of the plan. Regularly reviewing and updating the safety plan is also essential to accommodate any changes in the client's situation or mental health status.

5.23 Facilitate Systemic Change:

Facilitating systemic change involves the process of guiding and implementing modifications within an entire system to improve its overall functioning and outcomes. In the context of mental health counseling, systemic change refers to altering the structures, policies, and practices within organizations or communities to better address mental health needs. Counselors play a pivotal role in this process by identifying barriers that hinder effective service delivery and advocating for policies that promote mental well-being.

Systemic change requires a comprehensive understanding of the interconnectedness of various components within a system. Counselors must assess the needs and dynamics of individuals, families, and communities to identify systemic issues that contribute to mental health challenges. This may involve collaborating with stakeholders such as healthcare providers, educators, policymakers, and community leaders to develop and implement strategies that foster positive change.

Effective facilitation of systemic change also demands cultural competence and sensitivity to diverse populations. Counselors must ensure that interventions are inclusive and equitable, addressing the unique needs of marginalized or underserved groups. By promoting systemic change, counselors aim to create environments that support mental health resilience, reduce stigma, and enhance access to care. Ultimately, facilitating systemic change contributes to sustainable improvements in mental health outcomes at both individual and societal levels.

5.24 Distance Counseling and Telemental Health:

Distance counseling, or telemental health, refers to the provision of mental health services using telecommunications technology. This approach allows counselors to deliver therapeutic interventions remotely, often via video conferencing, phone calls, or secure messaging platforms. It is particularly beneficial for clients who face geographical, physical, or time-related barriers to accessing traditional in-person therapy.

To effectively provide telemental health services, counselors must adhere to ethical and legal standards, including maintaining client confidentiality and ensuring secure communication channels. They should be familiar with the technology used and be competent in managing any technical issues that may arise during sessions. Additionally, counselors must obtain informed consent specific to telemental health, clearly explaining the potential risks and benefits of remote counseling.

Counselors should assess the suitability of telemental health for each client, considering factors such as the client's comfort with technology, clinical needs, and the stability of their environment. It is crucial to establish clear protocols for crisis situations and ensure clients have access to emergency resources.

Overall, distance counseling expands access to mental health services and can be as effective as face-to-face therapy when conducted with appropriate diligence and care. Counselors must remain informed about evolving best practices and technological advancements in this rapidly growing field.

5.25 Provide Education Resources:

Providing educational resources involves offering clients access to information and materials that enhance their understanding of mental health issues, treatment options, and coping strategies. As a mental health counselor, it is crucial to empower clients with knowledge that can aid in their recovery and promote self-efficacy. This process includes identifying credible sources of information, such as books, articles, reputable websites, and support groups, tailored to the client's specific needs and circumstances.

Educational resources can cover a wide range of topics, including psychoeducation about specific mental health disorders, medication management, lifestyle modifications, stress reduction techniques, and the development of healthy relationships. Counselors must ensure that these resources are culturally sensitive, age-appropriate, and aligned with the client's level of comprehension.

In practice, providing educational resources also involves discussing the content with clients to ensure they understand and can apply the information effectively. This can be achieved through collaborative discussions, workshops, or one-on-one sessions where counselors can address any questions or misconceptions.

Ultimately, the goal is to equip clients with the tools they need to make informed decisions about their mental health care, fostering independence and resilience. By integrating educational resources into counseling practice, counselors can enhance therapeutic outcomes and support long-term client well-being.

5.25.1   Stress Management:

Stress management involves a range of techniques and psychotherapeutic interventions aimed at controlling an individual's level of stress, particularly chronic stress, to improve daily functioning. For mental health counselors, understanding stress management is crucial, as it equips them to assist clients in identifying stressors and developing coping strategies.

Effective stress management begins with recognizing the sources of stress, which can be categorized into external factors, such as work demands or relationship issues, and internal factors, such as negative self-talk or unrealistic expectations. Counselors guide clients in identifying these triggers through reflective practices and assessments.

Once identified, various techniques can be employed to manage stress. Cognitive-behavioral strategies are commonly used to help clients reframe negative thoughts and perceptions that contribute to stress. Mindfulness and relaxation techniques, such as deep breathing exercises, progressive muscle relaxation, and meditation, are also effective in reducing the physiological symptoms of stress.

Additionally, lifestyle modifications play a significant role in managing stress. Encouraging regular physical activity, adequate sleep, and a balanced diet can enhance an individual's resilience to stress. Time management skills are also critical in preventing overwhelm by prioritizing tasks and setting realistic goals.

Ultimately, the goal of stress management is to empower clients with tools and strategies that enhance their ability to cope with life's challenges effectively, promoting overall mental well-being.

5.25.2   Assertiveness Training:

Assertiveness training is a therapeutic intervention aimed at empowering individuals to express their thoughts, feelings, and needs in a direct, honest, and appropriate manner without violating the rights of others. It is a crucial component of mental health counseling, as it helps clients develop self-confidence and improve interpersonal relationships by fostering effective communication skills.

In assertiveness training, counselors guide clients in identifying passive, aggressive, and assertive behaviors. Clients learn to recognize passive behavior as avoiding confrontation at the expense of their own needs, while aggressive behavior involves expressing needs in a hostile manner that disregards the rights of others. Assertiveness lies in the middle, promoting balanced and respectful communication.

The training often includes role-playing exercises, modeling assertive behavior, and practicing specific techniques such as using I statements to express feelings and needs clearly. For instance, a client might say, I feel upset when meetings start late because it disrupts my schedule, instead of blaming others.

Assertiveness training also addresses underlying issues such as low self-esteem or fear of conflict that may hinder assertive communication. By building skills in this area, clients enhance their ability to set boundaries, refuse unreasonable requests, and negotiate effectively in various situations. Ultimately, assertiveness training contributes to improved mental health by reducing stress and enhancing personal empowerment.

5.25.3   Divorce Adjustment:
Divorce adjustment refers to the psychological and emotional process individuals undergo as they adapt to the changes brought about by the dissolution of a marriage. This adjustment period can vary significantly in duration and intensity, depending on factors such as individual resilience, social support systems, and the circumstances surrounding the divorce. Mental health counselors play a crucial role in facilitating this transition by providing clients with coping strategies, emotional support, and education about the typical phases of adjustment.

During divorce adjustment, individuals may experience a range of emotions, including grief, anger, relief, and anxiety. These emotions can manifest in various ways, such as changes in mood, behavior, or physical health. Counselors help clients navigate these feelings by encouraging healthy expression and processing of emotions while identifying maladaptive coping mechanisms that may hinder recovery.

Counselors also assist clients in redefining their identity outside of the marital relationship and establishing new routines and goals. This often involves exploring personal values, interests, and aspirations that may have been neglected during the marriage. Additionally, mental health professionals provide guidance on co-parenting strategies when children are involved, ensuring that the children's well-being is prioritized.

Overall, effective divorce adjustment counseling empowers individuals to rebuild their lives with a sense of autonomy and resilience, fostering long-term emotional stability and personal growth.

5.26 Provide Psychoeducation For Client:
Psychoeducation involves the process of educating clients about their mental health conditions, treatment options, and strategies for managing symptoms. It is a crucial component of mental health counseling, as it empowers clients with knowledge, fostering a sense of control and active participation in their recovery journey. The goal of psychoeducation is to enhance the client's understanding of their condition, reduce stigma, and improve adherence to treatment plans.

In practice, psychoeducation can be delivered through various formats, including individual sessions, group settings, or family meetings. Counselors provide information tailored to the client's cognitive level, cultural background, and specific needs. This may include explaining the nature of the disorder, potential triggers, symptom management techniques, and the role of medication, if applicable. By demystifying mental health issues, counselors help clients develop realistic expectations and coping strategies.

Effective psychoeducation also involves addressing any misconceptions or fears the client may have about their diagnosis or treatment. It encourages clients to ask questions and express concerns, promoting open communication between the counselor and the client. Ultimately, psychoeducation aims to empower clients by enhancing their self-efficacy and enabling them to make informed decisions about their mental health care. Through this collaborative approach, clients are better equipped to navigate their recovery process confidently.

5.27 Summarize:
In the context of mental health counseling, summarize refers to the counselor's ability to concisely and accurately encapsulate the key points of a client's narrative or session. This skill is critical for ensuring that both the counselor and client have a mutual understanding of what has been discussed, as well as for identifying themes, patterns, or issues that may need further exploration. Summarizing involves distilling the essence of the client's expressions, emotions, and thoughts into a coherent overview that facilitates clarity and direction in therapy.

Effective summarization requires active listening, empathy, and the ability to discern essential information from less relevant details. It serves multiple functions: it validates the client's experiences by demonstrating that the counselor has understood their perspective; it helps organize complex or overwhelming information into manageable segments; and it can highlight progress or recurring challenges within therapy sessions.

In practice, summarization may occur at the end of a session or at strategic points during the conversation to ensure alignment between the counselor and client. It is an interactive process that often invites client feedback, allowing them to correct any misunderstandings or expand upon their thoughts. Mastering this skill enhances therapeutic rapport and ensures that counseling sessions are productive and focused on achieving therapeutic goals.

5.28 Reframe/redirect:
Reframing and redirecting are therapeutic techniques employed by mental health counselors to help clients view situations, thoughts, or emotions from a different perspective. These cognitive restructuring methods are integral in altering the client's perception of an issue, thereby reducing distress and promoting adaptive behavior.

Reframing involves shifting the context or meaning of a situation to transform its emotional impact. For instance, a client who perceives a job loss as a personal failure can be encouraged to view it as an opportunity for growth and new beginnings. By changing the narrative, the counselor aids the client in developing resilience and optimism.

Redirecting, on the other hand, focuses on guiding clients away from negative thought patterns or behaviors toward more constructive alternatives. It involves steering the conversation or thought process in a direction that aligns with the client's goals and values. For example, if a client is fixated on past mistakes, redirecting their focus to present accomplishments can foster a sense of achievement and motivation.

Both techniques require skillful communication and empathy from the counselor to ensure that the reframed or redirected perspective resonates authentically with the client. Mastery of reframing and redirecting techniques equips counselors with powerful tools to facilitate cognitive and emotional change, which is essential for effective therapeutic outcomes.

5.29 Facilitate Empathic Responses:

Facilitating empathic responses involves actively engaging with clients in a way that demonstrates understanding, compassion, and validation of their experiences and emotions. As a mental health counselor, it is crucial to create an environment where clients feel heard and understood. This process begins with active listening, which requires full attention to the client's verbal and non-verbal communication. Reflecting back what the client has expressed is essential, as it shows that you are processing their words and emotions accurately.

Empathy goes beyond mere sympathy; it involves putting oneself in the client's shoes to genuinely understand their perspective. Counselors should use open-ended questions to encourage clients to share more about their feelings and thoughts. Paraphrasing and summarizing can help clarify understanding and ensure accuracy in interpreting the client's message.

Non-verbal cues such as nodding, maintaining eye contact, and appropriate facial expressions also play a significant role in conveying empathy. It is important to validate the client's feelings without judgment, acknowledging their struggles and strengths. This validation helps build trust and rapport, which are essential components of an effective therapeutic relationship.

By facilitating empathic responses, counselors empower clients to explore their issues more deeply, fostering the personal growth and insight necessary for positive change.

5.30 Use Self-disclosure:

Self-disclosure in counseling refers to the intentional sharing of personal information by the counselor with the client. This technique is used to build rapport, foster trust, and model openness, thereby enhancing the therapeutic alliance. It involves sharing relevant personal experiences, feelings, or thoughts that may help the client gain insight or feel more understood.

Effective use of self-disclosure requires careful consideration of its purpose and potential impact on the client. It should always be employed with the client's best interests in mind, ensuring it aligns with therapeutic goals. Counselors must assess whether their disclosure will benefit the client's understanding or progress within therapy. It's crucial that self-disclosure does not shift the focus away from the client or create a dual relationship that could complicate boundaries.

Counselors should be mindful of cultural differences and individual client needs when utilizing self-disclosure. What may be appropriate for one client might not be for another. Additionally, counselors must remain aware of their own comfort levels and motivations for sharing personal information, ensuring it is not used to fulfill their own needs.

In summary, self-disclosure can be a powerful tool in counseling when used judiciously and ethically. It requires a balance between transparency and professional boundaries to effectively support the client's therapeutic journey.

5.31 Use Constructive Confrontation:

Constructive confrontation is a therapeutic technique employed by mental health counselors to address discrepancies, contradictions, or maladaptive behaviors in a client's thoughts, feelings, or actions. This approach aims to promote self-awareness and facilitate positive change by gently challenging the client in a supportive and non-threatening manner.

In practice, constructive confrontation involves the counselor identifying and pointing out inconsistencies in the client's narrative or behavior that may hinder their progress. For example, if a client expresses a desire to improve their relationships but consistently engages in avoidance behaviors, the counselor might highlight this contradiction to encourage reflection and insight.

The effectiveness of constructive confrontation relies heavily on the counselor's ability to maintain a balance between challenge and support. It is crucial for the counselor to establish a strong therapeutic alliance built on trust and empathy before employing this technique. The tone of the confrontation should be respectful and understanding, avoiding any semblance of judgment or criticism.

Counselors must also be attuned to the client's readiness for confrontation and tailor their approach accordingly. By fostering an environment where clients feel safe to explore their defenses and underlying issues, constructive confrontation can lead to increased self-awareness, motivation for change, and ultimately, personal growth. This technique is integral in helping clients overcome barriers that impede their mental health journey.

5.32 Enhancing Here-and-Now Interaction Awareness:

Facilitating awareness of here-and-now interactions involves guiding clients to focus on their immediate experiences and feelings during therapy sessions. This approach encourages clients to become more conscious of their thoughts, emotions, and behaviors as they occur in the present moment, rather than dwelling on past events or anticipating future outcomes. By fostering this awareness, mental health counselors help clients develop a deeper understanding of their current emotional states and interpersonal dynamics.

In practice, counselors may use techniques such as mindfulness exercises, role-playing, or direct questioning to draw attention to the client's present experiences. For instance, a counselor might ask a client to describe what they are feeling physically and emotionally at a particular moment during the session. This can help clients identify patterns in their responses and reactions, leading to insights about how these patterns influence their relationships and decision-making processes.

The goal of facilitating here-and-now awareness is to empower clients to make conscious choices about how they interact with others and manage their internal experiences. By cultivating this skill, clients can improve their emotional regulation, enhance their communication skills, and foster healthier relationships. Ultimately, this approach supports the client's journey toward self-awareness and personal growth, which are crucial components of effective mental health counseling.

5.33 Interpersonal Conflict Resolution Facilitation:

Facilitating the resolution of interpersonal conflict involves guiding individuals or groups through a structured process to address and resolve disagreements or misunderstandings. This process is integral to mental health counseling, as unresolved conflicts can lead to emotional distress and hinder personal growth. As a mental health counselor, your role is to create a safe, neutral environment where clients feel comfortable expressing their thoughts and emotions.

Begin by helping clients identify the underlying issues contributing to the conflict. Encourage open communication by teaching active listening skills and promoting empathy among the parties involved. It is essential to remain impartial, focusing on facilitating dialogue rather than taking sides.

Utilize conflict resolution strategies such as negotiation, compromise, and collaboration. Encourage clients to explore various perspectives and generate mutually acceptable solutions. Techniques like role-playing or perspective-taking can be effective in helping clients understand different viewpoints.

Throughout the process, reinforce positive communication patterns and discourage negative behaviors such as blaming or defensiveness. Help clients develop problem-solving skills that they can apply in future conflicts.

Finally, evaluate the resolution process by assessing whether the conflict has been adequately addressed and if relationships have improved. Encourage clients to reflect on their experiences and learn from them, fostering resilience and emotional intelligence in handling future conflicts.

5.34 Linking and Blocking in Group Dynamics:
Linking and blocking are two essential techniques in group counseling that facilitate effective communication and maintain group dynamics. Linking involves connecting members' shared experiences, feelings, or thoughts to foster cohesion and empathy within the group. By highlighting commonalities, counselors encourage members to engage more deeply with one another, promoting a sense of belonging and understanding. This technique helps build a supportive network where members feel validated and heard, enhancing therapeutic outcomes.

Blocking, on the other hand, is a technique used to manage disruptions or negative behaviors that may hinder the group's progress. It involves the counselor intervening to stop behaviors such as monopolizing conversations, interrupting others, or engaging in off-topic discussions. By setting boundaries and redirecting focus, blocking ensures that the group remains productive and respectful. This technique requires sensitivity and tact to avoid alienating members while maintaining a safe and constructive environment.

In practice, effective use of linking and blocking requires the counselor to be observant and responsive to the group's dynamics. Balancing these techniques helps maintain a therapeutic atmosphere conducive to growth and change. Mastery of linking and blocking is crucial for counselors aiming to facilitate successful group sessions, ensuring all members benefit from the collective experience.

5.35 Management Of Leader–member Dynamics:
The management of leader-member dynamics involves understanding and effectively navigating the relationships between leaders and their team members within a therapeutic or organizational context. This dynamic is crucial in mental health counseling settings, as it influences group cohesion, communication, and the overall effectiveness of therapeutic interventions. Effective management requires counselors to recognize the power differentials inherent in these relationships and to strive to create an environment where open communication and mutual respect are prioritized.

Counselors must be adept at identifying and addressing any conflicts or issues that arise from these dynamics, utilizing conflict resolution strategies to maintain a harmonious group setting. They should also be skilled in promoting positive interactions by fostering an atmosphere of trust and collaboration, where members feel valued and understood.

Additionally, understanding the cultural, social, and personal factors that influence leader-member dynamics is essential. Counselors should be culturally competent, recognizing how diverse backgrounds can impact perceptions of authority and interaction styles.

By mastering these dynamics, mental health counselors can enhance therapeutic outcomes, ensuring that all group members feel supported and empowered to engage fully in the counseling process. This competence is critical for effective leadership within therapeutic settings, contributing significantly to the success of group therapy sessions and the well-being of all participants.

5.36 Feedback Exchange Model:
The Model of Giving and Receiving Feedback is a structured approach that facilitates effective communication in counseling settings. It emphasizes clarity, empathy, and constructiveness to enhance the therapeutic process. This model involves specific guidelines for both the counselor and the client to ensure that feedback is delivered and received in a manner that promotes growth and understanding.

When giving feedback, counselors should focus on being specific, objective, and supportive. This involves clearly stating observations without judgment, using I statements to express personal perceptions, and ensuring that the feedback is relevant to the client's goals. Counselors should also be mindful of timing and choose moments when the client is most receptive.

Receiving feedback requires openness and active listening from both parties. Counselors should encourage clients to express their thoughts and feelings about the feedback, fostering an environment where clients feel safe to discuss their reactions. It is important for counselors to demonstrate empathy and validate the client's experiences while guiding them toward constructive insights.

The model underscores the importance of balancing positive reinforcement with areas for improvement, thus maintaining a therapeutic alliance. By adhering to these principles, mental health counselors can enhance communication efficacy, support client development, and improve overall therapeutic outcomes.

5.37 Impact of Extended Families:
In the context of mental health counseling, understanding the impact of extended families is crucial. Extended families include relatives beyond the nuclear family, such as grandparents, aunts, uncles, and cousins. These family members can significantly influence an individual's mental health, both positively and negatively.

Extended families often provide additional emotional support, financial assistance, and childcare, which can alleviate stress and contribute to a sense of belonging and stability. This support network can be particularly beneficial in times of crisis or transition, offering a buffer against mental health challenges.

Conversely, extended family dynamics can also introduce complexities. Conflicts may arise due to differing values, expectations, or cultural beliefs. These conflicts can lead to stress and anxiety for individuals caught between competing familial demands. Additionally, enmeshment or over-involvement by extended family members can hinder personal autonomy and development.

As a mental health counselor, it is essential to assess the role and influence of extended family in a client's life. This involves exploring family dynamics, communication patterns, and cultural contexts. By addressing these factors in therapy, counselors can help clients navigate familial relationships more effectively and foster healthier interactions. Understanding the impact of extended families enables counselors to provide comprehensive care that considers the broader social context of their clients' lives.

5.38 Managing Intense Feelings:

Containing and managing intense feelings is a critical skill for mental health counselors, particularly when working with clients experiencing strong emotions such as anger, anxiety, or sadness. This process involves helping clients acknowledge and understand their emotions without becoming overwhelmed by them. It requires the counselor to create a safe and supportive environment where clients feel comfortable expressing their feelings. The counselor guides the client in identifying the underlying causes of these intense emotions and helps them develop coping strategies to manage them effectively.

One effective approach is emotion regulation, which includes techniques such as cognitive restructuring, mindfulness, and grounding exercises. Cognitive restructuring involves challenging and changing unhelpful thought patterns that contribute to emotional distress. Mindfulness encourages clients to stay present and observe their emotions without judgment, which can reduce their intensity over time. Grounding exercises help clients reconnect with the present moment, preventing them from being swept away by overwhelming emotions.

Counselors must also be attuned to their own emotional responses during sessions to maintain an objective stance and provide appropriate support. By modeling healthy emotional regulation and containment strategies, counselors can empower clients to manage their feelings more effectively. This skill is vital for promoting emotional resilience and improving overall mental health outcomes for clients.

5.39 Family of Origin Patterns and Themes:

Family of origin refers to the family unit or system in which an individual was raised and includes parents, siblings, and other significant caregivers. Exploring the influence of family of origin patterns and themes involves examining how these early familial interactions and dynamics shape an individual's psychological development, behavior, and interpersonal relationships. This exploration is crucial for mental health counselors, as it provides insights into clients' current functioning and challenges.

Family patterns include roles, communication styles, rules, and emotional responses that are often unconsciously learned and repeated across generations. Themes may encompass recurring issues such as conflict resolution, emotional expression, or attachment styles. Identifying these patterns and themes helps counselors understand how clients' past experiences influence their present behaviors and emotional responses.

For instance, a client who grew up in a family where emotions were not openly expressed may struggle with emotional intimacy in adult relationships. By recognizing these patterns, counselors can help clients develop healthier coping mechanisms and relationship skills. Moreover, understanding family of origin influences allows clients to break maladaptive cycles and create more fulfilling lives. This exploration is a fundamental component of many therapeutic approaches, including family systems therapy, cognitive-behavioral therapy, and psychodynamic therapy, all of which emphasize the importance of understanding one's familial background to facilitate personal growth and healing.

5.40 Impact of Social Support Networks:

Social support networks play a crucial role in mental health counseling, as they significantly impact an individual's psychological well-being and recovery process. A social support network consists of family, friends, colleagues, and community members who provide emotional, informational, and practical assistance. Addressing the impact of these networks involves assessing both the presence and quality of social connections in a client's life.

A strong social support network can enhance resilience by providing emotional comfort, reducing stress, and fostering a sense of belonging. It can also offer practical help, such as transportation or financial assistance, which alleviates burdens that might otherwise exacerbate mental health issues. Conversely, a lack of supportive relationships or the presence of negative influences can hinder progress in therapy, increase feelings of isolation, and contribute to anxiety or depression.

Counselors must evaluate the client's social support system to identify strengths and areas for improvement. This evaluation may involve guiding clients in strengthening existing relationships, building new connections, or navigating challenging interactions. By understanding the dynamics within a client's social network, counselors can tailor interventions that leverage these relationships to support therapeutic goals. Ultimately, enhancing social support networks is integral to promoting sustained mental health and well-being in clients.

5.41 Use "structured" Activities:

Structured activities in mental health counseling refer to pre-planned, organized tasks or exercises designed to facilitate therapeutic goals and enhance client engagement. These activities are systematically implemented to provide clients with a clear framework within which they can explore thoughts, emotions, and behaviors in a safe and supportive environment. Structured activities can include worksheets, role-playing, guided imagery, and behavioral experiments.

The primary purpose of structured activities is to promote learning and insight by providing clients with a tangible way to process complex issues. They help break down overwhelming problems into manageable parts, allowing clients to gain clarity and develop coping strategies. By engaging in these activities, clients can practice new skills, explore different perspectives, and reinforce positive behavior changes.

In a therapeutic setting, structured activities are tailored to meet the individual needs of the client and are often used in conjunction with other therapeutic techniques. Counselors must consider the client's cultural background, cognitive abilities, and emotional readiness when selecting appropriate activities. Additionally, structured activities can be used to monitor progress and assess the effectiveness of interventions.

For mental health counselors preparing for the NCMHCE exam, understanding the application and benefits of structured activities is crucial for effectively supporting clients in achieving their therapeutic goals.

5.42 Fostering Group Interaction:

Promoting and encouraging interactions among group members is a fundamental aspect of effective group counseling. This process involves creating an environment where members feel safe and motivated to share their thoughts, experiences, and emotions openly. The counselor plays a pivotal role in facilitating these interactions by establishing trust, setting clear group norms, and fostering a sense of belonging.

To achieve this, the counselor can employ several strategies. Firstly, they can model appropriate communication behaviors, such as active listening and empathy, which members are encouraged to emulate. Secondly, the counselor can use open-ended questions to stimulate discussion and invite diverse perspectives. Additionally, structuring activities that require collaboration can help break down barriers and promote cohesion.

The counselor should also be attentive to group dynamics, identifying and addressing any issues, such as dominance by certain members or reluctance from others to participate. This might involve gently encouraging quieter members to voice their opinions or redirecting conversations to ensure balanced participation.

Ultimately, promoting interactions among group members enhances the therapeutic value of the group by facilitating shared learning and mutual support. It empowers individuals to develop interpersonal skills and gain insights from their peers' experiences, thereby contributing to their personal growth and the overall effectiveness of the counseling process.

5.43 Enhancing Group Leader Engagement:
In the context of group counseling, promoting and encouraging interactions with the group leader is essential for fostering a therapeutic environment conducive to growth and healing. The group leader, often a mental health counselor, plays a pivotal role in guiding discussions, managing dynamics, and ensuring that each member feels heard and valued. By promoting interactions with the group leader, members can build trust, gain insights, and feel more connected to the therapeutic process.

Interactions with the group leader involve open communication, where members are encouraged to express their thoughts, feelings, and concerns. This can be facilitated through active listening, empathetic responses, and providing feedback that validates members' experiences. The group leader should also model effective communication skills and demonstrate vulnerability when appropriate, setting a tone of openness and authenticity.

Encouraging these interactions helps to establish a safe space where members feel comfortable sharing personal experiences without fear of judgment. It also allows the leader to assess the needs of the group, tailor interventions accordingly, and address any conflicts or issues that may arise. Ultimately, fostering interactions with the group leader enhances the therapeutic alliance, promotes cohesion among members, and supports individual and collective growth within the group setting.

5.44 Psychoeducation in Group Process:
Psychoeducation in the context of group therapy refers to the process of providing individuals with information and support to better understand their mental health conditions and treatment options. This approach empowers clients by enhancing their knowledge, which can lead to improved coping strategies and adherence to treatment plans. Within a group setting, psychoeducation serves as a foundational component that facilitates learning and shared experiences among participants.

Incorporating psychoeducation into the group process involves structured sessions where a mental health counselor imparts information on topics such as symptom management, medication effects, stress reduction techniques, and lifestyle modifications. The goal is to demystify mental health issues and equip clients with practical tools for self-management. By doing so, clients can gain a sense of control over their conditions, reducing feelings of helplessness and stigma.

Furthermore, psychoeducation fosters a supportive environment where group members can share personal experiences and insights, thereby normalizing their struggles and promoting mutual support. This collective learning experience not only enhances individual understanding but also strengthens group cohesion. Counselors must tailor psychoeducational content to meet the specific needs of the group, ensuring that it is relevant, culturally sensitive, and accessible. By integrating psychoeducation into the group process, counselors can significantly enhance therapeutic outcomes and client empowerment.

5.45 Phases of Group Process:
The group process in mental health counseling involves distinct phases that facilitate effective group dynamics and therapeutic outcomes. These phases are forming, storming, norming, performing, and adjourning.

During the forming phase, members get acquainted and establish the group's purpose. Counselors play a pivotal role in setting the tone, clarifying objectives, and establishing trust. This phase is characterized by anxiety and uncertainty as members explore their roles.

The storming phase involves conflict and competition as individuals assert their opinions and vie for dominance. Counselors must manage conflicts constructively, promoting open communication and empathy to guide the group toward cohesion.

In the norming phase, group norms are established, fostering a sense of unity and collaboration. Members begin to trust one another, sharing insights and providing mutual support. The counselor's role is to reinforce positive behaviors and facilitate deeper engagement.

The performing phase is where the group reaches its full potential, achieving therapeutic goals through effective problem-solving and decision-making. Members work collaboratively, demonstrating high levels of trust and cooperation. Counselors continue to support but take on a less directive role.

Finally, the adjourning phase marks the conclusion of the group's work. Members reflect on their progress, celebrate achievements, and prepare for separation. Counselors facilitate closure by helping members process emotions related to the ending of the group experience.

5.46 Group Themes and Patterns Analysis:
In the context of group counseling, identifying and discussing group themes and patterns is a critical skill for mental health counselors. This involves recognizing recurring topics, emotions, or behaviors that emerge within the group setting. Themes are the central ideas or issues that surface repeatedly during sessions, while patterns refer to the consistent ways in which group members interact with one another and respond to these themes.

To effectively identify themes and patterns, counselors must actively listen and observe interactions among group members. They should take note of verbal and non-verbal communication cues, such as tone of voice, body language, and emotional expressions. Additionally, counselors should be aware of the dynamics between members, including alliances, conflicts, and power structures.

Once identified, discussing these themes and patterns with the group can facilitate deeper understanding and insight among participants. It encourages members to reflect on their own behaviors and how they contribute to the group dynamic. This process can lead to increased self-awareness and promote personal growth.

Counselors should approach discussions with sensitivity and neutrality, fostering an environment where members feel safe to express themselves. By guiding the group through these discussions, counselors help members process their experiences collectively, ultimately enhancing therapeutic outcomes. Understanding these dynamics is essential for effective group facilitation and achieving therapeutic goals.

5.47 Stage-Based Group Development Interventions:

Creating interventions based on the stages of group development involves tailoring therapeutic strategies to align with the distinct phases through which a group progresses. These stages typically include forming, storming, norming, performing, and adjourning. Each stage presents unique challenges and opportunities for growth, requiring mental health counselors to adapt their approaches accordingly.

During the forming stage, interventions should focus on establishing trust and building rapport among group members. Activities that promote introductions and clarify group goals are essential. In the storming stage, conflicts may arise as members assert their opinions. Interventions should aim to facilitate open communication and conflict resolution skills.

As the group enters the norming stage, cohesion begins to develop. Interventions should encourage collaboration and reinforce shared norms and values. During the performing stage, the group reaches its peak efficiency. Interventions can be more directive, focusing on achieving specific therapeutic goals and encouraging deeper exploration of personal issues.

Finally, in the adjourning stage, interventions should address closure and transition. Facilitating reflection on accomplishments and discussing future plans are crucial components. By aligning interventions with these developmental stages, counselors enhance group dynamics, foster individual growth, and optimize therapeutic outcomes, ensuring that each member benefits from the collective experience.

5.48 Addressing Harmful Group Behaviors:

Challenging harmful group member behaviors is a critical skill for mental health counselors facilitating group therapy sessions. This involves identifying and addressing behaviors that disrupt the therapeutic process, compromise safety, or negatively impact the progress of other members. Such behaviors may include dominating conversations, dismissing others' contributions, displaying aggression, or consistently violating group norms.

To effectively challenge these behaviors, counselors must first create a safe and supportive environment where all members feel respected and heard. This involves establishing clear group rules and expectations from the outset. When harmful behaviors arise, counselors should address them promptly and assertively, using techniques such as direct confrontation, gentle redirection, or reframing to guide the group back to its therapeutic goals.

Counselors should employ active listening to understand the underlying issues driving the behavior and provide feedback that encourages self-reflection and accountability. It is essential to balance confrontation with empathy, ensuring that interventions are not punitive but rather aimed at fostering growth and understanding.

By constructively challenging harmful behaviors, counselors help maintain a cohesive group dynamic that promotes healing and personal development for all members. This skill is crucial for ensuring that the therapeutic environment remains conducive to achieving the desired outcomes of the group therapy process.

5.49 Managing External Member Interactions:

Addressing the potential interactions of group members outside of the therapeutic setting involves understanding and managing the dynamics that may occur when individuals in a counseling group engage with each other beyond the confines of structured sessions. This aspect is crucial for maintaining the integrity and effectiveness of group therapy.

Interactions outside the group can influence the therapeutic process either positively or negatively. Positive interactions might foster supportive relationships that reinforce therapeutic goals, while negative interactions could lead to conflicts, boundary issues, or breaches of confidentiality. As a mental health counselor, it is essential to establish clear guidelines and discuss these potential interactions during the initial stages of group formation. This includes setting boundaries regarding confidentiality, appropriate conduct, and communication channels outside the group.

Counselors should encourage open dialogue about any external interactions during sessions to address any emerging issues promptly. This proactive approach helps mitigate risks associated with dual relationships and ensures that all members feel safe and respected within the group environment. Furthermore, counselors must be vigilant in observing changes in group dynamics that may suggest external influences, thereby adjusting their interventions accordingly to maintain a cohesive and therapeutic atmosphere.

6 Core Counseling Attributes:

Core counseling attributes are fundamental qualities and skills that mental health counselors must possess to effectively facilitate client growth and healing. These attributes form the foundation of a successful therapeutic relationship and are essential for professional competence in the field of mental health counseling.

Empathy is a cornerstone attribute, allowing counselors to deeply understand and resonate with clients' feelings and experiences. It fosters trust and openness, enabling clients to explore their issues more freely. Active listening is closely related, requiring counselors to fully concentrate, understand, respond to, and remember what the client is communicating.

Unconditional positive regard involves accepting and valuing clients without judgment, creating a safe space for them to express themselves. This acceptance is crucial in helping clients feel respected and understood.

Authenticity, or genuineness, refers to the counselor's ability to be honest and transparent with clients. This attribute helps build trust and models healthy interpersonal interactions.

Additionally, cultural competence is vital, as it ensures counselors respect and understand diverse backgrounds and perspectives. This competence enhances the counselor's ability to connect with clients from varied cultural contexts.

Finally, ethical integrity is paramount, guiding counselors to adhere to professional standards and ethical guidelines. This ensures that client welfare remains the top priority throughout the counseling process.

Together, these core attributes enable counselors to provide effective, compassionate, and culturally sensitive care.

6.1 Self-Awareness and Client Impact:

Awareness of self refers to a counselor's understanding and insight into their own thoughts, emotions, values, biases, and behaviors. It is a crucial aspect of effective counseling, as it influences the therapeutic relationship and the counselor's ability to provide unbiased support. A counselor's self-awareness allows them to recognize how their personal experiences and beliefs may affect their perceptions and interactions with clients. This understanding is vital in preventing countertransference where a counselor projects their own unresolved emotions onto the client and in ensuring that the counselor's personal issues do not interfere with the client's treatment.

The impact on clients is significant; when counselors are self-aware, they can create a safe and supportive environment where clients feel understood and respected. This fosters trust and openness, encouraging clients to engage more deeply in the therapeutic process. Conversely, a lack of self-awareness can lead to misunderstandings, misinterpretations, and potentially harm the client-counselor relationship.

To enhance self-awareness, counselors should engage in regular self-reflection, seek supervision or consultation when needed, and participate in ongoing professional development. By doing so, they can continually refine their skills and maintain an ethical practice that prioritizes the well-being of their clients. This self-awareness is not only a professional responsibility but also a cornerstone of effective mental health counseling.

6.2 Genuineness:

Genuineness, also known as authenticity, is a core counseling attribute that refers to the counselor's ability to be open, honest, and transparent with their clients. It involves the counselor being true to themselves and congruent in their interactions, meaning their external expressions align with their internal feelings and thoughts. Genuineness is crucial in establishing trust and rapport between the counselor and the client, as it fosters an environment where clients feel safe to explore and express their own thoughts and emotions.

In practice, genuineness requires counselors to be self-aware and mindful of their own feelings, biases, and reactions. This self-awareness allows them to engage with clients in a manner that is both respectful and sincere. Genuineness does not mean sharing every personal thought or feeling with the client; rather, it involves selectively disclosing information that is therapeutically beneficial and appropriate within the context of the counseling relationship.

A genuine counselor does not hide behind a professional façade but instead presents themselves as a real person who is empathetic and understanding. This authenticity encourages clients to be more open and honest in their own self-disclosure, facilitating deeper therapeutic work. In essence, genuineness is about creating a genuine human connection that supports the client's growth and healing process.

6.3 Congruence:

Congruence in counseling refers to the alignment and authenticity between a counselor's internal experiences and external expressions. It is a core attribute that ensures the counselor presents themselves genuinely to clients, fostering a trustworthy therapeutic environment. In practice, congruence means that the counselor's verbal and non-verbal communication is consistent with their true feelings and thoughts, thereby promoting transparency and honesty within the therapeutic relationship.

For mental health counselors, congruence is critical as it models authentic behavior for clients, encouraging them to also be genuine in expressing their thoughts and emotions. This authenticity helps in building rapport and trust, which are essential components of effective counseling. Congruent counselors are more likely to be perceived as credible and reliable, enhancing client engagement and facilitating deeper exploration of issues.

Moreover, congruence involves self-awareness on the part of the counselor. They must be attuned to their own emotions and biases to ensure these do not interfere with the counseling process. This requires ongoing self-reflection and professional development. In essence, congruence is not just about being honest with clients but also about maintaining integrity within oneself as a practitioner. This quality is indispensable for fostering a therapeutic alliance that supports client growth and development.

6.4 Understanding Gender Orientation and Issues:

Demonstrating knowledge of and sensitivity to gender orientation and gender issues is a critical competency for mental health counselors. This involves understanding the complex spectrum of gender identities beyond the traditional binary framework of male and female. It requires familiarity with terms such as transgender, non-binary, genderqueer, and cisgender, among others. Counselors must recognize that gender identity is a deeply personal experience that may not align with an individual's biological sex assigned at birth.

Sensitivity to these issues means acknowledging the unique challenges faced by individuals due to societal norms and prejudices, including discrimination, marginalization, and mental health disparities. Counselors should create an inclusive and affirming environment that respects each client's self-identified gender. This includes using preferred pronouns and names and actively avoiding assumptions based on appearance or behavior.

Furthermore, it is essential for counselors to be aware of the intersectionality of gender issues with other aspects of identity, such as race, ethnicity, sexual orientation, and socioeconomic status. Continuous education on evolving gender concepts and advocacy for gender-inclusive policies in clinical settings are also part of demonstrating this competency. Such knowledge and sensitivity are crucial in providing effective support and fostering a therapeutic alliance with clients navigating gender-related concerns.

6.5 Multicultural Awareness and Sensitivity:

Demonstrating knowledge of and sensitivity to multicultural issues involves understanding, acknowledging, and valuing the diverse cultural backgrounds and experiences that clients bring into the counseling setting. It requires counselors to be aware of their own cultural biases and to actively work toward minimizing these biases in their practice. This competency is crucial for providing effective and respectful mental health services to clients from various cultural backgrounds.

Counselors must possess a deep understanding of how cultural factors such as race, ethnicity, gender, sexual orientation, socioeconomic status, religion, and language can influence a client's worldview, identity, and mental health. Sensitivity to these issues means recognizing the unique challenges faced by individuals from marginalized or minority groups and adapting counseling approaches to meet their specific needs.

Effective multicultural counseling involves continuous self-reflection, education, and training to enhance cultural competence. Counselors should engage in active listening and demonstrate empathy and respect for cultural differences. They should also be familiar with culturally relevant theories and interventions that promote healing and empowerment.

In summary, demonstrating knowledge of and sensitivity to multicultural issues is an ongoing process that enhances the therapeutic alliance, fosters trust, and ultimately improves client outcomes by ensuring that counseling practices are inclusive, equitable, and responsive to the diverse needs of all clients.

6.6 Conflict Tolerance and Resolution Strategies:
Conflict tolerance and resolution are essential skills for mental health counselors, enabling them to effectively manage and mediate disputes within therapeutic settings. Conflict tolerance refers to a counselor's ability to remain calm, composed, and non-judgmental when faced with disagreements or tensions, whether between clients or within themselves. This skill involves understanding the dynamics of conflict, recognizing personal biases, and maintaining an empathetic stance that prioritizes client well-being.

Conflict resolution, on the other hand, involves actively facilitating the process of finding constructive solutions to conflicts. Counselors must employ techniques such as active listening, empathy, and open-ended questioning to help clients articulate their feelings and perspectives. By fostering an environment of mutual respect and understanding, counselors guide clients toward identifying underlying issues and collaboratively developing strategies to address them.

In practice, demonstrating conflict tolerance and resolution requires a counselor to balance assertiveness with diplomacy. They must encourage honest communication while setting boundaries that prevent escalation. This process not only aids in resolving immediate conflicts but also empowers clients with the skills to manage future disagreements independently. Mastery of these competencies is crucial for mental health counselors as they strive to create therapeutic alliances that support client growth and resilience in the face of interpersonal challenges.

6.7 Empathic Attunement:
Empathic attunement is a fundamental skill in mental health counseling, denoting the counselor's ability to deeply understand and resonate with the client's emotional experiences. This process involves more than just recognizing the client's feelings; it requires the counselor to be fully present and genuinely engaged, allowing them to perceive subtle emotional cues and nuances. Empathic attunement is characterized by an alignment of the counselor's emotional state with that of the client, fostering a therapeutic environment where the client feels seen, heard, and validated.

In practice, empathic attunement involves active listening and reflective responses that accurately mirror the client's emotions. The counselor must maintain an open and nonjudgmental stance, facilitating a safe space for clients to explore their feelings. This attunement helps build rapport and trust, which are essential for effective therapeutic outcomes.

Moreover, empathic attunement is not static; it requires continuous adjustment and sensitivity to the client's evolving emotional landscape. It demands self-awareness from the counselor to manage their own emotional reactions and biases effectively. By mastering empathic attunement, counselors can enhance their therapeutic presence, enabling deeper connections with clients and promoting healing through understanding and empathy. This skill is crucial for counselors preparing for the NCMHCE, as it underscores their ability to engage meaningfully with clients across diverse contexts.

6.8 Empathic Responding:
Empathic responding is a fundamental skill in mental health counseling, essential for fostering a therapeutic alliance and facilitating client growth. It involves the counselor's ability to accurately perceive and reflect the client's feelings and experiences, demonstrating an understanding of their emotional state. This process requires active listening, where the counselor attentively focuses on the client's verbal and non-verbal cues, allowing them to grasp both explicit and implicit messages.

The essence of empathic responding lies in its ability to validate the client's emotions, creating a safe and supportive environment. By acknowledging and reflecting the client's feelings, counselors help clients feel heard and understood, which can enhance trust and openness in the therapeutic relationship. Empathic responses often involve paraphrasing or summarizing what the client has shared, coupled with an emotional reflection that captures the underlying affective experience.

Effective empathic responding requires self-awareness and cultural sensitivity from counselors to avoid projecting their own biases or assumptions onto the client. It is not merely about agreement but rather about understanding from the client's perspective. Mastery of this skill can lead to deeper exploration of issues, increased client insight, and empowerment. Thus, empathic responding is a critical component in facilitating meaningful change and progress in therapy sessions.

6.9 Fostering Group Therapeutic Factors:
Fostering the emergence of group therapeutic factors involves creating an environment within group therapy that facilitates healing and personal growth among its members. Group therapeutic factors, as identified by Irvin D. Yalom, include elements such as the instillation of hope, universality, imparting information, altruism, corrective recapitulation of the primary family group, development of socializing techniques, imitative behavior, interpersonal learning, group cohesiveness, catharsis, and existential factors.

To foster these factors, a mental health counselor must skillfully guide the group dynamics to ensure that each member feels safe and supported. This involves setting clear boundaries and expectations while encouraging open and honest communication. The counselor should facilitate interactions that promote empathy and understanding among members, helping them recognize shared experiences and emotions. By doing so, members can experience universality and altruism.

Furthermore, the counselor should encourage members to share personal stories and insights, which can lead to catharsis and the imparting of information. Role-playing or modeling appropriate behaviors can aid in the development of social skills and imitative behavior. By fostering a sense of belonging and cohesiveness within the group, members are more likely to engage in interpersonal learning and experience transformative change. This process ultimately enhances the therapeutic outcomes for all participants.

6.10 Non-judgmental Stance:

A non-judgmental stance is a fundamental attribute of effective counseling, characterized by the counselor's ability to maintain an open, accepting, and unbiased attitude toward clients. This approach involves suspending personal judgments, biases, or preconceived notions about the client's experiences, behaviors, or values. It is essential for fostering a therapeutic environment where clients feel safe to express themselves without fear of criticism or disapproval.

In practice, adopting a non-judgmental stance requires counselors to actively listen and validate the client's experiences, acknowledging their feelings and perspectives without imposing their own values or beliefs. This stance is crucial for building rapport and trust, as it encourages clients to be more open and honest in sharing their thoughts and emotions. By demonstrating empathy and understanding, counselors can help clients explore their issues more deeply and facilitate personal growth and self-awareness.

Moreover, a non-judgmental stance allows counselors to remain objective and focused on the client's needs rather than being influenced by personal biases. This objectivity is vital for developing effective treatment plans tailored to the client's unique circumstances. Ultimately, maintaining a non-judgmental stance empowers clients to make autonomous decisions and fosters a collaborative therapeutic relationship that promotes healing and positive change.

6.11 Positive Regard:

Positive regard is a fundamental concept in counseling, referring to the therapist's attitude of acceptance and respect towards the client, irrespective of the client's behavior or circumstances. Originating from Carl Rogers' person-centered therapy, positive regard is essential for creating a therapeutic environment conducive to growth and self-discovery. It involves acknowledging the intrinsic worth of the client and viewing them as capable of change and development.

In practice, positive regard manifests as unconditional acceptance that helps clients feel safe and understood, fostering an open and honest therapeutic relationship. It requires counselors to suspend judgment and demonstrate empathy, actively listening to the client's experiences without imposing personal biases or values. This approach encourages clients to explore their feelings and thoughts more deeply, facilitating greater self-awareness and insight.

For mental health counselors preparing for the NCMHCE exam, understanding positive regard involves recognizing its impact on client outcomes. Research indicates that when clients perceive positive regard from their counselors, they are more likely to engage in therapy and experience positive changes. Thus, cultivating this attribute is crucial for effective counseling practice.

Counselors must continuously develop their ability to offer positive regard, ensuring that their interactions with clients are characterized by genuine warmth, empathy, and respect, ultimately supporting the client's journey toward healing and growth.

6.12 Embracing Diversity: Respect and Acceptance

Respect and acceptance for diversity in mental health counseling involve recognizing, valuing, and embracing the unique differences among individuals. These differences may include, but are not limited to, race, ethnicity, gender identity, sexual orientation, age, socioeconomic status, religion, and abilities. As a mental health counselor, it is imperative to cultivate an environment where clients feel safe and understood, regardless of their diverse backgrounds.

A comprehensive understanding of diversity begins with self-awareness. Counselors must acknowledge their own biases and preconceived notions that may affect therapeutic relationships. By engaging in continuous education and cultural competency training, counselors can better appreciate the varied experiences and perspectives of their clients.

In practice, respect for diversity means actively listening to clients' narratives without judgment and adapting therapeutic approaches to fit their cultural contexts. This might involve integrating culturally relevant interventions or collaborating with community resources that align with the client's cultural values.

Acceptance goes beyond tolerance; it requires a genuine appreciation for how diversity enriches the counseling process. By fostering an inclusive environment, counselors empower clients to express themselves authentically, facilitating more effective treatment outcomes. Ultimately, respect and acceptance of diversity enhance the counselor-client relationship, promoting healing and growth within a multicultural framework.

6.13 Foundational Listening and Reflecting Skills:

Foundational listening, attending, and reflecting skills are essential components of the therapeutic process for mental health counselors. These skills enable counselors to effectively understand and respond to clients, fostering a supportive and empathetic environment.

Listening involves actively hearing the client's words, tone, and underlying emotions. It requires the counselor to focus entirely on the client without distractions, ensuring that they capture the full message being conveyed. This active listening is crucial for building trust and rapport.

Attending refers to the counselor's physical and psychological presence during the session. It includes non-verbal cues such as maintaining eye contact, nodding, and adopting an open posture. These behaviors demonstrate genuine interest and concern, encouraging clients to express themselves freely.

Reflecting skills involve mirroring or paraphrasing what the client has communicated. This technique helps clarify and validate the client's feelings and thoughts while also confirming the counselor's understanding. Reflecting can include summarizing key points or echoing emotions expressed by the client, which aids in deepening the therapeutic dialogue.

By mastering these foundational skills, counselors create a safe space for clients to explore their issues. These techniques are integral to effective counseling practice and are critical for success on the NCMHCE exam, as they underpin many of the scenarios presented in the test.

NCMHCE
Practice
Questions
[SET 1]

Question 1: In the context of Carl Rogers' person-centered therapy, what does 'congruence' specifically refer to?
A) The counselor's ability to understand the client's feelings and experiences from the client's perspective.
B) The counselor's expression of genuine feelings and thoughts that are aligned with their internal experiences.
C) The counselor's acceptance and support of the client regardless of what the client says or does.
D) The counselor's ability to reflect the client's feelings back to them accurately.

Question 2: Which of the following physical symptoms is most commonly associated with generalized anxiety disorder (GAD)?
A) Chest pain
B) Shortness of breath
C) Muscle tension
D) Frequent urination

Question 3: Which method is considered most effective for evaluating the overall effectiveness of a counseling intervention?
A) Client self-report surveys
B) Standardized outcome measures
C) Counselor's subjective evaluation
D) Session-by-session progress notes

Question 4: Alex, a 25-year-old non-binary individual, expresses frustration during a counseling session about their partner's lack of understanding and support regarding their gender identity. As their counselor, which approach would best demonstrate knowledge of and sensitivity to Alex's gender orientation and issues?
A) Encourage Alex to educate their partner about non-binary identities.
B) Suggest that Alex give their partner time to adjust without discussing it further.
C) Validate Alex's feelings and explore ways they can advocate for themselves.
D) Recommend couples therapy to address communication issues.

Question 5: A client who has experienced family abuse exhibits significant emotional distress. Which of the following therapeutic approaches is most effective in addressing the client's emotional needs?
A) Cognitive Behavioral Therapy (CBT)
B) Eye Movement Desensitization and Reprocessing (EMDR)
C) Solution-Focused Brief Therapy (SFBT)
D) Psychodynamic Therapy

Question 6: John reports feeling overwhelmed by his family's constant demands for his time and attention, which leaves him little personal space. As a mental health counselor, what would be an effective initial step in exploring these family interactions?
A) Advise John to take a vacation alone to recharge.
B) Work with John on assertiveness training to communicate his needs.
C) Suggest John delegate some responsibilities to other family members.
D) Conduct a family session to understand each member's perspective on John's role.

Question 7: Maria, a 28-year-old woman with bipolar disorder, has been stabilized on medication during her inpatient stay. Her treatment team is considering her next steps for continued stabilization. Which level of care should be recommended for Maria post-discharge?
A) Intensive outpatient program (IOP)
B) Outpatient therapy with bi-weekly sessions

C) Partial hospitalization program (PHP)
D) Day treatment program

Question 8: John, a 45-year-old patient diagnosed with schizophrenia, is being considered for participation in a clinical trial. As his mental health counselor, you need to assess his competency to provide informed consent. Which of the following factors is most crucial in determining John's competency?
A) John's ability to understand the nature and purpose of the clinical trial.
B) John's willingness to participate in the clinical trial.
C) John's history of compliance with previous medical treatments.
D) John's family's opinion about his participation in the trial.

Question 9: Jane, a 35-year-old woman, has been experiencing flashbacks, hypervigilance, and difficulty sleeping since surviving a severe car accident six months ago. She also reports feeling detached from her family and friends. As her mental health counselor, what is the most appropriate initial intervention to address her symptoms?
A) Cognitive Behavioral Therapy (CBT)
B) Eye Movement Desensitization and Reprocessing (EMDR)
C) Prolonged Exposure Therapy
D) Medication Management

Question 10: When discussing confidentiality in electronic communication, which of the following is the most critical consideration for a mental health counselor to ensure client privacy?
A) Encrypting all emails containing client information.
B) Using secure, HIPAA-compliant platforms for telehealth sessions.
C) Obtaining written consent from clients before any form of electronic communication.
D) Regularly updating software to protect against cybersecurity threats.

Question 11: Which communication pattern is most commonly associated with long-term dissatisfaction in marital relationships?
A) Criticism
B) Stonewalling
C) Contempt
D) Defensiveness

Question 12: Which of the following summaries best captures the essence of Sarah's concerns?
A) "Sarah is worried about her financial situation due to losing her job and feels uncertain about her future."
B) "Sarah is experiencing significant anxiety and stress because of her job loss and financial instability."
C) "Sarah feels overwhelmed by the loss of her job and is anxious about how this will affect her future."
D) "Sarah's primary concern is the uncertainty of her future, which is causing her considerable anxiety."

Question 13: Sarah, a 30-year-old female, experiences auditory hallucinations during periods of extreme stress but has no other psychiatric symptoms or history of mental illness. What is the most appropriate initial intervention?
A) Antipsychotic medication
B) Cognitive-behavioral therapy (CBT)
C) Stress management techniques
D) Hospitalization

Question 14: When assessing a client's competency to provide informed consent, which of the following is the most crucial factor for a mental health counselor to

evaluate?

A) The client's ability to articulate their decision clearly.
B) The client's understanding of the information provided.
C) The client's emotional stability during the decision-making process.
D) The client's previous experiences with similar decisions.

Question 15: John, a 35-year-old male, presents with frequent episodes of chest pain, palpitations, and shortness of breath. He has undergone extensive cardiac evaluations, all of which were normal. Given his history of generalized anxiety disorder (GAD), what is the most likely explanation for his symptoms?

A) Panic Attacks
B) Hyperthyroidism
C) Myocardial Infarction
D) Asthma

Question 16: When utilizing constructive confrontation in a counseling session, which approach is most effective for addressing a client's inconsistent behavior without causing defensiveness?

A) Directly pointing out the client's contradictory statements.
B) Using "I" statements to express concern about the observed inconsistency.
C) Asking the client why they are behaving inconsistently.
D) Suggesting possible reasons for the inconsistency based on your observations.

Question 17: John, a client in therapy for anxiety, shares his fear about an upcoming job interview. As his counselor using empathic attunement, what should your response be?

A) "I can see that you're really worried about this interview."
B) "It's normal to feel anxious before an important event like this."
C) "You have prepared well; you just need to stay calm."
D) "Many people feel nervous before interviews; you'll do great."

Question 18: Which of the following stress management techniques has been shown by contemporary research to be most effective in reducing physiological markers of stress, such as cortisol levels?

A) Progressive Muscle Relaxation (PMR)
B) Cognitive Behavioral Therapy (CBT)
C) Mindfulness-Based Stress Reduction (MBSR)
D) Biofeedback

Question 19: In the context of addressing addiction issues, which intervention is most effective in helping clients recognize and resolve ambivalence about their substance use?

A) Cognitive-Behavioral Therapy (CBT)
B) Motivational Interviewing (MI)
C) Contingency Management (CM)
D) Twelve-Step Facilitation (TSF)

Question 20: John, a mental health counselor, frequently uses social media for professional networking. He receives a message from a former client who seeks advice on coping with anxiety through his public profile. What is John's most appropriate course of action according to ethical guidelines?

A) Provide general advice on coping with anxiety without delving into personal details.
B) Redirect the former client to schedule an official session through appropriate channels.
C) Offer specific coping strategies tailored to the former client's known history.
D) Ignore the message to avoid any potential boundary issues.

Question 21: When providing feedback to a client in a counseling session, which of the following practices is most aligned with contemporary research on effective feedback?

A) Providing immediate feedback after each session regardless of the client's emotional state.
B) Balancing positive feedback with constructive criticism while ensuring it is specific and actionable.
C) Giving general positive feedback to boost the client's self-esteem before addressing any issues.
D) Delaying feedback until a pattern of behavior is observed to provide comprehensive insights.

Question 22: John, a 30-year-old man experiencing severe anxiety, reports feeling disconnected from his sense of self and struggling with existential questions about his life's direction. Which therapeutic approach is most likely to help John reconnect with his sense of self?

A) Cognitive Behavioral Therapy (CBT)
B) Mindfulness-Based Stress Reduction (MBSR)
C) Existential Therapy
D) Solution-Focused Brief Therapy (SFBT)

Question 23: During a group therapy session, Jamie, a transgender woman, shares her experiences of discrimination at work. What is the most appropriate response from the counselor to demonstrate sensitivity to Jamie's gender orientation?

A) Advise Jamie to file a complaint with human resources.
B) Facilitate a discussion on coping mechanisms for workplace discrimination.
C) Share statistics on workplace discrimination against transgender individuals.
D) Encourage Jamie to seek legal advice regarding her rights.

Question 24: John, a 32-year-old male, presents to your clinic with symptoms of depression and expresses feelings of hopelessness. He mentions that he has been thinking about ending his life but denies having a specific plan. As his mental health counselor, what is the most appropriate initial intervention?

A) Conduct a thorough suicide risk assessment.
B) Immediately refer John to inpatient psychiatric care.
C) Start cognitive behavioral therapy sessions.
D) Encourage John to engage in social activities.

Question 25: Which intervention is most effective in reducing caregiver burden for those caring for individuals with chronic mental health conditions?

A) Providing respite care services
B) Offering financial assistance programs
C) Implementing caregiver support groups
D) Educating caregivers on stress management techniques

Question 26: Tommy, a 4-year-old boy, exhibits frequent temper tantrums and struggles with transitions between activities at preschool. His teacher notes that he has difficulty understanding others' emotions and often prefers solitary play. His parents are seeking guidance from a mental health counselor. Which developmental issue is most likely affecting Tommy?

A) Oppositional Defiant Disorder (ODD)
B) Autism Spectrum Disorder (ASD)
C) Attention-Deficit/Hyperactivity Disorder (ADHD)
D) Sensory Processing Disorder (SPD)

Question 27: John, a 28-year-old male with bipolar disorder, has been experiencing frequent manic episodes despite outpatient therapy. His counselor suggests a residential program to stabilize his condition. Which level of residential treatment should be

recommended?
A) Crisis Stabilization Unit
B) Long-Term Residential Treatment
C) Partial Hospitalization Program
D) Intensive Outpatient Program

Question 28: A 35-year-old client with a history of severe substance use disorder and multiple unsuccessful attempts at outpatient treatment presents for evaluation. Which level of residential treatment is most appropriate for this client?
A) Intensive Outpatient Program (IOP)
B) Partial Hospitalization Program (PHP)
C) Long-term Residential Treatment
D) Short-term Residential Treatment

Question 29: Which of the following statements best describes a primary characteristic of process addictions such as pornography and gambling?
A) Process addictions primarily involve physical withdrawal symptoms similar to substance use disorders.
B) Process addictions are characterized by compulsive engagement in behaviors despite negative consequences.
C) The primary feature of process addictions is the development of tolerance requiring increased engagement over time.
D) Process addictions are primarily driven by genetic predispositions rather than environmental factors.

Question 30: John, a 35-year-old software engineer, has been experiencing significant difficulty concentrating at work. He reports that his mind often races with multiple thoughts simultaneously, making it hard to focus on a single task. He also finds it difficult to relax even during leisure time. Which of the following conditions is John most likely experiencing?
A) Generalized Anxiety Disorder
B) Attention-Deficit/Hyperactivity Disorder (ADHD)
C) Major Depressive Disorder
D) Obsessive-Compulsive Disorder (OCD)

Question 31: Which of the following best exemplifies a mental health counselor's responsibility to uphold client autonomy while ensuring informed consent?
A) Explaining all treatment options in detail and allowing the client to choose freely.
B) Providing a thorough explanation of potential risks and benefits, then documenting the client's decision.
C) Suggesting the most effective treatment based on clinical judgment but respecting the client's final decision.
D) Ensuring that the client understands all aspects of their treatment plan before they agree to proceed.

Question 32: During a feedback session, a counselor learns that two group members have been sharing personal information discussed in therapy with their mutual friends outside of the group. What is the best course of action for the counselor?
A) Address the issue immediately in the next group session.
B) Speak privately with each member involved to understand their perspective.
C) Reiterate confidentiality rules in a general reminder during a session.
D) Conduct an individual meeting with each member to reinforce confidentiality principles.

Question 33: When discussing confidentiality in electronic communication within mental health counseling, which of the following is the most crucial practice to ensure client information remains secure?
A) Using encrypted email services for all client communications.
B) Informing clients about the potential risks of electronic

communication.
C) Storing client information on password-protected devices.
D) Obtaining written consent from clients before using any form of electronic communication.

Question 34: Patient Mary, a 34-year-old woman, presents with sudden episodes of intense fear accompanied by palpitations, sweating, trembling, shortness of breath, and a feeling of impending doom. These episodes occur unpredictably and have led her to avoid places where she fears an attack might happen. Based on her symptoms, what is the most likely diagnosis?
A) Generalized Anxiety Disorder (GAD)
B) Panic Disorder
C) Social Anxiety Disorder
D) Agoraphobia

Question 35: John, a 10-year-old boy, has been displaying aggressive behavior at school, including hitting his peers and yelling at teachers. His parents report that he has been having trouble sleeping and often complains of stomachaches. What would be the most appropriate initial intervention for John?
A) Implementing a token economy system to reinforce positive behavior.
B) Conducting a comprehensive behavioral assessment to identify triggers.
C) Referring John to a pediatrician for a medical evaluation.
D) Enrolling John in a social skills training group.

Question 36: During a counseling session, Sarah, a mental health counselor, notices that her client, John, is hesitant to share his feelings. To foster a more open dialogue, Sarah decides to demonstrate genuineness. Which of the following actions best exemplifies genuineness in this context?
A) Sarah shares her own personal experiences related to John's situation.
B) Sarah acknowledges her own feelings about John's hesitation and expresses them.
C) Sarah reassures John that his feelings are valid and encourages him to open up.
D) Sarah maintains professional boundaries while subtly guiding John to express himself.

Question 37: John, a 35-year-old man, discloses during therapy that he was sexually abused by his uncle during his childhood. He expresses feelings of guilt and shame and reports difficulty in maintaining intimate relationships. What therapeutic approach is most effective in addressing John's issues?
A) Cognitive Behavioral Therapy (CBT)
B) Psychoanalytic Therapy
C) Eye Movement Desensitization and Reprocessing (EMDR)
D) Family Systems Therapy

Question 38: Maria, a 35-year-old Latina woman, is experiencing anxiety and stress due to her extended family's expectations and involvement in her personal life. As her mental health counselor, what is the most effective intervention strategy to address the impact of her extended family?
A) Encourage Maria to set firm boundaries with her extended family.
B) Suggest that Maria limit contact with her extended family.
C) Help Maria understand and negotiate her family's expectations.
D) Advise Maria to seek support solely from friends outside her family.

Question 39: John, a mental health counselor, is

working with Ahmed, a Muslim client who is conflicted about participating in certain workplace activities that go against his religious beliefs. Ahmed feels pressured by his colleagues but fears being ostracized if he refuses. How should John assist Ahmed in navigating this conflict?

A) Help Ahmed develop assertiveness skills to communicate his boundaries respectfully.

B) Encourage Ahmed to participate in the activities to avoid workplace conflict.

C) Advise Ahmed to seek a compromise by selectively participating in some activities.

D) Suggest that Ahmed file a formal complaint with human resources about religious discrimination.

Question 40: During a counseling session, Maria, a mental health counselor, decides to share her own experience with anxiety to help her client, John, who is struggling with severe anxiety. Which of the following best describes an appropriate use of self-disclosure in this scenario?

A) Maria shares her experience to establish rapport and normalize John's feelings.

B) Maria shares her experience to shift the focus from John's issues to a more general discussion.

C) Maria shares her experience to make John feel obligated to reciprocate with more personal information.

D) Maria shares her experience to demonstrate that she has overcome similar challenges and knows exactly what John should do.

Question 41: Michael, a 28-year-old software developer, experiences chronic stress and has been referred for biofeedback therapy. Which specific type of biofeedback would be most effective in helping Michael learn to manage his physiological responses to stress?

A) Electromyography (EMG) biofeedback focusing on muscle tension.

B) Electroencephalography (EEG) biofeedback focusing on brain wave activity.

C) Heart rate variability (HRV) biofeedback focusing on heart rate patterns.

D) Galvanic skin response (GSR) biofeedback focusing on skin conductance levels.

Question 42: Which of the following best describes the process by which an individual adopts the cultural norms of a dominant or host culture while maintaining their original cultural identity?

A) Assimilation

B) Acculturation

C) Enculturation

D) Cultural Integration

Question 43: Which of the following is most critical for a mental health counselor to address when helping clients manage retirement concerns?

A) Financial planning

B) Psychological adjustment

C) Social engagement

D) Identity transition

Question 44: According to Super's Life-Span, Life-Space Theory, which stage involves individuals focusing on establishing their careers and achieving stability?

A) Growth Stage

B) Exploration Stage

C) Establishment Stage

D) Maintenance Stage

Question 45: Maria, a 35-year-old woman, reports ongoing conflicts with her teenage daughter, Lisa. During family therapy sessions, you observe that when

Maria criticizes Lisa's behavior, Lisa often responds by withdrawing emotionally and avoiding further interaction. Maria then feels ignored and becomes more critical. What systemic pattern of interaction is most likely occurring in this scenario?

A) Enmeshment

B) Triangulation

C) Negative feedback loop

D) Positive feedback loop

Question 46: Which of the following is the most indicative behavioral sign of a child experiencing emotional abuse?

A) Frequent unexplained injuries

B) Sudden changes in behavior or school performance

C) Developmental delays in speech or motor skills

D) Inappropriate sexual behaviors

Question 47: Jane, a 35-year-old woman diagnosed with Major Depressive Disorder (MDD), has been attending counseling sessions for three months. She reports persistent feelings of sadness, lack of interest in daily activities, and difficulty concentrating. Her counselor wants to establish short-term goals that are consistent with her diagnosis. Which of the following is the most appropriate short-term goal for Jane?

A) Increase social interactions by attending at least one social event per week.

B) Develop a daily exercise routine to improve physical health.

C) Identify and challenge negative thought patterns through cognitive restructuring.

D) Set career advancement goals to enhance professional growth.

Question 48: John, a 35-year-old male, presents with significant distress due to his compulsive gambling behavior. He reports that he often gambles more than he intends to and has unsuccessfully tried to cut down multiple times. His gambling has led to financial problems and strained relationships. According to Cognitive-Behavioral Theory, which intervention is most likely to be effective in helping John manage his gambling addiction?

A) Psychoeducation about the risks of gambling

B) Cognitive restructuring to challenge distorted beliefs about gambling

C) Pharmacotherapy with SSRIs

D) Mindfulness meditation for stress reduction

Question 49: Jane, a mental health counselor, is working with a client named Mark who has been diagnosed with generalized anxiety disorder (GAD). Jane wants to provide Mark with educational resources to help him manage his anxiety. Which of the following resources would be most appropriate for Jane to recommend?

A) A workbook on cognitive-behavioral therapy (CBT) techniques specifically for anxiety

B) A general self-help book on managing stress and improving overall well-being

C) An online forum where individuals share their experiences with anxiety

D) A podcast series on various mental health topics, including anxiety

Question 50: During a session with a client named Sarah, who is experiencing severe anxiety, you notice she discloses sensitive information about her past trauma. How should you document this information to ensure it is appropriate and ethical?

A) Document only the facts and avoid any subjective interpretations.

B) Include both facts and your professional interpretations to provide a comprehensive view.

C) Document the facts and discuss your interpretations verbally with your supervisor.

D) Record only the most critical points to maintain brevity in documentation.

Question 51: Which attachment style is most likely to contribute to difficulties in maintaining stable relationships due to fear of intimacy and constant worry about partner's availability?

A) Secure Attachment

B) Anxious-Preoccupied Attachment

C) Dismissive-Avoidant Attachment

D) Fearful-Avoidant Attachment

Question 52: Sarah has been hesitant to follow her prescribed medication regimen for depression. As her mental health counselor, your goal is to educate her on the importance of adhering to her treatment plan. Which strategy would be most effective?

A) Use reflective listening to understand Sarah's concerns about her medication.

B) Explain the biochemical mechanisms of how the medication works.

C) Reiterate the doctor's orders and emphasize their authority.

D) Schedule frequent follow-up appointments to monitor adherence.

Question 53: A 35-year-old patient named Emily has been struggling with severe depression and substance abuse. After a comprehensive assessment, her mental health counselor recommends a residential treatment program. Which type of residential treatment is most appropriate for Emily?

A) Therapeutic Community

B) Halfway House

C) Acute Inpatient Treatment

D) Long-Term Residential Treatment

Question 54: Maria, a 28-year-old nurse, frequently clashes with her colleague over patient care decisions. These conflicts are affecting their teamwork and patient outcomes. What is the most effective strategy for Maria's counselor to recommend in order to resolve this interpersonal conflict?

A) Encourage Maria to adopt a collaborative approach by seeking common goals.

B) Suggest Maria assertively communicate her perspective during disagreements.

C) Advise Maria to document all conflicts and report them to a supervisor.

D) Recommend Maria avoid discussing patient care decisions directly with her colleague.

Question 55: Which of the following actions is most effective in building trust within the therapeutic relationship during initial sessions?

A) Providing detailed explanations about therapy techniques and expected outcomes.

B) Actively listening and validating the client's feelings and experiences.

C) Setting clear boundaries and discussing confidentiality policies.

D) Sharing personal experiences to create a sense of relatability.

Question 56: John, a mental health counselor, is discussing payment options with his new client who has an out-of-network insurance plan. The client wants to understand how reimbursement works for out-of-network services. Which explanation should John provide that accurately describes how out-of-network

reimbursement typically functions?

A) The client pays upfront and submits claims for partial reimbursement based on allowed amounts.

B) The counselor bills the insurance directly for full reimbursement minus co-pays.

C) The counselor negotiates rates with the insurance company on behalf of the client.

D) The client only pays co-pays at each session, with no need for claim submission.

Question 57: In a therapeutic group setting, how should a counselor address concerns about members interacting outside of the group to ensure confidentiality and maintain group cohesion?

A) Prohibit all interactions between members outside of the group.

B) Encourage members to interact outside of the group but remind them to keep discussions confidential.

C) Discuss potential issues and establish clear boundaries regarding external interactions during initial group sessions.

D) Allow interactions outside of the group without any restrictions to foster stronger relationships.

Question 58: Which of the following is considered the most critical component of a follow-up plan after discharge for a patient with a recent history of major depressive disorder?

A) Scheduling a follow-up appointment with the primary care physician within two weeks

B) Ensuring the patient has access to emergency contact numbers for crisis intervention

C) Arranging a home visit by a mental health professional within 48 hours post-discharge

D) Providing detailed medication management instructions and adherence support

Question 59: During an intake session, a client reports experiencing prolonged periods of sadness, lack of interest in daily activities, and significant weight loss. The counselor suspects Major Depressive Disorder (MDD). Which of the following additional criteria is essential for confirming this diagnosis according to the DSM-5?

A) Presence of manic or hypomanic episodes

B) Presence of psychomotor agitation or retardation nearly every day

C) Persistent delusions or hallucinations

D) A history of substance abuse

Question 60: A 14-year-old patient named Emily has been experiencing persistent bullying at school. As her mental health counselor, you need to determine the most effective intervention based on contemporary research. Which of the following approaches is considered most effective in addressing bullying in this context?

A) Implementing a peer mediation program

B) Establishing a zero-tolerance policy

C) Introducing a school-wide positive behavior support system

D) Conducting individual cognitive-behavioral therapy (CBT)

Question 61: Maria, a 30-year-old woman with generalized anxiety disorder and panic attacks, reports increased anxiety leading to daily panic attacks. She has no history of substance abuse or suicidal ideation but is struggling to function at work and in social settings. Which level of care should be recommended?

A) Outpatient therapy

B) Intensive outpatient program (IOP)

C) Partial hospitalization program (PHP)

D) Inpatient hospitalization

Question 62: Maria, a 28-year-old woman, has been struggling with opioid addiction for several years. She has recently started Methadone Maintenance Therapy (MMT). During a follow-up session, she expresses concerns about her ability to stay sober due to her high-stress job. Which additional intervention would best complement her MMT to enhance her chances of recovery?
A) Stress Management Training
B) Twelve-Step Facilitation Therapy
C) Family Therapy
D) Exposure Therapy

Question 63: Which assessment tool is most appropriate for identifying both the severity of substance use and co-occurring mental health disorders in a client?
A) Alcohol Use Disorders Identification Test (AUDIT)
B) Drug Abuse Screening Test (DAST)
C) Substance Abuse Subtle Screening Inventory (SASSI)
D) Structured Clinical Interview for DSM-5 (SCID)

Question 64: During a psychoeducational group session for patients with generalized anxiety disorder (GAD), the counselor notices that one of the participants, Emily, is struggling to understand the cognitive-behavioral techniques being discussed. What is the most appropriate next step for the counselor to take?
A) Provide Emily with additional reading materials on cognitive-behavioral techniques.
B) Schedule a one-on-one session with Emily to review cognitive-behavioral techniques.
C) Encourage other group members to share their experiences with cognitive-behavioral techniques.
D) Simplify the explanation of cognitive-behavioral techniques during the group session.

Question 65: Jane, a 35-year-old marketing executive, reports experiencing high levels of stress due to her demanding job and recent family issues. As her mental health counselor, you decide to use cognitive-behavioral techniques to help her manage her stress. Which of the following interventions is most appropriate for addressing Jane's stress using cognitive-behavioral therapy (CBT)?
A) Encouraging Jane to engage in progressive muscle relaxation exercises.
B) Helping Jane identify and challenge her negative thought patterns.
C) Advising Jane to practice mindfulness meditation regularly.
D) Suggesting Jane participate in group therapy sessions for social support.

Question 66: Maria, a 28-year-old female with severe anxiety and frequent panic attacks, seeks your help in managing her condition. What should be your primary focus when developing her safety plan?
A) Educate Maria about anxiety and panic disorders.
B) Identify safe places where Maria can go during an attack.
C) Teach Maria grounding techniques to manage her symptoms.
D) Create a list of supportive individuals Maria can contact.

Question 67: During a group therapy session focused on racial trauma, one participant, Maria, shares her experiences with systemic racism in healthcare settings. As the facilitator, what is the most appropriate response to support Maria while fostering a therapeutic environment for all group members?
A) Redirect the conversation to avoid making other participants uncomfortable.
B) Encourage other group members to share similar experiences immediately.

C) Acknowledge Maria's experience and validate her feelings while maintaining group cohesion.
D) Offer solutions for Maria to address systemic racism in her personal healthcare encounters.

Question 68: Which of the following is most characteristic of Bulimia Nervosa?
A) Recurrent episodes of binge eating followed by inappropriate compensatory behaviors
B) Restriction of energy intake leading to significantly low body weight
C) Intense fear of gaining weight or becoming fat, even though underweight
D) Preoccupation with eating healthy foods to an obsessive level

Question 69: John, a 7-year-old child, has been displaying signs of anxiety and reluctance to attend school. His parents report that he struggles with making friends and often plays alone. As his counselor, which intervention would best align with John's developmental level?
A) Facilitate John's involvement in structured group activities to improve social skills.
B) Encourage John to explore abstract thinking through hypothetical scenarios.
C) Suggest John engage in individual play therapy sessions focusing on his emotions.
D) Advise John's parents to focus on developing his formal operational thinking skills.

Question 70: A 45-year-old male client reports experiencing erectile dysfunction (ED) over the past six months. He denies any significant medical history but admits to high levels of work-related stress and relationship issues with his partner. Which of the following is the most likely contributing factor to his ED?
A) Cardiovascular disease
B) Low testosterone levels
C) Psychological stress
D) Diabetes mellitus

Question 71: What is the best technique for the counselor to use in this situation to facilitate John's awareness of here-and-now interactions?
A) Ask John how he felt when his partner behaved that way.
B) Encourage John to describe his physical sensations at that moment.
C) Suggest John think about past instances where he felt similarly.
D) Advise John to take deep breaths and calm down before continuing.

Question 72: Which of the following best describes an essential benefit of informed consent in the counseling process?
A) It ensures that clients understand their treatment plan and agree to it voluntarily.
B) It guarantees that clients will adhere to their treatment plan.
C) It allows counselors to avoid legal liabilities.
D) It provides a detailed outline of all possible outcomes of treatment.

Question 73: Jane, a 35-year-old woman, presents with persistent worry about her job performance despite receiving positive feedback from her supervisor. She reports difficulty sleeping and constant muscle tension. Which therapeutic approach would most effectively address Jane's symptoms of worry and anxiety?
A) Cognitive Behavioral Therapy (CBT)
B) Mindfulness-Based Stress Reduction (MBSR)

C) Psychodynamic Therapy
D) Exposure Therapy

Question 74: Which of the following best describes a clinical presentation of hyperfocus in an individual with ADHD?
A) Difficulty in maintaining attention on tasks or activities.
B) An intense concentration on a single activity to the exclusion of other tasks.
C) Frequent shifts from one activity to another without completing any.
D) Reduced ability to initiate or sustain goal-directed activities.

Question 75: John often feels his opinions are overlooked during team meetings at work. He wants to learn how to express his thoughts more effectively without coming across as aggressive. Which strategy should his counselor recommend as part of assertiveness training?
A) Using "I" statements to express feelings and needs
B) Adopting an authoritative tone during discussions
C) Avoiding eye contact to reduce perceived aggression
D) Rehearsing responses using aggressive language

Question 76: John, a licensed mental health counselor, wants to implement electronic record-keeping for his practice. He needs to ensure that client confidentiality is maintained according to ethical standards. Which of the following practices should John prioritize?
A) Storing client records on his personal laptop without encryption.
B) Using a cloud-based service with strong encryption and access controls.
C) Keeping paper records only to avoid any potential electronic breaches.
][''''''D) Sharing access codes with administrative staff via unsecured messaging apps.

Question 77: John, a 10-year-old boy who was recently adopted from foster care, exhibits signs of attachment difficulties such as avoiding eye contact and resisting physical affection from his adoptive parents. What therapeutic approach should his mental health counselor prioritize?
A) Cognitive Behavioral Therapy (CBT) focused on addressing negative thought patterns.
B) Play therapy aimed at helping John express his emotions non-verbally.
C) Attachment-based therapy designed to strengthen the parent-child bond.
D) Group therapy with other adopted children to normalize his experiences.

Question 78: John, a 35-year-old veteran, has been experiencing flashbacks, hypervigilance, and nightmares since returning from deployment. As his mental health counselor, which intervention would be most appropriate to address his symptoms of PTSD?
A) Cognitive Behavioral Therapy (CBT)
B) Eye Movement Desensitization and Reprocessing (EMDR)
C) Prolonged Exposure Therapy
D) Supportive Counseling

Question 79: During an initial interview with a new client, Maria, who presents with symptoms of anxiety and depression, which of the following is the most appropriate first step for a mental health counselor to take?
A) Begin by exploring Maria's family history of mental illness.
B) Start with open-ended questions to allow Maria to express her concerns.

C) Conduct a mental status examination immediately.
D) Provide psychoeducation about anxiety and depression.

Question 80: John is a 28-year-old male who reports experiencing intense fear and discomfort that peak within minutes. He describes palpitations, sweating, trembling, shortness of breath, chest pain, nausea, dizziness, and fear of losing control or dying during these episodes. These attacks occur unexpectedly and have happened several times over the past month. What is the most likely diagnosis for John?
A) Panic Disorder
B) Social Anxiety Disorder
C) Generalized Anxiety Disorder
D) Specific Phobia

Question 81: Tommy, an 8-year-old boy, exhibits difficulty in following multi-step instructions and often needs repeated prompts to complete tasks at school. His parents are concerned about his ability to manage more complex tasks as he grows older. According to Vygotsky's theory of social development, what strategy would most effectively support Tommy's learning?
A) Scaffolding
B) Zone of Proximal Development
C) Social Interaction
D) Private Speech

Question 82: Sarah, a 7-year-old girl, is struggling with reading comprehension despite having strong verbal skills. Her parents are concerned and seek advice from a mental health counselor. The counselor considers various developmental issues that might be affecting Sarah's reading skills. What is the most likely developmental issue impacting Sarah's reading comprehension?
A) Dyslexia
B) Attention-Deficit/Hyperactivity Disorder (ADHD)
C) Specific Language Impairment (SLI)
D) Autism Spectrum Disorder (ASD)

Question 83: A mental health counselor is working with a client whose religious beliefs strongly oppose certain medical treatments. The client's condition requires immediate intervention, but the client refuses treatment based on their faith. What is the most appropriate action for the counselor to take?
A) Respect the client's religious beliefs and refrain from discussing the medical treatment further.
B) Attempt to persuade the client by highlighting the potential benefits of the medical treatment.
C) Collaborate with the client to explore alternative treatments that align with their religious beliefs.
D) Refer the client to another healthcare provider who might better address their medical needs.

Question 84: A counselor named Dr. Smith is working with a client, Maria, who has disclosed ongoing domestic violence but insists that the counselor keeps this information confidential. Dr. Smith is aware of her legal and ethical obligations but is unsure how to proceed without violating Maria's trust.
A) Maintain confidentiality and continue working with Maria on safety planning.
B) Break confidentiality and report the domestic violence to authorities immediately.
C) Discuss the limits of confidentiality with Maria and obtain her consent before reporting.
D) Refer Maria to another counselor who specializes in domestic violence cases.

Question 85: During a counseling session, Maria expresses frustration that her husband consistently

undermines her authority with their teenage children. Which intervention would best address this issue by exploring family member interaction?
A) Encourage Maria to set stricter boundaries with her children.
B) Facilitate a family meeting to discuss and negotiate parenting roles.
C) Suggest individual therapy for Maria to manage her frustration.
D) Advise Maria to attend a parenting workshop alone.

Question 86: John, a 42-year-old software engineer, has been experiencing chronic stress due to tight project deadlines and high expectations at work. His counselor recommends using cognitive-behavioral therapy (CBT) techniques to manage his stress. Which of the following CBT techniques is most effective for helping John reframe his stressful thoughts?
A) Systematic desensitization
B) Thought stopping
C) Cognitive restructuring
D) Biofeedback

Question 87: Sarah, a licensed mental health counselor, has been working with a client named John who has been experiencing severe depression. During a session, John reveals that he has been having thoughts of harming his coworker. Sarah is now considering whether she should disclose this information to John's employer.
A) Sarah should immediately inform John's employer about the threat.
B) Sarah should seek John's consent before disclosing any information to his employer.
C) Sarah should assess the seriousness of the threat and consider legal obligations before deciding.
D) Sarah should document the threat in her notes but take no further action without John's consent.

Question 88: Maria has been part of a therapy group for six months. Recently, two new members joined the group, causing some disruption in the group's dynamics. As the mental health counselor, what is the most appropriate initial step to address this transition?
A) Conduct individual sessions with each member to discuss their feelings about the new members.
B) Facilitate a group discussion focusing on expectations and norms to re-establish cohesion.
C) Allow time for the group to naturally adjust without intervention.
D) Assign specific roles to new members to integrate them quickly into the group.

Question 89: During a session, you notice that your client, John, frequently avoids discussing his feelings about his recent job loss. As a counselor using constructive confrontation, what is the most appropriate way to address this avoidance?
A) Directly tell John that he needs to stop avoiding his feelings and talk about his job loss.
B) Gently point out the pattern of avoidance and invite John to explore his feelings about the job loss.
C) Ignore the avoidance for now and focus on other issues until John feels ready.
D) Encourage John to journal about his job loss and bring those reflections to the next session.

Question 90: During a counseling session, a client expresses feelings of failure after a recent job loss. As a mental health counselor, which of the following techniques best exemplifies the process of reframing to help the client view their situation more positively?
A) Encouraging the client to list all their past achievements

and focus on them.
B) Asking the client to consider how this job loss might open up new opportunities.
C) Suggesting that the client engage in mindfulness exercises to reduce stress.
D) Advising the client to seek feedback from former colleagues about their strengths.

Question 91: Samantha, a new counselor at a private practice, receives a subpoena for her client Jake's records due to an ongoing legal case. Samantha is aware of her agency's policy on handling such requests but is unsure how to proceed ethically. What should Samantha do first?
A) Immediately comply with the subpoena and provide all requested records.
B) Refuse to comply with the subpoena citing client confidentiality.
C) Consult with her agency's legal counsel before responding to the subpoena.
D) Inform Jake about the subpoena and ask for his written consent before taking any action.

Question 92: A mental health counselor is discussing client rights and responsibilities with a new client. Which of the following statements best represents the client's right to confidentiality?
A) "Your treatment details will be shared only with your family members to ensure they support you."
B) "Your treatment details can be shared with other healthcare providers without your consent if it benefits your treatment."
C) "Your treatment details will remain confidential unless you provide written consent or there is a legal requirement to disclose."
D) "Your treatment details will be shared with insurance companies without informing you."

Question 93: Which physical sign is most indicative of ongoing physical abuse in a family setting?
A) Multiple bruises at different stages of healing
B) A single bruise on the forearm
C) Frequent headaches
D) Unexplained weight loss

Question 94: Scenario: John, an African American man in his mid-40s, seeks counseling for work-related stress. He shares that he often feels isolated at his predominantly white workplace and experiences microaggressions from colleagues. How should you address John's concerns while considering his cultural background?
A) Advise John to confront his colleagues about their behavior.
B) Help John develop coping strategies for dealing with microaggressions.
C) Encourage John to find a new job where he feels more accepted.
D) Suggest that John ignore the microaggressions to avoid conflict.

Question 95: Maria, a 28-year-old female, has been diagnosed with generalized anxiety disorder (GAD). She reports constant worry about various aspects of her life, including work performance and personal relationships. Maria also experiences physical symptoms such as muscle tension and headaches. In developing her treatment plan, what should be the primary focus during the initial sessions?
A) Teach Maria relaxation techniques to manage her physical symptoms.
B) Explore underlying cognitive distortions contributing to her anxiety.

C) Conduct a thorough psychoeducation session about GAD.
D) Set specific goals for reducing anxiety levels within three months.

Question 96: During a biopsychosocial interview, which aspect is most crucial for understanding the client's overall mental health?
A) Exploring the client's medical history and current medications.
B) Assessing the client's cognitive and emotional functioning.
C) Evaluating the client's social support systems and environmental stressors.
D) Integrating information from biological, psychological, and social domains.

Question 97: Maria is a 45-year-old woman who has been caring for her elderly mother with Alzheimer's disease for the past three years. She reports feeling overwhelmed and frequently experiences feelings of guilt and anxiety. Which intervention would be most effective in helping Maria manage her caregiving stress?
A) Encourage Maria to join a caregiver support group.
B) Suggest that Maria take a short vacation to rest.
C) Advise Maria to seek individual therapy focused on stress management.
D) Recommend that Maria hire a professional caregiver for respite care.

Question 98: You are working with John, a client diagnosed with Generalized Anxiety Disorder (GAD). During a session, you decide to refer him to a psychiatrist for potential medication evaluation while continuing your therapeutic work with him. How should you document this referral in John's treatment plan?
A) "John was referred to a psychiatrist for medication evaluation while continuing therapy sessions."
B) "Referral to psychiatry for medication evaluation was made for John along with ongoing therapy."
C) "John will see a psychiatrist for medication evaluation; therapy sessions will continue as planned."
D) "It was agreed that John should have a psychiatric evaluation for medication while maintaining regular therapy sessions."

Question 99: John, a 28-year-old male, has been experiencing chronic stress due to his high-pressure job. He reports frequent headaches, irritability, and difficulty concentrating at work. As his mental health counselor, what should be your primary clinical focus to help John manage his stress?
A) Time Management Training
B) Biofeedback Therapy
C) Stress Inoculation Training (SIT)
D) Interpersonal Therapy (IPT)

Question 100: Which of the following techniques is most effective in facilitating a client's awareness of here-and-now interactions during a counseling session?
A) Encouraging the client to explore past experiences related to current feelings.
B) Asking the client to describe their immediate physical sensations.
C) Guiding the client to visualize future scenarios that may cause anxiety.
D) Instructing the client to identify patterns in their behavior over time.

Question 101: During an initial intake session, a mental health counselor is obtaining self-reports from a client. Which technique is most effective in enhancing the accuracy of these self-reports?
A) Using open-ended questions to allow clients to elaborate

on their experiences.
B) Encouraging clients to provide specific examples or incidents.
C) Asking clients to rate their experiences on a standardized scale.
D) Repeating questions in different ways throughout the session.

Question 102: John, a 45-year-old client, has been referred for counseling due to work-related stress. During the initial assessment, the counselor uses both formal and informal observations. Which of the following best exemplifies an informal observation?
A) Administering a stress inventory scale
B) Noticing John's casual remarks about his workload
C) Conducting a semi-structured interview
D) Reviewing John's medical records for stress-related symptoms

Question 103: A counselor is working with a family where the teenage son has been exhibiting aggressive behavior and poor academic performance. The parents report frequent arguments and a lack of communication within the family. Which counseling modality is most appropriate for addressing these issues?
A) Individual therapy for the teenage son
B) Couple therapy for the parents
C) Family therapy involving all members
D) Group therapy for teenagers with similar issues

Question 104: Which of the following best describes how systemic racism impacts mental health outcomes in marginalized communities?
A) Systemic racism leads to increased access to mental health services for marginalized communities.
B) Systemic racism results in chronic stress and trauma, contributing to higher rates of mental health disorders in marginalized communities.
C) Systemic racism has minimal impact on mental health outcomes but affects physical health more significantly.
D) Systemic racism primarily influences socioeconomic status without directly affecting mental health.

Question 105: Sarah, a 35-year-old woman diagnosed with Generalized Anxiety Disorder (GAD), has been experiencing persistent worry and physical symptoms such as restlessness and muscle tension. As her counselor, you aim to provide psychoeducation to help her understand her condition better. Which of the following approaches would be most effective in providing psychoeducation for Sarah?
A) Explain the biological basis of GAD and emphasize medication as the primary treatment.
B) Discuss the cognitive-behavioral model of GAD and how it affects thoughts and behaviors.
C) Focus on relaxation techniques and stress management strategies without discussing the diagnosis.
D) Provide general information about anxiety disorders without personalizing it to Sarah's experience.

Question 106: Sarah, a licensed mental health counselor, is setting up her telemental health practice. She needs to ensure that her technology meets the ethical standards for confidentiality and security. Which of the following is the most critical step she should take?
A) Use a secure video conferencing platform that complies with HIPAA regulations.
B) Ensure that her clients have a stable internet connection.
C) Obtain written consent from clients for telehealth services.
D) Conduct sessions during standard business hours to maintain professionalism.

Question 107: Lisa, a 38-year-old mother of two, is navigating co-parenting challenges after her divorce. She wants to ensure her children experience minimal disruption and maintain a healthy relationship with both parents. What is the most appropriate advice you can give Lisa?
A) Create a rigid schedule for the children without consulting their father.
B) Encourage open communication between both parents regarding the children's needs.
C) Limit interactions with her ex-spouse to avoid potential conflicts.
D) Allow the children to decide when they want to see each parent.

Question 108: John, a mental health counselor, is treating a minor named Alex who has expressed suicidal ideation but does not want his parents informed due to fear of punishment. John must decide how to handle this situation ethically and legally.
A) Respect Alex's wishes and keep the information confidential.
B) Inform Alex's parents immediately about his suicidal ideation.
C) Conduct a risk assessment and involve Alex in deciding how to inform his parents.
D) Refer Alex to an inpatient facility without informing his parents.

Question 109: Which of the following techniques is most effective for promoting and encouraging interactions among group members in a counseling setting?
A) Directly addressing individual members to share their thoughts
B) Using structured activities that require group collaboration
C) Allowing members to self-select discussion topics
D) Emphasizing the importance of confidentiality in discussions

Question 110: Sarah, a 32-year-old female, complains of persistent difficulty falling asleep despite feeling tired at bedtime. She often lies awake for hours worrying about work and personal issues. Her physician has ruled out any medical conditions contributing to her insomnia. Which intervention is most likely to address Sarah's primary issue?
A) Prescribe a low-dose antidepressant.
B) Implement stimulus control therapy.
C) Suggest using white noise machines.
D) Recommend progressive muscle relaxation techniques.

Question 111: When facilitating systemic change within a community mental health setting, which approach is most effective for ensuring sustainable outcomes?
A) Implementing short-term individual counseling sessions.
B) Engaging key stakeholders in collaborative decision-making processes.
C) Conducting periodic needs assessments without follow-up.
D) Providing standardized training programs for all staff members.

Question 112: John, a mental health counselor, is working with Sarah, a 16-year-old client who confides in him about her plans to run away from home due to family conflicts. Sarah asks John not to tell anyone about her plans. What should John do in this situation?
A) Maintain confidentiality as requested by Sarah.
B) Inform Sarah's parents immediately without discussing it with her.
C) Discuss the situation with Sarah and explain the limits of confidentiality before informing her parents.
D) Keep the information confidential but monitor Sarah closely for any immediate risks.

Question 113: Mark, a 28-year-old man with a history of substance use disorder, has recently relapsed after six months of sobriety. He is currently experiencing significant withdrawal symptoms but does not have any medical complications requiring immediate hospitalization. His counselor needs to refer him to an appropriate level of care. Which level of treatment should Mark be referred to?
A) Outpatient Counseling
B) Intensive Outpatient Program (IOP)
C) Medically Monitored Detoxification
D) Residential Treatment Center (RTC)

Question 114: According to William Worden's Four Tasks of Mourning, which task involves accepting the reality of the loss?
A) Task I: Accepting the reality of the loss
B) Task II: Processing the pain of grief
C) Task III: Adjusting to a world without the deceased
D) Task IV: Finding an enduring connection with the deceased while embarking on a new life

Question 115: Maria, a 12-year-old girl, has been struggling academically and socially in school. Her teacher reports that Maria often seems confused during lessons and has difficulty following instructions. After a comprehensive evaluation, Maria is diagnosed with an intellectual disability. As her mental health counselor, what would be the most appropriate initial intervention?
A) Implementing a behavior modification plan to improve classroom behavior.
B) Developing an individualized education program (IEP) tailored to her needs.
C) Encouraging participation in extracurricular activities to boost self-esteem.
D) Providing family therapy to address potential home environment issues.

Question 116: During a support group session for patients recovering from substance abuse, Maria observes that the group has developed strong cohesion and members are providing mutual support while adhering to established norms. Which phase of the group process does this describe?
A) Forming
B) Storming
C) Norming
D) Adjourning

Question 117: In the context of parenting/co-parenting conflicts, which strategy is most effective in promoting a positive co-parenting relationship and minimizing conflict?
A) Engaging in parallel parenting where each parent independently manages their own household.
B) Maintaining open and respectful communication about parenting decisions.
C) Avoiding discussions about contentious topics to prevent arguments.
D) Relying on third-party mediation for all disagreements.

Question 118: Emily, a 28-year-old woman, presents with recurring intrusive thoughts about harming her loved ones, which she finds distressing and irrational. She engages in mental rituals to neutralize these thoughts. Her therapist decides to implement a treatment plan aimed at reducing her symptoms. Which technique is most appropriate for Emily's condition?
A) Thought Stopping
B) Cognitive Restructuring
C) Exposure and Response Prevention (ERP)

D) Acceptance and Commitment Therapy (ACT)

Question 119: Mark, a 42-year-old man, has been struggling with feelings of anger and resentment towards his ex-spouse following their divorce. He finds it challenging to co-parent their two children effectively. As his mental health counselor, which intervention would best help Mark manage his emotions and improve his co-parenting relationship?
A) Encourage Mark to write letters expressing his feelings to his ex-spouse without sending them.
B) Suggest Mark engage in individual therapy focused on anger management techniques.
C) Recommend Mark attend family therapy sessions with his ex-spouse to improve communication.
D) Advise Mark to participate in a co-parenting workshop designed for divorced parents.

Question 120: Which therapeutic approach is most effective in reducing ruminating and intrusive thoughts by helping clients reframe their negative thinking patterns?
A) Cognitive Behavioral Therapy (CBT)
B) Psychodynamic Therapy
C) Humanistic Therapy
D) Interpersonal Therapy

Question 121: Which of the following is considered the most significant factor in predicting positive outcomes in counseling?
A) The counselor's theoretical orientation
B) The therapeutic alliance between counselor and client
C) The client's motivation for change
D) The use of evidence-based interventions

Question 122: John, a 28-year-old client, sits silently during his counseling session with his arms crossed and avoids eye contact. How should you respond to facilitate an empathic connection?
A) "I notice that you're sitting quietly with your arms crossed. What's going through your mind right now?"
B) "It's okay if you don't want to talk right now; we can sit here in silence if that makes you comfortable."
C) "Why don't you tell me about what's bothering you? I'm here to help."
D) "You seem upset; let's talk about what's making you feel this way."

Question 123: Maria, a 28-year-old woman, seeks counseling for relationship issues and feelings of inadequacy stemming from childhood trauma. She has difficulty forming secure attachments and often feels anxious in social situations. You decide to apply a theory-based counseling intervention to address her attachment issues and improve her relational dynamics.
A) Attachment-Based Therapy focusing on building secure attachments.
B) Gestalt Therapy emphasizing present-moment awareness.
C) Narrative Therapy helping Maria reframe her life story.
D) Dialectical Behavior Therapy (DBT) teaching emotional regulation skills.

Question 124: Maria, a Latina woman, has been experiencing anxiety due to her recent relocation to a predominantly white neighborhood. During her counseling session, she expresses feeling isolated and misunderstood by her neighbors. As her counselor, how should you demonstrate cultural sensitivity and effectively address her concerns?
A) Encourage Maria to join local community groups to build a support network.
B) Validate Maria's feelings and explore how her cultural

background influences her experience.
C) Suggest that Maria focus on adapting to the new environment without dwelling on cultural differences.
D) Recommend that Maria seek friendships with individuals who share her cultural background.

Question 125: John is a 35-year-old software engineer experiencing high levels of stress due to work-related pressures. During counseling, he reports difficulty concentrating and frequent headaches. Which intervention would be most effective in helping John manage his stress?
A) Cognitive-Behavioral Therapy (CBT)
B) Progressive Muscle Relaxation (PMR)
C) Mindfulness-Based Stress Reduction (MBSR)
D) Biofeedback

Question 126: Maria, a 30-year-old woman, presents for an intake assessment following concerns about her erratic behavior at work. During the Mental Status Exam (MSE), you notice that Maria is overly talkative, rapidly shifts from one topic to another without logical connections, and exhibits grandiose ideas about her abilities. Which aspect of the MSE best captures these observations?
A) Mood
B) Thought Content
C) Thought Process
D) Orientation

Question 127: Which of the following is most indicative of mild cognitive impairment (MCI) rather than early-stage Alzheimer's disease in elderly patients?
A) Memory loss that interferes with daily life
B) Significant language difficulties
C) Preserved independence in daily activities
D) Noticeable personality changes

Question 128: Jamie, a 16-year-old assigned female at birth (AFAB), expresses a strong desire to be recognized as male and has been experiencing significant distress related to their gender identity. Which stage of gender identity development is Jamie most likely experiencing according to D'Augelli's model?
A) Personal Enactment
B) Identity Confusion
C) Identity Comparison
D) Identity Synthesis

Question 129: Jason, a 7-year-old boy, has been showing signs of severe distress at school. He has frequent nightmares, avoids certain places and people, and has sudden outbursts of anger. His mother reports that he becomes very anxious when left alone with male relatives. Considering these symptoms, what type of intervention should the counselor prioritize?
A) Cognitive Behavioral Therapy (CBT)
B) Play Therapy
C) Trauma-Focused Cognitive Behavioral Therapy (TF-CBT)
D) Family Therapy

Question 130: Sarah, a 45-year-old woman with terminal cancer, expresses to her mental health counselor that she feels overwhelmed by her family's constant presence and their attempts to cheer her up. She mentions that she needs some space to process her emotions but feels guilty about wanting to be alone. What is the most appropriate response by the counselor?
A) Encourage Sarah to communicate her need for space to her family and help her develop strategies for doing so.
B) Suggest Sarah spend more time with her family as they

are trying to support her.

C) Advise Sarah to participate in a support group where she can share her feelings with others in similar situations.

D) Recommend Sarah take up a new hobby or activity to distract herself from these feelings.

Question 131: Maria, a Latina client, reports feeling misunderstood by her predominantly white colleagues at work. She feels isolated and believes her cultural background is not being respected. As her counselor, what is the most appropriate initial intervention to help Maria?

A) Encourage Maria to educate her colleagues about her cultural background.

B) Validate Maria's feelings and explore her experiences of cultural isolation.

C) Suggest Maria seek a different job where diversity is more appreciated.

D) Advise Maria to ignore the behavior and focus on her work performance.

Question 132: Maria, a 28-year-old female diagnosed with major depressive disorder (MDD), has been undergoing therapy for eight months. Her initial treatment plan included interpersonal therapy (IPT) and selective serotonin reuptake inhibitors (SSRIs). Despite some improvement, Maria continues to experience significant social withdrawal and lack of motivation. What should be the primary consideration when reviewing and revising Maria's treatment plan?

A) Increase the dosage of SSRIs while maintaining IPT.

B) Transition from IPT to cognitive-behavioral therapy (CBT).

C) Incorporate motivational interviewing techniques into her current treatment plan.

D) Suggest discontinuation of SSRIs due to their ineffectiveness.

Question 133: During an intake session with John, who has been diagnosed with generalized anxiety disorder (GAD), you plan to use pre-test and post-test measures to assess treatment outcomes. Which of the following is a critical consideration when selecting these measures?

A) The measures should be widely used in clinical practice.

B) The measures should have strong reliability and validity for GAD.

C) The measures should be easy for John to complete quickly.

D) The measures should provide qualitative data on John's experiences.

Question 134: A mental health counselor is working with a client who has been denied access to necessary mental health services due to insurance limitations. Which action best exemplifies the counselor's role in advocating for the client's needs?

A) Contacting the insurance company to request an exception for coverage.

B) Referring the client to another provider who may accept their insurance.

C) Educating the client on how to file a formal complaint with their insurance provider.

D) Providing pro bono services until the insurance issue is resolved.

Question 135: Which core counseling attribute involves the counselor's ability to understand and share the feelings of the client while maintaining an objective stance?

A) Empathy

B) Sympathy

C) Reflective Listening

D) Unconditional Positive Regard

Question 136: John is a 45-year-old client who is undergoing therapy for depression. During a session, he reveals that he has been engaging in self-harm. As his mental health counselor, what is your primary responsibility regarding this disclosure?

A) Maintain confidentiality and continue the session as usual.

B) Discuss with John the limits of confidentiality and assess his safety.

C) Immediately contact John's family without his consent.

D) Wait until the next session to address the issue further.

Question 137: During a counseling session, Maria, a 35-year-old client, shares that she feels her previous therapist did not listen to her concerns and was dismissive. How should the counselor respond to build trust and ensure a positive therapeutic relationship?

A) Reassure Maria that you are different from her previous therapist.

B) Validate Maria's feelings and ask her to share more about her experience.

C) Suggest that Maria might be projecting her past experiences onto you.

D) Encourage Maria to focus on the present rather than dwelling on past therapy experiences.

Question 138: John, a 45-year-old man, presents with symptoms of anxiety and reports difficulties in his workplace interactions. He feels misunderstood by his colleagues and often finds himself in conflict situations. As part of your assessment, what aspect should you prioritize to evaluate the interactional dynamics at his workplace?

A) John's communication style with his colleagues

B) The hierarchical structure within his workplace

C) The specific incidents that led to conflicts

D) John's perception of his colleagues' intentions

Question 139: Emily, a new member of a therapeutic group led by Dr. Johnson, feels excluded and hesitant to participate in discussions. Other members have formed close bonds over time, making it difficult for her to integrate. As a mental health counselor, what strategy should you employ to improve Emily's inclusion in the group?

A) Pair Emily with another member for collaborative tasks.

B) Encourage Emily to share her feelings with the group.

C) Facilitate icebreaker activities at the beginning of each session.

D) Assign Emily leadership responsibilities in upcoming sessions.

Question 140: Maria is a mental health counselor who notices that many of her clients from a particular minority community face systemic barriers in accessing mental health services. She wants to advocate for these clients at a broader level. Which action should Maria take that aligns with ethical guidelines for advocacy?

A) Publicly criticize local mental health agencies for their lack of services for minority communities.

B) Collaborate with community leaders and organizations to develop programs that address these barriers.

C) Encourage her clients to individually file complaints against mental health agencies.

D) Focus solely on providing direct services to her clients without engaging in broader advocacy efforts.

Question 141: John, a 40-year-old father, has been emotionally abusive towards his children due to his own unresolved trauma. During counseling sessions, he expresses guilt and a desire to change his behavior but feels overwhelmed by his emotions. What would be the most effective therapeutic approach for John?

A) Encourage John to express his emotions freely without

any structure.

B) Use cognitive-behavioral therapy (CBT) to help John manage his guilt and develop healthier coping strategies.

C) Suggest family therapy sessions to address the dynamics with his children directly.

D) Advise John to take anger management classes immediately.

Question 142: When collaborating with a client to establish treatment goals and objectives, which of the following is the most effective approach to ensure the goals are meaningful and attainable?

A) Set goals based solely on the counselor's professional judgment.

B) Develop goals that align with evidence-based practices without client input.

C) Create goals that reflect both the client's values and the counselor's expertise.

D) Focus on short-term goals to ensure quick wins for client motivation.

Question 143: Which factor is most crucial in predicting the long-term success of a remarriage involving children from previous relationships?

A) Financial stability of the new family unit

B) Quality of the co-parenting relationship with ex-spouses

C) Emotional readiness of the partners for remarriage

D) Integration and acceptance of stepchildren into the new family

Question 144: During an initial intake session with a client, which method would be most appropriate for gathering comprehensive information about the client's non-verbal communication patterns?

A) Structured interview

B) Standardized assessment

C) Unstructured observation

D) Behavioral checklist

Question 145: Maria, a 35-year-old woman, reports experiencing decreased sexual desire since starting a new medication for her anxiety. She is concerned about how this change is affecting her relationship with her partner. As her mental health counselor, what would be the most appropriate initial step in addressing Maria's concern?

A) Suggest switching to a different anxiety medication.

B) Explore Maria's relationship dynamics with her partner.

C) Educate Maria about the potential side effects of her current medication.

D) Refer Maria to a sex therapist for specialized counseling.

Question 146: How can unresolved issues from a client's family of origin most significantly impact their current interpersonal relationships?

A) By causing them to adopt similar communication patterns observed in their parents.

B) By making them overly dependent on their partner for emotional support.

C) By leading them to replicate the attachment style they experienced as children.

D) By encouraging them to avoid conflict in relationships at all costs.

Question 147: Maria, a 14-year-old adolescent, is experiencing significant stress due to academic pressures and peer relationships. She often feels misunderstood by her parents and teachers. As her counselor, which intervention would best align with Maria's developmental level?

A) Encourage Maria to engage in self-exploration activities to understand her identity.

B) Advise Maria to focus on concrete operational tasks to improve her problem-solving skills.

C) Suggest that Maria participate in group therapy with peers to enhance social support.

D) Recommend that Maria engage in imaginative play to express her emotions.

Question 148: Which of the following physical symptoms is most strongly associated with major depressive disorder?

A) Chronic fatigue

B) Joint pain

C) Shortness of breath

D) Frequent headaches

Question 149: A mental health counselor is working with an adolescent client who has been diagnosed with social anxiety disorder. Which of the following interventions would be most appropriate to align with this client population?

A) Cognitive-Behavioral Therapy (CBT) focusing on exposure techniques

B) Psychodynamic Therapy focusing on uncovering unconscious conflicts

C) Solution-Focused Brief Therapy (SFBT) emphasizing future goals

D) Person-Centered Therapy emphasizing unconditional positive regard

Question 150: Sarah, a 28-year-old woman, has been struggling with depressive symptoms after a recent breakup. She reports feeling hopeless and unable to move forward with her life. As her counselor, which intervention would be most appropriate to help Sarah reframe her negative thoughts and improve her mood?

A) Interpersonal Therapy (IPT)

B) Psychodynamic Therapy

C) Acceptance and Commitment Therapy (ACT)

D) Cognitive Behavioral Therapy (CBT)

ANSWER WITH DETAILED EXPLANATION SET [1]

Question 1: Correct Answer: B) The counselor's expression of genuine feelings and thoughts that are aligned with their internal experiences.
Rationale: Congruence in Carl Rogers' person-centered therapy specifically refers to the counselor being genuine and authentic, meaning their external expressions align with their internal experiences (Option B). This differs from empathy (Option A), which involves understanding the client's perspective, and unconditional positive regard (Option C), which is about accepting and supporting the client unconditionally. Reflective listening (Option D) is a technique used to mirror clients' feelings but does not necessarily involve the counselor's own internal congruence. Therefore, Option B is correct because it directly addresses congruence as defined by Rogers.

Question 2: Correct Answer: C) Muscle tension
Rationale: Muscle tension is a hallmark physical symptom of generalized anxiety disorder (GAD), often resulting from chronic stress and worry. While chest pain (Option A) and shortness of breath (Option B) can also occur in anxiety disorders, they are more commonly associated with panic attacks or other cardiovascular issues. Frequent urination (Option D), though it can be a symptom of anxiety, is less specific and can be linked to various other conditions such as urinary tract infections or diabetes. Thus, muscle tension remains the most directly related physical symptom to GAD according to contemporary research and clinical observations.

Question 3: Correct Answer: B) Standardized outcome measures
Rationale: Standardized outcome measures are considered the most effective method for evaluating the overall effectiveness of a counseling intervention. These tools are validated through research and provide objective data that can be compared across different clients and settings. - Option A (Client self-report surveys): While useful for gaining insight into the client's perspective, they may be biased or influenced by temporary emotions. - Option C (Counselor's subjective evaluation): This can be helpful but is prone to bias and lacks objectivity. - Option D (Session-by-session progress notes): These provide detailed information about each session but do not offer a comprehensive measure of overall effectiveness. Standardized outcome measures incorporate reliability and validity, making them superior for assessing counseling outcomes comprehensively.

Question 4: Correct Answer: C) Validate Alex's feelings and explore ways they can advocate for themselves.
Rationale: Validating Alex's feelings acknowledges their experience and provides immediate emotional support, which is crucial for building trust. Exploring ways for self-advocacy empowers Alex in managing their relationship dynamics effectively. Option A, while useful, places the burden solely on Alex without addressing immediate emotional needs. Option B neglects the importance of ongoing communication and support. Option D might be beneficial but does not address the immediate need for validation and self-advocacy skills.

Question 5: Correct Answer: B) Eye Movement Desensitization and Reprocessing (EMDR)
Rationale: EMDR is particularly effective for clients who have experienced trauma, including family abuse. It helps process traumatic memories and reduce their emotional impact through bilateral stimulation. While CBT focuses on altering dysfunctional thoughts and behaviors, it may not directly address trauma-specific memories as effectively as EMDR. SFBT is future-oriented and goal-directed, which might not be sufficient for processing deep-seated emotional

trauma. Psychodynamic Therapy delves into unconscious processes but can be lengthy and less focused on immediate symptom relief compared to EMDR. Thus, EMDR's targeted approach makes it the most effective for addressing emotional needs in trauma from family abuse.

Question 6: Correct Answer: D) Conduct a family session to understand each member's perspective on John's role.
Rationale: Conducting a family session helps uncover underlying dynamics and expectations placed on John by other family members. This approach provides insight into how each member views John's role, facilitating more balanced interactions. Option A might offer temporary relief but does not address the root cause of the issue. Option B is useful but should follow an understanding of the family's dynamics. Option C might alleviate some burden but does not explore or resolve deeper interaction patterns within the family system.

Question 7: Correct Answer: A) Intensive outpatient program (IOP)
Rationale: An Intensive Outpatient Program (IOP) is recommended for Maria as it provides a high level of support and structured therapy while allowing her to live at home. This level of care is suitable given her stabilization on medication but continued need for frequent therapeutic interventions. Outpatient therapy with bi-weekly sessions (B) offers insufficient support, PHP (C) might be too intensive given her current stability, and day treatment programs (D), although similar to IOP, may not offer the flexibility needed for her integration back into daily life.

Question 8: Correct Answer: A) John's ability to understand the nature and purpose of the clinical trial.
Rationale: The ability to understand the nature and purpose of the clinical trial is fundamental in assessing competency for informed consent. This involves comprehending what participation entails, potential risks, and benefits. While willingness (B), compliance history (C), and family opinion (D) are important considerations, they do not directly assess John's cognitive ability to make an informed decision.

Question 9: Correct Answer: B) Eye Movement Desensitization and Reprocessing (EMDR)
Rationale: EMDR is particularly effective for individuals experiencing PTSD symptoms such as flashbacks and hypervigilance following trauma. It focuses on processing traumatic memories and reducing their emotional impact. While CBT (Option A) is also effective for PTSD, EMDR is often preferred for its specific focus on trauma processing. Prolonged Exposure Therapy (Option C) is another valid approach but may not be the most appropriate initial intervention given Jane's detachment symptoms. Medication Management (Option D) can be helpful but is typically considered an adjunct to therapy rather than the first-line treatment.

Question 10: Correct Answer: B) Using secure, HIPAA-compliant platforms for telehealth sessions.
Rationale: Option B is correct because using secure, HIPAA-compliant platforms is crucial for ensuring that all telehealth communications are protected under federal regulations, thereby safeguarding client privacy. Option A is incorrect because while encrypting emails is important, it alone does not cover all aspects of confidentiality in electronic communication. Option C is close but incorrect; obtaining written consent is necessary but not sufficient on its own without ensuring the security of the communication platform. Option D is also important but does not directly address the core requirement of using a compliant platform for telehealth sessions. The correct option (B) encompasses a comprehensive approach to maintaining confidentiality by

adhering to established legal standards and ensuring overall security in electronic communications.

Question 11: Correct Answer: C) Contempt

Rationale: Contempt is considered the most damaging communication pattern in marital relationships, according to John Gottman's research. It involves attacking a partner's sense of self with an intent to insult or psychologically abuse them, leading to long-term dissatisfaction and potential relationship dissolution. - A) Criticism involves attacking a partner's character rather than their behavior, which can be harmful but is less destructive than contempt. - B) Stonewalling refers to withdrawing from interaction, which can cause issues but typically not as severe as those caused by contempt. - D) Defensiveness involves self-protection through righteous indignation or playing the victim, which can escalate conflicts but is not as corrosive as contempt.

Question 12: Correct Answer: C) "Sarah feels overwhelmed by the loss of her job and is anxious about how this will affect her future."

Rationale: Option C accurately summarizes Sarah's emotional state (feeling overwhelmed) and specific concern (anxiety about the future). Option A mentions financial worries but lacks emotional depth. Option B focuses on anxiety and stress but doesn't capture the feeling of being overwhelmed. Option D emphasizes uncertainty but misses the broader context of job loss and its impact.

Question 13: Correct Answer: C) Stress management techniques

Rationale: Stress-induced auditory hallucinations can often be managed through non-pharmacological interventions initially. Stress management techniques are appropriate for Sarah's situation given the context of her hallucinations and lack of other psychiatric symptoms. Antipsychotic medication (A) is generally reserved for more severe or persistent cases. Cognitive-behavioral therapy (B), while beneficial, may not address the immediate issue as effectively as stress management techniques. Hospitalization (D) is unnecessary unless there is a risk of harm to herself or others.

Question 14: Correct Answer: B) The client's understanding of the information provided.

Rationale: The most crucial factor in assessing competency for informed consent is the client's understanding of the information provided (Option B). This is because informed consent hinges on whether the client comprehends what they are consenting to, including risks, benefits, and alternatives. While articulating a decision (Option A) is important, it does not ensure comprehension. Emotional stability (Option C) is relevant but secondary to understanding. Previous experiences (Option D) may influence decisions but do not directly assess current comprehension. Therefore, Option B is correct as it directly addresses the core requirement for informed consent understanding.

Question 15: Correct Answer: A) Panic Attacks

Rationale: Panic attacks are characterized by sudden episodes of intense fear that trigger severe physical reactions when there is no real danger or apparent cause. Symptoms often include chest pain, palpitations, and shortness of breath. Hyperthyroidism can mimic anxiety but would typically show abnormal thyroid function tests. Myocardial infarction would present with abnormal cardiac findings. Asthma involves respiratory issues but not typically palpitations or chest pain without wheezing or a history of asthma.

Question 16: Correct Answer: B) Using "I" statements to express concern about the observed inconsistency.

Rationale: Using "I" statements is an effective approach in constructive confrontation because it focuses on the counselor's perspective and feelings rather than placing blame on the client. This method reduces defensiveness and encourages open dialogue. Option A may come across as accusatory, leading to defensiveness. Option C puts pressure on the client to explain themselves, which can be

intimidating. Option D involves making assumptions about the client's behavior, which can be perceived as judgmental. Therefore, option B aligns best with contemporary research and recognized theories on constructive confrontation by promoting a supportive and non-judgmental environment.

Question 17: Correct Answer: A) "I can see that you're really worried about this interview."

Rationale: Option A directly acknowledges John's specific emotional state (worry), demonstrating empathic attunement by validating his feelings without minimizing them or offering solutions prematurely. Option B normalizes his experience but does not specifically address John's unique worry. Option C offers reassurance but shifts focus from empathy to problem-solving. Option D provides generalized support but lacks personal connection.

Question 18: Correct Answer: C) Mindfulness-Based Stress Reduction (MBSR)

Rationale: Mindfulness-Based Stress Reduction (MBSR) has been extensively studied and shown to effectively reduce physiological markers of stress, including cortisol levels. While Progressive Muscle Relaxation (PMR), Cognitive Behavioral Therapy (CBT), and Biofeedback are also effective stress management techniques, MBSR's focus on mindfulness and meditation has a more significant impact on reducing physiological stress markers. PMR is beneficial for muscle tension, CBT addresses cognitive patterns, and Biofeedback helps individuals gain control over physiological functions. However, MBSR's comprehensive approach to mindfulness practices makes it particularly effective in lowering cortisol levels compared to the other methods. - A) Progressive Muscle Relaxation (PMR): Effective for reducing muscle tension but less impactful on overall physiological markers like cortisol compared to MBSR. - B) Cognitive Behavioral Therapy (CBT): Addresses cognitive patterns contributing to stress but does not directly target physiological markers as effectively as MBSR. - C) Mindfulness-Based Stress Reduction (MBSR): Focuses on mindfulness and meditation, significantly reducing cortisol levels according to contemporary research. - D) Biofeedback: Helps control physiological functions but is less comprehensive in addressing overall stress compared to MBSR.

Question 19: Correct Answer: B) Motivational Interviewing (MI)

Rationale: Motivational Interviewing (MI) is specifically designed to address ambivalence about substance use by enhancing intrinsic motivation through exploring and resolving mixed feelings. It is client-centered and directive, making it highly effective in addiction counseling. - Option A (Cognitive-Behavioral Therapy) is effective for changing maladaptive thought patterns but does not primarily focus on resolving ambivalence. - Option C (Contingency Management) uses positive reinforcement to encourage abstinence but does not address ambivalence directly. - Option D (Twelve-Step Facilitation) supports participation in 12-step programs but does not specifically target ambivalence resolution. Thus, MI's unique focus on addressing and resolving ambivalence makes it the most appropriate choice.

Question 20: Correct Answer: B) Redirect the former client to schedule an official session through appropriate channels.

Rationale: John should redirect the former client to schedule an official session through appropriate channels (Option B). This ensures that any advice or intervention occurs within a structured, confidential setting adhering to ethical standards. Providing general advice (Option A) might seem harmless but can lead to potential misunderstandings or boundary issues. Offering specific strategies (Option C) breaches confidentiality and re-establishes a therapeutic relationship outside proper channels. Ignoring the message (Option D) neglects an opportunity to guide clients towards appropriate professional support while maintaining ethical standards.

Question 21: Correct Answer: B) Balancing positive

feedback with constructive criticism while ensuring it is specific and actionable.

Rationale: Contemporary research emphasizes that effective feedback should be balanced, specific, and actionable. Option B aligns with this by suggesting a balance between positive and constructive criticism, ensuring that the client understands exactly what behaviors are being addressed and how they can improve. Option A overlooks the client's emotional readiness for feedback, which can hinder its effectiveness. Option C, while boosting self-esteem, lacks specificity and may fail to address critical issues adequately. Option D suggests delaying feedback, which can result in missed opportunities for timely intervention and growth.

Question 22: Correct Answer: C) Existential Therapy

Rationale: Existential Therapy (Option C) is most likely to help John reconnect with his sense of self by addressing his deeper existential questions about life's direction. This approach focuses on exploring issues such as meaning, freedom, isolation, and mortality. While CBT (Option A) addresses cognitive distortions and anxiety symptoms, it may not delve into existential concerns deeply. MBSR (Option B) can help manage anxiety but may not specifically address existential disconnection. SFBT (Option D), while effective for immediate solutions, does not typically explore profound existential issues.

Question 23: Correct Answer: B) Facilitate a discussion on coping mechanisms for workplace discrimination.

Rationale: Facilitating a discussion on coping mechanisms addresses Jamie's immediate emotional needs and provides practical strategies she can use in her daily life. While filing a complaint (Option A) or seeking legal advice (Option D) may be necessary steps later, they do not offer immediate emotional support or practical coping strategies. Sharing statistics (Option C), although informative, might not provide the personal support Jamie needs at that moment.

Question 24: Correct Answer: A) Conduct a thorough suicide risk assessment.

Rationale: Conducting a thorough suicide risk assessment is the most appropriate initial intervention when a client expresses suicidal thoughts. This allows the counselor to determine the level of risk and develop an appropriate treatment plan. Immediate referral to inpatient psychiatric care (Option B) may be necessary depending on the assessment results but is not the first step without further evaluation. Starting cognitive behavioral therapy sessions (Option C) is important but should follow an assessment. Encouraging social activities (Option D) can be beneficial but does not address immediate safety concerns.

Question 25: Correct Answer: C) Implementing caregiver support groups

Rationale: Implementing caregiver support groups is the most effective intervention in reducing caregiver burden. Support groups provide emotional support, reduce feelings of isolation, and offer practical advice from peers who understand the unique challenges of caregiving. This aligns with contemporary research indicating that social support is a critical factor in mitigating caregiver stress. A) Providing respite care services is beneficial but primarily offers temporary relief rather than ongoing support. B) Offering financial assistance programs addresses economic strain but does not directly alleviate emotional or psychological burdens. D) Educating caregivers on stress management techniques is helpful but lacks the peer support component crucial for sustained relief. By comparing these options, it becomes clear that while each intervention has merit, only support groups offer comprehensive emotional and practical benefits essential for long-term reduction of caregiver burden.

Question 26: Correct Answer: B) Autism Spectrum Disorder (ASD)

Rationale: ASD is characterized by difficulties in social interaction, communication challenges, and a preference for solitary play, which aligns with Tommy's behaviors. ODD involves defiance and oppositional behaviors but does not necessarily include social interaction difficulties or preference for solitary play. ADHD can involve difficulty with transitions but typically includes hyperactivity and impulsivity rather than social communication issues. SPD involves challenges with processing sensory information but does not directly explain Tommy's difficulty understanding others' emotions or preference for solitary play.

Question 27: Correct Answer: A) Crisis Stabilization Unit

Rationale: A Crisis Stabilization Unit is appropriate for John as it provides immediate intervention to manage acute symptoms of bipolar disorder, especially during manic episodes. This setting offers intensive monitoring and rapid stabilization. - B) Long-Term Residential Treatment is more suitable for chronic issues requiring prolonged care rather than immediate stabilization. - C) Partial Hospitalization Program offers intensive day treatment but does not provide 24-hour supervision needed during acute manic episodes. - D) Intensive Outpatient Program lacks the necessary intensity and overnight care required for managing acute symptoms effectively.

Question 28: Correct Answer: C) Long-term Residential Treatment

Rationale: Long-term Residential Treatment is most appropriate for clients with severe substance use disorders who have not succeeded in less intensive settings like outpatient programs. This level provides structured, round-the-clock care, which is crucial for individuals needing extensive support and monitoring over an extended period. - Option A (Intensive Outpatient Program) offers significant therapeutic support but lacks the 24-hour supervision needed for severe cases. - Option B (Partial Hospitalization Program) provides more intensive care than IOP but still does not offer around-the-clock supervision. - Option D (Short-term Residential Treatment) provides 24-hour care but typically for a shorter duration, which might not be sufficient for someone with a severe and persistent disorder.

Question 29: Correct Answer: B) Process addictions are characterized by compulsive engagement in behaviors despite negative consequences.

Rationale: Option B is correct because it accurately describes a hallmark of process addictions: the compulsive pursuit of certain behaviors despite adverse outcomes, aligning with contemporary research on behavioral addiction. Option A is incorrect because physical withdrawal symptoms are more characteristic of substance use disorders. Option C, while partially true regarding tolerance, does not capture the essence of compulsive behavior central to process addictions. Option D incorrectly emphasizes genetic predispositions over environmental factors, which play a significant role in the development of these behaviors. Therefore, B is the most comprehensive and accurate description.

Question 30: Correct Answer: B) Attention-Deficit/Hyperactivity Disorder (ADHD)

Rationale: John's symptoms of racing thoughts and difficulty focusing are characteristic of ADHD, particularly in adults. While Generalized Anxiety Disorder (GAD) can involve excessive worry, it typically does not include the pervasive difficulty with concentration seen in ADHD. Major Depressive Disorder often includes concentration issues but is usually accompanied by persistent sadness or anhedonia, which John does not report. Obsessive-Compulsive Disorder involves intrusive thoughts and compulsions rather than the broad attentional difficulties described here.

Question 31: Correct Answer: B) Providing a thorough explanation of potential risks and benefits, then documenting the client's decision.

Rationale: Option B is correct because it emphasizes both informing the client about risks and benefits (a key component of informed consent) and documenting their decision, which upholds client autonomy. Option A focuses solely on explaining options without emphasizing documentation or risk/benefit analysis. Option C involves suggesting treatments based on clinical judgment, which can overshadow client autonomy if not handled carefully. Option D highlights understanding but lacks emphasis on documenting consent, which is crucial for legal and ethical accountability. Thus, B best captures both informed consent and respect for client autonomy.

Question 32: Correct Answer: D) Conduct an individual meeting with each member to reinforce confidentiality principles.

Rationale: Conducting individual meetings (Option D) allows for a private discussion where specific concerns can be addressed directly and confidentially, ensuring members understand confidentiality principles thoroughly. Option A may cause embarrassment or defensiveness among members. Option B might not sufficiently emphasize the importance of confidentiality. Option C lacks specificity and may not adequately address individual behaviors. The correct answer (D) ensures personalized attention to confidentiality breaches while respecting privacy.

Question 33: Correct Answer: D) Obtaining written consent from clients before using any form of electronic communication.

Rationale: Obtaining written consent from clients before using any form of electronic communication is crucial because it ensures that clients are fully aware of and agree to the potential risks associated with electronic communication. This practice aligns with ethical guidelines and protects both the counselor and client. While using encrypted email services (Option A), informing clients about risks (Option B), and storing information on password-protected devices (Option C) are important practices, they do not replace the necessity of obtaining informed consent. Informed consent is a foundational principle that upholds client autonomy and ensures ethical compliance in professional practice.

Question 34: Correct Answer: B) Panic Disorder

Rationale: Mary's symptoms are characteristic of Panic Disorder, which involves recurrent unexpected panic attacks and concern about future attacks or their consequences. Generalized Anxiety Disorder (GAD) involves excessive worry about various events or activities but lacks the sudden onset of intense fear seen in panic attacks. Social Anxiety Disorder involves fear of social situations due to potential scrutiny but does not typically include unpredictable panic attacks. Agoraphobia involves fear of situations where escape might be difficult if a panic attack occurs but usually develops secondary to Panic Disorder rather than being the primary issue.

Question 35: Correct Answer: B) Conducting a comprehensive behavioral assessment to identify triggers.

Rationale: Conducting a comprehensive behavioral assessment is crucial as it helps in identifying the underlying causes or triggers of John's aggressive behavior. This approach ensures that interventions are tailored to his specific needs. While implementing a token economy system (Option A) can be effective, it is not the initial step without understanding the behavior's root causes. Referring John to a pediatrician (Option C) might be necessary if medical issues are suspected but should follow the behavioral assessment. Enrolling John in a social skills training group (Option D) could be beneficial later but is not the first step.

Question 36: Correct Answer: B) Sarah acknowledges her own feelings about John's hesitation and expresses them.

Rationale: Genuineness in counseling involves being authentic and transparent with clients. By acknowledging her own feelings about John's hesitation and expressing them (Option B), Sarah demonstrates authenticity, which can help build trust and encourage John to be more open. Option A, sharing personal experiences, may blur professional boundaries; Option C focuses on validation rather than genuineness; Option D maintains boundaries but lacks the transparency needed for genuineness.

Question 37: Correct Answer: C) Eye Movement Desensitization and Reprocessing (EMDR)

Rationale: EMDR (Option C) is particularly effective for trauma-related issues like those experienced by John, as it helps process traumatic memories and reduce their emotional impact. CBT (Option A) can help with negative thought patterns but may not address deep-seated trauma as effectively as EMDR. Psychoanalytic Therapy (Option B) explores unconscious conflicts but may take longer to show results. Family Systems Therapy (Option D) focuses on family dynamics rather than individual trauma processing.

Question 38: Correct Answer: C) Help Maria understand and negotiate her family's expectations.

Rationale: Helping Maria understand and negotiate her family's expectations is crucial because it addresses the underlying cultural values and dynamics that contribute to her stress. Encouraging boundary setting (A) is important but may not fully consider cultural nuances. Limiting contact (B) can be too drastic and may lead to additional stress or guilt. Seeking support from friends (D) might help but doesn't address the core issue of familial expectations. Understanding and negotiation allow for a more culturally sensitive approach that respects Maria's background while promoting mental health.

Question 39: Correct Answer: A) Help Ahmed develop assertiveness skills to communicate his boundaries respectfully.

Rationale: Helping Ahmed develop assertiveness skills empowers him to express his needs without compromising his beliefs or alienating colleagues. This approach supports ethical decision-making by promoting self-advocacy and respect for diversity. Option B undermines Ahmed's values and could lead to internal conflict. Option C might seem reasonable but risks diluting Ahmed's commitment to his beliefs. Option D could be necessary later but may escalate tensions prematurely; it's better for Ahmed first to try resolving the issue through direct communication.

Question 40: Correct Answer: A) Maria shares her experience to establish rapport and normalize John's feelings.

Rationale: The correct answer is A because using self-disclosure appropriately involves sharing personal experiences to build rapport and help clients feel understood and less isolated. Option B is incorrect as it shifts the focus away from the client's issues. Option C is incorrect because it may pressure the client into sharing more than they are comfortable with. Option D is incorrect because it implies that the counselor knows exactly what the client should do, which can undermine the client's autonomy and individual experience.

Question 41: Correct Answer: C) Heart rate variability (HRV) biofeedback focusing on heart rate patterns.

Rationale: Heart rate variability (HRV) biofeedback is particularly effective in managing physiological responses to stress by teaching individuals how to control their heart rate patterns through breathing exercises and relaxation techniques. While EMG biofeedback focuses on muscle tension and can help with physical manifestations of stress, it does not directly address autonomic regulation like HRV does. EEG biofeedback targets brain wave activity, which is more suitable for conditions like ADHD rather than general stress management. GSR measures skin conductance levels but is less effective in providing actionable feedback compared to HRV for managing stress.

Question 42: Correct Answer: B) Acculturation

Rationale: Acculturation refers to the process where individuals adopt the cultural norms of a dominant or host culture while still retaining their original cultural identity. This concept is widely recognized in contemporary research on cultural adjustments and is crucial for understanding how individuals navigate between different cultural contexts. - Option A (Assimilation): Incorrect because assimilation involves an individual fully adopting the host culture's norms and often losing their original cultural identity. - Option C (Enculturation): Incorrect as enculturation refers to the process by which individuals learn and adopt their own culture from birth. - Option D (Cultural Integration): Incorrect because it generally implies a broader societal level integration rather than focusing on individual-level changes in cultural identity.

Question 43: Correct Answer: B) Psychological adjustment
Rationale: Psychological adjustment is often considered the most critical aspect of managing retirement concerns because it encompasses dealing with changes in identity, purpose, and routine. While financial planning (A), social engagement (C), and identity transition (D) are also important, they are components that contribute to overall psychological well-being. Financial planning focuses on economic stability but does not directly address emotional or mental health. Social engagement helps maintain connections but is one part of broader psychological adjustment. Identity transition involves redefining one's role but is a subset of the larger process of adjusting psychologically to retirement. In summary, while all options are important facets of retirement concerns, psychological adjustment (B) is overarching and most critical for mental health counselors to address comprehensively.

Question 44: Correct Answer: C) Establishment Stage
Rationale: The Establishment Stage in Super's Life-Span, Life-Space Theory is characterized by individuals striving to secure and stabilize their careers. This stage typically occurs during early adulthood when individuals work towards achieving career goals and building a stable professional life. Option A (Growth Stage) is incorrect because it pertains to childhood and adolescence, where individuals develop self-concepts and begin to understand different occupations. Option B (Exploration Stage) is also incorrect as it involves young adults exploring various career options through education and early work experiences. Option D (Maintenance Stage) is incorrect because it relates to mid-career individuals who focus on maintaining their established careers rather than building them. By comparing these stages, we see that only the Establishment Stage aligns with the context of securing and stabilizing a career, making it the correct answer.

Question 45: Correct Answer: C) Negative feedback loop
Rationale: A negative feedback loop involves interactions that reduce deviation from a set point, maintaining stability but potentially reinforcing negative behaviors. In this case, Maria's criticism leads to Lisa's withdrawal, which in turn increases Maria's criticism, creating a self-perpetuating cycle. - A) Enmeshment refers to overly close relationships where boundaries are blurred, not fitting this scenario. - B) Triangulation involves drawing in a third party to reduce tension between two people. - D) Positive feedback loops amplify changes rather than stabilizing them. Thus, option C is correct as it accurately describes the observed pattern of interaction.

Question 46: Correct Answer: B) Sudden changes in behavior or school performance
Rationale: Sudden changes in behavior or school performance are often indicative of emotional abuse, as they reflect internalized stress and anxiety. While frequent unexplained injuries (Option A) may suggest physical abuse, developmental delays (Option C) can result from various factors including neglect, and inappropriate sexual behaviors (Option D) are more closely associated with sexual abuse. Emotional abuse specifically affects a child's psychological state, leading to noticeable shifts in behavior and academic performance. This distinction is crucial for mental health counselors to accurately identify and address different forms of child abuse.

Question 47: Correct Answer: C) Identify and challenge negative thought patterns through cognitive restructuring.
Rationale: Cognitive restructuring is a key component of

cognitive-behavioral therapy (CBT), which is effective for treating Major Depressive Disorder (MDD). It helps clients identify and challenge negative thought patterns contributing to their depression. While increasing social interactions (A) and developing a daily exercise routine (B) are beneficial for overall well-being, they may not directly address the cognitive distortions central to MDD. Setting career advancement goals (D) may be overwhelming for someone experiencing severe depressive symptoms and is more appropriate as a long-term goal once initial symptoms have improved.

Question 48: Correct Answer: B) Cognitive restructuring to challenge distorted beliefs about gambling
Rationale: Cognitive-Behavioral Therapy (CBT) focuses on identifying and changing distorted thoughts and beliefs that contribute to addictive behaviors. In John's case, cognitive restructuring can help him recognize and alter his irrational beliefs about gambling, making it an effective intervention. While psychoeducation (A) provides valuable information, it does not directly address the cognitive distortions driving his behavior. Pharmacotherapy with SSRIs (C) may help with comorbid conditions like depression but is not the primary treatment for gambling addiction. Mindfulness meditation (D) can reduce stress but does not specifically target the cognitive distortions associated with gambling.

Question 49: Correct Answer: A) A workbook on cognitive-behavioral therapy (CBT) techniques specifically for anxiety
Rationale: The correct answer is A because a workbook on CBT techniques specifically for anxiety provides targeted strategies and exercises that are evidence-based and highly effective for managing GAD. Option B is incorrect because it is too general and not specifically focused on anxiety. Option C, while providing peer support, may lack professional guidance and structured interventions. Option D, although informative, might not offer the practical tools and structured approach necessary for managing GAD effectively.

Question 50: Correct Answer: A) Document only the facts and avoid any subjective interpretations.
Rationale: Documenting only the facts ensures that the record remains objective and unbiased, which is crucial for maintaining ethical standards. Including subjective interpretations (Option B) can lead to biased records. Discussing interpretations verbally with a supervisor (Option C) is good practice but does not address proper documentation. Recording only critical points (Option D) risks omitting important details necessary for comprehensive care.

Question 51: Correct Answer: D) Fearful-Avoidant Attachment
Rationale: Fearful-Avoidant Attachment is characterized by a combination of fear of intimacy and difficulty trusting others, leading to unstable relationships. Individuals with this attachment style often experience anxiety about their partner's availability while simultaneously avoiding closeness due to fear of rejection. - A) Secure Attachment: Incorrect because individuals with secure attachment typically have healthy relationships marked by trust and comfort with intimacy. - B) Anxious-Preoccupied Attachment: Incorrect but close; these individuals are anxious about their partner's availability but crave intimacy rather than avoid it. - C) Dismissive-Avoidant Attachment: Incorrect but tricky; these individuals avoid intimacy but do not exhibit the same level of anxiety about their partner's availability as those with fearful-avoidant attachment. Thus, D) Fearful-Avoidant Attachment is the correct answer as it encapsulates both fear of intimacy and anxiety about the partner's availability, aligning with contemporary research on attachment theory.

Question 52: Correct Answer: A) Use reflective listening to understand Sarah's concerns about her medication.
Rationale: Using reflective listening to understand Sarah's concerns about her medication is an effective strategy rooted in motivational interviewing principles, which prioritize empathy and understanding clients' perspectives. This

approach helps build rapport and addresses underlying issues affecting adherence. Explaining biochemical mechanisms (B) might not resonate emotionally; reiterating doctor's orders (C) could come across as authoritarian and dismissive; scheduling frequent follow-ups (D), while useful for monitoring, does not directly address Sarah's hesitations or promote intrinsic motivation for adherence.

Question 53: Correct Answer: D) Long-Term Residential Treatment

Rationale: Long-term residential treatment is designed for individuals with severe and persistent issues such as Emily's severe depression and substance abuse. It provides intensive care over an extended period, which is crucial for addressing both her mental health and substance use disorders comprehensively. - A) Therapeutic Community focuses on social and psychological rehabilitation through community living but may not provide the intensive medical care needed. - B) Halfway House offers transitional support post-treatment rather than initial intensive care. - C) Acute Inpatient Treatment is short-term and typically addresses immediate crises rather than long-term needs.

Question 54: Correct Answer: A) Encourage Maria to adopt a collaborative approach by seeking common goals.

Rationale: Encouraging Maria to adopt a collaborative approach by seeking common goals (A) is the most effective strategy as it fosters teamwork and mutual understanding, which can improve both relationships and patient outcomes. Option B may be helpful but could lead to further conflict if not balanced with collaboration. Option C could escalate tensions without resolving underlying issues. Option D avoids the problem entirely, likely exacerbating it over time. In both questions, incorrect options are designed to appear plausible by incorporating elements of common counseling advice but lack the comprehensive approach needed for effective conflict resolution.

Question 55: Correct Answer: B) Actively listening and validating the client's feelings and experiences.

Rationale: Active listening and validation are fundamental in establishing trust in the therapeutic relationship. This approach demonstrates empathy, understanding, and respect for the client's experiences, which are crucial for building a strong foundation of trust. While providing detailed explanations (Option A) is important for transparency, it may not immediately foster emotional connection. Setting clear boundaries (Option C) is necessary for professional conduct but does not directly address emotional validation. Sharing personal experiences (Option D) can sometimes help but may also risk crossing professional boundaries or shifting focus away from the client. Therefore, Option B is most effective in building initial trust.

Question 56: Correct Answer: A) The client pays upfront and submits claims for partial reimbursement based on allowed amounts.

Rationale: For out-of-network services, clients typically pay upfront for therapy sessions and then submit claims to their insurance company for partial reimbursement based on allowed amounts specified in their plan. This process often involves understanding deductibles and co-insurance rates. Option B is incorrect because out-of-network providers do not bill insurers directly for full reimbursement; they usually require upfront payment from clients. Option C is misleading as counselors rarely negotiate rates with insurers for individual clients. Option D incorrectly suggests that clients only pay co-pays without needing to submit claims, which does not apply to out-of-network services.

Question 57: Correct Answer: C) Discuss potential issues and establish clear boundaries regarding external interactions during initial group sessions.

Rationale: Option C is correct because it involves proactively addressing potential issues by establishing clear boundaries at the outset. This approach helps maintain confidentiality and sets expectations for behavior outside the group, which is crucial for maintaining trust and cohesion

within the therapeutic setting. Option A is incorrect because prohibiting all interactions can be overly restrictive and may hinder natural relationship development, which can be beneficial for some therapeutic processes. Option B, while encouraging confidentiality, does not provide a structured framework or boundaries, potentially leading to misunderstandings or breaches in confidentiality. Option D is incorrect because allowing unrestricted interactions can compromise confidentiality and disrupt group dynamics if sensitive information is shared inappropriately.

Question 58: Correct Answer: C) Arranging a home visit by a mental health professional within 48 hours post-discharge

Rationale: Arranging a home visit by a mental health professional within 48 hours post-discharge is crucial because it ensures immediate support and assessment in the patient's living environment, which can significantly reduce the risk of relapse or self-harm. This approach aligns with contemporary research highlighting the importance of early intervention in preventing rehospitalization and promoting recovery. Option A, scheduling a follow-up appointment with the primary care physician within two weeks, is important but not as immediate or intensive as an early home visit. Option B, ensuring access to emergency contact numbers, is essential for crisis situations but does not provide proactive engagement. Option D, providing detailed medication management instructions, while vital for treatment adherence, lacks the immediate and personalized support that an early home visit offers.

Question 59: Correct Answer: B) Presence of psychomotor agitation or retardation nearly every day

Rationale: For a diagnosis of Major Depressive Disorder (MDD), the DSM-5 requires at least five symptoms to be present during the same 2-week period, with one of the symptoms being either depressed mood or loss of interest/pleasure. Psychomotor agitation or retardation nearly every day is one such symptom. Option A is incorrect because manic or hypomanic episodes would suggest a bipolar disorder rather than MDD. Option C is incorrect as persistent delusions or hallucinations are more indicative of psychotic disorders unless they occur exclusively during depressive episodes. Option D, while relevant in assessing overall mental health, is not a specific criterion for diagnosing MDD.

Question 60: Correct Answer: C) Introducing a school-wide positive behavior support system

Rationale: Contemporary research supports that a school-wide positive behavior support system is highly effective in addressing bullying because it promotes a positive school climate and reduces overall incidents of bullying through proactive strategies. Peer mediation programs (A) can be beneficial but are less comprehensive. Zero-tolerance policies (B) often fail to address underlying issues and can lead to negative consequences for students. Individual CBT (D) is helpful for victims but does not address systemic issues within the school environment.

Question 61: Correct Answer: B) Intensive outpatient program (IOP)

Rationale: An Intensive Outpatient Program (IOP) is suitable for Maria as it provides more structure than standard outpatient therapy while allowing her to maintain some daily activities such as work. IOP offers frequent sessions that can help manage her increased anxiety and panic attacks effectively. Outpatient therapy (A), though beneficial, might not provide enough support given her current distress levels. Partial hospitalization program (PHP) (C), though intensive, might be excessive since she does not have suicidal ideation or substance abuse issues. Inpatient hospitalization (D) is unnecessary as she isn't an imminent risk to herself or others.

Question 62: Correct Answer: A) Stress Management Training

Rationale: Stress Management Training is particularly effective in complementing Methadone Maintenance

Therapy (MMT) because it equips individuals with skills to handle stress without resorting to substance use. Twelve-Step Facilitation Therapy can provide peer support but does not specifically target stress management. Family Therapy can improve family dynamics but may not directly address Maria's job-related stress. Exposure Therapy is primarily used for treating phobias or PTSD and is not directly applicable to managing stress related to opioid addiction recovery.

Question 63: Correct Answer: D) Structured Clinical Interview for DSM-5 (SCID)

Rationale: The SCID is a comprehensive tool designed to diagnose mental disorders according to DSM-5 criteria, including substance use disorders. It allows clinicians to assess both the severity of substance use and co-occurring mental health disorders, making it highly suitable for dual diagnosis. Option A (AUDIT) focuses specifically on alcohol use and its severity but does not comprehensively assess other substances or mental health disorders. Option B (DAST) is similar but tailored to drug abuse and lacks a broader diagnostic scope. Option C (SASSI) provides insights into substance dependence but does not extensively cover co-occurring mental health conditions. Thus, SCID stands out as the most appropriate tool due to its comprehensive nature. Each option explained: - A) AUDIT: Effective for assessing alcohol use severity but limited in scope regarding other substances and mental health disorders. - B) DAST: Useful for screening drug abuse severity but lacks comprehensive assessment of co-occurring mental health issues. - C) SASSI: Provides subtle screening for substance dependence but does not fully address co-occurring mental health conditions. - D) SCID: Comprehensive in diagnosing both substance use and co-occurring mental health disorders, aligning with DSM-5 criteria. The SCID's detailed approach ensures an accurate and holistic understanding of a client's condition, making it superior in this context.

Question 64: Correct Answer: D) Simplify the explanation of cognitive-behavioral techniques during the group session.

Rationale: Simplifying the explanation during the group session ensures that all participants benefit from a clearer understanding, which aligns with the principles of psychoeducation in a group setting. While providing additional reading materials (Option A) or scheduling a one-on-one session (Option B) can be helpful, they do not address Emily's immediate needs within the group context. Encouraging other members to share their experiences (Option C) might help but could also lead to further confusion if not guided properly by the counselor. Simplifying explanations ensures inclusivity and immediate comprehension.

Question 65: Correct Answer: B) Helping Jane identify and challenge her negative thought patterns.

Rationale: Cognitive-behavioral therapy (CBT) primarily focuses on identifying and challenging negative thought patterns that contribute to stress. Option A (progressive muscle relaxation) and Option C (mindfulness meditation) are relaxation techniques that can be used within CBT but do not directly address cognitive restructuring. Option D (group therapy for social support) provides emotional support but does not specifically target cognitive processes. Therefore, helping Jane identify and challenge her negative thoughts is the most appropriate CBT intervention.

Question 66: Correct Answer: B) Identify safe places where Maria can go during an attack.

Rationale: The primary focus when developing a safety plan for someone with severe anxiety and panic attacks should be identifying safe places where they can go during an attack. This ensures that Maria has immediate refuge and feels secure during intense episodes. Educating her about the disorder (A), teaching grounding techniques (C), and creating a list of supportive individuals (D) are all important steps but follow after ensuring she has a safe environment to retreat to during an attack.

Question 67: Correct Answer: C) Acknowledge Maria's experience and validate her feelings while maintaining group cohesion.

Rationale: Acknowledging Maria's experience validates her feelings and helps build trust within the group while maintaining cohesion ensures that all participants feel supported. Redirecting the conversation (A) can invalidate Maria's experience. Encouraging immediate sharing (B) may overwhelm participants or shift focus prematurely. Offering solutions (D), though well-intentioned, might minimize her experience by focusing too quickly on problem-solving rather than emotional processing.

Question 68: Correct Answer: A) Recurrent episodes of binge eating followed by inappropriate compensatory behaviors

Rationale: Bulimia Nervosa is most accurately characterized by recurrent episodes of binge eating followed by inappropriate compensatory behaviors such as vomiting, fasting, or excessive exercise (Option A). This differentiates it from Anorexia Nervosa, which involves restriction of energy intake leading to significantly low body weight (Option B), and an intense fear of gaining weight despite being underweight (Option C). Orthorexia involves an unhealthy obsession with eating healthy foods (Option D), which is not a recognized clinical diagnosis but can overlap with other maladaptive behaviors. Option A is correct because it encapsulates the core diagnostic criteria for Bulimia Nervosa according to DSM-5.

Question 69: Correct Answer: A) Facilitate John's involvement in structured group activities to improve social skills.

Rationale: At age 7, John is in Erikson's stage of Industry vs. Inferiority and Piaget's concrete operational stage. Structured group activities help build social skills and a sense of competence among peers, addressing both his developmental needs and anxiety about school. Option B is more suited for adolescents who are developing abstract thinking skills. Option C may help with emotional expression but does not directly address the need for improved social interaction. Option D focuses on formal operational thinking, which typically develops later during adolescence.

Question 70: Correct Answer: C) Psychological stress

Rationale: Psychological stress is a significant contributing factor to erectile dysfunction, particularly in individuals without a notable medical history. High levels of work-related stress and relationship issues can lead to anxiety and reduced sexual performance. Cardiovascular disease (Option A) and diabetes mellitus (Option D) are also common causes of ED but are less likely given the absence of significant medical history. Low testosterone levels (Option B) can contribute to ED; however, psychological factors are more pertinent given the client's context of stress and relationship difficulties. Understanding these nuances helps distinguish between physiological and psychological etiologies in sexual functioning concerns.

Question 71: Correct Answer: B) Encourage John to describe his physical sensations at that moment.

Rationale: Encouraging John to describe his physical sensations focuses his attention on his immediate bodily experiences, enhancing his awareness of present emotions and reactions. This technique aligns with mindfulness practices that emphasize present-moment awareness. - A) Asking about past feelings directs attention away from current experiences. - C) Reflecting on past instances detracts from focusing on present emotions. - D) Advising deep breaths aims at calming rather than exploring current emotional states.

Question 72: Correct Answer: A) It ensures that clients understand their treatment plan and agree to it voluntarily.

Rationale: Informed consent is crucial as it ensures that clients are fully aware of their treatment plan and have agreed to it voluntarily. This fosters trust and transparency in the therapeutic relationship. Option B is incorrect because informed consent does not guarantee adherence; it only ensures understanding and voluntary participation. Option C is misleading; while informed consent can reduce legal risks, its primary purpose is client understanding and autonomy. Option D overstates the requirement; informed consent covers key aspects but not every possible outcome. Thus, option A correctly captures the essence of informed consent's benefit in counseling.

Question 73: Correct Answer: A) Cognitive Behavioral Therapy (CBT)

Rationale: Cognitive Behavioral Therapy (CBT) is considered the most effective approach for treating generalized anxiety disorder (GAD), which includes symptoms like persistent worry, sleep difficulties, and muscle tension. CBT focuses on identifying and challenging irrational thoughts and beliefs that contribute to anxiety. While MBSR can help with stress reduction, it does not specifically target the cognitive distortions central to GAD. Psychodynamic therapy explores unconscious conflicts but lacks the structured approach necessary for immediate symptom relief. Exposure therapy is more suited for phobias or PTSD rather than generalized worry.

Question 74: Correct Answer: B) An intense concentration on a single activity to the exclusion of other tasks.

Rationale: Hyperfocus is characterized by an individual's intense concentration on a single activity, often to the exclusion of other tasks. This state can be seen in individuals with ADHD when they become engrossed in activities that are highly stimulating or interesting to them. Option A describes general inattentiveness, which is more indicative of hypofocus. Option C describes distractibility and frequent task-switching, common in ADHD but not specific to hyperfocus. Option D refers to hypoactivity and lack of goal-directed behavior, which contrasts with the concept of hyperfocus where there is excessive focus on one particular task. Thus, B is the most accurate description of hyperfocus.

Question 75: Correct Answer: A) Using "I" statements to express feelings and needs

Rationale: Using "I" statements helps John communicate his feelings and needs clearly and respectfully, which is a core component of assertiveness training. This approach reduces defensiveness in others and promotes constructive dialogue. Adopting an authoritative tone (Option B) can come across as aggressive rather than assertive. Avoiding eye contact (Option C) can be perceived as passive or disinterested. Rehearsing responses using aggressive language (Option D) is counterproductive as it promotes aggression rather than assertiveness.

Question 76: Correct Answer: B) Using a cloud-based service with strong encryption and access controls.

Rationale: The correct answer is B) Using a cloud-based service with strong encryption and access controls. This approach ensures that client records are protected by robust security measures, complying with ethical standards for confidentiality in electronic communication. Option A is incorrect because storing unencrypted records on a personal laptop poses significant security risks. Option C, while avoiding electronic breaches, is impractical in modern practice settings where electronic records are standard. Option D compromises security by using unsecured messaging apps for sensitive information sharing.

Question 77: Correct Answer: C) Attachment-based therapy designed to strengthen the parent-child bond.

Rationale: Attachment-based therapy is specifically tailored to address attachment difficulties by focusing on strengthening the emotional bond between John and his adoptive parents. This approach directly targets the root of John's issues. Option A (CBT) may help with negative thought patterns but does not address attachment directly. Option B (Play Therapy) can aid in emotional expression but may not specifically target attachment issues. Option D (Group Therapy) might offer support but does not provide the individualized focus needed for attachment work.

Question 78: Correct Answer: B) Eye Movement Desensitization and Reprocessing (EMDR)

Rationale: EMDR is highly effective for treating PTSD as it helps reprocess traumatic memories. CBT and Prolonged Exposure Therapy are also effective but EMDR specifically targets the distressing memories with bilateral stimulation. Supportive Counseling is beneficial for general emotional support but lacks the targeted approach needed for PTSD.

Question 79: Correct Answer: B) Start with open-ended questions to allow Maria to express her concerns.

Rationale: The correct approach in an initial interview is to start with open-ended questions (Option B). This allows the client to share their thoughts and feelings freely, helping establish rapport and gather comprehensive information about their presenting issues. Option A (exploring family history) is important but should follow after establishing rapport. Option C (conducting a mental status examination) is crucial but typically comes later in the interview. Option D (providing psychoeducation) is beneficial but not appropriate as the first step before understanding the client's specific concerns.

Question 80: Correct Answer: A) Panic Disorder

Rationale: Panic Disorder is characterized by recurrent unexpected panic attacks involving intense fear and physical symptoms such as palpitations, sweating, trembling, shortness of breath, chest pain, nausea, dizziness, and fear of losing control or dying. John's description fits this profile perfectly. Social Anxiety Disorder involves intense fear or anxiety about social situations where one might be scrutinized by others but does not typically include unexpected panic attacks as described by John. Generalized Anxiety Disorder involves excessive anxiety and worry about various events or activities that are persistent but not necessarily accompanied by sudden panic attacks. Specific Phobia involves intense fear triggered by a specific object or situation but does not match John's experience of unexpected panic attacks.

Question 81: Correct Answer: A) Scaffolding

Rationale: Scaffolding involves providing structured support to help a child achieve a task they cannot complete independently. This aligns with Vygotsky's concept of the Zone of Proximal Development (B), which refers to the difference between what a child can do alone and what they can do with help; however, scaffolding specifically describes the method used within this zone. Social Interaction (C) is crucial for cognitive development but is broader than targeted instructional support. Private Speech (D), or self-talk, aids self-regulation but does not directly address how others can assist Tommy in managing complex tasks.

Question 82: Correct Answer: A) Dyslexia

Rationale: Dyslexia specifically affects reading and related language-based processing skills. Although Sarah has strong verbal skills, her difficulty with reading comprehension suggests dyslexia. ADHD can affect concentration but does not specifically target reading comprehension in children with strong verbal skills. SLI primarily impacts language acquisition rather than reading comprehension in isolation. ASD often involves broader social communication challenges beyond specific difficulties with reading comprehension.

Question 83: Correct Answer: C) Collaborate with the client to explore alternative treatments that align with their religious beliefs.

Rationale: The correct approach in this scenario is to collaborate with the client to find alternative treatments that respect their religious values while addressing their medical needs. This strategy demonstrates cultural competence and respects the client's autonomy, fostering a therapeutic alliance. Option A is incorrect because it may neglect urgent medical needs. Option B is inappropriate as it might be perceived as coercive and disrespectful of the client's beliefs. Option D could be seen as avoiding responsibility rather than finding an integrative solution within the therapeutic relationship. Thus, option C balances respect for religious values with clinical care.

Question 84: Correct Answer: C) Discuss the limits of confidentiality with Maria and obtain her consent before reporting.

Rationale: The correct approach is to discuss the limits of confidentiality with Maria and obtain her consent before reporting (Option C). This respects both legal mandates and ethical considerations by ensuring that Maria understands the necessity of reporting while maintaining her autonomy. Option A fails to address legal obligations for reporting domestic violence. Option B could damage trust without first attempting to gain consent, which is crucial in maintaining an ethical therapeutic relationship. Option D avoids addressing the immediate ethical and legal responsibilities directly.

Question 85: Correct Answer: B) Facilitate a family meeting to discuss and negotiate parenting roles.

Rationale: Facilitating a family meeting allows all members to express their perspectives and collaboratively establish clear and consistent parenting roles. This approach aligns with family systems theory, which emphasizes the importance of open communication and shared responsibilities. Option A focuses solely on Maria's actions without addressing the husband's behavior. Option C may help Maria individually but does not resolve the interaction issue within the family. Option D isolates Maria from the problem-solving process with her husband, failing to promote joint responsibility.

Question 86: Correct Answer: C) Cognitive restructuring

Rationale: Cognitive restructuring is a core CBT technique that helps individuals identify and challenge distorted or unhelpful thoughts, thereby reframing their stressful thoughts into more balanced ones. Systematic desensitization (A) is used primarily for phobias by gradually exposing individuals to anxiety-provoking stimuli. Thought stopping (B) aims to interrupt negative thought patterns but does not involve restructuring them. Biofeedback (D) focuses on physiological monitoring and control rather than cognitive processes.

Question 87: Correct Answer: C) Sarah should assess the seriousness of the threat and consider legal obligations before deciding.

Rationale: Ethical guidelines require counselors to balance confidentiality with duty to protect. Assessing the seriousness of the threat and considering legal obligations ensures that Sarah acts responsibly without breaching confidentiality unnecessarily. A) is incorrect because immediate disclosure without assessment may violate confidentiality. B) is incorrect as seeking consent may not be feasible in cases of imminent harm. D) is incorrect as documentation alone does not address potential danger.

Question 88: Correct Answer: B) Facilitate a group discussion focusing on expectations and norms to re-establish cohesion.

Rationale: Facilitating a group discussion helps address any concerns or anxieties about new members directly and allows for re-establishing group norms and expectations. This approach promotes open communication and supports smoother transitions by involving all members in the process. Option A may be useful but does not address group dynamics collectively. Option C risks prolonged disruption without guidance. Option D might expedite integration but could feel forced or artificial.

Question 89: Correct Answer: B) Gently point out the pattern of avoidance and invite John to explore his feelings about the job loss.

Rationale: Constructive confrontation involves addressing problematic behaviors or patterns in a way that is supportive and non-threatening. Option B is correct because it acknowledges John's avoidance without being confrontational, encouraging him to open up in a safe environment. Option A is too direct and may cause defensiveness. Option C avoids addressing the issue

entirely, which is not constructive. Option D suggests an alternative method but does not involve direct confrontation during the session.

Question 90: Correct Answer: B) Asking the client to consider how this job loss might open up new opportunities.

Rationale: Reframing involves changing the way an individual perceives a situation to alter its emotional impact. By asking the client to consider how the job loss might open up new opportunities (Option B), the counselor helps shift their perspective from negative to potentially positive. Option A, while helpful in boosting self-esteem, does not directly reframe the current situation. Option C focuses on stress reduction rather than altering perception. Option D is about gathering external validation, which does not change the client's internal view of their job loss. Thus, Option B is most aligned with reframing principles in cognitive-behavioral therapy.

Question 91: Correct Answer: C) Consult with her agency's legal counsel before responding to the subpoena.

Rationale: The correct answer is C because consulting legal counsel ensures compliance with legal requirements while protecting client rights. Option A may violate confidentiality without proper consideration. Option B could lead to legal repercussions for non-compliance. Option D involves Jake but does not address legal complexities adequately.

Question 92: Correct Answer: C) "Your treatment details will remain confidential unless you provide written consent or there is a legal requirement to disclose."

Rationale: Option C is correct because it accurately reflects the principle of client confidentiality in mental health counseling, which states that information should not be disclosed without the client's consent unless required by law. Option A is incorrect because sharing information with family members requires client consent. Option B is misleading as it overlooks the necessity of client consent even when sharing with other healthcare providers. Option D is incorrect because clients must be informed about disclosures to insurance companies. The key difference lies in understanding that confidentiality breaches require either client consent or legal mandates, which option C correctly states.

Question 93: Correct Answer: A) Multiple bruises at different stages of healing

Rationale: Multiple bruises at different stages of healing are highly indicative of ongoing physical abuse, as they suggest repeated trauma over time. This pattern is often seen in individuals who are subjected to regular physical violence. A single bruise on the forearm (Option B) could be accidental and does not necessarily indicate abuse. Frequent headaches (Option C) and unexplained weight loss (Option D) can be associated with stress or other medical conditions and are not specific enough to suggest physical abuse. Therefore, Option A is the most valid indicator in the context provided.

Question 94: Correct Answer: B) Help John develop coping strategies for dealing with microaggressions.

Rationale: Helping John develop coping strategies for dealing with microaggressions is essential as it empowers him to manage his stress while acknowledging the reality of his experiences. Advising confrontation (A) may not be safe or effective given workplace dynamics. Encouraging job change (C) is impractical without addressing underlying issues. Suggesting he ignore microaggressions (D) invalidates his experiences and can lead to further emotional harm. Therefore, option B provides a balanced approach that respects John's cultural context and supports his mental health.

Question 95: Correct Answer: B) Explore underlying cognitive distortions contributing to her anxiety.

Rationale: Addressing cognitive distortions is central to managing GAD as it targets the root cause of excessive worry. By identifying and challenging irrational thoughts, Maria can develop healthier thinking patterns that reduce anxiety. While relaxation techniques (A), psychoeducation (C), and goal-setting (D) are beneficial components of treatment, they are more effective when implemented after understanding the cognitive underpinnings of her anxiety. This approach aligns with contemporary cognitive-behavioral therapy principles.

Question 96: Correct Answer: D) Integrating information from biological, psychological, and social domains.

Rationale: The biopsychosocial model emphasizes the need to integrate information from biological, psychological, and social domains to fully understand a client's mental health. Option A (medical history and current medications) is important but focuses only on the biological aspect. Option B (cognitive and emotional functioning) addresses the psychological domain but ignores biological and social factors. Option C (social support systems and environmental stressors) highlights the social domain but neglects biological and psychological aspects. Only option D comprehensively captures all three essential components, making it the most accurate choice for conducting a thorough biopsychosocial interview.

Question 97: Correct Answer: A) Encourage Maria to join a caregiver support group.

Rationale: Joining a caregiver support group can provide Maria with emotional support from others who understand her situation, reducing feelings of isolation and guilt. While taking a vacation (Option B) may offer temporary relief, it does not address ongoing stress. Individual therapy (Option C) is beneficial but may not provide the peer support that can be crucial in caregiving contexts. Hiring a professional caregiver (Option D) can help reduce physical burden but may not address emotional needs effectively.

Question 98: Correct Answer: D) "It was agreed that John should have a psychiatric evaluation for medication while maintaining regular therapy sessions."

Rationale: Option D is correct because it indicates an agreement between you and John about the referral and continuation of therapy, which is essential in collaborative documentation. - Option A is incorrect because it does not specify an agreement or collaborative aspect. - Option B is too vague about who made the referral. - Option C lacks emphasis on mutual agreement or collaboration in decision-making.

Question 99: Correct Answer: C) Stress Inoculation Training (SIT)

Rationale: Stress Inoculation Training (SIT) is the most suitable primary clinical focus for John's chronic stress. SIT involves teaching coping skills to manage stressors effectively and has been shown to reduce symptoms like headaches and irritability. Time Management Training (A), while useful, does not directly address stress coping mechanisms comprehensively. Biofeedback Therapy (B) can help with physical symptoms but may not provide holistic stress management strategies. Interpersonal Therapy (IPT) (D), although beneficial for relational issues contributing to stress, does not specifically target stress management techniques as effectively as SIT.

Question 100: Correct Answer: B) Asking the client to describe their immediate physical sensations.

Rationale: Option B is correct because it directly engages the client's present-moment awareness, which is crucial for here-and-now interactions. This technique aligns with principles from Gestalt therapy and mindfulness, which emphasize present-moment experience. Option A, while valuable, focuses on past experiences rather than the present moment. Option C shifts attention to future anxieties rather than current experiences, detracting from here-and-now awareness. Option D involves recognizing patterns over time, which can be insightful but does not directly enhance immediate awareness. Thus, B is most aligned with facilitating here-and-now interactions effectively.

Question 101: Correct Answer: B) Encouraging clients to provide specific examples or incidents.

Rationale: Encouraging clients to provide specific examples or incidents (Option B) enhances the accuracy of self-reports by grounding their responses in concrete events, reducing ambiguity and recall bias. While open-ended questions (Option A) can elicit detailed information, they may also lead to vague or overly broad responses. Asking clients to rate their experiences on a standardized scale (Option C) provides quantitative data but may not capture nuanced details. Repeating questions in different ways (Option D) can help clarify inconsistencies but might also cause confusion or frustration. Therefore, Option B is the most effective technique for obtaining accurate self-reports.

Question 102: Correct Answer: B) Noticing John's casual remarks about his workload

Rationale: Informal observations involve gathering information from spontaneous interactions and casual remarks made by the client. In this case, noticing John's casual comments about his workload is an example of informal observation. Administering a stress inventory scale (A) is a formal method involving standardized measurement tools. Conducting a semi-structured interview (C), while less rigid than structured interviews, still follows a specific guide and is considered more formal than casual observation. Reviewing medical records (D) involves collecting documented information from other professionals, which is also a formal method of gathering data.

Question 103: Correct Answer: C) Family therapy involving all members

Rationale: Family therapy is most appropriate because it addresses systemic issues within the family unit, such as communication patterns and relational dynamics that contribute to the son's behavior. Individual therapy (Option A) would not address the broader family context. Couple therapy (Option B) focuses only on the parents' relationship and may miss issues involving the child. Group therapy (Option D) could provide peer support but would not directly address family-specific dynamics. - Option A (Individual therapy for the teenage son): While this might help address personal issues, it ignores systemic family dynamics. - Option B (Couple therapy for the parents): This focuses solely on parental relationships, missing out on child-parent interactions. - Option D (Group therapy for teenagers with similar issues): This offers peer support but lacks focus on specific family dynamics. Family therapy is validated by theories like Bowenian Family Systems Theory, which emphasizes understanding individual behavior within the context of family relationships.

Question 104: Correct Answer: B) Systemic racism results in chronic stress and trauma, contributing to higher rates of mental health disorders in marginalized communities.

Rationale: Option B is correct because contemporary research consistently shows that systemic racism contributes to chronic stress and trauma, which are significant risk factors for developing mental health disorders such as depression, anxiety, and PTSD. Option A is incorrect because systemic racism typically reduces access to quality mental health services rather than increasing it. Option C is misleading; while systemic racism does affect physical health, its impact on mental health is profound and well-documented. Option D oversimplifies the issue by suggesting that socioeconomic status is the primary influence, neglecting the direct psychological impacts of systemic racism.

Question 105: Correct Answer: B) Discuss the cognitive-behavioral model of GAD and how it affects thoughts and behaviors.

Rationale: Discussing the cognitive-behavioral model of GAD helps Sarah understand how her thoughts influence her feelings and behaviors, which is crucial for effective psychoeducation. This approach aligns with contemporary research that highlights cognitive-behavioral therapy (CBT) as an effective treatment for GAD. Option A is incorrect because emphasizing medication alone does not provide comprehensive psychoeducation. Option C is insufficient as it neglects the importance of understanding the diagnosis. Option D lacks personalization, which is essential for effective psychoeducation.

Question 106: Correct Answer: A) Use a secure video conferencing platform that complies with HIPAA regulations.
Rationale: The most critical step in ensuring confidentiality and security in telemental health is using a secure video conferencing platform that complies with HIPAA regulations. This ensures that client information is protected according to federal standards. While obtaining written consent (Option C) and ensuring stable internet (Option B) are important, they do not directly address the security of client data. Conducting sessions during standard business hours (Option D) relates more to professionalism than security.

Question 107: Correct Answer: B) Encourage open communication between both parents regarding the children's needs.
Rationale: Open communication between co-parents is crucial for ensuring that children's needs are met consistently and collaboratively. Creating a rigid schedule without consulting the other parent (Option A) can lead to conflict and instability for the children. Limiting interactions (Option C) might reduce conflict temporarily but doesn't support cooperative co-parenting. Allowing children to decide when they want to see each parent (Option D) places undue responsibility on them and can lead to inconsistency in their routines.

Question 108: Correct Answer: C) Conduct a risk assessment and involve Alex in deciding how to inform his parents.
Rationale: The correct course of action is conducting a risk assessment and involving Alex in deciding how to inform his parents (Option C). This approach balances legal requirements for protecting minors with ethical considerations for respecting client autonomy. Option A neglects legal obligations for safeguarding minors. Option B may breach trust without considering Alex's input or performing a proper risk assessment first. Option D bypasses necessary parental involvement without first evaluating the immediate risk or exploring less drastic measures.

Question 109: Correct Answer: B) Using structured activities that require group collaboration
Rationale: Structured activities that require group collaboration are highly effective in promoting interactions among group members because they create opportunities for shared experiences and mutual support. This technique is grounded in contemporary research, which shows that collaborative tasks can enhance cohesion and engagement within the group. Option A, while useful, may not equally involve all members. Option C can lead to uneven participation if some members dominate the discussion. Option D is important for creating a safe environment but does not directly facilitate interaction. Therefore, option B stands out as the most effective method for encouraging active participation and interaction among all group members.

Question 110: Correct Answer: B) Implement stimulus control therapy.
Rationale: Stimulus control therapy focuses on breaking the association between the bed and activities that are incompatible with sleep, such as worrying or lying awake. It aims to strengthen the bed-sleep connection by limiting time spent awake in bed. Prescribing a low-dose antidepressant (Option A) might help if depression were contributing to her insomnia but does not address her specific issue of anxiety-related wakefulness. White noise machines (Option C) can aid in creating a conducive sleep environment but do not target her anxiety directly. Progressive muscle relaxation techniques (Option D) can reduce anxiety but are less targeted than stimulus control therapy in modifying sleep-related behaviors.

Question 111: Correct Answer: B) Engaging key stakeholders in collaborative decision-making processes.
Rationale: Engaging key stakeholders in collaborative decision-making processes (Option B) is crucial for sustainable systemic change. This approach ensures that the needs and perspectives of all involved parties are considered, leading to more comprehensive and accepted interventions. In contrast, short-term individual counseling sessions (Option A) may address immediate needs but do not contribute to long-term systemic change. Periodic needs assessments without follow-up (Option C) fail to create actionable plans based on the findings. Standardized training programs for all staff members (Option D) are beneficial but may not address specific community needs or involve stakeholders in meaningful ways. Thus, Option B is the most effective strategy for facilitating sustainable systemic change.

Question 112: Correct Answer: C) Discuss the situation with Sarah and explain the limits of confidentiality before informing her parents.
Rationale: The correct answer is C because ethical guidelines require counselors to inform clients about the limits of confidentiality, especially when there is a risk of harm. This approach respects Sarah's autonomy while ensuring her safety. Option A is incorrect because it disregards potential harm. Option B is incorrect because it bypasses discussing confidentiality limits with Sarah. Option D is incorrect because it delays necessary intervention.

Question 113: Correct Answer: C) Medically Monitored Detoxification
Rationale: Medically Monitored Detoxification is most appropriate for Mark due to his significant withdrawal symptoms, which require medical supervision even though there are no immediate complications necessitating hospitalization. Outpatient Counseling (A) and Intensive Outpatient Program (B) do not provide the necessary medical oversight during detoxification. A Residential Treatment Center (D), while offering structured support, is more suitable for post-detox rehabilitation rather than initial detoxification.

Question 114: Correct Answer: A) Task I: Accepting the reality of the loss
Rationale: William Worden's model outlines four tasks that individuals must work through to cope with grief effectively. Task I involves accepting the reality of the loss, which is crucial as denial can hinder progress in mourning. Task II focuses on processing the pain associated with grief, while Task III involves adjusting to life without the deceased. Task IV is about finding a way to maintain a connection with the deceased while moving forward. Although all tasks are essential in managing grief, Task I specifically addresses accepting that the loss has occurred, making it foundational for subsequent tasks. - Option A (Correct): This is correct as per William Worden's Four Tasks of Mourning; accepting the reality of loss is indeed Task I. - Option B (Incorrect): Processing pain is important but is identified as Task II, not Task I. - Option C (Incorrect): Adjusting to a world without the deceased is critical but falls under Task III. - Option D (Incorrect): Finding an enduring connection while moving forward pertains to Task IV. Each option reflects critical aspects of Worden's model but only Option A correctly identifies Task I.

Question 115: Correct Answer: B) Developing an individualized education program (IEP) tailored to her needs.
Rationale: The most appropriate initial intervention for Maria is developing an individualized education program (IEP) tailored to her needs. An IEP is specifically designed to address the educational requirements of students with disabilities and ensure they receive the support necessary for academic success. While behavior modification plans (A), extracurricular activities (C), and family therapy (D) can be beneficial, they do not directly address the primary educational challenges posed by an intellectual disability as

effectively as an IEP does.

Question 116: Correct Answer: C) Norming

Rationale: The norming phase is marked by increased cohesion among group members who begin to support each other and adhere to established norms. This contrasts with forming (A), which involves initial orientation; storming (B), which includes conflict and power struggles; and adjourning (D), which pertains to disbandment after achieving goals. Therefore, norming best describes a scenario where cohesion and mutual support are evident. Each option has been carefully crafted to reflect different phases in the group process but only one option aligns perfectly with the given scenario based on recognized theories of group dynamics.

Question 117: Correct Answer: B) Maintaining open and respectful communication about parenting decisions.

Rationale: Maintaining open and respectful communication about parenting decisions is widely regarded as the most effective strategy for promoting a positive co-parenting relationship and minimizing conflict. This approach fosters mutual understanding and cooperation, which are essential for effective co-parenting. In contrast: - A) Parallel parenting can reduce direct conflict but often leads to inconsistent parenting approaches, which can confuse children. - C) Avoiding discussions about contentious topics may temporarily prevent arguments but does not address underlying issues, leading to unresolved tensions. - D) Relying on third-party mediation for all disagreements can be helpful in severe cases but is not sustainable for everyday decision-making. Thus, option B is correct because it encourages ongoing collaboration and problem-solving between parents.

Question 118: Correct Answer: C) Exposure and Response Prevention (ERP)

Rationale: ERP is highly effective for managing intrusive thoughts in OCD by exposing patients to their fears without engaging in neutralizing rituals, thereby reducing anxiety over time. Thought Stopping (option A) aims to interrupt intrusive thoughts but lacks strong evidence for effectiveness in OCD treatment. Cognitive Restructuring (option B), while useful for challenging irrational beliefs, does not specifically target the behavioral component of OCD as ERP does. Acceptance and Commitment Therapy (ACT; option D) helps patients accept their thoughts without acting on them but is less direct than ERP in addressing compulsive behaviors associated with OCD.

Question 119: Correct Answer: B) Suggest Mark engage in individual therapy focused on anger management techniques.

Rationale: Individual therapy focused on anger management techniques is the most appropriate intervention for Mark as it directly addresses his intense emotions of anger and resentment. By learning specific strategies to manage these feelings, he can better control his reactions and improve his interactions with his ex-spouse. While writing letters (A), attending family therapy sessions (C), and participating in a co-parenting workshop (D) are all valuable interventions, they do not specifically target anger management as effectively as individual therapy does.

Question 120: Correct Answer: A) Cognitive Behavioral Therapy (CBT)

Rationale: Cognitive Behavioral Therapy (CBT) is widely recognized for its effectiveness in addressing ruminating and intrusive thoughts by helping clients identify and reframe negative thinking patterns. CBT focuses on the interplay between thoughts, emotions, and behaviors, making it particularly suitable for treating conditions like anxiety disorders and depression where such thoughts are prevalent. Psychodynamic Therapy (Option B), while useful for exploring unconscious processes and past experiences, does not specifically target the reframing of negative thought patterns as directly as CBT. Humanistic Therapy (Option C) emphasizes personal growth and self-actualization but lacks the structured approach to cognitive restructuring found in

CBT. Interpersonal Therapy (Option D) focuses on improving interpersonal relationships and social functioning rather than directly addressing cognitive distortions. By comparing these approaches, it becomes clear why CBT is the most effective for this specific issue, despite the close relevance of other therapies.

Question 121: Correct Answer: B) The therapeutic alliance between counselor and client

Rationale: The therapeutic alliance between counselor and client is widely recognized as the most significant predictor of positive outcomes in counseling. Research consistently shows that a strong, collaborative relationship enhances treatment effectiveness regardless of the specific theoretical orientation or intervention used. While the counselor's theoretical orientation (Option A), client's motivation for change (Option C), and use of evidence-based interventions (Option D) are all important factors, they do not consistently predict outcomes as strongly as the therapeutic alliance does. This makes Option B the correct answer, emphasizing the importance of building a strong, trusting relationship with clients. - Option A (The counselor's theoretical orientation): While important, research indicates that no single theoretical orientation consistently predicts better outcomes across all clients. - Option C (The client's motivation for change): Although crucial, it is often influenced by the quality of the therapeutic alliance itself. - Option D (The use of evidence-based interventions): Effective but their success is heavily mediated by the strength of the therapeutic alliance.

Question 122: Correct Answer: A) "I notice that you're sitting quietly with your arms crossed. What's going through your mind right now?"

Rationale: Option A is the correct answer because it acknowledges John's non-verbal cues and invites him to share his thoughts without pressure. This approach demonstrates empathy by validating his current state and showing genuine interest in understanding his feelings. Option B might seem empathetic but could be perceived as avoidance rather than engagement. Option C directly asks John to talk about his issues without first acknowledging his non-verbal communication, which might feel intrusive. Option D assumes John is upset without exploring his actual feelings first, potentially leading to misinterpretation of his emotional state.

Question 123: Correct Answer: A) Attachment-Based Therapy focusing on building secure attachments.

Rationale: Attachment-Based Therapy is specifically designed to address issues stemming from early attachment disruptions by helping clients develop secure relationships and improve relational dynamics. This approach directly targets Maria's difficulties with forming secure attachments due to childhood trauma. Gestalt Therapy (B), while useful for increasing present-moment awareness, does not specifically focus on attachment issues. Narrative Therapy (C) can help reframe life stories but may not directly address attachment-related anxieties. Dialectical Behavior Therapy (D), although effective for emotional regulation, does not primarily focus on attachment issues that are central to Maria's concerns.

Question 124: Correct Answer: B) Validate Maria's feelings and explore how her cultural background influences her experience.

Rationale: Validating Maria's feelings and exploring how her cultural background influences her experience demonstrates a deep understanding of multicultural issues and sensitivity. This approach acknowledges the impact of cultural factors on mental health and fosters an inclusive therapeutic environment. Option A is helpful but does not directly address cultural sensitivity. Option C dismisses the importance of cultural differences, which is counterproductive. Option D might limit Maria's integration into the new community rather than helping her navigate it inclusively.

Question 125: Correct Answer: A) Cognitive-Behavioral

Therapy (CBT)

Rationale: Cognitive-Behavioral Therapy (CBT) is highly effective for managing stress as it helps individuals identify and change negative thought patterns that contribute to stress. While PMR, MBSR, and biofeedback are also effective, CBT specifically addresses the cognitive distortions that can exacerbate stress. PMR focuses on physical relaxation, MBSR emphasizes present-moment awareness, and biofeedback provides real-time physiological feedback. However, CBT's comprehensive approach to altering thought processes makes it particularly suitable for John's symptoms of concentration difficulties and headaches.

Question 126: Correct Answer: C) Thought Process

Rationale: Thought process refers to how thoughts are connected and organized. Maria's rapid speech and shifting topics without logical connections suggest a flight of ideas, which is characteristic of mania or hypomania. While mood (A), thought content (B), and orientation (D) are relevant aspects of the MSE, they do not specifically describe the disorganized thinking patterns observed in Maria's case.

Question 127: Correct Answer: C) Preserved independence in daily activities

Rationale: Mild cognitive impairment (MCI) is characterized by noticeable cognitive decline that does not significantly interfere with daily life and independence, whereas early-stage Alzheimer's disease typically involves more pronounced impairments that affect daily functioning. Option A describes memory loss, which can be present in both MCI and early Alzheimer's, making it less specific. Option B refers to significant language difficulties, which are more characteristic of Alzheimer's. Option D describes personality changes, which are also more commonly associated with Alzheimer's disease progression. Therefore, preserved independence in daily activities is the key distinguishing feature of MCI.

Question 128: Correct Answer: A) Personal Enactment

Rationale: According to D'Augelli's model of sexual orientation development, the "Personal Enactment" stage involves the individual beginning to express their true gender identity through behavior and self-presentation. Jamie's desire to be recognized as male and the distress associated with it indicate that they are actively working towards enacting their gender identity. - B) Identity Confusion: This stage is more about initial uncertainty and questioning of one's gender identity rather than active expression. - C) Identity Comparison: This involves comparing oneself to others but not necessarily enacting one's gender identity. - D) Identity Synthesis: This stage is where an individual fully integrates their gender identity into their overall sense of self, which Jamie has not yet achieved.

Question 129: Correct Answer: C) Trauma-Focused Cognitive Behavioral Therapy (TF-CBT)

Rationale: TF-CBT is specifically designed to address trauma-related symptoms in children like Jason's nightmares, avoidance behaviors, and anxiety around certain individuals. It integrates cognitive-behavioral principles with trauma-sensitive interventions to help children process their traumatic experiences safely. While CBT (Option A) can be effective for general anxiety and behavioral issues, TF-CBT is more specialized for trauma. Play Therapy (Option B) can be helpful but may not directly address trauma processing as effectively as TF-CBT. Family Therapy (Option D) can support the family system but might not provide the focused trauma intervention Jason needs immediately.

Question 130: Correct Answer: A) Encourage Sarah to communicate her need for space to her family and help her develop strategies for doing so.

Rationale: Encouraging Sarah to communicate her needs directly addresses the issue of feeling overwhelmed and respects her autonomy. It also helps reduce guilt by fostering open communication. Suggesting more family time (B) ignores Sarah's expressed need for space. Participating in a support group (C) may be beneficial but does not address

the immediate issue of feeling overwhelmed by family presence. Taking up a new hobby (D) might provide distraction but does not resolve the core issue of needing personal space.

Question 131: Correct Answer: B) Validate Maria's feelings and explore her experiences of cultural isolation.

Rationale: Validating Maria's feelings and exploring her experiences of cultural isolation is crucial as it acknowledges her lived experiences and fosters a therapeutic alliance. This approach aligns with culturally competent counseling practices, emphasizing empathy and understanding. Encouraging Maria to educate her colleagues (Option A) places undue burden on her without addressing her immediate emotional needs. Suggesting she seek a different job (Option C) might be premature without first understanding the depth of the issue. Advising her to ignore the behavior (Option D) dismisses her feelings and can exacerbate feelings of isolation.

Question 132: Correct Answer: C) Incorporate motivational interviewing techniques into her current treatment plan.

Rationale: The correct answer is C because incorporating motivational interviewing techniques can specifically target Maria's lack of motivation and social withdrawal while maintaining her current effective treatments. This approach aligns with contemporary research that supports integrating different therapeutic methods to address specific symptoms within a broader treatment plan. Option A may not be necessary if SSRIs are already at an effective dose. Option B ignores the benefits Maria might be receiving from IPT. Option D is premature without thorough evaluation of SSRIs' effectiveness and potential side effects.

Question 133: Correct Answer: B) The measures should have strong reliability and validity for GAD.

Rationale: When selecting pre-test and post-test measures, it is crucial that they possess strong reliability (consistency over time) and validity (accuracy in measuring what they intend to measure) specifically for generalized anxiety disorder. Option A, while important, does not guarantee that the measures are appropriate for GAD. Option C focuses on convenience rather than accuracy. Option D emphasizes qualitative data, which can be valuable but does not replace the need for reliable and valid quantitative measures essential for assessing treatment outcomes objectively.

Question 134: Correct Answer: A) Contacting the insurance company to request an exception for coverage.

Rationale: Contacting the insurance company directly to request an exception for coverage best exemplifies active advocacy on behalf of the client. This action demonstrates a direct intervention aimed at addressing and potentially resolving the barrier to accessing necessary services. Option B, referring the client to another provider, while helpful, does not address the systemic issue at hand and may not guarantee that the new provider will accept their insurance. Option C involves educating the client on self-advocacy, which is important but less direct than contacting the insurer directly. Option D, providing pro bono services, is generous but not sustainable or a long-term solution to addressing systemic barriers in healthcare access. Thus, option A is most aligned with proactive advocacy efforts as outlined in contemporary research and ethical guidelines in mental health counseling.

Question 135: Correct Answer: A) Empathy

Rationale: Empathy is the core counseling attribute where a counselor understands and shares the feelings of the client while maintaining an objective stance. Unlike sympathy (Option B), which involves feeling pity or sorrow for someone else's misfortune, empathy requires a deeper connection without losing objectivity. Reflective listening (Option C) is a technique used within empathetic interactions but does not encompass the full attribute of empathy. Unconditional positive regard (Option D) refers to accepting and supporting clients regardless of what they say or do, which is crucial but distinct from empathy. Therefore, empathy (Option A) is the correct answer as it encapsulates understanding and sharing feelings objectively.

Question 136: Correct Answer: B) Discuss with John the limits of confidentiality and assess his safety.

Rationale: When a client discloses self-harm, it is crucial to discuss the limits of confidentiality and assess their safety. This ensures that the client understands their rights while allowing the counselor to take necessary actions to protect them. Option A neglects immediate safety concerns. Option C breaches confidentiality without assessing immediate danger or obtaining consent. Option D delays addressing an urgent issue.

Question 137: Correct Answer: B) Validate Maria's feelings and ask her to share more about her experience.

Rationale: Validating Maria's feelings and asking her to share more about her experience demonstrates empathy and active listening, which are crucial for building trust in the therapeutic relationship. This approach acknowledges her past experiences without dismissing them. Option A is incorrect because simply reassuring without understanding does not build trust. Option C is incorrect as it may feel invalidating and dismissive. Option D is incorrect because it disregards the importance of addressing past negative experiences before moving forward.

Question 138: Correct Answer: A) John's communication style with his colleagues

Rationale: Prioritizing John's communication style with his colleagues (A) is essential in evaluating interactional dynamics because it directly influences how he interacts and resolves conflicts. Effective communication is foundational for healthy workplace relationships and can reveal potential areas for improvement. While understanding the hierarchical structure (B), specific incidents (C), and John's perception of his colleagues' intentions (D) are important, they do not offer as direct an insight into the dynamic nature of interactions as examining his communication style does. In both questions, incorrect options are designed to be closely related to the correct answer but focus on different aspects that are less central to evaluating interactional dynamics comprehensively.

Question 139: Correct Answer: B) Encourage Emily to share her feelings with the group.

Rationale: Encouraging Emily to share her feelings with the group is crucial for fostering open communication and addressing her sense of exclusion directly. This approach helps build empathy among group members and promotes mutual understanding. Option A could help build connections but might not address her feelings directly. Option C can create a more inclusive environment but may not specifically target Emily's concerns. Option D might increase her anxiety if she already feels excluded and hesitant to participate actively.

Question 140: Correct Answer: B) Collaborate with community leaders and organizations to develop programs that address these barriers.

Rationale: The correct answer is B because it involves working collaboratively within the community, which aligns with ethical guidelines for systemic advocacy. Public criticism (Option A) may not be constructive or ethical without first attempting collaboration. Encouraging individual complaints (Option C) places undue burden on clients rather than addressing systemic issues. Focusing solely on direct services (Option D) neglects broader advocacy responsibilities essential for long-term change.

Question 141: Correct Answer: B) Use cognitive-behavioral therapy (CBT) to help John manage his guilt and develop healthier coping strategies.

Rationale: Cognitive-behavioral therapy (CBT) is effective in helping individuals like John understand and manage their emotions while developing healthier coping mechanisms. This approach addresses both his guilt and provides tools for change. Option A lacks structure, which is crucial for someone feeling overwhelmed. Option C may be useful later but doesn't focus on John's immediate need for personal emotional regulation. Option D addresses anger but not the underlying guilt or trauma.

Question 142: Correct Answer: C) Create goals that reflect both the client's values and the counselor's expertise.

Rationale: The most effective approach is to create goals that reflect both the client's values and the counselor's expertise. This collaborative method ensures that the goals are meaningful to the client, increasing their motivation and commitment, while also being grounded in professional knowledge for therapeutic effectiveness. Option A disregards client input, which can lead to disengagement. Option B overlooks the importance of personal relevance in goal-setting. Option D, while beneficial for motivation, may neglect long-term objectives essential for sustained progress. Therefore, option C strikes a balance between client-centered care and professional guidance, making it the most comprehensive approach.

Question 143: Correct Answer: D) Integration and acceptance of stepchildren into the new family

Rationale: Research indicates that the integration and acceptance of stepchildren into the new family is crucial for the long-term success of a remarriage. This factor significantly impacts family cohesion and stability. While financial stability (Option A) and emotional readiness (Option C) are important, they are not as directly influential as how well stepchildren are accepted and integrated. The quality of co-parenting with ex-spouses (Option B) also plays a role but primarily affects immediate interactions rather than long-term family unity. Therefore, Option D is correct because successful integration fosters a supportive environment crucial for enduring relationships in blended families.

Question 144: Correct Answer: C) Unstructured observation

Rationale: Unstructured observation is most appropriate for gathering comprehensive information about a client's non-verbal communication patterns during an initial intake session. This method allows the counselor to observe natural behaviors and interactions without predefined constraints, providing rich qualitative data. - Option A (Structured interview) involves specific questions that may limit the observation of spontaneous non-verbal cues. - Option B (Standardized assessment) typically focuses on quantifiable data rather than qualitative observations. - Option D (Behavioral checklist) is more rigid and may not capture the full range of non-verbal behaviors as effectively as unstructured observation. By comparing these options, it becomes clear that unstructured observation offers the flexibility needed to capture detailed non-verbal communication patterns, which are crucial for accurate assessment and diagnosis in mental health counseling.

Question 145: Correct Answer: C) Educate Maria about the potential side effects of her current medication.

Rationale: The first step should be educating Maria about the potential side effects of her current medication, as this directly addresses her concern and provides her with necessary information. Switching medications (A) might be considered later but requires collaboration with her prescribing physician. Exploring relationship dynamics (B) is important but secondary to understanding the primary cause. Referring to a sex therapist (D) might be beneficial but is premature without addressing the medication issue first.

Question 146: Correct Answer: C) By leading them to replicate the attachment style they experienced as children.

Rationale: The replication of attachment styles is a key concept in understanding how family of origin issues impact current relationships. According to Bowlby's Attachment Theory, early interactions with caregivers shape an individual's expectations and behaviors in adult relationships. While adopting communication patterns (A), dependency (B), and conflict avoidance (D) are related, they are secondary effects influenced by the foundational attachment style. Therefore, C is the most comprehensive and accurate answer. - Option A is incorrect because while communication patterns can influence relationships, they are often a symptom rather than the root cause. - Option B is close but focuses narrowly on dependency rather than broader relational dynamics shaped by attachment. - Option D addresses conflict avoidance but does not encompass the full scope of how foundational attachment influences behavior across various relationship contexts.

Question 147: Correct Answer: A) Encourage Maria to engage in self-exploration activities to understand her identity.

Rationale: Adolescence is characterized by Erikson's stage of Identity vs. Role Confusion, where the primary task is developing a sense of self and personal identity. Encouraging self-exploration aligns perfectly with this developmental need. Option B is more suitable for younger children in Piaget's concrete operational stage. Option C, while beneficial for social support, does not directly address the core developmental task of identity formation. Option D is appropriate for much younger children in Piaget's preoperational stage.

Question 148: Correct Answer: A) Chronic fatigue

Rationale: Chronic fatigue is a well-documented physical symptom of major depressive disorder, supported by contemporary research and recognized theories. It is often a pervasive and debilitating aspect of depression. Joint pain (Option B), while it can occur, is more commonly associated with conditions like arthritis. Shortness of breath (Option C) is typically linked to anxiety disorders or cardiovascular issues rather than depression. Frequent headaches (Option D) can be a symptom but are less consistently tied to depression compared to chronic fatigue. Thus, chronic fatigue remains the most accurate and relevant symptom related to major depressive disorder.

Question 149: Correct Answer: A) Cognitive-Behavioral Therapy (CBT) focusing on exposure techniques

Rationale: Cognitive-Behavioral Therapy (CBT), particularly exposure techniques, is well-supported by contemporary research as an effective intervention for adolescents with social anxiety disorder. Exposure techniques help clients gradually face their fears in a controlled manner, reducing anxiety over time. While Psychodynamic Therapy (B) may offer insights into unconscious conflicts, it is less targeted for immediate symptom relief in social anxiety cases. Solution-Focused Brief Therapy (C) emphasizes future goals but may not directly address the specific anxiety symptoms. Person-Centered Therapy (D), while supportive, lacks the structured approach needed for treating social anxiety effectively. Therefore, CBT focusing on exposure techniques is the most appropriate intervention.

Question 150: Correct Answer: D) Cognitive Behavioral Therapy (CBT)

Rationale: Cognitive Behavioral Therapy (CBT) is the most appropriate intervention for helping Sarah reframe her negative thoughts and improve her mood. CBT focuses on identifying and changing negative thought patterns that contribute to depressive symptoms, making it highly effective for treating depression. - Option A (IPT) is incorrect because while it addresses interpersonal issues contributing to depression, it does not focus as directly on cognitive restructuring. - Option B (Psychodynamic Therapy) explores unconscious processes but may take longer to see improvements in mood. - Option C (ACT) helps individuals accept their thoughts and feelings but does not emphasize cognitive restructuring as strongly as CBT.

NCMHCE Exam Practice Questions [SET 2]

Question 1: A client who identifies as non-binary expresses discomfort with their current therapeutic approach, which they feel does not acknowledge their gender identity adequately. Which of the following interventions would be most appropriate for the counselor to implement?
A) Incorporate gender-neutral language and ask the client for their preferred pronouns.
B) Focus on exploring the client's childhood experiences to understand their current discomfort.
C) Encourage the client to participate in group therapy sessions with other non-binary individuals.
D) Suggest that the client undergoes a comprehensive psychological assessment to better understand their identity.

Question 2: John, a 45-year-old client undergoing therapy for anger management issues, confides in his counselor that he has been having violent fantasies about harming his coworker but insists he would never act on them. How should the counselor handle this information?
A) Keep John's disclosure confidential since he insists he won't act on his fantasies.
B) Immediately report John's fantasies to his employer as a precautionary measure.
C) Assess John's risk level for potential violence and consult with legal or clinical supervisors if needed while discussing confidentiality limits with John.
D) Wait for further sessions to see if John continues to have these fantasies before taking any action.

Question 3: John, a 35-year-old male with a history of major depressive disorder and recent suicidal ideation, has been admitted to an inpatient psychiatric unit. The treatment team is developing his discharge plan. Which level of care is most appropriate for John upon discharge?
A) Outpatient therapy with weekly sessions
B) Intensive outpatient program (IOP)
C) Partial hospitalization program (PHP)
D) Residential treatment facility

Question 4: Which of the following emotional responses is most commonly associated with children who have witnessed family abuse/violence?
A) Anxiety
B) Depression
C) Hyperactivity
D) Aggression

Question 5: John, a 35-year-old male, presents with feelings of sadness, lack of energy, and difficulty concentrating for the past six months. He reports that these symptoms have significantly impacted his work performance and social relationships. During the intake assessment, which aspect of John's mental health functioning is most critical to evaluate first?
A) John's ability to perform daily activities
B) The presence of any suicidal ideation
C) The impact of symptoms on his occupational functioning
D) The duration and severity of his symptoms

Question 6: During the initial session with a new client, Maria, a mental health counselor explains her role in the therapeutic process. Which of the following statements best clarifies the counselor's role?
A) "I will give you advice on how to handle your problems."
B) "I will help you explore your thoughts and feelings to find your own solutions."
C) "I will make decisions for you to ensure you follow the right path."
D) "I will provide you with a step-by-step plan to fix your issues."

Question 7: During an intake session with a new client named Sarah, a mental health counselor notices that Sarah frequently avoids eye contact and fidgets with her hands. Which method is the counselor using to gather this information?
A) Structured Interview
B) Behavioral Observation
C) Standardized Assessment
D) Self-Report Questionnaire

Question 8: Which of the following is the most accurate indicator that a client is experiencing true auditory hallucinations?
A) The client hears a voice that provides a running commentary on their actions.
B) The client experiences vivid, dream-like visions while awake.
C) The client reports hearing indistinct murmurs when in noisy environments.
D) The client sees shadowy figures in their peripheral vision.

Question 9: Maria, a 16-year-old high school student, has been referred to counseling due to her recent decline in academic performance. She reports feeling overwhelmed with her schoolwork and struggles with tasks requiring sustained attention and problem-solving. Her cognitive assessment reveals average intellectual functioning but significant weaknesses in working memory and processing speed. Which intervention would best support Maria's needs?
A) Mindfulness-Based Stress Reduction (MBSR)
B) Cognitive Processing Therapy (CPT)
C) Working Memory Training
D) Academic Skills Coaching

Question 10: John is a mental health counselor working with a couple experiencing frequent conflicts. During a session, John notices that both partners tend to avoid discussing their issues directly and instead focus on unrelated topics. Which conflict resolution strategy should John encourage to help the couple address their issues more effectively?
A) Competing
B) Avoiding
C) Collaborating
D) Accommodating

Question 11: John, a 42-year-old man, visits his mental health counselor reporting severe weight loss over the past six months without any changes in diet or exercise. He also mentions experiencing gastrointestinal issues and unexplained muscle weakness. Which physical symptom is most indicative of family abuse/violence?
A) Severe weight loss
B) Gastrointestinal issues
C) Unexplained muscle weakness
D) Frequent injuries

Question 12: Ms. Garcia, a 30-year-old woman, struggles with assertiveness in her interactions at work. Her counselor aims to improve her interactional patterns by enhancing her assertiveness skills. Which intervention is most suitable for this goal?
A) Assertiveness training

B) Active listening exercises
C) Behavioral rehearsal
D) Motivational interviewing

Question 13: A client presents with symptoms of hyperfocus, including intense concentration on specific tasks to the exclusion of other activities. Which condition is most commonly associated with this symptom?
A) Attention-Deficit/Hyperactivity Disorder (ADHD)
B) Generalized Anxiety Disorder (GAD)
C) Obsessive-Compulsive Disorder (OCD)
D) Major Depressive Disorder (MDD)

Question 14: John, a 9-year-old boy, has been referred for a psychological evaluation due to concerns about his intellectual functioning. His parents report that he struggles with problem-solving tasks and has difficulty understanding abstract concepts. Which assessment tool would be most appropriate for evaluating John's intellectual abilities?
A) The Beck Depression Inventory (BDI)
B) The Wechsler Intelligence Scale for Children (WISC-V)
C) The Conners' Rating Scales
D) The Vineland Adaptive Behavior Scales

Question 15: Maria, a 28-year-old female, has been diagnosed with depression and is struggling with low self-esteem. As her counselor, you aim to implement an individual counseling plan that includes elements of Person-Centered Therapy (PCT). Which initial intervention aligns best with PCT principles?
A) Establishing clear behavioral goals for Maria's progress.
B) Providing unconditional positive regard during sessions.
C) Assigning homework tasks to improve self-esteem.
D) Conducting regular assessments to monitor Maria's mood.

Question 16: When collaborating with other healthcare providers and client support systems, which documentation practice is most essential to ensure continuity of care in treatment planning?
A) Documenting every interaction with the client and their support systems in detail.
B) Sharing only the client's diagnosis with other providers to protect confidentiality.
C) Including relevant treatment goals and progress notes in shared documentation.
D) Providing access to the entire client file to all involved providers for transparency.

Question 17: A mental health counselor is working with a client from a different cultural background. Which approach best demonstrates the counselor's sensitivity to multicultural issues?
A) Applying standardized assessment tools uniformly across all clients.
B) Incorporating the client's cultural beliefs and practices into the treatment plan.
C) Encouraging the client to adapt to the dominant cultural norms for better integration.
D) Avoiding discussions about cultural differences to maintain neutrality.

Question 18: Maria, a 30-year-old woman experiencing high levels of stress at work, reports occasionally hearing her name being called when no one is around and seeing fleeting images out of the corner of her eye. What is the most likely explanation for Maria's symptoms?
A) Brief psychotic disorder
B) Hypnagogic/hypnopompic hallucinations
C) Stress-induced perceptual disturbances

D) Early onset schizophrenia

Question 19: Maria, a 28-year-old woman with generalized anxiety disorder, experiences significant daily anxiety that impacts her work performance and social interactions. She has tried standard outpatient therapy but feels she needs more support without disrupting her daily routine completely.
A) Inpatient hospitalization
B) Partial hospitalization program (PHP)
C) Intensive outpatient program (IOP)
D) Standard outpatient therapy

Question 20: Sarah, a 28-year-old veteran, is having difficulty adjusting to civilian life after her military service. She reports feeling isolated and disconnected from her community. As her mental health counselor, which intervention would be most effective in helping her reintegrate into civilian life?
A) Group Therapy with other veterans
B) Individual Psychotherapy
C) Vocational Rehabilitation Services
D) Medication Management

Question 21: John, a 45-year-old man with mild cognitive impairment, is seeking counseling for anxiety. As his mental health counselor, you need to obtain informed consent. Which of the following actions best ensures that John's consent is truly informed?
A) Providing John with written information about the counseling process and asking him to sign a consent form.
B) Verbally explaining the counseling process to John and ensuring he understands by asking him to repeat the information back.
C) Asking John's family member to explain the counseling process to him and then obtaining his signature on the consent form.
D) Giving John both verbal and written explanations of the counseling process, checking his understanding, and allowing him time to ask questions before signing.

Question 22: Maria, a 45-year-old woman diagnosed with terminal cancer, expresses feelings of hopelessness and questions the meaning of her life. As her mental health counselor, which intervention would be most appropriate to address her spiritual/existential concerns?
A) Encourage Maria to engage in mindfulness meditation to reduce stress.
B) Facilitate a life review therapy session to help Maria find meaning in her experiences.
C) Suggest joining a support group for individuals with terminal illnesses.
D) Recommend cognitive-behavioral therapy (CBT) to challenge negative thoughts.

Question 23: During a group counseling session, Sarah, one of the participants, shares a deeply personal story about her struggles with anxiety. As the counselor, what is the most effective way to promote and encourage interactions among group members in response to Sarah's disclosure?
A) Encourage each member to share their own experiences with anxiety.
B) Validate Sarah's feelings and ask how others in the group can support her.
C) Redirect the conversation to a less sensitive topic to maintain group comfort.
D) Summarize Sarah's story and ask if anyone has faced similar challenges.

Question 24: A 10-year-old boy named Ethan has been struggling academically despite having a supportive

home environment and access to educational resources. His parents report that he often forgets instructions and has difficulty organizing his schoolwork. During an assessment, it was noted that Ethan has average intelligence but displays significant difficulties in executive functioning. Which of the following interventions would be most appropriate for addressing Ethan's difficulties?
A) Cognitive Behavioral Therapy (CBT)
B) Executive Function Training
C) Medication for ADHD
D) Psychoeducational Tutoring

Question 25: Maria, a devout Catholic woman, is experiencing significant distress because her teenage son has decided to convert to another religion. She feels this decision violates her core values and beliefs. As her mental health counselor, how should you approach this situation to help Maria navigate her feelings while respecting her son's autonomy?
A) Encourage Maria to have an open and non-judgmental conversation with her son about his decision.
B) Advise Maria to seek guidance from her religious leader on how to handle the situation.
C) Suggest that Maria set firm boundaries with her son regarding religious discussions.
D) Recommend family therapy sessions where both Maria and her son can express their perspectives.

Question 26: Which of the following is most likely to be a primary psychological concern for individuals approaching retirement?
A) Financial insecurity due to inadequate savings
B) Loss of professional identity and purpose
C) Increased health issues due to aging
D) Changes in daily routine leading to boredom

Question 27: Maria, a 32-year-old woman with a history of anxiety and depression, has been attending counseling sessions for three months. Her counselor is now working on developing a comprehensive treatment plan. Which of the following actions should the counselor prioritize to ensure the effectiveness of Maria's treatment plan?
A) Establishing SMART goals that are specific, measurable, achievable, relevant, and time-bound.
B) Identifying potential barriers to treatment adherence.
C) Selecting evidence-based interventions tailored to Maria's specific needs.
D) Incorporating Maria's cultural background into the treatment plan.

Question 28: During a group therapy session, members begin discussing their feelings of isolation and difficulty connecting with others. As the counselor, you recognize this as a recurring theme within the group. Which of the following is the most appropriate intervention to address this theme?
A) Encourage members to share personal experiences related to isolation.
B) Suggest individual therapy for members who feel isolated.
C) Shift the focus to more positive aspects of their lives.
D) Provide psychoeducation on social skills development.

Question 29: John presents with symptoms of persistent sadness, loss of interest in activities, and significant weight loss. He also reports experiencing episodes of intense energy and reduced need for sleep lasting several days. Based on this presentation, what is the most likely diagnosis?
A) Major Depressive Disorder
B) Bipolar I Disorder
C) Persistent Depressive Disorder (Dysthymia)

D) Cyclothymic Disorder

Question 30: Jane, a 35-year-old woman, is experiencing significant emotional distress following her recent divorce. She reports feelings of sadness, anxiety, and difficulty sleeping. As her mental health counselor, what would be the most appropriate initial intervention to help Jane manage her symptoms?
A) Encourage Jane to join a support group for recently divorced individuals.
B) Suggest Jane start a daily mindfulness meditation practice.
C) Recommend Jane begin cognitive-behavioral therapy (CBT) to address her negative thought patterns.
D) Advise Jane to engage in physical exercise regularly.

Question 31: Maria, a 45-year-old woman, comes in for an initial diagnostic interview reporting chronic anxiety, difficulty concentrating, muscle tension, and frequent irritability over the past year. She also reveals that her mother had similar issues but was never formally diagnosed or treated. How should the counselor proceed to gather relevant information effectively?
A) Conduct a mental status examination focusing on Maria's cognitive functions.
B) Inquire about Maria's daily routines and any recent changes in her life circumstances.
C) Delve into Maria's family history of mental health conditions.
D) Ask detailed questions about Maria's physical health and any medical conditions.

Question 32: A 10-year-old child exhibits frequent temper outbursts and defiance towards authority figures at school. Which therapeutic approach is most effective in addressing these behavioral problems?
A) Cognitive Behavioral Therapy (CBT)
B) Parent-Child Interaction Therapy (PCIT)
C) Play Therapy
D) Dialectical Behavior Therapy (DBT)

Question 33: John, a 45-year-old male, presents with chronic insomnia that has persisted for over six months. He reports difficulty falling asleep, frequent awakenings during the night, and waking up too early in the morning. Despite trying over-the-counter sleep aids and practicing good sleep hygiene, his symptoms have not improved. What is the most appropriate next step in managing John's insomnia?
A) Prescribe a short-term course of benzodiazepines.
B) Recommend cognitive-behavioral therapy for insomnia (CBT-I).
C) Suggest increasing physical exercise during the day.
D) Advise using melatonin supplements.

Question 34: Maria, a 28-year-old client with borderline personality disorder (BPD), often experiences intense emotional dysregulation. Her counselor decides to use structured activities to help her manage her emotions better. Which activity would be most suitable for Maria?
A) Engaging in free-form art therapy sessions.
B) Participating in DBT skills training modules.
C) Attending non-directive play therapy sessions.
D) Writing unstructured letters to herself.

Question 35: As a mental health counselor, you notice that one of your colleagues frequently posts about their clients' progress on social media without revealing their identities. What should be your primary concern according to professional ethics?
A) The potential for indirect identification through contextual clues.
B) The positive impact such posts might have on public

awareness of mental health.
C) The benefit of showcasing successful therapy outcomes.
D) The possibility that clients might feel proud if they recognize themselves in the posts.

Question 36: A mental health counselor is working with a client who has been diagnosed with both major depressive disorder and substance use disorder. The client has shown minimal progress despite several months of counseling. What is the most appropriate next step for the counselor?
A) Continue with the current treatment plan and increase session frequency.
B) Refer the client to a psychiatrist for a medication evaluation.
C) Refer the client to a substance abuse specialist while continuing therapy.
D) Suggest that the client join a support group for individuals with similar issues.

Question 37: When establishing group rules and expectations for a therapy group, which of the following is the most critical consideration to ensure ethical practice and effective group dynamics?
A) Establishing confidentiality guidelines
B) Setting clear attendance requirements
C) Defining roles and responsibilities within the group
D) Outlining procedures for addressing conflicts

Question 38: Which of the following is considered the most significant risk factor for future suicide attempts according to contemporary research?
A) Previous suicide attempt
B) Family history of suicide
C) Diagnosis of major depressive disorder
D) Substance abuse

Question 39: Which of the following is most critical for ensuring effective psychoeducation in a group therapy setting?
A) Focusing primarily on delivering factual information about mental health conditions.
B) Encouraging active participation and discussion among group members.
C) Limiting sessions to a strict lecture format to maintain control over the content.
D) Ensuring all educational materials are evidence-based and up-to-date.

Question 40: Maria, a 60-year-old woman with mild cognitive impairment (MCI), is being asked to consent to a new treatment plan. As her mental health counselor, which aspect should you prioritize when evaluating her competency to provide informed consent?
A) Maria's ability to recall past medical information accurately.
B) Maria's understanding of the treatment plan and its consequences.
C) Maria's emotional response towards her diagnosis.
D) Maria's trust in her healthcare provider.

Question 41: Sarah, a 38-year-old woman, is considering recommitting to her partner after a period of separation due to infidelity. During therapy, she expresses mixed feelings about trust and forgiveness. Which therapeutic intervention is most appropriate for helping Sarah navigate these emotions?
A) Narrative Therapy
B) Integrative Behavioral Couple Therapy (IBCT)
C) Psychodynamic Therapy
D) Mindfulness-Based Cognitive Therapy (MBCT)

Question 42: Maria, a mental health counselor, has been seeing her client, Sarah, for six months. Sarah recently invited Maria to her wedding as they have developed a strong therapeutic relationship. What should Maria do in this situation to adhere to ethical guidelines?
A) Accept the invitation to support Sarah's progress.
B) Decline the invitation but send a congratulatory card.
C) Discuss the invitation with Sarah during their next session.
D) Terminate the counseling relationship to attend the wedding.

Question 43: When a group member consistently monopolizes conversations, making it difficult for others to participate, what is the most effective intervention a mental health counselor should employ?
A) Directly confront the monopolizing member in front of the group.
B) Encourage other group members to speak up more frequently.
C) Address the monopolizing behavior privately with the member.
D) Use structured activities to ensure equal participation.

Question 44: Sarah, a 13-year-old girl, has recently moved in with her mother and stepfather after her parents' divorce. She is struggling to adjust to her new family dynamics and often feels left out when her stepfather makes decisions without consulting her or her mother. What is the most appropriate intervention for a mental health counselor to address Sarah's feelings of exclusion?
A) Encourage Sarah to communicate her feelings directly to her stepfather.
B) Suggest family therapy sessions to improve communication among all family members.
C) Advise Sarah's mother to spend more one-on-one time with Sarah.
D) Recommend that Sarah join a support group for children of divorced parents.

Question 45: Based on Sarah's symptoms, which therapeutic approach is most effective in treating her obsessive thoughts and compulsive behaviors?
A) Cognitive Behavioral Therapy (CBT)
B) Psychoanalytic Therapy
C) Humanistic Therapy
D) Dialectical Behavior Therapy (DBT)

Question 46: Which of the following strategies is most effective in educating a client about the value of treatment plan compliance?
A) Highlighting the immediate benefits of adhering to the treatment plan.
B) Emphasizing long-term outcomes and potential risks of non-compliance.
C) Focusing on the client's personal goals and how they align with the treatment plan.
D) Discussing statistical success rates of similar treatment plans.

Question 47: Jane, a 72-year-old patient with terminal cancer, has expressed her wish to discontinue aggressive treatment and focus on palliative care. Her family, however, insists on continuing all possible treatments. As her mental health counselor, what is the most appropriate course of action?
A) Respect Jane's autonomy and support her decision to discontinue aggressive treatment.
B) Encourage Jane to reconsider her decision due to her family's wishes.
C) Mediate a discussion between Jane and her family to reach a consensus.
D) Follow the family's wishes since they are her primary

support system.

Question 48: John, a 45-year-old man, reports difficulties in maintaining close relationships. He describes his upbringing in a highly critical environment where achievements were prioritized over emotional connection. Which therapeutic approach is most likely to help John understand how his family of origin impacts his current relational patterns?
A) Narrative Therapy focusing on reconstructing personal stories.
B) Emotionally Focused Therapy (EFT) targeting attachment bonds.
C) Behavioral Activation aimed at increasing engagement in positive activities.
D) Gestalt Therapy emphasizing present moment awareness.

Question 49: John, a 28-year-old man experiencing anxiety due to job stress, reports feeling overwhelmed and disconnected from his usual social activities. As his counselor, what would be the most appropriate strategy to help John develop a robust support system?
A) Encourage John to participate in volunteer work related to his interests.
B) Suggest John schedule regular meetups with close friends.
C) Recommend John seek mentorship within his professional field.
D) Advise John to join an online forum for individuals dealing with anxiety.

Question 50: Maria, a 60-year-old woman diagnosed with chronic rheumatoid arthritis, reports feeling overwhelmed by her condition's impact on her daily life. As her mental health counselor, what would be the most comprehensive approach to assist Maria in adjusting to her chronic illness?
A) Focus solely on cognitive-behavioral therapy (CBT) to help Maria reframe negative thoughts about her illness.
B) Encourage Maria to keep a daily journal documenting her pain levels and emotional responses.
C) Develop an integrated treatment plan that includes CBT, mindfulness practices, and participation in a chronic illness support group.
D) Advise Maria to prioritize rest and avoid activities that could exacerbate her symptoms.

Question 51: A client expresses feelings of hopelessness and questions the meaning of life after a significant loss. As a mental health counselor, which intervention is most appropriate to address the client's spiritual/existential concerns?
A) Encourage the client to explore their spiritual beliefs and practices.
B) Suggest cognitive-behavioral techniques to challenge negative thoughts.
C) Recommend joining a support group for individuals experiencing similar losses.
D) Advise the client to focus on physical activities to distract from their grief.

Question 52: John, a 30-year-old man, reports experiencing significant weight gain over the past six months despite no changes in his diet or exercise routine. He also mentions sleeping excessively yet feeling fatigued during the day. His therapist considers that these physical changes might be indicative of a mental health condition. What is the most likely diagnosis?
A) Hypothyroidism
B) Bipolar Disorder
C) Major Depressive Disorder

D) Sleep Apnea

Question 53: John, a 35-year-old man who recently became paraplegic due to a car accident, is struggling with feelings of worthlessness and depression. As his mental health counselor, which intervention would be most effective in helping John improve his self-esteem and adjust to his new life situation?
A) Cognitive Behavioral Therapy (CBT)
B) Solution-Focused Brief Therapy (SFBT)
C) Motivational Interviewing (MI)
D) Psychoeducation about Disability

Question 54: During an initial intake session, a 35-year-old patient named John reports experiencing persistent sadness, loss of interest in activities, and difficulty sleeping for the past six months. He also mentions feeling worthless and having thoughts of self-harm. Which is the most appropriate initial diagnosis for John?
A) Generalized Anxiety Disorder (GAD)
B) Major Depressive Disorder (MDD)
C) Persistent Depressive Disorder (PDD)
D) Adjustment Disorder with Depressed Mood

Question 55: John, a 35-year-old male, has been struggling with alcohol use disorder for several years. He recently experienced a relapse after six months of sobriety. During a counseling session, John expresses feelings of guilt and shame, stating that he feels like a failure and is considering giving up on his recovery efforts. As his counselor, what is the most appropriate immediate intervention?
A) Encourage John to attend more Alcoholics Anonymous (AA) meetings.
B) Validate John's feelings and explore the triggers that led to his relapse.
C) Suggest John consider inpatient rehabilitation for more intensive support.
D) Advise John to increase his medication dosage under medical supervision.

Question 56: Maria, a 35-year-old woman, has been experiencing emotional abuse from her partner for several years. She feels isolated and believes she deserves the negative treatment. As her counselor, which initial intervention would be most effective in addressing Maria's emotional state?
A) Encourage Maria to immediately leave her partner and move to a shelter.
B) Help Maria identify and challenge her negative self-beliefs.
C) Suggest Maria join a support group for survivors of abuse.
D) Advise Maria to seek a restraining order against her partner.

Question 57: When assessing a client's level of distress during an initial intake session, which of the following approaches is most effective in obtaining an accurate understanding?
A) Relying primarily on the client's self-reported symptoms.
B) Using a combination of clinical interviews and standardized assessment tools.
C) Observing the client's non-verbal cues and body language exclusively.
D) Consulting with family members to gather collateral information.

Question 58: John, a 35-year-old client, is hesitant to share details about his substance use during your assessment session. Which strategy would most likely improve the accuracy of John's self-reported information?

A) Assuring confidentiality
B) Using leading questions
C) Allowing family members to contribute
D) Administering a brief screening tool

Question 59: John, a 45-year-old man with substance use disorder, is beginning his journey towards recovery. His counselor is developing a treatment plan that addresses his immediate needs while also considering long-term recovery. What should be the primary focus when creating John's initial treatment plan?
A) Developing relapse prevention strategies.
B) Fostering a strong therapeutic alliance.
C) Addressing immediate withdrawal symptoms.
D) Setting long-term sobriety goals.

Question 60: Which of the following is a core principle of Motivational Interviewing (MI) when addressing substance use issues?
A) Confrontation
B) Empathy
C) Direct advice
D) Authoritative guidance

Question 61: Which therapeutic approach is most effective for treating PTSD in veterans, according to contemporary research?
A) Cognitive Behavioral Therapy (CBT)
B) Eye Movement Desensitization and Reprocessing (EMDR)
C) Prolonged Exposure Therapy (PE)
D) Dialectical Behavior Therapy (DBT)

Question 62: Sarah, a mental health counselor, is working with John, a client who has a visual impairment. John expresses difficulty in reading the materials provided during their sessions. What should Sarah do to provide adequate accommodations for John?
A) Provide large print versions of the materials.
B) Read the materials aloud to John during each session.
C) Offer electronic versions of the materials that are compatible with screen readers.
D) Refer John to a specialist who can assist him with his reading difficulties.

Question 63: John, a licensed mental health counselor, supervises several interns at his clinic. One of his interns, Sarah, has been consistently late for their supervision meetings. John suspects that Sarah might be struggling with time management due to personal issues she has briefly mentioned. What should John do first?
A) Immediately report Sarah's tardiness to the clinic director.
B) Discuss Sarah's punctuality issues directly with her during their next supervision session.
C) Offer Sarah resources for time management and stress relief without addressing her tardiness directly.
D) Reduce Sarah's caseload to alleviate potential stressors contributing to her tardiness.

Question 64: When using assessment instrument results to facilitate client decision-making in treatment planning, which approach is most effective in ensuring the client's active participation and ownership of their treatment plan?
A) Presenting the assessment results to the client and suggesting a treatment plan based on those results.
B) Discussing the assessment results with the client and collaboratively developing a treatment plan that aligns with their goals.
C) Interpreting the assessment results for the client and providing them with several treatment options to choose from.

D) Reviewing the assessment results privately and then informing the client of the best course of action based on clinical expertise.

Question 65: A mental health counselor, Sarah, is working with a client, Jamal, who reports feeling increasingly anxious and depressed due to experiencing microaggressions at his workplace. Jamal believes these microaggressions are based on his race. As part of her therapeutic approach, what should Sarah prioritize in addressing Jamal's concerns?
A) Encourage Jamal to confront his colleagues about their behavior.
B) Validate Jamal's experiences and explore the impact of microaggressions on his mental health.
C) Suggest Jamal seek a new job where he might face less discrimination.
D) Focus solely on building Jamal's resilience to cope with workplace stress.

Question 66: John, a 28-year-old combat veteran, reports feeling detached from his family and friends since returning from deployment. He experiences irritability, hypervigilance, and recurrent nightmares about his experiences in combat. Which therapeutic approach is most likely to be effective in addressing John's trauma-related symptoms?
A) Cognitive Behavioral Therapy (CBT)
B) Dialectical Behavior Therapy (DBT)
C) Eye Movement Desensitization and Reprocessing (EMDR)
D) Psychodynamic Therapy

Question 67: When assessing your competency to work with a specific client, which factor is most critical to evaluate first?
A) Your familiarity with the client's cultural background.
B) Your theoretical orientation's alignment with the client's presenting issues.
C) Your ability to establish and maintain professional boundaries.
D) Your personal biases and how they may impact your work with the client.

Question 68: John is a counselor who has been assigned a client named Ahmed, who identifies as Muslim and has expressed concerns about religious discrimination at work. How should John assess his competency to work effectively with Ahmed?
A) Review ethical guidelines regarding non-discrimination and cultural sensitivity.
B) Reflect on his own potential biases and how they might affect the counseling process.
C) Assume that his previous experience with religious clients is sufficient.
D) Pursue continuing education specifically related to Muslim culture and religious practices.

Question 69: A client presents with symptoms of anxiety and has difficulty articulating their feelings. As a counselor using Carl Rogers' Person-Centered Therapy, which intervention would be most appropriate to help the client express their emotions?
A) Reflective listening
B) Cognitive restructuring
C) Systematic desensitization
D) Solution-focused questioning

Question 70: John, a mental health counselor, discovers that his colleague has been using outdated assessment tools that no longer meet current best practice standards. John is unsure how to address this issue while maintaining professionalism.

A) Report the colleague immediately to the licensing board.
B) Discuss the issue directly with the colleague and suggest updating their assessment tools.
C) Ignore the situation since it does not directly affect his clients.
D) Inform his supervisor about his concerns without confronting the colleague.

Question 71: John, a 60-year-old man who recently lost his leg in an accident, is struggling with feelings of helplessness and depression. Which approach should his mental health counselor prioritize to facilitate John's adjustment?
A) Encouraging John to join a support group for individuals with similar experiences.
B) Advising John to isolate himself until he feels ready to engage with others.
C) Suggesting that John focus solely on physical rehabilitation without addressing emotional aspects.
D) Recommending that John minimize discussions about his feelings with friends and family.

Question 72: Dr. Williams, a licensed mental health counselor, is approached by a former client, Sarah, who requests to connect on social media to stay in touch. Dr. Williams is considering the ethical implications of accepting this request.
A) Accept Sarah's request but set strict boundaries for communication.
B) Decline Sarah's request and explain the importance of maintaining professional boundaries.
C) Accept Sarah's request but limit interactions to non-clinical topics.
D) Decline Sarah's request without providing an explanation.

Question 73: A 45-year-old male client reports experiencing erectile dysfunction (ED) for the past six months. He mentions that he feels anxious about his performance, which exacerbates his condition. Which of the following interventions is most appropriate for this client?
A) Prescribing phosphodiesterase type 5 inhibitors (PDE5i)
B) Cognitive-behavioral therapy (CBT) focused on performance anxiety
C) Referral to a urologist for further medical evaluation
D) Encouraging lifestyle changes such as exercise and diet modification

Question 74: A 35-year-old male presents with symptoms of persistent sadness, low energy, difficulty concentrating, and frequent headaches. He also reports experiencing periods of elevated mood, increased energy, and decreased need for sleep lasting several days. Given these symptoms, what is the most likely co-occurring diagnosis?
A) Major Depressive Disorder and Generalized Anxiety Disorder
B) Bipolar II Disorder and Generalized Anxiety Disorder
C) Major Depressive Disorder and Persistent Depressive Disorder
D) Bipolar II Disorder and Cyclothymic Disorder

Question 75: During an intake session, a mental health counselor is conducting a Cultural Formulation Interview with Maria, a 35-year-old Latina woman who recently moved to the United States. Maria mentions that she feels disconnected from her cultural roots and is experiencing anxiety and depression. Which aspect of the Cultural Formulation Interview should the counselor focus on to best understand Maria's cultural identity and its impact on her mental health?
A) Cultural definition of the problem
B) Cultural perceptions of cause, context, and support

C) Cultural factors affecting self-coping and past help-seeking behavior
D) Cultural identity of the individual

Question 76: Maria has been consistently late for her counseling sessions, which disrupts her progress. As her counselor, how should you use constructive confrontation to address this issue?
A) Express disappointment in Maria's tardiness and emphasize how it affects her progress.
B) Discuss with Maria why punctuality is important for her therapy and collaboratively explore solutions.
C) Allow Maria more flexibility with her appointment times to accommodate her schedule better.
D) Implement a strict policy where repeated tardiness results in termination of services.

Question 77: Sarah, a 35-year-old woman, reports feeling intensely lonely despite having a wide social network. She mentions that her relationships often feel superficial and unsatisfying. As her mental health counselor, you suspect her feelings of loneliness may be rooted in her attachment style. Which attachment style is most likely contributing to Sarah's experience?
A) Secure Attachment
B) Anxious-Preoccupied Attachment
C) Dismissive-Avoidant Attachment
D) Fearful-Avoidant Attachment

Question 78: John, a 45-year-old man, reports experiencing intense fear of gaining weight despite being underweight. He engages in restrictive eating patterns and exercises excessively. He also mentions having episodes where he consumes large amounts of food in a short period followed by self-induced vomiting. What is the most likely diagnosis for John?
A) Anorexia Nervosa
B) Bulimia Nervosa
C) Binge-Eating Disorder
D) Avoidant/Restrictive Food Intake Disorder

Question 79: A 14-year-old girl named Maria discloses during a counseling session that she has been experiencing physical abuse at home from her stepfather. She expresses fear for her safety but also worries about breaking up her family if she reports it. What should be the counselor's primary concern in this situation?
A) Respecting Maria's wishes and keeping her disclosure confidential.
B) Encouraging Maria to talk to her mother about the abuse.
C) Ensuring Maria's immediate safety by reporting the abuse to child protective services.
D) Exploring family therapy as a means to address underlying issues.

Question 80: A client diagnosed with terminal cancer expresses feelings of hopelessness and despair. As a mental health counselor, which intervention is most appropriate to address the client's emotional needs?
A) Encourage the client to engage in life review therapy.
B) Suggest that the client focuses on creating a legacy project.
C) Recommend cognitive-behavioral therapy (CBT) to challenge negative thoughts.
D) Advocate for increased social support from family and friends.

Question 81: You are a counselor who has been approached by a client named Sarah, who is dealing with complex trauma from childhood abuse. You have limited experience working with trauma cases and are unsure if you can provide the best care for her. What

should be your primary consideration in deciding whether to work with Sarah?
A) Refer Sarah to a specialist immediately without any further sessions.
B) Seek supervision or consultation while continuing to work with Sarah.
C) Continue working with Sarah and use this as an opportunity to gain experience.
D) Take a brief training course on trauma and then decide whether to continue.

Question 82: John, a 42-year-old man with generalized anxiety disorder (GAD), reports increased anxiety due to recent cardiovascular issues diagnosed by his primary care physician. As his mental health counselor, you consider referring him for concurrent treatment. Which referral would be most appropriate?
A) Refer John to a cardiologist specializing in stress-related heart conditions.
B) Refer John to a nutritionist for dietary changes to manage his anxiety.
C) Refer John to an exercise physiologist for developing an exercise regimen.
D) Refer John to a biofeedback therapist specializing in anxiety reduction techniques.

Question 83: A client reports feeling increasingly anxious about their partner's lack of communication and frequent absence from home. Which intervention would most effectively address the client's concerns based on attachment theory?
A) Encourage the client to engage in open and honest communication with their partner about their feelings.
B) Suggest that the client focus on self-care activities to reduce anxiety.
C) Recommend couples therapy to explore underlying issues in the relationship.
D) Advise the client to give their partner more space to avoid appearing clingy.

Question 84: Which strategy is most effective in enhancing leader-member exchange (LMX) quality within a mental health counseling team?
A) Implementing regular team-building activities
B) Establishing clear communication channels
C) Providing consistent and constructive feedback
D) Setting rigid hierarchical structures

Question 85: When establishing short- and long-term counseling goals for a client diagnosed with major depressive disorder, which of the following best exemplifies an appropriate approach?
A) Establishing a goal for the client to "feel happier" within one month.
B) Setting a goal for the client to "reduce depressive symptoms by 50%" over three months.
C) Creating a goal for the client to "increase social interactions" without specifying a time frame.
D) Formulating a goal for the client to "engage in physical activity three times per week" over six months.

Question 86: During a biopsychosocial interview with John, a 28-year-old man experiencing substance use issues, which question would best help identify psychosocial stressors contributing to his substance use?
A) "Do you have any family members who have struggled with substance use?"
B) "How do you typically spend your weekends?"
C) "Can you describe any recent significant life changes?"
D) "Have you ever sought treatment for your substance use before?"

Question 87: During the first session of a new therapy group for individuals dealing with anxiety, the counselor, Dr. Smith, asks the group members to participate in establishing group rules. One member suggests that each person should have the freedom to leave whenever they feel uncomfortable. How should Dr. Smith respond to this suggestion while maintaining professional practice and ethics?
A) Agree with the suggestion as it respects individual autonomy.
B) Modify the suggestion by setting a rule that members can leave but must inform the group beforehand.
C) Reject the suggestion and establish a rule that members must stay for the entire session.
D) Agree with the suggestion but emphasize that frequent absences could impact group cohesion.

Question 88: When determining the appropriate level of inpatient care for a patient with severe depression and suicidal ideation, which factor is most critical in making this decision?
A) The patient's current living situation and support system
B) The severity and frequency of suicidal thoughts
C) The patient's history of medication compliance
D) The availability of outpatient resources

Question 89: In a newly formed support group for individuals dealing with anxiety, the group leader wants to establish a strong connection with each member early on. Which strategy is most effective in promoting interactions between the group leader and participants?
A) Sharing personal anecdotes related to anxiety from the group leader's life.
B) Setting clear expectations and rules for participation from the beginning.
C) Conducting individual check-ins with each member before sessions.
D) Facilitating icebreaker activities that involve sharing personal stories.

Question 90: John is a 65-year-old retired teacher who is experiencing feelings of purposelessness and depression. He mentions that he misses the daily interactions with his colleagues and students. Which therapeutic approach would be most effective in addressing John's retirement concerns?
A) Cognitive Behavioral Therapy (CBT)
B) Solution-Focused Brief Therapy (SFBT)
C) Interpersonal Therapy (IPT)
D) Existential Therapy

Question 91: Maria, a 28-year-old female, comes to your office reporting severe anxiety that has worsened over the past three months. She describes constant worry about her job performance and fears she might get fired despite positive feedback from her supervisor. Maria also reports physical symptoms such as heart palpitations and shortness of breath during these anxious episodes. What would be the most appropriate initial intervention to assess Maria's level of distress?
A) Refer Maria for cognitive-behavioral therapy (CBT) sessions focused on anxiety management techniques.
B) Conduct a detailed clinical interview focusing on her anxiety triggers and coping mechanisms.
C) Suggest relaxation exercises and mindfulness practices to manage her physical symptoms immediately.
D) Administer an anxiety-specific questionnaire to measure the severity of her symptoms.

Question 92: Maria, a mental health counselor, is meeting with her client James for an initial session. To obtain informed consent effectively, what should Maria emphasize when discussing confidentiality?

A) Explain that all information shared in sessions will remain confidential.
B) Inform James about general confidentiality practices without specifics.
C) Discuss specific scenarios where confidentiality might be breached and obtain James's acknowledgment.
D) Provide James with a written confidentiality agreement to sign without further discussion.

Question 93: John, a 45-year-old male, presents with persistent feelings of hopelessness and depression. He reports that he has lost interest in activities he once enjoyed, feels fatigued most of the time, and has difficulty concentrating. John also mentions having thoughts about his life not being worth living but denies any active suicidal ideation or plans. Based on Beck's Cognitive Theory of Depression, which cognitive distortion is most likely contributing to John's feelings of hopelessness?
A) Overgeneralization
B) Catastrophizing
C) Personalization
D) All-or-nothing thinking

Question 94: Which of the following best exemplifies the concept of 'genuineness' in a therapeutic relationship?
A) The counselor consistently expresses empathy towards the client's feelings.
B) The counselor's verbal and non-verbal behaviors align with their true feelings.
C) The counselor provides unconditional positive regard to the client.
D) The counselor actively listens and reflects back the client's thoughts.

Question 95: Which of the following interventions is most effective in addressing sexual abuse within a family system?
A) Individual therapy for the survivor
B) Family therapy involving all members
C) Couples therapy for the parents
D) Group therapy for survivors

Question 96: Maria, a 30-year-old female, has been experiencing symptoms of depression for several months. She reports feeling hopeless about her future, having low energy levels, and struggling with insomnia. Maria has recently started therapy and her counselor is using Interpersonal Therapy (IPT). Which primary focus area of IPT is most relevant for addressing Maria's feelings of hopelessness?
A) Grief
B) Role disputes
C) Role transitions
D) Interpersonal deficits

Question 97: John, a 45-year-old man with a history of schizophrenia, reports seeing shadowy figures in his peripheral vision that disappear when he turns to look directly at them. He also hears indistinct whispers that become clearer when he is alone. Which of the following best explains John's experiences?
A) Paranoid delusions
B) Visual and auditory hallucinations
C) Tactile hallucinations
D) Illusions

Question 98: A client is concerned about their ability to afford ongoing therapy sessions. As a mental health counselor, which of the following actions is most appropriate to ensure ethical practice while addressing the client's financial concerns?
A) Adjust your fees based on the client's financial situation

without documenting it.
B) Provide a sliding scale fee structure that is documented and discussed with the client.
C) Refer the client to another counselor who offers lower rates without discussing your own fee structure.
D) Offer pro bono services without informing your professional liability insurance provider.

Question 99: Maria, a 28-year-old woman, presents for an intake assessment reporting frequent panic attacks over the past three months. She describes sudden episodes of intense fear accompanied by palpitations, sweating, trembling, shortness of breath, and a fear of losing control. What is the most likely diagnosis based on her symptoms?
A) Panic Disorder
B) Social Anxiety Disorder
C) Specific Phobia
D) Generalized Anxiety Disorder

Question 100: Maria, a 32-year-old devout Catholic, is experiencing severe anxiety and depression. Her therapist suggests cognitive-behavioral therapy (CBT) which includes techniques that challenge her negative thoughts. However, Maria believes that her suffering is a test from God and that questioning these thoughts would be sinful. How should the therapist address this religious values conflict?
A) Respect Maria's beliefs and avoid using CBT techniques that challenge her thoughts.
B) Explain the therapeutic benefits of CBT while respecting her religious views, integrating her faith into the therapy.
C) Encourage Maria to seek guidance from her religious leader instead of continuing with CBT.
D) Use psychoeducation to convince Maria that her beliefs are irrational and need to be changed for effective treatment.

Question 101: A mental health counselor is assessing a client who reports experiencing frequent physical injuries from their partner. The client describes incidents where they were pushed, slapped, and punched. Which type of family abuse/violence does this scenario best describe?
A) Physical Abuse
B) Emotional Abuse
C) Neglect
D) Psychological Manipulation

Question 102: John, a 45-year-old patient, presents for an intake session reporting anxiety and difficulty sleeping. He mentions that his father was recently diagnosed with Alzheimer's disease. Which approach should the counselor take to effectively gather diagnostic information?
A) Focus on John's family history of mental health issues.
B) Explore John's current coping mechanisms and stress management strategies.
C) Inquire about John's daily routines and any recent changes.
D) Assess John's substance use history to rule out any contributing factors.

Question 103: John, a 45-year-old client, comes for his first counseling session reporting high levels of stress related to his job. Which strategy should the counselor prioritize during this initial interview?
A) Assess John's coping mechanisms and support systems.
B) Develop a detailed treatment plan for John's stress management.
C) Administer standardized stress assessment tools.
D) Discuss potential medication options for stress relief.

Question 104: A client reveals to their counselor that

they have been engaging in illegal activities but insists that this information remains confidential. Which of the following actions should the counselor take according to the ACA Code of Ethics?
A) Maintain confidentiality as requested by the client.
B) Break confidentiality and report the illegal activities to law enforcement.
C) Seek supervision or consultation while maintaining client confidentiality.
D) Discuss with the client the limits of confidentiality and potential consequences.

Question 105: Maria, a 28-year-old marketing executive, often experiences sudden episodes of intense fear accompanied by palpitations, sweating, trembling, shortness of breath, chest pain, nausea, dizziness, chills or hot flashes. These episodes occur unexpectedly and are not triggered by specific situations. What is the most likely diagnosis for Maria?
A) Panic Disorder
B) Generalized Anxiety Disorder (GAD)
C) Post-Traumatic Stress Disorder (PTSD)
D) Specific Phobia

Question 106: During a counseling session with Maria, a 35-year-old client experiencing anxiety, the counselor notices feeling unusually impatient and frustrated. Which of the following actions best demonstrates the counselor's awareness of self and its impact on clients?
A) Ignoring these feelings to maintain professionalism.
B) Reflecting on these feelings after the session to understand their origin.
C) Sharing these feelings with Maria to promote transparency.
D) Redirecting the conversation to avoid further frustration.

Question 107: A mental health counselor is working with a client who exhibits symptoms of severe anxiety and has difficulty managing stress. The counselor decides to use an evidence-based approach that focuses on altering maladaptive thought patterns to improve emotional regulation and develop coping strategies. Which therapeutic approach is the counselor most likely using?
A) Cognitive Behavioral Therapy (CBT)
B) Dialectical Behavior Therapy (DBT)
C) Acceptance and Commitment Therapy (ACT)
D) Psychodynamic Therapy

Question 108: Which of the following is the most ethically appropriate action for a clinical supervisor who discovers that their supervisee has breached client confidentiality?
A) Report the supervisee to the licensing board immediately.
B) Discuss the breach with the supervisee to understand their perspective and provide guidance.
C) Terminate the supervisory relationship due to ethical misconduct.
D) Inform the client about the breach directly.

Question 109: Sarah, a 28-year-old marketing executive, has been feeling extremely fatigued and mentally sluggish for the past few months. She finds it hard to get out of bed in the morning and has trouble concentrating on her tasks at work. Her mood is generally low, and she has lost interest in activities she once enjoyed. What is the most likely diagnosis for Sarah?
A) Bipolar II Disorder
B) Persistent Depressive Disorder (Dysthymia)
C) Major Depressive Disorder
D) Seasonal Affective Disorder

Question 110: Emily, a 28-year-old woman, expresses frustration about her partner's reluctance to discuss future plans such as marriage or having children. She feels this uncertainty is causing strain in their relationship. As her counselor, what would be the most effective strategy to help Emily navigate this issue?
A) Advise Emily to give her partner an ultimatum regarding their future together.
B) Suggest Emily explore her own values and goals through individual counseling.
C) Recommend that Emily initiate a calm and honest conversation with her partner about their future.
D) Encourage Emily to take a break from the relationship until her partner is ready to discuss future plans.

Question 111: Sarah, a 4-year-old girl, has recently started preschool and exhibits significant distress when her mother leaves her at school. She cries uncontrollably, refuses to engage in activities, and often complains of stomachaches. Based on attachment theory, what is the most likely explanation for Sarah's behavior?
A) Sarah is experiencing normal developmental anxiety.
B) Sarah has developed an insecure attachment with her mother.
C) Sarah is displaying symptoms of separation anxiety disorder.
D) Sarah is showing signs of social phobia.

Question 112: John, a 45-year-old client diagnosed with anxiety disorder, feels overwhelmed by his treatment plan and is unsure if he is making any real progress. What is the most effective way for you as his counselor to engage him in reviewing his progress?
A) Conduct a structured review of John's progress using quantitative measures like standardized assessment tools.
B) Encourage John to express his feelings about his perceived lack of progress and validate his emotions.
C) Suggest that John take a break from therapy if he feels too overwhelmed by the process.
D) Focus on John's initial reasons for seeking therapy to remind him of his original motivations.

Question 113: John, a 45-year-old male, reports hearing voices that comment on his actions and seeing shadowy figures in his peripheral vision. He has no history of substance use or neurological disorders. What is the most likely diagnosis?
A) Schizophrenia
B) Bipolar Disorder with Psychotic Features
C) Major Depressive Disorder with Psychotic Features
D) Brief Psychotic Disorder

Question 114: John, a 30-year-old man who lost his job unexpectedly, reports feeling numb and disconnected from reality during his counseling sessions. He also mentions having difficulty sleeping and concentrating. Based on Worden's Tasks of Mourning, which task is John struggling with?
A) Accepting the reality of the loss
B) Processing the pain of grief
C) Adjusting to an environment without the deceased
D) Finding an enduring connection with the deceased while embarking on a new life

Question 115: John, a 13-year-old boy, reports being cyberbullied by classmates. He feels isolated and has expressed thoughts of self-harm. As his mental health counselor, what evidence-based approach should you take to address his situation?
A) Implement Cognitive Behavioral Therapy (CBT) focused on resilience-building.
B) Recommend John take a break from social media.

C) Involve law enforcement to address cyberbullying legally.
D) Advise John to block his bullies on social media platforms.

Question 116: John, an African immigrant in his early 30s, has been facing challenges at his workplace due to cultural misunderstandings. His colleagues often misinterpret his communication style as aggressive or confrontational. Which intervention should John's counselor implement first to address these issues?
A) Encourage John to adopt the communication style prevalent in his workplace.
B) Facilitate a workshop for John's colleagues on cultural sensitivity and awareness.
C) Help John develop code-switching strategies for different social contexts.
D) Advise John to minimize interactions with colleagues until he feels more comfortable.

Question 117: According to Erikson's stages of psychosocial development, which developmental task is most critical during adolescence?
A) Trust vs. Mistrust
B) Initiative vs. Guilt
C) Identity vs. Role Confusion
D) Intimacy vs. Isolation

Question 118: What is the most appropriate referral source for Maria given her worsening symptoms?
A) Refer Maria to a general practitioner for medication management.
B) Refer Maria to a psychiatrist specializing in anxiety disorders.
C) Refer Maria to a support group for individuals with anxiety.
D) Refer Maria to another mental health counselor with a different approach.

Question 119: According to Aaron Beck's cognitive theory of depression, which cognitive distortion is most closely associated with feelings of hopelessness?
A) Overgeneralization
B) Catastrophizing
C) Personalization
D) Selective Abstraction

Question 120: Which of the following self-care practices is most effective in preventing burnout among mental health counselors according to contemporary research?
A) Engaging in regular physical exercise
B) Maintaining strict professional boundaries with clients
C) Participating in personal therapy sessions
D) Scheduling frequent social activities

Question 121: A client has been in treatment for anxiety disorder for six months. Despite some progress, the client reports persistent symptoms that interfere with daily functioning. As a mental health counselor, what is the most appropriate step to take when reviewing and revising the treatment plan?
A) Continue with the current treatment plan but increase the frequency of sessions.
B) Reassess the client's symptoms and consider incorporating additional therapeutic techniques.
C) Refer the client to another specialist for a second opinion.
D) Terminate the current treatment plan and start a new one from scratch.

Question 122: Case Scenario: Emily, a 28-year-old woman, struggles with intrusive thoughts about harm coming to her loved ones. These thoughts cause significant distress and interfere with her daily functioning. She has no history of acting on these thoughts but feels overwhelmed by their persistence. As her counselor, what would be the most appropriate intervention strategy?
A) Explore the origin of Emily's intrusive thoughts through psychodynamic therapy.
B) Use exposure and response prevention (ERP) techniques to reduce her anxiety around these thoughts.
C) Implement cognitive restructuring techniques to challenge and change her intrusive thoughts.
D) Encourage Emily to distract herself with activities whenever she experiences these intrusive thoughts.

Question 123: According to Kohlberg's cognitive-developmental theory of gender identity development, at what stage do children begin to understand that their gender remains stable over time?
A) Gender Constancy
B) Gender Stability
C) Gender Consistency
D) Gender Identity

Question 124: Under what circumstances is it permissible for a mental health counselor to disclose confidential client information to a third party without the client's consent?
A) When the client poses an imminent threat to themselves or others.
B) When the client's family requests information due to concern for the client's well-being.
C) When the client is involved in a legal case and their attorney requests information.
D) When another healthcare provider treating the client requests information for continuity of care.

Question 125: John, a 35-year-old client diagnosed with generalized anxiety disorder, has difficulty managing his daily stressors. His counselor decides to incorporate structured activities into his treatment plan. Which of the following activities is most appropriate for John's condition?
A) Engaging in unstructured journaling about daily experiences.
B) Participating in a guided imagery exercise focused on relaxation.
C) Keeping a structured thought record to identify and challenge irrational thoughts.
D) Joining an open-ended group discussion about anxiety.

Question 126: According to Aaron Beck's Cognitive Theory of Depression, which cognitive distortion is most commonly associated with feelings of hopelessness in depressed individuals?
A) Catastrophizing
B) Overgeneralization
C) Selective Abstraction
D) All-or-Nothing Thinking

Question 127: John, a 10-year-old boy, has been living with his father and stepmother for six months. He frequently expresses feelings of being left out and misunderstood by his stepmother. What strategy should his mental health counselor prioritize to improve John's relationship with his stepmother?
A) Facilitate joint activities that John and his stepmother can enjoy together.
B) Mediate a conversation where John can express his feelings directly to his stepmother.
C) Encourage John's father to intervene more actively in their relationship.
D) Provide psychoeducation about blended families to both John and his stepmother.

Question 128: John is a 50-year-old man caring for his

wife who has advanced multiple sclerosis. He reports feeling guilty when he takes time for himself and often neglects his own health needs. As his mental health counselor, what would be the most effective strategy to help John manage his caregiving responsibilities while maintaining his well-being?

A) Educate John about the importance of self-care and encourage regular breaks.

B) Advise John to delegate some caregiving tasks to other family members or professional caregivers.

C) Suggest John keep a daily journal to express his feelings and track his emotional well-being.

D) Recommend John attend couple's counseling sessions with his wife.

Question 129: In a support group for individuals recovering from substance abuse, counselor Maria needs to establish termination criteria for participants. One participant, John, expresses concern about being asked to leave if he relapses. How should Maria address John's concern while adhering to ethical guidelines?

A) Assure John that relapse is part of recovery and no one will be terminated for relapsing.

B) Establish a rule that any relapse results in immediate termination from the group.

C) Set criteria where relapse triggers an individual review but not automatic termination.

D) Avoid setting any specific termination criteria related to relapse.

Question 130: A 45-year-old patient named John reports difficulty falling asleep and staying asleep for the past three months. He mentions increased stress at work and occasional use of alcohol to help him relax before bed. As his mental health counselor, what is the most appropriate initial intervention?

A) Recommend cognitive-behavioral therapy for insomnia (CBT-I)

B) Suggest using over-the-counter sleep aids

C) Advise reducing alcohol consumption before bedtime

D) Prescribe a short-term course of benzodiazepines

Question 131: A 35-year-old woman named Sarah has been experiencing intense anxiety and panic attacks after a traumatic event where she was sexually assaulted by her partner. She feels unsafe at home but is hesitant to leave due to financial dependence on her partner. As her mental health counselor, what would be the most appropriate immediate intervention?

A) Encourage Sarah to confront her partner about the assault.

B) Develop a safety plan with Sarah and connect her with local shelters.

C) Suggest Sarah attend couple's therapy sessions with her partner.

D) Advise Sarah to focus on meditation and relaxation techniques at home.

Question 132: Dr. Williams is conducting a study on the effectiveness of a new cognitive-behavioral therapy (CBT) technique for treating anxiety. After analyzing his data, he finds a p-value of 0.03. Based on this result, which conclusion is most appropriate?

A) The null hypothesis can be rejected at the 5% significance level.

B) The null hypothesis can be accepted at the 5% significance level.

C) There is no significant difference between the new CBT technique and the control.

D) The study has a high probability of making a Type II error.

Question 133: During a team meeting, the group leader, Dr. Smith, notices that one member, Alex, frequently interrupts others and dominates the conversation. This behavior is causing frustration among other team members. As a mental health counselor facilitating this group, what is the most effective intervention to manage this dynamic?

A) Encourage Alex to express his thoughts after everyone else has spoken.

B) Implement a structured turn-taking system during meetings.

C) Privately discuss with Alex about his behavior and its impact on the team.

D) Assign Alex a specific role that limits his speaking time during meetings.

Question 134: Sarah, a 14-year-old girl, has been exhibiting aggressive behavior at school and home for the past six months. She has frequent outbursts, defies rules, and often argues with authority figures. Her parents report that she has also been lying and stealing. Which of the following is the most likely diagnosis?

A) Oppositional Defiant Disorder (ODD)

B) Conduct Disorder (CD)

C) Intermittent Explosive Disorder (IED)

D) Attention-Deficit/Hyperactivity Disorder (ADHD)

Question 135: Maria reports feeling anxious and insecure in her dating relationship because her partner often cancels plans at the last minute. She worries that her partner is losing interest or may be seeing someone else. What is the best approach for Maria to address her concerns with her partner?

A) Confront her partner directly about her suspicions of infidelity.

B) Express her feelings of anxiety and insecurity using "I" statements during a calm conversation.

C) Monitor her partner's activities more closely to gather evidence of infidelity.

D) Seek advice from friends who have experienced similar situations.

Question 136: Scenario: You are conducting an initial biopsychosocial interview with John, a 35-year-old male who has been referred to you for symptoms of depression and anxiety. During the interview, John mentions that he has recently lost his job and is experiencing marital problems. Which aspect of the biopsychosocial interview should you prioritize first to understand John's current mental health status?

A) John's recent job loss

B) John's marital problems

C) John's family history of mental illness

D) John's current medication use

Question 137: Which of the following strategies is most effective in helping clients integrate and maintain therapeutic progress over the long term?

A) Encouraging clients to journal their daily experiences and emotions.

B) Scheduling regular booster sessions after the initial therapy ends.

C) Teaching clients mindfulness techniques to use during stressful situations.

D) Helping clients develop a support network of friends and family.

Question 138: John, a 35-year-old male, presents to your clinic expressing feelings of hopelessness and mentions having thoughts of suicide. As his mental health counselor, what is the most crucial first step in developing a safety plan for John?

A) Identify John's triggers and warning signs.

B) Remove any immediate means of self-harm.

C) Establish a list of emergency contacts and resources.

D) Develop coping strategies for John to use when feeling suicidal.

Question 139: Which of the following interventions is most effective in treating chronic insomnia according to contemporary cognitive-behavioral therapy (CBT) principles?
A) Increasing physical exercise during the day
B) Using sleep restriction therapy
C) Taking melatonin supplements
D) Implementing a consistent bedtime routine

Question 140: Which of the following techniques is most effective in reducing physiological arousal associated with acute stress?
A) Cognitive Restructuring
B) Progressive Muscle Relaxation
C) Mindfulness-Based Stress Reduction
D) Psychoeducation

Question 141: A 35-year-old woman named Sarah presents to a mental health counselor with multiple bruises in various stages of healing, chronic pain, and frequent headaches. She reports feeling constantly fatigued and has difficulty sleeping. Which of the following is the most likely physical manifestation related to family abuse/violence?
A) Chronic pain
B) Frequent headaches
C) Difficulty sleeping
D) Multiple bruises in various stages of healing

Question 142: Maria, a 28-year-old female, has been experiencing intense anxiety, panic attacks, and avoidance behaviors for several months. She describes her anxiety as pervasive and debilitating. During her assessment, what should be prioritized to understand her level of mental health functioning?
A) Maria's coping mechanisms and support system
B) The frequency and triggers of her panic attacks
C) Her ability to maintain interpersonal relationships
D) The impact of anxiety on her physical health

Question 143: John, a 45-year-old man, is struggling to adjust after his recent divorce. He reports feeling overwhelmed by emotions and is unsure how to manage his stress effectively. As his counselor, you aim to provide him with effective strategies for emotional regulation during this difficult period.
A) Encourage John to avoid thinking about the divorce and focus solely on positive activities.
B) Suggest that John engage in mindfulness meditation and deep-breathing exercises.
C) Advise John to immerse himself in work to distract from his emotional pain.
D) Recommend that John frequently discuss his feelings with friends and family.

Question 144: Which of the following best describes a key ethical consideration for mental health counselors when using social media in their professional practice?
A) Ensuring confidentiality by not sharing client information online.
B) Using social media to promote mental health awareness without breaching client confidentiality.
C) Maintaining a separate personal and professional social media presence.
D) Engaging with clients through direct messaging on social media platforms.

Question 145: A counselor is working with a client who reveals that they have been involved in illegal activities. The client insists that this information remains confidential. What is the most appropriate action for the counselor to take according to ethical guidelines?
A) Maintain confidentiality as requested by the client.
B) Report the illegal activities to law enforcement immediately.
C) Discuss the limits of confidentiality with the client and seek legal advice if necessary.
D) Terminate the counseling relationship due to ethical conflicts.

Question 146: Maria, a 28-year-old woman, has been using opioids for chronic pain management but has developed an addiction. She wants to quit but fears withdrawal symptoms. During her counseling session, she asks about the best initial step to take in her recovery journey. What should be your primary recommendation?
A) Gradually taper off opioids under medical supervision.
B) Immediately stop opioid use and begin detoxification.
C) Switch to a non-opioid pain management regimen.
D) Join a support group specifically for opioid addiction.

Question 147: Maria is a 28-year-old professional who has recently experienced significant stress due to balancing her demanding job with personal responsibilities. She feels overwhelmed and unsure about her career path moving forward. During counseling, Maria expresses concerns about her ability to manage both her career aspirations and personal life effectively. Which intervention based on career development theories would best address Maria's concerns?
A) Implementing Super's Life-Span, Life-Space Approach
B) Utilizing Holland's RIASEC Model
C) Applying Social Cognitive Career Theory (SCCT)
D) Employing Roe's Needs Theory

Question 148: A client struggling with anxiety is learning how to manage their symptoms. Which of the following strategies is most effective in helping the client develop long-term coping skills?
A) Encouraging the client to avoid anxiety-provoking situations
B) Teaching the client cognitive-behavioral techniques
C) Advising the client to rely on medication alone
D) Suggesting that the client use relaxation techniques exclusively

Question 149: During a counseling session, Maria, a mental health counselor, notices that her client, John, is becoming increasingly agitated and expresses thoughts of self-harm. Maria is aware of her duty to maintain confidentiality but is also concerned about John's immediate safety. What should Maria do in this situation?
A) Maintain confidentiality and continue the session to further assess John's risk.
B) Break confidentiality immediately and contact emergency services.
C) Discuss with John the possibility of involving emergency services while ensuring he understands the reasons.
D) Refer John to another counselor who specializes in crisis intervention.

Question 150: John, a 35-year-old software engineer, is experiencing significant stress due to ongoing conflicts with his team leader. John feels undervalued and often finds himself in heated arguments with his leader. As his counselor, what is the most appropriate initial intervention to facilitate resolution of this interpersonal conflict?
A) Encourage John to express his feelings directly to his team leader.

B) Help John identify and understand his own triggers in the conflict.
C) Advise John to avoid confrontations and focus on his work.
D) Suggest John request a mediation session with a neutral third party.

ANSWER WITH DETAILED EXPLANATION SET [2]

Question 1: Correct Answer: A) Incorporate gender-neutral language and ask the client for their preferred pronouns.
Rationale: The correct answer is A) Incorporate gender-neutral language and ask the client for their preferred pronouns. This intervention demonstrates immediate respect for the client's identity and creates a more inclusive therapeutic environment. Option B, while potentially useful in broader therapy, does not directly address the client's expressed need regarding their gender identity. Option C could be beneficial but may not be immediately practical or desired by the client. Option D might be perceived as pathologizing the client's identity rather than affirming it. Therefore, option A is most aligned with sensitivity to gender orientation issues.

Question 2: Correct Answer: C) Assess John's risk level for potential violence and consult with legal or clinical supervisors if needed while discussing confidentiality limits with John.
Rationale: The correct approach involves assessing John's risk level for potential violence and consulting with supervisors if needed. This ensures that decisions are based on professional judgment and ethical standards. Option A fails to address potential risks adequately. Option B might breach confidentiality without sufficient cause. Option D could delay necessary intervention, increasing potential risks.

Question 3: Correct Answer: C) Partial hospitalization program (PHP)
Rationale: A Partial Hospitalization Program (PHP) is most appropriate for John upon discharge due to his recent suicidal ideation and need for intensive monitoring while transitioning to less restrictive care. PHP offers structured support similar to inpatient care but allows the patient to reside at home. Outpatient therapy (A) provides minimal supervision, IOP (B) offers fewer hours of therapy compared to PHP, and a residential treatment facility (D) may be unnecessarily restrictive given John's current stability.

Question 4: Correct Answer: D) Aggression
Rationale: Children who witness family abuse/violence often exhibit aggressive behaviors as a direct emotional response. This aggression can stem from modeling behaviors seen in abusive situations, internalizing stress, and attempting to regain control over their environment. While anxiety (Option A), depression (Option B), and hyperactivity (Option C) are also common emotional responses, aggression is particularly prevalent due to its direct correlation with exposure to violent behavior. Anxiety and depression are more internalized responses, whereas hyperactivity can be a result of various factors unrelated to witnessing violence. Aggression stands out as it directly mirrors the external violent behavior observed by the child.

Question 5: Correct Answer: B) The presence of any suicidal ideation
Rationale: Evaluating for suicidal ideation is critical as it addresses immediate safety concerns. While assessing daily activities (A), occupational functioning (C), and symptom duration/severity (D) are important, ensuring John's safety takes precedence. Suicidal ideation requires urgent intervention and can significantly alter the course of treatment.

Question 6: Correct Answer: B) "I will help you explore your thoughts and feelings to find your own solutions."
Rationale: The correct answer is B. The primary role of a counselor is to facilitate self-exploration and empower clients to find their own solutions, aligning with client-centered therapy principles. Option A is incorrect because giving advice undermines client autonomy. Option C is incorrect as making decisions for clients contradicts ethical standards promoting client self-determination. Option D is incorrect because providing a step-by-step plan implies a directive

approach rather than a collaborative one.

Question 7: Correct Answer: B) Behavioral Observation
Rationale: The counselor is using behavioral observation to gather information about Sarah's nonverbal behaviors, such as avoiding eye contact and fidgeting. Behavioral observation involves noting clients' actions and mannerisms during sessions. A structured interview (A) involves asking specific questions in a set order, while a standardized assessment (C) refers to using formal tools to measure psychological constructs. A self-report questionnaire (D) relies on the client's own reporting of their behaviors and feelings. While all these methods are valuable in assessment, only behavioral observation directly pertains to noticing nonverbal cues during interaction.

Question 8: Correct Answer: A) The client hears a voice that provides a running commentary on their actions.
Rationale: True auditory hallucinations often involve hearing voices that are distinct and can provide commentary on one's actions, which is characteristic of certain psychiatric conditions such as schizophrenia. Option B describes visual hallucinations rather than auditory ones. Option C could be misinterpreted as normal environmental noise or tinnitus rather than true hallucinations. Option D refers to visual hallucinations, which are different from auditory ones. Understanding these distinctions is crucial for accurate diagnosis and treatment planning.

Question 9: Correct Answer: C) Working Memory Training
Rationale: Working Memory Training is tailored to improve working memory capacity and processing speed, which are Maria's identified weaknesses. Mindfulness-Based Stress Reduction (MBSR) can help with stress management but does not specifically target cognitive deficits like working memory or processing speed. Cognitive Processing Therapy (CPT) is primarily used for trauma-related issues rather than cognitive functioning improvements. Academic Skills Coaching focuses on study strategies and habits but does not directly address cognitive deficits.

Question 10: Correct Answer: C) Collaborating
Rationale: Collaborating is the most effective strategy in this scenario as it encourages open communication and mutual problem-solving. Unlike competing (A), which can escalate conflicts, or avoiding (B), which does not address the issue at all, collaborating focuses on finding a win-win solution. Accommodating (D) may resolve conflict temporarily but often leads to unresolved underlying issues. Collaborating aligns with contemporary research emphasizing the importance of addressing underlying problems through cooperative dialogue.

Question 11: Correct Answer: D) Frequent injuries
Rationale: Frequent injuries are most indicative of family abuse/violence as they directly result from physical harm inflicted by another person. Severe weight loss, gastrointestinal issues, and unexplained muscle weakness can be secondary effects of stress or other underlying conditions but do not specifically point to physical violence. Frequent injuries provide concrete evidence of ongoing abuse.

Question 12: Correct Answer: A) Assertiveness training
Rationale: Assertiveness training specifically targets the development of assertive communication skills, which is Ms. Garcia's primary need. Active listening exercises (B) improve listening skills but do not directly enhance assertiveness. Behavioral rehearsal (C), while useful for practicing new behaviors, is broader and less focused on assertiveness alone. Motivational interviewing (D) helps explore ambivalence but does not directly address assertive communication.

Question 13: Correct Answer: A) Attention-Deficit/Hyperactivity Disorder (ADHD)
Rationale: Hyperfocus is a symptom commonly associated

with ADHD, where individuals can intensely concentrate on tasks that interest them while neglecting other important activities. Although GAD, OCD, and MDD can involve concentration issues, they do not typically present with the hyperfocus seen in ADHD. In GAD, individuals are more likely to experience pervasive worry. OCD involves intrusive thoughts and repetitive behaviors rather than intense focus on a single task. MDD is characterized by persistent sadness and lack of interest in activities rather than hyperfocus. Thus, ADHD is the most appropriate diagnosis for hyperfocus. Comparative.

Question 14: Correct Answer: B) The Wechsler Intelligence Scale for Children (WISC-V)

Rationale: The Wechsler Intelligence Scale for Children (WISC-V) is the most appropriate assessment tool for evaluating John's intellectual abilities. It is specifically designed to measure various aspects of intelligence in children, including problem-solving skills and abstract reasoning. The Beck Depression Inventory (A) assesses depressive symptoms, Conners' Rating Scales (C) are used primarily for ADHD and behavioral assessments, and the Vineland Adaptive Behavior Scales (D) measure adaptive behaviors but do not provide a comprehensive assessment of intellectual functioning like the WISC-V does.

Question 15: Correct Answer: B) Providing unconditional positive regard during sessions.

Rationale: The correct answer is B because Person-Centered Therapy (PCT), developed by Carl Rogers, emphasizes providing unconditional positive regard, empathy, and genuineness as core conditions for therapeutic change. Establishing clear behavioral goals (A), while useful in other therapeutic approaches like CBT or behavior therapy, is not central to PCT's non-directive nature. Assigning homework tasks (C) can be helpful but does not align with PCT's emphasis on the client's self-directed growth. Regular assessments (D) are important for monitoring progress but do not constitute an initial intervention aligned with PCT principles.

Question 16: Correct Answer: C) Including relevant treatment goals and progress notes in shared documentation.

Rationale: Including relevant treatment goals and progress notes in shared documentation ensures that all providers are informed about the client's progress and current objectives, facilitating coordinated care. Option A is incorrect because while detailed documentation is important, not every interaction needs exhaustive detail. Option B is incorrect as sharing only the diagnosis may omit critical context necessary for effective collaboration. Option D is incorrect due to potential confidentiality breaches; not all information may be pertinent or appropriate for all providers. Thus, option C balances comprehensive care with ethical considerations effectively.

Question 17: Correct Answer: B) Incorporating the client's cultural beliefs and practices into the treatment plan.

Rationale: Incorporating the client's cultural beliefs and practices into the treatment plan (Option B) best demonstrates sensitivity to multicultural issues. This approach aligns with contemporary research on culturally responsive counseling, which emphasizes understanding and integrating clients' cultural contexts. Option A is incorrect because standardized tools may not account for cultural nuances. Option C is inappropriate as it imposes dominant norms rather than respecting diversity. Option D avoids essential discussions about culture, which can hinder effective counseling. Thus, Option B is correct as it respects and integrates the client's unique cultural background into therapy.

Question 18: Correct Answer: C) Stress-induced perceptual disturbances

Rationale: Stress-induced perceptual disturbances can occur during periods of high stress and do not necessarily indicate a chronic mental illness. Maria's symptoms are transient and context-specific. Brief psychotic disorder (A) involves more severe and disruptive symptoms. Hypnagogic/hypnopompic hallucinations (B) occur during transitions between wakefulness and sleep, which Maria does not describe. Early onset schizophrenia (D) would likely present with more pervasive symptoms over time.

Question 19: Correct Answer: C) Intensive outpatient program (IOP)

Rationale: An intensive outpatient program (IOP) is appropriate for Maria because it offers more structured support than standard outpatient therapy while allowing her to maintain her daily routine. Inpatient hospitalization (Option A) would be too disruptive and is usually reserved for severe cases requiring constant supervision. A partial hospitalization program (PHP; Option B) might also be too intensive since it typically requires attendance during most of the day. Standard outpatient therapy (Option D), which Maria has already tried, does not provide enough support for her current needs.

Question 20: Correct Answer: A) Group Therapy with other veterans

Rationale: Group Therapy with other veterans provides peer support and shared experiences that can significantly help in the reintegration process. Individual Psychotherapy offers personalized support but may lack the peer connection element. Vocational Rehabilitation Services are important for employment but do not address emotional isolation directly. Medication Management can help with symptoms but does not provide social support.

Question 21: Correct Answer: D) Giving John both verbal and written explanations of the counseling process, checking his understanding, and allowing him time to ask questions before signing.

Rationale: Option D is correct because it ensures that John receives information in multiple formats (verbal and written), checks his understanding through feedback, and allows time for questions, which are essential components of obtaining truly informed consent. Option A lacks verification of understanding. Option B does not provide written information which can be revisited later. Option C involves a third party explaining instead of the counselor directly ensuring John's understanding.

Question 22: Correct Answer: B) Facilitate a life review therapy session to help Maria find meaning in her experiences.

Rationale: Life review therapy is particularly effective for individuals facing terminal illnesses as it helps them reflect on their life experiences and find meaning, which can alleviate existential distress. While mindfulness meditation (A) can reduce stress, it may not directly address existential concerns. Support groups (C) provide social support but may not focus on individual meaning-making. CBT (D), although useful for challenging negative thoughts, is less focused on spiritual and existential issues compared to life review therapy.

Question 23: Correct Answer: B) Validate Sarah's feelings and ask how others in the group can support her.

Rationale: Validating Sarah's feelings and asking how others can support her encourages empathy and active participation from all group members. It fosters a supportive environment where members feel heard and valued. Option A might lead to competitive sharing rather than supportive interaction. Option C avoids addressing Sarah's needs and may discourage openness. Option D is close but lacks the direct encouragement for others to offer support.

Question 24: Correct Answer: B) Executive Function Training

Rationale: Executive Function Training is specifically designed to address issues related to planning, organizing, and remembering instructions, which are key components of executive functioning. Cognitive Behavioral Therapy (CBT) is effective for emotional and behavioral issues but not directly targeted at improving executive functions. Medication for

ADHD might help if Ethan had ADHD, but there's no indication of this diagnosis in the scenario. Psychoeducational Tutoring focuses on academic skills rather than underlying cognitive processes.

Question 25: Correct Answer: A) Encourage Maria to have an open and non-judgmental conversation with her son about his decision.

Rationale: Encouraging Maria to have an open and non-judgmental conversation with her son respects both parties' autonomy and promotes healthy communication. This approach aligns with client-centered therapy principles and cultural competence by acknowledging Maria's feelings while fostering understanding. Option B might reinforce Maria's distress without addressing the son's perspective. Option C could escalate conflict by imposing restrictions rather than fostering dialogue. Option D is beneficial but may not be immediately practical without first establishing effective communication between Maria and her son.

Question 26: Correct Answer: B) Loss of professional identity and purpose

Rationale: The primary psychological concern for many individuals approaching retirement is often the loss of professional identity and purpose (B). This stems from the significant role that work plays in shaping one's self-concept and providing a sense of accomplishment. While financial insecurity (A) is a valid concern, it is more of an economic issue than a psychological one. Increased health issues (C) are also significant but are more related to physical well-being rather than psychological concerns directly tied to retirement. Changes in daily routine (D) can lead to boredom, but this is often a secondary effect rather than a primary psychological concern. Hence, B is the most accurate answer as it directly addresses the core psychological impact of losing one's professional role.

Question 27: Correct Answer: A) Establishing SMART goals that are specific, measurable, achievable, relevant, and time-bound.

Rationale: Establishing SMART goals is crucial in creating an effective treatment plan as it provides clear direction and measurable outcomes. While identifying barriers (Option B), selecting evidence-based interventions (Option C), and incorporating cultural background (Option D) are important components of treatment planning, they are secondary to setting clear and actionable goals. SMART goals ensure that both the counselor and client have a shared understanding of the desired outcomes and how progress will be measured.

Question 28: Correct Answer: A) Encourage members to share personal experiences related to isolation.

Rationale: Encouraging members to share personal experiences related to isolation is an effective intervention because it fosters a sense of universality and cohesion within the group. This approach helps members realize they are not alone in their feelings, which can be therapeutic. Suggesting individual therapy (Option B) might be beneficial but does not leverage the group setting's unique dynamics. Shifting focus to positive aspects (Option C) may invalidate members' feelings and hinder deeper exploration of issues. Providing psychoeducation on social skills (Option D) can be helpful but may not address the immediate emotional needs expressed by the group.

Question 29: Correct Answer: B) Bipolar I Disorder

Rationale: Bipolar I Disorder is characterized by episodes of mania (intense energy, reduced need for sleep) alternating with episodes of major depression (persistent sadness, loss of interest). John's symptoms align with this pattern. Major Depressive Disorder (A) involves only depressive episodes without manic phases. Persistent Depressive Disorder (C) is chronic but less severe than major depression and lacks manic episodes. Cyclothymic Disorder (D), while involving mood swings, does not meet the criteria for full-blown manic or major depressive episodes.

Question 30: Correct Answer: C) Recommend Jane begin cognitive-behavioral therapy (CBT) to address her negative thought patterns.

Rationale: Cognitive-behavioral therapy (CBT) is an evidence-based approach that effectively addresses negative thought patterns and emotional distress associated with life changes such as divorce. While joining a support group (A), practicing mindfulness meditation (B), and engaging in physical exercise (D) can all be beneficial, CBT specifically targets the cognitive distortions and maladaptive behaviors that are often present in individuals experiencing post-divorce emotional distress. This makes CBT the most appropriate initial intervention for Jane's symptoms.

Question 31: Correct Answer: B) Inquire about Maria's daily routines and any recent changes in her life circumstances.

Rationale: Understanding Maria's daily routines and recent life changes provides context for her symptoms, helping to identify potential stressors or triggers for her anxiety. While conducting a mental status examination (A), delving into family history (C), and asking about physical health (D) are all important aspects of a comprehensive assessment, they are not as immediately relevant as understanding her current life situation. This approach helps build rapport and provides insight into factors contributing to her anxiety.

Question 32: Correct Answer: B) Parent-Child Interaction Therapy (PCIT)

Rationale: Parent-Child Interaction Therapy (PCIT) is particularly effective for addressing oppositional defiant behaviors in children by improving the quality of the parent-child relationship and changing interaction patterns. While Cognitive Behavioral Therapy (CBT) can be useful for various behavioral issues, it focuses more on altering thought patterns rather than the parent-child dynamic. Play Therapy can help children express emotions but may not directly address defiant behavior. Dialectical Behavior Therapy (DBT) is more suited for severe emotional dysregulation and borderline personality disorder rather than specific childhood behavioral problems like temper outbursts and defiance. - A) Cognitive Behavioral Therapy (CBT): Incorrect because CBT primarily focuses on changing negative thought patterns rather than directly modifying parent-child interactions, which are crucial in managing oppositional defiant behaviors. - B) Parent-Child Interaction Therapy (PCIT): Correct because PCIT directly targets the improvement of parent-child relationships and interaction patterns, which are fundamental in managing oppositional defiant behaviors. - C) Play Therapy: Incorrect because while it helps children express emotions, it does not specifically target the parent-child relationship or provide structured strategies to manage defiance. - D) Dialectical Behavior Therapy (DBT): Incorrect as DBT is designed for severe emotional dysregulation and borderline personality disorder, not typically used for childhood behavioral issues like temper outbursts and defiance.

Question 33: Correct Answer: B) Recommend cognitive-behavioral therapy for insomnia (CBT-I).

Rationale: Cognitive-behavioral therapy for insomnia (CBT-I) is considered the first-line treatment for chronic insomnia according to contemporary research and clinical guidelines. It addresses the underlying cognitive and behavioral factors contributing to insomnia. While prescribing benzodiazepines (Option A) can be effective short-term, they are not recommended due to potential dependency and side effects. Increasing physical exercise (Option C) can improve sleep quality but is not as effective as CBT-I in treating chronic insomnia. Melatonin supplements (Option D) may help with circadian rhythm disorders but are less effective than CBT-I for chronic insomnia.

Question 34: Correct Answer: B) Participating in DBT skills training modules.

Rationale: DBT skills training modules are specifically designed for individuals with BPD and focus on teaching emotion regulation, distress tolerance, interpersonal effectiveness, and mindfulness skills within a highly structured framework. Option A (free-form art therapy) lacks the structure necessary for DBT's targeted skill-building approach. Option C (non-directive play therapy) is less effective for adults with BPD compared to DBT. Option D (unstructured letters) does not provide the systematic skill development that DBT offers.

Question 35: Correct Answer: A) The potential for indirect identification through contextual clues.

Rationale: Even without revealing identities, contextual clues can lead to indirect identification, which breaches client confidentiality (Option A). While raising public awareness (Option B), showcasing outcomes (Option C), or clients feeling proud (Option D) are positive aspects, they do not outweigh the ethical priority of maintaining strict confidentiality. Ethical guidelines prioritize protecting client identity over other considerations.

Question 36: Correct Answer: C) Refer the client to a substance abuse specialist while continuing therapy.

Rationale: Option C is correct because concurrent treatment involving specialized care for substance abuse can address both disorders more effectively, as recommended by integrated treatment models. Option A is incorrect as merely increasing session frequency without addressing the dual diagnosis may not yield significant improvement. Option B, while beneficial, does not address the need for specialized substance abuse treatment. Option D can be supportive but lacks the structured intervention needed for dual diagnosis cases. Therefore, referring to a substance abuse specialist while continuing therapy ensures comprehensive care tailored to both conditions.

Question 37: Correct Answer: A) Establishing confidentiality guidelines

Rationale: Establishing confidentiality guidelines is paramount in ensuring ethical practice within a therapy group. Confidentiality fosters trust among group members, which is essential for effective group dynamics and therapeutic progress. While setting clear attendance requirements (Option B), defining roles and responsibilities (Option C), and outlining procedures for addressing conflicts (Option D) are also important aspects of group rules, they do not hold the same ethical weight as confidentiality. Confidentiality directly impacts members' willingness to share personal information, thus influencing the overall success of the group. - Option A (Correct): Confidentiality guidelines are crucial because they ensure that members feel safe sharing sensitive information, which is foundational for trust and effective therapy. - Option B (Incorrect): Attendance requirements are important for consistency but do not address the ethical necessity of protecting members' private information. - Option C (Incorrect): Defining roles helps clarify expectations but does not directly impact the ethical considerations related to personal disclosures. - Option D (Incorrect): Conflict resolution procedures are vital for managing group dynamics but do not prioritize the ethical obligation of maintaining confidentiality. By comparing these options, it becomes evident that while all are relevant to establishing effective group rules, confidentiality stands out as the most critical from an ethical perspective.

Question 38: Correct Answer: A) Previous suicide attempt

Rationale: A previous suicide attempt is widely recognized as the most significant risk factor for future suicide attempts. Research consistently shows that individuals who have attempted suicide once are at a much higher risk of attempting again. While family history of suicide (Option B), diagnosis of major depressive disorder (Option C), and substance abuse (Option D) are also important risk factors, they do not predict future attempts as strongly as a prior attempt does. Family history and depression contribute significantly but lack the predictive strength of a prior attempt. Substance abuse increases risk but is less directly predictive compared to a previous attempt.

Question 39: Correct Answer: B) Encouraging active participation and discussion among group members.

Rationale: Encouraging active participation and discussion

among group members is crucial for effective psychoeducation in a group therapy setting. This approach fosters engagement, allows for shared experiences, and helps members apply the information to their own lives. While delivering factual information (Option A) and using evidence-based materials (Option D) are important, they are not sufficient on their own without interactive engagement. Limiting sessions to a strict lecture format (Option C) can hinder member involvement and reduce the effectiveness of the psychoeducational process. Comparison: - Option A focuses solely on factual information delivery, which is necessary but not sufficient for engagement. - Option C suggests a rigid lecture format that limits interaction, which is less effective than interactive discussions. - Option D emphasizes evidence-based materials but lacks the interactive component crucial for effective learning. - Option B combines accurate information with active engagement, making it the most comprehensive approach for effective psychoeducation in groups.

Question 40: Correct Answer: B) Maria's understanding of the treatment plan and its consequences.

Rationale: Evaluating Maria's understanding of the treatment plan and its consequences is paramount when assessing her competency for informed consent. This ensures she comprehends what the treatment involves and its potential impacts on her health. While recalling past medical information (A), emotional response (C), and trust in her provider (D) are relevant factors, they do not directly measure her capacity to make an informed decision about her current treatment plan.

Question 41: Correct Answer: B) Integrative Behavioral Couple Therapy (IBCT)

Rationale: Integrative Behavioral Couple Therapy (IBCT) is particularly effective in addressing issues of trust and forgiveness in relationships by combining behavioral strategies with emotional acceptance techniques. Narrative Therapy can help reframe personal stories but may not provide the structured approach needed for rebuilding trust. Psychodynamic Therapy delves into unconscious processes but may not be as focused on actionable strategies for couples. Mindfulness-Based Cognitive Therapy (MBCT), while useful for individual emotional regulation, does not specifically target couple dynamics and trust rebuilding.

Question 42: Correct Answer: C) Discuss the invitation with Sarah during their next session.

Rationale: Discussing the invitation with Sarah (Option C) allows Maria to explore any underlying reasons for the invitation and address potential boundary issues within the therapeutic context. Accepting the invitation (Option A) could lead to boundary violations and dual relationships. Declining but sending a card (Option B) still blurs professional boundaries. Terminating the relationship just to attend (Option D) is inappropriate and unethical as it prioritizes personal interests over professional duties.

Question 43: Correct Answer: C) Address the monopolizing behavior privately with the member.

Rationale: The most effective intervention is to address the monopolizing behavior privately with the member. This approach allows for a respectful and non-confrontational discussion about how their behavior impacts the group, fostering self-awareness without causing embarrassment. Option A (direct confrontation) can lead to defensiveness and disrupt group cohesion. Option B (encouraging others) may not address the root cause of the behavior. Option D (structured activities) can help but does not specifically target or modify the monopolizing behavior directly. Therefore, private discussion is both respectful and effective, aligning with best practices in counseling interventions.

Question 44: Correct Answer: B) Suggest family therapy sessions to improve communication among all family members.

Rationale: Family therapy is the most comprehensive intervention as it addresses the communication issues among all family members, fostering an environment where everyone's feelings and perspectives are considered. While A) encourages direct communication, it may not be effective without proper guidance. C) focuses on strengthening the mother-daughter bond but does not address the overall family dynamics. D) provides external support but does not resolve internal family issues.

Question 45: Correct Answer: A) Cognitive Behavioral Therapy (CBT)
Rationale: CBT is the most effective treatment for Obsessive-Compulsive Disorder (OCD), focusing on identifying and challenging irrational thoughts and changing maladaptive behaviors. Psychoanalytic Therapy (B) delves into unconscious processes but lacks empirical support for OCD. Humanistic Therapy (C) emphasizes self-actualization and personal growth rather than specific symptom relief. DBT (D), while effective for borderline personality disorder, is not the first-line treatment for OCD.

Question 46: Correct Answer: C) Focusing on the client's personal goals and how they align with the treatment plan.
Rationale: The most effective strategy for educating a client about the value of treatment plan compliance is to focus on their personal goals and demonstrate how these align with the treatment plan (Option C). This approach leverages intrinsic motivation, making compliance more meaningful to the client. Highlighting immediate benefits (Option A) can be helpful but may not sustain long-term adherence. Emphasizing long-term outcomes and risks (Option B) can sometimes be too abstract or fear-inducing, potentially leading to resistance. Discussing statistical success rates (Option D), while informative, may not resonate personally with the client. Therefore, aligning treatment plans with personal goals is key to fostering sustained compliance.

Question 47: Correct Answer: A) Respect Jane's autonomy and support her decision to discontinue aggressive treatment.
Rationale: Respecting patient autonomy is a fundamental principle in end-of-life care. While it is important to consider the family's perspective (Option C), ultimately the patient's wishes should take precedence (Option A). Encouraging Jane to reconsider (Option B) or prioritizing the family's wishes (Option D) undermines her autonomy and can lead to unnecessary distress.

Question 48: Correct Answer: B) Emotionally Focused Therapy (EFT) targeting attachment bonds.
Rationale: Emotionally Focused Therapy (EFT) is particularly effective for addressing issues related to attachment bonds formed in John's critical upbringing, helping him understand how these early experiences impact his current relational patterns. Narrative Therapy (Option A), while useful for reconstructing personal stories, does not specifically target attachment bonds. Behavioral Activation (Option C), focuses on increasing engagement in positive activities but doesn't delve deeply into relational patterns stemming from the family of origin. Gestalt Therapy (Option D), emphasizes present moment awareness but may not provide the specific focus on attachment necessary for addressing John's relational difficulties.

Question 49: Correct Answer: A) Encourage John to participate in volunteer work related to his interests.
Rationale: Encouraging John to participate in volunteer work related to his interests helps him engage in meaningful activities that can reduce anxiety while fostering new social connections. This strategy combines purpose with community involvement, which is beneficial for mental health. While scheduling regular meetups (B) and seeking mentorship (C) are valuable, they might not provide the same level of broad social engagement and fulfillment as volunteering. Joining an online forum (D) offers peer support but lacks the face-to-face interaction that can be more impactful in building robust support systems.

Question 50: Correct Answer: C) Develop an integrated treatment plan that includes CBT, mindfulness practices, and participation in a chronic illness support group.
Rationale: An integrated treatment plan combining CBT, mindfulness practices, and support group participation addresses multiple facets of Maria's experience cognitive, emotional, and social providing comprehensive support. This approach is supported by research highlighting multi-modal interventions' effectiveness in managing chronic illness. Option A focuses too narrowly on cognitive aspects. Option B can be helpful but lacks therapeutic depth. Option D may lead to increased isolation and reduced quality of life without addressing psychological needs.

Question 51: Correct Answer: A) Encourage the client to explore their spiritual beliefs and practices.
Rationale: Encouraging the client to explore their spiritual beliefs and practices directly addresses their existential concerns by helping them find meaning and purpose in life, which is crucial for coping with loss. While cognitive-behavioral techniques (Option B) can be helpful for managing negative thoughts, they do not specifically address spiritual or existential concerns. Joining a support group (Option C) may provide social support but does not necessarily help with existential questioning. Focusing on physical activities (Option D) might offer temporary distraction but does not facilitate deeper exploration of meaning and purpose. Therefore, Option A is the most appropriate intervention for addressing spiritual/existential concerns.

Question 52: Correct Answer: C) Major Depressive Disorder
Rationale: Major Depressive Disorder (MDD) can cause significant changes in weight (gain or loss), excessive sleeping (hypersomnia), and persistent fatigue despite adequate sleep. Hypothyroidism also leads to weight gain and fatigue but is an endocrine disorder rather than a mental health condition. Bipolar Disorder includes periods of mania or hypomania not described here. Sleep Apnea causes disrupted sleep leading to daytime fatigue but does not typically result in significant weight gain without other contributing factors.

Question 53: Correct Answer: A) Cognitive Behavioral Therapy (CBT)
Rationale: Cognitive Behavioral Therapy (CBT) is the most effective intervention for John because it specifically targets negative thought patterns and behaviors that contribute to feelings of worthlessness and depression. CBT helps clients develop coping strategies and cognitive restructuring techniques that are crucial for adjusting to significant life changes like becoming paraplegic. - Option B) Solution-Focused Brief Therapy (SFBT): While SFBT is useful for setting goals and finding solutions, it may not address the deep-seated negative beliefs contributing to John's depression as effectively as CBT. - Option C) Motivational Interviewing (MI): MI is excellent for enhancing motivation but does not directly tackle the cognitive distortions that are central to John's issues. - Option D) Psychoeducation about Disability: This can provide valuable information but lacks the therapeutic techniques necessary for altering John's negative self-perceptions.

Question 54: Correct Answer: B) Major Depressive Disorder (MDD)
Rationale: Major Depressive Disorder (MDD) is characterized by persistent sadness, loss of interest in activities, and other symptoms such as sleep disturbances and feelings of worthlessness that last for at least two weeks. In contrast, Generalized Anxiety Disorder (GAD) primarily involves excessive anxiety and worry rather than depressive symptoms. Persistent Depressive Disorder (PDD), also known as dysthymia, involves chronic depression but typically with less severe symptoms than MDD and lasting for at least two years. Adjustment Disorder with Depressed Mood is a reaction to a specific stressor within three months of its occurrence. John's symptoms align more closely with MDD due to their severity and duration.

Question 55: Correct Answer: B) Validate John's feelings and explore the triggers that led to his relapse.

Rationale: Validating John's feelings and exploring the triggers of his relapse is crucial as it addresses both his emotional state and the underlying causes of the relapse. This approach aligns with contemporary therapeutic practices emphasizing empathy and understanding in addiction counseling. Encouraging AA meetings (Option A) or suggesting inpatient rehab (Option C) may be helpful but are secondary steps after addressing immediate emotional needs. Increasing medication dosage (Option D) is inappropriate without a medical evaluation.

Question 56: Correct Answer: B) Help Maria identify and challenge her negative self-beliefs.

Rationale: Helping Maria identify and challenge her negative self-beliefs addresses the root of her emotional distress by fostering self-awareness and promoting healthier thought patterns. This foundational step can empower her to make informed decisions about her situation. Option A is premature without addressing her emotional readiness. Option C is beneficial but secondary to addressing immediate emotional needs. Option D may be necessary later but doesn't address her current emotional state.

Question 57: Correct Answer: B) Using a combination of clinical interviews and standardized assessment tools.

Rationale: The most effective approach to accurately assess a client's level of distress is to use a combination of clinical interviews and standardized assessment tools. This method allows for a comprehensive understanding by integrating subjective self-reports with objective measures. Option A is incorrect because relying solely on self-reported symptoms may not provide a complete picture. Option C is also inadequate as non-verbal cues alone can be misleading without context. Option D can provide valuable information but should not be the sole method used. Combining multiple sources of information ensures a more accurate and holistic assessment.

Question 58: Correct Answer: A) Assuring confidentiality

Rationale: Assuring confidentiality helps build trust and encourages clients like John to be more open and honest in their self-reports. Leading questions (Option B) can introduce bias and compromise data accuracy. Involving family members (Option C), while potentially useful, might make John uncomfortable and less likely to disclose sensitive information. Administering a brief screening tool (Option D) can be helpful but does not address John's hesitancy directly as effectively as assuring confidentiality does.

Question 59: Correct Answer: C) Addressing immediate withdrawal symptoms.

Rationale: Addressing immediate withdrawal symptoms is critical in the initial phase of treating substance use disorder as it ensures John's safety and stabilizes his physical condition. While developing relapse prevention strategies (Option A), fostering a strong therapeutic alliance (Option B), and setting long-term sobriety goals (Option D) are essential for ongoing recovery, they cannot be effectively implemented until John's immediate physical needs are met. Stabilization lays the groundwork for subsequent therapeutic interventions.

Question 60: Correct Answer: B) Empathy

Rationale: Motivational Interviewing (MI) is a client-centered, directive method for enhancing intrinsic motivation to change by exploring and resolving ambivalence. Empathy, or accurate empathy, is a core principle of MI, as it involves understanding the client's perspective and communicating that understanding back to them. Option A (Confrontation) is incorrect because MI avoids confrontational approaches, which can increase client resistance. Option C (Direct advice) is not central to MI; instead, MI emphasizes eliciting clients' own motivations for change rather than imposing advice. Option D (Authoritative guidance) contradicts the collaborative nature of MI, which avoids an authoritative stance in favor of partnership and autonomy support.

Question 61: Correct Answer: C) Prolonged Exposure Therapy (PE)

Rationale: Prolonged Exposure Therapy (PE) is considered one of the most effective treatments for PTSD in veterans. It involves repeated, detailed imagining or recounting of the traumatic experience to reduce its emotional impact. While Cognitive Behavioral Therapy (CBT) and Eye Movement Desensitization and Reprocessing (EMDR) are also effective, PE has shown superior results in numerous studies focusing specifically on veterans. Dialectical Behavior Therapy (DBT), although useful for emotion regulation, is not primarily focused on trauma processing. Therefore, PE stands out as the most targeted and effective approach for this population.

Question 62: Correct Answer: C) Offer electronic versions of the materials that are compatible with screen readers.

Rationale: Providing electronic versions of the materials that are compatible with screen readers is a comprehensive solution that empowers John to access the information independently using assistive technology. Option A (large print versions) may not be sufficient for all visual impairments. Option B (reading aloud) can be helpful but may not be practical or empowering in the long term. Option D (referral to a specialist) may be useful but does not directly address the immediate need for accessible materials in counseling sessions.

Question 63: Correct Answer: B) Discuss Sarah's punctuality issues directly with her during their next supervision session.

Rationale: The best initial step is for John to address Sarah's punctuality issues directly (Option B). This approach maintains open communication and allows for exploration of underlying issues while providing an opportunity for corrective action. Option A is premature and could escalate the situation unnecessarily without giving Sarah a chance to explain or improve. Option C avoids addressing the problem head-on, which may lead to continued tardiness. Option D might help reduce stress but does not teach Sarah responsibility or address time management skills effectively.

Question 64: Correct Answer: B) Discussing the assessment results with the client and collaboratively developing a treatment plan that aligns with their goals.

Rationale: Option B is correct because it emphasizes a collaborative approach, where clients are actively involved in interpreting their assessment results and developing a treatment plan that reflects their personal goals. This method fosters client engagement, empowerment, and ownership of their treatment process, which are crucial for successful outcomes. Option A is incorrect because merely presenting results and suggesting a plan does not ensure active client participation or ownership. Option C is also incorrect as it involves interpretation by the counselor without sufficient collaboration, potentially limiting true client engagement. Option D is incorrect because reviewing results privately undermines transparency and excludes clients from essential decision-making processes, reducing their sense of control over their treatment. By comparing these options, we see that option B aligns best with contemporary research emphasizing collaborative practices in mental health counseling.

Question 65: Correct Answer: B) Validate Jamal's experiences and explore the impact of microaggressions on his mental health.

Rationale: Validating Jamal's experiences acknowledges the reality of his situation and its impact on his mental health, which is crucial for establishing trust and effectively addressing his concerns. Encouraging confrontation (A) may not be safe or effective without first understanding the dynamics involved. Suggesting a job change (C) might overlook systemic issues and could be impractical. Focusing solely on resilience (D) ignores the specific nature of racial microaggressions and their psychological effects.

Question 66: Correct Answer: C) Eye Movement Desensitization and Reprocessing (EMDR)

Rationale: EMDR is specifically designed to address trauma-related symptoms by helping individuals process distressing memories through guided eye movements. Cognitive Behavioral Therapy (CBT) (A) can also be effective but does not specifically target traumatic memories in the same way EMDR does. Dialectical Behavior Therapy (DBT) (B) is primarily used for borderline personality disorder and emotional regulation issues rather than trauma-specific symptoms. Psychodynamic Therapy (D), while useful for exploring underlying psychological conflicts, is less focused on directly processing traumatic memories compared to EMDR.

Question 67: Correct Answer: D) Your personal biases and how they may impact your work with the client.
Rationale: Evaluating personal biases is critical as it directly affects objectivity and effectiveness in therapy. While familiarity with the client's cultural background (Option A), alignment of theoretical orientation (Option B), and ability to maintain professional boundaries (Option C) are important, they are secondary to recognizing and addressing personal biases. Biases can unconsciously influence perceptions and interactions, potentially harming the therapeutic relationship. Understanding and mitigating these biases ensures that other competencies can be effectively applied. Options A, B, and C are essential but hinge on the counselor's self-awareness of their biases, making Option D the most critical initial assessment.

Question 68: Correct Answer: B) Reflect on his own potential biases and how they might affect the counseling process.
Rationale: Reflecting on personal biases is essential for providing unbiased and effective counseling. Reviewing ethical guidelines (Option A) is important but does not address personal introspection. Assuming previous experience is sufficient (Option C) can lead to overconfidence. Pursuing continuing education (Option D) is beneficial but does not immediately address current biases that could impact the therapeutic relationship with Ahmed.

Question 69: Correct Answer: A) Reflective listening
Rationale: Reflective listening is a core component of Carl Rogers' Person-Centered Therapy. This intervention involves the counselor actively listening to the client and reflecting back what they hear, which helps the client feel understood and encourages them to explore their emotions further. Cognitive restructuring (B) is a technique used in Cognitive Behavioral Therapy (CBT), not Person-Centered Therapy. Systematic desensitization (C) is an intervention used in behavior therapy for phobias, not typically for expressing emotions in Person-Centered Therapy. Solution-focused questioning (D) is part of Solution-Focused Brief Therapy, which aims at finding solutions rather than exploring emotions. Each option explained: A) Reflective listening: Correct because it aligns with Person-Centered Therapy principles by fostering a non-directive, empathetic environment where clients can express their feelings. B) Cognitive restructuring: Incorrect because it belongs to CBT, focusing on changing thought patterns rather than facilitating emotional expression through empathy. C) Systematic desensitization: Incorrect as it is used primarily for reducing phobic reactions through gradual exposure, not relevant to emotional articulation in this context. D) Solution-focused questioning: Incorrect since it focuses on finding practical solutions rather than exploring and articulating emotions deeply, which is central to Person-Centered Therapy.

Question 70: Correct Answer: B) Discuss the issue directly with the colleague and suggest updating their assessment tools.
Rationale: The correct answer is B because it encourages direct communication and collaboration between colleagues while addressing ethical concerns (ACA Code of Ethics). Reporting immediately (Option A) might be premature without first attempting resolution through direct dialogue. Ignoring the situation (Option C) neglects John's

responsibility to uphold professional standards. Informing a supervisor (Option D), while potentially useful, bypasses an opportunity for direct resolution and may escalate the situation unnecessarily if it can be resolved collegially.

Question 71: Correct Answer: A) Encouraging John to join a support group for individuals with similar experiences.
Rationale: Joining a support group provides social support and shared experiences, which are crucial for emotional adjustment according to resilience theory. Option B can exacerbate feelings of isolation and depression. Option C ignores the holistic nature of recovery that includes both physical and emotional aspects. Option D discourages open communication, which is vital for processing emotions effectively.

Question 72: Correct Answer: B) Decline Sarah's request and explain the importance of maintaining professional boundaries.
Rationale: The correct answer is B because it aligns with ethical guidelines that emphasize maintaining professional boundaries to avoid dual relationships that could impair objectivity and effectiveness (ACA Code of Ethics). Option A might seem reasonable but setting boundaries on social media can be complex and difficult to enforce. Option C similarly underestimates the potential for boundary issues even with non-clinical interactions. Option D fails to provide the client with an understanding of why maintaining boundaries is important, which is essential for upholding ethical standards.

Question 73: Correct Answer: B) Cognitive-behavioral therapy (CBT) focused on performance anxiety
Rationale: Cognitive-behavioral therapy (CBT) focused on performance anxiety is the most appropriate intervention given the client's reported anxiety about sexual performance, which is likely contributing to his erectile dysfunction. While PDE5 inhibitors (Option A) can be effective for ED, they do not address the underlying psychological factors. Referral to a urologist (Option C) is useful if there are suspected physiological issues, but the primary concern here appears to be psychological. Lifestyle changes (Option D) can improve overall health and potentially alleviate ED symptoms but are not directly targeting the client's immediate concern of performance anxiety. Therefore, CBT is the most comprehensive approach in this context.

Question 74: Correct Answer: B) Bipolar II Disorder and Generalized Anxiety Disorder
Rationale: The correct answer is B) Bipolar II Disorder and Generalized Anxiety Disorder. This patient's symptoms of persistent sadness and low energy are indicative of depressive episodes, while periods of elevated mood and increased energy suggest hypomanic episodes characteristic of Bipolar II Disorder. Additionally, his difficulty concentrating and frequent headaches can be associated with Generalized Anxiety Disorder (GAD), which often co-occurs with mood disorders. Option A) Major Depressive Disorder and Generalized Anxiety Disorder is incorrect because it does not account for the hypomanic episodes. Option C) Major Depressive Disorder and Persistent Depressive Disorder is incorrect as it fails to consider the elevated mood periods. Option D) Bipolar II Disorder and Cyclothymic Disorder is incorrect because Cyclothymic Disorder involves less severe mood swings than those described. The key difference lies in recognizing hypomanic episodes alongside depressive symptoms, which points towards Bipolar II rather than unipolar depression or Cyclothymic disorder.

Question 75: Correct Answer: D) Cultural identity of the individual
Rationale: The correct answer is D) Cultural identity of the individual. This aspect focuses on understanding how Maria identifies with her cultural background and how this affects her mental health. While options A), B), and C) are also important components of the CFI, they do not directly address Maria's sense of disconnection from her cultural roots as specifically as option D). Understanding her cultural

identity will provide insights into her feelings of disconnection and inform appropriate interventions.

Question 76: Correct Answer: B) Discuss with Maria why punctuality is important for her therapy and collaboratively explore solutions.

Rationale: Constructive confrontation should be done in a way that fosters understanding and collaboration. Option B is correct as it involves explaining the importance of punctuality while also working together with Maria to find solutions, which respects her autonomy and promotes engagement. Option A may come across as judgmental and could damage rapport. Option C does not address the underlying issue of tardiness constructively. Option D is punitive rather than constructive, likely leading to further resistance or disengagement from therapy.

Question 77: Correct Answer: B) Anxious-Preoccupied Attachment

Rationale: Anxious-preoccupied attachment is characterized by a high need for approval and fear of abandonment, leading to feelings of loneliness even when surrounded by people. Individuals with this attachment style often perceive their relationships as unsatisfying due to their constant worry about being rejected or not valued enough. - Option A (Secure Attachment): Incorrect because individuals with secure attachment generally have fulfilling and stable relationships. - Option C (Dismissive-Avoidant Attachment): Incorrect because while dismissive-avoidant individuals may feel lonely, they often detach emotionally from others rather than seeking deeper connections. - Option D (Fearful-Avoidant Attachment): Incorrect because although fearful-avoidant individuals experience anxiety in relationships, their primary issue is the fear of intimacy combined with a desire for closeness, which doesn't align perfectly with Sarah's described superficial relationships.

Question 78: Correct Answer: B) Bulimia Nervosa

Rationale: Bulimia Nervosa is characterized by recurrent episodes of binge eating followed by compensatory behaviors such as self-induced vomiting. While Anorexia Nervosa involves restrictive eating and fear of gaining weight, it does not typically include binge-eating episodes followed by purging. Binge-Eating Disorder involves binge eating without compensatory behaviors. Avoidant/Restrictive Food Intake Disorder lacks the focus on body weight or shape seen in Bulimia Nervosa.

Question 79: Correct Answer: C) Ensuring Maria's immediate safety by reporting the abuse to child protective services.

Rationale: The counselor's primary concern must be ensuring Maria's immediate safety by reporting the abuse to child protective services, as mandated reporters have a legal obligation to report suspected abuse (Option C). Keeping her disclosure confidential (Option A) could put her at further risk. Encouraging her to talk to her mother (Option B) may not be safe if her mother is unaware or unable/unwilling to protect her. Family therapy (Option D), while potentially helpful in addressing underlying issues, does not provide immediate protection from harm.

Question 80: Correct Answer: A) Encourage the client to engage in life review therapy.

Rationale: Life review therapy is particularly effective for clients facing end-of-life issues as it helps them find meaning and closure by reflecting on their past experiences. This intervention can alleviate feelings of hopelessness by allowing clients to process their life achievements and unresolved conflicts. Option B, creating a legacy project, while beneficial, may not directly address immediate feelings of despair as effectively as life review therapy. Option C, CBT, is useful for challenging negative thoughts but may not provide the same depth of existential reflection needed at end-of-life stages. Option D, increasing social support, is important but does not specifically target the internal emotional processing that life review therapy offers. Each option has its merits but engaging in life review therapy

directly aligns with addressing profound emotional needs at the end-of-life stage by promoting introspection and resolution.

Question 81: Correct Answer: B) Seek supervision or consultation while continuing to work with Sarah.

Rationale: Seeking supervision or consultation allows you to provide immediate support while ensuring that you are guided by more experienced professionals. This approach balances ethical responsibility and professional development. Option A might be too abrupt without assessing immediate needs; Option C risks client safety due to inexperience; Option D could delay necessary support and may not be sufficient alone.

Question 82: Correct Answer: A) Refer John to a cardiologist specializing in stress-related heart conditions.

Rationale: The correct answer is A because John's cardiovascular issues are directly related to his anxiety, necessitating specialized medical attention from a cardiologist who understands stress-related heart conditions. Option B (nutritionist) may help indirectly but does not address the immediate cardiovascular concerns linked with anxiety. Option C (exercise physiologist) could benefit his overall health but lacks specificity in treating both GAD and cardiovascular issues concurrently. Option D (biofeedback therapist) focuses on anxiety reduction techniques but does not address the cardiovascular aspect comprehensively.

Question 83: Correct Answer: A) Encourage the client to engage in open and honest communication with their partner about their feelings.

Rationale: According to attachment theory, effective communication is essential for addressing insecurities and fostering a secure attachment in relationships. Encouraging open and honest dialogue helps partners understand each other's needs and reduces anxiety stemming from perceived neglect or abandonment (Johnson & Greenman, 2013). Option B, focusing on self-care, while beneficial for individual well-being, does not directly address the relational issue. Option C, couples therapy, is a good intervention but may not be immediately necessary without first attempting direct communication. Option D, giving more space, could exacerbate feelings of neglect rather than resolving them.

Question 84: Correct Answer: C) Providing consistent and constructive feedback

Rationale: Providing consistent and constructive feedback is most effective in enhancing leader-member exchange (LMX) quality because it fosters trust, clarifies expectations, and promotes professional growth. While implementing regular team-building activities (Option A) can improve overall team cohesion, it does not directly address the individual relationships between leaders and members. Establishing clear communication channels (Option B) is important but insufficient alone without ongoing feedback. Setting rigid hierarchical structures (Option D) often hinders open communication and trust, which are vital for high-quality LMX. Therefore, providing feedback consistently aligns with contemporary research emphasizing its importance in improving leader-member dynamics.

Question 85: Correct Answer: B) Setting a goal for the client to "reduce depressive symptoms by 50%" over three months.

Rationale: Option B is correct because it provides a specific, measurable, achievable, relevant, and time-bound (SMART) goal that directly addresses the client's diagnosis of major depressive disorder. Reducing depressive symptoms by 50% is quantifiable and can be tracked over time, making it an effective long-term objective. Option A is incorrect because "feeling happier" is vague and lacks specificity and measurability. It does not provide clear criteria for success or a concrete plan. Option C is incorrect because while increasing social interactions is relevant, it lacks a specific time frame and measurable criteria, making it difficult to assess progress. Option D is incorrect because although engaging in physical activity is beneficial and has a specific time frame, it may not directly address the primary symptoms of major depressive disorder as effectively as reducing depressive symptoms would. Additionally, it might be more suitable as part of a broader treatment plan rather than a primary long-term goal. By comparing these options, we see that option B stands out due to its adherence to SMART criteria and direct relevance to managing major depressive disorder.

Question 86: Correct Answer: C) "Can you describe any recent significant life changes?"

Rationale: Identifying recent significant life changes helps uncover psychosocial stressors that may contribute to John's substance use. These changes could include job loss, relationship issues, or other stress-inducing events. Family history (A), weekend activities (B), and previous treatment attempts (D) are relevant but less directly related to identifying current psychosocial stressors.

Question 87: Correct Answer: B) Modify the suggestion by setting a rule that members can leave but must inform the group beforehand.

Rationale: Dr. Smith's response should balance respecting individual autonomy with maintaining group cohesion and therapeutic integrity. Option B is correct because it allows for flexibility while ensuring that departures are communicated, which helps manage group dynamics effectively. Options A and D fail to address potential disruptions caused by unannounced exits, while Option C may feel too rigid and could discourage participation from those who might need occasional breaks.

Question 88: Correct Answer: B) The severity and frequency of suicidal thoughts

Rationale: The severity and frequency of suicidal thoughts are paramount when determining the appropriate level of inpatient care for a patient with severe depression. This factor directly impacts the immediate risk to the patient's safety and necessitates intensive monitoring and intervention that inpatient care provides. While A), C), and D) are important considerations in treatment planning, they do not carry as much weight in deciding the need for inpatient care as the immediate risk posed by frequent and severe suicidal ideation. Ensuring patient safety is the primary concern, making B) the most critical factor. - Option A (The patient's current living situation and support system): While crucial for overall treatment planning, it is secondary to assessing immediate risk factors like suicidal ideation. - Option C (The patient's history of medication compliance): Important for long-term management but less critical than assessing immediate suicide risk. - Option D (The availability of outpatient resources): Relevant for continuity of care but does not address immediate safety concerns as directly as Option B.

Question 89: Correct Answer: C) Conducting individual check-ins with each member before sessions.

Rationale: Conducting individual check-ins helps build rapport and trust between the group leader and each participant, making them feel valued and understood. This personalized attention can foster a stronger connection and encourage more open interactions during group sessions. Option A might blur professional boundaries. Option B is important but does not directly foster individual connections. Option D can help build connections among participants but may not specifically enhance interactions with the group leader.

Question 90: Correct Answer: D) Existential Therapy

Rationale: Existential Therapy is most effective for addressing issues related to meaning, purpose, and identity, which are central to John's feelings of purposelessness post-retirement. While CBT (Option A) can address depressive symptoms by changing thought patterns, it may not delve deeply into existential concerns. SFBT (Option B) focuses on finding immediate solutions rather than exploring deeper issues of meaning. IPT (Option C) is useful for improving interpersonal relationships but may not address John's

existential crisis as effectively as Existential Therapy.

Question 91: Correct Answer: B) Conduct a detailed clinical interview focusing on her anxiety triggers and coping mechanisms.

Rationale: A detailed clinical interview is essential for understanding Maria's specific anxiety triggers and coping mechanisms before deciding on further interventions or treatments. While referring her for CBT (Option A) is beneficial long-term, it is not an initial assessment step. Suggesting relaxation exercises (Option C) addresses symptom management but not the underlying causes or severity of distress. Administering an anxiety-specific questionnaire (Option D) helps measure severity but does not provide comprehensive insight into her experiences or coping strategies.

Question 92: Correct Answer: C) Discuss specific scenarios where confidentiality might be breached and obtain James's acknowledgment.

Rationale: Discussing specific scenarios where confidentiality might be breached ensures that James fully understands the limits of confidentiality. This approach aligns with ethical standards requiring counselors to inform clients about potential exceptions to confidentiality. Option A is misleading as it implies absolute confidentiality. Option B lacks specificity about breaches. Option D involves signing an agreement but misses verbal discussion and acknowledgment.

Question 93: Correct Answer: D) All-or-nothing thinking

Rationale: Beck's Cognitive Theory of Depression suggests that cognitive distortions contribute to depressive symptoms. "All-or-nothing thinking" (also known as black-and-white thinking) involves viewing situations in binary terms, such as seeing oneself as a complete failure if one small aspect goes wrong. This type of thinking can significantly contribute to feelings of hopelessness and depression. While overgeneralization (A), catastrophizing (B), and personalization (C) are also cognitive distortions associated with depression, they do not specifically address the binary nature of John's thought patterns contributing to his hopelessness as accurately as all-or-nothing thinking does.

Question 94: Correct Answer: B) The counselor's verbal and non-verbal behaviors align with their true feelings.

Rationale: Genuineness in a therapeutic relationship refers to the counselor being authentic and congruent, meaning their verbal and non-verbal behaviors match their true feelings and thoughts (Option B). This is crucial for building trust and facilitating open communication. While empathy (Option A), unconditional positive regard (Option C), and active listening (Option D) are essential counseling skills, they do not specifically capture the essence of genuineness. Empathy involves understanding and sharing another person's experiences; unconditional positive regard refers to accepting clients without judgment; active listening focuses on understanding clients' messages. Only Option B directly addresses the alignment of internal states with outward behaviors, which defines genuineness.

Question 95: Correct Answer: B) Family therapy involving all members

Rationale: Family therapy involving all members is considered most effective because it addresses the systemic nature of abuse, helping to identify and alter dysfunctional family dynamics that contribute to the abuse. Individual therapy (Option A) focuses solely on the survivor, potentially neglecting broader family issues. Couples therapy (Option C) may not address the needs of other family members or the survivor's trauma directly. Group therapy for survivors (Option D) offers peer support but lacks the comprehensive approach needed to address family dynamics. Contemporary research supports systemic interventions as crucial in treating and preventing further abuse within families.

Question 96: Correct Answer: C) Role transitions

Rationale: Interpersonal Therapy (IPT) focuses on addressing issues in four main areas: grief, role disputes, role transitions, and interpersonal deficits. Role transitions involve changes in life circumstances that can lead to feelings of hopelessness and depression due to the stress associated with adapting to new roles or losing old ones. Given Maria's symptoms and recent onset of therapy, focusing on role transitions (C) is most relevant for addressing her feelings of hopelessness. While grief (A), role disputes (B), and interpersonal deficits (D) are also important areas within IPT, they do not align as closely with Maria's reported experience of feeling hopeless about her future as role transitions do.

Question 97: Correct Answer: B) Visual and auditory hallucinations

Rationale: Visual and auditory hallucinations are sensory perceptions without external stimuli. John's experiences of seeing shadowy figures and hearing whispers align with this definition. Paranoid delusions (A) involve false beliefs rather than sensory misperceptions. Tactile hallucinations (C) involve sensations on the skin without external cause, which John does not report. Illusions (D) are misinterpretations of actual stimuli, whereas John's experiences lack real external stimuli.

Question 98: Correct Answer: B) Provide a sliding scale fee structure that is documented and discussed with the client.

Rationale: Option B is correct because providing a sliding scale fee structure aligns with ethical guidelines, ensuring transparency and documentation. This approach respects both the client's financial constraints and professional standards. Option A is incorrect because adjusting fees without documentation can lead to ethical issues and lacks transparency. Option C is not ideal as it avoids addressing the issue directly with your client and may not be in their best interest. Option D could have legal implications if not disclosed properly to your professional liability insurance provider, making it an unethical practice.

Question 99: Correct Answer: A) Panic Disorder

Rationale: Panic Disorder is characterized by recurrent unexpected panic attacks and ongoing concern about having more attacks or their implications. Maria's description of sudden episodes of intense fear with physical symptoms fits this diagnosis well. Social Anxiety Disorder involves fear or anxiety about social situations where one may be scrutinized by others but does not typically involve unexpected panic attacks. Specific Phobia pertains to an intense fear triggered by a specific object or situation. Generalized Anxiety Disorder involves excessive worry about various aspects of life rather than discrete panic attacks. Thus, Maria's presentation aligns best with Panic Disorder due to the nature and frequency of her symptoms.

Question 100: Correct Answer: B) Explain the therapeutic benefits of CBT while respecting her religious views, integrating her faith into the therapy.

Rationale: The correct approach is to explain the benefits of CBT while respecting Maria's religious views and integrating her faith into therapy. This approach acknowledges her beliefs without dismissing them and provides a way to incorporate them into treatment. Option A avoids addressing the core issue of her anxiety and depression. Option C might lead to discontinuation of necessary mental health treatment. Option D dismisses her beliefs outright, which could harm the therapeutic relationship.

Question 101: Correct Answer: A) Physical Abuse

Rationale: Physical abuse involves intentional acts causing physical harm such as hitting, slapping, or punching. Emotional abuse (B) refers to non-physical behaviors that harm emotional well-being, such as insults or threats. Neglect (C) involves failing to provide necessary care or protection. Psychological manipulation (D) includes tactics like gaslighting or coercion aimed at controlling someone's mental state. While all options are forms of family abuse/violence, only physical abuse directly involves causing physical injuries as described in the scenario.

Question 102: Correct Answer: B) Explore John's current coping mechanisms and stress management strategies.

Rationale: Exploring John's current coping mechanisms and stress management strategies is crucial in understanding how he is handling his father's diagnosis and its impact on his anxiety and sleep issues. While family history (Option A), daily routines (Option C), and substance use history (Option D) are important aspects of a comprehensive assessment, focusing on coping mechanisms directly addresses how John is managing his present challenges. This approach aligns with contemporary research emphasizing adaptive functioning and resilience in response to stressors. In both questions, incorrect options are crafted to be plausible but slightly less prioritized compared to the correct option. Each explanation clarifies why the correct option is more appropriate given the context, ensuring a thorough understanding of effective diagnostic interviewing techniques.

Question 103: Correct Answer: A) Assess John's coping mechanisms and support systems.

Rationale: During an initial interview, it is critical to assess John's coping mechanisms and support systems (Option A). This provides insight into how he currently manages stress and identifies areas where he may need additional support. Option B (developing a detailed treatment plan) should come after gathering sufficient information from the initial assessment. Option C (administering standardized assessment tools) can be useful but is secondary to understanding his current coping strategies. Option D (discussing medication options) might be necessary eventually but should not be prioritized without first comprehensively assessing his situation.

Question 104: Correct Answer: D) Discuss with the client the limits of confidentiality and potential consequences.

Rationale: According to the ACA Code of Ethics, counselors must inform clients about the limits of confidentiality, especially when it pertains to illegal activities that may pose a risk to others. While maintaining confidentiality is crucial (Option A), counselors are also obligated to discuss its limits (Option D). Reporting to law enforcement (Option B) might be necessary only if there's an imminent risk of harm, which isn't specified here. Seeking supervision (Option C) is good practice but does not address informing the client about confidentiality limits directly. Option D ensures ethical compliance by clarifying boundaries and potential legal implications to the client.

Question 105: Correct Answer: A) Panic Disorder

Rationale: Maria's symptoms are indicative of Panic Disorder, which is characterized by recurrent unexpected panic attacks sudden periods of intense fear with physical symptoms like palpitations and shortness of breath. - Option B (Generalized Anxiety Disorder) is incorrect as GAD involves chronic worry rather than sudden panic attacks. - Option C (Post-Traumatic Stress Disorder) is incorrect because PTSD requires exposure to a traumatic event and includes symptoms like flashbacks and avoidance. - Option D (Specific Phobia) is incorrect as it involves intense fear triggered by specific objects or situations rather than unexpected panic attacks. By carefully analyzing each option against the patient's presentation in both scenarios, we ensure that the correct answer stands out based on clinical criteria while making other options plausible but ultimately incorrect.

Question 106: Correct Answer: B) Reflecting on these feelings after the session to understand their origin.

Rationale: Reflecting on these feelings after the session helps the counselor understand their origin and manage their impact on future sessions. Ignoring feelings (Option A) may lead to unresolved issues affecting counseling efficacy. Sharing feelings (Option C) can shift focus from the client's needs, while redirecting conversation (Option D) avoids addressing underlying issues, both potentially harming therapeutic rapport.

Question 107: Correct Answer: A) Cognitive Behavioral

Therapy (CBT)
Rationale: Cognitive Behavioral Therapy (CBT) is an evidence-based approach that focuses on altering maladaptive thought patterns to improve emotional regulation and develop coping strategies. CBT is particularly effective for treating anxiety disorders by helping clients identify and challenge irrational thoughts and beliefs. Dialectical Behavior Therapy (DBT) also incorporates cognitive-behavioral techniques but is specifically designed for individuals with borderline personality disorder and focuses on emotion regulation, distress tolerance, interpersonal effectiveness, and mindfulness. Acceptance and Commitment Therapy (ACT) emphasizes accepting thoughts and feelings rather than changing them, while Psychodynamic Therapy explores unconscious processes influencing behavior. Thus, CBT is the most appropriate choice for this scenario. - Option B: Dialectical Behavior Therapy (DBT) - While DBT includes cognitive-behavioral techniques, it is primarily aimed at treating borderline personality disorder rather than general anxiety. - Option C: Acceptance and Commitment Therapy (ACT) - ACT focuses more on accepting thoughts and feelings rather than changing them, which differs from the primary goal of CBT. - Option D: Psychodynamic Therapy - This approach delves into unconscious processes affecting behavior, which contrasts with CBT's focus on altering conscious thought patterns. The key difference lies in the specific focus of each therapy; CBT directly targets maladaptive thoughts to manage anxiety effectively, aligning perfectly with the given scenario.

Question 108: Correct Answer: B) Discuss the breach with the supervisee to understand their perspective and provide guidance.
Rationale: Option B is correct because it aligns with ethical guidelines that emphasize education and remediation before punitive measures. Supervisors have a responsibility to help supervisees learn from their mistakes, providing guidance on how to avoid future breaches. Option A is incorrect because immediate reporting without understanding context may be premature. Option C is incorrect as termination should be a last resort after other corrective actions fail. Option D is incorrect because informing the client directly without first addressing it with the supervisee could undermine trust and bypass due process. The correct approach involves understanding, guiding, and remediating before escalating actions.

Question 109: Correct Answer: C) Major Depressive Disorder
Rationale: Sarah's symptoms align closely with Major Depressive Disorder (MDD), which includes fatigue, low mood, loss of interest in activities (anhedonia), and difficulty concentrating. Bipolar II Disorder involves periods of hypomania that Sarah does not report. Persistent Depressive Disorder (Dysthymia) features chronic depressive symptoms lasting for at least two years but may be less severe than those described by Sarah. Seasonal Affective Disorder typically occurs seasonally rather than continuously over several months.

Question 110: Correct Answer: C) Recommend that Emily initiate a calm and honest conversation with her partner about their future.
Rationale: Initiating an open conversation allows both partners to express their expectations and concerns, which is crucial for resolving uncertainties about the future. Giving an ultimatum (A) can lead to increased tension and may not foster constructive dialogue. Exploring personal values (B) is useful but does not directly address the relational issue at hand. Taking a break (D) might provide temporary relief but does not facilitate communication or resolution of the problem.

Question 111: Correct Answer: C) Sarah is displaying symptoms of separation anxiety disorder.
Rationale: Separation anxiety disorder (SAD) is characterized by excessive fear or anxiety concerning separation from attachment figures. This condition goes beyond normal developmental anxiety and includes physical symptoms like stomachaches. While an insecure attachment (Option B) may contribute to SAD, it does not fully explain the clinical severity of Sarah's symptoms. Normal developmental anxiety (Option A) does not usually result in such intense reactions. Social phobia (Option D) involves fear of social situations rather than separation from caregivers.

Question 112: Correct Answer: A) Conduct a structured review of John's progress using quantitative measures like standardized assessment tools.
Rationale: The correct answer is A because using standardized assessment tools provides an objective measure of John's progress, which can help him see tangible evidence of improvement. This method also aligns with evidence-based practices in mental health counseling. Option B is important for emotional validation but does not provide concrete evidence of progress. Option C could be counterproductive by interrupting continuity of care. Option D can be helpful but does not specifically address how to review current progress systematically.

Question 113: Correct Answer: A) Schizophrenia
Rationale: Schizophrenia is characterized by persistent auditory and visual hallucinations, often without a clear trigger. John's symptoms align with this diagnosis due to the chronic nature and lack of other underlying conditions. Bipolar Disorder with Psychotic Features (B) typically involves mood disturbances alongside psychosis but does not fit John's presentation without mood symptoms. Major Depressive Disorder with Psychotic Features (C) would require significant depressive symptoms in addition to hallucinations, which are not mentioned. Brief Psychotic Disorder (D) involves short-term psychosis lasting less than a month, which does not align with John's ongoing symptoms.

Question 114: Correct Answer: B) Processing the pain of grief
Rationale: John's symptoms of feeling numb and disconnected suggest he is struggling with processing the pain of grief according to Worden's Tasks of Mourning. This task involves confronting and working through emotional pain rather than avoiding or suppressing it. Accepting the reality of the loss (A) involves acknowledging that the loss has occurred; adjusting to an environment without the deceased (C) entails adapting to life changes after loss; finding an enduring connection with the deceased while embarking on a new life (D) involves maintaining a bond while continuing with life. John's difficulty sleeping and concentrating further supports that he is in emotional turmoil indicative of unprocessed grief.

Question 115: Correct Answer: A) Implement Cognitive Behavioral Therapy (CBT) focused on resilience-building.
Rationale: CBT is an evidence-based approach that helps individuals develop coping mechanisms and resilience, which are crucial for dealing with bullying's psychological impact. While taking a break from social media (Option B), involving law enforcement (Option C), and blocking bullies (Option D) can be parts of a broader strategy, they do not address John's emotional needs as comprehensively as CBT does. CBT targets the cognitive distortions that contribute to John's distress, promoting long-term mental health improvement.

Question 116: Correct Answer: C) Help John develop code-switching strategies for different social contexts.
Rationale: Code-switching involves adjusting one's communication style based on the social context, which can help John navigate workplace dynamics while retaining his cultural identity. Research shows that effective code-switching can improve interpersonal relationships and reduce misunderstandings. Option A suggests adopting a new communication style entirely, which may not be

sustainable or authentic for John. Option B addresses colleagues' behavior but does not empower John directly. Option D advises minimizing interactions, potentially exacerbating feelings of isolation and hindering professional growth. Each option was carefully crafted considering theories of acculturation (e.g., Berry's Model), emphasizing the importance of balancing cultural identities (biculturalism), understanding context-specific behaviors (code-switching), and recognizing potential pitfalls of complete assimilation or isolation strategies in cultural adjustments.

Question 117: Correct Answer: C) Identity vs. Role Confusion

Rationale: Erikson's theory posits that the primary developmental task during adolescence (approximately ages 12-18) is "Identity vs. Role Confusion." Adolescents explore different roles and ideas to develop a sense of personal identity, which is crucial for their future adult roles. - Option A (Trust vs. Mistrust) pertains to infancy, where the main task is developing trust based on the reliability of caregivers. - Option B (Initiative vs. Guilt) applies to early childhood, focusing on asserting control and initiating activities. - Option D (Intimacy vs. Isolation) relates to young adulthood, where forming intimate relationships is key. Thus, while all options are valid stages in Erikson's theory, only "Identity vs. Role Confusion" accurately corresponds to the critical developmental task during adolescence.

Question 118: Correct Answer: B) Refer Maria to a psychiatrist specializing in anxiety disorders.

Rationale: Referring Maria to a psychiatrist specializing in anxiety disorders is the most appropriate step given her worsening symptoms and severe panic attacks. Psychiatrists can provide specialized care, including medication management and advanced therapeutic techniques tailored to anxiety disorders. A general practitioner (Option A) may not have the specialized knowledge needed. While support groups (Option C) can be beneficial, they do not offer individualized treatment. Referring her to another counselor (Option D) might not address the need for potential medical intervention.

Question 119: Correct Answer: B) Catastrophizing

Rationale: Catastrophizing is a cognitive distortion where an individual expects or visualizes only negative outcomes, leading to feelings of hopelessness. This aligns with Aaron Beck's cognitive theory of depression, which posits that such distorted thinking patterns contribute significantly to depressive symptoms. Overgeneralization (A), while also a cognitive distortion, involves drawing broad negative conclusions based on limited evidence and does not directly relate to hopelessness as strongly as catastrophizing. Personalization (C) involves blaming oneself for events outside one's control, leading more to guilt than hopelessness. Selective abstraction (D) involves focusing on a single negative detail while ignoring other aspects, which can contribute to depression but is less directly tied to hopelessness compared to catastrophizing.

Question 120: Correct Answer: C) Participating in personal therapy sessions

Rationale: Contemporary research highlights that participating in personal therapy sessions is highly effective in preventing burnout among mental health counselors. Personal therapy provides a space for counselors to process their own emotions, receive support, and develop coping strategies. While engaging in regular physical exercise (Option A) and maintaining strict professional boundaries (Option B) are important aspects of self-care, they do not address the emotional processing and support that personal therapy offers. Scheduling frequent social activities (Option D) can improve social support but may not directly address professional stressors. Therefore, Option C is the most comprehensive approach to preventing burnout.

Question 121: Correct Answer: B) Reassess the client's symptoms and consider incorporating additional therapeutic techniques.

Rationale: Option B is correct because it emphasizes the importance of reassessing the client's symptoms to understand their current state better and considering additional therapeutic techniques that may address persistent issues more effectively. This approach aligns with contemporary research advocating for flexible and responsive treatment plans. Option A is incorrect because merely increasing session frequency without reassessing or modifying techniques might not address underlying issues effectively. Option C, while sometimes necessary, may not be the immediate best course of action without first attempting to modify the existing treatment plan based on new assessments. Option D is too drastic; terminating and starting anew disregards any progress made and can be destabilizing for the client. Thus, option B represents a balanced approach grounded in clinical best practices for revising treatment plans.

Question 122: Correct Answer: B) Use exposure and response prevention (ERP) techniques to reduce her anxiety around these thoughts.

Rationale: Exposure and response prevention (ERP) is a well-established technique for treating intrusive thoughts, particularly those associated with obsessive-compulsive disorder (OCD). ERP helps individuals confront their fears without engaging in compulsive behaviors, thereby reducing anxiety over time. - Option A (Psychodynamic therapy): While exploring origins can provide insights, it is not as immediately effective for symptom reduction as ERP. - Option C (Cognitive restructuring): Cognitive restructuring is useful but may not be as effective initially for OCD-related intrusive thoughts compared to ERP. - Option D (Distraction): Distraction can provide temporary relief but does not address the root cause or long-term management of intrusive thoughts like ERP does.

Question 123: Correct Answer: B) Gender Stability

Rationale: According to Kohlberg's cognitive-developmental theory, children reach the stage of "Gender Stability" around the age of 4-5 years. At this stage, they understand that their gender remains stable over time (e.g., boys grow up to be men). - A) Gender Constancy: This is a more advanced stage where children realize that gender remains the same across situations and despite superficial changes in appearance or activities. - C) Gender Consistency: This term is often used interchangeably with "Gender Constancy" but specifically emphasizes the permanence of gender regardless of external changes. - D) Gender Identity: This refers to the initial recognition and labeling of oneself as male or female, which typically occurs around age 2-3. The correct option, B) Gender Stability, is specific to understanding that one's gender remains stable over time, distinguishing it from other closely related concepts in Kohlberg's theory.

Question 124: Correct Answer: A) When the client poses an imminent threat to themselves or others.

Rationale: According to ethical guidelines and legal standards, mental health counselors are permitted to disclose confidential information without client consent if there is an imminent threat of harm to the client or others. This exception aligns with the duty to protect and is mandated by law in many jurisdictions. Option B is incorrect because family concern alone does not override confidentiality without explicit consent. Option C is incorrect unless there is a court order compelling disclosure. Option D is incorrect unless there is written consent from the client allowing such communication for continuity of care. The key difference lies in the immediate risk of harm, which justifies breaking confidentiality under specific conditions.

Question 125: Correct Answer: C) Keeping a structured thought record to identify and challenge irrational thoughts.

Rationale: Keeping a structured thought record is a core component of CBT, which is highly effective for treating generalized anxiety disorder. This activity helps clients identify irrational thoughts and replace them with more rational ones. Option A (unstructured journaling) lacks the structure necessary for targeted cognitive interventions. Option B (guided imagery) is beneficial but not as directly focused on cognitive restructuring. Option D (open-ended group discussion) may provide support but does not offer the same level of individualized cognitive intervention as keeping a structured thought record.

Question 126: Correct Answer: D) All-or-Nothing Thinking

Rationale: Aaron Beck's Cognitive Theory of Depression highlights that "All-or-Nothing Thinking," also known as black-and-white thinking, is a cognitive distortion where individuals see situations in only two categories rather than on a continuum. This type of thinking often leads to feelings of hopelessness because it allows no middle ground or possibility for improvement. Catastrophizing (Option A) involves expecting the worst possible outcome and can contribute to anxiety but is not directly linked to hopelessness in the same way. Overgeneralization (Option B) involves making broad conclusions based on a single event and can contribute to depression but does not specifically lead to hopelessness. Selective Abstraction (Option C) involves focusing on a single negative detail taken out of context and ignoring other information, which can exacerbate depressive symptoms but does not directly relate to the pervasive sense of hopelessness seen with all-or-nothing thinking. By understanding these nuances, mental health counselors can better identify and address the specific cognitive distortions contributing to their clients' feelings of hopelessness.

Question 127: Correct Answer: B) Mediate a conversation where John can express his feelings directly to his stepmother.

Rationale: Mediating a conversation allows John to voice his feelings in a safe environment, fostering empathy and understanding from his stepmother. This direct communication can help build trust and improve their relationship. - Option A (Facilitate joint activities that John and his stepmother can enjoy together) is beneficial but may not address underlying emotional issues directly. - Option C (Encourage John's father to intervene more actively in their relationship) could potentially undermine John's autonomy in resolving conflicts. - Option D (Provide psychoeducation about blended families to both John and his stepmother) is useful but may not be as immediately impactful as direct communication facilitated by a counselor.

Question 128: Correct Answer: A) Educate John about the importance of self-care and encourage regular breaks.

Rationale: Educating John about self-care and encouraging regular breaks addresses both his guilt and neglect of personal health by emphasizing that taking care of himself is essential for effective caregiving. Delegating tasks (Option B) is helpful but may not directly address John's feelings of guilt. Keeping a journal (Option C) can be beneficial for emotional expression but does not actively promote self-care practices. Couple's counseling (Option D), while valuable for relationship dynamics, may not focus sufficiently on John's individual need for self-care.

Question 129: Correct Answer: C) Set criteria where relapse triggers an individual review but not automatic termination.

Rationale: Maria should recognize relapse as a common part of recovery and provide supportive measures rather than punitive ones. Option C is correct because it allows for an individualized approach, ensuring that each case is reviewed on its merits without automatically excluding participants who relapse. Option A might lead to complacency about relapse consequences; Option B is too harsh and counterproductive; Option D lacks clarity and structure necessary for effective group management. Each option has been crafted based on principles of professional practice and ethics within mental health counseling, making them closely related yet distinct in their implications.

Question 130: Correct Answer: A) Recommend cognitive-behavioral therapy for insomnia (CBT-I)

Rationale: Cognitive-behavioral therapy for insomnia (CBT-I) is considered the first-line treatment for chronic insomnia according to contemporary research. It addresses both the cognitive and behavioral aspects contributing to insomnia without the side effects associated with medication. While reducing alcohol consumption (Option C) is beneficial, it does not address all factors contributing to John's insomnia. Over-the-counter sleep aids (Option B) and benzodiazepines (Option D) are not recommended as initial interventions due to potential dependency and side effects.

Question 131: Correct Answer: B) Develop a safety plan with Sarah and connect her with local shelters.

Rationale: Developing a safety plan and connecting Sarah with local shelters provides immediate protection and support, addressing her urgent need for safety. Confronting the partner (Option A) could escalate danger. Couple's therapy (Option C) is inappropriate in cases of abuse as it might not address power imbalances. While meditation (Option D) can be beneficial, it does not address the immediate risk to her safety.

Question 132: Correct Answer: A) The null hypothesis can be rejected at the 5% significance level.

Rationale: A p-value of 0.03 indicates that there is only a 3% probability that the observed results are due to chance if the null hypothesis were true. Since this p-value is less than the common alpha level of 0.05 (5%), we reject the null hypothesis, suggesting that there is a statistically significant effect of the new CBT technique on anxiety. Option B is incorrect because it misinterprets what a p-value less than 0.05 means. Option C is incorrect because it incorrectly states there is no significant difference when in fact there is. Option D is incorrect because it confuses Type I error (rejecting a true null hypothesis) with Type II error (failing to reject a false null hypothesis).

Question 133: Correct Answer: C) Privately discuss with Alex about his behavior and its impact on the team.

Rationale: The most effective intervention is to privately discuss with Alex about his behavior and its impact on the team. This approach addresses the issue directly while maintaining confidentiality and respect for Alex. It allows for an open dialogue where Alex can understand how his actions affect others and explore ways to modify his behavior. Option A might not fully address the underlying issue of interrupting others. Option B could be helpful but may not address individual accountability. Option D may seem like a solution but could be perceived as punitive rather than constructive.

Question 134: Correct Answer: B) Conduct Disorder (CD)

Rationale: Conduct Disorder (CD) is characterized by a pattern of behavior that violates the rights of others or major societal norms, including aggression, lying, stealing, and defiance. While ODD involves defiant behavior without severe violations of societal norms or rights of others, IED is marked by sudden episodes of impulsive aggression not typically accompanied by the other behaviors described. ADHD involves inattentiveness and hyperactivity rather than deliberate rule-breaking.

Question 135: Correct Answer: B) Express her feelings of anxiety and insecurity using "I" statements during a calm conversation.

Rationale: Using "I" statements allows Maria to express her feelings without blaming or accusing her partner, facilitating a constructive dialogue (Rosenberg, 2003). This method promotes understanding and empathy, which can help address underlying issues in their relationship dynamics. Option A is confrontational and may lead to defensiveness rather than resolution. Option C could increase anxiety and mistrust without resolving the core issue. Option D might offer support but lacks direct communication with her partner, which is essential for addressing relational concerns effectively.

Question 136: Correct Answer: A) John's recent job loss

Rationale: Prioritizing John's recent job loss is crucial as it is an immediate stressor that could be significantly contributing to his current symptoms of depression and anxiety. While marital problems (Option B), family history of mental illness (Option C), and current medication use (Option D) are also important, they do not provide as immediate a context for understanding his present mental state. Addressing the most pressing issue first allows for a more targeted and effective intervention strategy.

Question 137: Correct Answer: B) Scheduling regular booster sessions after the initial therapy ends.

Rationale: Scheduling regular booster sessions after the initial therapy ends is considered one of the most effective strategies for maintaining therapeutic progress over the long term. Booster sessions provide an opportunity for clients to review their progress, address any emerging issues, and reinforce coping strategies learned during therapy. This approach helps prevent relapse and ensures sustained improvement. Option A (Encouraging clients to journal their daily experiences and emotions) is beneficial for self-awareness but may not be sufficient on its own for long-term maintenance. Option C (Teaching clients mindfulness techniques) is useful in managing stress but does not specifically address ongoing integration and maintenance of therapeutic gains. Option D (Helping clients develop a support network) is important but is more about external support rather than structured follow-up. Thus, while each option has merit, B) Scheduling regular booster sessions provides a structured, ongoing mechanism directly aimed at sustaining therapeutic progress.

Question 138: Correct Answer: B) Remove any immediate means of self-harm.

Rationale: The most crucial first step in developing a safety plan for someone expressing suicidal ideation is to ensure their immediate safety by removing any means of self-harm. This action reduces the risk of an impulsive suicide attempt. While identifying triggers (A), establishing emergency contacts (C), and developing coping strategies (D) are essential components of a comprehensive safety plan, they come after ensuring that the individual is not in immediate danger.

Question 139: Correct Answer: B) Using sleep restriction therapy

Rationale: Sleep restriction therapy (SRT) is a key component of CBT for insomnia and has been shown to be highly effective in treating chronic insomnia. It involves limiting the amount of time spent in bed to match the actual amount of sleep, thereby increasing sleep efficiency. While increasing physical exercise (A), taking melatonin supplements (C), and implementing a consistent bedtime routine (D) can all contribute to better sleep hygiene, they are not as directly targeted or consistently effective as SRT in addressing chronic insomnia. Exercise and bedtime routines are supportive measures, and melatonin is more useful for circadian rhythm disorders rather than chronic insomnia specifically.

Question 140: Correct Answer: B) Progressive Muscle Relaxation

Rationale: Progressive Muscle Relaxation (PMR) is a highly effective technique for reducing physiological arousal associated with acute stress. It involves tensing and then slowly releasing different muscle groups, which helps to decrease muscle tension and lower overall stress levels. Cognitive Restructuring (Option A) focuses more on changing thought patterns rather than directly addressing physiological symptoms. Mindfulness-Based Stress Reduction (Option C), while beneficial for long-term stress management and overall well-being, does not target immediate physiological arousal as directly as PMR. Psychoeducation (Option D) provides valuable information but does not actively reduce physiological symptoms in the moment. Therefore, PMR is the most effective technique for immediate reduction of physiological arousal due to acute stress.

Question 141: Correct Answer: D) Multiple bruises in various stages of healing

Rationale: Multiple bruises in various stages of healing are a clear physical manifestation of ongoing physical abuse, as they indicate repeated trauma over time. While chronic pain, frequent headaches, and difficulty sleeping are also common in victims of family violence, they can be attributed to a variety of other causes such as stress or underlying medical conditions. The presence of bruises specifically points to direct physical harm.

Question 142: Correct Answer: A) Maria's coping mechanisms and support system

Rationale: Understanding Maria's coping mechanisms and support system is crucial as it provides insight into her resilience and resources available for managing anxiety. While assessing panic attack frequency/triggers (B), interpersonal relationships (C), and physical health impact (D) are relevant, identifying existing supports helps in formulating an effective intervention plan.

Question 143: Correct Answer: B) Suggest that John engage in mindfulness meditation and deep-breathing exercises.

Rationale: Mindfulness meditation and deep-breathing exercises are evidence-based strategies for managing stress and emotional regulation. Unlike avoidance (Option A), which can lead to unresolved emotions resurfacing later, mindfulness helps individuals process their feelings healthily. Immersing oneself in work (Option C) might provide temporary distraction but doesn't address underlying emotional issues. Frequent discussions with friends and family (Option D) can be beneficial but may not always provide the structured approach needed for effective emotional regulation.

Question 144: Correct Answer: B) Using social media to promote mental health awareness without breaching client confidentiality.

Rationale: Option B is correct because it encapsulates the dual responsibility of using social media for positive outreach while strictly adhering to confidentiality principles. Option A, while important, is too narrow as it focuses solely on not sharing client information, missing the broader context of promoting awareness. Option C, although relevant, does not directly address the ethical considerations specific to client interactions. Option D is incorrect as engaging with clients through direct messaging can easily lead to breaches in confidentiality and boundary issues. Thus, B comprehensively addresses the balance between leveraging social media for public good and maintaining ethical standards.

Question 145: Correct Answer: C) Discuss the limits of confidentiality with the client and seek legal advice if necessary.

Rationale: According to ethical guidelines, counselors are required to maintain client confidentiality but also must inform clients about its limits. In cases involving illegal activities, it is crucial for counselors to discuss these boundaries clearly with clients. Seeking legal advice ensures that the counselor's actions align with both ethical and legal standards. Option A overlooks the necessity of discussing confidentiality limits; Option B bypasses client consent and may violate trust; Option D is premature without exploring all ethical considerations first. Therefore, Option C is correct as it balances maintaining confidentiality with adhering to legal obligations.

Question 146: Correct Answer: A) Gradually taper off opioids under medical supervision.

Rationale: Gradually tapering off opioids under medical supervision is the safest initial step for Maria as it minimizes withdrawal symptoms and reduces the risk of severe complications. Immediate cessation (Option B) can lead to intense withdrawal symptoms and potential relapse. Switching to non-opioid pain management (Option C) is important but should follow a medically supervised tapering process. Joining a support group (Option D), while beneficial, should complement rather than replace medical supervision during tapering.

Question 147: Correct Answer: A) Implementing Super's Life-Span, Life-Space Approach

Rationale: Implementing Super's Life-Span, Life-Space Approach would best address Maria's concerns as it considers the integration of various life roles (e.g., worker, homemaker) across different stages of life. This approach helps individuals understand how to balance multiple roles and make informed decisions about their careers in relation to other life domains. Holland's RIASEC Model focuses more on personality-work environment fit rather than role balance; SCCT emphasizes self-efficacy but not explicitly role integration; Roe's Needs Theory focuses on early childhood experiences shaping career choices but does not address current role conflicts directly.

Question 148: Correct Answer: B) Teaching the client cognitive-behavioral techniques

Rationale: Cognitive-behavioral techniques (CBT) are evidence-based strategies that help clients identify and change negative thought patterns and behaviors, leading to long-term coping skills for managing anxiety. Option A, avoiding anxiety-provoking situations, may provide short-term relief but can reinforce avoidance behavior and does not address underlying issues. Option C, relying on medication alone, may be part of a treatment plan but should not be the sole strategy as it does not equip clients with coping skills. Option D, using relaxation techniques exclusively, can be helpful but is limited if not combined with other therapeutic approaches like CBT. Thus, teaching CBT is the most comprehensive and effective method for long-

term management.

Question 149: Correct Answer: C) Discuss with John the possibility of involving emergency services while ensuring he understands the reasons.

Rationale: The correct answer is C. Ethical guidelines emphasize balancing client confidentiality with the duty to protect clients from harm. By discussing the situation with John and explaining why emergency services might be needed, Maria respects his autonomy while addressing safety concerns. Option A fails to address immediate risk; Option B does not involve John in the decision-making process; Option D delays necessary intervention.

Question 150: Correct Answer: B) Help John identify and understand his own triggers in the conflict.

Rationale: The most appropriate initial intervention is to help John identify and understand his own triggers in the conflict (B). This self-awareness is crucial for managing emotional responses and contributes to more effective communication. Option A might escalate the conflict without prior self-reflection. Option C avoids addressing the issue, potentially worsening stress. Option D may be useful later but not as an initial step without understanding underlying issues.

NCMHCE Exam Practice Questions [SET 3]

Question 1: During a counseling session with a newly formed support group for individuals recovering from substance abuse, you observe that members are polite but hesitant to share personal experiences. What is the most appropriate intervention based on the group's current stage of development?
A) Encourage members to establish group norms and roles.
B) Facilitate conflict resolution among members.
C) Provide structured activities to build trust and rapport.
D) Promote open discussion about members' feelings and concerns.

Question 2: Which factor is most crucial for ensuring a successful remarriage or recommitment according to contemporary research?
A) Financial stability
B) Emotional readiness
C) Agreement on parenting styles
D) Social support

Question 3: John, a 35-year-old male, has been experiencing significant distress due to his eating habits. He often eats alone because he feels embarrassed by how much he eats and continues eating even when he is not hungry. He does not engage in any compensatory behaviors like vomiting or excessive exercise. What is the most likely diagnosis for John?
A) Bulimia Nervosa
B) Binge Eating Disorder
C) Anorexia Nervosa
D) Night Eating Syndrome

Question 4: Mary, a 60-year-old retired nurse, has been feeling anxious about her financial stability post-retirement. She reports constant worry about outliving her savings despite having a modest pension. Which intervention would best help Mary manage her anxiety related to financial concerns?
A) Financial Counseling
B) Mindfulness-Based Stress Reduction (MBSR)
C) Psychoeducation on Retirement Planning
D) Group Therapy

Question 5: Which of the following is considered the most reliable indicator of imminent risk for suicide in a client?
A) A detailed plan with access to means
B) A history of previous suicide attempts
C) Expressing feelings of hopelessness
D) Experiencing recent significant loss

Question 6: Which of the following physical symptoms is most commonly associated with major depressive disorder?
A) Chronic back pain
B) Persistent fatigue
C) Frequent headaches
D) Recurrent gastrointestinal distress

Question 7: Jessica, a 32-year-old African American woman, reports feeling consistently undervalued at her workplace despite her qualifications and contributions. She describes experiencing microaggressions from colleagues and a lack of support from her supervisor. As her mental health counselor, which approach would be most effective in addressing Jessica's experiences of racism and discrimination?
A) Cognitive Behavioral Therapy (CBT) focusing on challenging negative thought patterns.

B) Multicultural Counseling emphasizing cultural competence and validation of her experiences.
C) Solution-Focused Brief Therapy (SFBT) targeting immediate workplace concerns.
D) Psychoanalytic Therapy exploring unconscious biases and early life experiences.

Question 8: A 35-year-old male presents with persistent feelings of sadness, lack of interest in activities he once enjoyed, significant weight loss without dieting, insomnia, and fatigue. These symptoms have been present for over six months. What is the most likely diagnosis?
A) Major Depressive Disorder
B) Persistent Depressive Disorder (Dysthymia)
C) Bipolar II Disorder
D) Generalized Anxiety Disorder

Question 9: Sarah, a 28-year-old female, seeks counseling for alcohol dependency. You decide to use Motivational Interviewing (MI) to help her enhance her motivation to change. Which principle of MI focuses on helping Sarah recognize discrepancies between her current behavior and broader life goals?
A) Express Empathy
B) Develop Discrepancy
C) Roll with Resistance
D) Support Self-Efficacy

Question 10: Sarah, a 35-year-old woman, has been experiencing severe anxiety and flashbacks following a car accident six months ago. Despite attending regular therapy sessions, she continues to have difficulty sleeping and has started avoiding driving altogether. What is the most likely diagnosis for Sarah based on her symptoms?
A) Acute Stress Disorder
B) Generalized Anxiety Disorder
C) Post-Traumatic Stress Disorder
D) Adjustment Disorder

Question 11: Dr. Smith, a mental health counselor, is helping his client Emily who struggles with depressive episodes. He decides to provide her with educational resources to support her treatment plan. Which resource should Dr. Smith prioritize for Emily?
A) An online course on mindfulness-based stress reduction (MBSR)
B) A comprehensive guidebook on various types of depression
C) A video series featuring interviews with individuals who have overcome depression
D) An app designed to track mood and provide daily affirmations

Question 12: When evaluating systemic patterns of interaction within a family, which concept from Bowen's Family Systems Theory is crucial for understanding how anxiety can transfer across generations?
A) Differentiation of Self
B) Triangulation
C) Emotional Cutoff
D) Multigenerational Transmission Process

Question 13: According to William Worden's Tasks of Mourning, which task involves adjusting to a world without the deceased?
A) Accepting the reality of the loss
B) Processing the pain of grief

C) Adjusting to an environment in which the deceased is missing

D) Finding an enduring connection with the deceased while embarking on a new life

Question 14: Maria, a 65-year-old woman with advanced ALS, is struggling with anxiety about her impending death. As her mental health counselor, which approach would be most effective in helping her cope with these feelings?

A) Encourage her to focus on positive memories and gratitude exercises.

B) Help her develop a detailed plan for her remaining time and end-of-life arrangements.

C) Suggest she avoid thinking about death by engaging in distracting activities.

D) Recommend intensive psychotherapy sessions to explore deep-seated fears.

Question 15: In the context of counseling a client experiencing disenfranchised grief, which intervention is most appropriate to help them acknowledge and process their grief?

A) Encourage the client to participate in group therapy sessions where they can share their experiences.

B) Suggest that the client write letters expressing their feelings to the person they lost.

C) Recommend that the client engage in mindfulness meditation to help manage their emotions.

D) Advise the client to keep a daily journal documenting their emotional journey.

Question 16: When obtaining informed consent from a client for mental health counseling services, which of the following elements is most crucial to ensure that the consent is valid?

A) Providing detailed information about the counselor's qualifications and experience.

B) Ensuring that the client understands the potential risks and benefits of treatment.

C) Discussing the confidentiality limits and situations where confidentiality might be breached.

D) Confirming that the client voluntarily agrees to participate in counseling without any coercion.

Question 17: During a counseling session, Maria begins to exhibit feelings of intense anger towards her counselor, which seem disproportionate to the current interaction. The counselor recognizes this as a case of transference. Which of the following actions should the counselor take to effectively address this situation?

A) Confront Maria about her inappropriate behavior.

B) Explore Maria's past relationships to understand the source of these feelings.

C) Ignore Maria's anger and continue with the session.

D) Refer Maria to another counselor immediately.

Question 18: John, a 45-year-old Muslim man, is struggling with alcoholism but believes that admitting his problem would bring shame upon his family according to his cultural and religious values. His counselor needs to address this conflict effectively. What should be the counselor's best course of action?

A) Emphasize the importance of individual well-being over cultural expectations.

B) Suggest John keep his treatment confidential to avoid bringing shame upon his family.

C) Explore how John's faith can support his recovery process while acknowledging his concerns about family honor.

D) Encourage John to prioritize his recovery regardless of potential cultural consequences.

Question 19: When reviewing a client's records, which of the following actions best exemplifies adherence to professional practice and ethical standards?

A) Ensuring all entries are signed and dated by the counselor.

B) Regularly updating records with subjective observations.

C) Sharing client records with a multidisciplinary team without explicit consent.

D) Correcting any inaccuracies in the client's records promptly.

Question 20: During a Mental Status Exam (MSE), which component specifically assesses a patient's ability to understand and use language appropriately?

A) Thought Process

B) Insight

C) Judgment

D) Speech

Question 21: Emily, a mental health counselor, has a client named John who is unable to afford his sessions due to recent job loss. John expresses that he values the therapy but is financially strained. What should Emily do first in this situation?

A) Reduce John's session frequency to lower his overall cost.

B) Discuss sliding scale fees or payment plans based on John's current financial situation.

C) Refer John to community resources for free or low-cost counseling services.

D) Advise John to temporarily suspend therapy until he finds stable employment.

Question 22: Which cognitive-behavioral intervention is most effective in reducing the frequency and intensity of obsessive thoughts in individuals with Obsessive-Compulsive Disorder (OCD)?

A) Exposure and Response Prevention (ERP)

B) Cognitive Restructuring

C) Mindfulness-Based Cognitive Therapy (MBCT)

D) Habit Reversal Training

Question 23: Which cognitive-behavioral strategy is most effective for reducing the urge to engage in process addictions such as pornography or gambling?

A) Cognitive restructuring

B) Exposure and response prevention

C) Motivational interviewing

D) Mindfulness-based stress reduction

Question 24: Which of the following is the most accurate description of a counselor's duty to inform clients about the limits of confidentiality?

A) Counselors must inform clients that all information shared will remain confidential without exception.

B) Counselors must inform clients that confidentiality can be broken if there is a court order demanding disclosure.

C) Counselors must inform clients that confidentiality may be breached if there is a risk of harm to self or others, or if there is suspected child abuse.

D) Counselors must inform clients that confidentiality can be breached for any reason deemed necessary by the counselor.

Question 25: David, a 15-year-old adolescent, has been exhibiting behavioral problems at school and home. His parents are concerned about his recent withdrawal from family activities and aggressive behavior towards his younger siblings. As his counselor, what intervention modality would best address these issues?

A) Individual counseling for David

B) Group therapy with other adolescents

C) Family therapy involving David and his parents

D) Couple counseling for David's parents

Question 26: Maria, a 32-year-old woman, presents at the clinic with frequent headaches and anxiety. During the session, she mentions that her partner often belittles her and controls her finances. She seems hesitant when discussing her relationship but insists that everything is fine. As a mental health counselor, what should be your primary concern in this scenario?
A) Assessing Maria for signs of depression.
B) Exploring Maria's childhood trauma.
C) Evaluating Maria's risk for intimate partner violence.
D) Discussing stress management techniques with Maria.

Question 27: John frequently misses his counseling sessions and attributes it to being too busy with work. The counselor suspects this behavior might be a defense mechanism. Which defense mechanism is John most likely exhibiting?
A) Denial
B) Projection
C) Rationalization
D) Repression

Question 28: John, a 30-year-old man, comes for counseling due to feelings of existential crisis after losing his job. He expresses doubts about his life's purpose and mentions that he was raised with strong spiritual beliefs but has since become disconnected from them. What is the most effective approach for the counselor to take in this scenario?
A) Help John reconnect with his spiritual community as a source of support.
B) Discuss John's current beliefs and values without focusing on spirituality initially.
C) Encourage John to explore new spiritual or religious practices that align with his current worldview.
D) Guide John through an exploration of how his disconnection from spirituality may be impacting his sense of purpose.

Question 29: Which of the following factors is most likely to contribute to a successful attachment process in adopted children?
A) The age of the child at the time of adoption
B) The adoptive parents' socioeconomic status
C) The presence of pre-adoption trauma
D) The quality of post-adoption support

Question 30: Maria and Carlos are struggling with co-parenting after their separation. Maria feels overwhelmed by her work commitments and believes Carlos is not doing enough to support her with their two children. Carlos feels Maria is too critical of his efforts. As a mental health counselor, what strategy would be most effective in helping them improve their co-parenting relationship?
A) Encourage them to create a detailed schedule outlining each parent's responsibilities.
B) Suggest they hire a mediator to resolve their disputes.
C) Recommend they limit communication to essential matters only.
D) Advise them to attend family therapy sessions together with their children.

Question 31: Sarah, a mental health counselor, receives feedback from her supervisor about her tendency to dominate conversations during sessions. What would be an appropriate response from Sarah to model effective receiving of feedback?
A) Defend her approach by explaining why she dominates conversations.
B) Listen actively to the feedback without interrupting and

ask clarifying questions if needed.
C) Agree with everything her supervisor says without considering its applicability.
D) Dismiss the feedback as irrelevant since she believes her approach works well.

Question 32: John, a 45-year-old man, recently lost his leg in a car accident. He is struggling with feelings of anger, depression, and helplessness. As his mental health counselor, what would be the most effective initial intervention to help John adjust to his physical loss?
A) Encourage John to immediately start looking for new hobbies that do not require physical activity.
B) Facilitate a support group where John can share his feelings with others who have experienced similar losses.
C) Advise John to focus on positive affirmations and ignore negative thoughts.
D) Suggest John engage in physical therapy as soon as possible to regain some level of independence.

Question 33: Maria, a recent immigrant from Mexico, is experiencing significant stress and anxiety as she adjusts to life in the United States. She is struggling with language barriers, cultural differences, and a sense of isolation. Which of the following approaches should her mental health counselor prioritize to effectively support Maria's cultural adjustment?
A) Encourage Maria to fully assimilate into American culture by adopting its values and customs.
B) Help Maria develop bicultural skills to navigate both her native and new cultures effectively.
C) Advise Maria to maintain her native cultural practices exclusively to preserve her identity.
D) Suggest that Maria avoid interactions with individuals from her native culture to focus on integration.

Question 34: A 10-year-old child presents with significant limitations in intellectual functioning and adaptive behavior, which began before age 18. The child has an IQ score of 65 and struggles with daily living skills such as communication and social participation. Which of the following is the most likely diagnosis?
A) Specific Learning Disorder
B) Autism Spectrum Disorder
C) Intellectual Disability
D) Attention-Deficit/Hyperactivity Disorder

Question 35: Dr. Johnson, a mental health counselor, conducts virtual therapy sessions with his clients. During one session, his client mentions feeling unsafe at home due to domestic violence. Dr. Johnson is concerned about maintaining confidentiality while also ensuring his client's safety. What is Dr. Johnson's best course of action?
A) Immediately contact law enforcement to report the domestic violence.
B) Discuss a safety plan with the client and obtain their consent before taking further action.
C) Document the conversation and wait for further incidents before taking action.
D) Contact a family member of the client to discuss their concerns.

Question 36: A 35-year-old woman named Emily presents to your clinic with signs of physical abuse. She reports that her husband has been increasingly controlling and violent over the past year. Emily mentions that she often feels trapped and cannot leave because she fears for her safety and that of her children. Based on contemporary research, which phase of the Cycle of Violence is Emily most likely experiencing?
A) Tension-building phase

B) Acute battering incident
C) Honeymoon phase
D) Reconciliation phase

Question 37: Which of the following factors is most strongly associated with improved sleep quality according to contemporary research?
A) Regular physical exercise
B) Consistent sleep schedule
C) Reduction in caffeine intake
D) Use of white noise machines

Question 38: Maria, a 35-year-old client, is seeking counseling for anxiety related to her high-stress job. During your initial sessions, you aim to collaborate with her to establish treatment goals and objectives. Which of the following strategies would be most effective in ensuring that Maria's treatment goals are both meaningful and achievable?
A) Setting broad goals to allow flexibility in treatment.
B) Encouraging Maria to set highly ambitious goals to motivate progress.
C) Collaborating with Maria to create SMART goals tailored to her needs.
D) Allowing Maria to determine all goals independently without guidance.

Question 39: Sarah feels that her husband Mark often dismisses her concerns about their finances, leading to tension between them. The counselor advises Sarah to use "I" statements during their discussions. Which of the following is an example of an effective "I" statement?
A) "You never listen to me when I talk about our finances."
B) "I feel worried when our financial situation is uncertain."
C) "We need to fix our financial issues immediately."
D) "You should be more responsible with money."

Question 40: John, a 32-year-old male, has been experiencing persistent depressive symptoms for over six months. He reports feelings of hopelessness, lack of energy, and difficulty concentrating. He has tried medication in the past with limited success. During the intake session, John expresses a desire for a therapy that helps him understand and change his thought patterns.
A) Cognitive Behavioral Therapy (CBT)
B) Psychodynamic Therapy
C) Interpersonal Therapy (IPT)
D) Dialectical Behavior Therapy (DBT)

Question 41: Maria, a 65-year-old woman with terminal cancer, expresses feelings of hopelessness and contemplates ending her life. As her mental health counselor, what is the most appropriate initial intervention?
A) Validate her feelings and explore her reasons for wanting to end her life.
B) Immediately refer her to a psychiatrist for potential medication management.
C) Encourage her to focus on positive aspects of her life and distract from negative thoughts.
D) Develop a safety plan and discuss coping strategies for managing distress.

Question 42: A 10-year-old boy named Alex is brought to counseling by his mother. She reports that Alex has become increasingly withdrawn, has frequent nightmares, and is reluctant to go to school. Upon further inquiry, Alex reveals that he is being bullied by an older student at school who has also threatened him physically. What would be the most appropriate initial intervention for the counselor?

A) Encourage Alex to confront the bully directly in a safe manner.
B) Develop a safety plan with Alex and involve school authorities.
C) Focus on building Alex's self-esteem through individual therapy sessions.
D) Advise Alex's mother to consider changing schools immediately.

Question 43: John, a 45-year-old military veteran, seeks counseling for issues related to his combat experiences. He reports hypervigilance, irritability, and difficulty sleeping since returning home two years ago. What is the most appropriate initial step in assessing John's trauma?
A) Administering the Trauma Symptom Inventory (TSI)
B) Conducting a detailed clinical interview focused on his combat experiences
C) Using the Patient Health Questionnaire-9 (PHQ-9)
D) Implementing the Alcohol Use Disorders Identification Test (AUDIT)

Question 44: When using pre-test and post-test measures to assess outcomes in a mental health counseling intervention, which of the following is the most critical consideration to ensure valid results?
A) Ensuring the pre-test and post-test are administered by different clinicians to avoid bias.
B) Using standardized assessment tools for both pre-test and post-test.
C) Administering the post-test immediately after the intervention to capture immediate effects.
D) Comparing pre-test and post-test scores without considering any external variables that might influence the results.

Question 45: John, a 28-year-old veteran experiencing PTSD symptoms, seeks counseling to manage his condition. You plan to provide psychoeducation to help him cope with his symptoms. Which strategy should you prioritize to ensure John gains a thorough understanding of his PTSD?
A) Explain PTSD using complex medical terminology to emphasize its seriousness.
B) Use simple language to describe PTSD symptoms and relate them to John's experiences.
C) Focus solely on John's traumatic experiences without discussing symptom management.
D) Provide extensive literature on PTSD for John to read independently.

Question 46: Maria, a 38-year-old woman, has been experiencing decreased sexual desire since undergoing a mastectomy six months ago. She expresses feelings of unattractiveness and anxiety about her partner's perception of her body. Which therapeutic approach would be most beneficial for Maria's concerns?
A) Acceptance and Commitment Therapy (ACT).
B) Hormone replacement therapy.
C) Body image therapy combined with couples counseling.
D) Mindfulness-based stress reduction (MBSR).

Question 47: Maria, a 45-year-old woman who recently underwent a mastectomy due to breast cancer, is experiencing significant emotional distress. As her mental health counselor, you are working with her on adjusting to this physical loss. Which intervention is most likely to help Maria develop a healthier adjustment?
A) Encouraging Maria to focus solely on positive aspects of her life and avoid discussing her surgery.
B) Helping Maria identify and challenge negative thoughts about her body image and self-worth.

C) Advising Maria to rely heavily on family support without seeking external professional help.
D) Suggesting that Maria distract herself with work and hobbies to avoid thinking about her surgery.

Question 48: Maria, a mental health counselor, is explaining the limits of confidentiality to her client, Tom. Which statement accurately reflects Maria's legal obligation regarding informed consent?
A) "I need your verbal consent to share any information about our sessions with third parties."
B) "I can only disclose information if you provide written consent or in cases of suspected child abuse."
C) "I am required by law to obtain your written consent before sharing any details unless it's an emergency situation."
D) "Your informed consent allows me to share information freely with other healthcare providers involved in your care."

Question 49: Which type of social support is most directly associated with enhancing an individual's coping strategies by providing advice and guidance?
A) Emotional Support
B) Instrumental Support
C) Informational Support
D) Appraisal Support

Question 50: Dr. Smith, a licensed mental health counselor, receives a request for his client's records from a third party claiming to be an insurance provider. Dr. Smith knows that releasing such information requires careful consideration of ethical principles. What should Dr. Smith do?
A) Release the records immediately as requested by the insurance provider.
B) Refuse to release any information without first consulting with the client.
C) Verify the legitimacy of the request and obtain written consent from the client before releasing any records.
D) Release only non-sensitive parts of the records without consulting anyone.

Question 51: David, a 65-year-old man with advanced Alzheimer's disease, has an advance directive stating he does not want life-sustaining measures. However, during his current hospitalization for pneumonia, his daughter requests that all possible measures be taken to prolong his life. As his mental health counselor, what should you do?
A) Honor David's advance directive and advocate for withholding life-sustaining measures.
B) Suggest a temporary use of life-sustaining measures until David's condition stabilizes.
C) Recommend convening an ethics committee meeting to resolve the conflict.
D) Support the daughter's request as she is acting in David's best interest.

Question 52: John, a 60-year-old man, has been struggling since the death of his daughter in a car accident eight months ago. He frequently visits her grave and talks about feeling guilty for not being able to protect her. He also expresses difficulty in accepting her death and often avoids places they used to visit together. According to Worden's tasks of mourning, which task is John primarily struggling with?
A) To accept the reality of the loss
B) To process the pain of grief
C) To adjust to an environment without the deceased
D) To find an enduring connection with the deceased while moving on with life

Question 53: John, a 45-year-old male, presents with severe depression, suicidal ideation without a specific plan, and a history of substance abuse. He has supportive family members at home but has recently lost his job. What level of care is most appropriate for John?
A) Outpatient therapy
B) Intensive outpatient program (IOP)
C) Partial hospitalization program (PHP)
D) Inpatient hospitalization

Question 54: Maria, a 45-year-old woman, has recently been diagnosed with a terminal illness. She expresses feelings of hopelessness and questions the meaning of her life. As her mental health counselor, what is the most appropriate initial intervention to address her spiritual/existential concerns?
A) Encourage Maria to explore her religious beliefs and practices.
B) Help Maria identify sources of meaning and purpose in her life.
C) Refer Maria to a support group for individuals with terminal illnesses.
D) Discuss Maria's feelings about death and dying.

Question 55: John has decided to leave his support group due to relocation. As his mental health counselor, what is the best course of action to manage this transition within the group?
A) Inform the group immediately about John's departure and encourage them to share their feelings.
B) Gradually introduce the topic of John's departure over several sessions.
C) Wait until John has left before discussing his departure with the rest of the group.
D) Arrange a farewell session for John where he can express his thoughts and say goodbye.

Question 56: When reviewing a client's insurance benefits for mental health counseling services, which of the following is the most critical step to ensure accurate billing and reimbursement?
A) Verifying the client's coverage limits and copayment requirements.
B) Confirming the provider's network status with the insurance company.
C) Reviewing the client's deductible status and remaining balance.
D) Checking for pre-authorization requirements for specific services.

Question 57: Case Scenario: John, a 35-year-old male, presents with persistent ruminating thoughts about a recent job loss. Despite being aware of his qualifications and potential for future employment, he finds himself constantly replaying the events leading up to his termination and doubting his self-worth. As his counselor, what would be the most effective initial intervention to help John manage his ruminating thoughts?
A) Encourage John to engage in thought-stopping techniques whenever he begins to ruminate.
B) Suggest John write down his thoughts in a journal to gain perspective on them.
C) Teach John mindfulness meditation to help him focus on the present moment.
D) Recommend John challenge his negative thoughts with evidence-based counterarguments.

Question 58: John, a mental health counselor, is preparing to obtain informed consent from his new client, Sarah. Sarah has a history of anxiety and expresses concerns about understanding complex information. What is the most appropriate action John

should take to ensure that Sarah provides informed consent?
A) Provide Sarah with a detailed written document explaining all aspects of treatment.
B) Verbally explain the treatment process and ask Sarah if she has any questions.
C) Use simple language and visual aids to explain the treatment, then assess her understanding.
D) Refer Sarah to another counselor if she seems confused by the information.

Question 59: John, a 35-year-old man, presents with frequent episodes of rapid heartbeat, sweating, and shortness of breath. He reports that these symptoms often occur unexpectedly and are accompanied by feelings of impending doom. His medical history is unremarkable for cardiac issues. What is the most likely physical issue related to his anxiety?
A) Panic Attacks
B) Generalized Anxiety Disorder (GAD)
C) Hyperthyroidism
D) Myocardial Infarction

Question 60: When educating a client about transference, which of the following statements best explains how it relates to defense mechanisms?
A) Transference is a defense mechanism where clients project their feelings onto the therapist.
B) Transference involves redirecting feelings from past significant relationships onto the therapist.
C) Transference is a conscious process used by clients to manage anxiety.
D) Transference helps clients avoid painful emotions by shifting focus onto the therapist.

Question 61: Sarah, a 6-year-old girl, has been experiencing significant distress since her mother was hospitalized for a prolonged period. She has been showing signs of anxiety, including crying spells and reluctance to attend school. Based on Bowlby's Attachment Theory, what is the most likely explanation for Sarah's behavior?
A) Sarah is experiencing separation anxiety due to disrupted attachment with her primary caregiver.
B) Sarah is going through a normal developmental phase that involves fear of strangers.
C) Sarah is displaying symptoms of generalized anxiety disorder unrelated to her mother's absence.
D) Sarah is reacting to peer pressure at school which is causing her distress.

Question 62: Which of the following strategies is most effective in helping a client develop a robust support system?
A) Encouraging the client to join multiple social groups without assessing their interests.
B) Facilitating connections with community resources that align with the client's values and needs.
C) Advising the client to rely solely on family members for emotional support.
D) Suggesting that the client attend large community events to meet new people.

Question 63: John, an African American man, reports experiencing microaggressions at his workplace. He feels these incidents are affecting his mental health but is unsure how to address them. As his counselor, what would be the most culturally sensitive approach to help John?
A) Advise John to confront his colleagues directly about their behavior.
B) Help John develop coping strategies for dealing with microaggressions.

C) Suggest that John ignore the microaggressions to avoid conflict at work.
D) Encourage John to report the incidents to HR without discussing them further in therapy.

Question 64: Which of the following is considered a primary psychological impact of long-term exposure to interpersonal partner violence?
A) Increased self-esteem
B) Hypervigilance
C) Enhanced social skills
D) Improved problem-solving abilities

Question 65: When documenting a client's progress in therapy, which of the following is most important to include to ensure the documentation is both clinically useful and ethically sound?
A) A detailed narrative of every session.
B) The client's subjective reports and counselor's objective observations.
C) Only significant changes in the client's condition.
D) A summary of treatment goals discussed at the beginning of therapy.

Question 66: Mr. Smith, an 82-year-old man, presents with increased irritability, frequent falls, slowed movements, and difficulty sleeping. His family also notices changes in his handwriting and a shuffling gait. Considering these symptoms, what is the most likely diagnosis?
A) Parkinson's Disease
B) Lewy Body Dementia
C) Normal Pressure Hydrocephalus
D) Frontotemporal Dementia

Question 67: When exploring family member interactions, which of the following interventions is most effective in identifying patterns of communication and relational dynamics within the family system?
A) Genogram construction
B) Role-playing exercises
C) Narrative therapy techniques
D) Solution-focused brief therapy

Question 68: Sarah, a 45-year-old woman, recently lost her husband in a car accident. During her counseling sessions, she often expresses disbelief that her husband is gone and talks about him as if he were still alive. According to Kübler-Ross's stages of grief, which stage is Sarah most likely experiencing?
A) Denial
B) Anger
C) Bargaining
D) Depression

Question 69: During an initial intake session with a new client named Sarah, you need to gather comprehensive self-reported information about her mental health history. Which method would most effectively ensure the accuracy and depth of Sarah's self-report?
A) Structured clinical interview
B) Open-ended questionnaire
C) Standardized self-report inventory
D) Informal conversation

Question 70: During a group therapy session, one of the members, John, consistently interrupts others and dominates the conversation, preventing other members from sharing their experiences. As the counselor, what is the most appropriate initial intervention?
A) Directly confront John about his behavior in front of the group.
B) Speak with John privately after the session about his

behavior.
C) Gently redirect the conversation by encouraging other members to share.
D) Allow John to continue, hoping he will eventually self-regulate.

Question 71: Sarah is a 28-year-old female working in a high-stress corporate environment. She reports feeling overwhelmed by her workload and is considering leaving her job. As her mental health counselor, which of the following interventions would you recommend to help Sarah manage her occupational stress effectively?
A) Time Management Training
B) Job Redesign
C) Mindfulness-Based Stress Reduction (MBSR)
D) Assertiveness Training

Question 72: When obtaining informed consent from a client in mental health counseling, which of the following is most critical to ensure that the consent is valid?
A) Explaining the potential risks and benefits of the proposed treatment.
B) Ensuring the client understands their right to withdraw consent at any time.
C) Providing information about alternative treatment options.
D) Assessing the client's capacity to understand and make an informed decision.

Question 73: John, a 42-year-old man, discloses during a counseling session that his partner has been emotionally abusive for years, leading him to feel worthless and isolated. He mentions that his partner often uses manipulation tactics to maintain control over him. Which concept best explains John's experience according to contemporary research on family abuse/violence?
A) Learned helplessness
B) Stockholm syndrome
C) Gaslighting
D) Coercive control

Question 74: During an initial interview with a new client, Maria, who presents with symptoms of anxiety and depression, which of the following actions should the counselor prioritize to establish rapport and gather comprehensive information?
A) Begin by asking about Maria's family history of mental health issues.
B) Start with open-ended questions about Maria's current feelings and concerns.
C) Focus on discussing potential treatment plans to reassure Maria.
D) Conduct a thorough mental status examination immediately.

Question 75: A client consistently fails to attend scheduled therapy sessions despite expressing a strong desire to achieve their treatment goals. Which of the following is most likely a primary barrier affecting this client's goal attainment?
A) Lack of transportation
B) Fear of confronting painful emotions
C) Inadequate social support
D) Poor time management skills

Question 76: In a therapeutic setting, which of the following best demonstrates an empathic response from a counselor?
A) "I understand exactly how you feel."
B) "It sounds like you're feeling overwhelmed by your situation."
C) "You shouldn't feel this way; things will get better soon."

D) "I think you need to change your perspective on this issue."

Question 77: You are reviewing the client records of a patient named Sarah, who has been receiving counseling for anxiety and depression. During your review, you notice discrepancies in the documentation regarding her medication history. What is your best course of action?
A) Correct the discrepancies yourself based on what you know about Sarah's treatment.
B) Discuss the discrepancies with Sarah during her next session.
C) Consult with Sarah's prescribing physician to verify the correct medication history.
D) Ignore the discrepancies as they are likely minor and won't affect treatment.

Question 78: When addressing cultural considerations in mental health counseling, which of the following is the most effective approach to ensure culturally competent care?
A) Using standardized assessment tools for all clients regardless of their cultural background.
B) Applying a universal counseling approach that treats all clients equally.
C) Incorporating clients' cultural beliefs and practices into the treatment plan.
D) Avoiding discussions about culture to prevent making clients uncomfortable.

Question 79: Michael, a 35-year-old man, has been experiencing severe anxiety and panic attacks related to his high-stress job. During a counseling session, he expresses feelings of being overwhelmed and unable to manage his workload. As his counselor, which intervention would be most effective in helping Michael develop coping mechanisms for his anxiety?
A) Cognitive Behavioral Therapy (CBT)
B) Solution-Focused Brief Therapy (SFBT)
C) Dialectical Behavior Therapy (DBT)
D) Mindfulness-Based Stress Reduction (MBSR)

Question 80: Sarah, a 35-year-old woman, reports difficulty falling asleep and staying asleep. She mentions that she often uses her smartphone in bed to relax before attempting to sleep. As her mental health counselor, what would be the most appropriate initial recommendation based on contemporary sleep hygiene practices?
A) Limit smartphone use to 30 minutes before bedtime.
B) Turn off all electronic devices at least one hour before bedtime.
C) Use a blue light filter on the smartphone during evening hours.
D) Engage in relaxing activities such as reading or listening to soft music before bed.

Question 81: Mrs. Garcia, an 82-year-old woman, has been experiencing memory lapses and occasional confusion about time and place over the past year. She is still able to perform daily tasks independently but sometimes forgets appointments or where she placed items. What is the most appropriate diagnosis for her condition?
A) Normal Age-Related Memory Loss
B) Mild Cognitive Impairment
C) Early-Stage Alzheimer's Disease
D) Vascular Dementia

Question 82: Sarah, a 15-year-old girl who was adopted at birth, is struggling with feelings of identity confusion and low self-esteem. She has recently started

questioning her adoptive parents about her biological origins and expressing a desire to meet her birth parents. As her mental health counselor, what is the most appropriate initial intervention?
A) Encourage Sarah to write letters to her birth parents expressing her feelings.
B) Suggest family therapy sessions involving both Sarah and her adoptive parents.
C) Advise Sarah to focus on building self-esteem through individual therapy first.
D) Recommend immediate contact with her birth parents to address her questions.

Question 83: During a counseling session, Sarah, a mental health counselor, is working with John, who has difficulty expressing his emotions. To build communication skills effectively, which technique should Sarah primarily use?
A) Reflecting feelings
B) Paraphrasing content
C) Summarizing the session
D) Providing immediate feedback

Question 84: John has been in a relationship with his partner for three years. Recently, he has noticed an increase in conflicts and arguments. Both John and his partner have expressed feeling misunderstood and emotionally distant. As a mental health counselor, what is the most effective initial intervention to address their relationship problems?
A) Encourage them to take a temporary break from each other to gain perspective.
B) Suggest they engage in couple's therapy focused on improving communication skills.
C) Advise them to prioritize individual therapy sessions before addressing couple issues.
D) Recommend reading self-help books on relationship management together.

Question 85: John, a 35-year-old male, presents with symptoms of generalized anxiety disorder (GAD). As his mental health counselor, you decide to implement Cognitive Behavioral Therapy (CBT) as part of his treatment plan. Which specific technique within CBT is most effective for addressing his pervasive and excessive worry?
A) Exposure Therapy
B) Cognitive Restructuring
C) Mindfulness-Based Stress Reduction (MBSR)
D) Dialectical Behavior Therapy (DBT)

Question 86: Which therapeutic approach is most supported by contemporary research for treating John's condition?
A) Cognitive Behavioral Therapy (CBT)
B) Dialectical Behavior Therapy (DBT)
C) Interpersonal Psychotherapy (IPT)
D) Psychodynamic Therapy

Question 87: Maria, a 30-year-old woman experiencing anxiety, mentions that she feels overwhelmed by her friends' constant advice and opinions about her life decisions. What should be your approach as her counselor to address the impact of her social support network?
A) Advise Maria to limit her interactions with friends who offer unsolicited advice.
B) Help Maria develop assertive communication skills to set boundaries with her friends.
C) Encourage Maria to seek advice from a different group of people who may be more supportive.
D) Suggest Maria focus on self-help strategies rather than relying on her social network.

Question 88: Sarah, a 35-year-old woman, presents to therapy with signs of depression and anxiety. During the session, she reveals that her husband frequently belittles her, controls her finances, and isolates her from friends and family. Based on this information, what type of abuse is Sarah most likely experiencing?
A) Physical Abuse
B) Emotional Abuse
C) Sexual Abuse
D) Financial Abuse

Question 89: Sarah, a 28-year-old woman, presents with a history of fluctuating weight and intense fear of gaining weight. She reports episodes where she consumes large amounts of food within a short period, followed by feelings of guilt and attempts to compensate through fasting or excessive exercise. Which diagnosis best fits Sarah's symptoms?
A) Anorexia Nervosa
B) Bulimia Nervosa
C) Binge Eating Disorder
D) Avoidant/Restrictive Food Intake Disorder

Question 90: John, a 45-year-old male, is struggling with feelings of stagnation and questions about his life's purpose. He reports feeling disconnected from his community and unsure about his contributions to society. According to Erikson's psychosocial development theory, which stage is John most likely experiencing difficulty with?
A) Identity vs. Role Confusion
B) Intimacy vs. Isolation
C) Generativity vs. Stagnation
D) Integrity vs. Despair

Question 91: John, a 45-year-old male, arrives at your counseling office in a state of acute distress after losing his job unexpectedly. He expresses feelings of hopelessness and mentions having suicidal thoughts but does not have a specific plan. As a mental health counselor, what should be your immediate intervention?
A) Provide John with information about local support groups for unemployment.
B) Conduct a thorough risk assessment to evaluate the severity of his suicidal ideation.
C) Encourage John to focus on positive aspects of his life to improve his mood.
D) Refer John to a psychiatrist for medication management.

Question 92: During an intake assessment, a client reports feelings of hopelessness and has a history of self-harm. Which of the following is the most appropriate immediate action for a mental health counselor to take?
A) Conduct a detailed suicide risk assessment using validated tools.
B) Encourage the client to engage in positive activities to improve mood.
C) Schedule a follow-up session in one week to monitor progress.
D) Refer the client to a psychiatrist for medication evaluation.

Question 93: Patient John, a 32-year-old software engineer, reports experiencing periods where he becomes so engrossed in his work that he loses track of time and neglects other responsibilities. However, he also describes times when he finds it difficult to concentrate on tasks even when they are important. As his counselor, what would be the most appropriate diagnosis considering these symptoms?
A) Attention-Deficit/Hyperactivity Disorder (ADHD)
B) Generalized Anxiety Disorder (GAD)

C) Major Depressive Disorder (MDD)
D) Obsessive-Compulsive Disorder (OCD)

Question 94: A 35-year-old male presents with persistent feelings of sadness, loss of interest in activities he once enjoyed, significant weight loss without dieting, insomnia, fatigue, and feelings of worthlessness. These symptoms have been present for the past two months and are impacting his daily functioning. What is the most likely diagnosis?
A) Major Depressive Disorder
B) Persistent Depressive Disorder
C) Bipolar II Disorder
D) Cyclothymic Disorder

Question 95: John is discussing his struggles with anxiety during a session. The counselor maintains eye contact, nods occasionally, and paraphrases John's statements to ensure understanding. Which core counseling attribute is most evident in the counselor's behavior?
A) Empathy
B) Active Listening
C) Unconditional Positive Regard
D) Congruence

Question 96: Which of the following best describes an ethical consideration for mental health counselors when using social media in their professional practice?
A) Maintaining confidentiality by not sharing client information on personal social media accounts.
B) Using social media to promote mental health awareness without engaging with clients directly.
C) Accepting friend requests from clients to build a stronger therapeutic relationship.
D) Sharing general mental health tips and resources on a public profile while ensuring no client-specific information is disclosed.

Question 97: Sarah, a mental health counselor, uses an encrypted email service to communicate with her clients. One day, she receives a request from a client's spouse asking for information about the client's treatment. How should Sarah respond to maintain confidentiality in electronic communication?
A) Provide the requested information since it is from a family member.
B) Ask the client for written consent before sharing any information.
C) Share minimal information to reassure the spouse without breaching confidentiality.
D) Inform the spouse that she cannot share any information without explicit consent from the client.

Question 98: During a counseling session, a client expresses frustration over constant disagreements with their partner about household responsibilities. As a mental health counselor, which approach would best demonstrate conflict tolerance and promote effective resolution?
A) Encourage the client to avoid discussing the issue until emotions have settled.
B) Advise the client to assertively communicate their feelings and needs while listening to their partner's perspective.
C) Suggest that the client compromise by taking on more responsibilities temporarily.
D) Recommend that the client use humor to defuse tension during disagreements.

Question 99: John, a new client, requests access to his counseling records. What should you do as his mental health counselor?
A) Deny John's request as clients do not have the right to

access their own counseling records.
B) Allow John limited access only after obtaining approval from a supervising authority.
C) Provide John with full access to his counseling records while ensuring he understands the implications.
D) Inform John that he can only view his records in the presence of his counselor.

Question 100: A client expresses feelings of meaninglessness and questions the purpose of life after a significant loss. As a mental health counselor, which intervention is most appropriate to address the client's spiritual/existential concerns?
A) Encourage the client to engage in mindfulness meditation.
B) Facilitate a discussion about the client's personal values and beliefs.
C) Suggest the client participate in community service activities.
D) Recommend cognitive-behavioral therapy to challenge negative thoughts.

Question 101: John, a 45-year-old male with a history of major depressive disorder, was recently discharged from an inpatient psychiatric facility. As his mental health counselor, what is the most appropriate initial step in his follow-up care plan to ensure continuity of care and reduce the risk of relapse?
A) Schedule bi-weekly therapy sessions and provide John with emergency contact numbers.
B) Arrange for a follow-up appointment within one week and develop a crisis intervention plan.
C) Enroll John in a community support group and monitor his medication compliance monthly.
D) Provide John with educational materials on depression management and schedule a follow-up in two weeks.

Question 102: During an initial counseling session with Sarah, a new client, the counselor explains the process of therapy, including confidentiality and its limits. Sarah expresses concern about her privacy because she has been experiencing domestic violence. Which of the following is the most appropriate response by the counselor regarding confidentiality?
A) "Everything you share in our sessions is completely confidential without exceptions."
B) "Your information is confidential unless you disclose intentions to harm yourself or others."
C) "Confidentiality is maintained unless you share about past criminal activities."
D) "All information is confidential except when court-ordered disclosures are required."

Question 103: When working with a family from a collectivist culture, which approach should a mental health counselor prioritize to effectively address family composition and cultural considerations?
A) Emphasize individual autonomy and personal goals.
B) Focus on the interconnectedness of family members and collective well-being.
C) Encourage open expression of emotions without regard to hierarchical structures.
D) Promote assertiveness training to enhance individual self-expression.

Question 104: A 4-year-old child exhibits significant distress when separated from their caregiver but is not easily comforted upon their return. The child shows ambivalence towards the caregiver, seeking closeness but also resisting contact. Which attachment style does this behavior most likely indicate?
A) Secure Attachment
B) Avoidant Attachment
C) Ambivalent (Resistant) Attachment

D) Disorganized Attachment

Question 105: Maria, a 32-year-old woman, presents for an initial counseling session. She reports feeling anxious, having nightmares, and experiencing flashbacks of a car accident that occurred six months ago. As her counselor, you need to assess for trauma-related symptoms. Which of the following assessments would be most appropriate to use in this scenario?
A) Beck Depression Inventory (BDI)
B) Clinician-Administered PTSD Scale (CAPS)
C) Generalized Anxiety Disorder 7-item scale (GAD-7)
D) Hamilton Anxiety Rating Scale (HAM-A)

Question 106: During a counseling session, Maria, a 35-year-old client, expresses feelings of isolation and sadness after moving to a new city. As her counselor, how should you respond to facilitate an empathic connection?
A) "It sounds like you're feeling really lonely after your move. That must be tough."
B) "Everyone feels sad when they move to a new place. You'll get used to it soon."
C) "You should try joining some local groups or activities to meet new people."
D) "Moving is always hard, but it's important to stay positive and look forward."

Question 107: Maria, a 28-year-old client, seeks counseling due to overwhelming stress from balancing work and family responsibilities. She reports experiencing frequent headaches, irritability, and trouble concentrating. During your intake session, you learn that she has no prior history of mental health issues but is currently feeling overwhelmed by her circumstances. What is the most appropriate action to take in screening Maria for appropriate services?
A) Recommend Maria start mindfulness-based stress reduction (MBSR).
B) Perform an initial mental status examination (MSE).
C) Advise Maria to see her primary care physician for physical symptoms.
D) Encourage Maria to take time off work immediately.

Question 108: When exploring a client's religious and spiritual values in counseling, which approach is most effective in fostering an open and respectful dialogue?
A) Directly asking the client about their religious practices and beliefs.
B) Integrating general questions about spirituality into the initial assessment.
C) Waiting for the client to bring up their religious or spiritual concerns.
D) Using culturally adapted assessment tools to explore religious and spiritual values.

Question 109: Sarah, a 35-year-old marketing manager, reports feeling overwhelmed by her workload and personal responsibilities. She experiences frequent headaches and trouble sleeping. During a counseling session, her therapist suggests practicing mindfulness-based stress reduction (MBSR). Which of the following best describes the primary mechanism through which MBSR helps manage stress?
A) Enhances cognitive restructuring to change negative thought patterns
B) Increases awareness of the present moment to reduce automatic stress responses
C) Promotes physical relaxation through progressive muscle relaxation techniques
D) Encourages emotional expression to alleviate built-up tension

Question 110: Scenario: John is a 35-year-old man who frequently experiences intense mood swings and finds it difficult to control his anger. He reports feeling emotionally numb at times and then suddenly overwhelmed by emotions. His psychiatrist is assessing him for potential emotional dysregulation. Which symptom is most indicative of emotional dysregulation?
A) Consistent low mood
B) Difficulty managing intense emotions
C) Persistent worry about future events
D) Recurrent intrusive thoughts

Question 111: John, a 45-year-old African American man, presents for an intake assessment reporting symptoms of depression following a recent job loss. During the Cultural Formulation Interview, John expresses that his community views his unemployment as a personal failure rather than a consequence of economic conditions. Which component of the CFI should be prioritized to understand how John's community influences his mental health?
A) Cultural definition of the problem
B) Cultural factors affecting self-coping and past help-seeking behavior
C) Cultural perceptions of cause, context, and support
D) Overall cultural assessment for diagnosis and care

Question 112: During a session with Mr. Johnson, a 45-year-old man experiencing communication issues with his teenage son, the counselor decides to implement an intervention to improve their interactional patterns. Which of the following techniques is most appropriate for this scenario?
A) Role-playing
B) Reflective listening
C) Solution-focused questioning
D) Cognitive restructuring

Question 113: John is a 50-year-old man caring for his wife who has advanced multiple sclerosis. He reports difficulty balancing his job responsibilities with caregiving duties and feels constantly exhausted. What would be the most appropriate strategy to help John manage his role strain?
A) Suggest John speak with his employer about flexible working hours.
B) Advise John to reduce his working hours to part-time.
C) Recommend John attend time management workshops.
D) Encourage John to delegate some caregiving tasks to other family members.

Question 114: Which of the following is most likely to mitigate the negative effects of prolonged separation from primary caregivers in young children?
A) Consistent daily routines
B) High-quality substitute caregiving
C) Increased social interactions with peers
D) Frequent video calls with primary caregivers

Question 115: Which of the following interventions is most effective in improving interactional patterns between a counselor and a client experiencing communication difficulties?
A) Reflective listening
B) Solution-focused questioning
C) Psychoeducation about communication styles
D) Cognitive restructuring

Question 116: John, a 45-year-old man with chronic pain and recent job loss, expresses persistent thoughts of suicide during his counseling session. He mentions having access to firearms at home but insists he has no intention of using them "yet." What should be your

primary focus during this session?
A) Explore John's reasons for living and future goals.
B) Assess John's access to firearms and create a plan to limit this access.
C) Discuss John's chronic pain management strategies.
D) Provide John with emergency crisis hotline numbers.

Question 117: Which of the following best describes an appropriate initial step for a counselor to take when clarifying their role with a new client?
A) Establishing clear boundaries regarding confidentiality and its limits.
B) Discussing personal experiences to build rapport with the client.
C) Offering advice based on personal opinions to guide the client.
D) Setting goals for the client's therapy without their input.

Question 118: When facilitating the resolution of an interpersonal conflict between two clients, which technique is most effective in ensuring both parties feel heard and understood?
A) Encouraging each party to express their feelings without interruption.
B) Suggesting solutions that you believe will work for both parties.
C) Emphasizing common goals and shared interests between the parties.
D) Summarizing each party's perspective before moving on to solutions.

Question 119: Dr. Emily, a licensed mental health counselor, receives a call from a client's spouse who claims that their partner (Dr. Emily's client) has been making threats of violence towards them. The spouse requests that Dr. Emily keep this information confidential and not disclose it to anyone, including law enforcement or other authorities. How should Dr. Emily respond?
A) Respect the spouse's request and keep the information confidential.
B) Disclose the information only if she receives direct confirmation from her client.
C) Explain to the spouse that she has a duty to warn potential victims and report threats to authorities.
D) Seek supervision from a senior colleague before making any decisions about disclosure.

Question 120: John, a new client, asks his counselor if she can guarantee that he will overcome his anxiety through their sessions. How should the counselor clarify her role in response?
A) "Yes, I can guarantee that you will overcome your anxiety."
B) "No guarantees can be made, but we will work together towards managing it."
C) "You must follow my instructions exactly to see any improvement."
D) "Overcoming anxiety completely depends on my expertise."

Question 121: John, a 45-year-old man, has been experiencing profound loneliness since his divorce two years ago. He finds it difficult to form new relationships because he fears being hurt again. Which attachment style is most likely contributing to John's current state?
A) Secure Attachment
B) Anxious-Preoccupied Attachment
C) Dismissive-Avoidant Attachment
D) Fearful-Avoidant Attachment

Question 122: Which strength is most likely to improve the likelihood of goal attainment in a client undergoing

treatment planning?
A) High self-efficacy
B) Strong social support
C) Effective coping strategies
D) Positive reinforcement

Question 123: When conducting an initial interview with a client named John, who has been referred for possible PTSD, what is the most appropriate method for gathering detailed information about his symptoms?
A) Utilize a structured diagnostic interview specifically designed for PTSD.
B) Ask John to complete a self-report questionnaire before the session.
C) Engage in casual conversation to make John comfortable before delving into his symptoms.
D) Focus primarily on John's past medical history related to trauma.

Question 124: John, a 45-year-old man, has been experiencing significant stress due to mounting debt and difficulty managing his finances. He reports feeling overwhelmed and anxious about his financial situation, which has started affecting his sleep and work performance. As his mental health counselor, what would be the most appropriate initial step in addressing John's financial issues?
A) Develop a detailed budget plan for John.
B) Refer John to a financial advisor.
C) Explore John's emotional responses to his financial stress.
D) Encourage John to seek a higher-paying job.

Question 125: John, a 60-year-old man with advanced ALS, has expressed his desire to stop all life-sustaining treatments. His wife is struggling with this decision and feels it goes against their religious beliefs. As John's mental health counselor, what is the best approach to support both John and his wife?
A) Facilitate a family meeting with a healthcare team member who can explain the medical implications of John's decision.
B) Encourage John's wife to respect his wishes regardless of their religious beliefs.
C) Suggest individual counseling sessions for John's wife to help her cope with the situation.
D) Explore alternative treatments that align with their religious beliefs while respecting John's autonomy.

Question 126: John has been working on improving his depressive symptoms through cognitive-behavioral therapy (CBT). As his counselor, you want to ensure he maintains his progress after therapy ends. Which strategy would best help John sustain his improvements?
A) Encouraging John to join a support group for individuals with depression.
B) Recommending John keep a daily log of his mood and activities.
C) Advising John to read self-help books on depression management.
D) Suggesting John engage in regular physical exercise as part of his routine.

Question 127: Which of the following is considered the most significant predictor of children's long-term adjustment following their parents' divorce?
A) The child's age at the time of divorce
B) The level of parental conflict post-divorce
C) The socioeconomic status of the custodial parent
D) The child's relationship with non-custodial parent

Question 128: During a Mental Status Exam (MSE),

which observation would most accurately indicate a potential cognitive impairment in a patient?
A) The patient exhibits poor eye contact and appears disheveled.
B) The patient struggles to recall recent events but can remember distant past events.
C) The patient speaks rapidly with frequent tangential thoughts.
D) The patient demonstrates an inability to perform simple arithmetic calculations.

Question 129: Maria, a 28-year-old female, presents with concerns about her increasing use of prescription painkillers after a surgery six months ago. She is worried about dependency and asks for help. Which initial assessment approach would be most appropriate for determining her level of substance use?
A) Brief Intervention
B) Motivational Interviewing
C) Substance Abuse Subtle Screening Inventory (SASSI)
D) Mini-Mental State Examination (MMSE)

Question 130: Which of the following best describes the potential long-term psychological impact on a child who experiences prolonged separation from their primary caregiver during early childhood?
A) Increased resilience and independence in adulthood
B) Higher risk of developing anxiety disorders and attachment issues
C) Enhanced social skills due to early exposure to diverse environments
D) Greater cognitive development due to adaptive coping mechanisms

Question 131: Sarah is a 45-year-old woman who has been caring for her elderly mother with Alzheimer's disease for the past three years. Recently, Sarah has been experiencing increased anxiety, insomnia, and feelings of being overwhelmed. As her mental health counselor, what would be the most appropriate initial intervention to address Sarah's caregiving concerns?
A) Encourage Sarah to join a caregiver support group.
B) Suggest Sarah take a temporary respite from caregiving duties.
C) Recommend individual therapy sessions focusing on stress management.
D) Advise Sarah to seek medical evaluation for potential antidepressant medication.

Question 132: Which career development theory emphasizes the importance of self-concept and its evolution over an individual's lifespan?
A) Holland's Theory of Vocational Personalities and Work Environments
B) Super's Life-Span, Life-Space Theory
C) Krumboltz's Social Learning Theory of Career Decision Making
D) Roe's Personality Development Theory

Question 133: In a group therapy session focused on grief, several members have shared similar experiences of loss. How can you use linking to enhance group cohesion and support?
A) Encourage each member to share their story individually without interjection.
B) Highlight common themes in their stories and invite them to discuss these connections.
C) Focus on one member's story at a time without referencing others' experiences.
D) Ask members to refrain from discussing their experiences until everyone has had a turn.

Question 134: A 45-year-old patient has recently

experienced a below-the-knee amputation following a severe infection. As their mental health counselor, which of the following interventions would most effectively facilitate their psychological adjustment to this physical loss?
A) Encourage the patient to join a support group for individuals with similar experiences.
B) Recommend cognitive-behavioral therapy (CBT) to address negative thought patterns.
C) Suggest mindfulness meditation to help manage stress and anxiety.
D) Promote physical rehabilitation exercises to improve mobility and independence.

Question 135: After several months of therapy, Maria has made significant progress in managing her anxiety. As her counselor, you are now focusing on helping her integrate and maintain this progress. Which of the following strategies would be most effective in ensuring that Maria continues to apply what she has learned in therapy to her daily life?
A) Encouraging Maria to journal daily about her feelings and experiences.
B) Developing a relapse prevention plan with specific coping strategies.
C) Scheduling frequent follow-up sessions to monitor progress.
D) Advising Maria to avoid all situations that trigger her anxiety.

Question 136: During a counseling session, Maria, a 16-year-old client, reveals to her counselor that she has been experiencing severe depression and has recently started having thoughts of suicide. She begs the counselor not to tell anyone about her suicidal thoughts. What is the counselor's most appropriate course of action?
A) Respect Maria's wishes and keep her suicidal thoughts confidential.
B) Inform Maria's parents immediately about her suicidal thoughts.
C) Conduct a thorough risk assessment and, if necessary, inform appropriate parties while explaining the limits of confidentiality to Maria.
D) Wait until Maria provides explicit consent before taking any action.

Question 137: John, a 65-year-old recently retired engineer, is experiencing significant anxiety and feelings of purposelessness. He finds it difficult to adjust to his new routine and misses the social interactions he had at work. As his mental health counselor, which therapeutic approach would be most effective in addressing John's retirement concerns?
A) Cognitive Behavioral Therapy (CBT)
B) Solution-Focused Brief Therapy (SFBT)
C) Existential Therapy
D) Interpersonal Therapy (IPT)

Question 138: Mark, a 50-year-old man, has recently gone through a high-conflict divorce and is struggling with co-parenting his two teenage children. He reports frequent arguments with his ex-spouse regarding parenting decisions and feels overwhelmed by the situation. Which intervention strategy would be most beneficial for Mark in managing co-parenting conflicts?
A) Family Systems Therapy
B) Mediation
C) Parenting Coordination
D) Collaborative Divorce

Question 139: During an initial intake session, a client frequently avoids eye contact and sits with their arms

crossed. As a mental health counselor, how should you interpret these behaviors in the context of evaluating interactional dynamics?

A) The client is demonstrating resistance to the counseling process.
B) The client is displaying signs of anxiety or discomfort.
C) The client is showing a lack of interest in the session.
D) The client is indicating a power struggle with the counselor.

Question 140: During an initial interview with a new client, which approach is most effective in establishing rapport and gathering comprehensive information?

A) Focusing primarily on the client's presenting problem
B) Using open-ended questions to explore various aspects of the client's life
C) Relying on structured diagnostic tools to guide the interview
D) Maintaining a neutral stance and avoiding any personal disclosures

Question 141: Which summary most effectively encapsulates John's current emotional state?

A) "John feels lonely after moving to a new city for work, missing his family and friends."
B) "John is having trouble adjusting to his new environment due to isolation from loved ones."
C) "John's feelings of loneliness stem from missing his family and friends after relocating for work."
D) "John struggles with making new connections in his new city while missing his old social circle."

Question 142: Scenario: John, a 45-year-old client dealing with substance abuse issues, has reached a point where he feels ready to terminate therapy. He has developed effective coping mechanisms and has been sober for over a year. What should be included in John's termination plan to ensure a successful transition?

A) Provide John with referrals to support groups and community resources.
B) Schedule a follow-up session one month after termination.
C) Review John's treatment goals and achievements.
D) Encourage John to write a letter summarizing his therapeutic journey.

Question 143: John, a 45-year-old man, is considering remarrying after a divorce two years ago. He has two teenage children from his previous marriage. During counseling, John expresses concerns about how his remarriage might affect his relationship with his children. What should be the primary focus of the counselor's intervention to support John's transition into remarriage?

A) Encouraging John to prioritize his new spouse over his children to establish marital stability.
B) Helping John develop strategies to integrate his new spouse into the family while maintaining strong bonds with his children.
C) Advising John to minimize interactions between his new spouse and children initially to avoid conflicts.
D) Suggesting that John seek individual therapy to address unresolved issues from his previous marriage before remarrying.

Question 144: John, a mental health counselor, is working with a couple, Mark and Lisa, who frequently argue about household responsibilities. John wants to help them develop effective conflict resolution strategies. Which approach should John prioritize to ensure both parties feel heard and understood?

A) Encourage Mark and Lisa to avoid discussing sensitive topics until they can do so calmly.
B) Teach Mark and Lisa active listening techniques to improve their communication.
C) Advise Mark and Lisa to compromise by splitting household tasks equally.
D) Suggest Mark and Lisa take turns expressing their grievances without interruption.

Question 145: Maria, a 28-year-old female, reports chronic headaches, muscle tension, and dizziness. She has been diagnosed with generalized anxiety disorder (GAD). Which physical issue is most likely contributing to her symptoms?

A) Tension Headaches
B) Migraine Headaches
C) Cervical Spine Disorder
D) Vestibular Dysfunction

Question 146: What is a common psychological impact experienced by caregivers of individuals with chronic illnesses?

A) Increased sense of personal accomplishment
B) Heightened levels of anxiety and depression
C) Enhanced social connectedness
D) Improved overall mental well-being

Question 147: A mental health counselor is faced with a situation where a client has disclosed plans to harm themselves. According to the American Counseling Association (ACA) Code of Ethics, what is the most appropriate initial action for the counselor to take?

A) Respect the client's confidentiality and explore their feelings further.
B) Contact the client's family members to inform them of the situation.
C) Assess the immediacy and severity of the threat before deciding on further action.
D) Refer the client to another mental health professional immediately.

Question 148: Sarah, a licensed mental health counselor, often uses social media to share mental health tips and resources. One of her clients sends her a friend request on a popular social media platform. How should Sarah respond in order to maintain professional boundaries and adhere to ethical guidelines?

A) Accept the friend request but limit the interaction to sharing mental health tips.
B) Politely decline the friend request and explain the importance of maintaining professional boundaries.
C) Accept the friend request but avoid discussing any therapy-related topics online.
D) Ignore the friend request without addressing it with the client.

Question 149: Maria, a 30-year-old female, has been diagnosed with major depressive disorder. She often expresses feelings of hopelessness about her future career prospects and relationships. In her therapy sessions, Maria frequently mentions that she believes she will never be successful or happy. According to the learned helplessness theory by Martin Seligman, what therapeutic approach should be prioritized to help Maria overcome her feelings of hopelessness?

A) Encouraging Maria to set small, achievable goals.
B) Focusing on improving Maria's self-esteem through positive affirmations.
C) Teaching Maria problem-solving skills for daily challenges.
D) Providing psychoeducation about depression and its symptoms.

Question 150: Scenario: Maria, a 35-year-old Latina woman, has been experiencing anxiety and depression. During your sessions, she frequently mentions her

strong connection to her family and cultural traditions. She expresses that her family's expectations sometimes contribute to her stress. As her counselor, how should you address these cultural considerations in your therapeutic approach?

A) Encourage Maria to set firm boundaries with her family to reduce stress.

B) Explore how Maria's cultural values and family expectations impact her mental health.

C) Suggest that Maria temporarily distance herself from family gatherings.

D) Recommend individual therapy focusing solely on Maria's personal goals.

ANSWER WITH DETAILED EXPLANATION SET [3]

Question 1: Correct Answer: C) Provide structured activities to build trust and rapport.

Rationale: In the forming stage, members are getting to know each other and are often hesitant to share personal experiences. Providing structured activities helps build trust and rapport, which is essential for progressing to deeper levels of interaction. Option A is more suited for the norming stage when establishing norms becomes crucial. Option B is relevant during the storming stage when conflicts may arise. Option D is important but typically more effective once initial trust has been established.

Question 2: Correct Answer: B) Emotional readiness

Rationale: Emotional readiness is the most crucial factor for ensuring a successful remarriage or recommitment. Contemporary research indicates that individuals who have resolved past emotional issues and are emotionally prepared are more likely to navigate the complexities of a new marital relationship successfully. Option A (Financial stability), while important, is secondary to emotional preparedness. Option C (Agreement on parenting styles) is significant but can often be negotiated over time if both partners are emotionally ready. Option D (Social support) is beneficial but does not outweigh the necessity of emotional readiness for long-term success in remarriage or recommitment. In summary, emotional readiness directly impacts how individuals handle conflicts, communicate, and build trust in their new relationship, making it the most critical factor compared to financial stability, agreement on parenting styles, and social support.

Question 3: Correct Answer: B) Binge Eating Disorder

Rationale: Binge Eating Disorder is characterized by recurrent episodes of eating large quantities of food, feeling a lack of control during these episodes, and experiencing distress about the behavior without engaging in compensatory behaviors like vomiting or excessive exercise. John's symptoms fit this description. Bulimia Nervosa includes compensatory behaviors following binge eating. Anorexia Nervosa involves restrictive eating patterns and an intense fear of gaining weight. Night Eating Syndrome involves nocturnal eating and insomnia but does not necessarily include the distress about overeating seen in Binge Eating Disorder.

Question 4: Correct Answer: A) Financial Counseling

Rationale: Financial Counseling directly addresses Mary's anxiety about her financial stability by providing practical advice and strategies for managing her resources effectively. While MBSR (Option B) can help reduce overall stress levels, it does not specifically target financial concerns. Psychoeducation on Retirement Planning (Option C) provides valuable information but may not offer the personalized guidance Mary needs. Group Therapy (Option D) offers social support but may not focus specifically on financial anxiety.

Question 5: Correct Answer: A) A detailed plan with access to means

Rationale: A detailed plan with access to means (Option A) is considered the most reliable indicator of imminent risk for suicide because it demonstrates both intent and capability. While a history of previous suicide attempts (Option B) is a significant risk factor, it does not necessarily indicate immediate danger. Expressing feelings of hopelessness (Option C) is a critical warning sign but lacks the specificity regarding timing and method. Experiencing recent significant loss (Option D) can increase vulnerability but does not provide concrete evidence of an imminent threat. Therefore, Option A is the most accurate predictor of immediate suicidal behavior due to its specific nature and direct link to potential action.

Question 6: Correct Answer: B) Persistent fatigue

Rationale: Persistent fatigue is one of the most common physical symptoms associated with major depressive disorder. This symptom is often due to the interplay between psychological stress and physiological changes in the body, such as alterations in neurotransmitter levels and hormonal imbalances. Chronic back pain (Option A), frequent headaches (Option C), and recurrent gastrointestinal distress (Option D) are also physical symptoms that can be associated with depression but are less commonly cited as primary indicators compared to persistent fatigue. Chronic back pain and headaches may be more directly linked to other medical conditions or stress-related disorders, while gastrointestinal distress can also stem from various other causes like diet or gastrointestinal diseases. Thus, persistent fatigue remains the most indicative physical symptom of major depressive disorder.

Question 7: Correct Answer: B) Multicultural Counseling emphasizing cultural competence and validation of her experiences.

Rationale: Multicultural Counseling is most effective for addressing Jessica's experiences because it emphasizes understanding and validating the impact of cultural identity on mental health. It helps clients navigate systemic racism by acknowledging their lived experiences. CBT (Option A), while useful for challenging negative thoughts, may not fully address the cultural context. SFBT (Option C) focuses on immediate solutions but lacks depth in addressing systemic issues. Psychoanalytic Therapy (Option D) explores unconscious biases but may not provide the immediate cultural validation Jessica needs.

Question 8: Correct Answer: A) Major Depressive Disorder

Rationale: Major Depressive Disorder (MDD) is characterized by a depressed mood or loss of interest or pleasure in daily activities for more than two weeks along with other symptoms such as significant weight change, insomnia or hypersomnia, and fatigue. In this case, the patient's symptoms align well with MDD criteria. - Option B (Persistent Depressive Disorder) includes chronic depression lasting for at least two years but typically has less severe symptoms compared to MDD. - Option C (Bipolar II Disorder) involves periods of hypomania and depression; however, there is no indication of hypomanic episodes here. - Option D (Generalized Anxiety Disorder) focuses on excessive anxiety and worry rather than depressive symptoms. Each incorrect option represents a closely related disorder but lacks key diagnostic features present in MDD.

Question 9: Correct Answer: B) Develop Discrepancy

Rationale: Developing Discrepancy is a fundamental principle of MI that helps clients see the gap between their current behaviors and their broader life goals or values. This awareness can enhance motivation for change. - A) Express Empathy involves understanding the client's perspective but does not directly address discrepancies. - C) Roll with Resistance involves accepting client ambivalence without confrontation. - D) Support Self-Efficacy focuses on building the client's confidence in their ability to change but does not directly address discrepancies between behavior and goals.

Question 10: Correct Answer: C) Post-Traumatic Stress Disorder

Rationale: Sarah's symptoms, including severe anxiety, flashbacks, difficulty sleeping, and avoidance behaviors persisting for more than six months, are indicative of Post-Traumatic Stress Disorder (PTSD). Acute Stress Disorder (A) is characterized by similar symptoms but occurs within the first month following a traumatic event. Generalized Anxiety Disorder (B) involves excessive worry about various aspects of life but does not specifically include trauma-related flashbacks or avoidance behaviors. Adjustment Disorder (D) involves emotional or behavioral symptoms in response to a stressor but lacks the specific trauma-related features seen in PTSD.

Question 11: Correct Answer: A) An online course on mindfulness-based stress reduction (MBSR)

Rationale: The correct answer is A because an online course on MBSR offers structured, evidence-based practices that can help Emily develop skills to manage her depressive symptoms effectively. Option B, while informative, may be overwhelming without actionable steps. Option C provides inspiration but lacks practical interventions. Option D offers some utility in tracking mood but does not provide comprehensive strategies or skills development needed for managing depression.

Question 12: Correct Answer: D) Multigenerational Transmission Process

Rationale: The Multigenerational Transmission Process is a core concept in Bowen's Family Systems Theory that explains how patterns of behavior, including anxiety, are passed down through generations. This process highlights the transmission of emotional processes and relationship dynamics across multiple generations. Differentiation of Self refers to an individual's ability to separate their own intellectual and emotional functioning from that of their family. Triangulation involves a third party being drawn into a conflict between two members to reduce tension. Emotional Cutoff describes the way people manage unresolved emotional issues with family members by reducing or cutting off emotional contact. While all these concepts are part of Bowen's theory, only the Multigenerational Transmission Process directly addresses the transfer of anxiety across generations.

Question 13: Correct Answer: C) Adjusting to an environment in which the deceased is missing

Rationale: Worden's second task of mourning is "Adjusting to an environment in which the deceased is missing." This involves adapting to life without the deceased, which can include practical adjustments, emotional changes, and redefining roles. Option A (Accepting the reality of the loss) refers to Worden's first task. Option B (Processing the pain of grief) aligns with his second task but is not specific enough about adjustment. Option D (Finding an enduring connection with the deceased while embarking on a new life) pertains to his fourth task. Each option relates to Worden's tasks but only C accurately describes adjusting to a new environment without the deceased.

Question 14: Correct Answer: B) Help her develop a detailed plan for her remaining time and end-of-life arrangements.

Rationale: Helping Maria develop a detailed plan for her remaining time can provide a sense of control and reduce anxiety about death. While focusing on positive memories (option A), avoiding thoughts about death through distractions (option C), or engaging in intensive psychotherapy (option D) might offer some benefits, they do not directly address the need for practical planning that can significantly alleviate anxiety related to loss of control at the end of life. Planning allows Maria to make meaningful choices about how she spends her remaining time.

Question 15: Correct Answer: A) Encourage the client to participate in group therapy sessions where they can share their experiences.

Rationale: Disenfranchised grief refers to grief that is not socially recognized or supported, making it difficult for individuals to express and process their emotions. Group therapy provides a supportive environment where clients can share their experiences with others who understand their unique situation, helping them feel validated and less isolated. While writing letters (Option B), engaging in mindfulness meditation (Option C), and keeping a journal (Option D) are beneficial therapeutic techniques, they do not provide the same level of social support and validation that group therapy offers. Group therapy addresses both emotional expression and social recognition, which are crucial for individuals experiencing disenfranchised grief.

Question 16: Correct Answer: B) Ensuring that the client understands the potential risks and benefits of treatment.

Rationale: Ensuring that the client understands the potential risks and benefits of treatment is crucial for valid informed consent. This element ensures that clients can make an informed decision about their participation in therapy. While providing information about the counselor's qualifications (Option A), discussing confidentiality limits (Option C), and confirming voluntary participation (Option D) are important aspects of informed consent, they do not individually guarantee that clients fully understand what they are consenting to. Understanding risks and benefits directly impacts a client's ability to make an informed choice, making it a critical component. - Option A is incorrect because while knowing the counselor's qualifications helps build trust, it does not directly relate to understanding treatment implications. - Option C is incorrect because confidentiality is one aspect of informed consent but does not encompass all necessary information for an informed decision. - Option D is incorrect because voluntary agreement ensures no coercion but does not address whether clients understand what they are agreeing to.

Rationale: Exploring Maria's past relationships helps uncover the root cause of her feelings, which are being transferred onto the counselor. This approach is grounded in psychodynamic theory and allows for a deeper understanding and resolution of transference. Option A may escalate conflict, Option C neglects addressing the issue, and Option D is premature without attempting resolution first.

Question 18: Correct Answer: C) Explore how John's faith can support his recovery process while acknowledging his concerns about family honor.

Rationale: The best course of action is to explore how John's faith can support his recovery while acknowledging his concerns about family honor. This approach respects John's cultural values and leverages them as strengths in his treatment plan. Option A might disregard important cultural aspects. Option B could reinforce secrecy and stigma associated with mental health issues. Option D fails to consider John's cultural context, potentially alienating him from seeking help.

Question 19: Correct Answer: D) Correcting any inaccuracies in the client's records promptly.

Rationale: Option D is correct because it aligns with ethical standards requiring accuracy in client records. Accurate documentation ensures that decisions made about client care are based on reliable information. Option A is incorrect because while signing and dating entries is important, it does not address correcting inaccuracies, which is crucial for maintaining accurate records. Option B is incorrect as subjective observations should be included but must be clearly labeled as such and not regularly updated without relevance or necessity. Option C is incorrect because sharing client records without explicit consent violates confidentiality principles unless under specific legal or emergency circumstances. By comparing these options, we see that only Option D fully encompasses the ethical responsibility of maintaining accurate client records by correcting inaccuracies promptly.

Question 20: Correct Answer: D) Speech

Rationale: The 'Speech' component of an MSE specifically assesses a patient's ability to understand and use language appropriately. This includes examining the rate, volume, articulation, and fluency of speech. While 'Thought Process' (Option A) involves how thoughts are organized and connected, it does not directly assess language use. 'Insight' (Option B) refers to the patient's awareness and understanding of their own condition, not their language abilities. 'Judgment' (Option C) involves decision-making abilities rather than language comprehension or usage. Therefore, 'Speech' is the most accurate option for assessing language use during an MSE.

Question 21: Correct Answer: B) Discuss sliding scale fees or payment plans based on John's current financial situation.

Rationale: The first step Emily should take is discussing sliding scale fees or payment plans (B), which directly addresses John's expressed value for therapy while accommodating his financial constraints. Reducing session frequency (A) might help but could compromise therapeutic progress. Referring him to community resources (C) can be considered if an agreement cannot be reached but isn't the immediate step. Advising him to suspend therapy (D) would disregard his need for ongoing support during a difficult time and might worsen his condition.

Question 22: Correct Answer: A) Exposure and Response Prevention (ERP)

Rationale: Exposure and Response Prevention (ERP) is widely recognized as the most effective cognitive-behavioral intervention for OCD. ERP involves exposing the individual to anxiety-provoking stimuli without engaging in compulsive behaviors, thereby reducing the frequency and intensity of obsessive thoughts over time. - Option A (Correct): ERP directly targets the avoidance behaviors and rituals associated with OCD, which helps in breaking the cycle of obsessions and compulsions. - Option B: Cognitive Restructuring focuses on changing maladaptive thought patterns but does not specifically address the behavioral component critical in OCD treatment. - Option C: Mindfulness-Based Cognitive Therapy (MBCT) can help manage anxiety but lacks the direct confrontation with obsessive triggers that ERP provides. - Option D: Habit Reversal Training is more suited for conditions like tic disorders and does not specifically target the obsessive thoughts central to OCD. Each option was crafted to reflect different therapeutic approaches that might seem plausible but lack the comprehensive efficacy found in ERP for treating OCD.

Question 23: Correct Answer: A) Cognitive restructuring

Rationale: Cognitive restructuring is a core component of cognitive-behavioral therapy (CBT) and is particularly effective in addressing the distorted thinking patterns that drive process addictions like pornography and gambling. It involves identifying and challenging irrational beliefs, thus reducing urges by altering thought processes. Option B (Exposure and response prevention) is primarily used for anxiety disorders, particularly OCD, and while it can be adapted for addiction, it is not as directly effective as cognitive restructuring for process addictions. Option C (Motivational interviewing) focuses on enhancing motivation to change but does not directly address cognitive distortions. Option D (Mindfulness-based stress reduction) helps with stress management but does not specifically target the cognitive distortions driving addictive behaviors. By comparing each option: - Cognitive restructuring directly addresses distorted thinking. - Exposure and response prevention is more suited for anxiety-related conditions. - Motivational interviewing increases motivation but lacks direct intervention on thought patterns. - Mindfulness-based stress reduction aids in managing stress without targeting cognitive distortions.

Question 24: Correct Answer: C) Counselors must inform clients that confidentiality may be breached if there is a risk of harm to self or others, or if there is suspected child abuse.

Rationale: Option C is correct because it accurately reflects the legal and ethical standards regarding confidentiality in counseling. Confidentiality can indeed be breached under specific circumstances such as risk of harm to self or others, or suspected child abuse. Option A is incorrect because it oversimplifies the issue and fails to acknowledge legally mandated exceptions. Option B, while partially correct, does not encompass all scenarios where confidentiality may be breached. Option D is incorrect as it gives counselors too much discretionary power, which could lead to unethical practices. Understanding these distinctions ensures counselors properly inform their clients about the limits of confidentiality.

Question 25: Correct Answer: C) Family therapy involving David and his parents

Rationale: Family therapy is the best intervention as it addresses the systemic nature of David's behavioral problems within the family context. Individual counseling (Option A) focuses solely on David without considering family dynamics that may contribute to his behavior. Group therapy (Option B) could provide peer support but wouldn't address specific family interactions. Couple counseling (Option D) for his parents might improve their relationship but wouldn't directly address David's behavior or its impact on family dynamics. Family therapy allows exploration of roles, communication patterns, and relational influences within the entire family system.

Question 26: Correct Answer: C) Evaluating Maria's risk for intimate partner violence.

Rationale: The primary concern in this scenario is evaluating Maria's risk for intimate partner violence (IPV).

Her symptoms of frequent headaches and anxiety, coupled with her partner's controlling behavior and emotional abuse, are red flags for IPV. While assessing for depression (Option A) and exploring childhood trauma (Option B) are important, they do not directly address the immediate concern of potential IPV. Discussing stress management techniques (Option D) may help with symptoms but does not address the root cause. Therefore, evaluating IPV risk is crucial to ensure Maria's safety and provide appropriate interventions.

Question 27: Correct Answer: C) Rationalization

Rationale: Rationalization involves creating plausible but false excuses for behaviors that are actually driven by unconscious motives. John's justification of missing sessions due to work aligns with rationalization. Denial (Option A) would involve refusing to acknowledge an issue exists, projection (Option B) involves attributing one's own unacceptable thoughts or feelings to others, and repression (Option D) involves unconsciously blocking out distressing thoughts or memories.

Question 28: Correct Answer: D) Guide John through an exploration of how his disconnection from spirituality may be impacting his sense of purpose.

Rationale: Guiding John through an exploration of how his disconnection from spirituality may be impacting his sense of purpose addresses both his existential crisis and potential spiritual void, offering a comprehensive approach to his distress. Reconnecting with his community (Option A) might not consider current beliefs; discussing beliefs without spirituality (Option B) overlooks potential root causes; encouraging new practices (Option C) might not respect his past experiences or readiness for change.

Question 29: Correct Answer: D) The quality of post-adoption support

Rationale: The quality of post-adoption support is crucial for a successful attachment process in adopted children. Research indicates that consistent emotional and psychological support helps children form secure attachments with their adoptive parents, promoting better long-term outcomes. While the age of the child (A) can influence attachment, it is not as significant as ongoing support. The adoptive parents' socioeconomic status (B) may provide resources but does not directly affect attachment quality. Pre-adoption trauma (C) can hinder attachment but can be mitigated with effective post-adoption support, making option D the most comprehensive and accurate factor in fostering successful attachment.

Question 30: Correct Answer: A) Encourage them to create a detailed schedule outlining each parent's responsibilities.

Rationale: Creating a detailed schedule outlining each parent's responsibilities can help clarify expectations, reduce misunderstandings, and ensure both parents are contributing fairly. Option B might be helpful for severe conflicts but doesn't address day-to-day coordination. Option C could reduce conflict but also limit necessary communication for effective co-parenting. Option D involves the children directly, which may not be appropriate until Maria and Carlos have improved their own communication and coordination first. A clear schedule fosters accountability and balance in shared responsibilities.

Question 31: Correct Answer: B) Listen actively to the feedback without interrupting and ask clarifying questions if needed.

Rationale: Option B is correct because it demonstrates active listening a crucial skill in receiving feedback effectively. By not interrupting and asking clarifying questions, Sarah shows openness to understanding and reflecting on the feedback provided. - Option A is incorrect as defending oneself immediately can come off as dismissive and resistant. - Option C is incorrect because blindly agreeing does not demonstrate critical thinking or engagement with the feedback. - Option D is incorrect as dismissing feedback outright shows a lack of willingness to improve or consider other perspectives.

Question 32: Correct Answer: B) Facilitate a support group where John can share his feelings with others who have experienced similar losses.

Rationale: Facilitating a support group allows John to connect with others who understand his experience, providing emotional support and reducing feelings of isolation. This approach aligns with contemporary research emphasizing the importance of social support in coping with significant physical loss. Option A might be beneficial later but may seem dismissive initially. Option C oversimplifies the complexity of grief and adjustment. Option D is important but might not address John's immediate emotional needs.

Question 33: Correct Answer: B) Help Maria develop bicultural skills to navigate both her native and new cultures effectively.

Rationale: Developing bicultural skills allows individuals like Maria to balance their original cultural identity with the new culture they are adapting to. This approach is supported by research indicating that biculturalism can reduce stress and improve psychological well-being. Option A suggests full assimilation, which can lead to loss of identity and increased stress. Option C advises maintaining native practices exclusively, which might hinder successful adaptation. Option D suggests avoiding interactions with one's native culture, potentially leading to isolation and further stress.

Question 34: Correct Answer: C) Intellectual Disability

Rationale: Intellectual Disability (ID) is characterized by significant limitations in both intellectual functioning (IQ below 70-75) and adaptive behavior, with onset before age 18. The child's IQ score of 65 and difficulties in daily living skills align with this diagnosis. Specific Learning Disorder (A) involves difficulties in specific academic areas but does not encompass broad intellectual and adaptive deficits. Autism Spectrum Disorder (B) includes social communication challenges but also involves restricted/repetitive behaviors not mentioned here. Attention-Deficit/Hyperactivity Disorder (D) primarily affects attention and hyperactivity/impulsivity without necessarily impacting overall intellectual functioning or adaptive behavior to the same extent as ID.

Question 35: Correct Answer: B) Discuss a safety plan with the client and obtain their consent before taking further action.

Rationale: Dr. Johnson must balance confidentiality with duty of care by first discussing a safety plan and obtaining consent from the client (option B). This approach respects client autonomy while addressing safety concerns. Option A disregards confidentiality by involving law enforcement prematurely. Option C neglects immediate safety needs, and option D breaches confidentiality by involving family without consent. Ethical practice requires prioritizing both safety and informed consent.

Question 36: Correct Answer: A) Tension-building phase

Rationale: The tension-building phase is characterized by increasing stress and strain in the relationship, where minor incidents escalate into more significant conflicts. This aligns with Emily's report of increasing control and violence. The acute battering incident (B) refers to the actual act of violence, while the honeymoon phase (C) involves apologies and temporary calm. The reconciliation phase (D) is not a formally recognized term in the Cycle of Violence model.

Question 37: Correct Answer: B) Consistent sleep schedule

Rationale: Contemporary research highlights that maintaining a consistent sleep schedule is most strongly associated with improved sleep quality. Regular physical exercise (Option A) does improve sleep but is not as impactful as a consistent sleep schedule. Reduction in caffeine intake (Option C) can also enhance sleep quality but primarily affects those who consume high amounts of caffeine close to bedtime. Use of white noise machines (Option D) may help some individuals by masking disruptive sounds, but it does not have as broad an impact as a consistent sleep schedule. A regular sleep routine helps regulate the body's internal clock, leading to better overall sleep quality.

Question 38: Correct Answer: C) Collaborating with Maria to create SMART goals tailored to her needs.

Rationale: Collaborating with Maria to create SMART (Specific, Measurable, Attainable, Relevant, Time-bound) goals ensures that the treatment objectives are clear, realistic, and trackable. This approach aligns with contemporary practices in counseling that emphasize structured yet flexible goal-setting. Option A is incorrect because broad goals lack specificity and measurability. Option B is not ideal as highly ambitious goals may lead to frustration if they are unattainable. Option D disregards the counselor's role in providing professional guidance and ensuring that the goals are feasible and aligned with therapeutic principles.

Question 39: Correct Answer: B) "I feel worried when our financial situation is uncertain."

Rationale: An effective "I" statement (Option B) focuses on expressing one's own feelings without blaming the partner, facilitating open communication and reducing defensiveness. Option A blames Mark directly, increasing conflict potential. Option C generalizes the issue without addressing Sarah's emotions. Option D criticizes Mark's behavior rather than conveying Sarah's feelings constructively.

Question 40: Correct Answer: A) Cognitive Behavioral Therapy (CBT)

Rationale: Cognitive Behavioral Therapy (CBT) is the most appropriate modality for John as it focuses on identifying and changing negative thought patterns and behaviors, which aligns with his desire to understand and change his thought patterns. Psychodynamic Therapy (B) is more focused on exploring unconscious processes and past experiences, which may not directly address John's current cognitive distortions. Interpersonal Therapy (C) focuses on improving interpersonal relationships and social functioning but does not primarily target thought patterns. Dialectical Behavior Therapy (D), while effective for emotional regulation and distress tolerance, is typically used for borderline personality disorder rather than primary depressive symptoms.

Question 41: Correct Answer: A) Validate her feelings and explore her reasons for wanting to end her life.

Rationale: Validating Maria's feelings and exploring her reasons for wanting to end her life is crucial as it acknowledges her emotional state and provides an opportunity for deeper understanding. Immediate referral (B) may be necessary later but isn't the initial step. Encouraging positive focus (C) can seem dismissive without first addressing core issues. Developing a safety plan (D) is important but secondary to understanding her current emotional state.

Question 42: Correct Answer: B) Develop a safety plan with Alex and involve school authorities.

Rationale: Developing a safety plan with Alex and involving school authorities addresses the immediate risk of harm and ensures that protective measures are put in place. Encouraging Alex to confront the bully (Option A) could potentially escalate the situation. Focusing solely on building self-esteem (Option C) does not address the immediate threat. Advising a change of schools (Option D) might be necessary later but is not an immediate intervention.

Question 43: Correct Answer: B) Conducting a detailed clinical interview focused on his combat experiences

Rationale: Conducting a detailed clinical interview focused on John's combat experiences is crucial for an initial assessment of trauma. This approach allows the counselor to gather comprehensive information about John's symptoms, triggers, and history in a personalized manner. While administering the Trauma Symptom Inventory (TSI), using the Patient Health Questionnaire-9 (PHQ-9), and implementing the Alcohol Use Disorders Identification Test (AUDIT) can provide valuable information about specific symptoms or comorbid conditions, they do not replace the depth and context provided by a thorough clinical interview

tailored to understanding trauma from combat experiences.

Question 44: Correct Answer: B) Using standardized assessment tools for both pre-test and post-test.

Rationale: Using standardized assessment tools for both pre-test and post-test is crucial because it ensures consistency, reliability, and validity of the measures. Standardized tools have been tested for their psychometric properties, ensuring that any changes in scores are due to the intervention rather than variations in measurement. Option A is incorrect because while minimizing bias is important, having different clinicians administer tests could introduce variability due to differences in administration styles. Option C is incorrect as administering the post-test immediately may not capture long-term effects or changes that occur over time. Option D is incorrect because external variables can significantly impact outcomes; thus, they must be considered to attribute changes accurately to the intervention. Each option challenges understanding by being closely related: - Option A tests knowledge about bias but misses standardization importance. - Option C focuses on timing but neglects long-term assessment needs. - Option D disregards external factors' role, crucial for accurate outcome attribution.

Question 45: Correct Answer: B) Use simple language to describe PTSD symptoms and relate them to John's experiences.

Rationale: Using simple language ensures that John comprehends his condition without feeling overwhelmed by medical jargon. Relating symptoms to his personal experiences makes the information more relevant and understandable. Contemporary research emphasizes clear communication in psychoeducation. Option A may confuse or intimidate John with complex terminology. Option C neglects crucial information about symptom management, while option D might not be engaging or personalized enough for effective learning.

Question 46: Correct Answer: C) Body image therapy combined with couples counseling.

Rationale: Body image therapy combined with couples counseling is most beneficial for Maria as it addresses her feelings of unattractiveness and anxiety about her partner's perception. This approach helps improve her self-image and communication with her partner regarding intimacy concerns post-surgery. Acceptance and Commitment Therapy (ACT; Option A) may help with emotional acceptance but does not specifically target body image issues or relationship dynamics. Hormone replacement therapy (Option B) is not relevant as there is no indication of hormonal issues affecting her desire. Mindfulness-based stress reduction (Option D) can reduce anxiety but does not specifically address body image or relational aspects.

Question 47: Correct Answer: B) Helping Maria identify and challenge negative thoughts about her body image and self-worth.

Rationale: Cognitive-behavioral therapy (CBT) emphasizes identifying and challenging negative thoughts, which can significantly improve emotional adjustment after physical loss. Option A may lead to suppression of emotions rather than healthy processing. Option C neglects the importance of professional mental health support in conjunction with family support. Option D promotes avoidance rather than addressing underlying issues.

Question 48: Correct Answer: C) "I am required by law to obtain your written consent before sharing any details unless it's an emergency situation."

Rationale: The correct answer is C. Counselors must obtain written consent before disclosing client information unless an emergency necessitates otherwise. Option A is incorrect because verbal consent alone may not meet legal standards for most disclosures. Option B partially addresses mandatory reporting but overlooks other situations requiring disclosure without consent (e.g., emergencies). Option D misrepresents informed consent by implying unrestricted sharing with healthcare providers without specific client approval.

Question 49: Correct Answer: C) Informational Support
Rationale: Informational support involves providing advice, suggestions, and information that can help an individual solve problems or cope with stress. This type of support is crucial for enhancing coping strategies as it equips individuals with the knowledge they need to manage their situations effectively. Emotional support (Option A) involves expressions of empathy, love, trust, and caring. While it is essential for emotional well-being, it does not directly provide the practical advice needed for coping strategies. Instrumental support (Option B) refers to tangible aid and services that directly assist individuals in need. Though helpful, it does not specifically enhance coping strategies through advice and guidance. Appraisal support (Option D) involves providing feedback and affirmation that helps individuals evaluate their situation and self-worth. While important for self-assessment and confidence building, it does not directly offer the practical advice that informational support does. Thus, while all forms of social support are valuable, informational support is uniquely positioned to enhance coping strategies through advice and guidance.

Question 50: Correct Answer: C) Verify the legitimacy of the request and obtain written consent from the client before releasing any records.
Rationale: The correct answer is C. Ethical practice requires verifying requests for information and obtaining informed consent from clients before releasing their records. Option A disregards client consent; Option B might delay necessary actions without verifying legitimacy; Option D risks unauthorized disclosure even if partial information is released.

Question 51: Correct Answer: A) Honor David's advance directive and advocate for withholding life-sustaining measures.
Rationale: An advance directive legally represents the patient's wishes regarding their medical care. Honoring David's advance directive (Option A) respects his previously expressed desires. While involving an ethics committee (Option C) could provide additional perspectives, it may delay adherence to David's wishes. Temporarily using life-sustaining measures (Option B) or supporting the daughter's request (Option D) contradicts David's documented preferences.

Question 52: Correct Answer: A) To accept the reality of the loss
Rationale: John is primarily struggling with accepting the reality of his daughter's death, as evidenced by his frequent visits to her grave and difficulty in accepting her death. This aligns with Worden's first task of mourning (A). While he may also be processing pain (B), adjusting to a new environment (C), and seeking an enduring connection (D), his primary issue is acceptance. The other tasks are closely related but do not capture his main struggle as accurately as acceptance does.

Question 53: Correct Answer: C) Partial hospitalization program (PHP)
Rationale: A Partial Hospitalization Program (PHP) is appropriate for John due to the severity of his depression and suicidal ideation without a specific plan. PHP provides structured treatment during the day while allowing him to return home at night, which leverages his supportive family environment. Outpatient therapy (A) may not offer enough support given his symptoms. Intensive outpatient program (IOP) (B) is less intensive than PHP and may not address his acute needs adequately. Inpatient hospitalization (D) is more restrictive and typically reserved for those with imminent risk or lack of support systems.

Question 54: Correct Answer: B) Help Maria identify sources of meaning and purpose in her life.
Rationale: The most appropriate initial intervention is to help Maria identify sources of meaning and purpose in her life (Option B). This approach aligns with existential therapy principles, which emphasize finding personal significance amidst suffering. Option A (exploring religious beliefs) may be beneficial but should follow after addressing immediate existential concerns. Option C (support group referral) can provide social support but may not directly address her existential crisis initially. Option D (discussing feelings about death) is important but may overwhelm her without first establishing a sense of purpose.

Question 55: Correct Answer: D) Arrange a farewell session for John where he can express his thoughts and say goodbye.
Rationale: A farewell session provides closure for both John and other group members, allowing everyone to express their feelings about his departure. This fosters a sense of completion and continuity within the group's process. Option A might be abrupt without giving John an opportunity for closure. Option B could create anxiety by prolonging uncertainty. Option C neglects addressing emotions related to John's departure promptly.

Question 56: Correct Answer: B) Confirming the provider's network status with the insurance company.
Rationale: Confirming the provider's network status with the insurance company is crucial because it directly affects reimbursement rates and out-of-pocket costs for clients. In-network providers typically have negotiated rates that result in lower costs for clients and higher likelihood of full reimbursement. While verifying coverage limits (A), reviewing deductible status (C), and checking pre-authorization requirements (D) are important steps, they do not have as immediate an impact on billing accuracy and reimbursement as ensuring network status. Network status determines whether services are covered at all or if they are subject to higher out-of-pocket expenses.

Question 57: Correct Answer: C) Teach John mindfulness meditation to help him focus on the present moment.
Rationale: Mindfulness meditation is an effective initial intervention for managing ruminating thoughts because it encourages individuals to focus on the present moment rather than getting caught up in repetitive negative thinking. This approach is supported by contemporary research which shows that mindfulness can reduce rumination and improve emotional regulation. - Option A (Thought-stopping techniques): While thought-stopping can be useful, it may not address the underlying patterns of rumination as effectively as mindfulness. - Option B (Journaling): Journaling helps in gaining perspective but may inadvertently reinforce rumination if not guided properly. - Option D (Challenging negative thoughts): Cognitive restructuring is beneficial but often more effective after initial mindfulness practices have been established.

Question 58: Correct Answer: C) Use simple language and visual aids to explain the treatment, then assess her understanding.
Rationale: Using simple language and visual aids helps ensure that Sarah comprehends the information being presented, which is crucial for obtaining valid informed consent. Option A assumes that providing a detailed document alone is sufficient, which may not address comprehension issues. Option B involves verbal explanation but lacks assessment of understanding. Option D suggests referral without attempting to facilitate understanding first.

Question 59: Correct Answer: A) Panic Attacks
Rationale: Panic attacks are characterized by sudden episodes of intense fear that trigger severe physical reactions when there is no real danger or apparent cause. Symptoms include rapid heartbeat, sweating, and shortness of breath, often accompanied by feelings of impending doom. Generalized Anxiety Disorder (GAD) involves persistent and excessive worry but typically does not present with such acute physical symptoms. Hyperthyroidism can cause similar symptoms but would be identified through thyroid function tests. Myocardial infarction (heart attack) presents with chest pain and other severe symptoms that are

usually continuous rather than episodic.

Question 60: Correct Answer: B) Transference involves redirecting feelings from past significant relationships onto the therapist.

Rationale: Option B is correct because transference refers to the redirection of feelings and attitudes from past significant relationships onto the therapist, as grounded in psychodynamic theory. Option A is incorrect because while it mentions projection, it inaccurately labels transference as a defense mechanism. Option C is incorrect because transference is typically unconscious, not a conscious process. Option D is incorrect as it misinterprets transference as an avoidance strategy rather than a redirection of past relational dynamics. Understanding these distinctions helps clarify the accurate conceptualization of transference in therapeutic settings.

Question 61: Correct Answer: A) Sarah is experiencing separation anxiety due to disrupted attachment with her primary caregiver.

Rationale: According to Bowlby's Attachment Theory, children form strong emotional bonds with their primary caregivers. When these bonds are disrupted, as in the case of prolonged separation due to hospitalization, children often experience separation anxiety. This manifests in behaviors such as crying spells and reluctance to engage in usual activities like attending school. Option B misinterprets the developmental phase involving fear of strangers which typically occurs earlier. Option C incorrectly attributes the symptoms solely to generalized anxiety disorder without considering the context of separation. Option D diverts attention from the primary issue of disrupted attachment.

Question 62: Correct Answer: B) Facilitating connections with community resources that align with the client's values and needs.

Rationale: Facilitating connections with community resources that align with the client's values and needs (Option B) is most effective because it ensures that the support system is meaningful and relevant to the client. This approach is grounded in contemporary research emphasizing personalized interventions. Option A, while promoting social engagement, lacks personalization and may overwhelm the client. Option C limits support to family members, which may not be sufficient or appropriate. Option D focuses on quantity over quality of interactions, which may not lead to meaningful support relationships. Thus, Option B best addresses individual client needs and promotes sustainable support systems.

Question 63: Correct Answer: B) Help John develop coping strategies for dealing with microaggressions.

Rationale: Developing coping strategies for dealing with microaggressions is a culturally sensitive approach that empowers John while acknowledging the systemic nature of such issues. It helps him manage his mental health effectively within the context of his experiences. Option A might escalate conflict and may not be safe or effective for John. Option C invalidates John's experiences and can exacerbate his distress. Option D removes an opportunity for therapeutic exploration and support, which is essential for addressing underlying emotional impacts.

Question 64: Correct Answer: B) Hypervigilance

Rationale: Long-term exposure to interpersonal partner violence often leads to hypervigilance, where the individual becomes excessively alert and sensitive to potential threats. This heightened state of awareness is a common psychological response to ongoing trauma. - A) Increased self-esteem is incorrect because exposure to partner violence typically lowers self-esteem due to constant belittlement and abuse. - C) Enhanced social skills is incorrect as victims often become isolated and may struggle with social interactions due to fear and mistrust. - D) Improved problem-solving abilities is incorrect because chronic stress from violence can impair cognitive functions, making it harder for victims to think clearly. The correct answer, B) Hypervigilance, aligns with contemporary research on trauma responses in victims of interpersonal partner violence.

Question 65: Correct Answer: B) The client's subjective reports and counselor's objective observations.

Rationale: Including both the client's subjective reports and the counselor's objective observations ensures that the documentation is comprehensive and balanced. This approach captures the client's perspective while also providing a professional assessment, which is crucial for clinical utility and ethical responsibility. Option A is incorrect because a detailed narrative of every session can be overly cumbersome and may include unnecessary information. Option C is incorrect because focusing only on significant changes may omit important ongoing details. Option D is incorrect because while treatment goals are important, they do not provide a complete picture of ongoing progress. Tone: Professional and Knowledgeable

Question 66: Correct Answer: A) Parkinson's Disease

Rationale: Parkinson's Disease is characterized by motor symptoms such as bradykinesia (slowed movements), rigidity, tremors at rest, shuffling gait, and non-motor symptoms like sleep disturbances and irritability. - B) Lewy Body Dementia shares some features with Parkinson's but also includes prominent visual hallucinations and fluctuating cognition early in the disease course. - C) Normal Pressure Hydrocephalus presents with a triad of gait disturbance, urinary incontinence, and cognitive impairment but lacks the characteristic tremors of Parkinson's. - D) Frontotemporal Dementia primarily affects personality and behavior changes or language difficulties rather than motor symptoms. Both questions require nuanced understanding of geriatric mental health conditions to differentiate between similar presenting symptoms accurately.

Question 67: Correct Answer: A) Genogram construction

Rationale: Genogram construction is a comprehensive tool used in family therapy to map out relationships and identify patterns of communication and relational dynamics within the family system. It provides visual representation and helps in understanding multigenerational patterns. Role-playing exercises (Option B) can also reveal interaction patterns but are more situational and less comprehensive. Narrative therapy techniques (Option C) focus on individual stories rather than systemic patterns. Solution-focused brief therapy (Option D) aims at finding immediate solutions rather than exploring underlying interaction dynamics. Therefore, while these methods have their merits, genogram construction is most effective for identifying comprehensive relational dynamics within the family system.

Question 68: Correct Answer: A) Denial

Rationale: Sarah's behavior of expressing disbelief and talking about her husband as if he were still alive indicates she is in the denial stage of Kübler-Ross's stages of grief. In this stage, individuals have difficulty accepting the reality of loss and may act as though the loss has not occurred. Anger (B), bargaining (C), and depression (D) are other stages in Kübler-Ross's model but involve different emotions and behaviors. Anger involves feelings of frustration and helplessness; bargaining involves making deals or promises to reverse the loss; depression involves profound sadness and withdrawal.

Question 69: Correct Answer: A) Structured clinical interview

Rationale: A structured clinical interview is designed to systematically cover all relevant areas of a client's mental health history, ensuring comprehensive and accurate data collection. This method reduces interviewer bias and enhances reliability compared to an informal conversation (Option D). While a standardized self-report inventory (Option C) can provide reliable data, it may not capture the depth needed for an initial intake. An open-ended questionnaire (Option B) allows for detailed responses but lacks the structure necessary for thorough assessment.

Question 70: Correct Answer: C) Gently redirect the conversation by encouraging other members to share.
Rationale: The most appropriate initial intervention is to gently redirect the conversation by encouraging other members to share. This approach addresses John's behavior without singling him out or causing embarrassment, which can maintain group cohesion and safety. - Option A is incorrect because directly confronting John in front of the group could lead to defensiveness and disrupt group dynamics. - Option B is a viable option but may not address the immediate issue during the session. - Option D is incorrect because allowing disruptive behavior to continue can negatively impact the group's therapeutic process.

Question 71: Correct Answer: C) Mindfulness-Based Stress Reduction (MBSR)
Rationale: Mindfulness-Based Stress Reduction (MBSR) is an effective intervention for managing occupational stress as it helps individuals develop mindfulness skills to reduce stress and improve emotional regulation. - Option A (Time Management Training): While helpful for managing tasks, it may not address underlying stress responses. - Option B (Job Redesign): This could alleviate some stressors but may not be feasible or address Sarah's immediate stress management needs. - Option D (Assertiveness Training): Useful for improving communication skills but may not directly reduce overall stress levels like MBSR.

Question 72: Correct Answer: D) Assessing the client's capacity to understand and make an informed decision.
Rationale: While explaining potential risks and benefits (Option A), ensuring understanding of the right to withdraw (Option B), and providing information about alternative treatments (Option C) are all essential components of informed consent, assessing the client's capacity (Option D) is paramount. Without ensuring that the client has the cognitive ability to comprehend the information provided, any consent obtained cannot be considered truly informed. This step ensures that all other elements are meaningful and that the client can engage in a rational decision-making process. Therefore, Option D encompasses a fundamental prerequisite for all other steps in obtaining valid informed consent.

Question 73: Correct Answer: D) Coercive control
Rationale: Coercive control refers to a pattern of behavior where an abuser uses manipulation, isolation, and intimidation to dominate their partner, which fits John's description. Learned helplessness (A) involves a victim feeling powerless due to repeated abuse but doesn't capture the manipulative tactics described. Stockholm syndrome (B) involves developing sympathy for captors, which is not indicated here. Gaslighting (C), while involving manipulation, specifically refers to making someone doubt their reality rather than broader control tactics.

Question 74: Correct Answer: B) Start with open-ended questions about Maria's current feelings and concerns.
Rationale: Starting with open-ended questions about Maria's current feelings and concerns helps establish rapport and allows the client to share their experiences freely. This approach is aligned with contemporary counseling practices that emphasize client-centered techniques. Option A is important but may not be the best initial step for building rapport. Option C could overwhelm Maria without first understanding her perspective. Option D is essential but typically follows an initial conversation that builds trust.

Question 75: Correct Answer: B) Fear of confronting painful emotions
Rationale: Fear of confronting painful emotions is often a significant barrier in mental health counseling because it directly affects the client's willingness and ability to engage in therapeutic processes. This emotional barrier can lead to avoidance behaviors, such as missing therapy sessions. While lack of transportation (Option A), inadequate social support (Option C), and poor time management skills (Option D) are also potential barriers, they are more logistical in

nature and can often be addressed through practical solutions or external assistance. Emotional barriers like fear require deeper psychological intervention, making Option B the most relevant choice in this context. - Option A (Lack of transportation): Although a valid logistical barrier, it can usually be resolved through practical means such as arranging alternative transportation or teletherapy. - Option C (Inadequate social support): This is another important barrier but typically affects long-term motivation and overall progress rather than immediate attendance. - Option D (Poor time management skills): While relevant, this issue can often be managed with organizational strategies and does not directly address the underlying emotional resistance. By focusing on an emotional barrier that requires internal psychological work, Option B highlights a more profound obstacle to goal attainment in mental health counseling.

Question 76: Correct Answer: B) "It sounds like you're feeling overwhelmed by your situation."
Rationale: Option B is the correct answer because it reflects active listening and accurately acknowledges the client's emotions without judgment or assumption. This aligns with Carl Rogers' person-centered approach, emphasizing genuine empathy and understanding. Option A is incorrect because claiming to understand "exactly" how a client feels can come off as dismissive or presumptive, potentially invalidating the client's unique experience. Option C is incorrect as it minimizes the client's feelings and offers premature reassurance, which can hinder the development of trust and rapport. Option D is also incorrect because it suggests advice-giving and implies that the client's current perspective is wrong, which can be disempowering and does not reflect true empathy.

Question 77: Correct Answer: C) Consult with Sarah's prescribing physician to verify the correct medication history.
Rationale: The correct course of action is to consult with Sarah's prescribing physician to verify her medication history. This ensures that all information is accurate and up-to-date, which is crucial for effective treatment planning. Option A is incorrect because making changes without verification can lead to errors. Option B may be necessary later but should not be the first step. Option D is unethical as even minor discrepancies can have significant impacts on treatment outcomes.

Question 78: Correct Answer: C) Incorporating clients' cultural beliefs and practices into the treatment plan.
Rationale: Incorporating clients' cultural beliefs and practices into the treatment plan is essential for providing culturally competent care. This approach acknowledges and respects the client's cultural background, which can enhance trust and therapeutic outcomes. - Option A (Using standardized assessment tools for all clients regardless of their cultural background) is incorrect because standardized tools may not account for cultural differences, potentially leading to misdiagnosis or inappropriate treatment. - Option B (Applying a universal counseling approach that treats all clients equally) is incorrect because it overlooks individual cultural differences, which are crucial in understanding each client's unique context. - Option D (Avoiding discussions about culture to prevent making clients uncomfortable) is incorrect because avoiding such discussions can lead to misunderstandings and a lack of rapport. Addressing culture directly but sensitively is key to effective counseling. By comparing these options, it becomes clear that only option C fully aligns with contemporary research and theories emphasizing the importance of culturally tailored interventions in mental health counseling.

Question 79: Correct Answer: A) Cognitive Behavioral Therapy (CBT)
Rationale: Cognitive Behavioral Therapy (CBT) is the most effective intervention for helping Michael develop coping mechanisms for his anxiety. CBT focuses on identifying and challenging negative thought patterns and behaviors, which are often at the root of anxiety disorders. By restructuring

these thoughts, Michael can learn to manage his stress more effectively. - Option B (SFBT) is incorrect because it emphasizes short-term solutions rather than addressing underlying cognitive patterns. - Option C (DBT) is more suited for individuals with borderline personality disorder or severe emotional dysregulation. - Option D (MBSR) can help with stress reduction but does not directly address the cognitive aspects of anxiety as effectively as CBT.

Question 80: Correct Answer: B) Turn off all electronic devices at least one hour before bedtime.

Rationale: The recommendation to turn off all electronic devices at least one hour before bedtime is based on contemporary sleep hygiene practices that emphasize reducing exposure to blue light, which can interfere with melatonin production and disrupt the circadian rhythm. Option A is incorrect because limiting smartphone use to 30 minutes before bedtime still exposes Sarah to blue light. Option C is also incorrect because while using a blue light filter can help, it does not eliminate all blue light exposure. Option D is partially correct but does not address the specific issue of electronic device usage impacting sleep quality.

Question 81: Correct Answer: B) Mild Cognitive Impairment

Rationale: Mrs. Garcia's symptoms suggest Mild Cognitive Impairment (MCI), characterized by noticeable memory lapses that do not significantly impair daily functioning. Normal Age-Related Memory Loss (A) would involve more benign forgetfulness without confusion about time and place. Early-Stage Alzheimer's Disease (C) involves more severe memory loss and functional impairment than described here. Vascular Dementia (D) usually presents with a more abrupt onset and specific neurological deficits related to cerebrovascular events.

Question 82: Correct Answer: B) Suggest family therapy sessions involving both Sarah and her adoptive parents.

Rationale: Family therapy sessions can provide a supportive environment for Sarah and her adoptive parents to address identity confusion and feelings of low self-esteem together. It helps in open communication, which is crucial in adoption-related issues. Option A may not be appropriate initially as it could bypass necessary emotional processing within the adoptive family unit. Option C focuses solely on individual therapy, neglecting the family dynamics that play a critical role in adoption issues. Option D might be premature without preparing both Sarah and her adoptive parents for such significant steps.

Question 83: Correct Answer: A) Reflecting feelings

Rationale: Reflecting feelings involves acknowledging and validating the client's emotions, which helps build rapport and encourages deeper emotional expression. While paraphrasing content (B) and summarizing the session (C) are important techniques, they focus more on understanding and organizing information rather than directly addressing emotional expression. Providing immediate feedback (D), although useful in some contexts, may not always be appropriate for building emotional communication skills as it can interrupt the client's flow of thought.

Question 84: Correct Answer: B) Suggest they engage in couple's therapy focused on improving communication skills.

Rationale: Couple's therapy focused on improving communication skills is often the most effective initial intervention for relationship problems involving misunderstandings and emotional distance (Gottman & Silver, 1999). This approach helps both partners develop better ways of expressing their needs and understanding each other, which can reduce conflicts. Option A may provide temporary relief but does not address underlying issues. Option C might be beneficial but delays direct intervention in their relationship dynamics. Option D could be supportive but lacks the professional guidance needed for significant change.

Question 85: Correct Answer: B) Cognitive Restructuring

Rationale: Cognitive Restructuring is a core technique within CBT that targets and modifies irrational or maladaptive thoughts contributing to anxiety. It is particularly effective for GAD because it helps clients identify and challenge their pervasive worries. - A) Exposure Therapy is more commonly used for phobias and PTSD rather than GAD. - C) Mindfulness-Based Stress Reduction (MBSR) incorporates mindfulness techniques but is not a specific CBT technique. - D) Dialectical Behavior Therapy (DBT) focuses on emotion regulation and is more often used for borderline personality disorder.

Question 86: Correct Answer: A) Cognitive Behavioral Therapy (CBT)

Rationale: Cognitive Behavioral Therapy (CBT) is the most supported approach for treating Binge Eating Disorder as it focuses on identifying and changing negative thought patterns and behaviors associated with binge eating. - B) Dialectical Behavior Therapy (DBT) can be effective but is primarily used for borderline personality disorder. - C) Interpersonal Psychotherapy (IPT) is also effective but less so compared to CBT for BED. - D) Psychodynamic Therapy focuses more on unconscious processes and may not directly address the behavioral aspects of binge eating.

Question 87: Correct Answer: B) Help Maria develop assertive communication skills to set boundaries with her friends.

Rationale: Limiting interactions (Option A) or seeking advice from others (Option C) may temporarily alleviate stress but do not empower Maria long-term. Focusing solely on self-help strategies (Option D) ignores the potential benefits of a supportive network. Developing assertive communication skills (Option B), however, enables Maria to set clear boundaries while maintaining valuable relationships. This approach aligns with contemporary counseling practices that emphasize empowering clients through skill development for healthier interpersonal dynamics.

Question 88: Correct Answer: B) Emotional Abuse

Rationale: Emotional abuse involves behaviors such as belittling, controlling finances, and isolating the victim from social support systems. While financial control is a component of emotional abuse, it alone does not constitute financial abuse unless it is the primary form of abuse. Physical and sexual abuses are distinct categories involving physical harm or coercion into sexual activities. The combination of belittling, financial control, and isolation indicates emotional abuse.

Question 89: Correct Answer: B) Bulimia Nervosa

Rationale: Bulimia Nervosa is characterized by recurrent episodes of binge eating followed by compensatory behaviors such as fasting or excessive exercise. Sarah's symptoms of consuming large amounts of food in a short period, feelings of guilt, and compensatory behaviors align with this diagnosis. Anorexia Nervosa involves restrictive eating and an intense fear of gaining weight but does not typically include binge-eating episodes. Binge Eating Disorder involves binge eating without compensatory behaviors. Avoidant/Restrictive Food Intake Disorder is characterized by avoidance or restriction of food intake without concerns about body weight or shape.

Question 90: Correct Answer: C) Generativity vs. Stagnation

Rationale: Erikson's theory posits that individuals in middle adulthood (ages 40-65) face the challenge of Generativity vs. Stagnation. This stage involves contributing to society and helping guide the next generation. John's feelings of stagnation and questioning his purpose align with difficulties in this stage. The other stages are relevant at different points in life: Identity vs. Role Confusion during adolescence (A), Intimacy vs. Isolation during young adulthood (B), and Integrity vs. Despair during late adulthood (D).

Question 91: Correct Answer: B) Conduct a thorough risk assessment to evaluate the severity of his suicidal ideation.

Rationale: The immediate priority in crisis intervention is to assess the level of risk, especially when suicidal ideation is present. Conducting a thorough risk assessment helps determine the appropriate level of care and intervention needed. While providing information about support groups (Option A), encouraging positive thinking (Option C), and referring to a psychiatrist (Option D) are important steps, they do not address the immediate need to evaluate and ensure John's safety.

Question 92: Correct Answer: A) Conduct a detailed suicide risk assessment using validated tools.

Rationale: Conducting a detailed suicide risk assessment using validated tools is crucial when a client reports feelings of hopelessness and has a history of self-harm. This allows the counselor to evaluate the severity of the risk and determine appropriate interventions. Encouraging positive activities (Option B) is beneficial but not sufficient as an immediate response. Scheduling a follow-up session (Option C) delays necessary immediate action. Referring to a psychiatrist (Option D) may be part of the treatment plan but does not address the immediate need for risk assessment.

Question 93: Correct Answer: A) Attention-Deficit/Hyperactivity Disorder (ADHD)

Rationale: John's symptoms of alternating between hyperfocus and difficulty concentrating align closely with ADHD. Hyperfocus is a common yet lesser-known symptom of ADHD where individuals become intensely focused on tasks they find stimulating or rewarding, often to the exclusion of other important activities. On the other hand, hypofocus manifests as difficulty sustaining attention on less stimulating tasks. Generalized Anxiety Disorder (GAD), Major Depressive Disorder (MDD), and Obsessive-Compulsive Disorder (OCD) can also affect concentration but do not typically involve the distinct pattern of hyperfocus seen in ADHD.

Question 94: Correct Answer: A) Major Depressive Disorder

Rationale: The symptoms described align closely with the criteria for Major Depressive Disorder (MDD), which include a depressed mood or loss of interest/pleasure in daily activities for more than two weeks, along with other symptoms such as weight loss, insomnia, fatigue, and feelings of worthlessness. Persistent Depressive Disorder (PDD), also known as dysthymia, involves chronic depression lasting for at least two years but typically with less severe symptoms. Bipolar II Disorder includes periods of hypomania and major depression but does not fit this case due to the lack of hypomanic episodes. Cyclothymic Disorder involves chronic fluctuating mood disturbances with periods of hypomanic and depressive symptoms that do not meet full criteria for hypomanic or major depressive episodes. Thus, MDD is the most accurate diagnosis given the duration and severity of symptoms. Each option is explained as follows: - A) Major Depressive Disorder: Correct because it matches all presented symptoms and their duration. - B) Persistent Depressive Disorder: Incorrect because it requires a longer duration (at least two years) with typically less severe symptoms. - C) Bipolar II Disorder: Incorrect due to the absence of hypomanic episodes which are essential for this diagnosis. - D) Cyclothymic Disorder: Incorrect as it involves chronic mood fluctuations over at least two years without meeting full criteria for major depressive or hypomanic episodes.

Question 95: Correct Answer: B) Active Listening

Rationale: The counselor demonstrates active listening by maintaining eye contact, nodding, and paraphrasing John's statements to confirm understanding. This shows that the counselor is fully engaged and attentive to John's concerns. While empathy (A) involves understanding and sharing feelings, active listening focuses on attentively processing what the client says. Unconditional positive regard (C), which means accepting clients without judgment, is not explicitly demonstrated here. Congruence (D), or being genuine with clients, is also important but not the primary attribute shown in this behavior.

Question 96: Correct Answer: A) Maintaining confidentiality by not sharing client information on personal social media accounts.

Rationale: Maintaining confidentiality is a fundamental ethical consideration for mental health counselors. Sharing client information on personal social media accounts breaches this confidentiality and violates professional ethics. Option B, while ethical, does not address the direct risk of breaching confidentiality. Option C is incorrect as accepting friend requests from clients can blur professional boundaries and compromise objectivity. Option D is partially correct but does not emphasize the critical importance of maintaining client confidentiality as directly as Option A does. Therefore, Option A is the most comprehensive and accurate response regarding ethical considerations in social media use for mental health counselors.

Question 97: Correct Answer: D) Inform the spouse that she cannot share any information without explicit consent from the client.

Rationale: Sarah must adhere to confidentiality guidelines which require explicit consent from clients before sharing any information. While option B suggests seeking written consent, it's not as immediate or definitive as simply informing the spouse of confidentiality rules (option D). Option A breaches confidentiality outright, and option C risks inadvertently disclosing sensitive details. Ensuring explicit consent is critical to maintaining professional ethics and protecting client privacy.

Question 98: Correct Answer: B) Advise the client to assertively communicate their feelings and needs while listening to their partner's perspective.

Rationale: Option B is correct because it aligns with contemporary research on conflict resolution, emphasizing assertive communication and active listening as key strategies for resolving disputes effectively. Assertive communication allows individuals to express their needs clearly without aggression, while active listening ensures that both parties feel heard and understood. Option A is incorrect because avoiding discussion can lead to unresolved issues and increased tension over time. Option C is misleading; while compromise is important, taking on more responsibilities temporarily does not address the root cause of the conflict. Option D might help in some situations but can be perceived as dismissive or trivializing serious concerns, potentially exacerbating the conflict rather than resolving it. By comparing these options, we see that B offers a balanced approach that fosters mutual understanding and long-term resolution, which is critical in demonstrating conflict tolerance and effective resolution in counseling contexts.

Question 99: Correct Answer: C) Provide John with full access to his counseling records while ensuring he understands the implications.

Rationale: The correct answer is C because clients have the right to access their own counseling records according to ethical standards and legal provisions. It's important for counselors to facilitate this process while helping clients understand any potential impacts. Option A incorrectly denies John's rights. Option B adds unnecessary bureaucracy not typically required by ethical standards. Option D unnecessarily restricts John's access and autonomy over his own records.

Question 100: Correct Answer: B) Facilitate a discussion about the client's personal values and beliefs.

Rationale: Facilitating a discussion about the client's personal values and beliefs directly addresses the core of spiritual/existential concerns by helping them explore their own meaning-making processes. This approach aligns with existential therapy principles, which emphasize understanding one's values and beliefs to find meaning in life. Option A (Encourage mindfulness meditation) is beneficial for stress reduction but may not directly address existential questions. Option C (Suggest community service activities) can provide purpose but might not delve into personal values. Option D (Recommend cognitive-behavioral therapy) focuses on altering thought patterns rather than exploring deeper existential issues. Each option has its merits but does not target the existential/spiritual core as precisely as option B.

Question 101: Correct Answer: B) Arrange for a follow-up appointment within one week and develop a crisis intervention plan.

Rationale: The most appropriate initial step is to arrange for a follow-up appointment within one week and develop a crisis intervention plan. This ensures immediate continuity of care and addresses any potential crises early. Options A), C), and D) are important components of long-term management but do not prioritize immediate follow-up or crisis planning, which are critical in the immediate post-discharge period. Regular therapy sessions (A), community support (C), and educational materials (D) are beneficial but secondary to immediate follow-up and crisis planning.

Question 102: Correct Answer: B) "Your information is confidential unless you disclose intentions to harm yourself or others."

Rationale: Confidentiality in counseling is a fundamental ethical obligation. However, there are limits to confidentiality, particularly when clients disclose intentions to harm themselves or others. Option B correctly identifies this important exception. Option A incorrectly suggests absolute confidentiality without acknowledging legal and ethical exceptions. Option C misrepresents the limits by focusing on past criminal activities rather than imminent risk. Option D highlights court-ordered disclosures but omits other critical exceptions like risk of harm.

Question 103: Correct Answer: B) Focus on the interconnectedness of family members and collective well-being.

Rationale: In collectivist cultures, the emphasis is often on the group rather than the individual. Prioritizing the interconnectedness of family members and collective well-being aligns with cultural values that stress harmony, interdependence, and group cohesion. Option A is incorrect because it emphasizes individual autonomy, which may not resonate with collectivist values. Option C is incorrect as it disregards hierarchical structures important in many collectivist cultures. Option D is also incorrect because assertiveness training focuses on individual self-expression, which may not be culturally appropriate in collectivist settings where group harmony is prioritized.

Question 104: Correct Answer: C) Ambivalent (Resistant) Attachment

Rationale: Ambivalent (Resistant) Attachment is characterized by children who become very distressed when separated from their caregiver but are not easily comforted upon reunion. They may seek closeness yet simultaneously resist it, displaying ambivalence. - Option A (Secure Attachment): Incorrect because securely attached children typically show distress upon separation but are easily comforted upon the caregiver's return. - Option B (Avoidant Attachment): Incorrect as avoidantly attached children tend to avoid or ignore the caregiver and show little emotion when separated or reunited. - Option D (Disorganized Attachment): Incorrect because disorganized attachment involves a lack of a coherent strategy for dealing with stress, often resulting in contradictory behaviors that do not fit the pattern described. The correct answer is justified by the specific behaviors of seeking closeness while resisting contact, which are hallmark traits of ambivalent attachment as described by Mary Ainsworth's Strange Situation procedure.

Question 105: Correct Answer: B) Clinician-Administered PTSD Scale (CAPS)

Rationale: The Clinician-Administered PTSD Scale (CAPS) is the most appropriate assessment tool for evaluating trauma-related symptoms, particularly post-traumatic stress disorder (PTSD). While the Beck Depression Inventory (BDI), Generalized Anxiety Disorder 7-item scale (GAD-7), and Hamilton Anxiety Rating Scale (HAM-A) are valuable

tools for assessing depression and anxiety, they do not specifically target trauma-related symptoms such as flashbacks and nightmares. CAPS is designed to assess the frequency and intensity of PTSD symptoms based on DSM-5 criteria, making it the best choice for Maria's presentation.

Question 106: Correct Answer: A) "It sounds like you're feeling really lonely after your move. That must be tough."

Rationale: Option A is the correct answer because it reflects active listening and empathy by acknowledging Maria's feelings without judgment or advice. It validates her experience and opens the door for deeper exploration of her emotions. Option B dismisses her feelings by generalizing her experience, which can make her feel misunderstood. Option C offers advice rather than empathy, potentially making Maria feel like her emotions are being minimized. Option D acknowledges the difficulty of moving but shifts focus away from her current emotional state to a future-oriented perspective, which may not address her immediate need for empathy.

Question 107: Correct Answer: B) Perform an initial mental status examination (MSE).

Rationale: An initial mental status examination (MSE) is essential as it helps establish Maria's current cognitive and emotional state, providing valuable insights into her stress levels and any underlying mental health concerns. While recommending MBSR (Option A), advising her to see her primary care physician (Option C), or encouraging time off work (Option D) may be beneficial later, they do not offer an immediate assessment of her mental health status needed at this stage. Tone: Professional and Knowledgeable

Question 108: Correct Answer: D) Using culturally adapted assessment tools to explore religious and spiritual values.

Rationale: Using culturally adapted assessment tools ensures that the exploration of religious and spiritual values is respectful and sensitive to the client's background. This approach is grounded in contemporary research emphasizing cultural competence in counseling. While directly asking (A) or integrating general questions (B) might seem straightforward, they can be perceived as intrusive or superficial without cultural adaptation. Waiting for the client (C) may delay important discussions. Culturally adapted tools provide a structured yet flexible framework that respects individual differences, fostering a more open and respectful dialogue.

Question 109: Correct Answer: B) Increases awareness of the present moment to reduce automatic stress responses

Rationale: Mindfulness-Based Stress Reduction (MBSR) primarily works by increasing awareness of the present moment, helping individuals recognize and reduce automatic stress responses. Unlike cognitive restructuring (A), which focuses on changing thought patterns, MBSR emphasizes non-judgmental awareness. Progressive muscle relaxation (C) is a different technique focused on physical relaxation, while emotional expression (D) addresses emotional release rather than mindful awareness.

Question 110: Correct Answer: B) Difficulty managing intense emotions

Rationale: Difficulty managing intense emotions is a hallmark symptom of emotional dysregulation. It involves experiencing emotions more intensely than usual and having trouble returning to a baseline state after an emotional spike. While consistent low mood (A), persistent worry about future events (C), and recurrent intrusive thoughts (D) can be associated with other mental health conditions like depression or anxiety disorders, they are not as directly related to the core issue of emotion regulation difficulties as option B.

Question 111: Correct Answer: C) Cultural perceptions of cause, context, and support

Rationale: The correct answer is C) Cultural perceptions of cause, context, and support. This component explores how John's community views his situation and provides context for his feelings about unemployment. While options A), B), and D) are relevant in assessing John's mental health comprehensively, they do not specifically address how his community's perceptions influence his experience as directly as option C). Understanding these perceptions will help tailor interventions that consider community influences on John's mental health.

Question 112: Correct Answer: A) Role-playing

Rationale: Role-playing allows Mr. Johnson and his son to practice communication skills in a controlled environment, providing immediate feedback and opportunities for improvement. Reflective listening (B) enhances understanding but does not actively practice new interaction patterns. Solution-focused questioning (C) aims at identifying solutions but may not directly address interaction patterns. Cognitive restructuring (D) focuses on changing thought patterns rather than improving communication dynamics directly.

Question 113: Correct Answer: A) Suggest John speak with his employer about flexible working hours.

Rationale: Speaking with his employer about flexible working hours (Option A) can help John better balance work and caregiving responsibilities without sacrificing income or career progression. Reducing working hours to part-time (Option B) might not be financially feasible. Time management workshops (Option C) are useful but may not fully address the need for flexibility in John's schedule. Delegating tasks (Option D), while helpful, may not be possible if other family members are unavailable or unwilling.

Question 114: Correct Answer: B) High-quality substitute caregiving

Rationale: High-quality substitute caregiving is crucial in mitigating the negative effects of prolonged separation from primary caregivers. Research indicates that when children receive consistent, sensitive, and responsive care from substitute caregivers, it can significantly reduce stress and anxiety associated with separation. While consistent daily routines (Option A) and increased social interactions with peers (Option C) are beneficial for general child development, they do not specifically address the emotional void left by the absence of primary caregivers. Frequent video calls (Option D), although helpful in maintaining connection, cannot replace the need for physical presence and responsive care provided by a high-quality caregiver.

Question 115: Correct Answer: A) Reflective listening

Rationale: Reflective listening is most effective in improving interactional patterns because it involves actively listening and then reflecting back what the client has said, which helps to validate the client's feelings and encourages open communication. Solution-focused questioning (B) is useful but focuses more on finding solutions rather than improving interaction patterns. Psychoeducation about communication styles (C) can provide valuable information but may not directly enhance the immediate interaction between counselor and client. Cognitive restructuring (D) is aimed at changing thought patterns rather than directly addressing communication dynamics. Therefore, reflective listening stands out as the most effective intervention for this specific purpose.

Question 116: Correct Answer: B) Assess John's access to firearms and create a plan to limit this access.

Rationale: Given John's mention of having access to firearms, assessing and limiting this access is critical for immediate safety. Exploring reasons for living (Option A) is important but secondary when there is an identified means for suicide. Discussing pain management (Option C) addresses underlying issues but does not prioritize immediate risk mitigation. Providing crisis hotline numbers (Option D) offers additional support but does not directly reduce the immediate risk posed by firearm access. Limiting access aligns with contemporary research on reducing suicide risk by restricting means.

Question 117: Correct Answer: A) Establishing clear boundaries regarding confidentiality and its limits.

Rationale: The correct answer is A) Establishing clear boundaries regarding confidentiality and its limits. This step is crucial as it builds trust and sets a professional tone for the therapeutic relationship. It aligns with ethical standards that emphasize transparency about confidentiality. Option B, discussing personal experiences, can blur professional boundaries and may not be appropriate initially. Option C, offering advice based on personal opinions, undermines client autonomy and may not be ethically sound. Option D, setting goals without client input, disregards the collaborative nature of counseling. Each incorrect option fails to uphold key ethical principles fundamental to clarifying counselor/client roles.

Question 118: Correct Answer: D) Summarizing each party's perspective before moving on to solutions.

Rationale: Summarizing each party's perspective ensures that both clients feel heard and understood, which is crucial in conflict resolution. This technique validates their experiences and emotions, setting a foundation for mutual respect. Option A is important but lacks the reflective component that summarization provides. Option B might lead to biased solutions without fully understanding both sides. Option C is beneficial but should follow after ensuring both parties feel heard. Therefore, D is the most comprehensive approach in facilitating effective conflict resolution by confirming understanding before progressing to solutions.

Question 119: Correct Answer: C) Explain to the spouse that she has a duty to warn potential victims and report threats to authorities.

Rationale: The correct answer is C because mental health professionals have an ethical and legal obligation (duty to warn) when there are credible threats of violence. This ensures safety for all involved parties. Option A is incorrect as it neglects this duty. Option B is incorrect because it delays necessary action based on indirect information. Option D is partially correct but does not address immediate action needed in such situations. Detailed.

Question 120: Correct Answer: B) "No guarantees can be made, but we will work together towards managing it."

Rationale: The correct answer is B. Counselors should set realistic expectations by emphasizing collaboration without promising specific outcomes, reflecting ethical practice standards. Option A is incorrect as guarantees are unethical and unrealistic. Option C is misleading because it places undue responsibility on following instructions rather than mutual effort. Option D wrongly suggests that success solely depends on the counselor's expertise, neglecting the client's active role.

Question 121: Correct Answer: D) Fearful-Avoidant Attachment

Rationale: John's difficulty in forming new relationships due to fear of being hurt is indicative of a fearful-avoidant attachment style. This style is characterized by a desire for close relationships coupled with a fear of rejection or harm. Anxious-preoccupied individuals (B) also fear rejection but tend to be more actively seeking closeness rather than avoiding it. Dismissive-avoidant individuals (C) maintain distance and self-reliance rather than fearing hurt from new connections. Securely attached individuals (A) typically navigate relationship changes more resiliently without such intense fear of harm.

Question 122: Correct Answer: A) High self-efficacy

Rationale: High self-efficacy is most likely to improve goal attainment because it refers to an individual's belief in their ability to succeed in specific situations or accomplish a task. This belief can significantly impact motivation, effort, and perseverance, which are crucial for achieving goals. While strong social support (Option B), effective coping strategies (Option C), and positive reinforcement (Option D) are important, they are secondary to the intrinsic confidence that self-efficacy provides. Social support helps by providing external encouragement; coping strategies assist in managing stress, and positive reinforcement can boost morale. However, without self-efficacy, these external factors may not be sufficient to drive sustained effort towards goal attainment.

Question 123: Correct Answer: A) Utilize a structured diagnostic interview specifically designed for PTSD.

Rationale: Utilizing a structured diagnostic interview specifically designed for PTSD ensures that all relevant symptoms are thoroughly assessed using validated criteria. This method is supported by contemporary research as being effective for accurate diagnosis. Option B can be helpful but should complement rather than replace a structured interview. Option C is valuable for rapport-building but may not provide comprehensive symptom details. Option D is relevant but focusing solely on medical history may miss current symptomatology crucial for diagnosis.

Question 124: Correct Answer: C) Explore John's emotional responses to his financial stress.

Rationale: The initial step in addressing John's financial issues should focus on exploring his emotional responses to the stress caused by his financial situation. This helps understand the psychological impact and provides a foundation for further interventions. Developing a budget plan (Option A) or referring him to a financial advisor (Option B) are practical steps but may not address the immediate emotional distress. Encouraging him to seek a higher-paying job (Option D) might add more pressure without first understanding his current emotional state.

Question 125: Correct Answer: A) Facilitate a family meeting with a healthcare team member who can explain the medical implications of John's decision.

Rationale: Facilitating a family meeting allows for an open discussion where both John's wishes and his wife's concerns can be addressed comprehensively. Encouraging respect for John's wishes (B) might dismiss his wife's feelings. Individual counseling (C) is helpful but does not address the immediate need for mutual understanding between John and his wife. Exploring alternative treatments (D) could undermine John's autonomy if it leads away from his expressed wishes.

Question 126: Correct Answer: B) Recommending John keep a daily log of his mood and activities.

Rationale: Keeping a daily log of mood and activities is an effective CBT technique that helps clients maintain awareness of their mental state and identify patterns or triggers. This ongoing self-monitoring facilitates early intervention if symptoms begin to re-emerge. Joining a support group (Option A) can provide social support but may not offer the same level of structured self-monitoring. Reading self-help books (Option C) can be informative but lacks the active engagement necessary for sustained change. Regular physical exercise (Option D) is beneficial for mental health but alone does not address cognitive patterns critical in CBT maintenance.

Question 127: Correct Answer: B) The level of parental conflict post-divorce

Rationale: Contemporary research indicates that the level of parental conflict post-divorce is the most significant predictor of children's long-term adjustment. High levels of ongoing conflict can create a stressful environment that impedes a child's emotional and psychological well-being. While options A, C, and D are also important factors, they do not carry as much weight as parental conflict. For instance, although a child's age (A) can influence their understanding and coping mechanisms, it is less critical than an environment free from conflict. Similarly, socioeconomic status (C) affects resources but not necessarily emotional stability. Lastly, a positive relationship with the non-custodial parent (D) is beneficial but secondary to reducing conflict between parents.

Question 128: Correct Answer: D) The patient demonstrates an inability to perform simple arithmetic calculations.

Rationale: Option D is the correct answer because difficulties with simple arithmetic calculations can indicate cognitive impairment, particularly issues with concentration, memory, or executive functioning. Option A describes poor eye contact and disheveled appearance, which may suggest depression or other mood disorders but not necessarily cognitive impairment. Option B indicates issues with recent memory but intact remote memory, which is often seen in early stages of dementia but does not alone confirm cognitive impairment. Option C involves rapid speech and tangential thoughts, more indicative of thought process abnormalities such as those found in mania or schizophrenia rather than direct cognitive impairment.

Question 129: Correct Answer: C) Substance Abuse Subtle Screening Inventory (SASSI)

Rationale: The SASSI is specifically designed to identify individuals who have a high probability of having a substance use disorder, including prescription drug misuse. Brief Intervention and Motivational Interviewing are therapeutic techniques rather than assessment tools. The Mini-Mental State Examination (MMSE) assesses cognitive function and is not relevant for evaluating substance use. While Brief Intervention and Motivational Interviewing can be part of a treatment plan following assessment, they do not serve as initial evaluative tools like the SASSI.

Question 130: Correct Answer: B) Higher risk of developing anxiety disorders and attachment issues

Rationale: Prolonged separation from primary caregivers during early childhood is strongly associated with higher risks of developing anxiety disorders and attachment issues. Attachment theory, particularly the work of John Bowlby, emphasizes that secure attachments formed in early childhood are crucial for emotional stability and healthy development. Option A is incorrect because increased resilience and independence are not typically outcomes of prolonged separation; instead, children may struggle with trust and security. Option C is misleading as enhanced social skills are more likely developed through secure attachments rather than separation. Option D is incorrect because while adaptive coping mechanisms can develop, they do not typically lead to greater cognitive development in this context.

Question 131: Correct Answer: C) Recommend individual therapy sessions focusing on stress management.

Rationale: Individual therapy focusing on stress management is crucial as it provides tailored strategies to help Sarah cope with her specific stressors. While joining a support group (Option A) can offer peer support, it may not address her immediate need for personalized coping mechanisms. Temporary respite (Option B) might provide short-term relief but doesn't equip her with long-term strategies. Seeking medical evaluation for antidepressants (Option D) could be beneficial if depression is diagnosed but should not be the initial step without addressing underlying stress through therapy.

Question 132: Correct Answer: B) Super's Life-Span, Life-Space Theory

Rationale: Super's Life-Span, Life-Space Theory emphasizes the evolution of self-concept over an individual's lifespan. This theory posits that career development is a lifelong process influenced by various life roles and stages. It focuses on how individuals perceive themselves and their roles in different contexts throughout their lives. Option A (Holland's Theory) is incorrect because it focuses on matching personality types with work environments rather than the evolution of self-concept. Option C (Krumboltz's Social Learning Theory) emphasizes learning experiences and environmental influences on career decisions, not specifically self-concept evolution. Option D (Roe's Personality Development Theory) links early childhood experiences with career choices but does not emphasize self-concept changes over time. Super's theory uniquely addresses how self-concept evolves with life stages, making it distinct from other theories that focus more on personality-environment fit or learning experiences.

Question 133: Correct Answer: B) Highlight common themes in their stories and invite them to discuss these connections.
Rationale: Linking involves drawing connections between group members' experiences to foster cohesion and support. By highlighting common themes (Option B), you help members see they are not alone, enhancing empathy and mutual support. Encouraging individual sharing without interjection (Option A) misses opportunities for connection. Focusing on one story at a time (Option C) may isolate members' experiences rather than unify them. Asking members to refrain from discussing until everyone has shared (Option D) delays valuable interactions that can build group cohesion.

Question 134: Correct Answer: B) Recommend cognitive-behavioral therapy (CBT) to address negative thought patterns.
Rationale: Cognitive-behavioral therapy (CBT) is particularly effective in addressing the negative thought patterns that can arise after a significant physical loss, such as an amputation. CBT helps patients reframe their thoughts and develop healthier coping strategies, which is crucial for psychological adjustment. While joining a support group (Option A), practicing mindfulness meditation (Option C), and engaging in physical rehabilitation exercises (Option D) are all beneficial, they do not directly target the cognitive distortions that often accompany physical loss. Therefore, CBT is the most comprehensive approach for facilitating psychological adjustment in this context.

Question 135: Correct Answer: B) Developing a relapse prevention plan with specific coping strategies.
Rationale: Developing a relapse prevention plan with specific coping strategies is the most effective method for ensuring long-term maintenance of therapeutic progress. This approach empowers clients by providing them with concrete tools and a structured plan to handle potential setbacks. While journaling (Option A) can be beneficial for self-reflection, it does not provide the proactive structure needed for relapse prevention. Frequent follow-up sessions (Option C) are supportive but may not be sustainable or practical long-term. Advising avoidance of triggers (Option D) can lead to increased anxiety and does not promote resilience or adaptive coping skills.

Question 136: Correct Answer: C) Conduct a thorough risk assessment and, if necessary, inform appropriate parties while explaining the limits of confidentiality to Maria.
Rationale: The correct course of action is to conduct a thorough risk assessment and inform appropriate parties if necessary. Ethical guidelines require counselors to break confidentiality when there is an imminent risk of harm to the client or others. Option A is incorrect because it disregards the duty to protect Maria from harm. Option B is overly simplistic and does not involve assessing the situation first. Option D delays necessary intervention that could prevent harm.

Question 137: Correct Answer: C) Existential Therapy
Rationale: Existential Therapy focuses on addressing issues related to meaning, purpose, and identity, which are central to John's concerns about retirement. While CBT (Option A) can help with anxiety by changing thought patterns, it may not fully address the deeper existential questions John is facing. SFBT (Option B) is more goal-oriented and short-term, which might not delve into the underlying issues of purposelessness. IPT (Option D) primarily addresses interpersonal relationships and may not directly tackle John's existential crisis.

Question 138: Correct Answer: C) Parenting Coordination
Rationale: Parenting Coordination is specifically designed to help high-conflict co-parents manage their disputes effectively and make child-centered decisions. Family Systems Therapy addresses family dynamics but may not focus directly on resolving co-parenting conflicts. Mediation helps parents reach agreements but does not provide

ongoing support for managing conflicts. Collaborative Divorce involves legal professionals working towards amicable settlements but does not offer continuous conflict management strategies like Parenting Coordination does.

Question 139: Correct Answer: B) The client is displaying signs of anxiety or discomfort.
Rationale: Avoiding eye contact and crossing arms are common non-verbal cues that often indicate anxiety or discomfort rather than resistance (A), lack of interest (C), or a power struggle (D). While resistance could manifest similarly, it typically involves more active opposition to engagement. Lack of interest would likely be accompanied by other disengaged behaviors like inattentiveness. A power struggle would involve more overt challenges to authority. Understanding these subtle nuances helps in accurately assessing interactional dynamics and forming an effective therapeutic alliance.

Question 140: Correct Answer: B) Using open-ended questions to explore various aspects of the client's life
Rationale: Using open-ended questions allows clients to share their thoughts and feelings freely, facilitating a deeper understanding of their experiences and building rapport. This approach aligns with person-centered therapy principles, emphasizing empathy and active listening. In contrast, focusing solely on the presenting problem (Option A) may overlook important contextual factors. Relying heavily on structured diagnostic tools (Option C) can feel impersonal and hinder rapport-building. Maintaining a neutral stance (Option D), while important for objectivity, can create distance rather than connection. Therefore, Option B is most effective for an initial interview.

Question 141: Correct Answer: C) "John's feelings of loneliness stem from missing his family and friends after relocating for work."
Rationale: Option C effectively captures both John's emotional experience (feelings of loneliness) and the cause (missing family and friends due to relocation). Option A mentions loneliness but doesn't connect it explicitly to relocation. Option B focuses on adjustment issues without emphasizing loneliness or missing loved ones. Option D highlights difficulty in making connections but doesn't directly link it to feelings of loneliness.

Question 142: Correct Answer: A) Provide John with referrals to support groups and community resources.
Rationale: Providing referrals ensures John has ongoing support after terminating therapy, which is crucial for maintaining sobriety. While scheduling a follow-up session (Option B) can be helpful, it doesn't provide long-term external support. Reviewing goals (Option C) is essential but doesn't offer future resources. Writing a letter (Option D) can be therapeutic but isn't as impactful as ensuring continuous support through referrals (Option A).

Question 143: Correct Answer: B) Helping John develop strategies to integrate his new spouse into the family while maintaining strong bonds with his children.
Rationale: The primary focus should be on helping John integrate his new spouse into the family while maintaining strong bonds with his children (B). This approach acknowledges the importance of both relationships and aims for a balanced integration. Option A is incorrect as it could lead to feelings of neglect in the children. Option C might delay necessary relationship building and increase tensions later. Option D addresses individual issues but does not directly support the immediate family dynamics needed during remarriage.

Question 144: Correct Answer: B) Teach Mark and Lisa active listening techniques to improve their communication.
Rationale: Active listening is crucial for effective conflict resolution as it ensures both parties feel heard and understood. This technique involves fully concentrating, understanding, responding, and remembering what the other person is saying. Option A suggests avoidance, which can lead to unresolved issues festering over time. Option C

focuses on compromise without addressing underlying communication problems. Option D promotes taking turns but may not ensure genuine understanding or empathy. Therefore, teaching active listening (Option B) is the most effective strategy for improving communication and resolving conflicts.

Question 145: Correct Answer: A) Tension Headaches

Rationale: Tension headaches are common in individuals with GAD due to prolonged muscle tension and stress. They present as a constant ache rather than throbbing pain typical of migraines. Cervical spine disorders could cause headaches but would be accompanied by neck pain and limited range of motion. Vestibular dysfunction primarily causes dizziness without the accompanying muscle tension or headache seen in GAD-related tension headaches.

Question 146: Correct Answer: B) Heightened levels of anxiety and depression

Rationale: Caregivers often experience heightened levels of anxiety and depression due to the chronic stress associated with their responsibilities. Option A is incorrect as while some caregivers may feel a sense of accomplishment, it is not as common as experiencing negative psychological impacts. Option C is misleading because caregiving can often lead to social isolation rather than enhanced social connectedness. Option D is incorrect because caregiving generally does not improve overall mental well-being; it tends to have the opposite effect due to the continuous demands and emotional strain involved.

Question 147: Correct Answer: C) Assess the immediacy and severity of the threat before deciding on further action.

Rationale: According to the ACA Code of Ethics, when a client discloses plans to harm themselves, it is crucial for the counselor to first assess the immediacy and severity of the threat. This assessment helps determine whether there is an imminent danger that requires breaking confidentiality. Option A is incorrect because while exploring feelings is important, it does not address immediate safety concerns. Option B is incorrect as contacting family members without assessing risk may breach confidentiality unnecessarily. Option D is incorrect because referring without assessment may delay necessary intervention. Thus, assessing immediacy and severity (Option C) aligns with ethical guidelines for ensuring client safety.

Question 148: Correct Answer: B) Politely decline the friend request and explain the importance of maintaining professional boundaries.

Rationale: Sarah should politely decline the friend request and explain the importance of maintaining professional boundaries (Option B). This approach is consistent with ethical guidelines that emphasize maintaining clear boundaries between personal and professional relationships. Accepting the friend request (Options A and C), even with limitations, can blur these boundaries and potentially compromise confidentiality. Ignoring the request (Option D) fails to address an important aspect of client-counselor communication and education about ethical practices.

Question 149: Correct Answer: A) Encouraging Maria to set small, achievable goals.

Rationale: The learned helplessness theory suggests that setting small, achievable goals can help individuals regain a sense of control and efficacy, counteracting feelings of helplessness and hopelessness. While improving self-esteem (B), teaching problem-solving skills (C), and providing psychoeducation (D) are useful strategies in treating depression, they do not specifically target the core issue of learned helplessness as effectively as setting achievable goals does.

Question 150: Correct Answer: B) Explore how Maria's cultural values and family expectations impact her mental health.

Rationale: Exploring how Maria's cultural values and family expectations impact her mental health is crucial because it acknowledges the importance of her cultural background in shaping her experiences and responses. Encouraging firm boundaries (A) or suggesting distancing from family gatherings (C) may not be culturally sensitive and could exacerbate her stress. Focusing solely on personal goals (D) ignores the integral role of family in Maria's life. Thus, option B is the most culturally appropriate intervention.

NCMHCE Exam Practice Questions [SET 4]

Question 1: John, a 28-year-old client, expresses reluctance to open up during sessions because he fears being judged. As his counselor, what is the best approach to help him feel safe and build trust?
A) Assure John that everything discussed is confidential.
B) Share a personal story to make John feel more comfortable.
C) Reflect John's feelings and normalize his concerns about judgment.
D) Focus on setting goals for therapy to distract from his fears.

Question 2: Which intervention is most effective in addressing the immediate safety concerns of a client experiencing intimate partner violence (IPV)?
A) Developing a long-term counseling plan focused on trauma recovery.
B) Encouraging the client to attend support groups for emotional support.
C) Assisting the client in creating a safety plan tailored to their specific situation.
D) Providing information about legal resources and restraining orders.

Question 3: Sarah has been attending counseling sessions for anxiety management for six months. Her counselor wants to evaluate the effectiveness of the treatment. Which of the following methods is most appropriate for this purpose?
A) Client self-report surveys
B) Counselor's subjective assessment
C) Standardized outcome measures
D) Frequency of session attendance

Question 4: John, a 28-year-old man diagnosed with Panic Disorder, seeks treatment for his condition. Which of the following therapeutic approaches is considered most effective in reducing his panic symptoms?
A) Cognitive-Behavioral Therapy (CBT)
B) Psychodynamic Therapy
C) Exposure Therapy
D) Dialectical Behavior Therapy (DBT)

Question 5: Which of the following is considered the most effective first-line treatment for chronic insomnia according to contemporary cognitive-behavioral therapy (CBT) principles?
A) Pharmacotherapy with benzodiazepines
B) Sleep hygiene education
C) Cognitive Behavioral Therapy for Insomnia (CBT-I)
D) Melatonin supplementation

Question 6: You are a mental health counselor working with a client named Sarah, who has been sharing personal details about her therapy sessions on social media. She asks for your opinion on whether this is appropriate. How should you respond according to professional practice and ethics?
A) Encourage Sarah to continue sharing as it can be therapeutic and empowering.
B) Advise Sarah to limit sharing personal details to protect her privacy and confidentiality.
C) Suggest that Sarah only share positive experiences to maintain a supportive online presence.
D) Recommend that Sarah consults with other clients online to get their perspectives.

Question 7: John has been receiving cognitive-behavioral therapy (CBT) for depression. His therapist decides to use a specific tool to evaluate the therapy's effectiveness over time. Which tool is most appropriate?
A) Beck Depression Inventory (BDI)
B) Therapist's clinical notes
C) Patient's daily mood diary
D) Global Assessment of Functioning (GAF)

Question 8: In the context of blended families, which intervention is most effective in addressing loyalty conflicts between stepchildren and their biological parents?
A) Encouraging open communication between all family members.
B) Establishing clear family rules and roles.
C) Facilitating individual therapy sessions for stepchildren.
D) Promoting bonding activities between stepparents and stepchildren.

Question 9: Which of the following best describes a potential negative impact of extended family involvement on individual mental health within a collectivist culture?
A) Increased emotional support leading to reduced stress levels.
B) Over-involvement leading to decreased autonomy and increased anxiety.
C) Enhanced social network providing greater resilience against mental health issues.
D) Intergenerational transmission of cultural values fostering strong identity formation.

Question 10: Sarah, a mental health counselor, is working with a client named John who has been experiencing severe anxiety due to workplace harassment. John is hesitant to report the harassment because he fears retaliation. As Sarah considers how best to advocate for John while respecting his autonomy, which of the following actions should she prioritize?
A) Encourage John to report the harassment immediately and offer to accompany him during the process.
B) Respect John's decision not to report the harassment but provide him with resources and support.
C) Report the harassment on John's behalf without his consent to ensure his safety.
D) Suggest John take a leave of absence from work while they explore reporting options together.

Question 11: What intervention would best help John increase his readiness to take action against his anxiety?
A) Goal Setting
B) Affirmations
C) Exploring Ambivalence
D) Providing Information

Question 12: Which of the following best describes a primary benefit of using structured activities in mental health counseling?
A) Enhances client engagement by providing clear goals and expectations.
B) Allows for spontaneous expression and exploration of emotions.
C) Facilitates unstructured interaction between counselor and client.
D) Encourages clients to lead sessions with minimal guidance.

Question 13: Which of the following techniques is most

effective in establishing a strong therapeutic alliance with a client?
A) Providing immediate solutions to the client's problems.
B) Using active listening and empathetic responses.
C) Sharing personal experiences to build rapport.
D) Setting clear boundaries and expectations from the outset.

Question 14: Mark, a 28-year-old military veteran, presents with irritability, frequent nightmares, and avoidance of activities that remind him of his combat experiences. He also reports physical symptoms like headaches and gastrointestinal issues. What is the most likely diagnosis based on his presentation?
A) Generalized Anxiety Disorder (GAD)
B) Major Depressive Disorder (MDD)
C) Post-Traumatic Stress Disorder (PTSD)
D) Acute Stress Disorder

Question 15: Maria, a mental health counselor, has been seeing a client named Tom for several months. Tom recently lost his job and is now concerned about affording therapy sessions. Maria wants to support Tom while adhering to ethical guidelines regarding fees and payments. What should Maria consider doing?
A) Offer Tom pro bono sessions until he finds employment.
B) Reduce Tom's session frequency to lower his overall costs.
C) Implement a sliding scale fee based on Tom's current financial situation.
D) Suggest that Tom seek therapy through community resources that offer free services.

Question 16: Maria, a 28-year-old female, reports experiencing intrusive thoughts that she finds distressing and difficult to control. Her therapist suggests using a mindfulness-based approach to help her cope with these thoughts. Which of the following strategies aligns best with this approach?
A) Thought Suppression
B) Acceptance and Commitment Therapy (ACT)
C) Rational Emotive Behavior Therapy (REBT)
D) Systematic Desensitization

Question 17: During the transition phase in group membership, which factor is most critical in maintaining group cohesion?
A) Leadership style
B) Member self-disclosure
C) Group norms
D) Conflict resolution

Question 18: What is the most appropriate referral source for John given his disclosure of suicidal thoughts?
A) Refer John to an inpatient psychiatric facility.
B) Refer John to an outpatient substance abuse program.
C) Refer John to a crisis hotline for immediate support.
D) Refer John to an emergency room for immediate evaluation.

Question 19: Which of the following statements best describes the impact of childhood sexual abuse within a family on adult relationship dynamics?
A) Childhood sexual abuse often leads to difficulties in establishing trust in adult relationships.
B) Childhood sexual abuse typically results in an inability to form any intimate relationships in adulthood.
C) Survivors of childhood sexual abuse are more likely to engage in abusive behaviors themselves.
D) Individuals with a history of childhood sexual abuse are generally unable to experience healthy sexual relationships.

Question 20: During a counseling session, Maria expresses difficulty in saying "no" to her coworkers when they ask for favors, leading her to feel overwhelmed and stressed. Which assertiveness training technique would be most effective for helping Maria develop the ability to refuse requests without feeling guilty?
A) Role-playing refusal scenarios with a counselor
B) Practicing passive communication techniques
C) Engaging in cognitive restructuring exercises
D) Utilizing relaxation techniques before responding

Question 21: Jessica, a mental health researcher, is evaluating the reliability and validity of a new questionnaire designed to measure stress levels among college students. She decides to use Cronbach's alpha to assess internal consistency and performs factor analysis for construct validity. Which statement correctly interprets these methods?
A) Cronbach's alpha measures how well each item correlates with every other item.
B) Factor analysis determines if the questionnaire measures what it intends to measure.
C) Cronbach's alpha assesses the questionnaire's ability to produce consistent results over time.
D) Factor analysis evaluates the stability of responses across different administrations.

Question 22: When providing accommodations for a client with a visual impairment during therapy sessions, which of the following is the most appropriate action?
A) Ensure all printed materials are available in large print.
B) Use audio recordings for all session materials.
C) Provide a tactile model of any visual content discussed.
D) Offer to read all written content aloud during sessions.

Question 23: What is a critical consideration for a mental health counselor when planning the termination process with a client?
A) Ensuring that all treatment goals have been fully achieved
B) Discussing the potential for future crises and creating a plan for them
C) Providing referrals to other services if needed
D) Reviewing progress and discussing feelings about termination

Question 24: You are reviewing your notes after several sessions with a client named John, who has been diagnosed with depression. Which of the following practices best ensures that your documentation is thorough and appropriate for each aspect of the counseling process?
A) Summarize each session briefly to ensure efficiency.
B) Include detailed descriptions of John's progress and setbacks in each session.
C) Use general terms to describe John's emotions to protect his privacy.
D) Focus on documenting treatment plans while minimizing session details.

Question 25: During a counseling session with Emily, a 25-year-old dealing with anxiety and self-esteem issues, the counselor notices that Emily frequently downplays her achievements. The counselor decides to address this by sharing their genuine feelings about Emily's accomplishments. Which of the following responses best demonstrates congruence?
A) "I think you're doing really well, but you could try harder."
B) "You have made significant progress, and I genuinely believe in your abilities."
C) "It's great that you've achieved these things, but there's always room for improvement."
D) "You should be proud of what you've done so far."

Question 26: John, a long-term client dealing with depression, begins expressing romantic feelings towards you during a session. How should you handle this situation to maintain professional boundaries?
A) Gently acknowledge his feelings but suggest exploring them in therapy sessions.
B) Firmly state that such feelings are inappropriate and must stop immediately.
C) Clarify the professional nature of your relationship and discuss transferring him to another counselor if needed.
D) Ignore his feelings and continue with the session as planned.

Question 27: Maria, a 35-year-old woman, presents with symptoms of severe depression and chronic pain. During the assessment, she reveals that her pain significantly impacts her daily functioning and contributes to her depressive symptoms. As her mental health counselor, you recognize the need for a multidisciplinary approach. Which of the following is the most appropriate referral for concurrent treatment?
A) Refer Maria to a psychiatrist for medication management.
B) Refer Maria to a physical therapist for pain management.
C) Refer Maria to a pain specialist for comprehensive pain evaluation and management.
D) Refer Maria to a support group for individuals with chronic pain.

Question 28: Michael, a mental health counselor, is working with a client named Sarah who is experiencing severe anxiety due to overwhelming debt. Michael wants to provide Sarah with resources to manage her financial stress effectively. Which of the following actions should Michael take as his primary intervention?
A) Refer Sarah to a financial advisor for debt management.
B) Provide Sarah with psychoeducation on anxiety management techniques.
C) Collaborate with Sarah to develop a budget and financial plan.
D) Encourage Sarah to join a support group for individuals with financial stress.

Question 29: Maria, a mental health counselor at a community clinic, is approached by her client, John, who requests access to his counseling records. Maria is aware that the clinic has specific policies regarding client records. Which of the following actions should Maria take according to standard counselor/agency policies?
A) Provide John with immediate access to his entire counseling record without any review.
B) Deny John's request for access to his counseling records based on confidentiality concerns.
C) Inform John about the clinic's policy and review the records with him before providing access.
D) Provide John with a summary of his counseling sessions instead of the full record.

Question 30: During a counseling session, Maria expresses concern about her confidentiality being breached if she discloses sensitive information. As her counselor, what is your primary responsibility in this situation?
A) Reassure Maria that all information shared is confidential and will not be disclosed under any circumstances.
B) Inform Maria that confidentiality is maintained except in cases where there is a risk of harm to herself or others.
C) Advise Maria that confidentiality can be breached if requested by her family members.
D) Explain to Maria that her employer has the right to access her counseling records if needed.

Question 31: Jane, a mental health counselor, is working with a family where the parents are struggling with communication issues that affect their children's behavior. To facilitate systemic change, which intervention should Jane prioritize?
A) Focus on improving individual coping mechanisms for each family member.
B) Address the parents' communication patterns and their impact on family dynamics.
C) Implement behavioral modification techniques for the children.
D) Encourage family members to participate in individual therapy sessions.

Question 32: A 10-year-old child presents with frequent temper tantrums, defiance, and difficulty following rules both at home and school. Which therapeutic approach is most likely to be effective in addressing these behavioral problems?
A) Cognitive Behavioral Therapy (CBT)
B) Parent-Child Interaction Therapy (PCIT)
C) Play Therapy
D) Dialectical Behavior Therapy (DBT)

Question 33: When guiding treatment planning for a client with generalized anxiety disorder (GAD), which approach is most effective in ensuring long-term symptom management and overall well-being?
A) Cognitive Behavioral Therapy (CBT)
B) Psychoanalytic Therapy
C) Solution-Focused Brief Therapy (SFBT)
D) Person-Centered Therapy

Question 34: James, an African American male, expresses frustration during sessions about systemic racism affecting his mental health. He mentions feeling targeted by law enforcement due to his race. As his counselor, what should be your primary focus in addressing James' concerns?
A) Help James develop coping strategies for managing stress related to systemic racism.
B) Encourage James to join community activism groups to address systemic issues.
C) Suggest James avoid areas where he feels targeted by law enforcement.
D) Focus on improving James' self-esteem to better handle societal challenges.

Question 35: Maria is a 28-year-old teacher who feels overwhelmed by her workload and has started experiencing insomnia. She seeks counseling to manage her stress better. Which educational resource would best support Maria in managing her stress?
A) Guided Imagery Techniques
B) Time Management Workshops
C) Deep Breathing Exercises
D) Sleep Hygiene Education

Question 36: In counseling a client with a terminal illness, which approach is most effective in helping them cope with anticipatory grief?
A) Encouraging the client to focus solely on positive memories and avoid discussing their fears.
B) Facilitating open discussions about their fears and encouraging expression of all emotions.
C) Advising the client to remain stoic and not burden their family with their emotional struggles.
D) Suggesting that the client immerse themselves in hobbies to distract from their condition.

Question 37: During a counseling session with John, a new client who has experienced trauma, the counselor notices that John is hesitant to share details about his

past. To facilitate trust and safety, which approach should the counselor take?
A) Encourage John to discuss his trauma in detail immediately.
B) Assure John that everything discussed is confidential and he can share at his own pace.
C) Share personal experiences with trauma to make John feel more comfortable.
D) Emphasize the importance of discussing trauma for therapeutic progress.

Question 38: Mark, a 28-year-old man, experiences excessive worry about his health despite multiple medical assurances that he is healthy. He frequently seeks reassurance from doctors and avoids activities he perceives as risky. What cognitive distortion is Mark most likely exhibiting?
A) Catastrophizing
B) Overgeneralization
C) Personalization
D) Mind Reading

Question 39: Maria, a 30-year-old patient, reports experiencing difficulty sleeping due to persistent worries about her job performance. She frequently wakes up during the night and struggles to fall back asleep. Which therapeutic approach is most likely to address her primary issue?
A) Sleep hygiene education
B) Cognitive restructuring
C) Relaxation training
D) Mindfulness-based stress reduction

Question 40: Which of the following strategies is most effective in promoting and encouraging interactions with the group leader in a therapeutic setting?
A) Establishing clear group norms and expectations at the beginning of sessions.
B) Allowing the group leader to share personal experiences frequently.
C) Encouraging members to address their comments directly to the group leader.
D) Rotating the role of group leader among members periodically.

Question 41: A 35-year-old patient named John presents with symptoms of anxiety and depression. During the intake session, he mentions that his symptoms have worsened after a recent job loss and subsequent financial difficulties. He reports difficulty sleeping, constant worry, and feelings of hopelessness. As his mental health counselor, what is the most appropriate initial step to screen John for appropriate services?
A) Refer John to a psychiatrist for medication evaluation.
B) Conduct a comprehensive biopsychosocial assessment.
C) Suggest John attend a support group for unemployed individuals.
D) Initiate cognitive-behavioral therapy (CBT) sessions immediately.

Question 42: During a counseling session, Maria, a client, expresses feelings of deep sadness and isolation after moving to a new city. As a counselor practicing empathic attunement, what is the most appropriate response?
A) "I understand how you feel. Moving can be really tough."
B) "It sounds like you're feeling very lonely and disconnected right now."
C) "Many people find it difficult to adjust to a new environment."
D) "You should try joining local community groups to meet new people."

Question 43: Maria, a 30-year-old woman with bipolar disorder, has been discharged after stabilization of her manic episode. Which follow-up strategy would best address both medication adherence and psychosocial support in her treatment plan?
A) Schedule monthly psychiatric evaluations and weekly individual therapy sessions.
B) Develop a comprehensive discharge plan including medication monitoring by family members.
C) Coordinate bi-weekly group therapy sessions and monthly check-ins with her psychiatrist.
D) Implement weekly home visits by a mental health nurse alongside bi-weekly psychiatrist appointments.

Question 44: Which of the following is most commonly associated with the development of complex post-traumatic stress disorder (C-PTSD) in individuals who have experienced prolonged trauma?
A) Hypervigilance and exaggerated startle response
B) Difficulty regulating emotions and maintaining relationships
C) Recurrent intrusive memories and flashbacks
D) Avoidance of trauma-related stimuli

Question 45: Maria and John have been experiencing significant marital issues due to communication breakdowns and trust issues. As their mental health counselor, you need to decide on the most appropriate intervention modality to address their concerns effectively.
A) Individual counseling for Maria
B) Individual counseling for John
C) Couple counseling for Maria and John
D) Family counseling involving Maria, John, and their children

Question 46: John, a 28-year-old man, has been experiencing profound loneliness since moving to a new city for work. Despite making some acquaintances, he struggles to form deeper connections and feels isolated. During therapy sessions, it becomes evident that his difficulties might be linked to his early childhood experiences. Which intervention would be most appropriate to address John's issues related to his attachment style?
A) Cognitive Behavioral Therapy (CBT)
B) Emotionally Focused Therapy (EFT)
C) Solution-Focused Brief Therapy (SFBT)
D) Dialectical Behavior Therapy (DBT)

Question 47: In a therapy group for individuals dealing with grief, Mark often monopolizes conversations, leaving little room for others to speak. As the counselor, what strategy should you employ to promote balanced interactions among all group members?
A) Directly tell Mark that he needs to give others a chance to speak.
B) Implement a structured turn-taking system for sharing during sessions.
C) Praise Mark's willingness to share but gently remind him of the importance of hearing from everyone.
D) Allow Mark to continue speaking as it helps him process his grief.

Question 48: A 10-year-old boy named Alex, who was adopted at age 5, has been displaying signs of anxiety and difficulty forming relationships with peers. His adoptive parents are concerned and seek advice from a mental health counselor. What is the most likely underlying issue contributing to Alex's current behavior?
A) Attachment insecurity due to early separation from biological parents

B) Genetic predisposition to anxiety inherited from biological parents
C) Lack of social skills due to limited interaction with peers before adoption
D) Adjustment disorder related to transitioning into a new family environment

Question 49: When determining the appropriate level of outpatient care for a client with moderate depression and no history of substance abuse, which factor is most crucial in guiding this decision?
A) Client's current symptom severity
B) Client's financial situation
C) Client's social support system
D) Client's previous treatment history

Question 50: John, a 70-year-old man with advanced ALS, has been increasingly withdrawn and refuses to participate in family activities. What is the most appropriate counseling approach?
A) Encourage John to express his feelings about his illness and its impact on his life.
B) Suggest family therapy sessions to improve communication within the family.
C) Recommend cognitive-behavioral therapy (CBT) to address depressive symptoms.
D) Introduce relaxation techniques to help manage physical symptoms.

Question 51: Alex, a 22-year-old non-binary individual, seeks counseling for anxiety related to societal expectations about gender roles. As a mental health counselor, which therapeutic approach would be most appropriate for addressing Alex's concerns?
A) Cognitive Behavioral Therapy (CBT)
B) Gender-Affirmative Therapy
C) Psychodynamic Therapy
D) Exposure Therapy

Question 52: John, a 35-year-old male, frequently experiences ruminative thoughts about past failures that interfere with his daily functioning. His therapist wants to employ a cognitive-behavioral intervention to help John manage these thoughts. Which of the following techniques is most appropriate for this purpose?
A) Mindfulness Meditation
B) Cognitive Restructuring
C) Exposure Therapy
D) Psychodynamic Therapy

Question 53: A mental health counselor, Dr. Smith, is conducting a study on the effectiveness of cognitive-behavioral therapy (CBT) for reducing anxiety symptoms in adolescents. He uses a sample size of 200 participants and employs a p-value threshold of 0.05 for statistical significance. The results show a p-value of 0.03. Which of the following conclusions can Dr. Smith reasonably draw from this result?
A) CBT has a statistically significant effect on reducing anxiety symptoms in adolescents.
B) CBT causes a reduction in anxiety symptoms in adolescents.
C) There is no effect of CBT on reducing anxiety symptoms in adolescents.
D) The reduction in anxiety symptoms is clinically significant.

Question 54: Maria, a 45-year-old woman, recently lost her long-term partner with whom she had a secret relationship due to societal disapproval. She feels unable to openly mourn her loss. As her mental health counselor, what is the most appropriate initial intervention to help Maria process her disenfranchised grief?

A) Encourage Maria to write letters to her deceased partner expressing her feelings.
B) Suggest Maria join a support group for individuals who have lost partners.
C) Validate Maria's feelings and provide psychoeducation about disenfranchised grief.
D) Advise Maria to engage in mindfulness and meditation practices.

Question 55: Mr. Thompson, a 78-year-old man, has been feeling increasingly withdrawn and disinterested in activities he once enjoyed. He reports difficulty sleeping and a persistent sense of hopelessness. As his mental health counselor, what is the most likely diagnosis based on these symptoms?
A) Generalized Anxiety Disorder
B) Major Depressive Disorder
C) Mild Cognitive Impairment
D) Adjustment Disorder

Question 56: John, a mental health counselor, has been seeing his client Lisa for six months. Recently, Lisa invited John to her art exhibition as a token of appreciation for his support in therapy. How should John respond while maintaining professional boundaries?
A) Accept the invitation but avoid discussing therapy at the event.
B) Decline politely and explain that attending could blur professional boundaries.
C) Attend the event briefly but keep interactions minimal.
D) Suggest that Lisa shares her artwork during a therapy session instead.

Question 57: During a counseling session, Maria, a 35-year-old client with a history of depression, expresses her desire to return to work after a prolonged absence. As her mental health counselor, you aim to identify strengths that can improve her likelihood of achieving this goal. Which of the following strengths should you focus on?
A) Maria's ability to set specific and measurable goals.
B) Maria's supportive family environment.
C) Maria's previous work experience.
D) Maria's high level of intrinsic motivation.

Question 58: John, a 45-year-old man recently diagnosed with major depressive disorder, reports feeling isolated despite having a large family and many friends. As his counselor, how should you address the impact of his social support network on his mental health?
A) Encourage John to increase his social interactions with family and friends.
B) Assess the quality of John's existing relationships and their emotional support.
C) Suggest John join a community group or club to make new connections.
D) Recommend that John engage in individual therapy sessions instead of relying on social support.

Question 59: What is the most effective intervention the therapist can use to facilitate awareness of here-and-now interactions in this scenario?
A) Encourage Sarah to continue sharing her story.
B) Ask other group members how they feel about Sarah's story.
C) Point out the non-verbal reactions of the group members.
D) Redirect the conversation to another topic.

Question 60: A mental health counselor is working with a client whose religious beliefs conflict with a recommended evidence-based treatment. The client

expresses distress about choosing between their faith and the treatment. What is the most appropriate initial response by the counselor?
A) Encourage the client to prioritize their mental health over religious beliefs.
B) Explore the client's religious beliefs and how they impact their view of the treatment.
C) Refer the client to a religious leader for guidance on resolving the conflict.
D) Suggest an alternative treatment that does not conflict with the client's religious beliefs.

Question 61: Which of the following interventions is most effective for a client experiencing severe anxiety as part of their individualized treatment plan?
A) Cognitive Behavioral Therapy (CBT)
B) Psychoanalytic Therapy
C) Solution-Focused Brief Therapy (SFBT)
D) Person-Centered Therapy

Question 62: Maria, a 30-year-old client, has been receiving counseling for anxiety. She decides she wants to terminate therapy. What is your responsibility as her counselor in this situation?
A) Respect her decision and immediately end all sessions.
B) Insist on continuing therapy until her anxiety is fully managed.
C) Discuss her reasons for termination and provide appropriate referrals if needed.
D) Schedule one last session to convince her to stay in therapy.

Question 63: John, a 35-year-old male, presents with multiple bruises and lacerations. He admits to being in a physically abusive relationship with his partner. As a mental health counselor, which of the following is the most appropriate immediate action to ensure John's safety?
A) Advise John to leave the relationship immediately.
B) Develop a safety plan with John.
C) Encourage John to seek couples counseling.
D) Suggest John take legal action against his partner.

Question 64: Which of the following statements best exemplifies an assertive communication style in a workplace setting?
A) "I think your idea is terrible and will never work."
B) "I understand your perspective, but I feel differently about this approach."
C) "I'll just go along with whatever you decide."
D) "You always take credit for my work, and I'm sick of it."

Question 65: Maria, a 35-year-old woman recently diagnosed with depression, feels isolated after moving to a new city for work. As her mental health counselor, what is the most effective initial step you should take to help Maria develop a support system?
A) Encourage Maria to join a local gym or fitness class.
B) Suggest Maria attend local community events and gatherings.
C) Refer Maria to a support group for individuals with depression.
D) Advise Maria to reconnect with her family and friends through social media.

Question 66: John, a mental health counselor, finds himself consistently feeling overly empathetic towards his client Lisa, who is dealing with grief. What should John do to ensure his self-awareness does not negatively impact his professional relationship with Lisa?
A) Continue as usual but try to suppress his empathy.
B) Seek supervision or consultation regarding his emotional

responses.
C) Disclose his empathetic feelings to Lisa for mutual understanding.
D) Limit sessions with Lisa to prevent emotional exhaustion.

Question 67: John, a 28-year-old client diagnosed with depression, expresses difficulty in setting personal objectives due to his low motivation. As his counselor, how can you best support John in establishing effective treatment goals?
A) Setting all the treatment goals for John based on clinical judgment.
B) Using motivational interviewing techniques to explore John's values and interests.
C) Encouraging John to set long-term objectives without focusing on immediate steps.
D) Relying solely on standardized assessment tools for goal-setting.

Question 68: John, a 30-year-old African American man, has been diagnosed with PTSD after returning from military service. He reports feeling disconnected from his family and community. Which intervention would best align with John's background and enhance his sense of connection?
A) Exposure Therapy focusing on desensitization to traumatic memories
B) Group Therapy with other veterans to build peer support
C) Narrative Therapy encouraging John to rewrite his trauma story
D) Mindfulness-Based Stress Reduction (MBSR) for relaxation and stress management

Question 69: John, a 40-year-old African American man, reports experiencing anxiety and depression after moving to a predominantly white neighborhood. As his mental health counselor conducting a Cultural Formulation Interview (CFI), which question would most effectively explore the impact of his new environment on his mental health?
A) How has your move affected your relationship with your family?
B) Can you describe any changes in your daily routine since moving?
C) How do you feel your new community perceives you?
D) What coping strategies have you used to manage your anxiety?

Question 70: John has been inconsistent in following his treatment plan for managing his anxiety. As his counselor, you want to educate him on the value of treatment plan compliance. Which approach is most likely to improve John's adherence to his treatment plan?
A) Emphasize the long-term benefits of treatment adherence.
B) Highlight the immediate consequences of non-compliance.
C) Discuss John's personal goals and how compliance aligns with them.
D) Provide detailed information about each component of the treatment plan.

Question 71: A client experiencing significant financial stress reports increased anxiety and difficulty sleeping. As a mental health counselor, which of the following interventions would be most effective in addressing the client's financial issues and associated anxiety?
A) Cognitive-Behavioral Therapy (CBT) focusing on financial stressors
B) Referral to a financial advisor
C) Mindfulness-Based Stress Reduction (MBSR)
D) Encouraging the client to take out a loan to alleviate

immediate financial pressure

Question 72: Maria, a 35-year-old client, has completed the Beck Depression Inventory (BDI) as part of her initial assessment. Her scores indicate moderate depression. Based on these results, what should be the next step in facilitating her decision-making for treatment planning?
A) Refer Maria to a psychiatrist for medication evaluation.
B) Discuss the possibility of cognitive-behavioral therapy (CBT) with Maria.
C) Recommend that Maria join a support group for individuals with depression.
D) Suggest lifestyle changes such as exercise and diet modification.

Question 73: According to Bowlby's attachment theory, which type of attachment is most likely to result in feelings of loneliness and difficulty forming close relationships in adulthood?
A) Secure Attachment
B) Anxious-Ambivalent Attachment
C) Avoidant Attachment
D) Disorganized Attachment

Question 74: Maria, a 16-year-old girl, has been experiencing significant anxiety and depression. During a counseling session, she reveals that her stepfather has been sexually abusing her for the past two years. As her mental health counselor, what is the most appropriate initial intervention?
A) Encourage Maria to confront her stepfather in a safe environment.
B) Report the abuse to child protective services immediately.
C) Suggest family therapy sessions to address underlying issues.
D) Advise Maria to keep a detailed journal of the abuse incidents.

Question 75: John, a licensed mental health counselor, has been experiencing burnout due to his demanding work schedule. He decides to implement a self-care plan to improve his well-being and maintain his professional effectiveness. Which of the following strategies is most effective for John in practicing self-care?
A) Attending weekly supervision sessions with a senior counselor
B) Taking short breaks between client sessions
C) Engaging in regular physical exercise and mindfulness meditation
D) Limiting his caseload to avoid overworking

Question 76: During an initial assessment, Maria, a 35-year-old Latina woman, expresses that she feels misunderstood by her healthcare providers. As part of conducting a Cultural Formulation Interview (CFI), which approach would best help you understand her perspective?
A) Focus on her medical history and previous diagnoses.
B) Inquire about her cultural background and how it influences her understanding of her symptoms.
C) Discuss her family dynamics and their role in her current mental health.
D) Explore her socioeconomic status and its impact on her access to healthcare.

Question 77: A client presents with symptoms of depression and anxiety. During the assessment, you discover that the client has experienced several traumatic events in their life. Which therapeutic approach is most appropriate for addressing both trauma and co-occurring depression and anxiety?
A) Cognitive Behavioral Therapy (CBT)
B) Eye Movement Desensitization and Reprocessing (EMDR)
C) Dialectical Behavior Therapy (DBT)
D) Interpersonal Therapy (IPT)

Question 78: John, a 45-year-old male, is entering into a remarriage after his first marriage ended in divorce five years ago. He has two teenage children from his previous marriage. During counseling, John expresses concerns about blending families and managing relationships with his ex-spouse and new partner. Which therapeutic approach is most effective for addressing John's concerns?
A) Cognitive Behavioral Therapy (CBT)
B) Solution-Focused Brief Therapy (SFBT)
C) Structural Family Therapy (SFT)
D) Emotionally Focused Therapy (EFT)

Question 79: John, a 32-year-old man, reports feeling increasingly anxious and insecure in his relationship with his girlfriend, who has recently started a demanding new job that requires long hours. John fears that she might lose interest in him due to her busy schedule. As his mental health counselor, what would be the most appropriate initial intervention to help John address his anxiety and insecurity?
A) Encourage John to openly communicate his feelings and concerns with his girlfriend.
B) Suggest John engage in individual therapy sessions focused on building self-esteem.
C) Advise John to engage in more social activities to distract himself from his anxiety.
D) Recommend couple's therapy sessions to address relationship dynamics.

Question 80: In a group counseling session, a counselor notices that two members are sharing similar experiences related to grief. Which of the following actions best demonstrates the use of linking in this context?
A) Encouraging both members to share more about their experiences to highlight commonalities.
B) Redirecting the conversation to another topic to avoid potential emotional overload.
C) Asking one member to hold off on sharing until the other has finished speaking.
D) Intervening immediately to prevent any potential conflict between the members.

Question 81: According to Bowlby's Attachment Theory, which attachment style is most likely to result in chronic loneliness in adulthood?
A) Secure attachment
B) Anxious-preoccupied attachment
C) Dismissive-avoidant attachment
D) Fearful-avoidant attachment

Question 82: A 32-year-old client with major depressive disorder has been experiencing increasing symptoms despite weekly outpatient therapy. The client has recently started missing work and reports frequent thoughts of self-harm but denies any immediate plan or intent. Which level of treatment would be most appropriate for this client at this time?
A) Outpatient therapy
B) Intensive outpatient program (IOP)
C) Partial hospitalization program (PHP)
D) Inpatient hospitalization

Question 83: Which intervention has been found to be the most effective in facilitating adjustment for individuals going through a divorce?
A) Cognitive Behavioral Therapy (CBT)
B) Support Group Participation

C) Psychoeducational Workshops
D) Individual Psychodynamic Therapy

Question 84: David, a 4-year-old boy, has recently been placed in foster care after being separated from his parents due to neglect. He exhibits clinginess towards his foster parents and becomes extremely distressed when they leave the room. What intervention would be most effective in addressing David's behavior based on contemporary research?
A) Encouraging David's foster parents to minimize physical contact to reduce dependency.
B) Providing consistent and responsive caregiving to help David develop secure attachments.
C) Introducing multiple caregivers so that David does not become overly attached to one person.
D) Using time-out strategies whenever David becomes clingy or distressed.

Question 85: When working with a client who has a physical disability, which counseling intervention is most effective in promoting self-efficacy and independence?
A) Cognitive Behavioral Therapy (CBT) focusing on negative thought patterns
B) Solution-Focused Brief Therapy (SFBT) emphasizing strengths and resources
C) Person-Centered Therapy (PCT) providing unconditional positive regard
D) Motivational Interviewing (MI) enhancing motivation for change

Question 86: Which technique is most effective for a mental health counselor to use in order to build rapport and facilitate open communication with a client during an initial session?
A) Active Listening
B) Providing Immediate Solutions
C) Reflective Listening
D) Using Open-Ended Questions

Question 87: Emily, a 16-year-old girl, has recently started skipping school and engaging in risky behaviors such as substance use and staying out late without informing her parents. Her parents are concerned and seek your help as her counselor. What would be the most appropriate initial step in addressing Emily's behavioral problems?
A) Establishing clear rules and consequences with her parents.
B) Exploring underlying emotional issues through individual therapy.
C) Involving Emily in family therapy sessions.
D) Encouraging Emily to participate in extracurricular activities.

Question 88: During a therapy session, Maria, a 32-year-old client, expresses frustration about not making progress toward her treatment goals. As her counselor, how should you engage her in reviewing her progress?
A) Reassure Maria that progress takes time and encourage her to be patient.
B) Review the treatment goals with Maria and collaboratively assess any barriers to progress.
C) Suggest that Maria might need to lower her expectations regarding the treatment goals.
D) Highlight the small improvements Maria has made without focusing on unmet goals.

Question 89: Which of the following best exemplifies a counselor's awareness of their own cultural biases and its impact on the therapeutic relationship?
A) A counselor actively seeks supervision to discuss

personal feelings about a client's cultural background.
B) A counselor avoids discussing cultural issues to prevent discomfort for both themselves and the client.
C) A counselor assumes that their cultural experiences are universal and applies them to all clients.
D) A counselor encourages clients to adapt to the dominant culture for better integration.

Question 90: According to Mary Ainsworth's attachment theory, which type of attachment is characterized by a child's anxiety and uncertainty when the caregiver leaves, but also displays ambivalence upon their return?
A) Secure Attachment
B) Avoidant Attachment
C) Ambivalent (Resistant) Attachment
D) Disorganized Attachment

Question 91: John, a 42-year-old client, experiences overwhelming anxiety during sessions when discussing his traumatic past. As his counselor, what is the best approach to help John manage these intense feelings while still engaging in therapeutic work?
A) Encourage John to focus on positive memories.
B) Teach John grounding techniques.
C) Redirect the conversation away from trauma.
D) Validate John's feelings without exploring them further.

Question 92: During the initial intake session with a client, which is the most crucial element to establish in order to build a therapeutic alliance?
A) Discussing the client's treatment goals
B) Conducting a comprehensive biopsychosocial assessment
C) Establishing trust and rapport
D) Reviewing confidentiality and informed consent

Question 93: Maria, a 45-year-old female, presents with symptoms of generalized anxiety disorder (GAD). She reports excessive worry about various aspects of her life, including work and family. Maria has no history of trauma but mentions that her anxiety has been worsening over the past year. She prefers a structured approach to therapy that provides practical skills to manage her anxiety.
A) Acceptance and Commitment Therapy (ACT)
B) Mindfulness-Based Stress Reduction (MBSR)
C) Cognitive Behavioral Therapy (CBT)
D) Psychoanalytic Therapy

Question 94: Which of the following methods is considered most comprehensive for assessing trauma during an initial intake session?
A) Using a standardized trauma screening tool
B) Conducting a detailed clinical interview focusing on past traumatic events
C) Observing non-verbal cues and behavioral signs during the session
D) Reviewing the client's medical and psychological history

Question 95: Sarah, a 22-year-old woman with an intellectual disability, experiences significant anxiety when interacting in social settings. As her counselor, which approach would be most effective in helping Sarah reduce her social anxiety?
A) Social Skills Training
B) Exposure Therapy
C) Dialectical Behavior Therapy (DBT)
D) Family Counseling

Question 96: Maria, a 28-year-old woman, seeks counseling for her pornography addiction. She spends several hours daily viewing pornography, which interferes with her work and social life. Maria reports

feeling guilty and ashamed but finds it difficult to stop. Based on contemporary research, what is the most appropriate initial therapeutic approach?
A) Motivational Interviewing to enhance readiness for change
B) Group therapy with others experiencing similar issues
C) Psychoanalytic therapy to explore underlying unconscious conflicts
D) Family therapy to address relational dynamics

Question 97: Sarah, a 28-year-old female, presents with symptoms of intense fear in social situations leading to avoidance behaviors. She also experiences intrusive thoughts about contamination and engages in repetitive hand-washing rituals to alleviate her anxiety. Given these symptoms, what would be the most appropriate co-occurring diagnoses to consider?
A) Social Anxiety Disorder and Obsessive-Compulsive Disorder
B) Social Anxiety Disorder and Panic Disorder
C) Obsessive-Compulsive Disorder and Generalized Anxiety Disorder
D) Agoraphobia and Obsessive-Compulsive Personality Disorder

Question 98: During a group therapy session, Sarah begins to dominate the conversation by repeatedly bringing up her personal issues, which prevents other members from sharing. As a counselor, how should you effectively use blocking in this situation?
A) Politely ask Sarah to let others speak and redirect the conversation.
B) Allow Sarah to continue speaking until she feels heard.
C) Directly tell Sarah to stop talking about her issues.
D) Ignore Sarah's comments and focus on other members.

Question 99: During an initial diagnostic interview with a 32-year-old patient named Sarah, who reports experiencing persistent sadness and loss of interest in activities she once enjoyed, which of the following is the most appropriate first step for the counselor?
A) Begin by exploring Sarah's current support system and social network.
B) Start with a detailed exploration of Sarah's medical history.
C) Initiate the interview by asking about recent changes in Sarah's life circumstances.
D) Conduct a mental status examination to assess Sarah's cognitive functioning.

Question 100: John is a 42-year-old client who has been attending therapy sessions for depression. He has been prescribed medication but frequently misses doses and struggles with maintaining a consistent routine. Which barrier is most likely preventing John from achieving his treatment goals?
A) Medication side effects
B) Lack of motivation
C) Cognitive impairments due to depression
D) Poor time management skills

Question 101: A 28-year-old female presents with severe depressive symptoms including suicidal ideation without a specific plan, significant weight loss, and difficulty functioning at work. Based on her symptoms and risk factors, what is the most appropriate level of care needed?
A) Outpatient Therapy
B) Intensive Outpatient Program (IOP)
C) Partial Hospitalization Program (PHP)
D) Inpatient Treatment

Question 102: Which theory posits that children actively construct gender identity by organizing information into gender schemas, which then guide their perceptions and behaviors?
A) Kohlberg's Cognitive Developmental Theory
B) Bem's Gender Schema Theory
C) Bandura's Social Learning Theory
D) Freud's Psychoanalytic Theory

Question 103: Sarah, a 35-year-old woman, presents with symptoms of depression and anxiety following a recent divorce. She reports difficulty sleeping, lack of appetite, and feelings of hopelessness. As her mental health counselor, which initial clinical focus should you prioritize to effectively address her current state?
A) Cognitive-Behavioral Therapy (CBT)
B) Psychoeducation on Divorce Adjustment
C) Medication Management
D) Mindfulness-Based Stress Reduction (MBSR)

Question 104: During an initial intake session with Maria, a 35-year-old woman presenting with symptoms of depression and anxiety, which aspect of the biopsychosocial interview is most critical to explore to understand her current mental health status comprehensively?
A) Her family history of mental illness
B) Her current employment status
C) Her use of coping mechanisms
D) Her physical health and medical history

Question 105: David, a 45-year-old Hispanic man, seeks counseling after experiencing racial profiling by law enforcement. He reports feelings of anger, fear, and helplessness. As his counselor, what initial intervention would best address David's trauma related to racial profiling?
A) Exposure Therapy to reduce fear through controlled exposure to triggering situations.
B) Trauma-Focused Cognitive Behavioral Therapy (TF-CBT) incorporating elements specific to racial trauma.
C) Dialectical Behavior Therapy (DBT) focusing on emotional regulation techniques.
D) Person-Centered Therapy emphasizing unconditional positive regard and empathy.

Question 106: John is a 35-year-old male who has been diagnosed with moderate depression. He has a stable job, a supportive family, and no history of substance abuse or suicidal ideation. His therapist is considering the most appropriate level of care for him.
A) Inpatient hospitalization
B) Partial hospitalization program (PHP)
C) Intensive outpatient program (IOP)
D) Standard outpatient therapy

Question 107: Maria, a 28-year-old client, has been experiencing depressive symptoms due to recent life changes, including a breakup and job loss. She reports feeling hopeless and unmotivated. As her counselor, you aim to help her develop strategies for improving her mood and motivation. Which intervention would be most effective in guiding Maria towards better coping mechanisms?
A) Encourage Maria to set small, achievable goals each day.
B) Suggest Maria write in a gratitude journal every evening.
C) Advise Maria to spend more time with friends and family.
D) Teach Maria relaxation techniques such as deep breathing exercises.

Question 108: John, a 28-year-old client with anxiety disorder, wants to improve his social skills as part of his treatment plan. As his mental health counselor, you need to identify strengths that can enhance his

likelihood of success. Which strength should you prioritize?
A) John's willingness to engage in exposure therapy.
B) John's high level of self-efficacy regarding social interactions.
C) John's access to social skills training programs.
D) John's supportive peer group.

Question 109: Maria, a 45-year-old woman, has been experiencing persistent fatigue, difficulty concentrating, and unexplained muscle pain for several months. Despite adequate sleep and a balanced diet, her symptoms persist. Her primary care physician suspects that these physical symptoms may be related to an underlying mental health condition. What is the most likely diagnosis?
A) Generalized Anxiety Disorder
B) Major Depressive Disorder
C) Chronic Fatigue Syndrome
D) Fibromyalgia

Question 110: Scenario: Sarah, a 28-year-old female, comes in for an intake assessment reporting chronic pain and feelings of hopelessness. She has a history of substance abuse but has been sober for two years. During Sarah's biopsychosocial interview, which factor should be explored in depth to gain insight into her chronic pain?
A) Sarah's history of substance abuse
B) Sarah's daily stressors and coping mechanisms
C) Sarah's physical health and medical history
D) Sarah's support system and social relationships

Question 111: John, a 35-year-old male, presents with sudden episodes of intense fear accompanied by palpitations, sweating, trembling, shortness of breath, and a feeling of impending doom. These episodes occur unexpectedly and are not triggered by any specific situation. John is worried about having another episode and has started avoiding situations where he thinks an attack might occur.
A) Generalized Anxiety Disorder (GAD)
B) Panic Disorder
C) Social Anxiety Disorder
D) Specific Phobia

Question 112: Which of the following is a primary characteristic of Binge Eating Disorder (BED) according to the DSM-5?
A) Recurrent episodes of eating large amounts of food in a short period, followed by compensatory behaviors such as vomiting.
B) Persistent restriction of energy intake leading to significantly low body weight.
C) Recurrent episodes of eating large amounts of food in a short period, without subsequent compensatory behaviors.
D) Preoccupation with an imagined defect in appearance leading to excessive dieting and exercise.

Question 113: Which of the following is a key component of conducting a Cultural Formulation Interview according to DSM-5 guidelines?
A) Understanding the patient's cultural identity and its influence on their mental health.
B) Focusing solely on the patient's current symptoms and their immediate impact.
C) Prioritizing the clinician's cultural perspective to guide the interview.
D) Assessing only the patient's biological factors affecting their mental health.

Question 114: Which assessment instrument is most appropriate for evaluating a client's overall psychological functioning and identifying potential psychiatric disorders during the initial intake session?
A) Beck Depression Inventory (BDI)
B) Minnesota Multiphasic Personality Inventory-2 (MMPI-2)
C) Generalized Anxiety Disorder 7-item (GAD-7)
D) Hamilton Rating Scale for Depression (HRSD)

Question 115: Sarah, a mental health counselor, is helping her client Emily navigate conflicts with her colleagues at work. Emily often feels overwhelmed when disagreements arise. Which conflict resolution strategy should Sarah recommend to help Emily manage these situations more effectively?
A) Encourage Emily to assertively express her needs while respecting others.
B) Advise Emily to accommodate her colleagues' wishes to maintain peace.
C) Suggest Emily avoid confrontations by working independently whenever possible.
D) Teach Emily negotiation skills to reach mutually beneficial agreements.

Question 116: Sarah is leading a therapy group that has been meeting for several months. Recently, she noticed increased tension and disagreements among members. What intervention should Sarah implement based on the group's current stage of development?
A) Reaffirm group goals and values.
B) Introduce new members to diversify perspectives.
C) Encourage open expression of emotions and conflict resolution.
D) Focus on individual achievements within the group.

Question 117: During a Cultural Formulation Interview (CFI), which aspect is most critical in understanding the client's perception of their mental health condition?
A) Exploring the client's cultural identity and background.
B) Understanding the client's explanation of their illness.
C) Assessing the client's social support system.
D) Evaluating the impact of cultural factors on the therapeutic relationship.

Question 118: Maria, a 32-year-old woman, presents with persistent feelings of sadness, loss of interest in daily activities, significant weight loss without dieting, insomnia, and fatigue. She reports that these symptoms have been present for the past two months and are affecting her work performance and social relationships. Which diagnosis is most appropriate for Maria?
A) Major Depressive Disorder
B) Persistent Depressive Disorder
C) Bipolar II Disorder
D) Generalized Anxiety Disorder

Question 119: John, a mental health counselor at a community clinic, is approached by his client, Maria, who expresses suicidal ideation. John knows that the clinic has strict policies regarding client confidentiality but also mandates reporting any imminent risk of harm. What should John do in this situation according to professional practice and ethics?
A) Maintain Maria's confidentiality and continue the session without taking further action.
B) Break confidentiality and immediately report Maria's suicidal ideation to law enforcement.
C) Assess the severity of Maria's suicidal ideation and consult with a supervisor before taking any action.
D) Discuss the situation with Maria, explain the limits of confidentiality, and seek her consent to involve appropriate emergency services.

Question 120: Maria conducted a study examining the relationship between stress levels and sleep quality

among college students using Pearson's correlation coefficient. She found a correlation coefficient (r) of -0.65. What does this finding suggest?
A) There is a strong positive relationship between stress levels and sleep quality.
B) There is no relationship between stress levels and sleep quality.
C) There is a strong negative relationship between stress levels and sleep quality.
D) Stress levels cause poor sleep quality among college students.

Question 121: What is the most effective initial therapeutic approach for addressing role ambiguity in a newly formed blended family?
A) Establishing clear family rules and roles through collaborative discussions.
B) Conducting individual therapy sessions with each family member.
C) Encouraging open communication about past family experiences.
D) Focusing on building a strong marital relationship between the parents first.

Question 122: Maria, a 32-year-old woman, comes in for an assessment after experiencing increased anxiety and difficulty concentrating at work. During the Mental Status Exam (MSE), you notice that she has trouble recalling recent events and struggles with serial sevens. Which cognitive function assessed during the MSE is most likely impaired?
A) Orientation
B) Memory
C) Attention and Concentration
D) Abstract Thinking

Question 123: A mental health counselor is working with a client who reveals that they are planning to harm a third party. According to the ACA Code of Ethics, what is the most appropriate action for the counselor to take?
A) Maintain client confidentiality and continue to work with the client to reduce their risk of harm.
B) Immediately report the threat to law enforcement and notify the potential victim.
C) Consult with a supervisor or legal counsel before taking any action.
D) Document the threat in the client's record and monitor the situation closely.

Question 124: Maria, a 32-year-old woman, seeks counseling for anxiety and relationship issues. During sessions, it becomes evident that her family of origin had rigid roles and a lack of emotional expression. Which intervention would most effectively address the influence of these family patterns on Maria's current issues?
A) Cognitive Behavioral Therapy (CBT) focusing on identifying and changing negative thought patterns.
B) Family Systems Therapy to explore and reframe family roles and communication styles.
C) Solution-Focused Brief Therapy (SFBT) emphasizing quick resolution of present problems.
D) Psychodynamic Therapy focusing on unconscious processes and early childhood experiences.

Question 125: After conducting an initial assessment with a new client named Sarah, who is experiencing symptoms of depression, you decide to use pre-test and post-test measures to evaluate the effectiveness of the cognitive-behavioral therapy (CBT) intervention over eight weeks. Which of the following best describes the primary purpose of using these measures?
A) To identify Sarah's baseline functioning and monitor her progress over time.
B) To compare Sarah's symptoms with those of other clients in the practice.
C) To determine the specific cause of Sarah's depressive symptoms.
D) To establish a therapeutic alliance with Sarah through regular assessments.

Question 126: John, a 45-year-old man with a high-stress job, complains of waking up multiple times during the night and feeling unrefreshed in the morning. He consumes caffeine throughout the day to stay alert. As his mental health counselor, what would be the most effective advice regarding his caffeine consumption?
A) Limit caffeine intake to no more than two cups of coffee per day.
B) Avoid caffeine after lunchtime.
C) Replace caffeinated beverages with decaffeinated options after 3 PM.
D) Gradually reduce overall caffeine consumption over several weeks.

Question 127: John, a licensed mental health counselor, is beginning therapy with a new client named Sarah. During the initial session, John needs to inform Sarah about the legal aspects of their counseling relationship. Which of the following statements should John include to ensure he meets his legal and ethical obligations?
A) "I am required by law to keep everything you say confidential unless you give me written permission to share it."
B) "I must maintain your confidentiality, but there are exceptions such as if you disclose intent to harm yourself or others."
C) "Your confidentiality is guaranteed in all circumstances except when court-ordered."
D) "Everything you share with me is confidential unless it involves illegal activities."

Question 128: During a counseling session, Maria, a 35-year-old client, begins to express intense anger about her recent job loss. As her counselor, you notice her becoming increasingly agitated. Which intervention is most appropriate to help Maria contain and manage her intense feelings in this moment?
A) Encourage Maria to describe her feelings in detail.
B) Guide Maria through a deep breathing exercise.
C) Allow Maria to vent without interruption.
D) Suggest that Maria take a short break from discussing the topic.

Question 129: When screening a client presenting with severe depression and suicidal ideation, which of the following actions should a mental health counselor prioritize to ensure appropriate services are provided?
A) Refer the client to an outpatient therapy program for weekly counseling sessions.
B) Conduct a comprehensive risk assessment and refer the client to an inpatient psychiatric facility.
C) Suggest that the client join a support group for individuals with depression.
D) Recommend that the client start medication management with their primary care physician.

Question 130: Jane, a 35-year-old woman, has been experiencing severe depression and anxiety that have not improved with outpatient therapy and medication management. She has had multiple hospitalizations in the past year due to suicidal ideation. Her therapist believes she needs a higher level of care. Which level of treatment is most appropriate for Jane at this point?
A) Intensive Outpatient Program (IOP)
B) Partial Hospitalization Program (PHP)

C) Inpatient Psychiatric Hospitalization
D) Residential Treatment Center (RTC)

Question 131: John, a 35-year-old client, is struggling with anxiety that affects his daily functioning. As his counselor, you aim to help him develop effective coping strategies. During a session, John expresses that he often feels overwhelmed at work and doesn't know how to manage his stress levels. Which of the following interventions would be most appropriate to guide John in developing skills to manage his anxiety?
A) Encourage John to practice mindfulness meditation daily.
B) Advise John to avoid stressful situations at work whenever possible.
C) Suggest that John engage in regular physical exercise.
D) Teach John cognitive-behavioral techniques to reframe negative thoughts.

Question 132: During a supervision session, Maria, a mental health counselor-in-training, discusses her struggle with maintaining professional boundaries with a client who frequently shares personal stories about their own life. How should Maria's supervisor address this issue?
A) Advise Maria to share less about her own life to maintain professional boundaries.
B) Encourage Maria to set clear boundaries with the client and discuss the importance of maintaining them.
C) Suggest that Maria terminate sessions with the client if boundaries cannot be maintained.
D) Recommend that Maria seek personal therapy to explore her own boundary issues.

Question 133: John, an African American man working in a predominantly white corporate environment, reports feeling misunderstood and marginalized by his colleagues. He often experiences microaggressions but struggles with how to address them without escalating tensions. What strategy should his counselor recommend?
A) Encouraging John to confront his colleagues directly about their behavior.
B) Advising John to document instances of microaggressions for future reference.
C) Suggesting John seek mentorship from other African American professionals within or outside the company.
D) Recommending John ignore the microaggressions to avoid conflict.

Question 134: Sarah, a 15-year-old girl, has recently moved in with her mother and stepfather after her parents' divorce. She is experiencing difficulty adjusting to the new family structure and often argues with her stepfather. As her mental health counselor, what is the most effective initial intervention to help Sarah adjust?
A) Encourage open communication between Sarah and her stepfather.
B) Suggest individual therapy sessions for Sarah to process her feelings.
C) Recommend family therapy sessions to address blended family dynamics.
D) Advise Sarah's mother to spend more one-on-one time with her.

Question 135: Under which circumstance is a mental health counselor permitted to breach client confidentiality without explicit consent?
A) When a client discloses intentions to commit a crime in the future.
B) When a client reveals past criminal activities that have not been prosecuted.
C) When a client expresses suicidal ideation with a detailed plan and means to execute it.

D) When a client requests information to be shared with their family members.

Question 136: John, a 28-year-old client, has completed the Generalized Anxiety Disorder 7-item (GAD-7) scale during his intake session. His scores suggest severe anxiety. How should his counselor use this information to facilitate John's decision-making regarding his treatment?
A) Suggest John start mindfulness meditation practices immediately.
B) Discuss initiating pharmacotherapy alongside counseling sessions.
C) Recommend an intensive outpatient program (IOP).
D) Propose regular weekly individual therapy sessions focusing on anxiety management techniques.

Question 137: A client, Maria, is struggling with low self-esteem and frequently expresses negative thoughts about her capabilities. As her counselor, you decide to use the reframe/redirect technique. Which of the following responses best exemplifies this approach?
A) "I understand you're feeling down about your abilities, but everyone has strengths and weaknesses."
B) "It sounds like you're really hard on yourself. Let's explore some of your recent achievements."
C) "Why do you think you feel this way about your capabilities?"
D) "Let's focus on what you can do rather than what you can't."

Question 138: During the "storming" stage of group development, what is the most appropriate intervention for a mental health counselor to implement?
A) Establish clear group norms and roles.
B) Facilitate team-building activities.
C) Encourage open communication and conflict resolution.
D) Provide closure and reflect on group achievements.

Question 139: During a biopsychosocial interview, which aspect is most crucial to explore when assessing a client's social context?
A) The client's family medical history
B) The client's current living situation
C) The client's past psychological treatment
D) The client's dietary habits

Question 140: Maria, a 35-year-old Latina woman, recently moved to the United States and is experiencing difficulty adjusting to her new environment. She feels isolated and has trouble communicating with her coworkers due to language barriers. Which intervention would be most effective in helping Maria adjust culturally?
A) Encouraging Maria to join a community group that shares her cultural background.
B) Advising Maria to focus solely on learning English to improve communication.
C) Suggesting Maria avoid interactions with people from her own culture to adapt faster.
D) Recommending Maria seek individual therapy to address her feelings of isolation.

Question 141: Which of the following behavioral indicators is most commonly associated with emotional abuse in children?
A) Frequent unexplained injuries
B) Extreme withdrawal or fearfulness
C) Sudden changes in academic performance
D) Inappropriate sexual behaviors

Question 142: Maria, a 28-year-old woman, complains of persistent muscle tension, headaches, and fatigue. She

mentions that she feels constantly on edge and has difficulty sleeping. What is the most likely diagnosis considering her physical symptoms related to anxiety?
A) Generalized Anxiety Disorder (GAD)
B) Chronic Fatigue Syndrome
C) Tension-Type Headache
D) Fibromyalgia

Question 143: During an intake session, Maria, a 35-year-old woman, reports ongoing conflicts with her partner. She describes their communication as often leading to misunderstandings and escalating arguments. As a mental health counselor evaluating the interactional dynamics, what should you focus on to gain a comprehensive understanding of their issues?
A) The frequency and duration of their arguments
B) The content of their arguments
C) The underlying emotional triggers during their interactions
D) The roles each partner assumes during conflicts

Question 144: Which of the following scenarios would legally justify Sarah breaching confidentiality?
A) John expresses a desire to harm himself.
B) John reveals he has committed a crime in the past.
C) John discloses plans to harm another person.
D) John requests that his therapy records be shared with his spouse.

Question 145: John, a client dealing with anxiety about his job performance, often says he is not good enough and fears losing his job. How would you use reframe/redirect to help him?
A) "It's normal to feel anxious about work; many people experience this."
B) "Can you tell me more about why you think you're not good enough?"
C) "Think about times when you've received positive feedback at work."
D) "Let's discuss strategies to improve your performance at work."

Question 146: John, a 35-year-old male with a history of generalized anxiety disorder (GAD), has been in therapy for six months. Initially, his treatment plan included cognitive-behavioral therapy (CBT) and medication management. Recently, John has reported significant improvement in his anxiety symptoms but has started experiencing depressive symptoms. As his mental health counselor, what is the most appropriate step to take when reviewing and revising his treatment plan?
A) Continue with CBT and medication management without any changes.
B) Discontinue CBT and focus solely on medication management for depressive symptoms.
C) Integrate an additional therapeutic approach targeting depressive symptoms while continuing CBT.
D) Refer John to a psychiatrist for a complete reassessment of his mental health condition.

Question 147: John is providing distance counseling to

a client who lives in another state. He needs to ensure he is practicing legally and ethically. What should be his primary consideration?
A) Verify licensure requirements in both his state and the client's state.
B) Ensure he has malpractice insurance covering interstate practice.
C) Inform his client about potential limitations of telemental health.
D) Schedule regular check-ins with his supervisor about interstate cases.

Question 148: Dr. Smith, a licensed mental health counselor at an outpatient facility, learns that one of her clients, Sarah, has started working at the same facility in an administrative role. According to agency policies and professional ethics, what should Dr. Smith do?
A) Continue counseling Sarah but avoid discussing work-related topics during sessions.
B) Immediately terminate counseling sessions with Sarah due to a conflict of interest.
C) Discuss the situation with Sarah and seek supervision or consultation from a colleague.
D) Transfer Sarah's case to another counselor without informing her of the reason.

Question 149: When working with a couple experiencing significant communication issues, which conflict resolution strategy is most effective for helping them understand each other's perspectives and fostering empathy?
A) Mediation
B) Reflective Listening
C) Problem-Solving Negotiation
D) Compromise

Question 150: Maria, a mental health counselor, is working with the Rodriguez family, who recently immigrated from Mexico. The parents are concerned about their teenage son, Juan, who is struggling academically and socially. They believe that Juan's problems are due to his lack of respect for family traditions and cultural values. Maria wants to address these concerns while being culturally sensitive.
A) Emphasize the importance of Juan adapting to American culture to improve his academic performance.
B) Encourage the family to maintain their cultural traditions while helping Juan integrate into American society.
C) Suggest that the parents adopt more American parenting styles to better support Juan.
D) Focus on individual counseling for Juan to address his academic and social issues separately from his family's concerns.

ANSWER WITH DETAILED EXPLANATION SET [4]

Question 1: Correct Answer: C) Reflect John's feelings and normalize his concerns about judgment.
Rationale: Reflecting John's feelings and normalizing his concerns helps him feel understood and accepted, which are key components of building trust in the therapeutic relationship. This approach validates his emotions without minimizing them. Option A, while important for confidentiality, does not directly address his fear of judgment. Option B may blur professional boundaries and shift focus away from John's concerns. Option D attempts to distract rather than address underlying fears, which can undermine trust-building efforts.

Question 2: Correct Answer: C) Assisting the client in creating a safety plan tailored to their specific situation.
Rationale: Assisting the client in creating a safety plan tailored to their specific situation is the most effective intervention for addressing immediate safety concerns. A safety plan includes practical steps that can help the client avoid danger and know what to do in an emergency. This approach prioritizes immediate physical safety, which is crucial before addressing longer-term psychological impacts. Option A (Developing a long-term counseling plan focused on trauma recovery) is important but secondary to ensuring immediate safety. Option B (Encouraging the client to attend support groups for emotional support) offers valuable emotional support but does not directly address urgent safety needs. Option D (Providing information about legal resources and restraining orders) is useful but may not offer immediate protection without an actionable plan in place.

Question 3: Correct Answer: C) Standardized outcome measures
Rationale: Standardized outcome measures (Option C) are considered the most valid method for evaluating counseling effectiveness because they provide objective, reliable, and validated data on client progress. Client self-report surveys (Option A), while useful, can be biased by the client's perception. The counselor's subjective assessment (Option B) lacks objectivity and can be influenced by personal biases. Frequency of session attendance (Option D) does not directly measure therapeutic outcomes but rather engagement level.

Question 4: Correct Answer: A) Cognitive-Behavioral Therapy (CBT)
Rationale: Cognitive-Behavioral Therapy (CBT) is widely recognized as the most effective treatment for Panic Disorder. It focuses on changing maladaptive thought patterns and behaviors associated with panic attacks. Psychodynamic Therapy explores unconscious processes influencing behavior but lacks robust evidence for treating Panic Disorder specifically. Exposure Therapy is a component of CBT that helps patients face feared situations but is not as comprehensive alone as CBT for treating panic symptoms. Dialectical Behavior Therapy (DBT), while effective for emotion regulation in Borderline Personality Disorder, is not specifically tailored to address the cognitive distortions central to Panic Disorder.

Question 5: Correct Answer: C) Cognitive Behavioral Therapy for Insomnia (CBT-I)
Rationale: Cognitive Behavioral Therapy for Insomnia (CBT-I) is widely recognized as the most effective first-line treatment for chronic insomnia. Unlike pharmacotherapy with benzodiazepines (Option A), which can lead to dependency and other side effects, CBT-I addresses the underlying cognitive and behavioral factors contributing to insomnia. Sleep hygiene education (Option B) is a component of CBT-I but is not sufficient on its own as a standalone treatment. Melatonin supplementation (Option D) can help regulate sleep-wake cycles but does not address the root psychological causes of insomnia. Therefore, CBT-I remains the gold standard based on contemporary research and clinical guidelines.

Question 6: Correct Answer: B) Advise Sarah to limit sharing personal details to protect her privacy and confidentiality.
Rationale: Professional practice and ethics emphasize the importance of client confidentiality and privacy. Encouraging or suggesting specific types of sharing (Options A, C, D) may inadvertently compromise Sarah's privacy or lead to boundary issues. Advising her to limit sharing (Option B) aligns with ethical guidelines, ensuring her confidentiality is maintained while respecting her autonomy.

Question 7: Correct Answer: A) Beck Depression Inventory (BDI)
Rationale: The Beck Depression Inventory (BDI; Option A) is a standardized tool specifically designed to measure the severity of depression symptoms, making it highly appropriate for evaluating CBT's effectiveness. Therapist's clinical notes (Option B), while informative, are subjective and not standardized. The patient's daily mood diary (Option C), though useful for tracking day-to-day changes, lacks the rigor and validation of standardized tools. The Global Assessment of Functioning (GAF; Option D), although comprehensive, assesses overall functioning rather than focusing specifically on depression symptoms.

Question 8: Correct Answer: A) Encouraging open communication between all family members.
Rationale: Encouraging open communication between all family members is crucial in addressing loyalty conflicts as it allows each member to express their feelings and concerns, fostering understanding and reducing tension. While establishing clear family rules (Option B) is important, it does not directly address emotional conflicts. Individual therapy (Option C) can be beneficial but may not resolve issues within the family dynamic itself. Promoting bonding activities (Option D) is helpful but might not address underlying loyalty conflicts without open dialogue. Thus, Option A is the most comprehensive approach to resolving loyalty conflicts in blended families.

Question 9: Correct Answer: B) Over-involvement leading to decreased autonomy and increased anxiety.
Rationale: In collectivist cultures, extended families often play a significant role in an individual's life. While this can provide emotional support (Option A), enhance social networks (Option C), and foster identity formation through cultural values (Option D), over-involvement can lead to decreased personal autonomy and increased anxiety (Option B). This is because individuals may feel pressured by family expectations and lack personal space to make independent decisions. Options A, C, and D describe positive impacts that are also true but do not address the potential negative impact as precisely as Option B does.

Question 10: Correct Answer: B) Respect John's decision not to report the harassment but provide him with resources and support.
Rationale: The correct answer is B because it respects John's autonomy while still providing him with necessary support and resources. Encouraging immediate reporting (Option A) may not consider John's readiness or fear of retaliation. Reporting without consent (Option C) violates confidentiality and autonomy. Suggesting a leave of absence (Option D) might not address the root issue and could be seen as avoiding advocacy responsibilities.

Question 11: Correct Answer: C) Exploring Ambivalence
Rationale: Exploring ambivalence helps clients like John understand their mixed feelings about change, which is a critical step in increasing readiness for action. By addressing both sides of his ambivalence, John can move towards resolving these conflicts and become more committed to

making changes. - Goal Setting (A) is useful once readiness is established but may be premature if ambivalence remains. - Affirmations (B) are supportive statements that reinforce client strengths but do not directly address ambivalence. - Providing Information (D) can increase knowledge but does not necessarily resolve internal conflicts about change.

Question 12: Correct Answer: A) Enhances client engagement by providing clear goals and expectations.

Rationale: Structured activities are designed to enhance client engagement by providing clear goals and expectations, which help clients understand the purpose of each session and stay focused. Option B is incorrect because spontaneous expression is more characteristic of unstructured activities. Option C is misleading as structured activities are meant to provide a framework rather than facilitate unstructured interaction. Option D is also incorrect as structured activities involve more guidance from the counselor rather than allowing clients to lead sessions independently. Structured activities are grounded in contemporary research that emphasizes goal-oriented interventions for effective counseling outcomes.

Question 13: Correct Answer: B) Using active listening and empathetic responses.

Rationale: Active listening and empathetic responses are fundamental in establishing a strong therapeutic alliance as they validate the client's feelings and experiences, fostering trust and understanding. Providing immediate solutions (Option A) may undermine the client's sense of autonomy. Sharing personal experiences (Option C) can blur professional boundaries and shift focus away from the client. Setting clear boundaries (Option D) is important but does not directly address emotional connection and empathy, which are crucial for building a strong alliance. Thus, Option B is the most effective technique based on contemporary counseling theories and research.

Question 14: Correct Answer: C) Post-Traumatic Stress Disorder (PTSD)

Rationale: Mark's symptoms of irritability, nightmares, avoidance behavior, and physical issues are indicative of PTSD, particularly given his history of combat experiences. GAD (Option A) involves chronic anxiety but lacks the specific trauma-related triggers seen in PTSD. MDD (Option B) includes depressive symptoms but does not typically involve avoidance or trauma-specific triggers. Acute Stress Disorder (Option D) has similar symptoms to PTSD but occurs within one month of the traumatic event; Mark's ongoing issues suggest a longer duration consistent with PTSD.

Question 15: Correct Answer: C) Implement a sliding scale fee based on Tom's current financial situation.

Rationale: Implementing a sliding scale fee aligns with ethical guidelines by considering the client's ability to pay while ensuring access to necessary services. Option A might not be sustainable or fair to other clients needing similar accommodations. Option B reduces service frequency but doesn't address affordability directly. Option D could disrupt continuity of care and may not be necessary if an adjusted fee can be agreed upon between Maria and Tom..

Question 16: Correct Answer: B) Acceptance and Commitment Therapy (ACT)

Rationale: Acceptance and Commitment Therapy (ACT) focuses on accepting intrusive thoughts without trying to change or suppress them, which aligns well with mindfulness principles. Thought suppression (A) often exacerbates intrusive thoughts by making them more persistent. Rational Emotive Behavior Therapy (REBT) (C), while effective in addressing irrational beliefs, does not emphasize acceptance in the same way ACT does. Systematic desensitization (D), primarily used for phobias and anxiety disorders, involves gradual exposure rather than acceptance of intrusive thoughts. Each option was crafted to be closely related to the correct answer by including elements common in therapeutic settings but differing in their primary focus or theoretical foundation.

Question 17: Correct Answer: C) Group norms

Rationale: Group norms are fundamental in maintaining group cohesion during transitions because they provide a consistent framework for behavior and expectations within the group. These norms help members understand their roles and responsibilities, facilitating smoother transitions and reducing anxiety associated with changes in membership. - A) Leadership style: While important, leadership style alone cannot maintain cohesion if the group's norms are not well-established. - B) Member self-disclosure: This can enhance trust but is less effective without clear norms guiding interactions. - D) Conflict resolution: Essential for addressing issues, but it relies on established norms to be effective. Thus, while leadership style, self-disclosure, and conflict resolution are significant, they are all underpinned by the overarching influence of group norms in maintaining cohesion during transitions.

Question 18: Correct Answer: A) Refer John to an inpatient psychiatric facility.

Rationale: Given John's disclosure of frequent suicidal thoughts, referring him to an inpatient psychiatric facility is crucial as it provides intensive monitoring and comprehensive care necessary for his safety and well-being. An outpatient substance abuse program (Option B) does not offer the level of supervision required for someone with active suicidal ideation. A crisis hotline (Option C), while helpful in emergencies, is not sufficient for ongoing care. Referring him to an emergency room (Option D) might provide immediate evaluation but lacks long-term treatment planning essential for his condition.

Question 19: Correct Answer: A) Childhood sexual abuse often leads to difficulties in establishing trust in adult relationships.

Rationale: A) Correct. Contemporary research indicates that survivors of childhood sexual abuse frequently struggle with trust issues in their adult relationships due to the betrayal experienced during their formative years. This affects their ability to form secure attachments and maintain healthy interpersonal connections. B) Incorrect. While some survivors may struggle with intimacy, it is not accurate to generalize that they are unable to form any intimate relationships. Many survivors work through their trauma and can establish meaningful connections with appropriate support and therapy. C) Incorrect. Although there is some risk for intergenerational transmission of abusive behaviors, it is not a definitive outcome for all survivors. Many do not perpetuate the cycle of abuse and instead become advocates against it. D) Incorrect. While some individuals may face challenges in their sexual lives due to past trauma, many can experience healthy sexual relationships through therapy and healing processes. It is an overgeneralization to state that they are generally unable to have healthy sexual experiences.

Question 20: Correct Answer: A) Role-playing refusal scenarios with a counselor

Rationale: Role-playing refusal scenarios with a counselor is an effective assertiveness training technique as it allows Maria to practice saying "no" in a safe environment, receive feedback, and build confidence. Passive communication techniques (Option B) do not address assertiveness directly. Cognitive restructuring exercises (Option C) focus more on changing thought patterns rather than behavior practice. Relaxation techniques (Option D) may help manage stress but do not specifically teach assertive communication skills.

Question 21: Correct Answer: B) Factor analysis determines if the questionnaire measures what it intends to measure.

Rationale: Factor analysis is used to examine construct validity by identifying whether items group together as expected based on theoretical constructs (Option B). Cronbach's alpha measures internal consistency by assessing how well items correlate with each other (Option A), not over time (Option C). Option D confuses factor analysis with test-retest reliability.

Question 22: Correct Answer: C) Provide a tactile model of any visual content discussed.

Rationale: Providing a tactile model of any visual content discussed is the most appropriate action because it directly addresses the client's need to access visual information through alternative sensory input, aligning with contemporary research on multisensory learning and accessibility. Option A (large print materials) and Option B (audio recordings) are useful but may not fully meet the needs of someone who relies heavily on tactile information. Option D (reading aloud) is helpful but does not provide an interactive or comprehensive way to understand visual content. Thus, C offers the most effective accommodation by engaging the client's sense of touch for better comprehension.

Question 23: Correct Answer: D) Reviewing progress and discussing feelings about termination

Rationale: Reviewing progress and discussing feelings about termination is essential because it helps clients process their emotions about ending therapy, ensures they recognize their achievements, and prepares them for future challenges. Option A is incorrect as treatment goals may not always be fully achieved; readiness for termination depends more on stability and self-efficacy. Option B is close but focuses more on crisis planning rather than the emotional aspect of termination. Option C is also important but secondary to discussing feelings and progress, which are central to a smooth transition out of therapy.

Question 24: Correct Answer: B) Include detailed descriptions of John's progress and setbacks in each session.

Rationale: Detailed descriptions of progress and setbacks provide a comprehensive view of John's therapeutic journey, essential for ongoing assessment and treatment planning. Summarizing sessions briefly (Option A) may omit critical details. Using general terms (Option C) can lead to vague records that are not useful for precise interventions. Focusing solely on treatment plans (Option D), while minimizing session details, fails to capture the full scope of John's experience and therapeutic response. By creating these nuanced questions with closely related incorrect options, we challenge candidates to apply their knowledge critically and comprehensively.

Question 25: Correct Answer: B) "You have made significant progress, and I genuinely believe in your abilities."

Rationale: Option B best demonstrates congruence as it reflects the counselor's genuine feelings and belief in Emily's progress without any reservation or contradiction. It aligns with Carl Rogers' principle of being authentic and transparent with clients. Option A introduces doubt ("but you could try harder"), which undermines the authenticity. Option C also includes a contradictory statement ("but there's always room for improvement"), which can be perceived as less genuine. Option D is positive but lacks the personal conviction and belief expressed in Option B.

Question 26: Correct Answer: C) Clarify the professional nature of your relationship and discuss transferring him to another counselor if needed.

Rationale: Maintaining professional boundaries is crucial in counseling relationships. By clarifying the nature of your relationship and discussing the possibility of transferring John to another counselor, you uphold ethical standards and protect both parties from potential harm. Option A could lead John to believe his feelings are acceptable within the therapeutic context. Option B may come across as harsh and could damage the therapeutic alliance. Option D ignores an important issue that needs addressing for ethical practice.

Question 27: Correct Answer: C) Refer Maria to a pain specialist for comprehensive pain evaluation and management.

Rationale: The correct answer is C because a pain specialist can provide an in-depth evaluation and a multifaceted approach to managing chronic pain, which is crucial given its impact on Maria's depression. Option A (psychiatrist) focuses solely on medication management without addressing the root cause of her chronic pain. Option B (physical therapist) addresses physical aspects but lacks the comprehensive approach needed. Option D (support group) offers emotional support but not professional medical intervention necessary for complex cases like Maria's.

Question 28: Correct Answer: C) Collaborate with Sarah to develop a budget and financial plan.

Rationale: The primary intervention should directly address the root cause of Sarah's anxiety her overwhelming debt. Collaborating with Sarah to develop a budget and financial plan empowers her by providing practical steps towards managing her debt, which can alleviate her anxiety. While referring her to a financial advisor (A) or encouraging her to join a support group (D) are beneficial, they do not offer immediate personal empowerment and actionable steps as effectively as option C. Providing psychoeducation on anxiety management techniques (B) addresses symptoms but not the underlying financial issue.

Question 29: Correct Answer: C) Inform John about the clinic's policy and review the records with him before providing access.

Rationale: According to standard counselor/agency policies, clients have the right to access their records. However, it is essential for counselors to inform clients about agency policies and review the records with them to ensure understanding and address any potential concerns. Option A is incorrect because immediate access without review can lead to misinterpretation. Option B is incorrect as clients generally have a right to their records unless there are specific legal or ethical reasons not to provide them. Option D is partially correct but does not fully align with standard practices which involve reviewing the full record with the client.

Question 30: Correct Answer: B) Inform Maria that confidentiality is maintained except in cases where there is a risk of harm to herself or others.

Rationale: The correct answer is B because it aligns with ethical guidelines and legal requirements concerning client confidentiality. Confidentiality must be maintained unless there are exceptions such as risk of harm to self or others. Option A is incorrect because it falsely guarantees absolute confidentiality. Option C is incorrect as family members do not have the right to breach confidentiality without consent. Option D is incorrect because an employer does not have automatic access to counseling records without proper authorization.

Question 31: Correct Answer: B) Address the parents' communication patterns and their impact on family dynamics.

Rationale: Addressing the parents' communication patterns and their impact on family dynamics (Option B) is crucial because it targets the root cause affecting all members. Systemic change in counseling often involves altering interaction patterns within the system (the family). While focusing on individual coping mechanisms (Option A), behavioral modification (Option C), and individual therapy sessions (Option D) can be beneficial, they do not directly address the systemic issue of poor communication affecting everyone.

Question 32: Correct Answer: B) Parent-Child Interaction Therapy (PCIT)

Rationale: Parent-Child Interaction Therapy (PCIT) is specifically designed for young children with disruptive behaviors such as temper tantrums and defiance. It focuses on improving the quality of the parent-child relationship and changing parent-child interaction patterns. Cognitive Behavioral Therapy (CBT) can be effective but is generally more suitable for older children and adolescents. Play Therapy is beneficial for younger children but may not directly address behavioral compliance issues as effectively as PCIT. Dialectical Behavior Therapy (DBT) is primarily used for older adolescents and adults with severe emotional regulation issues, making it less appropriate for this scenario. - A) Cognitive Behavioral Therapy (CBT): While CBT can be effective in modifying thoughts and behaviors, it is generally more suitable for older children and adolescents rather than younger children with defiance issues. - B) Parent-Child Interaction Therapy (PCIT): This approach directly targets parent-child interactions and has been shown to be highly effective in managing disruptive behaviors in young children. - C) Play Therapy: Although useful for younger children, Play Therapy may not focus sufficiently on rule-following and compliance compared to PCIT. - D) Dialectical Behavior Therapy (DBT): DBT focuses on emotional regulation and is more appropriate for older adolescents or adults with severe emotional dysregulation rather than young children with behavioral compliance issues. The key differences lie in the target age group, specific focus on parent-child dynamics, and direct applicability to defiant behaviors, making PCIT the most suitable option.

Question 33: Correct Answer: A) Cognitive Behavioral Therapy (CBT)

Rationale: Cognitive Behavioral Therapy (CBT) is widely recognized as the most effective approach for treating generalized anxiety disorder (GAD). CBT focuses on identifying and changing maladaptive thought patterns and behaviors, which are central to managing GAD symptoms. Psychoanalytic Therapy (Option B) delves into unconscious processes and past experiences but lacks strong empirical support for treating GAD specifically. Solution-Focused Brief Therapy (Option C) emphasizes short-term goals rather than addressing the underlying cognitive distortions associated with GAD. Person-Centered Therapy (Option D) provides a supportive environment but does not offer structured techniques to directly target anxiety symptoms. Therefore, while all these therapies have their merits, CBT stands out due to its robust evidence base for effectively managing GAD over the long term.

Question 34: Correct Answer: A) Help James develop coping strategies for managing stress related to systemic racism.

Rationale: Helping James develop coping strategies for managing stress related to systemic racism addresses his immediate mental health needs while acknowledging the impact of systemic issues on his well-being. This approach is rooted in trauma-informed care and resilience-building strategies. Encouraging community activism (Option B) can be empowering but may not address his immediate emotional distress. Suggesting avoidance of certain areas (Option C) may reinforce fear and does not provide long-term solutions. Focusing solely on self-esteem (Option D) overlooks the broader context of systemic racism affecting his mental health.

Question 35: Correct Answer: D) Sleep Hygiene Education

Rationale: Sleep hygiene education is crucial for someone like Maria who is experiencing insomnia due to stress. It provides practical strategies to improve sleep quality, which can significantly reduce stress levels. While guided imagery techniques, time management workshops, and deep breathing exercises are beneficial for overall stress management, they do not directly address the specific issue of insomnia as effectively as sleep hygiene education does. This targeted approach helps Maria establish healthy sleep routines that can alleviate both her insomnia and associated stress.

Question 36: Correct Answer: B) Facilitating open discussions about their fears and encouraging expression of all emotions.

Rationale: Option B is correct because contemporary research supports that facilitating open discussions about fears and encouraging the expression of all emotions helps clients process anticipatory grief effectively. This approach aligns with theories such as Kübler-Ross's stages of grief,

emphasizing the importance of acknowledging all emotions. Option A is incorrect because avoiding fears can lead to unresolved grief. Option C is incorrect as remaining stoic can isolate the client emotionally. Option D may provide temporary distraction but does not address underlying emotional needs, making it less effective in long-term coping.

Question 37: Correct Answer: B) Assure John that everything discussed is confidential and he can share at his own pace.

Rationale: Assuring John of confidentiality and allowing him to share at his own pace creates a safe environment conducive to building trust. This approach respects John's autonomy and acknowledges his readiness, which are crucial for trauma survivors. Option A may overwhelm him, Option C risks boundary issues, and Option D may pressure him prematurely.

Question 38: Correct Answer: A) Catastrophizing

Rationale: Mark's excessive worry about his health despite medical reassurances indicates catastrophizing, where he imagines the worst possible outcomes without evidence. Overgeneralization involves drawing broad conclusions from a single event, which does not align with Mark's specific health concerns. Personalization refers to blaming oneself for events outside one's control, which is not evident in this scenario. Mind reading involves assuming others' thoughts or intentions without evidence; Mark's issue revolves around his own health fears rather than assumptions about others' thoughts.

Question 39: Correct Answer: B) Cognitive restructuring

Rationale: Cognitive restructuring focuses on identifying and changing maladaptive thought patterns that contribute to anxiety and insomnia. In Maria's case, her worries about job performance are likely exacerbating her sleep difficulties, making cognitive restructuring the most effective approach. Sleep hygiene education (Option A), while helpful, primarily addresses behaviors rather than thoughts. Relaxation training (Option C) can reduce physical tension but may not fully address cognitive aspects of anxiety. Mindfulness-based stress reduction (Option D) helps with overall stress but may not specifically target maladaptive thoughts as effectively as cognitive restructuring.

Question 40: Correct Answer: A) Establishing clear group norms and expectations at the beginning of sessions.

Rationale: Establishing clear group norms and expectations at the beginning of sessions is crucial as it sets a foundation for open communication, trust, and a structured environment where members feel safe to interact. This approach aligns with contemporary research emphasizing the importance of structure in therapeutic settings. Option B) Allowing the group leader to share personal experiences frequently can blur professional boundaries and shift focus away from members' issues, making it less effective. Option C) Encouraging members to address their comments directly to the group leader may inhibit peer interactions, which are vital for group dynamics. Option D) Rotating the role of group leader among members can undermine consistency and authority, leading to confusion and reduced efficacy in managing group processes. In summary, while all options might seem beneficial, A) Establishing clear group norms and expectations is supported by evidence as a foundational strategy for promoting effective interactions with the group leader.

Question 41: Correct Answer: B) Conduct a comprehensive biopsychosocial assessment.

Rationale: Conducting a comprehensive biopsychosocial assessment is crucial as it provides a holistic understanding of John's condition by considering biological, psychological, and social factors. This approach ensures that all aspects of his life contributing to his anxiety and depression are evaluated before deciding on further interventions. Referring to a psychiatrist (Option A), suggesting a support group (Option C), or initiating CBT (Option D) might be necessary steps later but are premature without an initial comprehensive assessment.

Question 42: Correct Answer: B) "It sounds like you're feeling very lonely and disconnected right now."

Rationale: Option B demonstrates empathic attunement by accurately reflecting Maria's emotional state, showing that the counselor is truly attuned to her feelings. Option A, while supportive, is more about the counselor's understanding rather than Maria's specific emotions. Option C generalizes her experience instead of focusing on her unique feelings. Option D offers advice rather than empathetic reflection, which can come across as dismissive.

Question 43: Correct Answer: D) Implement weekly home visits by a mental health nurse alongside bi-weekly psychiatrist appointments.

Rationale: Implementing weekly home visits by a mental health nurse alongside bi-weekly psychiatrist appointments provides both medication adherence monitoring and psychosocial support, ensuring comprehensive care. Option A) lacks frequent enough contact for effective medication monitoring. Option B) places responsibility on family members without professional oversight. Option C), while providing group therapy support, does not offer the same level of direct monitoring as home visits combined with psychiatric appointments. Weekly home visits ensure close supervision and immediate intervention if issues arise, making it the most robust strategy for Maria's needs.

Question 44: Correct Answer: B) Difficulty regulating emotions and maintaining relationships

Rationale: Complex post-traumatic stress disorder (C-PTSD) is often associated with prolonged trauma exposure, such as childhood abuse or domestic violence. Unlike PTSD, which may focus more on hypervigilance (A), intrusive memories (C), and avoidance (D), C-PTSD involves significant difficulties in emotional regulation and interpersonal relationships (B). This distinction is crucial as it highlights the chronic nature of C-PTSD. Hypervigilance, intrusive memories, and avoidance are more typical of standard PTSD symptoms but do not encapsulate the broader relational and emotional dysregulation seen in C-PTSD.

Question 45: Correct Answer: C) Couple counseling for Maria and John

Rationale: Couple counseling is the most appropriate intervention as it directly addresses the relational dynamics between Maria and John. Individual counseling (Options A and B) would not focus on their interaction patterns or communication issues as a couple. Family counseling (Option D) might involve other family members who are not central to the marital issues at hand. Couple counseling provides a structured environment where both partners can work on communication skills, rebuild trust, and understand each other's perspectives.

Question 46: Correct Answer: B) Emotionally Focused Therapy (EFT)

Rationale: Emotionally Focused Therapy (EFT) is particularly effective for addressing issues related to attachment styles as it focuses on creating secure emotional bonds and understanding underlying emotional needs. EFT helps clients explore their attachment history and develop healthier relationship patterns. - Option A (Cognitive Behavioral Therapy): Incorrect because while CBT can address negative thought patterns contributing to loneliness, it doesn't specifically target the emotional aspects of attachment styles. - Option C (Solution-Focused Brief Therapy): Incorrect because SFBT focuses on finding immediate solutions rather than exploring deep-seated attachment issues. - Option D (Dialectical Behavior Therapy): Incorrect because DBT is primarily used for emotional regulation and borderline personality disorder rather than addressing core attachment-related problems. Each option has been crafted considering its theoretical relevance but only EFT directly targets the foundational issues related to John's described difficulties with forming deeper connections due to early childhood experiences.

Question 47: Correct Answer: C) Praise Mark's willingness to share but gently remind him of the importance of hearing from everyone.

Rationale: Praising Mark while reminding him of the group's need for balanced participation maintains a positive atmosphere and encourages equitable interaction. Option A could make Mark feel singled out and defensive. Option B is practical but may feel too rigid, limiting natural conversation flow. Option D neglects other members' needs and does not foster group cohesion.

Question 48: Correct Answer: A) Attachment insecurity due to early separation from biological parents

Rationale: Attachment insecurity is a common issue among adopted children, particularly those who experienced early separation from their biological parents. This can lead to difficulties in forming secure relationships and increased anxiety. While genetic predisposition (B), lack of social skills (C), and adjustment disorder (D) are relevant considerations, they do not fully explain the depth of attachment-related issues stemming from early childhood experiences.

Question 49: Correct Answer: A) Client's current symptom severity

Rationale: The most crucial factor in determining the appropriate level of outpatient care is the client's current symptom severity. This directly impacts the intensity and type of treatment required. While financial situation (Option B), social support system (Option C), and previous treatment history (Option D) are important considerations, they do not primarily dictate the level of care needed. Symptom severity helps clinicians gauge whether standard outpatient therapy is sufficient or if more intensive services like intensive outpatient programs (IOP) are necessary. This ensures that clients receive care tailored to their immediate clinical needs. - Option A (Correct): Symptom severity is critical as it determines how intensive the treatment needs to be. - Option B: Financial situation can affect access to services but does not determine clinical necessity. - Option C: Social support is important for recovery but secondary to clinical needs in determining care level. - Option D: Previous treatment history provides context but does not override current clinical assessment.

Question 50: Correct Answer: A) Encourage John to express his feelings about his illness and its impact on his life.

Rationale: Encouraging John to express his feelings about his illness helps him process emotions and fosters open communication. Family therapy (B), CBT (C), and relaxation techniques (D) are beneficial but secondary; they should follow after addressing John's need for emotional expression. Understanding his perspective provides a foundation for further therapeutic interventions.

Question 51: Correct Answer: B) Gender-Affirmative Therapy

Rationale: Gender-Affirmative Therapy focuses specifically on validating and supporting an individual's gender identity while addressing societal pressures and expectations. It is tailored to help clients like Alex navigate anxiety related to societal norms around gender roles. - A) Cognitive Behavioral Therapy (CBT): While effective for general anxiety, it may not address the specific nuances of gender-related stress. - C) Psychodynamic Therapy: This approach delves into unconscious processes but may not provide immediate support for navigating current societal expectations. - D) Exposure Therapy: Typically used for phobias and PTSD, this is less relevant for addressing ongoing societal pressures related to gender roles. Each option was crafted considering its relevance and potential applicability in similar contexts but with key differences making the correct answer stand out due to its specific alignment with contemporary research and recognized theories in gender identity development.

Question 52: Correct Answer: B) Cognitive Restructuring

Rationale: Cognitive restructuring is a core component of cognitive-behavioral therapy (CBT) that helps individuals identify and challenge irrational or maladaptive thoughts. This technique is particularly effective for managing ruminative thoughts by replacing them with more balanced thinking patterns. Mindfulness meditation (A) can be beneficial but is more aligned with mindfulness-based therapies rather than CBT. Exposure therapy (C) is typically used for anxiety disorders and phobias, not primarily for ruminative thoughts. Psychodynamic therapy (D), while useful for exploring underlying issues, does not directly address the cognitive distortions associated with rumination.

Question 53: Correct Answer: A) CBT has a statistically significant effect on reducing anxiety symptoms in adolescents.

Rationale: A p-value of 0.03 indicates that there is less than a 3% chance that the observed effect is due to random variation alone, thus it meets the threshold for statistical significance ($p < 0.05$). However, statistical significance does not imply causation (Option B), nor does it comment on clinical significance (Option D). Option C is incorrect as the p-value indicates an effect exists.

Question 54: Correct Answer: C) Validate Maria's feelings and provide psychoeducation about disenfranchised grief.

Rationale: Validating Maria's feelings and providing psychoeducation about disenfranchised grief helps her understand that her emotions are normal and that she is not alone in experiencing this type of grief. This approach lays a foundation for further therapeutic work by normalizing her experience and reducing feelings of isolation. While writing letters (A), joining a support group (B), and mindfulness practices (D) can be beneficial later in the therapy process, they do not address the immediate need for validation and understanding of her unique situation.

Question 55: Correct Answer: B) Major Depressive Disorder

Rationale: Mr. Thompson's symptoms of withdrawal, disinterest in activities, sleep difficulties, and hopelessness are hallmark signs of Major Depressive Disorder (MDD). Generalized Anxiety Disorder (A) involves excessive worry rather than pervasive hopelessness. Mild Cognitive Impairment (C) primarily affects memory and cognitive function without the profound emotional symptoms seen here. Adjustment Disorder (D) involves emotional or behavioral symptoms in response to a specific stressor but typically lacks the depth of depressive symptoms described.

Question 56: Correct Answer: B) Decline politely and explain that attending could blur professional boundaries.

Rationale: Maintaining professional boundaries is crucial in counseling to prevent dual relationships that could impair objectivity and professionalism. Option B appropriately addresses this by declining the invitation and explaining potential boundary issues. Option A risks blurring boundaries despite avoiding therapy discussions at the event. Option C still involves crossing professional lines by attending. Option D shifts focus back to therapy but doesn't address boundary concerns adequately.

Question 57: Correct Answer: D) Maria's high level of intrinsic motivation.

Rationale: Intrinsic motivation is a critical strength that significantly enhances the likelihood of goal attainment because it drives individuals to pursue goals for personal satisfaction and fulfillment rather than external rewards. While setting specific and measurable goals (Option A), having a supportive family environment (Option B), and previous work experience (Option C) are all important factors, intrinsic motivation is particularly powerful in maintaining long-term commitment and resilience in the face of challenges. Research shows that intrinsic motivation is strongly linked to sustained effort and perseverance, which are essential for achieving complex goals like returning to work after depression.

Question 58: Correct Answer: B) Assess the quality of John's existing relationships and their emotional support.

Rationale: While increasing social interactions (Option A) or joining new groups (Option C) might seem beneficial, they do not address the core issue of the quality of existing relationships. Individual therapy (Option D) may be helpful but does not directly address the social support network's impact. Assessing the quality of John's relationships (Option B) is critical as it focuses on understanding whether these relationships provide meaningful emotional support, which is essential for improving mental health outcomes according to contemporary research.

Question 59: Correct Answer: C) Point out the non-verbal reactions of the group members.

Rationale: Pointing out non-verbal reactions helps bring attention to immediate interactions within the group, fostering awareness of here-and-now dynamics. This intervention encourages members to reflect on their feelings and behaviors in real-time, which is essential for facilitating present-moment awareness. - A) Encouraging Sarah to continue sharing focuses on her narrative rather than group dynamics. - B) Asking others how they feel shifts focus from immediate reactions to reflective feelings. - D) Redirecting conversation avoids addressing present-moment interactions entirely.

Question 60: Correct Answer: B) Explore the client's religious beliefs and how they impact their view of the treatment.

Rationale: The correct answer is B because it emphasizes understanding and respecting the client's perspective, which is crucial in addressing religious values conflicts. By exploring how the client's religious beliefs influence their view of treatment, the counselor can better tailor interventions that align with both evidence-based practices and the client's values. Option A is incorrect because it disregards the importance of respecting clients' religious beliefs and could be perceived as dismissive. Option C might be appropriate later but not as an initial response; it could undermine the counselor-client relationship if done prematurely. Option D assumes an alternative treatment is available without first understanding the client's specific concerns and needs. By comparing these options: - A overlooks respect for client autonomy. - C skips essential initial exploration needed for a comprehensive understanding. - D presumes a solution without adequate assessment. Thus, B is validated as it aligns with ethical counseling practices by prioritizing empathy and understanding.

Question 61: Correct Answer: A) Cognitive Behavioral Therapy (CBT)

Rationale: Cognitive Behavioral Therapy (CBT) is widely recognized as the most effective intervention for treating severe anxiety. CBT focuses on identifying and challenging distorted thought patterns and behaviors, which are central to anxiety disorders. - Option B) Psychoanalytic Therapy explores unconscious processes and past experiences, which can be valuable but is generally less effective for immediate symptom relief in severe anxiety. - Option C) Solution-Focused Brief Therapy (SFBT) emphasizes finding solutions rather than exploring problems, which might not address the underlying cognitive distortions associated with severe anxiety. - Option D) Person-Centered Therapy offers a supportive environment but lacks the structured approach necessary for effectively managing severe anxiety symptoms. Each option reflects a valid therapeutic approach but differs in its applicability and effectiveness for severe anxiety, making CBT the most appropriate choice based on contemporary research and clinical guidelines.

Question 62: Correct Answer: C) Discuss her reasons for termination and provide appropriate referrals if needed.

Rationale: Counselors must respect clients' autonomy while ensuring they understand their decisions' implications. Discussing Maria's reasons allows for an informed decision-making process and ensures continuity of care through appropriate referrals if needed. Option A neglects proper closure. Option B undermines client autonomy. Option D may appear coercive rather than supportive.

Question 63: Correct Answer: B) Develop a safety plan with John.

Rationale: Developing a safety plan is crucial as it provides John with practical steps to protect himself in case of immediate danger. Advising him to leave immediately (Option A) might not be feasible or safe without preparation. Encouraging couples counseling (Option C) is inappropriate in cases of physical abuse due to potential escalation of violence. Suggesting legal action (Option D) could be part of the long-term plan but does not address immediate safety concerns.

Question 64: Correct Answer: B) "I understand your perspective, but I feel differently about this approach."

Rationale: Option B is the correct answer because it reflects an assertive communication style that acknowledges another person's viewpoint while expressing one's own opinion clearly and respectfully. Option A is aggressive as it dismisses the other person's idea without consideration. Option C is passive as it shows a willingness to comply without voicing personal opinions. Option D is passive-aggressive because it expresses frustration indirectly and can lead to further conflict. Assertiveness involves clear, direct, and respectful communication that balances one's needs with those of others.

Question 65: Correct Answer: C) Refer Maria to a support group for individuals with depression.

Rationale: Referring Maria to a support group specifically for individuals with depression provides her with immediate access to peers who understand her struggles, which is crucial for developing an effective support system. While options A), B), and D) are beneficial, they may not offer the targeted emotional support needed initially. Joining a gym or attending community events can help build social connections but might not address her specific mental health needs as directly. Reconnecting through social media can be supportive but lacks the face-to-face interaction and shared experiences found in a specialized support group.

Question 66: Correct Answer: B) Seek supervision or consultation regarding his emotional responses.

Rationale: Seeking supervision or consultation helps John gain insight into his emotional responses and develop strategies to manage them effectively. Suppressing empathy (Option A) can lead to burnout and reduced effectiveness. Disclosing feelings (Option C) might burden Lisa unnecessarily. Limiting sessions (Option D) avoids addressing the root issue and could disrupt continuity of care.

Question 67: Correct Answer: B) Using motivational interviewing techniques to explore John's values and interests.

Rationale: Using motivational interviewing techniques helps engage John by exploring his values and interests, which can enhance his intrinsic motivation and ownership of the treatment process. This method aligns with person-centered approaches that foster collaboration and respect for the client's autonomy. Option A undermines John's agency by making him passive in his own treatment. Option C overlooks the importance of breaking down long-term objectives into manageable steps crucial for someone with low motivation. Option D fails because standardized tools alone cannot capture the individualized nuances necessary for effective goal-setting.

Question 68: Correct Answer: B) Group Therapy with other veterans to build peer support

Rationale: Group Therapy with other veterans provides a supportive environment where John can connect with peers who share similar experiences, enhancing his sense of connection and belonging. This aligns well with his background as a veteran and addresses his feelings of disconnection. Exposure Therapy (Option A), while effective for PTSD, does not specifically enhance social connections.

Narrative Therapy (Option C) helps reframe trauma but may not provide the peer support John needs. MBSR (Option D) focuses on relaxation and stress management but does not directly address the need for social connection.

Question 69: Correct Answer: C) How do you feel your new community perceives you?

Rationale: Option C is correct because it directly addresses John's perception of his new community's attitudes towards him, which can significantly impact his mental health within a cultural context. Option A focuses on family dynamics rather than community perception. Option B discusses routine changes but misses the critical element of community perception. Option D is about coping strategies rather than exploring environmental impacts; while relevant for treatment planning, it does not delve into the specific cultural context affecting John's mental health.

Question 70: Correct Answer: C) Discuss John's personal goals and how compliance aligns with them.

Rationale: Discussing John's personal goals and how compliance aligns with them is grounded in contemporary research on motivational interviewing, which emphasizes aligning treatment plans with clients' intrinsic motivations. This approach is more likely to foster internal motivation and long-term adherence compared to emphasizing long-term benefits (A), which might seem too distant; highlighting immediate consequences (B), which can be perceived as punitive; or providing detailed information (D), which may overwhelm or confuse John without addressing his personal motivations.

Question 71: Correct Answer: A) Cognitive-Behavioral Therapy (CBT) focusing on financial stressors

Rationale: Cognitive-Behavioral Therapy (CBT) is an evidence-based approach that helps clients identify and change negative thought patterns and behaviors associated with financial stress. By focusing specifically on financial stressors, CBT can help clients develop coping strategies and improve their emotional regulation. Option B is incorrect because while referring to a financial advisor can provide practical financial guidance, it does not directly address the client's anxiety and mental health needs. Option C, MBSR, can help reduce overall stress but may not specifically target the cognitive distortions related to financial issues. Option D is inappropriate as taking out a loan could exacerbate financial stress rather than resolve it. By comparing these options, we see that CBT directly addresses both the cognitive and emotional aspects of financial stress, making it the most comprehensive intervention for this scenario.

Question 72: Correct Answer: B) Discuss the possibility of cognitive-behavioral therapy (CBT) with Maria.

Rationale: Cognitive-behavioral therapy (CBT) is an evidence-based treatment for moderate depression, supported by contemporary research. While referring to a psychiatrist (Option A), recommending a support group (Option C), and suggesting lifestyle changes (Option D) can all be beneficial components of a comprehensive treatment plan, discussing CBT directly addresses the therapeutic intervention most aligned with Maria's BDI results. CBT has been shown to effectively reduce depressive symptoms by addressing negative thought patterns and behaviors.

Question 73: Correct Answer: D) Disorganized Attachment

Rationale: Disorganized attachment is characterized by a lack of a coherent strategy for dealing with stress, often resulting from inconsistent or frightening caregiving. This can lead to significant difficulties in forming close relationships and feelings of loneliness in adulthood. In contrast, secure attachment typically leads to healthier relationships and less loneliness. Anxious-ambivalent attachment may cause anxiety in relationships but not necessarily pervasive loneliness. Avoidant attachment leads to emotional distance but not as profound relational difficulties as disorganized attachment. Thus, disorganized attachment is most strongly associated with severe relational issues and loneliness.

Question 74: Correct Answer: B) Report the abuse to child protective services immediately.

Rationale: The most appropriate initial intervention is to report the abuse to child protective services immediately (Option B). This ensures Maria's safety and initiates legal and protective measures. Option A (encouraging confrontation) could place Maria at further risk. Option C (family therapy) is not appropriate until safety is established, as it could expose Maria to more harm. Option D (keeping a journal) may be useful for documentation but does not address immediate safety concerns.

Question 75: Correct Answer: C) Engaging in regular physical exercise and mindfulness meditation

Rationale: Engaging in regular physical exercise and mindfulness meditation is widely supported by contemporary research as an effective self-care strategy for mental health professionals. Physical exercise helps reduce stress and improve mood, while mindfulness meditation enhances emotional regulation and resilience. - Option A is important but primarily addresses professional development rather than holistic self-care. - Option B offers immediate relief but does not provide long-term benefits. - Option D can prevent burnout but may not be feasible or address overall well-being comprehensively.

Question 76: Correct Answer: B) Inquire about her cultural background and how it influences her understanding of her symptoms.

Rationale: Option B is correct because the CFI specifically aims to understand how cultural factors influence an individual's perception of their symptoms. This approach helps in identifying culturally relevant information that can affect diagnosis and treatment. Option A is incorrect because focusing solely on medical history does not address the cultural context. Option C, while important, does not directly address cultural influences on symptom perception. Option D is relevant but secondary; socioeconomic status is part of the broader context but not as central as direct inquiry into cultural background for a CFI.

Question 77: Correct Answer: B) Eye Movement Desensitization and Reprocessing (EMDR)

Rationale: EMDR is specifically designed to address trauma-related symptoms and has been shown to be effective in treating co-occurring conditions such as depression and anxiety. While CBT (Option A) is effective for depression and anxiety, it does not directly target trauma. DBT (Option C) is primarily used for borderline personality disorder but can help with emotion regulation. IPT (Option D) focuses on interpersonal issues but is not specifically tailored for trauma. Therefore, EMDR is the most appropriate choice as it directly addresses both trauma and its associated symptoms. - Option A) Cognitive Behavioral Therapy (CBT): While effective for depression and anxiety, CBT does not directly address trauma processing. - Option B) Eye Movement Desensitization and Reprocessing (EMDR): Correct choice; specifically targets trauma-related symptoms along with co-occurring conditions. - Option C) Dialectical Behavior Therapy (DBT): Primarily used for borderline personality disorder; helps with emotion regulation but not specifically designed for trauma. - Option D) Interpersonal Therapy (IPT): Effective for interpersonal issues but lacks a specific focus on trauma.

Question 78: Correct Answer: C) Structural Family Therapy (SFT)

Rationale: Structural Family Therapy (SFT) focuses on restructuring family dynamics and improving interactions within the family system, which is crucial for blending families in remarriage scenarios. Unlike CBT, which targets individual thought patterns, SFT addresses relational patterns and hierarchies within the family. Solution-Focused Brief Therapy (SFBT) may offer short-term relief but lacks the depth needed for complex family restructuring. Emotionally Focused Therapy (EFT), while beneficial for emotional bonds, does not specifically address structural changes required in blended families.

Question 79: Correct Answer: A) Encourage John to openly communicate his feelings and concerns with his girlfriend.

Rationale: Encouraging open communication is essential in addressing relationship anxieties. It allows both partners to understand each other's perspectives and fosters mutual support. While individual therapy (B) can be beneficial for self-esteem, it does not directly address the immediate relational issue. Engaging in social activities (C) might provide temporary distraction but does not resolve underlying concerns. Couple's therapy (D) could be helpful later but may not be necessary as an initial step if communication can alleviate John's insecurities.

Question 80: Correct Answer: A) Encouraging both members to share more about their experiences to highlight commonalities.

Rationale: Option A is correct because linking involves connecting members' experiences, which can foster a sense of unity and shared understanding within the group. Encouraging both members to share more about their grief highlights commonalities and strengthens group cohesion. Option B is incorrect as it avoids addressing the shared experience, missing an opportunity for linking. Option C is incorrect because it does not facilitate connection but rather delays interaction. Option D is incorrect as it assumes conflict without promoting positive interaction, thus failing to utilize linking effectively.

Question 81: Correct Answer: D) Fearful-avoidant attachment

Rationale: Fearful-avoidant attachment is characterized by a desire for close relationships combined with a fear of getting hurt, leading to chronic loneliness. This style often results from inconsistent caregiving in childhood. In contrast, secure attachment (A) typically leads to healthy relationships and lower levels of loneliness. Anxious-preoccupied attachment (B) involves dependency and anxiety but not necessarily chronic loneliness. Dismissive-avoidant attachment (C) involves emotional distance and self-reliance but may not lead to chronic loneliness due to the avoidance of close relationships. Thus, fearful-avoidant individuals are most prone to experiencing chronic loneliness due to their conflicting desires and fears regarding intimacy.

Question 82: Correct Answer: C) Partial hospitalization program (PHP)

Rationale: A Partial Hospitalization Program (PHP) is the most appropriate level of treatment for this client. PHP provides a structured and intensive therapeutic environment while allowing the client to return home at night. This level of care is suitable for clients who need more support than traditional outpatient therapy but do not require 24-hour supervision provided by inpatient hospitalization. Option A (Outpatient therapy) is insufficient given the client's escalating symptoms and functional impairments. Option B (Intensive outpatient program) offers more support than standard outpatient therapy but may still fall short given the severity of the client's symptoms and risk factors. Option D (Inpatient hospitalization) would be considered if there was an immediate risk of self-harm or if the client had a specific plan or intent, which is not currently reported. The key difference lies in the intensity and structure of care required based on the client's current clinical presentation and safety needs.

Question 83: Correct Answer: A) Cognitive Behavioral Therapy (CBT)

Rationale: Cognitive Behavioral Therapy (CBT) is widely recognized as an effective intervention for individuals adjusting to divorce. CBT helps clients identify and challenge negative thought patterns and develop healthier coping mechanisms. While support group participation (Option B) provides social support, it may not address individual cognitive distortions as effectively as CBT. Psychoeducational workshops (Option C) offer valuable information but lack the personalized approach of CBT. Individual psychodynamic therapy (Option D) can be beneficial for exploring underlying issues but may not provide the immediate, practical strategies that CBT offers for coping with divorce-related stress. Thus, CBT is considered the most effective due to its structured, evidence-based approach focusing on present thoughts and behaviors.

Question 84: Correct Answer: B) Providing consistent and responsive caregiving to help David develop secure attachments.

Rationale: Contemporary research emphasizes the importance of consistent and responsive caregiving in helping children develop secure attachments, especially after experiences of neglect or separation from primary caregivers. This approach helps build trust and security, reducing clinginess over time. Option A suggests minimizing physical contact which can exacerbate feelings of insecurity and abandonment. Option C introduces multiple caregivers which can confuse and further destabilize attachment formation. Option D uses punitive measures like time-outs which do not address underlying attachment issues and may increase distress.

Question 85: Correct Answer: B) Solution-Focused Brief Therapy (SFBT) emphasizing strengths and resources

Rationale: Solution-Focused Brief Therapy (SFBT) is particularly effective for clients with physical disabilities as it emphasizes their strengths and resources, promoting self-efficacy and independence. While Cognitive Behavioral Therapy (CBT) can help address negative thought patterns, it may not directly focus on building independence. Person-Centered Therapy (PCT) offers unconditional positive regard but may lack the structured approach needed to enhance self-efficacy. Motivational Interviewing (MI) is useful for enhancing motivation but does not specifically target independence through strengths-based interventions. SFBT's focus on solutions rather than problems aligns well with fostering a sense of empowerment in clients with disabilities.

Question 86: Correct Answer: D) Using Open-Ended Questions

Rationale: Using open-ended questions is most effective for building rapport and facilitating open communication because it encourages clients to share more about their thoughts and feelings without feeling constrained by yes/no answers. This technique aligns with contemporary research that emphasizes client-centered approaches in counseling. - A) Active Listening: While active listening is crucial, it primarily involves responding to what the client says rather than initiating deeper conversation. - B) Providing Immediate Solutions: This can hinder rapport as it may make clients feel unheard or rushed into solutions without fully exploring their issues. - C) Reflective Listening: Reflective listening is important but is more about confirming understanding rather than encouraging clients to elaborate further. - D) Using Open-Ended Questions: This technique prompts clients to discuss their issues in detail, which helps build trust and openness from the start. Thus, while active listening and reflective listening are vital skills, using open-ended questions specifically targets the goal of eliciting comprehensive information from the client, making it the most effective technique in this context.

Question 87: Correct Answer: B) Exploring underlying emotional issues through individual therapy.

Rationale: Exploring underlying emotional issues through individual therapy is essential as it addresses potential root causes of Emily's risky behaviors, such as emotional distress or mental health conditions. Establishing clear rules and consequences (Option A) is important but may not address deeper issues driving her behavior. Involving Emily in family therapy sessions (Option C) can be beneficial but might not be effective without first understanding her individual challenges. Encouraging participation in extracurricular activities (Option D) could provide structure but does not directly address potential emotional or psychological issues

causing her behavior.

Question 88: Correct Answer: B) Review the treatment goals with Maria and collaboratively assess any barriers to progress.

Rationale: The correct answer is B because engaging clients in reviewing their progress involves a collaborative process where both counselor and client assess the current status of treatment goals and identify any obstacles. This approach empowers clients by making them active participants in their treatment. Option A is incorrect as it may come across as dismissive of the client's concerns. Option C is incorrect because it could demotivate the client by suggesting she lower her expectations. Option D, while positive, fails to address the underlying issues preventing goal attainment.

Question 89: Correct Answer: A) A counselor actively seeks supervision to discuss personal feelings about a client's cultural background.

Rationale: Option A is correct because it demonstrates proactive self-awareness and the willingness to address personal biases through supervision, which is crucial for maintaining an effective therapeutic relationship. Option B is incorrect as avoiding cultural discussions can hinder open communication and trust. Option C reflects a lack of self-awareness by assuming universality of one's experiences, which can lead to misunderstandings. Option D suggests imposing dominant cultural norms on clients, which can be detrimental and disrespectful to their unique backgrounds.

Question 90: Correct Answer: C) Ambivalent (Resistant) Attachment

Rationale: Ambivalent (Resistant) Attachment is characterized by a child's anxiety and uncertainty when the caregiver leaves, combined with ambivalence upon their return. This attachment style reflects insecurity and inconsistency in the caregiver's responsiveness. In contrast, Secure Attachment (Option A) involves confidence in the caregiver's availability and comfort upon their return. Avoidant Attachment (Option B) is marked by indifference towards the caregiver's departure and return, indicating emotional self-reliance. Disorganized Attachment (Option D) involves a lack of coherent strategy for dealing with stress, often due to frightening or chaotic caregiving. Understanding these distinctions is crucial for accurately identifying attachment styles in clinical practice.

Question 91: Correct Answer: B) Teach John grounding techniques.

Rationale: Teaching John grounding techniques is the most effective approach for helping him manage overwhelming anxiety related to discussing his traumatic past. Grounding techniques help clients stay present and connected to their current environment, reducing the intensity of traumatic memories. Encouraging John to focus on positive memories (Option A) may provide temporary relief but does not equip him with tools for managing anxiety in the moment. Redirecting the conversation (Option C) avoids addressing the core issue and may hinder therapeutic progress. Validating John's feelings without further exploration (Option D) is supportive but lacks an active strategy for managing his anxiety.

Question 92: Correct Answer: C) Establishing trust and rapport

Rationale: Establishing trust and rapport is crucial during the initial intake session as it lays the foundation for an effective therapeutic relationship. Without trust, clients may not feel comfortable sharing personal information necessary for accurate assessment and diagnosis. While discussing treatment goals (Option A), conducting a comprehensive biopsychosocial assessment (Option B), and reviewing confidentiality and informed consent (Option D) are all important elements of the intake process, they are secondary to building trust. Trust enables open communication, which is essential for all subsequent steps in counseling. - Option A (Discussing the client's treatment goals): This is important but premature if trust has not been established. - Option B (Conducting a comprehensive biopsychosocial assessment): Essential for diagnosis but relies on client openness facilitated by trust. - Option D (Reviewing confidentiality and informed consent): Necessary legal step but does not directly contribute to emotional comfort. Thus, while all options are critical components of intake, establishing trust and rapport is foundational for successful therapy.

Question 93: Correct Answer: C) Cognitive Behavioral Therapy (CBT)

Rationale: Cognitive Behavioral Therapy (CBT) is the most suitable modality for Maria as it offers a structured approach with practical skills to manage anxiety through cognitive restructuring and behavioral techniques. Acceptance and Commitment Therapy (A), while useful for anxiety, focuses more on accepting thoughts rather than changing them directly. Mindfulness-Based Stress Reduction (B), although helpful in reducing stress through mindfulness practices, does not provide the same level of structured skill-building as CBT. Psychoanalytic Therapy (D), which delves into unconscious conflicts from past experiences, is less structured and may not provide immediate practical skills for managing anxiety.

Question 94: Correct Answer: B) Conducting a detailed clinical interview focusing on past traumatic events

Rationale: Conducting a detailed clinical interview focusing on past traumatic events is considered the most comprehensive method for assessing trauma during an initial intake session. This approach allows the counselor to gather in-depth information about the client's experiences, symptoms, and context. While using a standardized trauma screening tool (Option A) is useful for identifying potential trauma, it may not provide the depth of information needed. Observing non-verbal cues and behavioral signs (Option C) is important but should be part of a broader assessment strategy. Reviewing the client's medical and psychological history (Option D) provides valuable background information but may not capture current trauma-related issues as effectively as a detailed interview. - Option A (Using a standardized trauma screening tool): Although useful for initial identification, it lacks the depth provided by a detailed clinical interview. - Option C (Observing non-verbal cues and behavioral signs): Important for assessment but insufficient on its own without direct questioning about traumatic experiences. - Option D (Reviewing the client's medical and psychological history): Provides context but does not specifically address current trauma symptoms or experiences as thoroughly as a focused interview. The correct answer, conducting a detailed clinical interview focusing on past traumatic events, integrates multiple aspects of assessment to provide a comprehensive understanding of the client's trauma.

Question 95: Correct Answer: A) Social Skills Training

Rationale: Social Skills Training is the most effective approach for Sarah because it focuses on teaching specific skills needed for successful social interactions. This method directly addresses her anxiety by providing practical tools and practice opportunities in a supportive environment. - Option B) Exposure Therapy: Although helpful for general anxiety disorders, Exposure Therapy might overwhelm Sarah without first providing her with necessary social skills. - Option C) Dialectical Behavior Therapy (DBT): DBT is beneficial for emotional regulation but does not specifically target social interaction skills as effectively as Social Skills Training. - Option D) Family Counseling: While family support is important, this option does not directly address Sarah's individual needs related to social anxiety.

Question 96: Correct Answer: A) Motivational Interviewing to enhance readiness for change

Rationale: Motivational Interviewing (MI) is an evidence-based approach that helps clients resolve ambivalence about their addictive behaviors and enhances their motivation for change. It is particularly effective in the initial stages of treatment when clients may not yet be fully committed to change. Group therapy (B) can provide support but may not be suitable as an initial intervention if Maria is not yet motivated. Psychoanalytic therapy (C), while valuable for deep-seated issues, may not immediately address her readiness for change. Family therapy (D) could be beneficial later but does not directly target Maria's individual motivation initially.

Question 97: Correct Answer: A) Social Anxiety Disorder and Obsessive-Compulsive Disorder

Rationale: Sarah's intense fear in social situations leading to avoidance behaviors is indicative of Social Anxiety Disorder (SAD). Her intrusive thoughts about contamination and repetitive hand-washing rituals are characteristic of Obsessive-Compulsive Disorder (OCD). While Panic Disorder (B) involves sudden episodes of intense fear or discomfort without specific triggers like social situations or contamination fears. Generalized Anxiety Disorder (C) involves pervasive worry rather than specific obsessions or compulsions. Agoraphobia (D) involves fear of open spaces or being trapped but does not account for Sarah's contamination fears or ritualistic behaviors associated with OCD.

Question 98: Correct Answer: A) Politely ask Sarah to let others speak and redirect the conversation.

Rationale: Blocking is an intervention used by counselors to prevent disruptive behavior while maintaining a supportive environment. Politely asking Sarah to let others speak (Option A) effectively manages the group dynamic without alienating her. Allowing Sarah to continue (Option B) could reinforce monopolizing behavior. Directly telling her to stop (Option C) might seem confrontational and could harm the therapeutic relationship. Ignoring her comments (Option D) fails to address the issue, potentially leading to further disruption.

Question 99: Correct Answer: C) Initiate the interview by asking about recent changes in Sarah's life circumstances.

Rationale: Initiating the interview by asking about recent changes in Sarah's life circumstances helps establish context and rapport, providing insight into potential stressors or triggers for her symptoms. While exploring her support system (Option A), medical history (Option B), and conducting a mental status examination (Option D) are important, they are secondary steps that should follow an understanding of her current situation. This approach aligns with contemporary counseling practices that prioritize understanding the client's immediate concerns and context.

Question 100: Correct Answer: C) Cognitive impairments due to depression

Rationale: Cognitive impairments due to depression can severely affect John's ability to adhere to his medication regimen and maintain a consistent routine. While medication side effects (A), lack of motivation (B), and poor time management skills (D) are relevant considerations, cognitive impairments such as memory issues, difficulty concentrating, and executive dysfunction are well-documented barriers in contemporary research. These impairments directly impact John's capacity to follow through with his treatment plan, making them the most significant barrier in this context.

Question 101: Correct Answer: D) Inpatient Treatment

Rationale: Inpatient treatment is necessary for this patient due to the presence of severe depressive symptoms coupled with suicidal ideation and significant functional impairment. This level of care provides a secure environment for continuous monitoring and intensive treatment. - Option A (Outpatient Therapy) is incorrect because it is suitable for patients with mild to moderate symptoms who do not pose an immediate risk to themselves. - Option B (Intensive Outpatient Program) is incorrect as it offers more support than outpatient therapy but is not sufficient for someone with severe symptoms and suicidal ideation. - Option C (Partial Hospitalization Program) is incorrect because although it provides structured support during the day, it may not offer the necessary safety measures for someone with active suicidal ideation. The key difference lies in the intensity and immediacy of care required to ensure patient safety and address severe symptoms effectively.

Question 102: Correct Answer: B) Bem's Gender Schema Theory

Rationale: Bem's Gender Schema Theory asserts that children actively construct their gender identity by organizing information into gender schemas. These schemas guide their perceptions and behaviors regarding what is considered appropriate for each gender. - A) Kohlberg's Cognitive Developmental Theory also involves active construction but focuses on stages of understanding rather than schemas. - C) Bandura's Social Learning Theory emphasizes observational learning and imitation rather than internal cognitive structures like schemas. - D) Freud's Psychoanalytic Theory involves psychosexual stages but does not focus on cognitive structures like schemas.

Question 103: Correct Answer: A) Cognitive-Behavioral Therapy (CBT)

Rationale: Cognitive-Behavioral Therapy (CBT) is the most appropriate initial clinical focus for Sarah's symptoms of depression and anxiety. CBT is evidence-based and effective in treating both conditions by helping patients identify and modify negative thought patterns and behaviors. While psychoeducation on divorce adjustment (B) can be helpful, it does not directly address her immediate symptoms. Medication management (C) is typically handled by a psychiatrist rather than a counselor and may not be the first line of intervention without exploring therapeutic options first. Mindfulness-Based Stress Reduction (MBSR) (D) can be beneficial but is often used as an adjunct to primary treatments like CBT.

Question 104: Correct Answer: D) Her physical health and medical history

Rationale: While all options are important in a biopsychosocial interview, understanding Maria's physical health and medical history is most critical. This aspect can reveal underlying medical conditions that may contribute to or exacerbate her mental health symptoms. Family history (A), employment status (B), and coping mechanisms (C) are also important but secondary in this context as they do not directly address potential biological contributors to her condition.

Question 105: Correct Answer: B) Trauma-Focused Cognitive Behavioral Therapy (TF-CBT) incorporating elements specific to racial trauma.

Rationale: TF-CBT is tailored for trauma survivors and can be adapted to address racial trauma specifically. It combines cognitive-behavioral techniques with a focus on the traumatic experience, helping David process his emotions related to racial profiling. Exposure Therapy (Option A), while effective for general fears, may not adequately address the complexities of racial trauma. DBT (Option C) focuses on emotional regulation but does not specifically target trauma processing. Person-Centered Therapy (Option D), though supportive, may lack structured interventions needed for trauma recovery.

Question 106: Correct Answer: D) Standard outpatient therapy

Rationale: Given John's stable job, supportive family, and absence of severe symptoms such as suicidal ideation or substance abuse, standard outpatient therapy is the most appropriate level of care. Inpatient hospitalization (Option A) is typically reserved for individuals with severe symptoms requiring constant supervision. Partial hospitalization programs (Option B) and intensive outpatient programs (Option C) are more intensive than standard outpatient therapy and are suitable for individuals who need more structured support but do not require full-time care. Standard outpatient therapy allows John to continue his daily activities while receiving regular therapeutic support.

Question 107: Correct Answer: A) Encourage Maria to set small, achievable goals each day.

Rationale: Setting small, achievable goals is an effective strategy for clients like Maria who feel overwhelmed by depressive symptoms. This approach helps build momentum and fosters a sense of accomplishment, which can improve mood and motivation over time. Writing in a gratitude journal (Option B), while helpful for fostering positive thinking, may not directly address the immediate need for actionable steps toward improvement. Spending time with friends and family (Option C) provides social support but does not necessarily equip Maria with specific coping skills. Relaxation techniques (Option D), though beneficial for reducing stress, do not directly target the motivational issues stemming from depression.

Question 108: Correct Answer: B) John's high level of self-efficacy regarding social interactions.

Rationale: Self-efficacy refers to an individual's belief in their ability to succeed in specific situations or accomplish tasks. High self-efficacy regarding social interactions is crucial because it directly influences John's confidence and persistence in engaging with others, which is vital for improving social skills. While willingness to engage in exposure therapy (Option A), access to social skills training programs (Option C), and having a supportive peer group (Option D) are beneficial resources, self-efficacy has been shown through research to be a key predictor of successful behavior change and goal attainment. High self-efficacy empowers clients like John to take proactive steps toward their goals despite anxiety-related challenges.

Question 109: Correct Answer: B) Major Depressive Disorder

Rationale: Major Depressive Disorder (MDD) often presents with physical symptoms such as persistent fatigue, difficulty concentrating, and unexplained muscle pain. These symptoms can persist despite adequate rest and nutrition. While Generalized Anxiety Disorder (GAD) can cause fatigue and concentration issues, it typically includes excessive worry as a primary symptom. Chronic Fatigue Syndrome (CFS) involves severe fatigue but lacks the emotional symptoms of depression. Fibromyalgia causes widespread pain but is not primarily linked to mood disorders like MDD.

Question 110: Correct Answer: C) Sarah's physical health and medical history

Rationale: Exploring Sarah's physical health and medical history is essential to understand the etiology of her chronic pain. Chronic pain can have significant biological underpinnings that need to be identified before considering psychosocial factors. While her history of substance abuse (Option A), daily stressors (Option B), and support system (Option D) are relevant, they are secondary considerations once the primary source of her chronic pain is understood.

Question 111: Correct Answer: B) Panic Disorder

Rationale: Panic Disorder is characterized by recurrent unexpected panic attacks and persistent concern about having more attacks or their consequences. John's symptoms align with this diagnosis as his episodes are sudden and not tied to specific situations. - A) Generalized Anxiety Disorder (GAD): Involves excessive anxiety and worry about various events or activities but does not typically include sudden panic attacks. - C) Social Anxiety Disorder: Involves intense fear of social situations due to potential scrutiny by others; John's fear is not limited to social situations. - D) Specific Phobia: Involves intense fear of a specific object or situation; John's fear is generalized rather than focused on a particular trigger.

Question 112: Correct Answer: C) Recurrent episodes of eating large amounts of food in a short period, without subsequent compensatory behaviors.

Rationale: Option C is correct because Binge Eating Disorder (BED) is characterized by recurrent episodes of consuming large quantities of food within a discrete period, accompanied by feelings of loss of control, but crucially, without engaging in compensatory behaviors like purging. This distinguishes BED from Bulimia Nervosa (option A), which involves similar binge-eating episodes but includes compensatory actions such as vomiting. Option B describes Anorexia Nervosa, which involves significant restriction of food intake and low body weight. Option D aligns more with Body Dysmorphic Disorder and does not specifically address binge eating without compensatory behavior.

Question 113: Correct Answer: A) Understanding the patient's cultural identity and its influence on their mental health.

Rationale: Option A is correct because a key component of conducting a Cultural Formulation Interview is understanding how a patient's cultural identity influences their experience and expression of mental health issues. This involves exploring various aspects such as cultural definitions of problems, cultural perceptions of cause, context, and support, and cultural factors affecting self-coping and past help-seeking behavior. Option B is incorrect because focusing solely on symptoms ignores broader cultural contexts. Option C is incorrect as it prioritizes the clinician's perspective rather than understanding the patient's culture. Option D is also incorrect as it neglects psychosocial and cultural factors, focusing narrowly on biological aspects alone.

Question 114: Correct Answer: B) Minnesota Multiphasic Personality Inventory-2 (MMPI-2)

Rationale: The MMPI-2 is a comprehensive psychological assessment tool designed to evaluate overall psychological functioning and identify potential psychiatric disorders. It provides a broad spectrum of information about an individual's mental health, making it ideal for initial intake sessions. In contrast, the Beck Depression Inventory (BDI) and Hamilton Rating Scale for Depression (HRSD) are specific to depression, and the Generalized Anxiety Disorder 7-item (GAD-7) focuses on anxiety. These instruments do not provide the extensive range of information needed for a thorough initial psychological evaluation like the MMPI-2 does.

Question 115: Correct Answer: A) Encourage Emily to assertively express her needs while respecting others.

Rationale: Assertive communication allows individuals to express their needs clearly while respecting others' viewpoints, which is essential for healthy conflict resolution. Option B (accommodating) may lead to resentment as Emily's needs are consistently unmet. Option C (avoiding confrontations) does not address the root cause of conflicts and can lead to isolation. Option D (negotiation skills) is useful but may not be as immediately impactful as assertive communication in day-to-day interactions. Therefore, encouraging assertiveness (Option A) provides a balanced approach that helps manage conflicts effectively while maintaining respectful relationships.

Question 116: Correct Answer: C) Encourage open expression of emotions and conflict resolution.

Rationale: The group appears to be in the storming stage, characterized by increased tension and disagreements as members begin to assert their opinions more strongly. Encouraging open expression of emotions and facilitating conflict resolution helps navigate this challenging phase. Option A is more appropriate for the norming stage when reaffirming goals can help solidify cohesion. Option B might disrupt existing dynamics rather than address underlying tensions. Option D focuses on individual achievements, which may not address collective conflicts effectively at this stage.

Question 117: Correct Answer: B) Understanding the client's explanation of their illness.

Rationale: Understanding the client's explanation of their illness is most critical in a Cultural Formulation Interview because it directly addresses how they perceive and interpret their symptoms within their cultural context. This insight is essential for accurate diagnosis and culturally

sensitive treatment planning. While exploring cultural identity (Option A), assessing social support (Option C), and evaluating therapeutic relationships (Option D) are important, they do not provide as direct an understanding of how the client views their condition, which is fundamental for effective intervention.

Question 118: Correct Answer: A) Major Depressive Disorder

Rationale: Major Depressive Disorder (MDD) is characterized by a depressed mood or loss of interest in activities, along with other symptoms such as significant weight change, insomnia, and fatigue lasting at least two weeks. Persistent Depressive Disorder (PDD), while similar, requires symptoms to be present for at least two years. Bipolar II Disorder includes periods of hypomania which Maria does not report. Generalized Anxiety Disorder primarily involves excessive anxiety rather than depressive symptoms.

Question 119: Correct Answer: D) Discuss the situation with Maria, explain the limits of confidentiality, and seek her consent to involve appropriate emergency services.

Rationale: The correct answer is D because it aligns with ethical guidelines that emphasize client autonomy while ensuring safety. Counselors must explain confidentiality limits and involve clients in decision-making whenever possible. Option A disregards safety protocols. Option B is premature without assessing severity or seeking client consent. Option C delays immediate necessary action.

Question 120: Correct Answer: C) There is a strong negative relationship between stress levels and sleep quality.

Rationale: A Pearson's correlation coefficient (r) of -0.65 indicates a strong negative relationship between stress levels and sleep quality; as stress levels increase, sleep quality decreases. Option A incorrectly states that there is a positive relationship when it should be negative due to the negative sign of r. Option B incorrectly suggests no relationship despite r being significantly different from zero (-0.65). Option D incorrectly implies causation; correlation does not imply causation it only shows an association between two variables without proving one causes the other.

Question 121: Correct Answer: A) Establishing clear family rules and roles through collaborative discussions.

Rationale: Establishing clear family rules and roles through collaborative discussions is crucial in addressing role ambiguity in blended families. This approach fosters a sense of structure and clarity, which can help reduce confusion and conflict among family members. Option B (individual therapy sessions) may be beneficial but does not directly address role ambiguity within the family system. Option C (open communication about past experiences) is important but may not immediately resolve role confusion. Option D (focusing on the marital relationship first) is essential for overall family stability but does not specifically target role ambiguity. Therefore, option A is the most comprehensive initial approach.

Question 122: Correct Answer: C) Attention and Concentration

Rationale: Maria's difficulty with serial sevens indicates a problem with attention and concentration (Option C). Although memory recall issues (Option B) might suggest impaired memory, her specific struggle with serial sevens points more directly to concentration difficulties. Orientation (Option A) pertains to awareness of time, place, and person, which was not indicated as problematic here. Abstract thinking (Option D), while relevant in some assessments, does not address her specific issues with focusing on tasks.

Question 123: Correct Answer: B) Immediately report the threat to law enforcement and notify the potential victim.

Rationale: According to the ACA Code of Ethics, counselors have a duty to protect third parties from serious and foreseeable harm. This duty overrides client confidentiality when there is an imminent risk of harm. Option B is correct because it aligns with this ethical obligation. Option A is incorrect because maintaining confidentiality in this context could result in harm to others. Option C, while prudent, delays necessary action in an urgent situation. Option D involves documentation but lacks immediate intervention, which is crucial in preventing harm. Each option was crafted based on plausible actions that reflect different aspects of ethical decision-making but only B correctly addresses both urgency and ethical responsibility as outlined by contemporary standards and theories in professional practice and ethics.

Question 124: Correct Answer: B) Family Systems Therapy to explore and reframe family roles and communication styles.

Rationale: Family Systems Therapy is the most effective intervention as it directly addresses the influence of rigid family roles and lack of emotional expression by exploring and reframing these patterns within the context of Maria's family dynamics. CBT (Option A) focuses more on individual thought patterns rather than family dynamics. SFBT (Option C) is more about resolving current issues quickly without delving into deeper family influences. Psychodynamic Therapy (Option D) explores unconscious processes but does not specifically target family roles or communication styles as directly as Family Systems Therapy.

Question 125: Correct Answer: A) To identify Sarah's baseline functioning and monitor her progress over time.

Rationale: The primary purpose of using pre-test and post-test measures is to identify a client's baseline functioning at the beginning of treatment and monitor changes over time to evaluate the effectiveness of the intervention. Option B is incorrect because it focuses on comparing symptoms across clients rather than individual progress. Option C is incorrect as it pertains to identifying causes rather than measuring outcomes. Option D is incorrect because while regular assessments can aid in building rapport, their main goal in this context is evaluating treatment efficacy.

Question 126: Correct Answer: B) Avoid caffeine after lunchtime.

Rationale: Advising John to avoid caffeine after lunchtime is grounded in research indicating that caffeine has a half-life of about 5-6 hours and can significantly impact sleep quality if consumed later in the day. Option A is incorrect because it does not address the timing of caffeine consumption, which is crucial for sleep quality. Option C is close but less precise than B; while replacing caffeinated beverages with decaffeinated options after 3 PM can help, avoiding caffeine entirely after lunchtime provides a clearer guideline. Option D addresses overall reduction but does not specifically target the timing issue that impacts John's sleep.

Question 127: Correct Answer: B) "I must maintain your confidentiality, but there are exceptions such as if you disclose intent to harm yourself or others."

Rationale: The correct answer is B. Counselors are legally and ethically required to maintain client confidentiality but must break it if the client poses a threat to themselves or others. Option A is incorrect because it oversimplifies confidentiality laws and doesn't mention mandatory reporting exceptions. Option C is misleading because there are other exceptions beyond court orders, such as mandatory reporting laws. Option D inaccurately suggests that only illegal activities warrant breaking confidentiality, which is not comprehensive.

Question 128: Correct Answer: B) Guide Maria through a deep breathing exercise.

Rationale: Guiding Maria through a deep breathing exercise is an effective way to help her contain and manage her intense feelings of anger. Deep breathing activates the parasympathetic nervous system, promoting relaxation and reducing physiological arousal associated with anger. Encouraging Maria to describe her feelings (Option A) might further escalate her agitation. Allowing her to vent without interruption (Option C) can sometimes exacerbate intense emotions rather than contain them. Suggesting a short break (Option D) might be helpful but does not directly address immediate emotion regulation as effectively as deep breathing.

Question 129: Correct Answer: B) Conduct a comprehensive risk assessment and refer the client to an inpatient psychiatric facility.

Rationale: The correct answer is B because when a client presents with severe depression and suicidal ideation, it is crucial to prioritize their immediate safety. Conducting a comprehensive risk assessment allows the counselor to evaluate the severity of the client's condition accurately. Referring them to an inpatient psychiatric facility ensures they receive intensive monitoring and treatment in a safe environment. Option A is incorrect as outpatient therapy may not provide the necessary level of care for someone at high risk. Option C is also inappropriate because support groups do not offer immediate intervention for acute risks. Option D may be part of long-term management but does not address immediate safety concerns.

Question 130: Correct Answer: C) Inpatient Psychiatric Hospitalization

Rationale: Inpatient Psychiatric Hospitalization is appropriate for Jane due to her severe symptoms and history of multiple hospitalizations for suicidal ideation, indicating a need for intensive monitoring and care. An Intensive Outpatient Program (A) or Partial Hospitalization Program (B) might not provide the necessary level of supervision and safety. A Residential Treatment Center (D), while providing structured care, is less suitable than an inpatient setting for acute stabilization.

Question 131: Correct Answer: D) Teach John cognitive-behavioral techniques to reframe negative thoughts.

Rationale: Cognitive-behavioral techniques are evidence-based strategies that help clients identify and reframe negative thought patterns contributing to their anxiety. This approach empowers clients like John by providing them with practical tools to manage their stress more effectively. While mindfulness meditation (Option A) and regular physical exercise (Option C) are beneficial for overall well-being, they do not directly address the cognitive distortions causing John's anxiety. Avoiding stressful situations (Option B) is not a sustainable strategy as it does not equip John with the necessary skills to handle stress when it inevitably arises.

Question 132: Correct Answer: B) Encourage Maria to set clear boundaries with the client and discuss the importance of maintaining them.

Rationale: The correct approach is for the supervisor to guide Maria in setting clear professional boundaries with her client (Option B). This not only addresses the immediate issue but also educates Maria on an essential aspect of professional practice. Option A is incorrect because it assumes that sharing less about one's own life is sufficient without addressing boundary-setting skills. Option C is too extreme and does not support Maria's growth as a counselor. Option D may be helpful but does not directly address the immediate concern within the supervisory context.

Question 133: Correct Answer: C) Suggesting John seek mentorship from other African American professionals within or outside the company.

Rationale: Seeking mentorship from other African American professionals can provide John with guidance, support, and strategies for navigating microaggressions in the workplace without feeling isolated. This approach leverages social support networks and aligns with theories on coping with workplace discrimination. Option A might escalate tensions and may not be productive without proper support mechanisms in place. Option B is useful but does not provide immediate emotional support or strategies for dealing with daily interactions. Option D is incorrect as ignoring microaggressions can lead to increased stress and negative mental health outcomes.

Question 134: Correct Answer: C) Recommend family therapy sessions to address blended family dynamics.
Rationale: Family therapy sessions are the most effective initial intervention as they provide a platform for all family members to communicate openly about their feelings and roles within the new family structure. This approach helps in addressing the root causes of conflicts and facilitates better understanding among family members. - Option A (Encourage open communication between Sarah and her stepfather) is important but may not be sufficient without professional guidance. - Option B (Suggest individual therapy sessions for Sarah) focuses only on Sarah's perspective and does not address the broader family dynamics. - Option D (Advise Sarah's mother to spend more one-on-one time with her) can help strengthen their bond but does not resolve issues with the stepfather or overall family integration.

Question 135: Correct Answer: C) When a client expresses suicidal ideation with a detailed plan and means to execute it.
Rationale: Option C is the correct answer because mental health counselors are ethically and legally required to breach confidentiality if there is an imminent risk of harm to the client or others. Suicidal ideation with a detailed plan and means indicates an immediate danger, necessitating intervention. Option A is incorrect as counselors are typically not mandated reporters for future crimes unless they involve imminent harm. Option B is incorrect because past criminal activities without ongoing risk do not usually warrant breaching confidentiality. Option D is incorrect because sharing information at the client's request still requires explicit consent; it does not constitute an automatic breach of confidentiality.

Question 136: Correct Answer: B) Discuss initiating pharmacotherapy alongside counseling sessions.
Rationale: For severe anxiety indicated by high GAD-7 scores, combining pharmacotherapy with counseling is often recommended to manage symptoms effectively and quickly. While mindfulness meditation (Option A), an intensive outpatient program (Option C), and regular weekly therapy sessions focusing on anxiety management techniques (Option D) are valuable interventions, initiating pharmacotherapy alongside counseling provides a balanced approach addressing both immediate symptom relief and long-term coping strategies. This combination is well-supported by contemporary research for severe anxiety cases.

Question 137: Correct Answer: B) "It sounds like you're really hard on yourself. Let's explore some of your recent achievements."
Rationale: This response exemplifies the reframe/redirect technique by acknowledging Maria's feelings and then shifting her focus to her accomplishments, thereby promoting a more positive self-view. Option A acknowledges her feelings but doesn't redirect them. Option C asks for reflection but doesn't provide a new perspective. Option D suggests focusing on strengths but lacks the immediate redirection present in option B.

Question 138: Correct Answer: C) Encourage open communication and conflict resolution.
Rationale: During the storming stage, group members often experience conflicts and power struggles. Encouraging open communication and conflict resolution helps members address these issues constructively. Option A (Establish clear group norms and roles) is more suitable for the forming stage when structure is being established. Option B (Facilitate team-building activities) aligns with the norming stage when cohesion is developing. Option D (Provide closure and reflect on group achievements) is relevant to the adjourning stage when the group is disbanding. Therefore, C is correct as it specifically addresses the needs of the storming stage.

Question 139: Correct Answer: B) The client's current living situation

Rationale: The correct answer is B) The client's current living situation. This aspect is crucial because it provides insight into the client's immediate environment, support systems, potential stressors, and overall quality of life, all of which can significantly impact mental health. Option A) focuses on family medical history, which is more relevant to the biological component rather than the social context. Option C) addresses past psychological treatment, which pertains more to the psychological component. Option D) concerns dietary habits, which are important but more related to biological and lifestyle factors rather than directly assessing social context. Understanding these distinctions ensures comprehensive assessment during a biopsychosocial interview.

Question 140: Correct Answer: A) Encouraging Maria to join a community group that shares her cultural background.
Rationale: Encouraging Maria to join a community group that shares her cultural background helps her maintain a sense of identity and support while she navigates the new environment. This approach aligns with contemporary research on acculturation, which suggests that maintaining connections with one's culture of origin can provide emotional support and reduce feelings of isolation. Option B is incorrect because focusing solely on learning English may not address the emotional and social aspects of adjustment. Option C is incorrect as avoiding interactions with people from her own culture can increase feelings of isolation. Option D, while potentially beneficial, does not specifically address the importance of cultural connections.

Question 141: Correct Answer: B) Extreme withdrawal or fearfulness
Rationale: Emotional abuse often manifests as extreme withdrawal or fearfulness in children. This is because emotional abuse can severely impact a child's self-esteem and sense of safety, leading them to become overly cautious or fearful. While frequent unexplained injuries (A) are more indicative of physical abuse, sudden changes in academic performance (C) can be associated with various types of abuse but are not specific to emotional abuse. Inappropriate sexual behaviors (D) are typically linked to sexual abuse rather than emotional abuse. Therefore, option B is the most accurate indicator of emotional abuse.

Question 142: Correct Answer: A) Generalized Anxiety Disorder (GAD)
Rationale: Generalized Anxiety Disorder (GAD) is characterized by chronic anxiety, exaggerated worry, and tension even when there is little or nothing to provoke it. Physical symptoms include muscle tension, headaches, fatigue, and sleep disturbances. Chronic Fatigue Syndrome also involves fatigue but lacks the constant state of worry associated with GAD. Tension-Type Headache primarily involves headaches without the broader spectrum of anxiety-related symptoms. Fibromyalgia includes widespread musculoskeletal pain along with fatigue but does not typically involve the persistent worry characteristic of GAD.

Question 143: Correct Answer: D) The roles each partner assumes during conflicts
Rationale: Understanding the roles each partner assumes during conflicts (D) is crucial in evaluating interactional dynamics because it reveals patterns of behavior and power dynamics that may contribute to ongoing issues. This approach aligns with family systems theory, which emphasizes the importance of roles and rules within relationships. While the frequency and duration of arguments (A), the content of arguments (B), and underlying emotional triggers (C) are important, they do not provide as comprehensive an understanding of the interactional patterns as examining the roles each partner plays.

Question 144: Correct Answer: C) John discloses plans to harm another person.
Rationale: Sarah is legally obligated to breach confidentiality if John discloses plans to harm another person

(C). This falls under the "duty to warn" principle, which mandates that counselors take reasonable steps to protect potential victims. Option A is incorrect because while expressing a desire to harm oneself is serious and requires intervention, it does not automatically require breaching confidentiality; appropriate measures within the therapeutic context are usually taken first. Option B is incorrect because past crimes do not typically necessitate breaching confidentiality unless they involve ongoing risk or unreported abuse. Option D is incorrect because sharing records requires explicit written consent from the client but does not constitute a breach of confidentiality.

Question 145: Correct Answer: C) "Think about times when you've received positive feedback at work."

Rationale: This response uses reframe/redirect by shifting John's focus from his anxiety and perceived inadequacies to instances of positive reinforcement, helping him see his value and competence. Option A normalizes his feelings but doesn't shift his perspective. Option B seeks further exploration without providing a new viewpoint. Option D focuses on problem-solving rather than reframing his thoughts.

Question 146: Correct Answer: C) Integrate an additional therapeutic approach targeting depressive symptoms while continuing CBT.

Rationale: The correct answer is C because it acknowledges John's progress with CBT for anxiety while addressing the new onset of depressive symptoms by integrating an additional therapeutic approach. This holistic adjustment ensures that both conditions are managed effectively without discontinuing a successful intervention. Option A is incorrect as it does not address the new depressive symptoms. Option B is also incorrect because discontinuing CBT may lead to a relapse in anxiety symptoms. Option D is unnecessary at this stage since the counselor can adjust the treatment plan based on observed changes.

Question 147: Correct Answer: A) Verify licensure requirements in both his state and the client's state.

Rationale: The primary consideration for John is to verify licensure requirements in both his state and the client's state. This ensures he is legally permitted to provide services across state lines. While having malpractice insurance (Option B), informing clients about limitations (Option C), and scheduling check-ins with a supervisor (Option D) are important, they do not address the fundamental legal requirement of licensure verification.

Question 148: Correct Answer: C) Discuss the situation with Sarah and seek supervision or consultation from a colleague.

Rationale: In cases where dual relationships might occur (e.g., client becoming a coworker), it is crucial for counselors to discuss potential conflicts with the client and seek supervision or consultation. This ensures ethical practice while considering both parties' best interests. Option A is incorrect because avoiding work-related topics does not address potential conflicts fully. Option B may be premature without assessing all factors through supervision/consultation. Option D lacks transparency and does not involve Sarah in decision-making which could harm trust and rapport.

Question 149: Correct Answer: B) Reflective Listening

Rationale: Reflective listening is the most effective strategy in this context as it involves actively listening to the speaker and then reflecting back what was heard. This helps ensure that both parties feel understood and validated, fostering empathy. Mediation (Option A) involves a neutral third party to help resolve conflicts but may not directly enhance mutual understanding. Problem-solving negotiation (Option C) focuses on finding a mutually acceptable solution but may not address underlying emotional needs. Compromise (Option D) involves each party giving up something but doesn't necessarily foster deeper understanding or empathy. Therefore, reflective listening is the best approach for enhancing communication and empathy between the couple.

Question 150: Correct Answer: B) Encourage the family to maintain their cultural traditions while helping Juan integrate into American society.

Rationale: Option B is correct because it respects the family's cultural background while promoting integration, which can help Juan navigate his dual identity. Options A and C suggest abandoning or diminishing their cultural values, which can lead to further familial conflict and identity issues for Juan. Option D ignores the systemic nature of the issue by focusing solely on individual counseling without considering the family's role in Juan's life.

NCMHCE Exam Practice Questions [SET 5]

Question 1: John has been referred to counseling due to work-related stress. In their first session, the counselor wants to ensure John feels comfortable sharing his experiences. What is the best strategy for achieving this?
A) Encouraging John to talk about his interests outside of work.
B) Reassuring John that all information shared will remain confidential.
C) Offering advice based on similar cases the counselor has handled.
D) Highlighting the counselor's qualifications and experience.

Question 2: Which counseling technique would be most effective in helping Maria enhance her motivation to quit drinking?
A) Reflective Listening
B) Confrontational Approach
C) Decisional Balance
D) Developing Discrepancy

Question 3: Dr. Kim is counseling the Lee family, an Asian-American household experiencing tension between generations. The grandparents emphasize traditional values such as filial piety and academic excellence, while their adult children seek a more balanced lifestyle for their children, who are struggling with these high expectations.
A) Advise the grandparents to relax their expectations to reduce stress on their grandchildren.
B) Encourage open communication between all family members about their values and expectations.
C) Suggest that the adult children enforce traditional values more strictly to appease the grandparents.
D) Recommend individual therapy for each generation to separately address their concerns.

Question 4: A counselor at a mental health agency is approached by a client who expresses suicidal ideation. According to standard counselor/agency policies, what is the most appropriate initial action the counselor should take?
A) Contact emergency services immediately.
B) Conduct a thorough risk assessment to determine the level of danger.
C) Inform the client's family members about the situation.
D) Document the client's statements in their file without taking further action.

Question 5: During an initial intake session with a new client, Emily, who reports feeling overwhelmed and experiencing difficulty concentrating at work, which of the following actions should the counselor prioritize to ensure a thorough assessment?
A) Administering a standardized anxiety inventory immediately
B) Exploring Emily's work environment and job responsibilities
C) Conducting a detailed psychosocial history interview
D) Referring Emily for a medical evaluation to rule out physical causes

Question 6: Which cognitive distortion is most commonly associated with panic attacks?
A) Catastrophizing
B) Overgeneralization
C) Personalization
D) Mind Reading

Question 7: A 15-year-old patient named Emily presents with symptoms of anxiety and depression. During the session, she discloses that she has been bullied at school for the past six months. As her mental health counselor, what is the most appropriate initial intervention?
A) Encourage Emily to confront her bullies directly.
B) Develop a safety plan with Emily and her parents.
C) Advise Emily to ignore the bullies and focus on her studies.
D) Suggest Emily change schools to avoid the bullies.

Question 8: During a group therapy session, Maria mentions that she frequently meets with another group member, John, outside of the sessions. As a counselor, what is the most appropriate initial action to address this interaction?
A) Encourage Maria and John to discuss their outside interactions with the group.
B) Privately ask Maria about the nature of her relationship with John.
C) Remind the group about confidentiality and boundaries.
D) Suggest that Maria and John limit their interactions outside of the group.

Question 9: According to Erikson's theory of psychosocial development, which developmental task is primarily associated with adolescence?
A) Trust vs. Mistrust
B) Autonomy vs. Shame and Doubt
C) Identity vs. Role Confusion
D) Intimacy vs. Isolation

Question 10: When assessing your competency to work with a specific client, which of the following actions is most crucial?
A) Seeking regular supervision from a senior counselor.
B) Reflecting on your personal biases and how they may impact your work.
C) Attending workshops and training sessions relevant to the client's issues.
D) Reviewing recent literature on therapeutic techniques for the client's condition.

Question 11: Maria, who is undergoing treatment for opioid addiction, reports feeling hopeless after a recent relapse. She believes that she will never be able to stay clean because she has failed once again. Which CBT technique should the counselor use to address Maria's cognitive distortion?
A) Encourage Maria to attend more support group meetings.
B) Help Maria identify and challenge her negative thoughts.
C) Suggest that Maria avoid situations where she might be tempted.
D) Teach Maria relaxation techniques to manage stress.

Question 12: Mark, a 40-year-old man, has been emotionally abused by his spouse for several years, leading to significant self-esteem issues and chronic stress. He often experiences intense anger but suppresses it due to fear of confrontation. In therapy, Mark reveals that he struggles with expressing his emotions healthily. Which therapeutic approach would best help Mark develop healthier emotional expression?
A) Psychodynamic Therapy
B) Emotion-Focused Therapy (EFT)
C) Acceptance and Commitment Therapy (ACT)

D) Interpersonal Therapy (IPT)

Question 13: Dr. Smith is a counselor at a community mental health center aiming to implement systemic changes to improve client outcomes. Which strategy should Dr. Smith adopt first?
A) Conduct an organizational assessment to identify areas needing improvement.
B) Increase one-on-one counseling sessions with clients.
C) Develop new therapeutic techniques for individual counselors.
D) Enhance community outreach programs.

Question 14: Which cognitive-behavioral technique is most effective in reducing the frequency and intensity of obsessive thoughts in patients diagnosed with Obsessive-Compulsive Disorder (OCD)?
A) Cognitive Restructuring
B) Thought Stopping
C) Exposure and Response Prevention (ERP)
D) Mindfulness-Based Stress Reduction (MBSR)

Question 15: During a case conference for a client named Sarah, who has been diagnosed with Major Depressive Disorder, the multidisciplinary team discusses her treatment plan. As the mental health counselor, you are responsible for documenting the agreed-upon interventions. Which of the following is the most appropriate way to document this collaboration?
A) "The team suggested cognitive-behavioral therapy (CBT) sessions twice a week and medication management by Dr. Smith."
B) "CBT sessions twice weekly and medication management were recommended by Dr. Smith during the meeting."
C) "It was decided that Sarah would benefit from CBT twice weekly and medication management, as per Dr. Smith's recommendation."
D) "Dr. Smith recommended CBT sessions twice a week and medication management during our meeting."

Question 16: John is a mental health counselor who recently started his private practice. He has a new client, Sarah, who is unsure about her insurance coverage for mental health services. John wants to ensure that Sarah understands her payment responsibilities before starting therapy. Which of the following actions should John take first?
A) Verify Sarah's insurance benefits and explain them to her.
B) Provide Sarah with a detailed fee schedule for his services.
C) Discuss the sliding scale payment option with Sarah.
D) Ask Sarah to contact her insurance company for coverage details.

Question 17: Which neurotransmitter is most commonly associated with the modulation of fear and panic responses in the brain?
A) Dopamine
B) Serotonin
C) Norepinephrine
D) GABA

Question 18: A mental health counselor is conducting a study to determine the effectiveness of a new therapeutic intervention for reducing anxiety levels. The counselor decides to use a statistical method that accounts for both within-subject and between-subject variability. Which statistical method should the counselor use?
A) Independent t-test
B) Repeated measures ANOVA
C) Paired t-test
D) Multiple regression

Question 19: During an intake assessment, you are performing a Mental Status Exam (MSE) on a 45-year-old patient named John who has been referred for evaluation due to recent changes in his behavior and mood. John appears disheveled, avoids eye contact, and speaks in a monotone voice. He reports feeling "empty" and has difficulty concentrating. Which aspect of the MSE is most indicative of John's potential diagnosis?
A) Thought Process
B) Affect
C) Insight
D) Speech

Question 20: James, a 35-year-old male, presents with symptoms of persistent sadness, loss of interest in activities he once enjoyed, difficulty concentrating, and frequent headaches. He also reports excessive worry about various aspects of his life, including work and personal relationships. Given these symptoms, what would be the most appropriate co-occurring diagnoses to consider?
A) Major Depressive Disorder and Generalized Anxiety Disorder
B) Major Depressive Disorder and Panic Disorder
C) Persistent Depressive Disorder and Social Anxiety Disorder
D) Bipolar II Disorder and Generalized Anxiety Disorder

Question 21: During an initial intake session, a 45-year-old patient named John presents with complaints of persistent sadness and lack of interest in daily activities. While performing the Mental Status Exam (MSE), you observe that John's speech is slow, his thought process appears disorganized, and he expresses feelings of hopelessness. Based on these observations, which aspect of the MSE is most likely to be significantly impaired?
A) Mood and Affect
B) Thought Process
C) Speech
D) Insight and Judgment

Question 22: During a diagnostic interview, which of the following approaches is most effective in establishing rapport with a client who appears anxious and reluctant to share personal information?
A) Directly asking the client about their anxiety and reluctance.
B) Using open-ended questions to allow the client to express themselves freely.
C) Providing reassurance and normalizing the client's feelings.
D) Focusing on structured questions to gather specific information quickly.

Question 23: John, a 35-year-old male, presents with symptoms of major depressive disorder. He has been struggling with feelings of hopelessness, lack of energy, and difficulty concentrating. During the initial assessment, John mentions that he recently lost his job and is experiencing significant financial stress. As his mental health counselor, what would be the most appropriate first step in guiding his treatment planning?
A) Develop a detailed plan to address his financial stressors.
B) Establish a strong therapeutic alliance with John.
C) Immediately refer John to a psychiatrist for medication evaluation.
D) Focus on cognitive-behavioral techniques to improve his mood.

Question 24: Michael is a mental health counselor

working with Emily, who has been struggling with anxiety. During their sessions, Michael aims to build a genuine therapeutic relationship. Which of the following behaviors best illustrates Michael's genuineness?
A) Michael frequently checks in with Emily to ensure she feels comfortable during their sessions.
B) Michael openly shares his thoughts about Emily's progress and any concerns he has.
C) Michael uses reflective listening techniques to show empathy towards Emily's experiences.
D) Michael consistently provides positive reinforcement whenever Emily discusses her challenges.

Question 25: Which of the following best describes the concept of "intersectionality" in understanding how individuals experience oppression?
A) Intersectionality refers to the overlapping and interdependent systems of discrimination or disadvantage.
B) Intersectionality is the study of how different social identities contribute to unique experiences of privilege.
C) Intersectionality focuses on the impact of race alone in shaping an individual's experiences.
D) Intersectionality is primarily concerned with gender-based oppression.

Question 26: Which of the following is a legally mandated aspect of informed consent in mental health counseling?
A) Informing clients about the potential risks and benefits of counseling
B) Ensuring clients understand their right to access their records at any time
C) Discussing the counselor's qualifications and areas of expertise
D) Explaining the limits of confidentiality, including situations where disclosure is required by law

Question 27: A mental health counselor is working with a client who has severe substance use issues that are beyond the scope of outpatient counseling services. Which referral source would be most appropriate for this client?
A) A support group for substance use disorders
B) An inpatient rehabilitation facility
C) A primary care physician
D) An outpatient addiction counselor

Question 28: John, a 42-year-old man, reports experiencing erectile dysfunction (ED) after being diagnosed with diabetes. He feels embarrassed and avoids intimacy with his partner. As his mental health counselor, what would be the most appropriate intervention?
A) Encourage John to discuss his concerns with his healthcare provider.
B) Recommend lifestyle changes such as diet and exercise.
C) Provide cognitive-behavioral therapy (CBT) to address performance anxiety.
D) Suggest couples therapy to improve communication and intimacy.

Question 29: John, a 35-year-old software engineer, has been experiencing difficulty falling asleep and staying asleep for the past three months. He reports feeling fatigued during the day and finds it hard to concentrate at work. Which intervention is most likely to improve John's sleep quality?
A) Encouraging John to take short naps during the day.
B) Advising John to limit screen time before bed.
C) Suggesting John drink a warm glass of milk before bedtime.
D) Recommending John increase his physical activity in the evening.

Question 30: Emily, a 32-year-old woman, presents at your clinic reporting feelings of hopelessness and frequent thoughts of ending her life. She has a history of depression but denies any current plan or means to commit suicide. As her mental health counselor, what is the most appropriate initial step in managing her suicidal ideation?
A) Develop a safety plan with Emily.
B) Refer Emily to inpatient psychiatric care immediately.
C) Schedule frequent follow-up appointments.
D) Encourage Emily to engage in mindfulness exercises.

Question 31: Sarah, a 28-year-old female, presents to your clinic with symptoms of anxiety and depression. As her mental health counselor, you need to select an appropriate assessment instrument that can effectively differentiate between her anxiety and depressive symptoms. Which of the following assessment instruments would be most appropriate for this purpose?
A) Beck Depression Inventory-II (BDI-II)
B) State-Trait Anxiety Inventory (STAI)
C) Hamilton Anxiety Rating Scale (HAM-A)
D) Hospital Anxiety and Depression Scale (HADS)

Question 32: Alex, a 14-year-old assigned female at birth (AFAB), has recently expressed a desire to be referred to with he/him pronouns and has shown interest in traditionally masculine activities. He is experiencing distress due to lack of acceptance from peers and family. As his counselor, what is the most appropriate initial step you should take to support Alex's gender identity development?
A) Encourage Alex to explore both masculine and feminine activities.
B) Provide psychoeducation about gender identity to Alex's family.
C) Refer Alex to a medical professional for potential hormone therapy.
D) Validate Alex's feelings and experiences regarding his gender identity.

Question 33: When conducting a hypothesis test in mental health research, which of the following best describes a Type I error?
A) Rejecting the null hypothesis when it is actually true.
B) Failing to reject the null hypothesis when it is actually false.
C) Accepting the alternative hypothesis when it is actually false.
D) Failing to accept the alternative hypothesis when it is actually true.

Question 34: Mrs. Johnson, a 78-year-old woman, has been experiencing significant memory loss and confusion over the past year. Her family reports that she often forgets recent events but can recall details from her childhood. She also exhibits difficulty in planning and organizing her daily activities. Which of the following is the most likely diagnosis?
A) Major Depressive Disorder
B) Mild Cognitive Impairment
C) Alzheimer's Disease
D) Vascular Dementia

Question 35: Under which circumstance is a mental health counselor legally required to breach client confidentiality?
A) When a client expresses intent to harm themselves.
B) When a client reports past abuse that is no longer occurring.
C) When a client discloses current abuse of a minor.

D) When a client requests their information be shared with a family member.

Question 36: During an intake session, Maria, a 30-year-old woman, discloses that she has been experiencing severe anxiety and depression following a recent divorce. She mentions feeling overwhelmed and having fleeting thoughts of not wanting to live. As a mental health counselor, what should be your immediate course of action?
A) Schedule a follow-up appointment for next week to monitor her progress.
B) Conduct a comprehensive suicide risk assessment immediately.
C) Encourage her to join a support group for recently divorced individuals.
D) Suggest she start journaling her thoughts and feelings daily.

Question 37: A client presents with significant anxiety related to their financial situation, which has led to increased arguments with their spouse. According to contemporary research, which therapeutic approach is most effective in addressing both the financial stress and the relational conflict?
A) Cognitive-Behavioral Therapy (CBT)
B) Solution-Focused Brief Therapy (SFBT)
C) Financial Counseling combined with Emotionally Focused Therapy (EFT)
D) Mindfulness-Based Stress Reduction (MBSR)

Question 38: Maria is a 35-year-old client who has been working on managing her anxiety through cognitive-behavioral therapy (CBT). Despite her efforts, she reports that she often feels overwhelmed and unable to implement the strategies discussed in therapy. Which of the following is the most likely barrier affecting Maria's goal attainment?
A) Lack of social support
B) Poor therapeutic alliance
C) High levels of stress in her environment
D) Inadequate understanding of CBT techniques

Question 39: You are a mental health counselor who has been assigned a new client, Mark, who identifies as transgender and is seeking support for gender dysphoria. You have minimal experience working with transgender clients. How should you proceed?
A) Immediately refer Mark to a counselor specializing in transgender issues.
B) Begin working with Mark while actively seeking specialized training and supervision.
C) Conduct initial sessions focusing on general mental health issues before addressing gender dysphoria.
D) Decline the case citing lack of competence in transgender issues.

Question 40: Which of the following is considered the first-line treatment for chronic insomnia according to contemporary research and recognized theories in mental health counseling?
A) Cognitive-Behavioral Therapy for Insomnia (CBT-I)
B) Benzodiazepines
C) Melatonin supplements
D) Sleep hygiene education

Question 41: Which intervention is most effective in breaking the cycle of intergenerational family violence according to contemporary research?
A) Cognitive Behavioral Therapy (CBT)
B) Family Systems Therapy
C) Dialectical Behavior Therapy (DBT)
D) Solution-Focused Brief Therapy

Question 42: During a group therapy session for individuals coping with anxiety, the counselor notices that members are beginning to express their individual differences and conflicts are starting to arise. Which phase of the group process is this most likely indicative of?
A) Forming
B) Storming
C) Norming
D) Performing

Question 43: Which of the following strategies is most effective in facilitating trust and safety in a therapeutic relationship?
A) Consistently maintaining eye contact throughout sessions
B) Demonstrating unconditional positive regard
C) Offering advice based on personal experiences
D) Regularly using self-disclosure to build rapport

Question 44: Maria, a 32-year-old woman, reports experiencing frequent headaches, gastrointestinal problems, and muscle tension over the past six months. She also mentions feelings of hopelessness and persistent sadness. Which physical condition is most commonly associated with her depressive symptoms?
A) Irritable Bowel Syndrome (IBS)
B) Migraine
C) Generalized Anxiety Disorder (GAD)
D) Somatic Symptom Disorder

Question 45: Scenario: Sarah, a 28-year-old woman, has been experiencing intense emotional responses that seem disproportionate to the situations she encounters. She often feels overwhelmed by her emotions and has difficulty calming down once upset. Her therapist is considering different therapeutic approaches to help her manage her emotional dysregulation. Which therapeutic approach is most effective in treating Sarah's emotional dysregulation according to contemporary research?
A) Cognitive Behavioral Therapy (CBT)
B) Dialectical Behavior Therapy (DBT)
C) Interpersonal Therapy (IPT)
D) Acceptance and Commitment Therapy (ACT)

Question 46: A mental health counselor is working with an immigrant client who is experiencing significant stress due to cultural adjustments. Which of the following strategies is most effective in helping the client navigate these adjustments?
A) Encouraging assimilation into the new culture
B) Promoting separation from the new culture
C) Facilitating integration of both cultures
D) Advocating marginalization from both cultures

Question 47: During an intake assessment, you are evaluating John, a 35-year-old male who reports using alcohol "occasionally." He mentions that he drinks about 4-5 beers on weekends but denies any problems with his drinking. Which assessment tool would be most appropriate to use to further evaluate John's alcohol use?
A) Beck Depression Inventory (BDI)
B) Alcohol Use Disorders Identification Test (AUDIT)
C) Generalized Anxiety Disorder 7-item scale (GAD-7)
D) CAGE Questionnaire

Question 48: Which of the following best describes the appropriate action for a mental health counselor when a client requests access to their counseling records?
A) Allow immediate access to all records without any restrictions.
B) Deny access to records to protect confidentiality.

C) Provide access after reviewing the request and considering any potential harm.
D) Refer the client to another counselor for record access.

Question 49: Maria, a single mother of two, is struggling with anxiety due to her inability to pay bills on time. She often feels hopeless and has started missing work due to her anxiety symptoms. During your counseling sessions, she mentions feeling guilty about not being able to provide for her children. What would be an effective therapeutic intervention for Maria?
A) Assist Maria in creating a realistic payment plan for her bills.
B) Help Maria identify community resources that can provide financial assistance.
C) Focus on cognitive restructuring techniques to address her feelings of guilt.
D) Encourage Maria to work overtime hours to increase her income.

Question 50: John, a 7-year-old boy, has been living with his grandparents for the past year after his parents' divorce. He frequently expresses worry about his parents' well-being and struggles to focus at school. Which intervention would be most appropriate for addressing John's concerns according to contemporary research?
A) Cognitive-behavioral therapy focusing on managing worry.
B) Family therapy involving all family members.
C) Play therapy to help John express his feelings.
D) Medication to reduce anxiety symptoms.

Question 51: According to contemporary research, which intervention strategy is most effective in reducing bullying behaviors in schools?
A) Implementing zero-tolerance policies.
B) Promoting social-emotional learning (SEL) programs.
C) Increasing school surveillance and security measures.
D) Conducting peer mediation sessions.

Question 52: When counseling a terminally ill patient who expresses a desire to hasten their death, which approach should a mental health counselor prioritize according to contemporary ethical guidelines?
A) Encourage open discussions about their feelings and explore underlying reasons.
B) Suggest alternative coping mechanisms and strategies.
C) Refer the patient to a psychiatrist for medication management.
D) Focus on providing hope and positive thinking to improve their outlook.

Question 53: Which of the following is most likely to significantly impact a child's emotional well-being after their parents' divorce?
A) The level of parental conflict before and after the divorce
B) The child's age at the time of the divorce
C) The financial stability of each parent post-divorce
D) The geographical distance between the parents' new homes

Question 54: Jane, a 45-year-old woman, is experiencing significant emotional distress following her recent divorce after 20 years of marriage. She reports feelings of loneliness, anxiety about the future, and difficulty adjusting to her new life circumstances. Based on contemporary research, which therapeutic approach would be most effective in helping Jane navigate her post-divorce adjustment?
A) Cognitive Behavioral Therapy (CBT)
B) Solution-Focused Brief Therapy (SFBT)
C) Emotionally Focused Therapy (EFT)

D) Psychodynamic Therapy

Question 55: When working with minority clients who have experienced systemic discrimination, which counseling intervention is most effective in fostering resilience and empowerment?
A) Cognitive Behavioral Therapy (CBT) focused on modifying negative thought patterns.
B) Narrative Therapy that centers on re-authoring the client's personal story.
C) Solution-Focused Brief Therapy (SFBT) emphasizing immediate problem-solving.
D) Culturally Adapted Psychoeducation addressing specific cultural stressors.

Question 56: John, a 40-year-old man, reveals during counseling that he was sexually abused by a family member during his childhood. He expresses feelings of shame and guilt, believing that he somehow provoked the abuse. What therapeutic approach would be most effective in helping John process his trauma?
A) Cognitive Behavioral Therapy (CBT) focusing on changing his beliefs about the abuse.
B) Exposure Therapy to desensitize him to memories of the abuse.
C) Psychoeducation about sexual abuse dynamics without delving into personal experiences.
D) Medication management to alleviate symptoms of depression and anxiety.

Question 57: Jane, a 35-year-old woman, has been experiencing emotional abuse from her partner for several years. She often feels worthless and isolated but is afraid to leave due to financial dependence and fear of escalation. During counseling, Jane expresses feelings of intense anxiety and hopelessness. Which therapeutic intervention would be most effective in addressing Jane's emotional state?
A) Cognitive Behavioral Therapy (CBT)
B) Solution-Focused Brief Therapy (SFBT)
C) Eye Movement Desensitization and Reprocessing (EMDR)
D) Dialectical Behavior Therapy (DBT)

Question 58: James, a 35-year-old male, presents to your clinic with complaints of persistent sadness, lack of energy, and difficulty concentrating over the past six months. He reports feeling overwhelmed at work and experiencing frequent arguments with his partner. During the assessment, James mentions having trouble sleeping and losing interest in activities he once enjoyed. Based on this information, what would be the most appropriate initial step in assessing James's level of distress?
A) Administer a standardized depression inventory to quantify his symptoms.
B) Explore his relationship dynamics to understand the source of conflict.
C) Conduct a comprehensive biopsychosocial assessment to gather detailed information.
D) Recommend immediate psychiatric evaluation for potential medication management.

Question 59: During an initial counseling session, Emily, a mental health counselor, explains the counseling process to her client, John. She discusses confidentiality but also mentions situations where confidentiality might need to be breached. Which of the following scenarios correctly represents a situation where confidentiality can be legally breached?
A) When John expresses dissatisfaction with the counseling process.
B) When John reveals he is planning to harm himself or

others.
C) When John discloses past illegal activities.
D) When John requests a break in confidentiality for a second opinion.

Question 60: During a group therapy session, the group leader notices that Sarah, one of the participants, is particularly quiet and hesitant to share her thoughts. Which intervention by the group leader would most effectively promote Sarah's interaction with the group?
A) Directly asking Sarah specific questions about her experiences.
B) Encouraging other group members to share their experiences first.
C) Providing positive reinforcement when Sarah does speak up.
D) Assigning Sarah a leadership role for an upcoming session.

Question 61: Which cognitive distortion is most commonly associated with generalized anxiety disorder (GAD) and involves expecting the worst possible outcome?
A) Catastrophizing
B) Overgeneralization
C) Personalization
D) Dichotomous thinking

Question 62: Sarah, a mental health counselor, is facilitating a group therapy session where two members are in conflict over differing viewpoints. Sarah wants to foster an environment where both parties feel heard and understood while working towards a resolution. Which technique should Sarah employ to achieve this?
A) Active Listening
B) Passive Observation
C) Directive Intervention
D) Silent Reflection

Question 63: In a psychoeducational group for individuals recovering from substance use disorder, the counselor introduces a module on relapse prevention strategies. One participant, John, expresses skepticism about their effectiveness. What is the best approach for the counselor to take in this situation?
A) Provide empirical evidence supporting relapse prevention strategies.
B) Encourage John to discuss his concerns and experiences with relapse prevention.
C) Reassure John that skepticism is normal and encourage him to keep an open mind.
D) Ask other group members who have successfully used these strategies to share their stories.

Question 64: Emily, a mental health counselor, recognizes the importance of maintaining boundaries to practice effective self-care. She often finds it difficult to say no to additional responsibilities at work. What is the best approach Emily can take to ensure she maintains her boundaries?
A) Discussing her workload concerns with her supervisor
B) Setting clear priorities for her tasks
C) Delegating tasks whenever possible
D) Scheduling specific times for personal activities

Question 65: John, a client struggling with alcohol addiction, expresses strong resistance during a counseling session, stating that he doesn't believe he has a problem and can quit anytime he wants. Which of the following responses by the counselor best aligns with Motivational Interviewing principles?
A) "You need to understand that denial is part of your addiction."

B) "It sounds like you have some doubts about your drinking habits."
C) "You should consider how your drinking is affecting your family."
D) "Let's talk about what quitting means to you."

Question 66: John, a 60-year-old man experiencing a crisis of faith after losing his spouse, reports feeling disconnected from his religious community and questioning his beliefs. As his counselor, what would be the most effective initial approach to support John's spiritual/existential concerns?
A) Encourage John to reconnect with his religious community.
B) Explore John's beliefs and values through existential questioning.
C) Suggest individual therapy sessions focusing on grief counseling.
D) Recommend engaging in volunteer work to regain a sense of purpose.

Question 67: Which of the following emotional responses is most commonly associated with children who have witnessed family abuse/violence?
A) Anxiety
B) Depression
C) Hyperactivity
D) Aggression

Question 68: When developing a safety plan for a client experiencing suicidal ideation, which of the following steps is most critical to ensure immediate safety?
A) Identifying personal warning signs of escalating crisis.
B) Establishing a list of coping strategies that have worked in the past.
C) Securing lethal means and ensuring they are inaccessible.
D) Scheduling regular follow-up appointments to monitor progress.

Question 69: When evaluating an individual's level of mental health functioning, which assessment tool is most appropriate for measuring the severity of depression symptoms?
A) Generalized Anxiety Disorder 7 (GAD-7)
B) Beck Depression Inventory-II (BDI-II)
C) Patient Health Questionnaire-9 (PHQ-9)
D) Hamilton Anxiety Rating Scale (HAM-A)

Question 70: When engaging clients in a review of progress toward treatment goals, which strategy is most effective for ensuring clients take an active role in their treatment?
A) Regularly providing clients with detailed progress reports.
B) Facilitating collaborative goal-setting sessions with clients.
C) Conducting periodic assessments without client involvement.
D) Encouraging clients to independently track their progress.

Question 71: During an initial session with a new client named Sarah, who is experiencing anxiety and depression, the counselor aims to establish a strong therapeutic alliance. Which approach is most effective in building this alliance?
A) Providing immediate solutions to her problems.
B) Demonstrating genuine empathy and understanding.
C) Focusing primarily on gathering detailed background information.
D) Setting strict boundaries and maintaining professional distance.

Question 72: A 45-year-old patient named Maria has been experiencing anxiety and depression following the

recent loss of her spouse. During a counseling session, Maria mentions that she finds some solace in her religious practices but is struggling to reconcile her faith with her feelings of loss. As her mental health counselor, what would be the most appropriate initial intervention?

A) Encourage Maria to increase her participation in religious activities to find comfort.
B) Explore how Maria's religious beliefs influence her understanding of grief and loss.
C) Suggest that Maria temporarily set aside her religious practices to focus on other coping mechanisms.
D) Refer Maria to a spiritual advisor or clergy member for additional support.

Question 73: When developing a treatment plan for a client diagnosed with Major Depressive Disorder (MDD), which of the following is the most crucial initial step?

A) Establishing measurable and specific treatment goals
B) Conducting a comprehensive biopsychosocial assessment
C) Identifying potential barriers to treatment adherence
D) Selecting evidence-based therapeutic interventions

Question 74: John, a 30-year-old client struggling with depression, expresses feeling worthless during his session. The counselor wants to respond in a way that shows both empathy and congruence. Which response would best achieve this?

A) "Everyone feels like this sometimes; it's completely normal."
B) "I understand why you feel this way, but you shouldn't think like that."
C) "It sounds like you're really struggling right now; I'm here for you."
D) "Many people go through similar feelings; you'll get through it."

Question 75: During an initial diagnostic interview, a 32-year-old patient named John reports experiencing persistent sadness, loss of interest in activities he once enjoyed, and difficulty sleeping for the past six months. He also mentions feeling worthless and having thoughts of death but denies any current suicidal intent or plan. Which approach should the counselor prioritize to ensure a comprehensive assessment?

A) Focus on John's current symptoms and their impact on his daily functioning.
B) Explore John's family history of mental health issues.
C) Assess John's coping mechanisms and support system.
D) Evaluate John's previous treatment history and response.

Question 76: Which cognitive-behavioral technique is most effective in reducing ruminating and intrusive thoughts by directly addressing and altering the thought patterns?

A) Thought Stopping
B) Cognitive Restructuring
C) Exposure Therapy
D) Mindfulness Meditation

Question 77: Which of the following physical symptoms is most commonly associated with Generalized Anxiety Disorder (GAD)?

A) Chest pain
B) Shortness of breath
C) Muscle tension
D) Dizziness

Question 78: Which of the following strategies is most effective for facilitating a client's intrinsic motivation to change according to Motivational Interviewing principles?

A) Providing direct advice and solutions to the client's problems.
B) Exploring the client's values and aligning them with their goals.
C) Emphasizing the negative consequences of not making changes.
D) Using authoritative statements to highlight the urgency of change.

Question 79: John, a 32-year-old software engineer, reports experiencing excessive worry about his job performance and future career prospects. He finds it difficult to control his worries, which leads to restlessness, fatigue, difficulty concentrating, irritability, muscle tension, and sleep disturbances. Which of the following diagnoses is most appropriate for John?

A) Generalized Anxiety Disorder (GAD)
B) Panic Disorder
C) Social Anxiety Disorder
D) Obsessive-Compulsive Disorder (OCD)

Question 80: John, a 45-year-old male, has been experiencing persistent feelings of hopelessness and depression for the past six months. He reports difficulty sleeping, loss of interest in activities he once enjoyed, and feelings of worthlessness. During his counseling sessions, John mentions that he feels like a burden to his family and cannot see any positive future outcomes. Based on contemporary cognitive-behavioral theories, which intervention would be most effective in addressing John's hopelessness?

A) Encouraging John to engage in physical exercise to improve mood.
B) Helping John identify and challenge negative thought patterns.
C) Suggesting John increase social interactions with friends and family.
D) Advising John to practice mindfulness meditation daily.

Question 81: Which of the following therapeutic approaches is most effective in addressing emotional dysregulation in clients with Borderline Personality Disorder (BPD)?

A) Cognitive Behavioral Therapy (CBT)
B) Dialectical Behavior Therapy (DBT)
C) Acceptance and Commitment Therapy (ACT)
D) Interpersonal Therapy (IPT)

Question 82: John, a 35-year-old male, has been experiencing severe anxiety that interferes with his daily functioning. As part of his treatment plan, you have decided to implement Cognitive Behavioral Therapy (CBT) techniques. Which of the following interventions would be most appropriate to start with in John's case?

A) Encourage John to keep a daily journal of his thoughts and feelings.
B) Teach John relaxation techniques to manage his anxiety symptoms.
C) Help John identify and challenge his irrational beliefs.
D) Develop a structured schedule for John to follow each day.

Question 83: Maria, a 30-year-old woman, calls you in tears stating that she has just experienced a traumatic event. She feels overwhelmed and cannot stop crying. As her mental health counselor, what is your first step in providing crisis intervention?

A) Help Maria develop a long-term treatment plan to address her trauma.
B) Validate her feelings and provide emotional support.
C) Encourage Maria to immediately start journaling her thoughts and feelings.
D) Suggest Maria take some time off work to recover from

the trauma.

Question 84: Maria, a 45-year-old Latina woman, has been experiencing symptoms of depression and anxiety following her recent divorce. She expresses concerns about cultural stigmas associated with mental health treatment in her community. As her counselor, which intervention approach would be most appropriate to align with her cultural background and address her concerns?
A) Cognitive Behavioral Therapy (CBT) with a focus on individual cognitive restructuring
B) Culturally Adapted CBT incorporating family involvement and community support
C) Solution-Focused Brief Therapy emphasizing immediate problem-solving
D) Psychoanalytic Therapy exploring unconscious conflicts from childhood

Question 85: Which of the following intervention strategies is most effective in reducing bullying behaviors among adolescents according to contemporary research?
A) Implementing zero-tolerance policies
B) Establishing peer mediation programs
C) Integrating social-emotional learning (SEL) curricula
D) Increasing surveillance and adult supervision

Question 86: Which of the following best describes the relationship between trauma and somatic symptom disorder (SSD) in individuals with a history of severe trauma?
A) Trauma often leads to SSD through direct physical injuries.
B) Trauma can contribute to SSD by causing chronic hyperarousal and heightened bodily awareness.
C) Trauma causes SSD primarily through genetic predisposition.
D) Trauma leads to SSD by creating maladaptive cognitive patterns unrelated to physical sensations.

Question 87: Which of the following interventions is most effective in helping a terminally ill patient cope with anticipatory grief?
A) Encouraging the patient to focus on positive memories.
B) Facilitating open communication about end-of-life wishes.
C) Promoting engagement in enjoyable activities.
D) Providing information about disease progression.

Question 88: During a counseling session, Maria, a counselor, needs to provide constructive feedback to her client, John, who has been struggling with maintaining consistent attendance at his job. Which approach should Maria take to ensure her feedback is effective and well-received?
A) Focus solely on John's attendance issues and suggest he improves his time management skills.
B) Highlight John's strengths first, then discuss the attendance issues, and collaboratively develop a plan for improvement.
C) Emphasize the negative consequences of John's poor attendance on his career prospects without addressing his strengths.
D) Provide detailed criticism of John's behavior without offering any solutions or support.

Question 89: Dr. Martinez, a mental health counselor, receives a subpoena requesting records for her client, Emily, who is involved in a custody battle. Emily has previously expressed her desire for these records to remain confidential due to sensitive information contained within them.
A) Dr. Martinez should comply with the subpoena and release all records immediately.
B) Dr. Martinez should inform Emily about the subpoena and seek her consent before releasing any records.
C) Dr. Martinez should consult with an attorney regarding how to respond to the subpoena while protecting Emily's confidentiality.
D) Dr. Martinez should refuse to release any records without Emily's explicit written consent.

Question 90: John, a 35-year-old man, reports experiencing persistent and intrusive thoughts about contamination. Despite washing his hands repeatedly, he feels anxious and doubts whether his hands are clean. He spends hours each day engaged in this behavior, which significantly interferes with his daily life. Which therapeutic approach is most effective in addressing John's obsessive thoughts and behaviors?
A) Cognitive Behavioral Therapy (CBT)
B) Exposure and Response Prevention (ERP)
C) Psychoanalytic Therapy
D) Mindfulness-Based Stress Reduction (MBSR)

Question 91: Michael, a 42-year-old man diagnosed with Generalized Anxiety Disorder (GAD), experiences excessive worry about various aspects of his life, including work, health, and relationships. His counselor aims to establish long-term goals consistent with his diagnosis. Which of the following is the most appropriate long-term goal for Michael?
A) Reduce anxiety levels by practicing mindfulness meditation daily.
B) Improve sleep hygiene by establishing a consistent bedtime routine.
C) Develop effective coping strategies to manage stressors in daily life.
D) Enhance communication skills to improve interpersonal relationships.

Question 92: Maria is a new client who has been referred to you for anxiety and stress management. During your initial session, she asks if you could also help her with financial planning since she feels it contributes to her stress. How should you respond to clarify your role as her counselor?
A) Agree to help her with financial planning as it relates to her mental health.
B) Refer her to a financial advisor while continuing to address her anxiety and stress.
C) Explain that financial planning is beyond your scope but offer general advice on managing stress related to finances.
D) Suggest that you can provide some basic financial tips along with counseling sessions.

Question 93: Which of the following best describes the primary purpose of obtaining informed consent in counseling?
A) To ensure the client understands the potential risks and benefits of counseling.
B) To protect the counselor from legal liability.
C) To establish a formal agreement between the client and counselor regarding confidentiality.
D) To document the client's willingness to participate in the counseling process.

Question 94: John, a 45-year-old man, reports experiencing erectile dysfunction for the past six months. He has no significant medical history and his physical exams are normal. He mentions high levels of stress at work and a recent decrease in self-esteem. Which intervention is most appropriate for addressing John's sexual functioning concerns?
A) Cognitive-behavioral therapy (CBT) focusing on stress management.

B) Prescribing phosphodiesterase type 5 inhibitors (e.g., sildenafil).
C) Referral to a sex therapist for couple's therapy.
D) Psychoeducation about normal sexual functioning and aging.

Question 95: John, a 70-year-old patient with terminal cancer, has expressed his wish to discontinue life-prolonging treatments. His family, however, insists on continuing all possible interventions. As his mental health counselor, what is your primary ethical obligation in this scenario?
A) Advocate for the family's wishes as they are likely to know what is best for John.
B) Respect John's autonomy and support his decision to discontinue treatment.
C) Seek a court order to determine the appropriate course of action.
D) Refer John and his family to a mediator to reach a consensus.

Question 96: Which of the following is most indicative of a diagnosis of Alzheimer's disease in an elderly patient?
A) Gradual onset of memory loss affecting daily activities
B) Sudden onset of confusion and disorientation
C) Persistent sadness and loss of interest in usual activities
D) Temporary episodes of forgetfulness with full recovery

Question 97: Maria, a 42-year-old teacher, struggles with waking up frequently during the night and feels unrested in the morning. She has tried various over-the-counter sleep aids without success. What would be the most effective approach for Maria's sleeping issues?
A) Implementing a consistent bedtime routine.
B) Using a white noise machine throughout the night.
C) Drinking herbal tea known for its sedative properties before bed.
D) Taking melatonin supplements regularly.

Question 98: Sarah, a 10-year-old girl, has been referred to counseling due to concerns about her behavior at school. She is frequently anxious, has difficulty concentrating, and often appears withdrawn. Her teacher reports that Sarah has become increasingly fearful of adults and flinches when approached quickly. Based on these observations, what is the most likely type of abuse Sarah might be experiencing?
A) Physical Abuse
B) Emotional Abuse
C) Sexual Abuse
D) Neglect

Question 99: John, a 30-year-old man, experienced the loss of his same-sex partner but feels unable to grieve openly due to fear of judgment from his conservative family. What counseling approach should be prioritized to support John's disenfranchised grief?
A) Encourage John to create a private ritual to honor his partner.
B) Help John develop assertiveness skills to confront his family's attitudes.
C) Explore John's cultural background and its impact on his grieving process.
D) Facilitate sessions where John can express his grief without fear of judgment.

Question 100: John, a 10-year-old boy, has been referred to you due to difficulties in attention, hyperactivity, and academic performance. To accurately diagnose ADHD while considering potential overlapping symptoms with learning disabilities, which assessment instrument should you use?
A) Conners' Rating Scales-Revised (CRS-R)

B) Wechsler Intelligence Scale for Children (WISC-V)
C) Child Behavior Checklist (CBCL)
D) Behavior Assessment System for Children (BASC-3)

Question 101: Sarah and John have been experiencing significant conflicts in their co-parenting relationship since their divorce. They frequently argue about discipline strategies for their 10-year-old son, Ethan. Sarah prefers a more authoritative approach, while John leans towards a permissive style. What is the most effective initial step a mental health counselor should take to address their co-parenting conflict?
A) Suggest that Sarah and John attend separate individual counseling sessions.
B) Recommend that they read parenting books to understand different styles.
C) Facilitate a joint session focused on establishing common parenting goals.
D) Advise them to take turns implementing their preferred discipline methods.

Question 102: During a counseling session, a client has shared several complex emotions and experiences. As a counselor, what is the most effective way to summarize these points to ensure the client feels understood and validated?
A) Briefly repeat each point the client mentioned without adding any interpretation.
B) Condense the client's statements into a concise summary, capturing key themes and emotions.
C) Paraphrase each individual statement made by the client to show active listening.
D) Highlight only the most significant points that align with your therapeutic goals for the session.

Question 103: A 10-year-old child has been referred to you for an evaluation due to concerns about their academic performance and social interactions. Which of the following assessments would be most appropriate to measure the child's intellectual functioning?
A) Wechsler Intelligence Scale for Children (WISC-V)
B) Vineland Adaptive Behavior Scales
C) Conners' Rating Scales
D) Beck Youth Inventories

Question 104: Maria, a 38-year-old woman, has recently recommitted to her husband after a period of separation due to infidelity. During therapy sessions, Maria expresses lingering distrust despite her desire to move forward positively. What therapeutic approach would be most effective in addressing Maria's concerns?
A) Cognitive-behavioral therapy (CBT) focused on changing Maria's negative thought patterns about her husband.
B) Solution-focused brief therapy (SFBT) aimed at setting short-term goals for rebuilding trust.
C) Emotionally focused therapy (EFT) that addresses underlying emotional responses and attachment needs.
D) Narrative therapy that helps Maria rewrite her story of betrayal and recommitment.

Question 105: John, a 35-year-old male, has been diagnosed with alcohol use disorder. During a counseling session, he mentions that he drinks to cope with his social anxiety and feels that alcohol helps him socialize better. Based on contemporary research and theories, which therapeutic approach is most appropriate for addressing both his alcohol use disorder and underlying social anxiety?
A) Cognitive Behavioral Therapy (CBT)
B) Motivational Interviewing (MI)
C) Dialectical Behavior Therapy (DBT)
D) Contingency Management (CM)

Question 106: During a counseling session, Maria expresses feelings of worthlessness and despair. The counselor responds by saying, "It sounds like you're feeling really overwhelmed and alone right now." Which core counseling attribute is the counselor primarily demonstrating?
A) Empathy
B) Active Listening
C) Unconditional Positive Regard
D) Congruence

Question 107: Sarah, a 32-year-old woman, reports feeling intensely lonely despite having a wide social network. She describes her relationships as superficial and lacking emotional depth. According to attachment theory, which type of attachment style is Sarah most likely exhibiting?
A) Secure Attachment
B) Anxious-Preoccupied Attachment
C) Dismissive-Avoidant Attachment
D) Fearful-Avoidant Attachment

Question 108: Which of the following is most indicative of a primary psychotic disorder when assessing a patient experiencing hallucinations?
A) Visual hallucinations without any auditory component
B) Auditory hallucinations commanding the patient to perform actions
C) Tactile hallucinations in absence of substance use
D) Olfactory hallucinations with no apparent medical cause

Question 109: A 12-year-old client presents with anxiety and difficulty in social situations. According to Erikson's stages of psychosocial development, which intervention would be most appropriate to align with the client's developmental level?
A) Encouraging autonomy by allowing the client to make independent decisions.
B) Fostering a sense of industry by engaging the client in group activities and providing positive reinforcement.
C) Promoting identity exploration through discussions about personal values and future goals.
D) Developing trust by establishing a consistent and supportive therapeutic relationship.

Question 110: Maria, a 28-year-old woman, reports frequent physical assaults by her spouse but expresses fear about leaving due to financial dependence and threats from her partner. As her counselor, what should be your primary focus during the initial sessions?
A) Empower Maria by helping her gain financial independence.
B) Validate Maria's feelings and provide emotional support.
C) Assist Maria in finding a safe shelter or temporary housing.
D) Encourage Maria to confront her spouse about the abuse.

Question 111: During an intake session, Maria, a mental health counselor, learns that her new client, David, has a hearing impairment and uses American Sign Language (ASL). What is the most appropriate accommodation Maria should provide to ensure effective communication?
A) Use written notes for all communications.
B) Learn basic ASL phrases to communicate with David.
C) Schedule sessions with an ASL interpreter present.
D) Encourage David to lip-read during sessions.

Question 112: During a family therapy session with the Johnson family, the counselor observes that the teenage daughter frequently interrupts her mother with derogatory comments and displays aggressive body language. The mother appears visibly distressed but does not address her daughter's behavior. What dynamic is most likely occurring in this family?
A) Parental Neglect
B) Sibling Rivalry
C) Child-to-Parent Violence
D) Covert Parental Alienation

Question 113: John, a 45-year-old man, reports during an intake session that he has been having frequent arguments with his partner and has felt increasingly angry. He admits to having violent thoughts towards his partner but insists he would never act on them. What should be your primary concern as his mental health counselor?
A) Assess for underlying mental health conditions contributing to his anger.
B) Develop an anger management plan with John to help him manage his emotions.
C) Conduct an immediate risk assessment for potential relationship violence.
D) Refer John to couples therapy to address relationship issues.

Question 114: During a group therapy session, the counselor notices that members are consistently avoiding discussing their feelings about a recent conflict within the group. Instead, they focus on superficial topics. What is the most likely theme emerging in this group?
A) Trust
B) Avoidance
C) Cohesion
D) Conflict Resolution

Question 115: Jamie, a 16-year-old assigned male at birth (AMAB), has been exploring their gender identity and identifies as non-binary. Jamie reports feeling isolated at school due to lack of understanding from peers and teachers. What intervention should you prioritize as Jamie's counselor?
A) Advocate for Jamie by educating school staff about non-binary identities.
B) Suggest Jamie join an online support group for non-binary teens.
C) Focus on building Jamie's resilience through individual counseling sessions.
D) Encourage Jamie to conform temporarily for easier social interactions.

Question 116: Scenario: Sarah, a 35-year-old client, has been in therapy for anxiety and depression for two years. She has made significant progress and is now discussing termination with her therapist. During the final sessions, Sarah expresses mixed feelings about ending therapy. What is the most appropriate action for the therapist to take during the termination process with Sarah?
A) Reassure Sarah that she can return to therapy anytime if she feels the need.
B) Emphasize Sarah's progress and encourage her to maintain it independently.
C) Discuss potential future stressors and how Sarah might handle them.
D) Gradually reduce session frequency before final termination.

Question 117: Maria, a 17-year-old high school student, is facing significant stress regarding her future career choices and personal identity. She feels torn between different paths and struggles with self-definition. Which developmental issue is Maria most likely encountering?
A) Autonomy vs. Shame and Doubt
B) Initiative vs. Guilt

C) Industry vs. Inferiority
D) Identity vs. Role Confusion

Question 118: When providing educational resources to a client diagnosed with generalized anxiety disorder (GAD), which approach is most effective in ensuring the client understands and utilizes the information?
A) Providing printed handouts with detailed explanations about GAD.
B) Offering interactive online modules tailored to GAD management.
C) Referring the client to a local support group for individuals with anxiety disorders.
D) Scheduling regular follow-up sessions to review and discuss educational materials.

Question 119: During a crisis intervention session with a client who has just experienced a traumatic event, what should be the counselor's primary focus?
A) Exploring the client's past traumatic experiences.
B) Establishing immediate safety and stabilization.
C) Developing long-term coping strategies.
D) Encouraging the client to express their feelings in detail.

Question 120: In a group therapy session with five members, Sarah consistently takes on a leadership role and dominates discussions. The other members often seem disengaged or reluctant to participate actively. What pattern might be affecting the group's dynamics?
A) Role Fixation
B) Group Cohesion
C) Communication Breakdown
D) Power Imbalance

Question 121: Lisa, a counselor, informs her client, Mark, about the potential risks and benefits of therapy during their first session. Which statement accurately reflects an appropriate disclosure about the risks involved in therapy?
A) Therapy guarantees complete resolution of all psychological issues.
B) Therapy may lead to emotional discomfort as difficult topics are addressed.
C) Therapy sessions will always result in immediate positive changes.
D) Therapy eliminates the need for any other medical treatments.

Question 122: During an initial interview with a new client, which of the following should be the primary focus for a mental health counselor to establish an effective therapeutic relationship?
A) Gathering detailed family history
B) Establishing rapport and trust
C) Conducting a comprehensive mental status examination
D) Discussing potential treatment goals

Question 123: During a therapy session with Emily, who is dealing with grief after losing a parent, Dr. Smith considers sharing his own similar loss. What should Dr. Smith primarily consider before deciding to disclose his personal experience?
A) Whether his disclosure will shift the session's focus onto his own experiences.
B) Whether his disclosure will make Emily feel obligated to support him emotionally.
C) Whether his disclosure will be relevant and beneficial for Emily's therapeutic process.
D) Whether his disclosure will demonstrate that he has experienced similar pain and understands exactly what Emily feels.

Question 124: Sarah, a 45-year-old woman, recently lost her husband to a sudden heart attack. She has been experiencing intense sadness, withdrawal from social activities, and difficulty concentrating at work for the past six months. Her symptoms are starting to impact her daily functioning significantly. As her mental health counselor, which diagnosis is most appropriate for Sarah based on her current symptoms?
A) Major Depressive Disorder
B) Normal Grief
C) Complicated Grief
D) Adjustment Disorder with Depressed Mood

Question 125: When is it most appropriate for a mental health counselor to use self-disclosure during a counseling session?
A) When the client seems reluctant to share personal information.
B) When the counselor feels that sharing their own experiences will build rapport.
C) When the self-disclosure is relevant to the client's situation and can facilitate the therapeutic process.
D) When the client directly asks about the counselor's personal life.

Question 126: Which of the following approaches is most effective in facilitating adjustment for a patient experiencing significant physical loss due to a chronic illness?
A) Encouraging the patient to focus solely on positive aspects of their life.
B) Promoting active engagement in rehabilitation and adaptive activities.
C) Advising the patient to avoid discussing their condition with others.
D) Suggesting the patient rely primarily on medication for emotional stability.

Question 127: Which treatment modality is considered most effective for individuals with co-occurring substance use and mental health disorders?
A) Cognitive Behavioral Therapy (CBT)
B) Dialectical Behavior Therapy (DBT)
C) Integrated Dual Disorder Treatment (IDDT)
D) Motivational Interviewing (MI)

Question 128: John, a 35-year-old man, presents with symptoms of anxiety and depression following a recent job loss. He reports feeling worthless and has difficulty managing his emotions. As his counselor, you decide to apply a theory-based counseling intervention to help John develop healthier coping mechanisms and improve his self-esteem.
A) Cognitive Behavioral Therapy (CBT) focusing on restructuring negative thought patterns.
B) Person-Centered Therapy emphasizing unconditional positive regard.
C) Solution-Focused Brief Therapy (SFBT) concentrating on future goals.
D) Psychodynamic Therapy exploring unconscious conflicts from past experiences.

Question 129: John, a 16-year-old high school student, has been identified as both a victim and perpetrator of bullying. As his mental health counselor, which of the following interventions should you prioritize based on contemporary research and theories?
A) Social skills training
B) Group therapy sessions
C) Family counseling
D) School-based anti-bullying curriculum

Question 130: Maria, a 45-year-old woman with a history of bipolar disorder, reports experiencing intense

suicidal ideation over the past week. She has access to means and has expressed specific plans for self-harm. What is the most appropriate immediate action for her mental health counselor?
A) Develop a safety plan with Maria.
B) Contact her family members for support.
C) Arrange for immediate hospitalization.
D) Increase the frequency of therapy sessions.

Question 131: Maria, a 30-year-old woman experiencing severe depression, is concerned about confidentiality as she begins therapy. To obtain her informed consent effectively while addressing her concerns about confidentiality, which approach should you take?
A) Reassuring Maria verbally that all information will remain confidential unless she poses a risk to herself or others.
B) Providing Maria with a detailed written document outlining confidentiality policies and having her sign it without further discussion.
C) Explaining confidentiality policies verbally, giving Maria a written document for reference, discussing any concerns she has in detail, and then obtaining her signature.
D) Asking Maria to read through confidentiality policies online before coming to her first session and then obtaining her verbal agreement.

Question 132: Which therapeutic approach is most effective in treating Generalized Anxiety Disorder (GAD) by addressing both cognitive distortions and behavioral avoidance?
A) Cognitive Behavioral Therapy (CBT)
B) Acceptance and Commitment Therapy (ACT)
C) Dialectical Behavior Therapy (DBT)
D) Mindfulness-Based Stress Reduction (MBSR)

Question 133: A counselor named Dr. Smith is working with a client named John who has expressed suicidal ideation but does not have an immediate plan or intent to harm himself. John also mentioned a history of severe depression and past suicide attempts. What is Dr. Smith's most ethical course of action?
A) Maintain confidentiality but monitor John's condition closely.
B) Break confidentiality and contact John's family immediately.
C) Conduct a thorough risk assessment and develop a safety plan with John.
D) Refer John to an inpatient psychiatric facility without his consent.

Question 134: During a telehealth session with her client, Sarah, a mental health counselor named Dr. Jane receives a request from Sarah to email her session notes. Dr. Jane is aware of the ethical guidelines regarding confidentiality in electronic communication. What is the most appropriate action for Dr. Jane to take?
A) Email the session notes using her personal email account.
B) Use an encrypted email service to send the session notes.
C) Share the session notes through a social media private message.
D) Refuse to send the session notes electronically due to confidentiality concerns.

Question 135: Maria, a licensed mental health counselor, has a new client who is concerned about the cost of therapy sessions. The client has insurance but is unsure about what their plan covers. Maria needs to review the client's insurance benefits to provide accurate information. Which of the following steps should Maria prioritize to ensure she accurately reviews the client's insurance benefits?

A) Contact the insurance company directly to verify coverage details.
B) Review the client's insurance policy documents provided by the client.
C) Use a third-party verification service to check insurance benefits.
D) Ask the client to call their insurance company for details.

Question 136: John, a 35-year-old male, has been struggling with compulsive gambling for several years. He often finds himself preoccupied with thoughts of gambling and experiences restlessness when trying to cut back. Recently, he has started lying to his family about his gambling habits. As his counselor, what would be the most appropriate initial intervention based on contemporary research?
A) Encourage John to attend a support group like Gamblers Anonymous.
B) Suggest John engage in mindfulness-based stress reduction techniques.
C) Recommend John undergo Cognitive Behavioral Therapy (CBT).
D) Advise John to seek medication management for impulse control.

Question 137: Sarah, a client with anxiety, expresses fear about being judged during sessions. Which strategy should her counselor use to facilitate trust and safety?
A) Reassure Sarah that her feelings are valid and she will not be judged.
B) Suggest that Sarah write down her thoughts before sharing them verbally.
C) Immediately challenge Sarah's negative thoughts about judgment.
D) Focus on relaxation techniques before addressing her fears.

Question 138: John, a 10-year-old boy, has been referred to counseling due to frequent temper tantrums that seem disproportionate to the situation. His parents note that these outbursts occur several times a week and are often triggered by minor frustrations. There is no history of physical aggression towards others or destruction of property. What is the most appropriate diagnosis?
A) Intermittent Explosive Disorder (IED)
B) Disruptive Mood Dysregulation Disorder (DMDD)
C) Oppositional Defiant Disorder (ODD)
D) Bipolar Disorder

Question 139: In a counseling group for individuals dealing with anxiety, Sarah frequently makes negative comments about herself and others, which seems to be affecting group morale. What is the best course of action for you as a counselor?
A) Ignore Sarah's comments and focus on positive aspects of other members' contributions.
B) Address Sarah's behavior immediately in front of the group by explaining its impact.
C) Encourage Sarah to explore her feelings in a one-on-one session after addressing her behavior briefly in the group.
D) Ask another group member to provide feedback to Sarah about her comments.

Question 140: Which of the following best exemplifies the importance of clarifying counselor/client roles at the beginning of therapy?
A) It establishes a power dynamic where the counselor is seen as an authority figure.
B) It helps in setting clear boundaries and expectations, reducing potential misunderstandings.
C) It allows the client to dictate the terms and conditions of therapy sessions.
D) It minimizes the need for ongoing communication about

roles throughout therapy.

Question 141: John, a 15-year-old boy, is experiencing significant stress due to loyalty conflicts between his biological father and his stepmother. He feels guilty when he enjoys activities with his stepmother because he believes it betrays his father. What should a mental health counselor prioritize in their approach to help John?
A) Encourage John to openly discuss his feelings with both his biological father and stepmother.
B) Focus on helping John understand that it is normal to have positive relationships with both parents and stepparents.
C) Advise John's biological father and stepmother to avoid putting John in situations where he has to choose sides.
D) Recommend individual counseling for John to explore his feelings privately.

Question 142: Sarah, a 35-year-old woman, presents with persistent sadness, loss of interest in daily activities, significant weight loss without dieting, insomnia, fatigue, and feelings of worthlessness. These symptoms have been present for the past three months and are significantly impairing her social and occupational functioning. What is the most likely diagnosis for Sarah?
A) Major Depressive Disorder
B) Persistent Depressive Disorder (Dysthymia)
C) Bipolar II Disorder
D) Generalized Anxiety Disorder

Question 143: Which of the following techniques is most effective for a mental health counselor to help a client contain and manage intense feelings during a session?
A) Cognitive Restructuring
B) Grounding Techniques
C) Guided Imagery
D) Progressive Muscle Relaxation

Question 144: John, a 45-year-old man, reports feeling isolated and fearful after his partner started monitoring his phone calls and restricting his interactions with friends. He downplays these actions as "normal relationship issues." What should be your initial step as a mental health counselor?
A) Encouraging John to improve communication with his partner.
B) Validating John's feelings and educating him about IPV.
C) Suggesting couples therapy to address relationship issues.
D) Advising John to focus on self-care activities.

Question 145: Sarah, a 16-year-old girl who was adopted as an infant, has recently been struggling with her sense of identity and expressing feelings of not belonging. Her adoptive parents are seeking guidance on how best to support her during this time. What is the most appropriate explanation for Sarah's current struggles?
A) Normal adolescent development exacerbated by adoption status
B) Lack of cultural integration within her adoptive family
C) Unresolved grief over loss of biological family
D) Peer pressure influencing her perception of self-worth

Question 146: John, a 45-year-old male, presents to his mental health counselor with complaints of persistent fatigue, unexplained weight gain, and chronic pain in his joints. He has been feeling low for several months and struggles to find motivation for daily activities. Which physical issue is most likely related to John's depression?
A) Hypothyroidism
B) Chronic Fatigue Syndrome
C) Fibromyalgia
D) Sleep Apnea

Question 147: John, a 28-year-old African American man, feels overwhelmed by his extended family's involvement in his decision-making processes. As his mental health counselor, what would be the most appropriate first step in addressing this issue?
A) Explore John's feelings about his family's involvement.
B) Advise John to assert his independence from his family.
C) Encourage John to have an open conversation with his family about boundaries.
D) Suggest John avoid discussing personal decisions with his family.

Question 148: A 35-year-old female client presents with symptoms of Borderline Personality Disorder (BPD), including emotional dysregulation, impulsivity, and unstable interpersonal relationships. Which modality of treatment is most appropriate for addressing her condition?
A) Cognitive Behavioral Therapy (CBT)
B) Dialectical Behavior Therapy (DBT)
C) Psychodynamic Therapy
D) Person-Centered Therapy

Question 149: In the context of empathic attunement, which of the following best describes a counselor's ability to resonate deeply with a client's emotional state?
A) Reflective Listening
B) Active Listening
C) Emotional Resonance
D) Cognitive Empathy

Question 150: You have been assigned a new client, Maria, who has recently immigrated from Mexico and is experiencing symptoms of depression. As a counselor, how should you assess your competency to work with Maria effectively?
A) Reflect on your past experiences with clients from diverse backgrounds.
B) Evaluate your knowledge of Mexican culture and its impact on mental health.
C) Seek supervision or consultation to discuss potential cultural issues.
D) Assume that general counseling skills will be sufficient to address Maria's needs.

ANSWER WITH DETAILED EXPLANATION SET [5]

Question 1: Correct Answer: B) Reassuring John that all information shared will remain confidential.
Rationale: Reassuring John about confidentiality is essential for creating a safe space where he feels comfortable sharing personal experiences. This assurance helps build trust and encourages openness. While discussing interests outside of work (Option A) can help build rapport, it may not address John's immediate concerns about privacy. Offering advice based on similar cases (Option C) might make John feel less unique or understood. Highlighting qualifications (Option D), while important for credibility, does not directly address John's need for confidentiality assurance.

Question 2: Correct Answer: D) Developing Discrepancy
Rationale: Developing discrepancy involves helping clients see the gap between their current behaviors and their broader goals or values. This technique is central to motivational interviewing and can effectively enhance Maria's motivation by making her aware of how her alcohol use conflicts with her personal goals. - Reflective Listening (A) is also important in motivational interviewing but primarily serves to build rapport rather than directly enhancing motivation. - Confrontational Approach (B) is generally not recommended as it can lead to resistance rather than motivation. - Decisional Balance (C) involves weighing pros and cons of change, which is useful but less direct in creating the internal conflict needed for change compared to developing discrepancy.

Question 3: Correct Answer: B) Encourage open communication between all family members about their values and expectations.
Rationale: Option B is correct as it promotes dialogue and mutual understanding among family members, essential in addressing intergenerational conflicts in a culturally sensitive manner. Option A may seem beneficial but could be perceived as disrespectful to traditional values. Option C reinforces rigid adherence to tradition without considering the children's well-being. Option D separates rather than integrates perspectives within the family unit, missing an opportunity for holistic resolution through shared understanding.

Question 4: Correct Answer: B) Conduct a thorough risk assessment to determine the level of danger.
Rationale: The correct initial action for a counselor when a client expresses suicidal ideation is to conduct a thorough risk assessment (Option B). This step is crucial to evaluate the immediacy and severity of the threat and determine appropriate interventions. Option A (Contact emergency services immediately) may be necessary if the risk assessment indicates an immediate threat, but it is not always the first step. Option C (Informing family members) can breach confidentiality unless there is an immediate risk or prior consent has been given. Option D (Documenting without further action) fails to address the urgency of suicidal ideation. Therefore, conducting a risk assessment aligns with ethical guidelines and ensures appropriate follow-up actions based on assessed risk levels.

Question 5: Correct Answer: C) Conducting a detailed psychosocial history interview
Rationale: Conducting a detailed psychosocial history interview is crucial during an initial intake session as it provides comprehensive information about the client's background, current situation, and potential stressors. This approach helps in identifying underlying issues that may contribute to the presenting problem. While administering an anxiety inventory (A), exploring work environment (B), and referring for medical evaluation (D) are important steps, they should follow after obtaining a holistic understanding through the psychosocial history.

Question 6: Correct Answer: A) Catastrophizing
Rationale: Catastrophizing involves imagining the worst possible outcome and is closely linked to panic attacks, where individuals often believe that they are experiencing a life-threatening event. Overgeneralization (Option B) involves making broad conclusions based on limited evidence but does not specifically relate to the acute fear seen in panic attacks. Personalization (Option C) is when individuals attribute external events to themselves without basis, which is more related to anxiety disorders rather than panic attacks. Mind Reading (Option D) involves assuming others' thoughts, which is more associated with social anxiety than panic attacks. Thus, A) Catastrophizing is the most accurate answer due to its direct link with the intense fear experienced during panic attacks.

Question 7: Correct Answer: B) Develop a safety plan with Emily and her parents.
Rationale: Developing a safety plan is crucial as it provides immediate support and ensures Emily's safety, addressing both her emotional and physical well-being. Encouraging confrontation (Option A) can escalate the situation, ignoring (Option C) may not address underlying issues, and changing schools (Option D) might not be feasible or solve the root problem. The safety plan involves collaboration with parents, which is essential for a supportive environment.

Question 8: Correct Answer: C) Remind the group about confidentiality and boundaries.
Rationale: The most appropriate initial action is to remind the group about confidentiality and boundaries (Option C). This reinforces important group norms without singling out individuals initially. Option A could prematurely expose personal details without consent. Option B might be seen as intrusive and could breach privacy. Option D assumes that their interactions are problematic without fully understanding their nature. The correct answer (C) ensures that all members are aware of essential guidelines while maintaining a non-confrontational approach.

Question 9: Correct Answer: C) Identity vs. Role Confusion
Rationale: Erikson's theory posits that the primary developmental task during adolescence (approximately ages 12-18) is "Identity vs. Role Confusion". During this stage, individuals explore their personal identity and sense of self. Failure to establish a clear identity may lead to role confusion. - Option A (Trust vs. Mistrust): This stage occurs in infancy (0-1 year). It involves developing trust when caregivers provide reliability, care, and affection. - Option B (Autonomy vs. Shame and Doubt): This stage occurs in early childhood (1-3 years). It focuses on developing a sense of personal control over physical skills and a sense of independence. - Option D (Intimacy vs. Isolation): This stage occurs in young adulthood (18-40 years). It involves forming intimate, loving relationships with other people. The correct answer is C because it directly aligns with the adolescent period defined by Erikson's framework, whereas the other options pertain to different life stages with distinct developmental tasks.

Question 10: Correct Answer: B) Reflecting on your personal biases and how they may impact your work.
Rationale: Reflecting on personal biases is crucial because it directly impacts the counselor-client relationship and ensures ethical practice. While seeking supervision (Option A), attending workshops (Option C), and reviewing literature (Option D) are all important for professional development, they do not address the immediate need for self-awareness in relation to a specific client. Personal biases can affect judgment and interaction, making self-reflection essential for

providing unbiased and effective care. - Option A is important but secondary to understanding one's own biases. - Option C enhances skills but does not address personal bias directly. - Option D is valuable for knowledge but does not ensure unbiased application of techniques. Reflecting on biases ensures that counselors remain aware of potential prejudices that could hinder their effectiveness with clients from diverse backgrounds or with differing issues.

Question 11: Correct Answer: B) Help Maria identify and challenge her negative thoughts.

Rationale: Option B is correct as it directly addresses Maria's cognitive distortion by helping her recognize and reframe her negative thoughts, which is a core component of CBT. Option A focuses on increasing support but does not tackle the underlying cognitive issue. Option C addresses behavioral strategies rather than cognitive processes. Option D provides stress management skills but does not specifically target the distorted thinking related to relapse.

Question 12: Correct Answer: B) Emotion-Focused Therapy (EFT)

Rationale: Emotion-Focused Therapy (EFT) would best help Mark develop healthier emotional expression as it specifically aims to enhance awareness and understanding of emotions, facilitating healthier ways of experiencing and expressing them. EFT focuses on helping clients process their emotions constructively within a safe therapeutic environment. Psychodynamic Therapy explores unconscious processes but may not provide immediate strategies for emotion regulation. Acceptance and Commitment Therapy (ACT) emphasizes acceptance of emotions and committed action towards values but does not focus as directly on changing emotional expression patterns. Interpersonal Therapy (IPT) targets interpersonal issues but may not address the internal emotional processes as effectively as EFT.

Question 13: Correct Answer: A) Conduct an organizational assessment to identify areas needing improvement.

Rationale: Conducting an organizational assessment (Option A) is essential as it provides a comprehensive understanding of current practices and identifies areas needing improvement. This foundational step enables informed decision-making for systemic changes. Increasing one-on-one sessions (Option B), developing new techniques (Option C), and enhancing outreach programs (Option D) are beneficial but secondary actions that should follow after understanding the broader organizational context through an assessment.

Question 14: Correct Answer: C) Exposure and Response Prevention (ERP)

Rationale: Exposure and Response Prevention (ERP) is considered the most effective cognitive-behavioral technique for reducing obsessive thoughts in patients with OCD. ERP involves exposing the patient to anxiety-provoking stimuli without allowing them to engage in their usual compulsive behaviors, thereby reducing the anxiety associated with obsessive thoughts over time. Option A, Cognitive Restructuring, involves changing maladaptive thought patterns but does not specifically target the avoidance behaviors central to OCD. Option B, Thought Stopping, is less effective as it can sometimes reinforce obsessions by focusing attention on them. Option D, Mindfulness-Based Stress Reduction (MBSR), helps manage stress but does not directly address the avoidance behaviors characteristic of OCD. By comparing these options, ERP stands out as it directly targets both exposure to anxiety-provoking stimuli and prevention of compulsive responses, making it uniquely suited for treating OCD.

Question 15: Correct Answer: C) "It was decided that Sarah would benefit from CBT twice weekly and medication management, as per Dr. Smith's recommendation."

Rationale: Option C is correct because it clearly states the decision made collaboratively by the team while attributing specific recommendations to Dr. Smith. This ensures clarity

in documentation and reflects collaborative decision-making. - Option A is incorrect because it implies that only Dr. Smith suggested interventions without indicating team agreement. - Option B is incorrect as it lacks clarity about who made the recommendation. - Option D is close but does not emphasize collaborative decision-making; it focuses solely on Dr. Smith's input.

Question 16: Correct Answer: A) Verify Sarah's insurance benefits and explain them to her.

Rationale: Verifying Sarah's insurance benefits ensures that both John and Sarah have a clear understanding of what services are covered and any out-of-pocket costs. This step helps prevent misunderstandings about payment responsibilities. Option B is incorrect because providing a fee schedule without understanding the insurance coverage may lead to confusion. Option C is less relevant initially since it assumes financial need without verifying coverage first. Option D places the responsibility on the client, which can be overwhelming and may not ensure accurate information.

Question 17: Correct Answer: C) Norepinephrine

Rationale: Norepinephrine plays a crucial role in the body's fight-or-flight response, which is activated during states of fear and panic. It is involved in increasing heart rate, blood pressure, and glucose release from energy stores, preparing the body for rapid action. While dopamine (A) is involved in reward and pleasure pathways, serotonin (B) regulates mood and anxiety but is not as directly involved in acute fear responses. GABA (D) is an inhibitory neurotransmitter that reduces neuronal excitability throughout the nervous system, often having a calming effect rather than initiating a panic response. By focusing on norepinephrine's specific role in activating physiological changes during fear and panic, we can see why it is more directly related to these states compared to dopamine, serotonin, or GABA.

Question 18: Correct Answer: B) Repeated measures ANOVA

Rationale: The repeated measures ANOVA is the appropriate statistical method when accounting for both within-subject and between-subject variability in studies involving repeated measurements on the same subjects. This method allows researchers to control for individual differences by comparing changes within subjects over time. The independent t-test (Option A) compares means between two independent groups, not accounting for within-subject variability. The paired t-test (Option C) is used for comparing means within the same group but does not handle multiple time points or conditions as effectively as repeated measures ANOVA. Multiple regression (Option D) examines relationships between variables but does not specifically address within-subject variability in repeated measures designs.

Question 19: Correct Answer: B) Affect

Rationale: Affect refers to the observable expression of emotions. John's monotone voice and report of feeling "empty" indicate a flat or blunted affect, which is often associated with depression or other mood disorders. While thought process (A), insight (C), and speech (D) are important aspects of the MSE, they do not directly address the emotional expression that is critical in diagnosing mood disorders.

Question 20: Correct Answer: A) Major Depressive Disorder and Generalized Anxiety Disorder

Rationale: The combination of persistent sadness, loss of interest in activities, and difficulty concentrating are hallmark symptoms of Major Depressive Disorder (MDD). The excessive worry about various aspects of life aligns with Generalized Anxiety Disorder (GAD). While Panic Disorder (B) involves sudden episodes of intense fear or discomfort, it does not encompass the generalized worry seen in GAD. Persistent Depressive Disorder (C) is characterized by chronic depression but does not fully account for the intensity of James's symptoms. Bipolar II Disorder (D) includes hypomanic episodes which are not indicated in

James's presentation.

Question 21: Correct Answer: B) Thought Process

Rationale: The primary concern in this scenario is John's disorganized thought process, which is a critical component of the MSE. While slow speech (Option C) and feelings of hopelessness (Option A) are also significant observations, they are secondary to the disorganization in thought processes when considering diagnosis and treatment planning. Insight and judgment (Option D), though important, are not as directly relevant to the immediate observations described.

Question 22: Correct Answer: C) Providing reassurance and normalizing the client's feelings.

Rationale: Providing reassurance and normalizing the client's feelings (Option C) is most effective in establishing rapport with an anxious and reluctant client. This approach helps in reducing anxiety by making the client feel understood and accepted. Directly asking about anxiety (Option A) may increase discomfort. Open-ended questions (Option B) are generally useful but may overwhelm an anxious client initially. Structured questions (Option D) can seem impersonal and may hinder rapport-building. Establishing trust through reassurance creates a safe environment for more open communication later in the interview.

Question 23: Correct Answer: B) Establish a strong therapeutic alliance with John.

Rationale: Establishing a strong therapeutic alliance is crucial as it forms the foundation for effective treatment planning. Building trust ensures that John feels supported and understood, which can significantly enhance engagement and outcomes. While addressing financial stressors (A), considering medication (C), and using cognitive-behavioral techniques (D) are important components of treatment, they should follow after establishing rapport and trust. Without a strong therapeutic alliance, these interventions may not be as effective.

Question 24: Correct Answer: B) Michael openly shares his thoughts about Emily's progress and any concerns he has.

Rationale: Genuineness involves being honest and open with clients about one's thoughts and feelings. By sharing his thoughts on Emily's progress and any concerns (Option B), Michael demonstrates authenticity, fostering a trusting therapeutic relationship. Option A is about ensuring comfort rather than genuineness; Option C focuses on empathy rather than transparency; Option D emphasizes positive reinforcement without the element of openness critical for genuineness.

Question 25: Correct Answer: A) Intersectionality refers to the overlapping and interdependent systems of discrimination or disadvantage.

Rationale: Intersectionality, a term coined by Kimberlé Crenshaw, highlights how various forms of discrimination (e.g., race, gender, class) intersect and create unique dynamics and effects. Option A is correct because it captures this comprehensive view. Option B is incorrect as it mentions privilege without emphasizing oppression. Option C is too narrow by focusing solely on race, neglecting other intersecting identities. Option D incorrectly limits intersectionality to gender-based oppression alone. Understanding intersectionality requires recognizing the complexity and multiplicity of oppressive structures beyond single-axis frameworks.

Question 26: Correct Answer: D) Explaining the limits of confidentiality, including situations where disclosure is required by law

Rationale: Option D is correct because it addresses a critical legal aspect of informed consent: counselors must inform clients about the limits of confidentiality, such as mandatory reporting requirements for abuse or threats. This ensures clients are aware that certain disclosures may be necessary by law. Option A is incorrect but tricky because while informing clients about risks and benefits is part of

informed consent, it does not specifically address a legally mandated aspect like confidentiality limits. Option B is also incorrect but close because although clients have rights to their records, this falls under client rights rather than a specific legal requirement tied to informed consent. Option C is incorrect yet plausible because discussing qualifications can build trust but isn't a legally mandated part of informed consent like explaining confidentiality limits. The correct answer (D) encompasses essential legal obligations that protect both client and counselor within the therapeutic relationship.

Question 27: Correct Answer: B) An inpatient rehabilitation facility

Rationale: The correct answer is B) An inpatient rehabilitation facility. This option is most appropriate because it provides a structured and intensive treatment environment necessary for severe substance use issues, which are beyond what outpatient services can handle. Option A, a support group, while beneficial, does not offer the intensive treatment required for severe cases. Option C, a primary care physician, can provide medical oversight but lacks specialized addiction treatment capabilities. Option D, an outpatient addiction counselor, might be suitable for less severe cases but not when intensive intervention is needed. The key difference lies in the level of care and structure provided by an inpatient rehabilitation facility compared to other options, making it the most appropriate referral for severe substance use issues.

Question 28: Correct Answer: A) Encourage John to discuss his concerns with his healthcare provider.

Rationale: Encouraging John to discuss his concerns with his healthcare provider is crucial because ED can be directly linked to diabetes management and may require medical intervention. Lifestyle changes (B), CBT (C), and couples therapy (D) are all valuable interventions but should follow after ensuring that John's medical condition is properly managed. Addressing the medical aspect first ensures that any underlying physiological issues are identified and treated appropriately.

Question 29: Correct Answer: B) Advising John to limit screen time before bed.

Rationale: Limiting screen time before bed is crucial because exposure to blue light from screens can suppress melatonin production, making it harder to fall asleep. This recommendation aligns with contemporary research on sleep hygiene. Option A is incorrect because napping during the day can disrupt nighttime sleep. Option C is based on an old wives' tale and lacks strong scientific support. Option D is misleading; while physical activity is beneficial for sleep, doing it too close to bedtime can have a stimulating effect, making it harder to fall asleep.

Question 30: Correct Answer: A) Develop a safety plan with Emily.

Rationale: Developing a safety plan is an immediate and practical step that involves collaboratively identifying coping strategies and resources for support. It directly addresses the urgency of suicidal ideation without escalating to inpatient care prematurely. While referring to inpatient care (Option B) might be necessary if there were an imminent risk, it is not warranted here due to the absence of a specific plan or means. Scheduling frequent follow-ups (Option C) is important but secondary to immediate safety planning. Mindfulness exercises (Option D) can be beneficial long-term but do not address immediate safety concerns.

Question 31: Correct Answer: D) Hospital Anxiety and Depression Scale (HADS)

Rationale: The Hospital Anxiety and Depression Scale (HADS) is specifically designed to assess both anxiety and depression simultaneously, making it highly effective in differentiating between these two constructs. The Beck Depression Inventory-II (BDI-II) focuses solely on depressive symptoms, while the State-Trait Anxiety Inventory (STAI) measures anxiety without addressing depression. The

Hamilton Anxiety Rating Scale (HAM-A) is primarily used for assessing the severity of anxiety symptoms but does not include depressive symptomatology.

Question 32: Correct Answer: D) Validate Alex's feelings and experiences regarding his gender identity.

Rationale: Validating Alex's feelings and experiences is crucial as it helps build trust and provides emotional support, which is essential for his mental well-being. Encouraging exploration (Option A) might be beneficial later but does not address immediate emotional needs. Providing psychoeducation to the family (Option B) is important but secondary to validating Alex first. Referring for hormone therapy (Option C) may be premature without addressing immediate psychological support.

Question 33: Correct Answer: A) Rejecting the null hypothesis when it is actually true.

Rationale: A Type I error occurs when researchers reject a true null hypothesis, meaning they believe there is an effect or difference when there actually isn't one. This type of error is also known as a "false positive." Option B describes a Type II error, which involves failing to reject a false null hypothesis (a "false negative"). Options C and D are incorrect because they misrepresent the definitions of Type I and Type II errors. Understanding these errors is crucial for evaluating research findings and their implications accurately.

Question 34: Correct Answer: C) Alzheimer's Disease

Rationale: Alzheimer's Disease is characterized by progressive memory loss, particularly affecting recent memories while older memories remain intact longer. Mrs. Johnson's symptoms of significant memory loss, confusion, and difficulty with planning are consistent with this diagnosis. - A) Major Depressive Disorder can cause memory issues but typically includes other symptoms like persistent sadness or loss of interest, which are not mentioned here. - B) Mild Cognitive Impairment involves slight but noticeable declines in cognitive abilities that do not interfere significantly with daily life. - D) Vascular Dementia is related to cerebrovascular issues and often presents with a more stepwise progression and focal neurological signs, unlike the gradual decline seen in Alzheimer's.

Question 35: Correct Answer: C) When a client discloses current abuse of a minor.

Rationale: The correct answer is C) When a client discloses current abuse of a minor. Mental health counselors are mandated reporters and are legally required to breach confidentiality if there is an ongoing risk of harm, such as current abuse of a minor. Option A is incorrect because while self-harm intentions may warrant breaking confidentiality, it depends on the severity and immediacy of the threat. Option B is incorrect because past abuse without ongoing risk does not typically require breaching confidentiality. Option D is incorrect because sharing information at the client's request involves obtaining explicit consent rather than breaching confidentiality. Understanding these distinctions is crucial for ethical decision-making in counseling practice.

Question 36: Correct Answer: B) Conduct a comprehensive suicide risk assessment immediately.

Rationale: Conducting a comprehensive suicide risk assessment immediately is crucial when a client expresses thoughts of not wanting to live. This step ensures that the counselor can evaluate the severity of Maria's suicidal ideation and determine the appropriate level of care. Scheduling a follow-up appointment (A) delays necessary intervention, while encouraging support groups (C) or journaling (D) are supportive measures but do not address the immediate risk.

Question 37: Correct Answer: C) Financial Counseling combined with Emotionally Focused Therapy (EFT)

Rationale: Financial Counseling combined with Emotionally Focused Therapy (EFT) is particularly effective because it addresses both financial literacy and emotional connection within relationships. Contemporary research supports this integrative approach as it helps clients develop practical financial skills while also improving communication and emotional intimacy, thus reducing relational conflict. - Option A (CBT) is incorrect as it primarily focuses on changing individual thought patterns rather than addressing relational dynamics directly. - Option B (SFBT) is useful for short-term solutions but may not provide the depth needed for complex issues like financial stress intertwined with relational conflict. - Option D (MBSR) helps manage stress but does not specifically target financial literacy or relationship dynamics. This comprehensive approach ensures clients receive holistic support, addressing both the practical and emotional aspects of their issues.

Question 38: Correct Answer: C) High levels of stress in her environment

Rationale: High levels of stress in Maria's environment can significantly impede her ability to implement CBT strategies effectively. While lack of social support (A), poor therapeutic alliance (B), and inadequate understanding of CBT techniques (D) are all potential barriers, contemporary research indicates that environmental stress is a critical factor that can overwhelm coping mechanisms and hinder progress. Stress affects cognitive functions and emotional regulation, making it difficult for clients like Maria to apply therapeutic techniques consistently.

Question 39: Correct Answer: B) Begin working with Mark while actively seeking specialized training and supervision.

Rationale: Starting work with Mark while pursuing specialized training and supervision ensures that he receives timely support while you enhance your competency. Option A might neglect the urgency of his needs; Option C could avoid addressing his primary concern; Option D fails to utilize available resources for immediate support.

Question 40: Correct Answer: A) Cognitive-Behavioral Therapy for Insomnia (CBT-I)

Rationale: Cognitive-Behavioral Therapy for Insomnia (CBT-I) is widely recognized as the first-line treatment for chronic insomnia due to its effectiveness in addressing the underlying cognitive and behavioral factors contributing to sleep issues. Unlike benzodiazepines (Option B), which can lead to dependence and have side effects, CBT-I provides long-term benefits without such risks. Melatonin supplements (Option C) may help regulate sleep-wake cycles but are not as effective as CBT-I in treating chronic insomnia. Sleep hygiene education (Option D), while important, is typically considered an adjunctive approach rather than a standalone treatment. Thus, CBT-I remains the gold standard.

Question 41: Correct Answer: A) Cognitive Behavioral Therapy (CBT)

Rationale: Cognitive Behavioral Therapy (CBT) is considered one of the most effective interventions for breaking the cycle of intergenerational family violence. CBT helps individuals identify and change maladaptive thought patterns and behaviors that contribute to abusive dynamics. It is evidence-based and has been shown to reduce symptoms of trauma, anxiety, and depression, which are often prevalent in victims and perpetrators of family violence. Family Systems Therapy (Option B) focuses on family dynamics but may not address individual cognitive distortions as effectively as CBT. Dialectical Behavior Therapy (Option C) is beneficial for emotional regulation but is less targeted towards breaking cycles of violence specifically. Solution-Focused Brief Therapy (Option D) emphasizes immediate solutions rather than addressing underlying cognitive patterns contributing to long-term change. Each option was carefully chosen for its relevance to therapeutic interventions used in cases of family abuse/violence but only CBT has robust evidence supporting its effectiveness in this specific context.

Question 42: Correct Answer: B) Storming

Rationale: The storming phase is characterized by the emergence of individual differences and conflicts as group members start to assert their opinions and personalities. This phase is crucial for growth but can be challenging. In contrast, forming (A) involves initial orientation and getting acquainted, norming (C) focuses on developing cohesion and establishing norms, while performing (D) involves working efficiently towards goals. Thus, storming accurately describes the scenario where conflicts are arising.

Question 43: Correct Answer: B) Demonstrating unconditional positive regard

Rationale: Demonstrating unconditional positive regard is a core principle in Carl Rogers' person-centered therapy, which emphasizes accepting clients without judgment. This approach helps create a safe and trusting environment. While maintaining eye contact (Option A) can be important, it must be balanced and culturally sensitive. Offering advice based on personal experiences (Option C) can undermine client autonomy. Regularly using self-disclosure (Option D) may shift focus away from the client and can be inappropriate if overused. Unconditional positive regard consistently supports trust and safety by ensuring clients feel valued and understood without conditions or biases.

Question 44: Correct Answer: D) Somatic Symptom Disorder

Rationale: Somatic Symptom Disorder involves experiencing significant physical symptoms that are distressing or result in significant disruption of daily life without a clear medical cause. These symptoms are often related to psychological factors such as depression. While IBS (A), Migraine (B), and GAD (C) can present with similar physical complaints, they are not as directly linked to the manifestation of depressive symptoms as Somatic Symptom Disorder (D). This disorder specifically highlights the connection between psychological distress and physical symptomatology.

Question 45: Correct Answer: B) Dialectical Behavior Therapy (DBT)

Rationale: Dialectical Behavior Therapy (DBT) is specifically designed to treat individuals with emotional dysregulation. It combines cognitive-behavioral techniques with mindfulness practices, focusing on teaching skills in distress tolerance, emotion regulation, interpersonal effectiveness, and mindfulness. While CBT (A), IPT (C), and ACT (D) can be beneficial for various mental health issues, DBT has been shown through contemporary research to be particularly effective for managing emotional dysregulation due to its structured approach targeting this specific issue.

Question 46: Correct Answer: C) Facilitating integration of both cultures

Rationale: Facilitating integration of both cultures (Option C) is considered most effective as it allows clients to retain their original cultural identity while also adapting to the new culture, promoting psychological well-being. Encouraging assimilation (Option A) can lead to loss of cultural identity and increased stress. Promoting separation (Option B) can result in social isolation and hinder adjustment. Advocating marginalization (Option D) typically leads to poor mental health outcomes as it involves rejecting both cultures. Integration balances maintaining one's cultural heritage with adapting to the new environment, fostering resilience and well-being.

Question 47: Correct Answer: B) Alcohol Use Disorders Identification Test (AUDIT)

Rationale: The AUDIT is specifically designed to assess alcohol consumption, drinking behaviors, and alcohol-related problems. The Beck Depression Inventory (BDI) assesses depressive symptoms, the Generalized Anxiety Disorder 7-item scale (GAD-7) evaluates anxiety levels, and the CAGE Questionnaire is a brief screening tool for identifying potential alcohol problems but lacks the comprehensive nature of the AUDIT. Therefore, while the CAGE Questionnaire is related, it does not provide as detailed an assessment as the AUDIT.

Question 48: Correct Answer: C) Provide access after reviewing the request and considering any potential harm.

Rationale: The correct answer is C because it aligns with ethical guidelines that emphasize both client autonomy and protection from potential harm. Counselors must balance transparency with professional judgment regarding what information might be harmful if disclosed. Option A is incorrect because unrestricted access may not consider potential harm. Option B is incorrect as it disregards client rights to their information. Option D is misleading; referral isn't typically necessary unless there are specific circumstances warranting it. Thus, option C represents a balanced, ethical approach grounded in contemporary practice standards.

Question 49: Correct Answer: C) Focus on cognitive restructuring techniques to address her feelings of guilt.

Rationale: Cognitive restructuring techniques can help Maria reframe her negative thoughts and feelings of guilt about her financial situation. This intervention addresses the root cause of her anxiety and helps improve her overall mental health. Assisting with a payment plan (Option A) or identifying community resources (Option B) are important but secondary steps that do not directly address her emotional distress. Encouraging overtime work (Option D) could exacerbate her anxiety without first managing her current emotional state.

Question 50: Correct Answer: B) Family therapy involving all family members.

Rationale: Family therapy can address the systemic issues contributing to John's anxiety by involving all family members in the therapeutic process. This approach aligns with contemporary research that highlights the importance of addressing family dynamics in cases of separation-related distress. Cognitive-behavioral therapy (Option A) may help manage worry but does not address underlying family issues. Play therapy (Option C) can be beneficial but may not be sufficient alone for complex family dynamics. Medication (Option D) should be considered only after other interventions have been explored due to potential side effects and long-term implications.

Question 51: Correct Answer: B) Promoting social-emotional learning (SEL) programs.

Rationale: Contemporary research indicates that promoting social-emotional learning (SEL) programs is the most effective intervention strategy in reducing bullying behaviors in schools. SEL programs focus on developing students' emotional intelligence, empathy, and conflict-resolution skills, which are crucial in preventing bullying. Zero-tolerance policies (Option A) often fail because they do not address the underlying causes of bullying and can lead to negative consequences such as increased suspensions. Increasing school surveillance (Option C) may deter some incidents but does not foster a positive school climate or address root issues. Peer mediation sessions (Option D) can be helpful but are generally less effective than comprehensive SEL programs that integrate these skills into daily interactions. The key difference lies in SEL's holistic approach, which equips students with lifelong skills for managing emotions and relationships, making it a more sustainable solution compared to punitive or reactive measures.

Question 52: Correct Answer: A) Encourage open discussions about their feelings and explore underlying reasons.

Rationale: According to contemporary ethical guidelines, mental health counselors should prioritize encouraging open discussions about the patient's feelings and exploring underlying reasons for their desire to hasten death. This approach respects the patient's autonomy while ensuring that any psychological distress or unmet needs are addressed. Option B is close but does not emphasize understanding the underlying reasons. Option C might be necessary but is not the primary approach in this context. Option D, while well-meaning, may overlook critical emotional and psychological factors driving the patient's request. - Option A (Correct): Encourages an open dialogue, which is crucial for understanding and addressing the complex emotions involved in end-of-life decisions. - Option B: While suggesting coping mechanisms is important, it does not directly address the patient's immediate concerns or reasons behind their desire. - Option C: Referring to a psychiatrist can be part of a comprehensive care plan but is not the primary step in addressing the expressed desire. - Option D: Focusing solely on hope and positive thinking may invalidate the patient's feelings and fail to address deeper issues. This detailed explanation ensures clarity on why option A is prioritized according to contemporary ethical guidelines, distinguishing it from other closely related options.

Question 53: Correct Answer: A) The level of parental conflict before and after the divorce

Rationale: Research indicates that high levels of parental conflict both before and after a divorce are significantly correlated with negative emotional outcomes in children. This is supported by family systems theory, which emphasizes the importance of stable and low-conflict environments for children's emotional development. While options B, C, and D can also affect a child's well-being, they do not have as direct or consistent an impact as ongoing parental conflict. Option B (the child's age) can influence how they process the divorce but is less critical than conflict levels. Option C (financial stability) affects practical aspects but not necessarily emotional well-being directly. Option D (geographical distance) can influence logistics but does not have as strong an emotional impact compared to ongoing conflict.

Question 54: Correct Answer: A) Cognitive Behavioral Therapy (CBT)

Rationale: Cognitive Behavioral Therapy (CBT) is highly effective for addressing post-divorce emotional distress by helping individuals reframe negative thought patterns and develop coping strategies. While Solution-Focused Brief Therapy (SFBT) emphasizes solutions rather than problems, it may not fully address underlying cognitive distortions contributing to Jane's distress. Emotionally Focused Therapy (EFT) focuses more on attachment issues within relationships rather than individual adjustment post-divorce. Psychodynamic Therapy explores unconscious processes but may not provide the immediate coping mechanisms that CBT offers.

Question 55: Correct Answer: D) Culturally Adapted Psychoeducation addressing specific cultural stressors

Rationale: Culturally Adapted Psychoeducation is considered most effective because it directly addresses the unique cultural stressors faced by minority clients, fostering resilience and empowerment through relevant information and strategies. While CBT (A) can help modify negative thought patterns, it may not fully address cultural context. Narrative Therapy (B) is useful for re-authoring personal stories but may lack specific cultural relevance. SFBT (C) focuses on immediate problem-solving but may overlook deeper cultural issues. Therefore, option D is best aligned with contemporary research emphasizing culturally sensitive interventions.

Question 56: Correct Answer: A) Cognitive Behavioral Therapy (CBT) focusing on changing his beliefs about the abuse.

Rationale: CBT helps John reframe distorted beliefs about the abuse, reducing feelings of shame and guilt. Exposure Therapy (Option B), while useful for some trauma cases, might retraumatize him without proper processing of underlying beliefs. Psychoeducation (Option C), though informative, lacks personal engagement necessary for deep healing. Medication management (Option D) can alleviate symptoms but does not address core cognitive distortions related to trauma. In both questions, each incorrect option is designed to appear plausible but lacks crucial elements necessary for effectively addressing the specific needs presented in each scenario. This ensures that only those

with a deep understanding of contemporary theories and research can identify the correct answer.

Question 57: Correct Answer: A) Cognitive Behavioral Therapy (CBT)

Rationale: Cognitive Behavioral Therapy (CBT) is most effective in addressing Jane's emotional state as it focuses on identifying and altering negative thought patterns that contribute to feelings of worthlessness and anxiety. CBT helps clients develop healthier coping mechanisms by challenging distorted cognitions and promoting positive behavioral changes. While Solution-Focused Brief Therapy (SFBT) emphasizes solutions rather than problems, it may not address underlying cognitive distortions as effectively as CBT. EMDR is primarily used for trauma processing, which may not be directly applicable to Jane's situation unless specific traumatic events are identified. Dialectical Behavior Therapy (DBT) is effective for emotion regulation but is more commonly used for borderline personality disorder or severe emotional dysregulation.

Question 58: Correct Answer: C) Conduct a comprehensive biopsychosocial assessment to gather detailed information.

Rationale: Conducting a comprehensive biopsychosocial assessment is crucial as it allows for gathering detailed information about James's psychological state, social environment, and biological factors that may contribute to his distress. While administering a standardized depression inventory (Option A) is important for quantifying symptoms, it does not provide a holistic view. Exploring relationship dynamics (Option B) is relevant but too narrow for an initial step. Recommending immediate psychiatric evaluation (Option D) may be premature without understanding the full context of his distress.

Question 59: Correct Answer: B) When John reveals he is planning to harm himself or others.

Rationale: Confidentiality is a fundamental aspect of counseling; however, there are exceptions where it can be legally breached. One such exception is when a client poses a threat to themselves or others (Option B). This is supported by ethical guidelines and laws that prioritize safety over confidentiality. Option A is incorrect as dissatisfaction does not warrant breaching confidentiality. Option C is tricky but incorrect because past illegal activities do not necessitate breaking confidentiality unless they involve ongoing risk. Option D involves client consent but does not constitute a legal breach scenario.

Question 60: Correct Answer: C) Providing positive reinforcement when Sarah does speak up.

Rationale: Providing positive reinforcement when Sarah speaks up encourages her to continue participating by reinforcing her behavior positively. This approach is grounded in behavioral theory, which suggests that positive reinforcement increases the likelihood of repeated behavior. Option A might put undue pressure on Sarah and make her more uncomfortable. Option B does not directly address encouraging Sarah's participation. Option D could be overwhelming for someone who is already hesitant to engage.

Question 61: Correct Answer: A) Catastrophizing

Rationale: Catastrophizing is a cognitive distortion where an individual expects the worst possible outcome, often associated with GAD. It involves magnifying potential negative outcomes, leading to heightened anxiety. Overgeneralization (B) involves making broad interpretations from a single event, while Personalization (C) refers to taking responsibility for events outside one's control. Dichotomous thinking (D), or black-and-white thinking, involves seeing situations in extremes. Although all these distortions can contribute to anxiety, catastrophizing is most directly linked to GAD due to its focus on anticipating disastrous outcomes. By comparing the options: - A) Catastrophizing: Directly linked to GAD as it involves expecting catastrophic outcomes. - B) Overgeneralization: While it contributes to anxiety, it does not specifically involve expecting the worst. -

C) Personalization: Involves self-blame but not necessarily expecting catastrophic outcomes. - D) Dichotomous thinking: Involves seeing things in black-and-white terms but not specifically anticipating disasters. Each option is relevant but only A directly addresses the core aspect of GAD related to expecting the worst possible outcome.

Question 62: Correct Answer: A) Active Listening
Rationale: Active listening is crucial for ensuring both parties feel heard and understood. This technique involves fully concentrating, understanding, responding, and remembering what the other person says. Passive observation (B) does not engage the parties directly, while directive intervention (C) may impose solutions rather than facilitate mutual understanding. Silent reflection (D), although useful for self-awareness, does not actively contribute to resolving interpersonal conflicts in real-time. Active listening aligns with principles of emotional intelligence and cognitive behavioral therapy by promoting empathy and effective communication.

Question 63: Correct Answer: B) Encourage John to discuss his concerns and experiences with relapse prevention.
Rationale: Encouraging John to discuss his concerns allows him to voice his skepticism and provides an opportunity for dialogue and clarification within the group context, which is essential in psychoeducation. Providing empirical evidence (Option A) might address his skepticism but does not engage him actively in the process. Reassuring John (Option C) addresses his feelings but may not fully resolve his concerns. Asking other members to share their stories (Option D) can be helpful but might not directly address John's specific doubts. Engaging him in discussion fosters a supportive environment where concerns are openly addressed.

Question 64: Correct Answer: D) Scheduling specific times for personal activities
Rationale: Scheduling specific times for personal activities ensures that Emily commits to her self-care routine, making it less likely that she will overextend herself with additional responsibilities. This approach directly addresses boundary maintenance by prioritizing personal time. - Option A helps address workload concerns but may not guarantee boundary maintenance. - Option B is essential for task management but does not specifically address personal time. - Option C can alleviate workload but does not ensure that Emily maintains boundaries for self-care.

Question 65: Correct Answer: B) "It sounds like you have some doubts about your drinking habits."
Rationale: Option B aligns with Motivational Interviewing principles by expressing empathy and reflecting the client's ambivalence without judgment. This approach encourages self-exploration and minimizes resistance. Option A confronts the client directly, which can increase resistance. Option C introduces external consequences prematurely, potentially causing defensiveness. Option D pushes for a discussion about quitting before establishing rapport and understanding the client's perspective.

Question 66: Correct Answer: B) Explore John's beliefs and values through existential questioning.
Rationale: Existential questioning helps clients like John explore their beliefs and values deeply, facilitating understanding and resolution of their spiritual crisis. Reconnecting with his religious community (A) might be beneficial later but does not address the immediate internal conflict. Grief counseling (C), while important, focuses more on loss rather than existential concerns. Volunteer work (D) can provide purpose but may not directly resolve the spiritual disconnection John feels.

Question 67: Correct Answer: D) Aggression
Rationale: Children who witness family abuse/violence often exhibit aggressive behaviors as a direct emotional response. This aggression can stem from modeling behaviors seen in abusive situations, internalizing stress, and attempting to regain control over their environment. While anxiety (Option A), depression (Option B), and hyperactivity (Option C) are also common emotional responses, aggression is particularly prevalent due to its direct correlation with exposure to violent behavior. Anxiety and depression are more internalized responses, whereas hyperactivity can be a result of various factors unrelated to witnessing violence. Aggression stands out as it directly mirrors the external violent behavior observed by the child.

Question 68: Correct Answer: C) Securing lethal means and ensuring they are inaccessible.
Rationale: Securing lethal means and ensuring they are inaccessible is crucial for immediate safety when dealing with suicidal ideation. This step directly addresses the risk of self-harm by reducing access to methods that could be used for suicide. While identifying personal warning signs (Option A), establishing coping strategies (Option B), and scheduling follow-up appointments (Option D) are essential components of a comprehensive safety plan, they do not provide the same immediate reduction in risk as securing lethal means. Ensuring that potentially dangerous items are not accessible can prevent impulsive actions during moments of crisis, thereby providing an immediate safeguard. - Option A is important for recognizing when a crisis may escalate but does not directly mitigate immediate risk. - Option B helps in managing distress but does not address the direct threat posed by accessible lethal means. - Option D is vital for ongoing support but is less critical than securing lethal means in preventing imminent harm.

Question 69: Correct Answer: B) Beck Depression Inventory-II (BDI-II)
Rationale: The Beck Depression Inventory-II (BDI-II) is specifically designed to measure the severity of depression symptoms. While the PHQ-9 also assesses depression, it is more commonly used in primary care settings for initial screening rather than detailed severity measurement. The GAD-7 and HAM-A are both focused on anxiety disorders, making them inappropriate for evaluating depression severity. Understanding these distinctions requires knowledge of the specific purposes and applications of these tools within mental health assessments.

Question 70: Correct Answer: B) Facilitating collaborative goal-setting sessions with clients.
Rationale: Facilitating collaborative goal-setting sessions with clients is the most effective strategy as it actively involves them in their treatment process. This approach aligns with contemporary research emphasizing client empowerment and shared decision-making, which enhances motivation and commitment to treatment goals. Option A (Regularly providing clients with detailed progress reports) is incorrect because while informative, it is more passive and does not engage clients actively in the review process. Option C (Conducting periodic assessments without client involvement) fails to involve the client directly, thus missing the opportunity for engagement and collaboration. Option D (Encouraging clients to independently track their progress) places too much responsibility on the client without sufficient support from the counselor, which can lead to inconsistent engagement. In contrast, option B ensures that both counselor and client work together, fostering a sense of ownership and accountability in the client's treatment journey. This method has been shown to improve outcomes by making clients feel more invested in their progress.

Question 71: Correct Answer: B) Demonstrating genuine empathy and understanding.
Rationale: Demonstrating genuine empathy and understanding is crucial in establishing a strong therapeutic alliance. This approach helps build trust and rapport, making the client feel heard and valued. While providing immediate solutions (Option A) might seem helpful, it can undermine the client's sense of autonomy. Gathering detailed background information (Option C) is important but should not overshadow the need for empathy in the initial stages.

Setting strict boundaries (Option D) is necessary for professionalism but can hinder the development of a warm, trusting relationship if overemphasized.

Question 72: Correct Answer: B) Explore how Maria's religious beliefs influence her understanding of grief and loss.

Rationale: Exploring how Maria's religious beliefs influence her understanding of grief and loss allows the counselor to integrate her spiritual values into the therapeutic process. This approach respects her faith while addressing her emotional struggles, facilitating a more holistic healing process. Encouraging increased participation (Option A) might not address underlying conflicts; suggesting setting aside practices (Option C) could be dismissive of her faith; referring to a spiritual advisor (Option D) might be premature without first understanding the role of religion in her life.

Question 73: Correct Answer: B) Conducting a comprehensive biopsychosocial assessment

Rationale: Conducting a comprehensive biopsychosocial assessment is the most crucial initial step in developing a treatment plan for a client with Major Depressive Disorder. This assessment helps gather detailed information about the client's biological, psychological, and social factors that may influence their condition and treatment. Without this foundational assessment, it would be challenging to establish accurate treatment goals, identify barriers, or select appropriate interventions. While establishing goals (Option A), identifying barriers (Option C), and selecting interventions (Option D) are essential components of treatment planning, they all rely on the thorough understanding gained from the initial comprehensive assessment. - Option A is incorrect because setting goals without a complete understanding of the client's condition might lead to unrealistic or irrelevant objectives. - Option C is incorrect because identifying barriers is important but should follow after understanding the client's overall situation through an assessment. - Option D is incorrect because selecting interventions requires knowledge from the biopsychosocial assessment to ensure they are tailored to the client's specific needs. By comparing these options, it becomes clear that while each step is important in its own right, conducting a comprehensive biopsychosocial assessment is foundational and must precede other steps in effective treatment planning.

Question 74: Correct Answer: C) "It sounds like you're really struggling right now; I'm here for you."

Rationale: Option C demonstrates congruence by acknowledging John's feelings directly and offering support without minimizing his experience. This response aligns with the counselor's internal empathy and external expression of support. Option A normalizes John's feelings but lacks personal connection and may come off as dismissive. Option B acknowledges John's feelings but contradicts them by suggesting he shouldn't feel that way, which is incongruent. Option D offers some reassurance but generalizes John's experience rather than addressing it personally.

Question 75: Correct Answer: A) Focus on John's current symptoms and their impact on his daily functioning.

Rationale: The primary goal during an initial diagnostic interview is to understand the patient's current symptoms and how they affect daily functioning. This helps in formulating an accurate diagnosis and treatment plan. While exploring family history (B), assessing coping mechanisms (C), and evaluating previous treatment history (D) are important, they are secondary to understanding the immediate clinical picture. Focusing on current symptoms provides a foundation for further exploration into other areas.

Question 76: Correct Answer: B) Cognitive Restructuring

Rationale: Cognitive restructuring is a core component of cognitive-behavioral therapy (CBT) aimed at identifying and challenging maladaptive thought patterns, making it highly effective for reducing ruminating and intrusive thoughts. Thought stopping (A) involves interrupting negative thoughts but does not alter the underlying cognitive patterns.

Exposure therapy (C), while useful for anxiety disorders, focuses on desensitization rather than directly changing thought processes. Mindfulness meditation (D) helps in managing thoughts by promoting present-moment awareness but does not specifically target altering thought patterns. Thus, cognitive restructuring is most effective because it directly addresses and modifies dysfunctional thinking.

Question 77: Correct Answer: C) Muscle tension

Rationale: Muscle tension is a hallmark physical symptom of Generalized Anxiety Disorder (GAD). While chest pain, shortness of breath, and dizziness can also occur in anxiety disorders, they are more commonly associated with panic attacks or other specific anxiety disorders rather than GAD. Muscle tension reflects the chronic nature of GAD, where individuals often experience persistent worry and physiological arousal. Chest pain and shortness of breath might suggest cardiac issues or panic attacks, whereas dizziness can be linked to various conditions including vestibular disorders. Thus, muscle tension stands out as the most consistent physical manifestation specifically tied to GAD.

Question 78: Correct Answer: B) Exploring the client's values and aligning them with their goals.

Rationale: Exploring the client's values and aligning them with their goals (Option B) is a core principle of Motivational Interviewing (MI). It helps clients find personal reasons for change, enhancing intrinsic motivation. Providing direct advice (Option A) can be less effective as it may not align with the client's internal motivations. Emphasizing negative consequences (Option C) often leads to resistance rather than motivation. Using authoritative statements (Option D) can undermine client autonomy, which is counterproductive in MI. The correct approach focuses on eliciting and reinforcing the client's own motivations for change, making Option B the most valid choice.

Question 79: Correct Answer: A) Generalized Anxiety Disorder (GAD)

Rationale: John's symptoms align closely with Generalized Anxiety Disorder (GAD), characterized by chronic and excessive worry about various aspects of life. The key features include difficulty controlling worry and associated symptoms such as restlessness, fatigue, difficulty concentrating, irritability, muscle tension, and sleep disturbances. - Option B (Panic Disorder) is incorrect because it primarily involves sudden episodes of intense fear or discomfort (panic attacks), not chronic worry. - Option C (Social Anxiety Disorder) is incorrect as it involves intense fear or anxiety about social situations where one might be scrutinized by others. - Option D (Obsessive-Compulsive Disorder) is incorrect because OCD involves recurrent obsessions or compulsions that are time-consuming or cause significant distress.

Question 80: Correct Answer: B) Helping John identify and challenge negative thought patterns.

Rationale: Cognitive-behavioral therapy (CBT) is highly effective for treating hopelessness by helping individuals identify and challenge negative thought patterns. While physical exercise (A), increasing social interactions (C), and mindfulness meditation (D) can also be beneficial for depression, they do not directly address the cognitive distortions contributing to John's feelings of hopelessness as effectively as CBT does.

Question 81: Correct Answer: B) Dialectical Behavior Therapy (DBT)

Rationale: Dialectical Behavior Therapy (DBT) is specifically designed to address emotional dysregulation, particularly in clients with Borderline Personality Disorder (BPD). DBT incorporates strategies from cognitive-behavioral therapy but adds components like mindfulness and dialectical strategies to manage intense emotions effectively. While Cognitive Behavioral Therapy (CBT) can help with some aspects of emotional regulation, it does not specifically target the complex emotional patterns seen in BPD as effectively as DBT. Acceptance and Commitment Therapy (ACT) focuses on accepting emotions rather than changing them, which might not be sufficient for severe dysregulation seen in BPD. Interpersonal Therapy (IPT) addresses relational issues but lacks specific techniques for managing emotional dysregulation. - A) Cognitive Behavioral Therapy (CBT): Effective for many disorders but lacks the specific focus on emotional regulation techniques crucial for BPD. - C) Acceptance and Commitment Therapy (ACT): Emphasizes acceptance over change, which may not be sufficient for severe emotional dysregulation. - D) Interpersonal Therapy (IPT): Focuses on interpersonal relationships rather than directly addressing emotional regulation skills. Thus, DBT remains the most validated and targeted approach for treating emotional dysregulation in BPD.

Question 82: Correct Answer: C) Help John identify and challenge his irrational beliefs.

Rationale: The correct answer is C because CBT primarily focuses on identifying and challenging irrational beliefs that contribute to anxiety. While options A, B, and D are useful interventions within a broader treatment plan, they are not the primary focus of CBT when initially addressing severe anxiety. Journaling (A) can help track thoughts but does not directly challenge irrational beliefs. Relaxation techniques (B) are beneficial for symptom management but do not address cognitive distortions. A structured schedule (D) can improve daily functioning but does not target the underlying cognitive processes contributing to anxiety.

Question 83: Correct Answer: B) Validate her feelings and provide emotional support.

Rationale: In an acute crisis situation, the first step is often to provide emotional support and validate the individual's feelings. This helps stabilize them emotionally before moving on to other interventions. Developing a long-term treatment plan (Option A), encouraging journaling (Option C), or suggesting time off work (Option D) are all useful strategies but are not appropriate as initial responses in an acute crisis. Immediate emotional support is crucial for helping Maria feel heard and understood during this overwhelming time.

Question 84: Correct Answer: B) Culturally Adapted CBT incorporating family involvement and community support

Rationale: Culturally Adapted CBT is designed to align with the client's cultural background by integrating culturally relevant elements such as family involvement and community support. This approach addresses Maria's concerns about cultural stigmas by involving her support system and making therapy more acceptable within her cultural context. While CBT focusing on individual cognitive restructuring (Option A) is effective, it may not fully address cultural factors. Solution-Focused Brief Therapy (Option C) emphasizes immediate problem-solving but may overlook deeper cultural issues. Psychoanalytic Therapy (Option D) focuses on unconscious conflicts from childhood, which may not directly address Maria's current cultural concerns.

Question 85: Correct Answer: C) Integrating social-emotional learning (SEL) curricula

Rationale: Integrating social-emotional learning (SEL) curricula has been shown to be highly effective in reducing bullying behaviors among adolescents. SEL programs teach skills such as empathy, self-regulation, and conflict resolution, which are crucial for creating a positive school climate and reducing bullying. - A) Implementing zero-tolerance policies can lead to increased suspensions without addressing underlying issues. - B) Establishing peer mediation programs can help but may not be as comprehensive as SEL curricula. - D) Increasing surveillance and adult supervision might deter bullying temporarily but does not address the root causes or equip students with necessary skills. Thus, while all options have merit, SEL curricula provide a more holistic and sustainable approach according to contemporary research.

Question 86: Correct Answer: B) Trauma can contribute to

SSD by causing chronic hyperarousal and heightened bodily awareness.

Rationale: Option B is correct because contemporary research indicates that trauma can lead to chronic hyperarousal, which in turn heightens bodily awareness and contributes to somatic symptom disorder (SSD). This is grounded in theories of trauma that emphasize the role of the autonomic nervous system and its impact on bodily perception. Option A is incorrect as it simplifies the relationship by attributing SSD directly to physical injuries rather than the complex interplay of psychological factors. Option C is incorrect because while genetic predisposition can play a role, it does not primarily explain the connection between trauma and SSD. Option D misrepresents the relationship by suggesting that cognitive patterns unrelated to physical sensations are the primary cause, which overlooks the significant role of heightened bodily awareness due to hyperarousal.

Question 87: Correct Answer: B) Facilitating open communication about end-of-life wishes.

Rationale: Facilitating open communication about end-of-life wishes helps patients process their emotions and make informed decisions, which is crucial in managing anticipatory grief. Option A, while beneficial for emotional well-being, does not directly address anticipatory grief. Option C can improve quality of life but may not effectively address the deeper emotional processing required for anticipatory grief. Option D provides necessary information but lacks the emotional support aspect critical for coping with anticipatory grief. Therefore, option B is the most comprehensive intervention for this specific issue.

Question 88: Correct Answer: B) Highlight John's strengths first, then discuss the attendance issues, and collaboratively develop a plan for improvement.

Rationale: Option B is correct because it follows the "sandwich" model of giving feedback starting with positive reinforcement (John's strengths), addressing areas needing improvement (attendance issues), and ending with a collaborative approach to problem-solving. This method increases receptiveness and motivation for change. - Option A is incorrect as it focuses only on the problem without acknowledging strengths, which can demotivate John. - Option C is incorrect because emphasizing negatives without recognizing positives can lead to defensiveness. - Option D is incorrect since it lacks constructive elements and support for change.

Question 89: Correct Answer: C) Dr. Martinez should consult with an attorney regarding how to respond to the subpoena while protecting Emily's confidentiality.

Rationale: Consulting with an attorney helps ensure that Dr. Martinez complies with legal requirements while safeguarding Emily's privacy as much as possible. A) is incorrect because immediate compliance may breach confidentiality without considering legal protections or objections. B) is partially correct but incomplete without legal consultation for proper guidance. D) is incorrect as outright refusal may lead to legal repercussions against Dr. Martinez.

Question 90: Correct Answer: B) Exposure and Response Prevention (ERP)

Rationale: ERP is a specific type of CBT that is considered the gold standard for treating Obsessive-Compulsive Disorder (OCD). It involves exposing the patient to the source of their anxiety without allowing them to perform their compulsive behavior. This method helps reduce the anxiety associated with obsessive thoughts over time. While CBT (option A) is also effective, ERP specifically targets OCD more directly. Psychoanalytic Therapy (option C) focuses on uncovering unconscious conflicts but lacks empirical support for treating OCD. Mindfulness-Based Stress Reduction (option D) can help manage stress but does not directly address compulsive behaviors as effectively as ERP.

Question 91: Correct Answer: C) Develop effective coping strategies to manage stressors in daily life.

Rationale: Developing effective coping strategies is crucial for managing Generalized Anxiety Disorder (GAD). It involves learning techniques such as problem-solving, relaxation exercises, and time management, which can help reduce overall anxiety levels. Practicing mindfulness meditation daily (A) and improving sleep hygiene (B) are helpful but are more specific interventions rather than comprehensive long-term goals. Enhancing communication skills (D) can be beneficial but may not directly address the pervasive worry characteristic of GAD as effectively as developing broad coping strategies.

Question 92: Correct Answer: B) Refer her to a financial advisor while continuing to address her anxiety and stress.

Rationale: It is essential for counselors to maintain clear boundaries regarding their professional roles. While acknowledging the impact of financial stress on mental health, referring Maria to a financial advisor ensures that she receives expert advice in that area while you continue focusing on her anxiety and stress management. This approach adheres to ethical guidelines and clarifies the counselor's role. Options A and D blur professional boundaries by implying dual roles, which can lead to ethical dilemmas. Option C, although close, still involves offering advice outside the counselor's expertise.

Question 93: Correct Answer: A) To ensure the client understands the potential risks and benefits of counseling.

Rationale: The primary purpose of obtaining informed consent is to ensure that clients are fully aware of the potential risks and benefits associated with counseling. This aligns with ethical standards emphasizing client autonomy and informed decision-making. Option B is incorrect because while informed consent can help protect against legal liability, this is not its primary purpose. Option C is partially correct but focuses too narrowly on confidentiality rather than a broader understanding of risks and benefits. Option D is also partially correct but emphasizes documentation over comprehension. Therefore, option A is most accurate as it encompasses understanding both risks and benefits comprehensively.

Question 94: Correct Answer: A) Cognitive-behavioral therapy (CBT) focusing on stress management.

Rationale: Cognitive-behavioral therapy (CBT) focusing on stress management is the most appropriate intervention as it directly addresses the psychological factors contributing to John's erectile dysfunction. CBT can help John manage his stress and improve his self-esteem, which are likely impacting his sexual functioning. While prescribing medication (Option B) might be considered, it does not address the underlying psychological issues. Referral to a sex therapist (Option C) could be beneficial but is more appropriate if relationship issues were identified. Psychoeducation (Option D) might help but is insufficient as a standalone intervention.

Question 95: Correct Answer: B) Respect John's autonomy and support his decision to discontinue treatment.

Rationale: The primary ethical obligation is to respect the patient's autonomy, especially when they are competent to make their own decisions. While involving family members (option A), seeking legal intervention (option C), or mediation (option D) might seem reasonable, they do not prioritize John's expressed wishes as directly as option B does. Autonomy is a fundamental principle in medical ethics that underscores the importance of respecting patients' rights to make decisions about their own healthcare.

Question 96: Correct Answer: A) Gradual onset of memory loss affecting daily activities

Rationale: Alzheimer's disease is characterized by a gradual onset of memory loss that progressively worsens and significantly affects daily activities. This distinguishes it from other conditions like delirium (sudden onset of confusion and disorientation), depression (persistent sadness and loss of interest), and transient episodes of forgetfulness (which do not lead to progressive decline).

Recognizing the gradual progression and impact on daily living is key to identifying Alzheimer's disease. - Option A is correct because Alzheimer's disease typically presents with a slow, progressive decline in memory that interferes with daily life. - Option B describes delirium, which has an acute onset and fluctuating course, often due to an underlying medical condition. - Option C refers to depression, which can cause cognitive impairment but is primarily characterized by mood disturbances. - Option D suggests benign forgetfulness or mild cognitive impairment without significant progression or impact on daily functioning.

Question 97: Correct Answer: A) Implementing a consistent bedtime routine.

Rationale: Establishing a consistent bedtime routine helps regulate the body's internal clock and improves overall sleep quality by creating predictable cues for relaxation and sleep onset. Option B might help some people but isn't universally effective and doesn't address underlying habits. Option C may provide temporary relief but lacks robust evidence for long-term efficacy. Option D can be useful for some individuals but isn't recommended as a first-line treatment due to potential side effects and variability in effectiveness.

Question 98: Correct Answer: A) Physical Abuse

Rationale: Sarah's symptoms fearfulness of adults, flinching when approached quickly, and anxiety are strongly indicative of physical abuse. These behaviors are consistent with a child who has experienced physical harm and is now hyper-vigilant around potential threats. Emotional abuse (Option B) can also cause anxiety and withdrawal but is less likely to cause fear of physical contact. Sexual abuse (Option C) might lead to similar symptoms but often includes additional signs such as inappropriate sexual behavior or knowledge. Neglect (Option D) typically results in poor hygiene or developmental delays rather than fearfulness of adults.

Question 99: Correct Answer: D) Facilitate sessions where John can express his grief without fear of judgment.

Rationale: Providing a safe space for John to express his grief without fear of judgment is crucial in addressing disenfranchised grief. This approach prioritizes creating an environment where John feels understood and supported in expressing his emotions fully. While private rituals (A), assertiveness training (B), and exploring cultural background (C) are valuable components of therapy, they do not directly address the immediate need for an accepting space where John can freely mourn his loss.

Question 100: Correct Answer: A) Conners' Rating Scales-Revised (CRS-R)

Rationale: Conners' Rating Scales-Revised (CRS-R) is specifically designed to assess ADHD symptoms across multiple settings and includes input from parents and teachers. This comprehensive approach makes it suitable for distinguishing ADHD from other potential issues such as learning disabilities. The Wechsler Intelligence Scale for Children (WISC-V) assesses cognitive abilities but does not directly address ADHD symptoms. The Child Behavior Checklist (CBCL) provides a broad overview of behavioral issues but lacks specificity for ADHD diagnosis. The Behavior Assessment System for Children (BASC-3) is useful but less targeted than CRS-R in identifying ADHD-specific behaviors.

Question 101: Correct Answer: C) Facilitate a joint session focused on establishing common parenting goals.

Rationale: Facilitating a joint session focused on establishing common parenting goals helps both parents align their approaches and understand each other's perspectives, fostering cooperation and consistency in parenting. Option A may not address the immediate co-parenting issue effectively. Option B might provide valuable information but lacks direct intervention. Option D could lead to inconsistency and confusion for the child. Joint sessions encourage collaboration and mutual understanding, which are crucial in resolving co-parenting conflicts.

Question 102: Correct Answer: B) Condense the client's

statements into a concise summary, capturing key themes and emotions.

Rationale: Option B is correct because effective summarization involves condensing multiple points into a coherent summary that captures key themes and emotions, ensuring the client feels understood. Option A is incorrect because merely repeating points lacks synthesis and may not convey understanding. Option C, while demonstrating active listening, doesn't provide an overarching summary. Option D focuses on the counselor's perspective rather than fully validating the client's experience. Summarizing should prioritize the client's narrative over therapeutic goals at this stage.

Question 103: Correct Answer: A) Wechsler Intelligence Scale for Children (WISC-V)

Rationale: The Wechsler Intelligence Scale for Children (WISC-V) is specifically designed to assess a child's intellectual functioning and cognitive abilities, making it the most appropriate choice in this context. The Vineland Adaptive Behavior Scales measure adaptive behaviors rather than intellectual functioning. Conners' Rating Scales are used primarily for assessing ADHD and related behavioral issues. Beck Youth Inventories focus on emotional and social functioning rather than cognitive abilities. Thus, while all options are relevant to psychological assessment, only WISC-V directly measures intellectual functioning as required in this scenario.

Question 104: Correct Answer: C) Emotionally focused therapy (EFT) that addresses underlying emotional responses and attachment needs.

Rationale: Emotionally focused therapy (EFT) is most effective as it targets underlying emotional responses and attachment needs (C), which are crucial in rebuilding trust after infidelity. CBT (A) may help change thought patterns but might not fully address deep-seated emotional issues. SFBT (B) focuses on short-term goals but may overlook deeper emotional healing necessary for long-term trust rebuilding. Narrative therapy (D), while helpful in reframing experiences, may not sufficiently address immediate emotional needs essential for trust restoration.

Question 105: Correct Answer: A) Cognitive Behavioral Therapy (CBT)

Rationale: Cognitive Behavioral Therapy (CBT) is considered highly effective for treating co-occurring disorders such as alcohol use disorder and social anxiety. CBT helps individuals identify and change negative thought patterns and behaviors contributing to their substance use. While Motivational Interviewing (MI) is useful in enhancing motivation for change, it does not specifically target the underlying social anxiety. Dialectical Behavior Therapy (DBT) is more focused on emotional regulation and may not directly address social anxiety. Contingency Management (CM) involves providing tangible rewards for positive behaviors but does not address the cognitive aspects of social anxiety.

Question 106: Correct Answer: A) Empathy

Rationale: The counselor's response demonstrates empathy by accurately reflecting Maria's feelings and showing understanding. Empathy involves recognizing and validating the client's emotions. While active listening (B) is also crucial in this context, it pertains more to attentively hearing what the client says rather than reflecting emotions. Unconditional positive regard (C) is about accepting the client without judgment, which isn't explicitly shown here. Congruence (D) involves being genuine and transparent with clients, which doesn't directly apply to this scenario.

Question 107: Correct Answer: C) Dismissive-Avoidant Attachment

Rationale: Sarah's description of her relationships as superficial and lacking emotional depth aligns with characteristics of a dismissive-avoidant attachment style. Individuals with this attachment style often maintain emotional distance and prioritize independence over close connections. In contrast, anxious-preoccupied individuals crave closeness and fear abandonment (B), fearful-avoidant individuals desire intimacy but fear rejection (D), and securely attached individuals generally have healthy, emotionally fulfilling relationships (A). Thus, the dismissive-avoidant attachment style best explains Sarah's experience.

Question 108: Correct Answer: B) Auditory hallucinations commanding the patient to perform actions

Rationale: Auditory hallucinations, especially those that command the patient to perform actions, are highly indicative of a primary psychotic disorder such as schizophrenia. Visual hallucinations (Option A) can occur in various conditions, including delirium or substance use disorders. Tactile hallucinations (Option C) are often associated with substance use, particularly stimulants like cocaine. Olfactory hallucinations (Option D), while concerning, are less specific and can be linked to neurological conditions such as temporal lobe epilepsy. Therefore, Option B is most indicative of a primary psychotic disorder due to its specificity and severity. - Option A: Visual hallucinations alone are not as strongly indicative of a primary psychotic disorder; they can occur in other contexts. - Option C: Tactile hallucinations are more commonly linked to substance use rather than primary psychotic disorders. - Option D: Olfactory hallucinations can be related to neurological issues and are less specific for primary psychotic disorders. - Correct Option B is supported by contemporary research indicating that command auditory hallucinations are a hallmark symptom of schizophrenia and other primary psychotic disorders.

Question 109: Correct Answer: B) Fostering a sense of industry by engaging the client in group activities and providing positive reinforcement.

Rationale: According to Erikson's stages of psychosocial development, a 12-year-old is typically in the "Industry vs. Inferiority" stage. During this stage, children need to develop a sense of competence and achievement through social interactions and productive activities. Option B aligns with this developmental need by fostering industry through group activities and positive reinforcement. Option A is more appropriate for younger children in the "Autonomy vs. Shame and Doubt" stage (ages 1-3). Option C is relevant for adolescents in the "Identity vs. Role Confusion" stage (ages 12-18). Option D pertains to infants in the "Trust vs. Mistrust" stage (birth to 1 year). Thus, while all options are based on Erikson's theory, only Option B aligns correctly with the developmental level of a 12-year-old client.

Question 110: Correct Answer: C) Assist Maria in finding a safe shelter or temporary housing.

Rationale: Ensuring Maria's immediate safety is paramount, hence finding safe shelter or temporary housing is critical. While empowering her financially (Option A) is important for long-term independence, it does not address immediate danger. Validating feelings and providing emotional support (Option B) are necessary but secondary to physical safety. Encouraging confrontation (Option D) can escalate the risk of harm and is not advisable in abusive situations. Each option was crafted considering common counseling practices and potential misconceptions. The correct answers focus on immediate physical safety, aligning with best practices for handling family abuse/violence cases.

Question 111: Correct Answer: C) Schedule sessions with an ASL interpreter present.

Rationale: Scheduling sessions with an ASL interpreter ensures accurate and effective communication between Maria and David. Option A (written notes) might not capture nuanced emotional content effectively. Option B (learning basic ASL phrases) is insufficient for complex therapeutic dialogue. Option D (lip-reading) can be unreliable and exhausting for individuals with hearing impairments. The presence of a qualified ASL interpreter respects David's communication needs and fosters an inclusive therapeutic environment.

Question 112: Correct Answer: C) Child-to-Parent Violence

Rationale: Child-to-parent violence involves aggressive behaviors by a child towards their parent, leading to distress or harm. The mother's visible distress and lack of response suggest an established pattern of such behavior. Parental neglect refers to a parent's failure to provide for their child's needs, which is not indicated here. Sibling rivalry involves conflicts between siblings rather than between a child and parent. Covert parental alienation typically involves one parent manipulating a child against the other parent without overt aggression from the child. Each option has been carefully crafted to challenge understanding: - A) Parental neglect might seem plausible if misinterpreted as the mother's failure to discipline. - B) Sibling rivalry could confuse those who do not focus on the specific parent-child dynamic. - D) Covert parental alienation could mislead those thinking about indirect forms of family manipulation rather than direct aggression. By focusing on these nuances, we ensure that only those with a comprehensive understanding can identify the correct answer.

Question 113: Correct Answer: C) Conduct an immediate risk assessment for potential relationship violence.

Rationale: Conducting an immediate risk assessment for potential relationship violence is paramount when a client admits to having violent thoughts towards their partner. This step ensures that any imminent danger can be identified and addressed promptly. Assessing underlying mental health conditions (A), developing an anger management plan (B), or referring to couples therapy (D) are important but secondary actions that do not directly address the immediate safety concern.

Question 114: Correct Answer: B) Avoidance

Rationale: Avoidance is the most likely theme emerging in this scenario as the group members are not addressing their feelings about the conflict and instead are focusing on superficial topics. Trust (Option A) would involve open sharing of feelings, which is not happening here. Cohesion (Option C) would imply a strong sense of unity and shared goals, which is contradicted by the avoidance behavior. Conflict Resolution (Option D) would involve addressing and working through conflicts, which is also not occurring.

Question 115: Correct Answer: A) Advocate for Jamie by educating school staff about non-binary identities.

Rationale: Educating school staff about non-binary identities can create a more inclusive environment for Jamie, reducing isolation and fostering acceptance. While joining a support group (Option B) can provide peer support, it does not address the broader school environment. Building resilience (Option C) is beneficial but secondary to creating an inclusive environment. Encouraging conformity (Option D) undermines Jamie's authentic self-expression and can lead to further distress.

Question 116: Correct Answer: D) Gradually reduce session frequency before final termination.

Rationale: Gradually reducing session frequency helps Sarah transition smoothly out of therapy while still feeling supported. It allows her to apply coping strategies independently while knowing she has access to support if needed. Option A is incorrect because it may give false reassurance without addressing immediate concerns. Option B, while important, lacks a practical plan for transitioning out of therapy. Option C is also crucial but should be part of an overall strategy that includes gradually reducing sessions (Option D).

Question 117: Correct Answer: D) Identity vs. Role Confusion

Rationale: During adolescence (ages 12-18), according to Erikson's theory, individuals face the challenge of Identity vs. Role Confusion as they explore various roles and ideas to form a personal identity and direction for their future. Maria's struggle with career choices and self-definition indicates this stage's typical issues. The other stages occur earlier in life: Autonomy vs. Shame and Doubt during early childhood (A), Initiative vs. Guilt during preschool years (B), and Industry vs. Inferiority during school-age years (C).

Question 118: Correct Answer: B) Offering interactive online modules tailored to GAD management.

Rationale: Offering interactive online modules tailored to GAD management is most effective as it engages clients actively, allowing them to learn at their own pace while reinforcing key concepts through interactive elements. This method aligns with contemporary research emphasizing active learning and technology-enhanced education. - Option A (Providing printed handouts) is less effective because it relies on passive learning, which may not engage clients as deeply or accommodate different learning styles. - Option C (Referring to a local support group) provides social support but does not directly address individualized educational needs. - Option D (Scheduling regular follow-ups) is important for reinforcement but does not replace the need for comprehensive initial education through interactive means. The correct option leverages modern educational tools that cater specifically to the client's condition and learning preferences, ensuring better understanding and retention of information.

Question 119: Correct Answer: B) Establishing immediate safety and stabilization.

Rationale: The primary focus during the initial phase of crisis intervention is to ensure the client's immediate safety and stabilization. This involves assessing any imminent risks and providing support to help the client regain a sense of control. Exploring past traumas (Option A) or developing long-term coping strategies (Option C) are important but secondary steps that come after stabilization. Encouraging detailed expression of feelings (Option D) can be part of the process but is not as crucial as ensuring safety first. Immediate safety is paramount according to contemporary research on crisis intervention principles.

Question 120: Correct Answer: D) Power Imbalance

Rationale: Power Imbalance is the pattern affecting the group's dynamics as Sarah's dominant behavior leads to disengagement from other members. Role Fixation (Option A), while related, implies individuals are stuck in specific roles without necessarily causing disengagement from others. Group Cohesion (Option B) suggests unity and active participation from all members, which is not evident here. Communication Breakdown (Option C), although relevant, typically implies a lack of effective communication overall rather than one person dominating discussions.

Question 121: Correct Answer: B) Therapy may lead to emotional discomfort as difficult topics are addressed.

Rationale: Ethical practice requires counselors to inform clients about both the benefits and risks of therapy. Option B correctly highlights that therapy can involve emotional discomfort as clients work through challenging issues. This transparency helps manage expectations and prepare clients for the therapeutic process. Option A is incorrect as therapy cannot guarantee complete resolution of all issues. Option C is misleading because therapy does not always yield immediate results; progress can take time. Option D falsely suggests that therapy alone suffices without other medical interventions, which may not be true for all clients depending on their needs.

Question 122: Correct Answer: B) Establishing rapport and trust

Rationale: Establishing rapport and trust is crucial during an initial interview as it sets the foundation for a therapeutic relationship. Without trust, clients may not feel comfortable sharing sensitive information necessary for accurate assessment and diagnosis. While gathering detailed family history (Option A), conducting a comprehensive mental status examination (Option C), and discussing potential treatment goals (Option D) are important, they are secondary to building rapport. Rapport ensures that subsequent interactions are productive and that clients are more likely to engage in the therapeutic process. Contemporary research highlights the importance of client-counselor relationships in successful therapy outcomes.

Question 123: Correct Answer: C) Whether his disclosure will be relevant and beneficial for Emily's therapeutic process.

Rationale: The correct answer is C because self-disclosure should always serve the client's therapeutic needs by being relevant and beneficial. Option A is close but not entirely correct; while shifting focus is important, relevance and benefit are primary concerns. Option B highlights an important consideration but doesn't address whether the disclosure aids therapy. Option D is incorrect as it assumes exact understanding of Emily's feelings, which can invalidate her unique experience.

Question 124: Correct Answer: C) Complicated Grief

Rationale: Sarah's symptoms are indicative of Complicated Grief (CG), characterized by prolonged and intense grief that disrupts daily functioning. Unlike Major Depressive Disorder (A), CG is specifically linked to the loss and includes persistent yearning or preoccupation with the deceased. Normal Grief (B) does not typically impair daily functioning for such an extended period. Adjustment Disorder with Depressed Mood (D) might fit if her symptoms were less severe and more transient, but her prolonged and intense reaction aligns more with CG.

Question 125: Correct Answer: C) When the self-disclosure is relevant to the client's situation and can facilitate the therapeutic process.

Rationale: The correct answer is C. Self-disclosure should be used when it is directly relevant to the client's situation and has the potential to enhance the therapeutic process. This approach ensures that self-disclosure remains purposeful and beneficial rather than distracting or self-serving. Option A is incorrect because using self-disclosure primarily to encourage a reluctant client can risk shifting focus away from the client's issues. Option B, while building rapport is important, using personal experiences indiscriminately may blur professional boundaries. Option D may lead to boundary issues as not all personal questions from clients should be answered; discretion is necessary.

Question 126: Correct Answer: B) Promoting active engagement in rehabilitation and adaptive activities.

Rationale: Promoting active engagement in rehabilitation and adaptive activities is considered most effective because it encourages patients to regain a sense of control and competence, which are crucial for psychological adjustment. This approach aligns with contemporary research emphasizing the importance of active coping strategies and participation in meaningful activities. In contrast: A) Encouraging the patient to focus solely on positive aspects can lead to avoidance of necessary emotional processing. C) Advising the patient to avoid discussing their condition can isolate them from valuable social support networks. D) Suggesting reliance primarily on medication neglects the benefits of psychological and social interventions essential for holistic adjustment. Each option is crafted to challenge understanding: - Option A is incorrect because while positivity is beneficial, exclusive focus can hinder emotional processing. - Option C is incorrect as it undermines the role of social support, which is critical according to research. - Option D fails to acknowledge that medication alone cannot address all aspects of psychological adjustment.

Question 127: Correct Answer: C) Integrated Dual Disorder Treatment (IDDT)

Rationale: Integrated Dual Disorder Treatment (IDDT) is specifically designed to address both substance use and mental health disorders simultaneously, making it the most effective modality for individuals with co-occurring conditions. Cognitive Behavioral Therapy (CBT) and Dialectical Behavior Therapy (DBT) are effective for various mental health issues but may not comprehensively address the complexity of co-occurring disorders. Motivational Interviewing (MI) is useful in enhancing motivation for change but does not provide the integrated approach necessary for treating dual disorders. Therefore, IDDT is superior due to its comprehensive and simultaneous focus on both types of disorders.

Question 128: Correct Answer: A) Cognitive Behavioral Therapy (CBT) focusing on restructuring negative thought patterns.

Rationale: Cognitive Behavioral Therapy (CBT) is an evidence-based approach that helps clients identify and challenge negative thought patterns and beliefs, which can lead to improved emotional regulation and self-esteem. This approach is particularly effective for anxiety and depression. Person-Centered Therapy (B), while beneficial for creating a supportive environment, may not directly address the cognitive distortions contributing to John's symptoms. Solution-Focused Brief Therapy (C) is future-oriented but may not address the underlying negative thoughts impacting John's current state. Psychodynamic Therapy (D) explores unconscious conflicts, which can be insightful but may not provide the immediate cognitive restructuring needed for John's situation.

Question 129: Correct Answer: A) Social skills training

Rationale: Social skills training is prioritized because it addresses both John's victimization and perpetration by improving his interpersonal skills, which can reduce aggressive behaviors and enhance his ability to form positive relationships. Group therapy sessions (B) can be supportive but may not directly target the skill deficits contributing to John's behavior. Family counseling (C) is important but secondary to addressing John's immediate social skill needs. A school-based anti-bullying curriculum (D) benefits the broader student population but does not provide individualized support necessary for John's dual role as victim and perpetrator.

Question 130: Correct Answer: C) Arrange for immediate hospitalization.

Rationale: Given Maria's specific plans for self-harm and access to means, arranging for immediate hospitalization is crucial to ensure her safety. Developing a safety plan (Option A) is important but insufficient given the severity of her ideation and plans. Contacting family members (Option B) can provide support but does not address immediate safety concerns. Increasing therapy sessions (Option D) may be part of long-term management but does not mitigate acute risk.

Question 131: Correct Answer: C) Explaining confidentiality policies verbally, giving Maria a written document for reference, discussing any concerns she has in detail, and then obtaining her signature.

Rationale: Option C is correct because it combines verbal explanation with written documentation and an opportunity for discussion key elements in ensuring informed consent while addressing confidentiality concerns. Option A does not provide written documentation. Option B lacks interactive discussion about concerns. Option D relies solely on self-directed reading without direct interaction or confirmation of understanding.

Question 132: Correct Answer: A) Cognitive Behavioral Therapy (CBT)

Rationale: Cognitive Behavioral Therapy (CBT) is widely recognized as the most effective treatment for Generalized Anxiety Disorder (GAD). It addresses cognitive distortions by challenging irrational thoughts and promotes behavioral changes through exposure techniques, reducing avoidance behaviors. Acceptance and Commitment Therapy (ACT), while also addressing cognitive elements, focuses more on accepting thoughts rather than changing them. Dialectical Behavior Therapy (DBT) is primarily used for borderline personality disorder but includes mindfulness and emotional regulation skills that can be beneficial for anxiety. Mindfulness-Based Stress Reduction (MBSR) emphasizes mindfulness practices to reduce stress but does not specifically target cognitive distortions or behavioral avoidance as comprehensively as CBT does. - Option A)

CBT is correct because it directly targets both cognitive distortions and behavioral avoidance, making it highly effective for GAD. - Option B) ACT is incorrect because it focuses on acceptance of thoughts rather than altering them, which is a nuanced difference from CBT. - Option C) DBT is incorrect as it is mainly designed for borderline personality disorder, although it includes components that can help with anxiety. - Option D) MBSR is incorrect because it primarily uses mindfulness techniques without specifically addressing cognitive distortions or avoidance behaviors in the way CBT does. This differentiation clarifies why CBT stands out among these therapies for treating GAD effectively.

Question 133: Correct Answer: C) Conduct a thorough risk assessment and develop a safety plan with John.
Rationale: Conducting a thorough risk assessment and developing a safety plan is the most ethical approach because it respects John's autonomy while addressing the potential risk. Monitoring alone (Option A) may be insufficient without a clear understanding of John's current state. Breaking confidentiality immediately (Option B) could violate ethical guidelines unless there is imminent danger, which isn't indicated here. Referring John to an inpatient facility without consent (Option D) is premature without assessing the level of risk first.

Question 134: Correct Answer: B) Use an encrypted email service to send the session notes.
Rationale: The correct answer is B) Use an encrypted email service to send the session notes. This ensures that the information is securely transmitted and maintains client confidentiality. Option A is incorrect because using a personal email account does not guarantee encryption and security. Option C is incorrect as sharing sensitive information through social media violates confidentiality protocols. Option D, while cautious, overlooks secure methods available for electronic communication that comply with ethical guidelines.

Question 135: Correct Answer: A) Contact the insurance company directly to verify coverage details.
Rationale: The most reliable way for Maria to ensure she accurately reviews the client's insurance benefits is by contacting the insurance company directly. This step allows her to obtain up-to-date and precise information regarding coverage details, co-pays, deductibles, and any limitations or exclusions. While reviewing policy documents (Option B) can provide some information, it may not be as current or comprehensive. Using a third-party verification service (Option C) might introduce errors or delays. Asking the client to call their insurance company (Option D) could lead to miscommunication or incomplete information.

Question 136: Correct Answer: C) Recommend John undergo Cognitive Behavioral Therapy (CBT).
Rationale: Cognitive Behavioral Therapy (CBT) is widely recognized as an effective treatment for process addictions like gambling. It helps individuals identify and modify distorted thinking patterns and maladaptive behaviors associated with their addiction. While support groups (A), mindfulness techniques (B), and medication management (D) can be beneficial adjuncts, CBT remains the primary evidence-based intervention for compulsive gambling.

Question 137: Correct Answer: A) Reassure Sarah that her feelings are valid and she will not be judged.
Rationale: Reassuring Sarah validates her emotions and establishes a non-judgmental space essential for trust. This foundational step addresses her immediate concern directly. Option B might help later but does not address the current fear directly. Option C could seem confrontational too early in therapy. Option D is useful but secondary to addressing her primary concern of judgment first.

Question 138: Correct Answer: B) Disruptive Mood Dysregulation Disorder (DMDD)
Rationale: DMDD is characterized by severe temper outbursts that are disproportionate to the situation and occur frequently, typically three or more times per week. This disorder also includes a persistently irritable or angry mood between outbursts. IED involves impulsive aggression but doesn't include persistent irritability. ODD features defiance and argumentative behavior without the severe mood dysregulation seen in DMDD. Bipolar Disorder involves mood swings between mania/hypomania and depression but does not primarily feature frequent temper outbursts as seen in DMDD.

Question 139: Correct Answer: B) Address Sarah's behavior immediately in front of the group by explaining its impact.
Rationale: Addressing Sarah's behavior immediately in front of the group by explaining its impact helps maintain a supportive environment and sets clear boundaries for acceptable behavior. It also provides an opportunity for learning for all group members. - Option A is incorrect because ignoring harmful behavior can allow it to persist and affect group morale further. - Option C might be useful later but does not address immediate harm caused during sessions. - Option D places undue responsibility on another member and could lead to conflict or discomfort within the group.

Question 140: Correct Answer: B) It helps in setting clear boundaries and expectations, reducing potential misunderstandings.
Rationale: Clarifying counselor/client roles at the beginning of therapy is crucial for setting clear boundaries and expectations, which helps reduce potential misunderstandings (Option B). This practice ensures both parties are aware of their responsibilities, promoting a safe and effective therapeutic environment. Option A is incorrect because establishing a power dynamic can hinder the therapeutic alliance. Option C is misleading as it implies an imbalance where clients dictate terms, which is not conducive to effective therapy. Option D is incorrect because ongoing communication about roles may still be necessary to address evolving dynamics in therapy. Thus, Option B accurately reflects contemporary research and recognized theories on role clarification in counseling.

Question 141: Correct Answer: B) Focus on helping John understand that it is normal to have positive relationships with both parents and stepparents.
Rationale: Helping John understand that it is normal and healthy to have positive relationships with both his biological father and stepmother directly addresses his loyalty conflict by normalizing his emotions. A), while promoting open communication, may put undue pressure on John. C) is important but does not empower John with coping strategies. D), although beneficial for personal exploration, does not specifically address normalizing dual loyalties within blended families.

Question 142: Correct Answer: A) Major Depressive Disorder
Rationale: Major Depressive Disorder (MDD) is characterized by a period of at least two weeks during which there is either depressed mood or loss of interest or pleasure in nearly all activities. The symptoms described by Sarah persistent sadness, loss of interest, significant weight loss, insomnia, fatigue, and feelings of worthlessness are classic indicators of MDD. Persistent Depressive Disorder (Dysthymia) involves chronic depression lasting for at least two years but typically with less severe symptoms than MDD. Bipolar II Disorder includes periods of hypomania along with depressive episodes but does not fit Sarah's symptom profile since she has not reported any hypomanic episodes. Generalized Anxiety Disorder involves excessive anxiety and worry about various events or activities but does not primarily feature the depressive symptoms Sarah exhibits.

Question 143: Correct Answer: B) Grounding Techniques
Rationale: Grounding techniques are highly effective for helping clients manage intense feelings because they focus on bringing the client's attention back to the present moment,

thereby reducing overwhelming emotions. This technique is particularly useful in cases of anxiety, trauma, or dissociation. - A) Cognitive Restructuring involves changing negative thought patterns but does not immediately address intense emotional states. - C) Guided Imagery can be helpful for relaxation but may not be effective in moments of acute emotional distress. - D) Progressive Muscle Relaxation helps reduce physical tension but may not sufficiently address immediate emotional intensity. Grounding techniques stand out as they offer immediate relief by anchoring clients in the present, making them the most appropriate choice for managing intense feelings during a session.

Question 144: Correct Answer: B) Validating John's feelings and educating him about IPV.

Rationale: The initial step should be validating John's feelings and educating him about intimate partner violence (IPV). His description of isolation and fear due to his partner's controlling behavior indicates potential IPV. Improving communication (Option A), suggesting couples therapy (Option C), or advising self-care activities (Option D) might be beneficial later but do not address the immediate need to recognize and understand IPV. Validating his experience helps build trust and opens the door for further discussion about safety planning and resources.

Question 145: Correct Answer: A) Normal adolescent development exacerbated by adoption status

Rationale: Adolescence is a critical period for identity formation, and adopted adolescents often face additional challenges as they integrate their adoption status into their self-concept. While lack of cultural integration (B), unresolved grief (C), and peer pressure (D) can contribute to identity struggles, they do not capture the unique intersection of normal adolescent development with the complexities introduced by adoption.

Question 146: Correct Answer: A) Hypothyroidism

Rationale: Hypothyroidism can present with symptoms such as fatigue, weight gain, and joint pain, which are also common in depression. While Chronic Fatigue Syndrome (B), Fibromyalgia (C), and Sleep Apnea (D) can have overlapping symptoms with depression, Hypothyroidism is particularly relevant due to its direct impact on mood and energy levels through hormonal imbalance. Depression is often linked with thyroid dysfunctions, making Hypothyroidism the most likely physical issue in this scenario.

Question 147: Correct Answer: A) Explore John's feelings about his family's involvement.

Rationale: Exploring John's feelings about his family's involvement is essential as it helps uncover underlying emotions and beliefs that influence his experience. Advising independence (B) might be premature without understanding these feelings. Encouraging open conversation (C) is important but should come after initial exploration of feelings. Suggesting avoidance (D) can lead to unresolved issues and further strain relationships. Understanding John's emotional landscape provides a foundation for more tailored interventions that respect familial bonds while addressing individual needs.

Question 148: Correct Answer: B) Dialectical Behavior Therapy (DBT)

Rationale: Dialectical Behavior Therapy (DBT) is the most appropriate treatment modality for Borderline Personality Disorder (BPD) due to its focus on emotional regulation, distress tolerance, and interpersonal effectiveness. CBT is effective for various disorders but does not specifically target the unique challenges of BPD as DBT does. Psychodynamic Therapy explores unconscious processes but lacks the structured skills training essential for BPD. Person-Centered Therapy provides a supportive environment but does not offer the specific strategies needed to manage BPD symptoms effectively. - A) Cognitive Behavioral Therapy (CBT): While CBT addresses dysfunctional thinking patterns and behaviors, it does not specifically cater to the emotional dysregulation seen in BPD. - B) Dialectical Behavior Therapy (DBT): DBT combines cognitive-behavioral techniques with mindfulness practices tailored for BPD, making it the most effective choice. - C) Psychodynamic Therapy: This approach delves into unconscious conflicts but lacks the practical skills training that DBT provides for managing BPD symptoms. - D) Person-Centered Therapy: Although it offers unconditional positive regard and empathy, it does not provide structured interventions necessary for treating BPD. This detailed explanation helps clarify why DBT is superior in this context compared to other modalities.

Question 149: Correct Answer: C) Emotional Resonance

Rationale: Emotional resonance refers to the counselor's ability to connect deeply with the client's emotions, experiencing a shared sense of feeling. This goes beyond just understanding or reflecting what the client says; it involves an intuitive grasp of their emotional experience. Reflective listening (A) and active listening (B) are important skills but focus more on accurately hearing and summarizing the client's words rather than deeply resonating with their emotions. Cognitive empathy (D) involves understanding another's perspective intellectually but does not necessarily include an emotional connection. Therefore, emotional resonance is the most accurate term describing deep empathic attunement.

Question 150: Correct Answer: C) Seek supervision or consultation to discuss potential cultural issues.

Rationale: Seeking supervision or consultation is crucial for ensuring cultural competence when working with clients from diverse backgrounds. While reflecting on past experiences (Option A) and evaluating knowledge of Mexican culture (Option B) are important, they may not provide the comprehensive support needed. Assuming that general counseling skills are sufficient (Option D) overlooks the specific cultural nuances that can impact treatment.

Made in the USA
Monee, IL
27 September 2024

66746118R00109